British Thrillers,
1950–1979

British Thrillers, 1950–1979

845 Films of Suspense, Mystery, Murder and Espionage

Franz Antony Clinton

McFarland & Company, Inc., Publishers
Jefferson, North Carolina

All photographs are from the author's collection.

LIBRARY OF CONGRESS CATALOGUING-IN-PUBLICATION DATA

Names: Clinton, Franz Antony, author.
Title: British thrillers, 1950–1979 : 845 films of suspense, mystery, murder and espionage / Franz Antony Clinton.
Description: Jefferson, North Carolina : McFarland & Company, Inc., Publishers, 2020 | Includes bibliographical references, filmography, and index.
Identifiers: LCCN 2020036769 | ISBN 9780786410323 (paperback : acid free paper) ∞
ISBN 9781476640679 (ebook)
Subjects: LCSH: Thrillers (Motion pictures)—Great Britain—Reviews. | Spy films—Great Britain—Reviews. | Detective and mystery films—Great Britain—Reviews.
Classification: LCC PN1995.9.S87 C58 2020 | DDC 791.43/6556—dc23
LC record available at https://lccn.loc.gov/2020036769

BRITISH LIBRARY CATALOGUING DATA ARE AVAILABLE

ISBN (print) 978-0-7864-1032-3
ISBN (ebook) 978-1-4766-4067-9

© 2020 Franz Antony Clinton. All rights reserved

No part of this book may be reproduced or transmitted in any form or by any means, electronic or mechanical, including photocopying or recording, or by any information storage and retrieval system, without permission in writing from the publisher.

Front cover image: 1958 British thriller *Kill Her Gently* (Fortress Film Productions/Columbia Pictures UK)

Printed in the United States of America

McFarland & Company, Inc., Publishers
Box 611, Jefferson, North Carolina 28640
www.mcfarlandpub.com

To the memories
of Brian Clemens (1931–2015)
and
Jimmy Sangster (1927–2011),
two great maestros of the British thriller

Acknowledgments

I would like to extend my thanks to the following: my partner Miriam Lekich for her fantastic work preparing the electronic images as well as for her unending patience and support; home video expert Brian Rake for help with some rare films, and for double-checking certain key information; Ian Caunce for helping bring added illustrative life to the book by making available some great publicity material; the BBC Archives; BFI National Archive; Kit Parker of "Kit Parker Films" for help with one particular bit of research in the U.S.; Salman Sobe for his generous hospitality during the many hours I spent reviewing the manuscript at his Cinnamon Village café in north London; Alan Milford for his invaluable suggestions during the finalization of the manuscript; Peter Jones for undertaking the majority of the proofreading; and my sister Corina (cheers, "Splogg") for additional proofreading. Regarding viewing material, I'd like to extend a massive thanks to Ade Miller for allowing me access to his vast collection of films, which helped fill many gaps. Also, I'm eternally grateful to my parents for having always supported me in my interests.

I am also extremely grateful to the following for help with an unfinished past project from which this current book emerged: legendary screenwriter Brian Clemens (1931–2015) for his help and encouragement, not to mention an interview and foreword (parts of which are reproduced in the current preface and introduction); Janet Moat for facilitating access to so many pressbooks in so little time during her tenure at the British Film Institute library; producer John I. Phillips (1925–2004) for help accessing materials pertaining to his many 1960s B movies for Butcher's Film Distributors; film historian Richard Dacre in connection with certain movie stills; and Lawrence Rogoff for allowing me access to the many rare films he'd taped off the television over the years.

Table of Contents

Acknowledgments — vi
Preface — 1
Introduction — 7

1. Espionage — 15
2. Mystery and Murder — 57
3. The Psychological and the Psychopathic — 114
4. Focus on Crime Solvers — 155
5. The Business of Crime — 199
6. Suspense — 258
7. Merton Park's Edgar Wallace B-Movie Series — 289
8. Action/Adventure — 306

Filmography — 337
Appendix I. British Thrillers from Selected Production Companies — 395
Appendix II. Hollywood Actors in British B Thrillers — 399
Appendix III. Sources for the Edgar Wallace Series — 403
Appendix IV. Selected Listings — 405
Appendix V. British and U.S. Video Retitlings — 407
Appendix VI. British-Made U.S. TV Movies — 411
Appendix VII. Supposed Alternate U.S. Titles — 413
Appendix VIII. "Ad"dendum — 415
Selected Bibliography — 417
Index of Names — 419
Index of Film Titles — 442

Preface

For those seeking vicarious cinematic thrills but who are squeamish when it comes to the horror genre, thrillers are the perfect solution. The broad variety within the thriller universe should ensure there is something to suit everyone, from those who enjoy unraveling clues in a whodunit, or untangling the complex webs of intrigue spun in a Cold War spy thriller, to those who would rather endure the unbearable tension of a race against time, or the violent action in a gangster thriller. And for those who do enjoy the aforementioned horror genre, there are plenty of chills to be found in some of the more terrifying psycho-killer thrillers.

Speaking of the horror genre, I myself became interested in British thrillers (especially of the "B" variety) at a young age through what I *thought* was a horror film. It was back in 1975 when a TV listing for a late-night showing of a movie called *The Night of the Full Moon* had me imagining what type of werewolf antics might be in store. Already a budding horror film fan, and having recently watched the American TV movie *Moon of the Wolf* (1972), I couldn't wait to see this enticingly titled picture and was figuring out how I would convince my parents to let me stay up for what was a particularly late broadcast. As it turned out, I couldn't convince them, and it wasn't until some time later that I discovered *The Night of the Full Moon* was nothing more than a fairly run-of-the-mill B-movie spy thriller with not a werewolf in sight!

A 1953 B movie in which, despite the promising title, there's not a werewolf in sight.

However, back at the time, the film's lack of mentions in reference books just helped add to my curiosity. At one point I found it listed—just the title—in an edition of *The British Film & Television Year Book* (edited by Peter Noble), a volume which referred to many more intriguing titles (all B movies as it turned out), most of which I'd never heard of and could only hope to one day see. Some of these, such as *Cover Girl Killer* (1959), *Out of the Fog* (1962) and *Don't Talk to Strange Men* (1962), have since gained a fair amount of recognition and have had DVD releases; others, like *At the Stroke of Nine* (1957), *The Child and the Killer* (1959) and *Doomsday at Eleven* (1962), are nowhere to be found, having been out of circulation for decades. Anyhow, my interest in such films had begun; indeed, the original idea for this book was to include only British B thrillers from 1950 to 1966, but the scope was subsequently widened to also include "A" thrillers and to cover a longer time period. (One aspect of the original idea, namely to highlight Hollywood actors in British B thrillers, can be found in Appendix II.)

What makes a thriller a thriller? Usually, thrillers are concerned with some type of crime such as murder or espionage, with the added presence of at least some of the following elements: mystery, suspense, cat-and-mouse play, danger, double-crossing, intrigue, excitement, unease and surprise. My criteria for what constitutes a thriller includes that the above ingredients are used in a fictional or semi-fictional plot that features characters functioning in a reasonably plausible setting. (This does not necessarily preclude the fact that the twists and turns common in thrillers often require that characters react in unrealistic ways in order to service the plot.) Consequently, horror films are not really thrillers as, even though they may contain suspense, danger and excitement, the focus is more on the horror, fantasy and supernatural (monsters, vampires, ghosts, etc.), therefore forgoing plausibility.

Because thrillers cover quite a broad range of themes, they are often described with a qualifying word; thus we have the terms "mystery thriller," "murder thriller," "spy thriller," "psychological thriller," "suspense thriller," "crime thriller," "detective thriller" and others, which can encompass scenarios including whodunits, Cold War shenanigans, deadly mind games, chases, heists, blackmail plots and police procedurals. "Comedy thriller" is a term used when a significant amount of humor is integrated with any of the above types, but would not include out-and-out comedies like *Carry On Spying* (1964). Some films with a science fiction theme, such as *Spaceways* (1952) and *Escapement* (1957), can be counted as thrillers because the scientific elements do not overwhelm the more traditional elements of murder, mystery and intrigue. War films can also be thrillers if the war is used as a backdrop to more thriller-like intrigues, such as in *Where Eagles Dare* (1968) or *The Eagle Has Landed* (1976).

This book is intended to be a thorough compendium of British thriller films—specifically main features and B movies—from 1950 to 1979, a fascinating period that I consider a golden age of the genre due to the sheer volume and variety of productions therein. The term "B movie" (also sometimes called supporting feature, second feature or programmer) refers to the lower-budget films that were made for showing on the bottom half of double bills. ("Co-features," which had marginally higher budgets than the typical B movie and were intended to be paired on double bills with a film of equal status, are also commonly referred to—and were often also treated—as B movies.) The book does not cover short films, TV movies (with the exception of those in Appendix VI) or films with thriller aspects that were made for children (such as from the Children's Film Foundation). Also not included are theatrically released features edited together from TV episodes, e.g., *King of the Underworld* (1952) and *Murder at Scotland Yard* (1954), both of which were made up of segments from the unaired series *Inspector Morley Investigates*; and fare such as the late 1960s offerings *The Fiction-Makers* and *Vendetta for the Saint*, both originally two-part episodes of Roger Moore's *The Saint* series.

The following are examples of British films involving crime that are often regarded as thrillers but which were not included in the book as I felt they did not meet the overall criteria: *Marilyn* (noir-style marital melodrama), *The Flesh Is Weak* (prostitution drama), *A Place to Go* (kitchen sink–style drama), *Repulsion* (dark psychological drama about a descent into insanity), *Blowup* (deliberately inconclusive mystery focusing on the nature of reality), *10 Rillington Place* (bleak biographical account of true-life serial killer), *Something to Hide* (depressing psychological drama).

Given the book's focus on British contributions to the thriller film universe, a word or two should be mentioned as to particular aspects within that universe at which the British excel. When one thinks about American thrillers, it may be noir movies or slasher films that come to mind; with the Italians it may be the *giallos* or the slew of James Bond imitations from the 1960s; the French have their often darkly humorous crime thrillers with that inescapable sense of Gallic doom. In the case of British thrillers, mystery and murder prevail, with espionage running a close second. "Britishness," when it comes to murder, is perhaps best summed up by the words of Brian Clemens, one of the most creative screenwriters in the genre, in an excerpt from his foreword to an earlier, unfinished incarnation of this book:

> There are two kinds of movies we Brits do better than Hollywood: the costume drama (because most of the locations are still standing) and the thriller. The roots for the latter go back through Agatha Christie, Daphne Du Maurier and Ruth Rendell et al. to Arthur Conan Doyle and Wilkie Collins, but are fuelled by the reality of our own special criminology. I have always advocated that if there were an Olympics for murder, Britain would get the Gold. Every time! In America they have slayings, but WE have something deeper

and more satisfying. It may have something to do with Victorian repressions (or even maybe Shakespeare), but undeniably we have always produced murderers with an unerring sense of drama. What could be more theatrical than the legend of Jack the Ripper: stalking fog-shrouded, cobblestoned streets—slashing and disembowelling—and all to the distant, jolly sound of the hurdy-gurdy? Hitchcock was well aware of this legacy, and much of his work, from *The Lodger* to *Frenzy*, contains sly references to the wonderful art of murder and mayhem we British have honed to grisly perfection.

Hitchcock, in a 1972 interview with Sheridan Morley, had also cited Doyle, and he further included John Buchan (*The 39 Steps*) in regard to the "first class [British] literature" that got him into thrillers in the first place.

Within the eight themed chapters of this book, titles of the main films covered appear in bold type for easy browsing and are the original British release titles. Coverage of films includes a synopsis/review and in some cases a quote from a contemporary review. Where a film was an adaptation, the source (novel, play, etc.) may be mentioned, although it was not my intention to do so in all such cases. Selected original publicity taglines are scattered throughout the chapters and appear as italicized subheadings in quotation marks, in each case relating to the film immediately following. The year assigned to a film is the original British copyright year (where such was present) as shown on the film itself, but in any case is intended to reflect a time when production had finished and a film was essentially ready to be, or ready to go through the process of being, released. As the book starts from 1950, films released in that year but which have a 1949 copyright, such as *The Blue Lamp*, *Stage Fright*, *Golden Salamander* and *Your Witness*, are not included. Other 1950 releases such as *Torment* and *The 20 Questions Murder Mystery*, which contain no copyright year but which were rated in 1949 by the British Board of Film Censors (subsequently known as the British Board of Film

Classification) and thus essentially ready for release in that year, are also not included. Within sections or subsections of the book, films have been sorted in order of year, with those falling within the same year further sorted chronologically based on the date they were rated by the British Board of Film Censors. (Note: The only time chronology is broken is when a film and its remake or sequel are covered consecutively.) In the very few cases where a film was unavailable to view, information for the synopses was compiled from a variety of sources including release scripts and pressbooks.

An alphabetically arranged filmography has been included to provide additional details for all the main films covered in the preceding chapters. Each entry is numbered (for the purpose of the Index of Names) and contains the film title, year, production company details, color or B&W, running time, director, producer, screenplay, photography, music and a selection of cast members. When it came to B movies featuring Hollywood stars, it was quite common for British production companies to work in association with producers in the U.S., although this was hardly if ever mentioned in the credits of the films themselves (British prints) or in British publicity. Where the involvement of such companies was possible to ascertain (through U.S. publicity, U.S. film prints, etc.), this information has been included in parentheses following the British production company name, e.g., Hammer Film Productions (in association with Lippert Pictures [U.S.]). In cases where a film has no credit for music composer but does contain a credit for musical direction, then this name has been used instead. Some films contain no music credits at all. Running times given are for the longest known (as far as I could establish) original theatrical release versions, which are not necessarily always the original British theatrical release versions (the 1958 B movie *Kill Her Gently*, for example, was seen outside Britain in a 73-minute version, whereas at home it was cut down to 63 minutes). Any mentions about different length versions of films will be made in the main entries within the first eight chapters. Where there are differences in the way someone's first name/names has been credited, such as director of photography Walter J. Harvey, who was also sometimes billed as James Harvey, Jimmy Harvey, Jimmy W. Harvey and Walter Harvey, I have used just one name (usually the most commonly known) across the board for uniformity. Where someone has had a change of surname during their career, or has been billed under a pseudonym, I have used their commonly known name followed by the billed name in parentheses. All alternate names are shown in the Index of Names. Also, I have endeavored to correct any names that were misspelled on actual film prints or elsewhere.

The Filmography also includes alternate British titles as well as titles used for U.S. distribution. In cases where a film has multiple U.S. titles, it can be assumed that the first title listed was the principal theatrical and/or television title, and was possibly also used for subsequent video and/or DVD releases. If a U.S. title is followed by the description "TV only," this means that the title in question was, as far as I could reasonably ascertain, only ever used for television broadcast, which does not rule out the possibility that other titles (including the British title) appearing in the entry were also used for release on that medium. Needless to say, if no U.S. title is listed in a given entry, then the British title would have been the principal title for U.S. distribution (if indeed the film was distributed in the U.S. at all). In general, the presence in any given entry of a U.S. title or titles does not exclude the possibility that the film's original British title was also used for U.S. distribution; e.g., *Eyewitness* (1956) was shown on U.S. television as both *Peril in the Night* and *Eyewitness*, while *Assault* (1970), which over the years had five alternate titles in the U.S., was also distributed there as *Assault*. Any reference to "video" within this book refers to videocassette releases and not to DVD. New titles that were used for British and U.S. video releases can be found in Appendix V, one of eight appendices that I hope readers will find interesting and useful.

Lastly, there are two indexes. The first (Index of Names) is for locating names (actors, directors, etc.) in the Filmography and refers to the film entry numbers therein. The second (Index of Film Titles) refers to page numbers and points to the reviews/synopses within chapters 1-8. So, for example, if a reader wants to find out what thrillers a particular actor starred in, this can be done via the Index of Names; reviews/synopses for the films can then be located in the Index of Film Titles.

Introduction

A Perilous World

Welcome to the exciting, mysterious and dangerous world of the British thriller, to which this book is your guided tour. Most of us who enjoy a good thriller welcome the opportunity to escape into a realm of assorted perils and uncertainties. The world of the thriller is one of murder, mystery, danger, suspense and excitement, a world populated by opportunist murderers, deranged psychopaths and unprincipled gangsters, not to mention treacherous spies, nasty blackmailers, scheming counterfeiters, unbalanced kidnappers and dishonest cops. It's a world where the danger is not from some marauding Frankenstein's creature, bloodthirsty vampire or shadowy ghost, but from our fellow man—or woman; a world in which, after hours, city streets become a playground for criminals, a playground in which we face being stranded simply by missing the last bus home. The average person, just by being in the wrong place at the wrong time, faces possible immersion in this otherwise hidden domain. We are only a step away from a street of shadows. It is only through luck that we avoid it.

In the realm of the thriller, things are not always as they seem. For instance, ponder those late-night clubs in London's Soho district, where smiling faces and friendly greetings conceal shady dealings behind closed doors; or the forced cordiality of family members gathered at a gloomy ancestral estate where murder occurs almost as soon as the will is read. And how about that dimly lit train compartment, where a well-dressed passenger—seemingly asleep—lurches forward to reveal a knife protruding from their back. Consider those sinister figures from the London underworld, on whose attire the crimson markings are not part of some fashion design statement, but rather the bloody remnants of a deadly shoot-out. Contemplate the naked edge of a razor—a razor not used for shaving. Take a trip to the serene and secretive British countryside, where isolated and seemingly innocuous houses are in fact hives of criminal activity where counterfeiting and smuggling are the norm. Then there's the charm of the curious, sleepy British village—a charm that evaporates as night falls and a murderer becomes restless.

While experiencing the "thrill" of a thriller, the excitement is in trying to figure out how we would react in a particular situation. As ordinary people mixed up in extraordinary events, how would we manage? Consider, if you will, the possibility of unusual situations that could take you away from the safety and comfort of your everyday life. What if you found clues pointing to your spouse being a murderer? How would you react to seeing a passenger being strangled on a passing train? If you are a detective, are you up to the task of catching that ruthless criminal playing deadly cat-and-mouse games with you? What if you are cycling through rural France on a pleasant sunlit afternoon, only to find that murderers don't always wait until dark? What if you were witness to a murder and the murderer came after you? Hopefully, you will not find yourself in such situations in real life; however, you are most cordially invited to experience them through the unique world of the British thriller film, preferably in the comfort of your own home. Just don't forget to lock the doors and windows!

A Golden Age

In the period covered by this book, 1950 to 1979, the British film industry produced hundreds of thrillers that collectively comprise the full spectrum of the genre's styles, from traditional favorites such as mystery and spy thrillers to the roots and early development of the modern gangster and psycho thriller. Fairly recent to the start of the period was World War II, with this and the Nazi legacy providing plenty of material for thrillers throughout the period; hidden Nazi treasure was the subject of films like *The House of the Seven Hawks* (1959), *The Bay of Saint Michel* (1963) and *Bear Island* (1979). The ensuing Cold War provided material for a plethora of movies such as *The Man in the Road* (1956), *The Spy Who Came in from the Cold* (1965) and *Spy Story* (1976).

In short, the sheer volume and variety of films produced during the three decades qualifies the era as a veritable "Golden Age of British Thrillers."

1950s to 1960s

Some of the standout thrillers of the 1950s, which was by far the busiest of the three decades, include *Seven Days to Noon* (1950), *The Clouded Yellow* (1950), *Footsteps in the Fog* (1955), *The Ladykillers* (1955), *The Long Arm* (1956), *Hell Drivers* (1957), *Chase a Crooked Shadow* (1957), *The Snorkel* (1958), *Tiger Bay* (1959) and *SOS Pacific* (1959).

"B" Hive

From 1950 and halfway into the 1960s, the hive of activity that was the British B movie industry yielded a staggering number of thrillers. Although B movies were made cheaply and quickly, the opportunities they provided for some imaginative directors who had fallen from A-list status, such as Lance Comfort, as well as for new filmmakers looking to prove themselves, resulted in some high quality films. To make the most of their low budgets, B-movie makers often employed extensive and cost-effective location shooting which now provides fascinating viewing for film historians.

When one begins examining the wide and wonderful world of the British B thriller, it's amazing to see just how many of them featured U.S. or U.S.-based actors. Enterprising British production companies often made deals with American organizations in order to secure established Hollywood stars for lead roles, thus helping film sales at home as well as ensuring healthy theatrical distribution in the U.S. Also, the upshot of a British Government initiative known as the Eady Plan, which came into effect in 1950 to help boost domestic film production, made it more profitable for U.S. companies to make films in England as opposed to exporting their homegrown product, which was subject to hefty British tariffs at the time. The plan required that most of the budget be spent on British or British-based casts and crews, which still left enough money to employ Hollywood stars and also sometimes an American director.

The vast array of well-known actors who crossed the Atlantic to appear in British B thrillers includes Dane Clark, Howard Duff, Larry Parks, Faith Domergue, Dan Duryea, Richard Denning, Phyllis Kirk, Scott Brady, Zachary Scott, Hillary Brooke, Lex Barker, Pat O'Brien and many others (see Appendix II: Hollywood Actors in British B Thrillers). And among the U.S. companies involved (by way of arranging finance, signing up Hollywood stars, setting up U.S. distribution deals, etc.) in British B thriller production were: Lippert Pictures (Robert L. Lippert), who had a well-known association with Hammer Film Productions; Amalgamated Productions, run by London-born, New York–based Richard Gordon together with his American partner, Charles F. Vetter; and Todon Productions, headed by producer Tony Owen with his Hollywood actress wife Donna Reed (Todon was derived from **To**ny-**Don**na).

A cheaper way of giving films that transatlantic feel was to employ American actors who were resident in England, such as William Sylvester, who established his career in the UK before eventually moving back to the States where he worked mainly in television, including the classic 1973 TV movie *Don't Be Afraid of the Dark* and a recurring role in the 1976 sci-fi show *Gemini Man*; and John Crawford, who moved to England during the 1950s for a few years before returning home (in the early 1960s) to much TV work and some memorable character roles in big-screen outings like *Night Moves* (1975) and as the mayor in *The Enforcer* (1976). It was also quite common to employ Canadian actors to play lead characters in 1950s British B thrillers. Two particularly prominent examples were Paul Carpenter and Lee Patterson, both of whom were based in England for many years. Carpenter, an amiable actor and singer, was usually the easy-going hero (often a reporter), but could also play a great villain as evidenced in 1956's *No Road Back*. It would have been too easy to always cast the handsome Patterson as a good guy, and thankfully producers recognized his often quirky style, leading to edgy and flawed characters in films such as *The Flying Scot* (1957) and *Cat and Mouse* (1958). Such was the demand for product with a transatlantic flavor that even Irish actor Dermot Walsh found himself being cast as an American detective in *The Blue Parrot* (1953). Of course, Britain was not without its own homegrown B-movie leading men, the most popular of which included John Bentley, Ronald Howard, Donald Houston, Peter Reynolds and Conrad Phillips. The aforementioned (British-based) Irishman Dermot Walsh was equally popular as a lead in such films. Recognition should also be made of the many talented and reliable character actors, such as Anton Diffring, Ferdy Mayne, Peter Illing, Eric Pohlmann, George Pastell, Marne Maitland and Martin Benson, who played the foreign criminal masterminds populating British B thrillers.

Two standout production companies when it came to making films using Hollywood actors were Tempean Films and Hammer Film Productions. Hammer secured their stateside stars mainly through production deals with the aforementioned U.S.-based Lippert Pictures, while Tempean for the most part worked through then London-based U.S. movie producer Bob Goldstein. (Goldstein had once been a talent scout and vice-president of Universal-International Pictures, for which his twin brother, Leonard, before his untimely death in 1954, had produced films featuring many of the stars—Mark Stevens, Scott Brady, Alex Nicol, etc.—that would later appear in Tempean's output.) Tempean was run by Robert S. Baker and Monty Berman, who also operated under other company names such as Mid-Century Film Productions and Cipa Productions. Baker occasionally directed in the early days, while Berman was cinematographer on the majority of their films. Interviewed in Brian McFarlane's *An Autobiography of British Cinema* (London: Methuen, 1997), Baker spoke about the market demand for thrillers, saying "It's easy to hook an audience with a thriller, not so easy to hook them on a romantic plot. It was demand, basically. Thrillers were easier to sell and therefore easier to set up." Baker and Berman's films were very Americanized, often in the noir style, with the most obvious example being *Impulse* (1954) starring Arthur Kennedy. *Bond of Fear* (1956) stood out as a great example of a B movie shot almost entirely on location. John Gilling, a director and screenwriter, was one of the more noteworthy contributors to Baker and Berman's impressive output. Hammer, the production arm of distributor Exclusive Films, made over two dozen B thrillers prior to their color rebooting of the classic Universal monster movies. Like in the case of Tempean, many of these were in the American style and included several noir offerings, most notably *The House Across the Lake* (1953). The legendary Terence Fisher was a prominent director of Hammer's B thrillers before going on to be one of the main driving forces behind their horror/monster output.

The Danziger brothers (Edward J. Danziger and Harry Lee Danziger) were entrepreneurial American producers who had made a few films in the U.S., including *Jigsaw* (1949) and *So Young So Bad* (1950), before moving to England in the early 1950s. For the next decade, a busy filming schedule yielded many hours of episodic television and dozens of B movies, mostly thrillers, all made swiftly on ultra-low budgets. While never as polished as those of Tempean or Hammer, many of their B pictures remain notable for the ingenuity and resourcefulness of the prolific Brian Clemens who, as chief screenwriter, proved to be one of the brothers' greatest assets. The Danzigers secured Clemens right at the start of his career and provided him with opportunities to hone the creative skills that would later lead to major success, especially on television where he became the driving force behind such classic series as *The Avengers*, *Thriller* and *The Professionals*. Clemens recalled, "It was a learning curve denied to most British writers: the Danzigers nomadically roamed from studio to studio, often inheriting sets from more illustrious productions, and so would come to me and instruct, 'we want a thriller that is set in the Old Bailey, Madame Tussaud's and a submarine!'"[1] The pseudonymous Eldon Howard, in reality one Mrs. Guggenheim (Edward J. Danziger's mother-in-law), often featured alongside Clemens in the writing credits. However, it appears that, for reasons that remain unclear, her involvement was purely nominal, with Clemens himself stating, "I never worked with Eldon Howard and as far as I know she didn't do anything for any script."[2] The Danzigers eventually left the film industry in the early 1960s to concentrate on their other major interest, namely the hotel business. Among their better productions were *The Depraved* (1957), *The Great Van Robbery* (1958), *Return of a Stranger* (1961) and *The Pursuers* (1962); in fact, out of the very few Danziger B thrillers that had theatrical releases in the U.S., *The Great Van Robbery* was probably the widest distributed, playing regularly on double bills (mostly at drive-ins) as support to classics such as *West Side Story* (1961), *Dr. No* (1962) and *Irma La Douce* (1963).

Director Montgomery Tully, whose film work consisted almost exclusively of B movies, made many thrillers including several for Anglo Amalgamated Film Distributors at their Merton Park production unit. The best of these were for producer Alec C. Snowden and included *The Counterfeit Plan* and *Man in the Shadow*, two 1957 offerings with Zachary Scott in tremendously villainous mode. Later, in partnership with producer-writer Maurice J. Wilson, he turned out several efficient thrillers—highlighted by the excellent *The Third Alibi* (1961)—for Eternal Films. Another notable director of B thrillers was the industrious Charles Saunders, who often worked with producer Guido Coen. Among their better collaborations were *Kill Her Gently* (1958), whose title Walter Winchell once amusingly described as "grimly polite,"[3] and *Naked Fury* (1959).

Butcher's Film Distributors (formerly

---

1. Excerpt from Brian Clemens' foreword to an earlier, unfinished incarnation of this book.
2. Told to the author by Brian Clemens in a 1998 interview.
3. From the widely syndicated show business observations of Walter Winchell, in this case taken from the "Broadway Beat" column of the *Sarasota Journal* (October 3, 1958).

known as Butcher's Film Service), who had been around for decades, made many B thrillers from 1956 to 1964 through their own production unit. As was the case with the Danziger productions, very few of the films were released theatrically in the U.S.; of those that were, *The Breaking Point* (1960), under its stateside title *The Great Armored Car Swindle*, had the best distribution, playing mainly at drive-ins as support to such diverse fare as *The Flesh Eaters* (1964) and *Dr. Strangelove* (1964). The Butcher's movies had been pretty much forgotten in England until they were resurrected on late-night television in the 1990s, whereupon viewers haunting the graveyard slots were treated to regular showings of a broadcast package that included brisk offerings such as *Mark of the Phoenix* (1957), *Serena* (1962) and *Smokescreen* (1964). Also in the package was 1959's superior *Cover Girl Killer* (actually a Parroch Films production but for which Butcher's had held distribution rights), which features a pre–*Steptoe and Son* Harry H. Corbett as a serial killer in pebble glasses, a character that fans of the actor had thought lost forever in some dusty film vault. Terry Bishop, the director of that film, which has since achieved semi-cult status, had started in documentaries and subsequently had a short-lived movie career that nevertheless yielded a few interesting and individual B thrillers.

Some of the best British B thrillers were made in the last few years before the heyday of British B movies in general came to an end (around 1966). Vernon Sewell's two 1961 gems *The Man in the Back Seat* and *Strongroom* are almost certainly the director's most accomplished low-budget efforts, while *Tomorrow at Ten* (1962) stands tall among director Lance Comfort's always excellent output. Parroch-McCallum Productions (producer Jack Parsons and actor/writer/producer Neil McCallum) continued the trend of importing U.S. actors in five impressive pictures between 1963 and 1964, the highlights of which—*Walk a Tightrope* and *Do You Know This Voice?*—feature Dan Duryea at his villainous best. Finally, the superb *Act of Murder* (1964) was the standout among the 47 B movies in Merton Park's high-quality and fondly remembered "Edgar Wallace" series (1960–1965).

Queens of the "B" Hive

British B movie thrillers, particularly those in the noir style, offered an impressive array of femme fatales. Visiting Hollywood actresses Hillary Brooke, Barbara Payton and Faith Domergue played them to perfection, but there were many British actresses who were able to give their American counterparts a good run for their money. Among them were one-time "Miss Great Britain" Anne Heywood making a sucker out of an American Army officer in *The Depraved* (1957); the lovely Lisa Daniely using her seductive charms to lure a former trapeze artist into a daring heist in *High Jump* (1958); and Barbara Shelley who, before going on to play the ultimate femme fatale in 1964's Hammer horror *The Gorgon*, had been an evil schemer in both *The End of the Line* (1957) and *Blind Corner* (1963).

1960s to 1970s

Agatha Christie and the Two Best Secret Agents in the World

Agatha Christie's elderly amateur sleuth Miss Marple made her big-screen debut in MGM's 1961 comedy thriller *Murder She Said*, starring the inimitable Margaret Rutherford. The film was directed by George Pollock, who went on to make three more Rutherford/Marple films as well as the similarly styled *Kill or Cure* (1962) with the delightful Terry-Thomas as a blundering private detective. Pollock also directed 1965's *Ten Little Indians*, a hugely entertaining version of one of Christie's most famous stories, for independent producer Harry Alan

Towers. Towers had a knack for picking up rights to popular literary material; to this end he also produced thrillers based on characters created by pulp authors Edgar Wallace and Sax Rohmer, in the latter case including a successful series of five Fu Manchu films. Fu, an evil Chinese mastermind, was supposedly the inspiration for Dr. Julius No, the villain in Ian Fleming's sixth James Bond novel *Dr. No*, which producers Harry Saltzman and Albert R. Broccoli brought to the big screen in 1962. The film was the start of the phenomenally successful Bond franchise, and it wasn't long before producers in Europe and the U.S. jumped on the "superspy" bandwagon, churning out scores of films during the decade; in Europe's case, leading to what became known as the Eurospy genre. *Films and Filming* (November 1962), in trying to make sense of what they called *Dr. No*'s "concoction of sex and sadism," concluded that "the British cinema will never be the same again." Not content with having introduced moviegoers to the best secret agent in the world, Britain was also responsible for *The 2nd Best Secret Agent in the Whole Wide World*, which was the U.S. title of 1965's *Licensed to Kill*, the first in a short-lived series of Bond thriller spoofs starring Tom Adams as a superspy named Charles Vine.

Less regarded than their horror movies, but just as effective in their own way, were the many psychological thrillers produced by the ever-enterprising Hammer Film Productions throughout the 1960s and into the early 1970s. The driving force behind most of these was Jimmy Sangster, whose brilliantly labyrinthine scripts kept audiences guessing about characters' identities and motivations. The first few films were crisply shot in black and white and, although *Psycho* is often cited as their influence, the films owe just as much if not more to the 1955 French thriller *Les Diaboliques* as they do to Hitchcock.

It is also worth mentioning that the exciting, groovy and fashionable quality that made the 1960s the "swinging" sixties was reflected in several thrillers including *Kaleidoscope* (1966), *Hammerhead* (1968) and *Salt & Pepper* (1968).

For Adults Only

The 1970s saw a peak in the more overt type of adult British thriller which mainly featured psychopathic villains (often serial killers) with sexual perversions, voyeuristic tendencies or fetishistic inclinations. This trend had actually started over a decade earlier with examples such as *Peeping Tom* (1960) and *The Very Edge* (1962), as well as some surprisingly effective B movies including *The Impersonator* (1960) and *Don't Talk to Strange Men* (1962). However, by the 1970s, an increasingly lenient censor allowed filmmakers more freedom to explore controversial subject matter, resulting in more sordid and explicit content finding its way into British thrillers. Two notable figures from this era were Brian Clemens and Sidney Hayers. Clemens was the driving force behind the women-in-peril chillers *And Soon the Darkness* (1970) and *Blind Terror* (1971), while Hayers, probably best-known for directing the classic 1962 horror/supernatural movie *Night of the Eagle*, gave us the lurid trio *Assault* (1970), *Revenge* (1971) and *Deadly Strangers* (1974). Alfred Hitchcock also made a contribution with his stylistically old-fashioned, and yet modern—in terms of explicit content—shocker, *Frenzy* (1972).

Director Pete Walker, particularly in his collaborations with writer David McGillivray, challenged the British censor and critics alike, not to mention audiences, with some truly disturbing (for the time) horror thrillers, dealing with subjects such as cannibalism, mental illness and torture. A self-confessed maker of mischief, Walker was at his best when turning establishment figures—such as a judge in *House of Whipcord* (1974) and a priest in *House of Mortal Sin* (1975)—into purveyors of terror. Actress Sheila Keith, who was to Walker what Robert De Niro was to Martin Scorsese, turned in some memorably terrifying performances in films that have since achieved cult status.

Crime Thriller Updates, Action Adaptations and New Interpretations

British crime thrillers were sharply updated in the 1970s, with "X" ratings being handed out left, right and center due to more realistic violence, language and occasional nudity. Gone were the polite law enforcers of the past, these being replaced by the likes of the boozing rough-and-tumble flying squad detectives of the two *Sweeney* movies. Good guys of old were quickly being replaced with a plethora of morally ambiguous characters like the anti-hero Jack Carter in the bleak and brilliant *Get Carter* (1971), which holds its place as the first true modern British gangster thriller. This landmark film, which gave rise to other standout gangster movies such as *The Long Good Friday* (1979), has extended its influence through to 2000's *Sexy Beast* and beyond.

The 1970s also saw many action-adventure thrillers adapted from the works of best-selling authors including Alistair MacLean (*Puppet on a Chain, Fear Is the Key,* etc.), Frederick Forsyth (*The Day of the Jackal* and *The Odessa File*) and Wilbur Smith (*Gold*). Throughout the decade, the steadily declining British film industry resulted in a corresponding decline in the production of British thrillers, but this didn't affect the diversity of material on offer, and before the close of the 1970s we had contributions from directors Sam Peckinpah and Don Siegel, a John Wayne cop movie, the start of a new franchise featuring Agatha Christie's Poirot, and remakes of classics like *The Spiral Staircase, The Big Sleep* and *The Lady Vanishes*.

1

Espionage

Espionage thrillers can be separated into two categories—those that are based on the more realistic activities of those engaged in spying, and those that involve the fantastical adventures of glamorous and indestructible secret agents. This chapter has therefore been split into the respective sections "Spies" and "Super Secret Agents." The "Spies" section, made up mainly of Cold War thrillers but also including some World War II films such as 1955's semi-fictional *The Man Who Never Was*, features everything from double and triple agents, missions behind the Iron Curtain, deadly Soviet spy rings, kidnapped scientists, secret formulas, defections, not to mention depictions of the often boring drudgery and red tape involved in the everyday world of government intelligence departments. Here can be found many adaptations of works by luminaries such as Graham Greene, John Le Carré and Len Deighton. The "Super Secret Agents" section features the thrilling antics of author Ian Fleming's James Bond as well as other super-spies who followed in his wake.

Spies

"Caught in a blaze of intrigue!"

Partly inspired by the fearless hero, Frank Conway, of her young nephew's favorite radio show, British entomologist Frances Gray (Margaret Lockwood) agrees to carry out a **Highly Dangerous** (1950) mission for her government. The assignment entails traveling to an East European country to investigate an installation believed to be breeding insects that could be used for biological warfare. While there, Frances is captured by the secret police and given a truth drug, only to be released after revealing nothing. However, the drug has a strange effect that leaves Frances temporarily believing she is the aforementioned Frank Conway, this giving her the confidence to carry out a daring break-in at the installation to obtain vital insect specimens. Lockwood gives an engaging performance in this light-hearted Eric Ambler-scripted romp, which also notably involves an amiable American reporter (U.S. star Dane Clark) and a sinister secret police chief (Marius Goring).

Set in 1930s London, **Secret People** (1951) features an emotionally charged performance by Valentina Cortesa as Maria, a kind-hearted refugee from a tyrannical South European country who gets drawn into helping in an assassination plot. The target is a visiting dictator named General Galbern (Hugo Schuster), the man responsible for the murder of Maria's pacifist freedom-fighter father back in their homeland; the plotters are a violent revolutionary organization including Maria's old flame and erstwhile ally of her father's, Louis (Serge Reggiani). When a time bomb meant for Galbern kills an innocent woman instead, the conscience-stricken Maria confesses her involvement to the police and is placed in a witness protection-type program to save her from the vengeance-seeking conspirators. Audrey Hepburn, whose next film, *Roman*

Holiday (1953), would catapult her to superstardom, plays Maria's kid sister—a dancer (the actress gets to show off her real-life dancing skills)—who in the end also becomes entangled with the revolutionaries, this having tragic consequences when Maria intervenes.

Some effective London locations feature in the B movie *Escape Route* (1952), in which undercover FBI agent Steve Rossi (Hollywood legend George Raft) arrives in England to track down the mysterious head (Clifford Evans) of an organization responsible for smuggling kidnapped Western scientists behind the Iron Curtain. In what turned out to be her last film role, Sally Gray plays a British Intelligence operative also on the criminal's trail who teams up with Steve (including romantically) for an adventure that culminates in an exciting dockside climax where hero and villain slug it out on a hydraulic elevator platform. Fans of Raft should enjoy the film even though, as somewhat truthfully asserted by the *Monthly Film Bulletin* (January 1953), it's "a poor imitation of an American type second-feature thriller."

Set in Cornwall, *Deadly Nightshade* (1952) features Emrys Jones as John Barlow, an escaped convict on the run who learns of his uncanny resemblance to a local artist named Robert Matthews (also Jones). With the police closing in, Barlow plans to temporarily assume Matthews' identity (which will entail holding the artist captive in his own coastal cottage) but things go awry and he ends up accidentally killing the man. Notwithstanding, Barlow goes ahead with the deception; however, he later learns that Matthews was a communist agent involved in acts of sabotage, and becomes entangled with the man's dangerous cohorts. This fast-paced B movie also stars Zena Marshall as Barlow's ex-girlfriend, who gets involved in the story

Light-hearted capers behind the Iron Curtain.

through a coincidence concerning one of Matthews' sabotage plots, and Joan Hickson as Matthews' sharp-tongued housekeeper. Jones would again play a fugitive convict in the 1962 Edgar Wallace B thriller *On the Run*.

The fairly exciting suspenser **The Net** (1953) unfolds at a heavily guarded British research station where dedicated (to the detriment of his marriage) aviation expert Professor Heathley (James Donald) has developed a high-speed jet aircraft known as the M7. The main thriller aspect involves a doctor (Noel Willman)—actually a foreign agent—at the facility, and the circumstances that lead to him taking part in a test flight with Heathley, whereupon he attempts to steal the M7 by forcing Heathley at gunpoint to fly it behind the Iron Curtain. Phyllis Calvert is top-billed as the otherwise occupied Heathley's neglected wife, who finds temporary romantic distraction in one of her husband's charming colleagues, played in characteristically smooth fashion by Herbert Lom; and Robert Beatty registers strongly as the facility's security chief. Both the special effects and sound effects depicting the M7 in action were highly impressive for their time.

*"No man dared cross him …
or his gunsights!"*

In the lively **Rough Shoot** (1953), an unassuming Joel McCrea plays Bob Taine, an American Lieutenant Colonel in England who becomes involved in a British Intelligence operation to smash an enemy spy ring. Roland Culver plays a top British official in the, as he calls it, "cloak and dagger department," while Herbert Lom steals the show as a flamboyant former Polish commandant in his employ. McCrea's fellow Hollywoodian, Evelyn Keyes, plays Taine's wife, who also gets mixed up in the affair which culminates in the rounding up of the spies at Madame Tussaud's wax museum in London. The title pertains to the film's opening where Taine mistakenly believes he has killed a man while out rough shooting, this being the catalyst for his involvement in the adventure.

At the outset of **Counterspy** (1953), an accountant, Frank Manning (Dermot Walsh), is tricked into taking a package—containing details of a secret metal alloy formula—to an apartment where he finds a dead body. This proves to be just the beginning of an adventure that sees him tangling with a ruthless gang of spies seeking the formula. Manning gets captured by the gang, but not before securing the package by posting it to his home address, which leads to his wife (Walsh's then real-life wife Hazel Court) becoming embroiled in the dangerous shenanigans. This light-hearted B movie, described by the *Monthly Film Bulletin* (September 1953) as "a conventional but quite lively spy thriller," features pleasant performances by the two leads and a spirited finale that takes place in a fake nursing home used by the gang as a cover.

Set in an atmospherically photographed post-war Berlin, **The Man Between** (1953) stars James Mason as Ivo Kern, a haunted former Nazi and now East Sector black marketeer. Previously thought dead by his wife Bettina (Hildegarde Neff), a German national now remarried to British army doctor Martin (Geoffrey Toone) in the Western Sector, Ivo has recently turned up in an attempt—on behalf of racketeer Halendar (Aribert Waescher)—to pressure (via blackmail) Bettina into aiding in the kidnap of one of her husband's colleagues wanted in East Germany. Things are further complicated when Martin's visiting sister, Susanne (Claire Bloom), strikes up a friendship with Ivo, only to be captured by Halendar in mistake for Bettina, on whom further pressure was to have been exerted. When Halendar decides that he can use Susanne in his plan, the not irredeemable Ivo, who has by now decided to give up his life of crime, takes it upon himself to rescue her in the hope that this heroic deed will gain him some leniency with the West Berlin authorities.

The last 40 minutes detail an elaborate

escape to the Western Sector, during which Ivo and Susanne fall in love—but don't expect a happy ending. The striking Neff shines during the first half in a complex role, and Mason and Bloom have great chemistry in all their scenes together. Berlin proves to be just as dramatic a backdrop as had been Belfast and Vienna, respectively, in the director's (Carol Reed) earlier classics *Odd Man Out* (1947) and *The Third Man* (1949).

The most intriguing thing about the B movie *The Night of the Full Moon* (1953) may well be its title, which the plot certainly does not live up to. Made by the same team as *The Straw Man* (another B thriller), the film tells of an American secret agent, Dale Merritt (Philip Saville), who crash-lands his plane in the English countryside while en route to London with a vital formula stolen from a foreign power. Events mainly unfold at a remote farmhouse whose occupants—including the eccentric owner (Everley Gregg), her niece (Kathleen Byron) and the latter's hard-drinking husband (Dermot Walsh)—shelter the agent and, after some initial distrust, attempt to help him escape from pursuing enemy spies who blockade the place. The jovial-mannered character actor George Woodbridge plays a local police constable pivotal to the story's outcome. Reviews at the time were fairly scathing, with the *Kinematograph Weekly* (April 8, 1954) describing the picture as "fifth-rate" as well as "unintentionally funny and seldom thrilling."

> *"Catches you by the throat—
> and never lets go."*

The British-Italian co-production *The Stranger's Hand* (1953) is based on a story by Graham Greene, who also had a hand in the film's production. Eight-year-old Roger

Kathleen Byron in *The Night of the Full Moon* (1953).

(Richard O'Sullivan), the son of divorced parents, is sent by his aunt to a hotel in Venice to be reunited with his father, Major Court (Trevor Howard), a British Security Service agent he has not seen for three years. Some twenty minutes before the reunion, Court is kidnapped by an enemy agent who keeps him drugged while preparing to transport him to an Iron Curtain country. The bulk of the plot concerns the resourceful young boy's attempts to find his father with the help of a sympathetic hotel receptionist (Alida Valli) and her American boyfriend (Richard Basehart), the latter instrumental in Court's eventual rescue. A nice performance by O'Sullivan (a future sitcom star of the 1970s) and some atmospheric locations highlight this otherwise unremarkable affair, whose Italian title is *La mano dello straniero*.

The Master Plan (1954) begins with U.S. Army major Tom Brent (Hollywood's Wayne Morris in his first of five British B thrillers) arriving at NATO headquarters in Central Europe to assist his old friend Colonel Cleaver (Norman Wooland) in connection with security issues. As the story unfolds, Brent's susceptibility to blackouts (the result of a war injury) sees him become easy prey for enemy agents who kidnap and then hypnotize him into photographing top-secret information for them; and there's also a mystery concerning the identity of a traitor at the headquarters. Tilda Thamar has a key role as Cleaver's fiancée in this slow-paced but interesting production based on Harald Bratt's *Operation Northstar*, a teleplay filmed for both British and Canadian TV in 1953, and later for American TV as a 1960 episode of *The United States Steel Hour*. The movie's most interesting of its many double-bill pairings in the U.S. was with *Gow*, a sincere silent-era anthropological documentary (about the disappearing tribal customs of the South Seas Islands) which by the 1950s was being exploited as a "shockumentary" with correspondingly sensational taglines like "see what actually happens at a cannibal sacrificial ceremony!" Also known as *Gow, the Headhunter* and *Cannibal Island*, it's a real curiosity in which *King Kong* makers Merian C. Cooper and Ernest B. Schoedsack were involved as cameramen.

"The track of the monkey led to Mystery.... Mayhem.... Murder!"

In the B movie **Little Red Monkey** (1954), a gang of communist agents is busy assassinating key scientists engaged in the advancement of Western weapons capabilities. One of their intended targets, Dushenko (Arnold Marle), an escapee from behind the Iron Curtain, has arrived in London, from where he is due to be escorted to America by U.S. State Department agent Bill Locklin (a sharp performance by key Hollywood thriller actor Richard Conte). The plot largely details the gang's efforts to eliminate Dushenko, but its main attraction is a gimmicky puzzle involving the titular primate (the mysterious chief assassin's pet), which is sighted at the scene of every killing. Based on a 1953 BBC TV serial of the same name and distinguished by a catchy theme tune, the film also stars the ever-lovely Rona Anderson as a Scotland Yard detective's (Russell Napier) niece who falls in love with Locklin.

Another BBC television serial, *The Teckman Biography*, was adapted for the big screen as **The Teckman Mystery** (1954). British test pilot Martin Teckman (Michael Medwin), supposedly dead after a top-secret aircraft he was flying crashed, is actually alive and well, albeit on the run from subversive foreign agents out to get him for having sabotaged their plans (in which he was initially complicit) to steal the plane. The typically convoluted Francis Durbridge story sees an author (John Justin) become tangled up in the affair when asked to write a biography of the supposedly deceased Teckman. Margaret Leighton has a key role as Teckman's sister, whose coincidental meeting with the author at the film's start proves to not have been so coincidental after all, as is made clear in a dramatic climactic twist.

The brisk B movie **Secret Venture** (1954)

was made back-to-back with, and by the same team—including U.S. star Kent Taylor—as, another B thriller, namely *Track the Man Down*. The impeccably groomed Taylor plays Ted O'Hara, an American adventurer who accidentally comes into possession of a briefcase belonging to a scientist, Professor Henrik (Hugo Schuster), as a result of both men traveling on the same flight to London. Henrik is subsequently kidnapped in order to obtain his new secret jet fuel formula which just happens to be contained—in coded form—in the briefcase, thus leading to O'Hara being sought by the kidnappers. The American is soon embroiled in a dangerous adventure involving international spies, Scotland Yard and Henrik's secretary (Jane Hylton), who may or may not be implicated in the kidnapping. There's some impressive use of London locations including the South Bank area by the River Thames, where a chase across Hungerford Bridge ends in a punch-up between O'Hara and one of the crooks (Martin Boddey) which is nowhere near the "terrifying fight" as promised in the film's pressbook.

Donald Houston stars as sturdy Cornish fisherman Albert Pascoe in the pleasantly diverting B movie **Doublecross** (1955). In exchange for £100, Albert agrees to ferry Dmitri (Anton Diffring), Clifford (Allan Cuthbertson) and Dmitri's wife Anna (Delphi Lawrence) to France, unaware that the trio are engaged in espionage and are planning to smuggle stolen documents (concerning radar predictors) behind the Iron Curtain. During the voyage, Albert's life becomes in danger from Dmitri and Clifford after he learns too much. However, using his wits, he manages to trick the two men, leaving them stranded in a cove from where they can be later picked up by the authorities. He then returns to safety with Anna, who'd decided to have nothing more to do with her husband after discovering he'd killed a man during the theft of the documents. There are some nice touches of humor surrounding Albert's favorite pastime of salmon poaching and the frustrated attempts of a local fisheries officer (a nice turn by William Hartnell) to catch him in the act.

"A simple political thriller of modest pretensions" was how the *Monthly Film Bulletin* (February 1956) described **Flight from Vienna** (1955), a B movie in which Hungarian security chief Sandor Kosice (Theodore Bikel) escapes from the Iron Curtain into Austria seeking political asylum. With nothing to offer the West, he is treated with caution by British Intelligence in Vienna, one of whose operatives (John Bentley) tells him he may be granted asylum in exchange for returning to Hungary and effecting the escape of a scientist who does have something to offer the West. Kosice manages to successfully (if not very excitingly) extract the scientist as well as his own wife (he was unable to bring her the first time around), eventually gaining asylum following a last-ditch attempt on his life by a Hungarian assassin.

*"A thrill-a-minute story
behind today's atomic headlines."*

Sentenced to death for murdering a woman, senior civil servant Robert Pitt (Andre Morell) declares—**They Can't Hang Me** (1955). According to Pitt, who we learn has been a go-between for a ring of spies passing Western secrets into Eastern Europe, the reason they can't hang him is because he has certain information that could be of vital importance to Britain's security. In exchange for this information, which concerns the identity of Britain's most wanted spy as well as the imminent theft of top secret atomic equipment to be smuggled behind the Iron Curtain, Pitt demands that his sentence be annulled. Terence Morgan, as a no-nonsense Scotland Yard Special Branch officer attempting to uncover the information without relying on Pitt, gives a certain drive to the film, which is occasionally hindered by some unnecessary comic relief involving his neglected fiancée (Yolande Donlan).

In the light-hearted B movie **Cloak Without Dagger** (1955), fashion writer Kyra

(Mary Mackenzie) stays at a London hotel where she finds old flame Felix (Philip Friend) working as a floor waiter. During World War II, Felix was a Military Intelligence agent whose attempt to capture a top spy was unintentionally foiled by Kyra. Coincidentally, Kyra sees the very same spy at the hotel and, with the help of the house detective (a dryly humorous Leslie Dwyer), makes amends for the past by becoming instrumental in his capture, learning along the way that Felix is still in fact an agent working undercover on the case. A fairly routine story is enlivened by the two likeable leads, with action alternating between the hotel and a weapons facility from where the spy plans to steal top-secret information.

Based to some extent on true events, ***The Man Who Never Was*** (1955) tells of an ingenious British Naval Intelligence plan designed to fool the Germans about the imminent Allied invasion of Sicily in 1943. The scheme entails the strategic placement of a corpse—with the fictional identity of a Royal Marine officer named "William Martin"—for the Nazis to find, hoping they will be hoodwinked into believing, because of false information contained on the body, that Greece will be invaded instead. The first half depicts in great detail the careful planning and implementation of the scheme, with the thriller elements really kicking in during the second half when O'Reilly, a cunning Irish Nazi spy (Stephen Boyd in his first prominent movie role), is deployed to validate the authenticity of "William Martin" following discovery of the body. Clifton Webb and Robert Flemyng are excellent as the naval officers behind the scheme, and Gloria Grahame has a pivotal role as a woman whose part in the plan (involving the composition of a love letter to be found in the fictional Marine's effects) places her in potential danger from O'Reilly.

"Would his captive mind betray his secret?"

One night, while driving along a lonely English country lane, a man (Derek Farr) sees a body lying in his path, little knowing it has been placed there by a gang lying in wait. Stopping to investigate, he is knocked unconscious and taken away by the gang, but not before his car (with the body from the road placed inside) is set on fire to make it appear as if he has died in a crash. All this happens in the pre-credits sequence of ***The Man in the Road*** (1955), which is followed by the man waking up with amnesia in a nursing home, where he is told he's an accountant named Ivan Mason and shown documentation to prove it. However, it's all in fact part of an elaborate scheme by communist agents aimed at getting the man—actually a scientist called James Paxton—to Russia where his secrets can be extracted by the Soviets. Donald Wolfit, as the mastermind behind the plot, and Cyril Cusack, as an alcoholic doctor, stand out among the solid cast, which also includes U.S. star Ella Raines (in what would be her last film) as a local writer who helps Paxton out of his predicament.

Brussels is the setting for the eventful B movie ***Mark of the Phoenix*** (1957). A murderous gang of spies steal a secret alloy in liquid form and then force a jeweler to mold it into a cigarette case so that it can be smuggled into East Berlin and sold for $1 million. An international jewel thief, Chuck Martin (Sheldon Lawrence), gets caught up in the proceedings when one of the gang members uses him in an attempt to secure the million dollars for himself. Anton Diffring is cast against type as a good guy (a charming Belgian police inspector), and Julia Arnall plays the spy gang boss' (Eric Pohlmann) ex-girlfriend, who falls for Chuck. The title refers to the head of a phoenix engraved on the cigarette case. By the time of its belated 1959 British theatrical release, the film had already been seen on U.S. television, dating at least as far back as October 4, 1957, when it was broadcast on Oklahoma's KWTV as a late-night "Million Dollar Movie."

The opening credits of ***Count Five and Die*** (1957) inform us that the film is "a true story from the annals of the OSS." Major

Derek Farr and Ella Raines in *The Man in the Road* (1956).

Howard (Nigel Patrick) and Captain Ranson (Jeffrey Hunter), representing British and U.S. Military Intelligence respectively, head a unit—using a fake film company as a cover—whose task is to relay certain false information to German Intelligence so as to mislead them regarding the location of the D-Day invasion. Part of the plot involves sending unwitting agents into enemy territory in the hope they will be captured and, under torture, divulge said false information which they themselves have been led to believe is true (see *Circle of Deception* for a more detailed examination of this particular idea). Patrick and Hunter play off each other nicely, and the film, whose action is mostly confined to interior sets, also stars Swiss actress Annemarie Duringer as the unit's radio operator (actually a German spy).

The Man Who Wouldn't Talk (1957) begins with two Americans—scientist Dr. Frank Smith (Anthony Quayle) and secret agent Eve Trent (Zsa Zsa Gabor)—traveling to London on a government mission to obtain vital information from Professor Horvad (Leonard Sachs), an Iron Curtain scientist attending a London conference. After receiving the information (detailing the development of a vaccine to counteract a supercharged virus which Horvad regrets having helped the Russians create), Smith, who has promised to relay it no one except a specified scientist in the U.S., finds himself charged with murder when Eve is shot dead in mysterious circumstances. Top-billed Anna Neagle plays a brilliant attorney taking up Smith's defense, a tough task owing to the latter's initial refusal to take the witness stand as this could mean revealing the scientific secrets and breaking his promise to Horvad. A satisfying conclusion (involving a flashback that reveals the truth about Eve's shooting) and some engrossing courtroom scenes compensate for an overall lack of excitement and suspense.

By the time he appeared in ***The Secret Man*** (1958), U.S. actor Marshall Thompson was working mostly in television, where he would eventually find lasting fame in the long-running series *Daktari*. In what is the least remembered of his three British B movies for independent filmmakers Richard Gordon and Charles F. Vetter's Amalgamated Productions/Producers Associates (the other two being the cheesy but undeniably entertaining sci-fi flicks *Fiend Without a Face* [1957] and *First Man into Space* [1958]), Thompson plays Canadian physicist Dr. Clifford Mitchell, inventor of the Q7 missile at Britain's Rushwell research station. The story sees Mitchell recruited (in rather unorthodox fashion) by Scotland Yard's Special Branch to help investigate leakages at Rushwell in an attempt to identify the mysterious boss of a spy ring. Anne Aubrey and Magda Miller provide contrasting feminine appeal as Mitchell's fiancée and a blonde spy respectively, but even they couldn't stop the film from receiving the dreaded "BOMB" rating in *Leonard Maltin's Movie Guide*, which referred to it as "unremittingly dull."

The Two-Headed Spy (1958) of the title is Alex Scotland (Jack Hawkins), a real-life character on whose exploits this well-paced adventure is based. A British Army officer and Intelligence operative, Scotland, having infiltrated the German Army during World War I, has managed to keep up his deception to become a respected high-ranking general in the Nazi war machine. Hawkins is brilliant in a suitably somber performance as the clever spy who, throughout World War II, relays invaluable information to the Allies. Felix Aylmer and Gia Scala play Alex's contacts, he an antique clock dealer who gets arrested and tortured to death by the Gestapo, and she an attractive singer who also ends up dead, this time at the hands of Alex's young aide (Erik Schumann) after he discovers his boss' duplicity. In a tense finale, Alex is forced to make a daring escape behind British lines, and finally makes it safely back to England after an absence of many years.

*"Mystery with a twist of menace ...
and laced with laughter!"*

Beautifully shot on authentic Cuban locations just after the Castro takeover, but set during Batista's reign, ***Our Man in Havana*** (1959) is a wry comedy thriller scripted by Graham Greene from his own imaginative novel of the same name. Alec Guinness is on fine form as Englishman Jim Wormold, an unassuming Havana-based vacuum cleaner salesman and single father who, struggling to support his extravagant teenage daughter, allows himself to be recruited into the British Secret Service for $150 per month plus expenses. Left to his own devices, and with no idea how to operate as a spy, Wormold creates a fictitious network of sub-agents for whom he claims regular salaries, while also sending false intelligence—including diagrams (for which he gains inspiration from vacuum cleaner designs) of a supposed enemy installation in the mountains—to his London paymasters. Delighted by his progress, they in turn send Wormold his own secretary-assistant (Hollywood's Maureen O'Hara), but it's not long before his deception begins to unravel, and the so far lighthearted shenanigans take a dark turn when Wormold becomes targeted for death by an enemy assassin. The great cast also includes Burl Ives and Ernie Kovacs in crucial roles, and there's some pleasant music courtesy of The Hermanos Deniz Cuban Rhythm Band.

In ***Beyond the Curtain*** (1960), Karin Von Seefeldt (Eva Bartok), an East German refugee now working as an air stewardess, finds herself back behind the Iron Curtain when her plane is forced down for violating air space. Obligated by the authorities to remain in East Germany, she ends up being used by the secret police in their efforts to locate her brother (George Mikell), wanted for his role in an attempt to overthrow the

A British flying officer (Richard Greene) rescues his girlfriend (Eva Bartok) from East Germany in *Beyond the Curtain* (1960).

government. The latter stages of the story see Karen rescued by her English boyfriend, a flying officer played by Richard Greene in his first film role following a four-year stint playing the hero in TV's *The Adventures of Robin Hood*. Directed without frills by Compton Bennett (who'd helmed a couple of *Robin Hood*'s final season episodes), this engaging B movie also features Marius Goring as an old family friend of Karin's found to be in league with the secret police.

Another B movie, this one not so engaging, is the leaden and excessively talky **Highway to Battle** (1960), which unfolds in London shortly before the outbreak of World War II. The thin plot has two Gestapo agents (Ferdy Mayne and Peter Reynolds) arrive in London to investigate a German diplomat's (George Mikell from the previous film) failure to return to Berlin when scheduled. The diplomat, a disillusioned Nazi Party member, has gone into hiding after taking the decision to defect, and the agents are soon attempting to track him down lest he should leak secrets about Hitler's plan to invade Poland. Much of the story takes place in London's German Embassy, where the ambassador (Gerard Heinz) also runs afoul of the agents after they correctly sense a slight wavering in his once staunch support for the Führer.

Mikell also appeared, albeit in a tiny uncredited part (as a German officer), in the compelling *Circle of Deception* (1960), another World War II story this time set in 1944 just prior to the D-Day landings. In one of his earliest films, Bradford Dillman gives an emotionally charged performance as Paul Raine, a Canadian lieutenant picked by British Intelligence for a special mission behind enemy lines in occupied France. What he doesn't know is that the plan is for him to be captured by the Germans and tortured to the point where he will crack and reveal information which he has been led to believe is true, but which is in fact false and intended to mislead the enemy regarding the Allied invasion. The cold-hearted intelligence chief (Harry Andrews) in charge of operations tasks his assistant, Lucy Bowen (actress-model Suzy Parker), with getting to know Paul so as to assess the man's psychological suitability for the assignment. Lucy and Paul soon fall in love (Dillman and Parker actually hooked up for real and went on to marry in 1963) but are forced to separate when it comes time for the latter to embark on his mission, whereupon he is captured as planned.

The eventual torture scenes are quite grueling for the time and involve a powerful moment where Paul decides to end his life with a standard-issue cyanide pill (concealed in a false tooth), only to discover it is ineffective—another trick by his British masters to ensure he will submit to his captors. Events are told in one long flashback bookended by scenes in Tangier involving an emotional post-war reunion between Paul, now a broken man due to his experience, and Lucy, who had always held moral qualms about the mission. The makers, 20th Century–Fox, had previously dramatized the story (by Alec Waugh) as a 1956 episode—titled "Deception"—of their U.S. TV show *The 20th Century–Fox Hour*, with Trevor Howard and Linda Darnell in the leads.

A small-scale production from the Boulting brothers, **Suspect** (1960) centers around a London research laboratory where Professor Sewell (Peter Cushing on fine form) and his team of scientists—including Bob Marriott (Tony Britton) and Lucy Byrne (Virginia Maskell)—have developed virulent bugs that could be utilized to stamp out the bubonic plague and typhus. Having decided to publish the findings, Sewell is shocked when the government's Ministry

Bradford Dillman stars in a gripping World War II story.

of Defence, worried that the bugs may end up being used for germ warfare by a hostile power, effectively makes publication impossible by placing the research on the Official Secrets List. A foolhardy attempt by Bob to secretly defy the government almost results in the findings getting into the hands of a dangerous spy network, which he ultimately becomes instrumental in smashing. The movie, to some extent correctly noted by the *Monthly Film Bulletin* (December 1960) as resembling "nothing so much as a prestige TV play," features an intense performance by Ian Bannen in a pivotal role as Lucy's former fiancé, now a bitter and dependent double amputee attempting to scupper a developing romance between Lucy and Bob. That wonderful character actor, Thorley Walters, shines as a bumbling but wily security agent keeping tabs on the scientists in case of any leaks.

The B movie *The Long Shadow* (1961) starts with the escape of a mother, her young son and the latter's nursemaid from communist Hungary (amid an uprising) into Austria, during which the mother is shot dead. The boy, whose father is a Hungarian rebel leader named Korbanyi, is subsequently sought by Cernik (Jan Konrad) of the Russian Embassy in Vienna, who wants to use the child to either negotiate with or blackmail Korbanyi. Susan Hampshire plays a Swedish Red Cross worker protecting the boy after the nursemaid is captured by Cernik's agents, and the adventure also involves two heroic Americans, one of them an agent (Bill Nagy) working on instructions from the American consulate and the other a foreign correspondent (John Crawford). *Leonard Maltin's Movie Guide* awarded the film a paltry one-and-a-half-star rating, calling it a "flabby espionage caper."

*"They seek the awesome
secrets of destruction!"*

Extensive London locations are used to great effect in director Robert Tronson's vérité-style B movie *The Traitors* (1962). A British Intelligence operative (the authoritative Patrick Allen) and an American NATO security officer (James Maxwell) team up to spearhead the uncovering of a communist spy ring, whose existence is discovered following the leakage of atomic-powered rocket engine secrets from a research facility. Essentially a procedural, the film goes into great detail regarding the surveillance and pursuit of the spies, whose number include a doctor (Jeffrey Segal) and a respected Foreign Office official (Mark Singleton), with events leading to an exciting climactic bust at a public swimming pool. The production was deemed so realistic that the British Security Service reportedly asked for a copy in order to study its depiction of spy-tailing techniques.

Dead Man's Evidence (1962) stars Conrad Phillips as David Baxter, a British Intelligence MI7 agent assigned to investigate a dead frogman found on a beach in Ireland. A distinctive ring on the body suggests the man is a fellow agent who'd gone missing while working with Baxter on a mission to root out a traitor in the department. During his inquiries, Baxter meets, among others, the woman who found the body (Jane Griffiths) and a news photographer (Veronica Hurst). An intriguing and complex series of events finally lead to the revelation that the assignment has all along been an elaborate set-up by MI7 designed to expose the real traitor—Baxter himself! All in all, a well-filmed B movie with good performances (especially Phillips playing against type) and a script that the *Monthly Film Bulletin* (October 1962) noted "scatters its red herrings ingeniously."

A British-German co-production, *The Devil's Agent* (1962) is an episodic affair that begins in Austria, 1950, and concerns Viennese wine salesman and ex–Army Intelligence officer George Droste (a fine performance by Peter Van Eyck). After getting tricked by old friend Baron Von Staub (Christopher Lee) and his sister Countess Cosimano (Helen Cherry)—both Soviet agents—into running an illicit errand for them, George ends up held by U.S. Intelligence and blackmailed into joining the communists as a double agent for the Americans. There follows a series of adventures, including daring missions in Budapest and Berlin, during which George sells both sides out, leading to him being marked for death by the Russians. Be prepared for a decidedly downbeat ending, although some shorter versions (including the 77-minute British theatrical cut) conclude on a happy note. The film, whose German title is *Im Namen des Teufels*, also stars Macdonald Carey as a U.S. Intelligence chief and Marianne Koch as a Hungarian refugee with whom George falls in love.

Despite some initial intrigue, ***The Man Who Finally Died*** (1962) becomes, as the *Monthly Film Bulletin* (December 1963) put it, an "exceedingly complicated thriller" that "scarcely warrants the trouble in working out its plot convolutions." The always watchable Stanley Baker plays jazz musician Joe Newman, a naturalized German-born British citizen lured via a mysterious telephone call—supposedly from his father, Kurt Deutsch, a German officer he thought had died on the Russian front during World War II—to the sleepy Bavarian town of Königsbaden. The phone call was actually engineered by a crafty communist agent (Niall MacGinnis) who wishes to use Joe as a pawn to locate one of two escapees from East Germany. The escapee in question is either Deutsch (it transpires he did not die in the war after all but had been taken prisoner by the Russians) or a famous rocket scientist going under Deutsch's identity; if in fact the latter, then the communists want the man back behind the Iron Curtain. There's lots of mystery involving the efforts of certain townsfolk, including an ex-Nazi doctor (Peter Cushing) and a belligerent police chief (Eric Portman), to protect the fugitive (ultimately revealed to be the scientist), this involving staging a fake funeral for him under Deutsch's name, which causes much consternation to Joe as he tries to find out what became of the real Deutsch.

Baker looks suitably cool (his character has a thing about wearing dark glasses—including indoors) even if his performance is less compelling than usual, and the excellent cast also includes Mai Zetterling who, although playing a key role, is unfortunately given very little to do. Direction by Quentin Lawrence is proficient (he had also directed the likewise titled 1959 ATV television serial on which the film was based), and the black-and-white photography is never less than striking.

"Meet secret agent 909 ... as he blasts open a master plan of counter-espionage!"

In the unpretentious and well-structured B movie ***Master Spy*** (1962), Iron Curtain scientist Boris Turganev (a suitably impassive Stephen Murray) requests and is granted political asylum in England while visiting the country for a conference. He is subsequently permitted to continue his work in neutron physics at a rural research facility but is soon (as was his plan all along) leaking information to local landowner Paul Skelton (Alan Wheatley in familiar villainous mode), actually a communist spy master. Circumstances involving two researchers (June Thorburn and John Carson) lead to the capture of Skelton and Turganev, this being followed by a neat twist revealing the latter's true role in the affair. Some good atmosphere is provided by scenes in and around the research facility.

Another B movie, ***Echo of Diana*** (1963), tells an intriguing though often confusing story about a network of spies attempting to capture a British Security agent, Phillip Scott (Dermot Walsh), on behalf of an Eastern European government from which he has gained vital secret information. Walsh is billed as a "guest artist" and doesn't actually appear until the end of the film, his character spending the preceding time undercover after faking his own death in a plane crash (depicted in the pre-credits sequence). The focus of the plot is Phillip's wife Joan (Australian actress Betty McDowall), who for security reasons cannot be told that her husband is alive and ends up getting abducted by the spies in an effort to draw him out. Also starring are McDowall's fellow Australian, Vincent Ball, as a journalist who's not all he seems, and Geoffrey Toone as a British Security chief. The "Diana" of the title is part of a coded message in a newspaper ad used by the chief to impart information about Phillip to fellow agents.

In the comedy thriller **Hide and Seek** (1963), Ian Carmichael plays David Garrett, a Cambridge astrophysicist who, through an ingenious scheme involving (among others) a Londoner named Maggie (Janet Munro), is lured to a mansion on the Yorkshire coast. There, he comes face to face with the mastermind behind the scheme, Marek (Curt Jürgens). Having already sold Garrett to a country behind the Iron Curtain, Marek now plans to have him forcibly transferred there in a submarine. However, helped by Maggie, who has by now fallen for him, Garrett manages to outsmart the villain and remain firmly on British soil. Director Cy Endfield tries hard but in the end is defeated by a script which *Films and Filming* (August 1964) called "neither comic nor thrilling."

The efficient B movie **Shadow of Fear** (1963) stars Paul Maxwell as American oil prospector Bill Martin who, while preparing to fly to London from Baghdad, is persuaded by a British Intelligence agent to carry with him a vital secret message for delivery to MI5. Upon arriving in London, Bill is tricked into handing over the message (concerning Middle East rocket bases) to a gang of spies headed by Sharp (John Arnatt). Ensuing events see Bill and his girlfriend Barbara (Clare Owen) agreeing to become decoys in a dangerous MI5 plan designed to trap the gang. The film, which *The Daily Cinema* (January 27–28, 1964) described as a "neatly contrived cloak-and-dagger yarn," also stars Eric Pohlmann as the spy network's contact in Baghdad.

The real-life Portland spy case is the basis for **Ring of Spies** (1963), a semidocumentary directed with a keen eye for detail by Robert Tronson. Henry Houghton (a top-notch performance by Bernard Lee), a disgruntled employee at the British Navy's Underwater Weapons Establishment, is targeted by a Soviet espionage network who persuade him to betray top-secret information. In order to obtain the necessary data, Henry plays up to and secures the cooperation of spinster Elizabeth Gee (Margaret Tyzack), the person responsible for the keys to a safe containing the secrets. In exchange for large sums of cash, Houghton and Gee are soon handing over documents to master spy Gordon Lonsdale (a smooth William Sylvester), who photographs them and arranges for the information to be sent to Russia via a powerful transmitter. However, the authorities get wind of the traitorous goings-on as a result of Henry splashing around his new-found income. The film is notable for making use of locations (in and around London) where the real spies actually operated.

"The most fantastic spy story ever revealed!"

In her review for New York's *Daily News* (June 4, 1964), Kate Cameron concluded that **The Secret Door** (1963) "shows signs of having been made cheaply and in a hurry." The U.S.-British B movie was produced in association with Fifeshire Motion Pictures, owned by super-successful broadcast industry figure Joel Aldred, a Canadian who'd been one of America's highest paid and most recognized television commercial announcers (he also provides some narration for the movie). The producer—also a skilled vocalist and writer of the title song, "Lisboa"—is another Canadian, Charles Baldour, with the film's main star, Hollywood's Robert Hutton, acting as associate producer. (As it happens, Hutton and Baldour were brothers-in-law through their respective spouses, siblings Bridget and Betty Carr.)

Things begin in America just after

the Pearl Harbor attack in 1941, with convicted safecrackers Joe Adams (Hutton) and Edward Brentano (Peter Allenby) being released into the custody of U.S. Naval Intelligence. The idea is that their special skills be put to use on a dangerous mission that will require them cracking open a safe at the Japanese Embassy in Lisbon to photograph the Japanese naval code. Once in Lisbon (the film was shot on authentic locations there), a plan to access the Embassy requires the two men to crawl through a labyrinth of sewers, a sequence about which Hutton (in a quote from Allied Artists' pressbook) said: "I've had to do a lot of things in picture-making, but crawling through that sewer—it seemed it was 10 miles long, but actually I only covered about a quarter of a mile in it—was the toughest job I've been called upon to do." Sandra Dorne plays Sonia, a duplicitous Russian woman trading in stolen government secrets who helps in the plan in order to get the naval code for her own ends, which involves financially baiting Brentano into double-crossing Adams. Her own subsequent double-cross of Brentano has disastrous consequences for both of them, not to mention her equally duplicitous husband (Peter Illing). Adams endures being captured and held aboard a Japanese freighter before ultimately making it to safety and securing a presidential pardon.

Hutton, who several years earlier had made two films—the engagingly bizarre sci-fi horror flick *The Man Without a Body* and the thriller *Man from Tangier* (both B movies dated 1957)—in England, would later semi-permanently move there as a result of *The Secret Door*. In an interview conducted by Tom Weaver (published in *Science Fiction Stars and Horror Heroes* [Jefferson, NC: McFarland, 1991]), Hutton explained: "After shooting the picture [*The Secret Door*] we had to go up to London to do the scoring and editing and so forth, and while I was there I was offered quite a bit of work. And so I stayed on." His first film during that stay was another B thriller, *The Sicilians* (1964), although he's probably better remembered from the period for his horror and sci-fi fare like *The Vulture* (1966), *Torture Garden* (1967) and *They Came from Beyond Space* (1967).

In the spoofy **Hot Enough for June** (1964), bumbling out-of-work writer Nicholas Whistler (a delightful Dirk Bogarde) accepts a job with a glass manufacturing company and is sent on a business trip to Prague behind the Iron Curtain. However, the glass company is actually a front for a British Intelligence department, who are manipulating Whistler into acting as their unwitting courier in a covert mission. Starting out as a parody of the James Bond franchise (there's even a direct reference to 007), the film later adopts a more serious tone when Whistler learns the truth and goes on the run after falling afoul of Czech security services. Robert Morley and Leo McKern are entertaining as, respectively, a pompous British Intelligence officer and gruff Czech police chief, while Sylva Koscina plays the latter's beautiful daughter and romantic interest for Whistler. A 78-minute cut was used for theatrical release in the U.S., where the movie is known as *Agent 8¾* (some early publicity material bore the title *Agent 008¾*).

> "His past was dangerous…
> his future EXPLOSIVE!"

The rare B movie *The Runaway* (1964) seems to have had its largest audience in Australia where, under the title *Escape from Fear*, it frequently played from 1965 through to the early 1970s as support to films such as *Major Dundee* (1965) and *The Green Berets* (1968). In a rare leading role, bit-part actor Alex Gallier plays Andrian Peshkin, a Polish-born industrial chemist working at Trans Ocean Laboratories in England who stumbles on a formula for a synthetic chemical used by the Russians in ballistic missiles but as yet unperfected by the British. This leads to him being menaced by a Soviet hatchet man (Denis Shaw) sent to ensure that the formula will never become of

Cold War spy spoofery with Dirk Bogarde on fine form.

benefit to Britain, and also to avenge Peshkin's betrayal in 1940 when, as a Paris-based Russian agent, he had absconded to South America with a large sum of Soviet cash. In what was her final role, Greta Gynt gets top-billing as Peshkin's wife, and the story, partly told in flashback, also prominently involves an MI5 officer played by Paul Williamson. One of two B thrillers (see also *Delayed Flight*) made back-to-back by producer Bill Luckwell at the then Hammer Films-owned Bray Studios.

Even if *The New York Times* (December 3, 1964) was correct in calling it "thumpingly mediocre," **Night Train to Paris** (1964) is nevertheless worth a watch if only for the novelty of seeing Leslie Nielsen in a British B movie. Set on New Year's Eve, the fast-moving story sees London-based ex–U.S. Intelligence agent Alan Holiday (Nielsen) become responsible for delivering a computer tape (containing vital Western European defense secrets) to Paris on an overnight boat train full of partygoers. Eric Pohlmann plays a pursuing enemy agent who murders one of said partygoers so as to use their bear costume as a disguise, with a ludicrous climactic fight between Alan and the bear-suited villain anticipating an equally ridiculous grapple between Nielsen and a grizzly in the "nature-on-the-rampage" thriller *Day of the Animals* (1977). Also starring is Alizia Gur (1960's Miss Israel) as a femme fatale. Produced by Lippert Films for 20th Century–Fox, the picture, which *TNYT* went on to say "adds up to a mighty dull choo-choo," commonly featured on U.S. double bills with other 1964 Fox fare such as *The Visit* and *Goodbye Charlie*. However, its most apt booking was as locomotive bedfellow to *Von Ryan's Express* (1965) on an early October 1965 double bill at the Portola Entertainment Center (Portola, California).

Harry Palmer

Harry Palmer, a bespectacled working-class British Intelligence operative with a liking for cookery and classical music, was played by Michael Caine in a trio of films based on novels by Len Deighton. Colonel Ross, the Machiavellian head of Palmer's

A rare leading role for bit-part actor Alex Gallier in *The Runaway* (1964).

department at London's Ministry of Defence, is played in all three films by Guy Doleman.

The first and best of the trilogy, ***The Ipcress File*** (1965), features many of the personnel (including producer Harry Saltzman and composer John Barry) from the James Bond films, while at the same time successfully achieving its intended goal of being the antithesis of that franchise. The story concerns a plot by communist agents in England to abduct and brainwash important scientists so as to render them useless in their respective fields of expertise. Palmer is assigned to investigate, which entails being seconded to a department run by Major Dalby (a superb Nigel Green), and ends up kidnapped and subjected to some of the brainwashing himself. His eventual escape leads to a neat twist in which a key character is unmasked as a traitor in league with the enemy agents.

In contrast to the excitement, glamour, fast cars and beautiful people found in the Bond universe, the world of *The Ipcress File* is one of drudgery, red tape, public transport and civil servants aspiring for a pay rise. However, in its own way it's just as stylized as the Bond films, and is beautifully photographed by Otto Heller with some interesting psychedelic visuals during the brainwashing scenes. Caine gives an iconic performance, and among all the intrigues are some interesting observations about the social disparity between the rank-and-file Palmer (we learn he's an army sergeant effectively being forced to undertake intelligence work through blackmail in connection with past shady activities) and his upper-middle-class superiors. Gordon Jackson and Sue Lloyd are on fine form as Palmer's fellow operatives, the latter also providing some romantic interest, and the evocative and influential soundtrack, which features the distinctive

Michael Caine (right) and Nigel Green in *The Ipcress File* (1965).

sound of the Hungarian dulcimer (cimbalom), remains the quintessential spy movie score. If anyone was wondering, IPCRESS is the acronym for the brainwashing technique (in full, the Induction of Psychoneuroses by Conditioned Reflex under Stress).

The second film of the trio, **Funeral in Berlin** (1966), is also the most complex, featuring two intriguing and cleverly intertwined plot lines. Firstly, Palmer is sent to Berlin to organize the defection of Soviet Intelligence officer Colonel Stok (a gloriously hammy Oscar Homolka), this involving Palmer's contact Johnny Vulkan (Paul Hubschmid) and a racketeer, Kreutzman (Gunter Meisner), the latter paid by Palmer to smuggle the colonel out of East Berlin in a coffin; however, the whole defection saga is revealed to be a ruse by Stok in a plan to eliminate Kreutzman. Secondly, identity papers supplied to Palmer in connection with the "defection" lead to the discovery that Vulkan is not all he seems, and the story shifts gears into a race between Israeli Intelligence agents (their leader played by Eva Renzi) and an ex–Nazi (actually Vulkan) to get hold of said identity papers, which can provide access to a Swiss bank account holding over $2 million in Jewish funds stolen by the Germans during World War II. The witty and well-constructed screenplay is expertly directed by Guy Hamilton (*Goldfinger*), and there are plenty of atmospherically bleak Berlin locations.

The final film, **Billion Dollar Brain** (1967), concerns a plot by communist-hating Texas oil magnate General Midwinter (a larger-than-life Ed Begley) to instigate, and then support militarily with his own private army, an anti–Soviet uprising in Latvia which could spark off World War III. Palmer, having left the intelligence service, is now working as a low-rent private detective (his dingy office has a photo of Humphrey Bogart), but it's not long before he's blackmailed back into service by Colonel Ross in order to infiltrate Midwinter's organization. Also starring are Karl Malden as a duplicitous operative of Midwinter's, Françoise Dorléac (in her final role before her tragic death) as a beguiling Russian agent, and Oscar Homolka reprising his role as Colonel Stok from the previous film. The "Billion Dollar Brain" is a sophisticated supercomputer (at the heart of Midwinter's operations) whose workings we are first introduced to in the superb title sequence by James Bond titles designer Maurice Binder, who can't resist putting Palmer in a couple of 007-like poses. Director Ken Russell, in what was just his second feature film, steers a clear course through the frequently complex goings-on, and there's an exhilarating climax—inspired by "The Battle on the Ice" sequence from Sergei Eisenstein's 1938 historical epic *Alexander Nevsky*—in which Midwinter's troops are destroyed by Russian forces on Latvia's frozen wastelands.

Caine returned as Harry Palmer in the internationally produced mid–1990s TV movies *Bullet to Beijing* and *Midnight in Saint Petersburg*, neither of which is based on Len Deighton material.

> *"The book the world could not lay down is now a motion picture."*

"Discourages us from supposing that the life of a real spy might just possibly be exciting" was one of Gordon Gow's (author of *Suspense in the Cinema*) observations in his *Films and Filming* (March 1966) review of **The Spy Who Came in from the Cold** (1965), an intelligent, powerful and totally engrossing tale that really gets down to the nitty-gritty of Cold War espionage. The complex but never confusing story sees British Intelligence agent Alec Leamas (Richard Burton) pose as a defector as part of a scheme to bring down a brilliant East German counter-espionage chief (Peter Van Eyck) by convincing the latter's second-in-command (Oskar Werner) that his boss is a traitor. However, all is not as it seems, and Alec is in fact being used as a pawn by his British controllers, whose real objective is revealed in a surprising twist. Burton, in an Oscar-nominated performance, is mesmerizing while at the same time being careful to never dominate the proceedings, thus allowing plenty of room for his co-stars to shine; among these are Claire Bloom as a naïve assistant librarian and member of the British Communist Party, who becomes another pawn in the plot, and Cyril Cusack as Alec's Intelligence chief. There's some great dialogue, particularly during an angry and self-hating admission by Alec about the squalid realities of the Cold War game, and the whole thing is masterfully photographed in black and white by Oswald Morris.

In **City of Fear** (1966), Canadian journalist Mike Foster (Paul Maxwell) is cleverly tricked by communist agents into helping a scientist (Albert Lieven) escape from Hungary, the plan being for Mike to be arrested so that he can then be used as an exchange hostage for an important Russian spy held by the Americans. Described by *The Daily Cinema* (October 10, 1966) as "implausible but mildly suspenseful," the film gives top billing to Hollywood's Terry Moore as a beautiful fashion expert becoming mixed up in the adventure while on business in Budapest. Harry Alan Towers, who wrote and produced, later reused the *City of Fear* title for a 2000 straight-to-video production which again featured a journalist in Eastern Europe but this time with a different storyline.

The Quiller Memorandum (1966), a somewhat simplified adaptation of Elleston Trevor's novel of the same name (also known as *The Berlin Memorandum*), is highlighted by superb location work, a haunting atmosphere and a beautiful John Barry score. A rather miscast though still very good George Segal stars as Quiller, a secret agent working for British Intelligence to uncover the headquarters of a neo–Nazi group in Berlin. The head of the group, Oktober (Max Von Sydow), in turn uses Quiller as a pawn in an attempt to discover the location of the latter's control base, run by Pol (Alec Guinness, armed with some of the best lines from Harold Pinter's screenplay). There's a brilliantly filmed car-tailing sequence (that thankfully does not rely on the usual back projection effects), and the film builds considerable suspense in the extended and well-choreographed climax in which our hero outwits several of Oktober's henchmen to get safely back to base. The enigmatic Senta Berger plays a schoolteacher helping (and romancing) our hero, although there is much more to her character than initially meets the eye. The Quiller character was later played by Michael Jayston in the 1975 BBC TV series *Quiller*.

A strong James Mason performance is the driving force behind the slow but absorbing ***The Deadly Affair*** (1966), an adaptation of John Le Carré's first novel *Call for the Dead* but with the lead character's name changed from George Smiley to Charles Dobbs due to rights issues. Circumstances (involving his dismissive superior) lead to aging British Intelligence operative Dobbs (Mason) initiating his own private investigation into what he deems the suspicious death—officially determined to be suicide—of top Foreign Office official Samuel Fennan (Robert Flemyng). Helped by a colleague (Kenneth Haigh) and a tough retired police inspector (Harry Andrews), Dobbs begins to unravel the truth—that Fennan was murdered in connection with having discovered his wife's (Simone Signoret) involvement in a communist spy network. Events lead to a clever trap being set for the network's mysterious leader, whose suspected presence in London just happens to coincide with a visit to the capital by Dobbs' old friend Dieter Frey (Maximilian Schell), a one-time Allied agent under Dobbs' command during World War II.

The film's original British "X" rating was probably due to the one or two instances of brutal violence, the most startling of which comes when the normally staid Dobbs suddenly transforms into a deadly unarmed killing machine in the tense climax. Andrews and Signoret are both excellent, with the latter providing emotional gravitas as a world-weary concentration camp survivor, while the expert photography and carefully chosen London locations combine to create an appropriately dreary atmosphere over which Quincy Jones' bossa nova score works surprisingly well. The only weakness is the tiresome depiction of Dobbs' troubled home life with a younger and serially unfaithful wife (Harriet Andersson), one of whose affairs explains the movie's title.

> *"He played both ends against the middle ... and came out the only authentic hero-villain of World War II!"*

Set during World War II and based on real-life events, the Anglo-French co-production ***Triple Cross*** (1966) tells the incredible tale of how Eddie Chapman (Christopher Plummer), a cocksure British safecracker with the notorious "Gelignite Gang," becomes a spy for German Intelligence before then becoming a double agent for the British. During his exploits, Chapman fools the Nazis enough to be awarded an Iron Cross and ultimately supplies the British with crucial information that helps save London from a V-1 rocket attack. Director Terence Young had previously made three James Bond films, so it's no surprise to find Chapman possessing a "Bondian" prowess with the ladies (one of them a beautiful countess played by Romy Schneider); in fact, even the title music conjures up the 007 franchise. However, none of this suits the story (taken from the 1953 book *The Eddie Chapman Story* by Frank Owen), and the film is mostly underwhelming despite a decent performance by Plummer. Yul Brynner appears in a supporting role as Chapman's German intelligence handler.

Brynner's next film saw him take the lead role—or more precisely, roles—as ***The Double Man*** (1967), an entertaining yarn nicely filmed in the Austrian Tyrol. The charismatic actor stars as Dan Slater, a CIA agent who travels to the picturesque Austrian resort of St. Anton upon news of his teenage son's death there in an apparent skiing accident. In fact, the young man was murdered by communist agents in order to lure Slater to the resort, the idea being to liquidate him and put in his place a plastic surgery–created double so as to infiltrate the CIA. Slater manages to avoid his planned demise and spends the rest of the film pursued by the agents, including his double. Anton Diffring plays the mastermind behind the scheme, while other key roles are filled by Britt Ekland and Clive Revill. The latter, as an ex–British Intelligence operative and old friend of Slater's, features in the tense finale during which he holds both the real and fake Slaters at gunpoint, unable to tell who is who; in a neat twist, the double gives himself away by saying something the real Slater would never say.

Van Heflin is well cast in *The Man Outside* (1967) as William Maclean, a world-weary and wrongfully (as it happens) discredited CIA agent in London. The particularly convoluted plot has Maclean become embroiled in shady acquaintance George Venaxas' (Ronnie Barker) scheme to sell a defector—a top man in Soviet International Intelligence recently smuggled into the country—to the CIA for $50,000. A dangerous adventure ensues, during which Maclean is sought by Scotland Yard after being framed for a murder by a Russian security chief (Peter Vaughan) intent on capturing the defector. Also starring in what *Variety* (May 8, 1968) called a "modest but well conceived thriller" are Charles Gray as a supercilious British financier involved in bankrolling clandestine CIA operations (although he's secretly working for Russian interests) and Austrian actress Heidelinde Weis as Venaxas' innocent sister, who gets caught up in the intrigue.

The Naked Runner (1967) is an intricate and suspenseful adaptation of Francis Clifford's clever source novel of the same name. British Intelligence requires the assassination of an international spy but does not wish to use one of its regular operatives for

Van Heflin was in the better half of this double bill of British thrillers from Trio Films/Group W Films.

the job. Sam Laker (Frank Sinatra), a former OSS agent and now an award-winning furniture designer, is deemed perfect for the job but would never willingly become involved. An elaborate deception (involving intelligence operatives played by Peter Vaughan, Derren Nesbitt and Nadia Gray) is therefore put into motion with the aim of manipulating Laker into carrying out the assassination. Director Sidney J. Furie (reunited with his director of photography from 1965's *The Ipcress File*) indulges in the use of trademark close-ups, unusual camera angles and generally flashy visuals, while securing excellent performances from all concerned. According to *The Daily Cinema* (July 14, 1967), it's not a film "that spy fans—or Sinatra fans—will need urging twice to see."

Set in Saigon during the Vietnam War, *Some May Live* (1967) stars Martha Hyer as Kate Meredith, an American decoder at a U.S. Army Intelligence unit run by Colonel Woodward (Joseph Cotten). Personal circumstances lead to Kate confessing to Woodward that she has been leaking information to her husband John (Peter Cushing), a British journalist and communist spy. She then cooperates with Woodward by giving John (who subsequently defects to Red China) false information concerning the timing of a planned invasion of North Vietnam by U.S. and Australian troops. Also prominently involved is Woodward's assistant, Captain Elliott Thomas (John Ronane), who's in love with Kate and ends up murdering John's contact man (Alec Mango) after the latter tries to force Kate and her young son to also defect. This all leads to a melodramatic conclusion in which Kate is compelled to take the blame for the murder in connection with preserving the secrecy of the invasion plans. Made in British studios and intercut with travelog-style footage of Saigon, this rather lackluster affair went straight to television in the U.S., airing as both *Some May Live* and *In Saigon: Some May Live*.

"*A mission that follows its rules to the letter: K for Kill*"

In ***Assignment K*** (1967), Philip Scott (suavely played by Stephen Boyd) is for all intents and purposes an executive with a London-based toy company; in his true capacity as a top secret agent, he reports to Harris (Michael Redgrave) at a British Intelligence section known as Department K. During his latest mission, which entails visits to Germany and Austria and concerns the retrieval of microfilm containing Russia's missile tracking secrets, Philip falls in love with Toni (Camilla Sparv), only for her to be kidnapped by an enemy organization headed by Smith (Leo McKern) in an effort to force Philip into betraying his contacts. A couple of twists (involving Toni and Harris) ensue in this colorful but rather tepid adventure that lacks character motivation. Geoffrey Bayldon has a neat cameo as Philip's gadget supplier, billed as "The Boffin," who provides the agent with an explosive device to use against Smith in the climax.

The stylish ***Sebastian*** (1967) stars Dirk Bogarde as the whimsical brainiac of the title, an Oxford math professor turned codebreaker for a British Secret Service bureau in London. The story follows the character's ups and downs, which include a love affair with a new recruit—the flighty Becky (Susannah York)—to his all-female team of cryptographers. An incident involving a security breach by trusted staffer Elsa (the ever-radiant Lilli Palmer) leads to Sebastian quitting his job, abandoning Becky and returning to Oxford. Just over a year later, he agrees to temporarily return to the bureau to decode a mysterious signal from a Soviet satellite. During this time, he is nearly killed by an enemy agent in a trap baited by an ex-girlfriend (a washed-up pop singer played by Janet Munro) while, on a more positive note, he discovers he's the father of a baby son (it turns out Becky was pregnant), the sound of whose plastic rattle provides him with an idea as to how to crack the satellite code. The episodic proceedings, which alternate between seriousness and frivolity, also feature John Gielgud as Sebastian's superior, and are accompanied by a catchy Jerry Goldsmith soundtrack.

Amicus Productions, best remembered for their horror anthologies such as *Dr. Terror's House of Horrors* (1964) and *Tales from the Crypt* (1972), made a one-off excursion into the spy genre with **Danger Route** (1967). The result is a much darker and more cynical view of the espionage world than that initially suggested by the opening James Bond-esque theme song. Richard Johnson is perfectly cast as Jonas Wilde, a world-weary British Secret Service assassin whose preferred method of killing is a commando blow to the neck. The complex story concerns Wilde's unit being cleverly manipulated by a double agent into carrying out assassinations beneficial to the Soviets; this means that the unwitting Wilde has for some time been used as a pawn, and it's no different with his latest assignment, namely the liquidation of a Czech germ-warfare scientist hoping to defect to the West. The 15-minute section dealing with the liquidation is the best part of the film and features Diana Dors in a key role as housekeeper of a country mansion where the scientist is to be terminated. Very few of the characters, including Wilde's girlfriend (Carol Lynley) and a fellow agent (Gordon Jackson) turn out to be who they seem in this above-average adaptation of Andrew York's 1966 novel *The Eliminator*.

The Limbo Line (1968) concerns an international communist organization that kidnaps Russian defectors and returns them home for forced re-education. Hollywood's Craig Stevens (probably best remembered as TV's *Peter Gunn*) plays a veteran British Intelligence agent who, despite having fallen in love with the organization's latest target, a beautiful London-based ballerina (Kate O'Mara), nevertheless allows her to be kidnapped, using her as a pawn in a plan to smash the outfit. Polish-born Vladek Sheybal is in great form as the Communist Party member in charge of the nefarious operations (which include the use of a tour bus and a modified fuel tanker in the smuggling of victims through Amsterdam and Germany), and Norman Bird also shines as the hero's resourceful assistant. The most unexpected thing in an otherwise fairly predictable adventure is the decidedly downbeat conclusion.

> "A double agent ... ordered to kill ... himself!"

The most memorable thing about **A Dandy in Aspic** (1968) is its creative title sequence featuring a marionette (as if to foreshadow manipulations of the main character during the film) and a cool Quincy Jones theme tune. British Intelligence operative Alexander Eberlin (Laurence Harvey) is actually a double agent, a Russian yearning to return home but forbidden to do so by his Soviet controllers. Eberlin finds himself in a dilemma when tasked by his British masters with the elimination of a mysterious Russian assassin known as Krasnevin. The problem is that Eberlin and Krasnevin are in fact one and the same, Krasnevin being Eberlin's Russian codename. Ensuing complications, including the murder by Eberlin's Soviet comrades of a British agent whom they attempt to pass off as "Krasnevin," culminate in a twist ending in which the surprising true reason for Eberlin's assignment is revealed.

Some superbly photographed London and West Berlin locations provide an atmospheric backdrop to events, which also feature Tom Courtenay as a ruthless British spy and Mia Farrow in a romantic role of no real consequence. Harvey is as captivating as ever in a tricky role, and no doubt just as tricky was his decision to take over directorial duties from the legendary Anthony Mann after the latter died early on during production (the film remains wholly credited to Mann, however). Harvey would go on to direct just one more film, *Welcome to Arrow Beach* (1973; aka *Tender Flesh*), a fascinating and almost completely neglected/forgotten U.S.-produced cannibalism-themed shocker in which he also starred, and which proved to be his swansong.

Gene Barry and Joan Collins in *Subterfuge* (1968).

Subterfuge (1968) stars Gene Barry as U.S. Special Agent Michael Donovan, in London to help find a traitor in a British Security organization. Donovan cozies up to Anne Langley (Joan Collins, sporting a wide variety of the "in" fashions of the day) in order to learn more about her husband Peter (Tom Adams), one of those suspected of being the turncoat. Ensuing events see Peter, who it transpires is the traitor (it's not difficult to guess), faking his own death and attempting to leave the country with the reluctant Anne and their young son, this leading to a showdown with Donovan. Barry is a listless hero in this boring and flatly scripted yarn, which is briefly enlivened by Suzanna Leigh as a memorably sadistic member of a foreign spy organization. The film was made by pioneering London-based video production services company Intertel (VTR Services) Limited (they of the famous Beatles promotional videos that became known as the "Intertel Promos") as part of a deal with U.S. production-distribution outfit Commonwealth United Entertainment, and it was the first live-action feature film to be shot using the Add-a-Vision system, an early form of video assist technology.

Tom Courtenay is well cast as ***Otley*** (1968), a perpetually unemployed London antique dealer caught up in intrigue following the murder of one of his former clients, Lambert (Edward Hardwicke). It turns out that Lambert was working for a government approved counter-intelligence group (one of them a character played by enigmatic French actress Romy Schneider) and had been blackmailing one of their operatives who was about to defect to an enemy group. Otley just happened to be at Lambert's apartment at the time he was murdered, and had purloined the man's antique tobacco holder which, unbeknownst to him, conceals a small tape recorder with details of the blackmail. His possession of the artifact soon leads to him becoming enmeshed in a dangerous adventure involving Lambert's assassin, played brilliantly by Leonard Rossiter, and the two aforementioned groups. The complicated and mostly light-hearted shenanigans feature some great locations, not the least of which is London's Portobello Road with its famous antiques market, and there's a hilarious sequence in which Otley takes a driving test that turns into a hectic car chase.

The British-U.S. co-production *The Most Dangerous Man in the World* (1969) stars Gregory Peck as John Hathaway, an American scientist sent by Western Intelligence into Red China to steal a climate-resistant crop-growing formula before it can be used by the Chinese to monopolize world food production. To enable him to broadcast back to base, a transmitter is surgically implanted into Hathaway's skull, but what his controllers do not tell him is that the transmitter also contains an explosive device to be detonated in the event of his capture. The effective opening titles—comprising images of Communist China accompanied by an atmospheric and stirring Jerry Goldsmith theme—are promising, but what follows is mostly lethargic until a relatively exciting climax in which the Russians aid the West by rescuing Hathaway at the Sino-Soviet border. Keye Luke (Master Po from the *Kung Fu* TV series), plays the formula's inventor, while Anne Heywood, despite second-billing, has only a tiny role of little consequence.

Somewhat loosely adapted from John Le Carré's novel of the same name, *The Looking Glass War* (1969) stars cult *Wild in the Streets* actor Christopher Jones as Leiser, a young Polish refugee guaranteed asylum in England in exchange for undertaking a dangerous mission (investigating a suspected missile site) in East Germany. After weeks of training, Leiser penetrates the East German border, but his killing of a sentry proves to be the catalyst for a string of events that ultimately have disastrous consequences for him. Ralph Richardson and Anthony Hopkins play, respectively, a British Intelligence chief and his assistant, while romantic interest is provided by Pia Degermark as a young German woman helping Leiser during his ill-fated mission. *The New York Times* (February 5, 1970) accurately described both the film and Jones' James Dean–like performance as "odd, mannered and unconvincing."

"Every day he lives, somebody else dies."

The Executioner (1970) casts George Peppard as John Shay, a British MI5 agent who it's explained was raised in the U.S., thereby saving Peppard from having to adopt a British accent. Shay becomes the executioner of the title when he unofficially liquidates Adam Booth (Keith Michell), a colleague he believes leaked information to the Russians which led to the drastic failure of a top-secret mission in Vienna. Later events in Greece see Shay captured by KGB agents, one of whom (Peter Dyneley) tells him something he didn't want to hear—namely that Booth was innocent. The KGB also capture Booth's wife (Joan Collins), a former lover of Shay's, and attempt to exchange her (in a plan that involves using Shay as a pawn) for a British scientist (George Baker), the latter playing a crucial role in a story where at times, as pointed out by *Films and Filming* (December 1970), "events become a little too complex for their own good." The film is essentially one long flashback that culminates in a violent climactic shootout (connected with the planned exchange, and whose horrific aftermath had already been shown in the striking opening sequence), with a cynical closing scene revealing some surprising final truths about Booth and the Vienna mission. The great cast also includes Judy Geeson as Shay's long-suffering girlfriend and Nigel Patrick as an MI5 chief.

In the British-French co-production

Catch Me a Spy (1971), a corrupt British businessman (Patrick Mower) is paid £50,000 by Russian agents in a scheme that entails romancing and marrying London-based French teacher Fabienne (Marlène Jobert) and then being arrested on fake espionage charges while in Eastern Europe. The plan is for the Russians to exchange him for one of their British-held spies, this to be expedited by Fabienne's uncle (Trevor Howard), a high-ranking British Government official, who will do so for the sake of his naïve niece's happiness. Nicely woven into the sometimes hard-to-follow story is Andrej (top-billed Kirk Douglas), a smuggler of banned Russian manuscripts ultimately responsible for Fabienne learning that she'd been used by her husband, and whose actions see him end up with both Fabienne and the £50,000. Douglas and the charming Jobert have a nice chemistry in what is a largely forgettable light-hearted adventure.

> *"The superstar from Shaft is back ... waging an ice-cold war on your nerves."*

While still in the very early days of his movie career, Richard Roundtree played tough diplomat Dick Shannon in ***Embassy*** (1972), a film whose sheer drive, according to the *Monthly Film Bulletin* (April 1972), "is enough to compensate for its faults and its evidently modest budget." Shannon gets involved when a defecting Soviet Union Foreign Service official (Max Von Sydow) requests and is granted political asylum at the U.S. Embassy in Beirut, whereupon arrangements, which become fraught with difficulties, are made to transfer him to America. The highlight of the film is the great Chuck Connors as a psychopathic KGB assassin who, posing as a U.S. Air Force colonel, infiltrates the embassy in an attempt to liquidate the defector. The fantastic cast also includes Ray Milland as the U.S. Ambassador to Lebanon and Broderick Crawford as a gruff security man. The movie was made in between Roundtree's first two Shaft hits, *Shaft* (1971) and *Shaft's Big Score* (1972), but not released in the U.S. until after the latter.

At the start of ***Innocent Bystanders*** (1972), a brilliant Russian scientist, Aaron Kaplan (Vladek Sheybal), escapes from a Siberian prison camp before going into hiding in Turkey. A generously mustachioed Stanley Baker plays John Craig, a sexually impotent (due to psychological problems resulting from a previous mission) middle-aged British Intelligence agent assigned to locate Kaplan on behalf of the Americans, who want the scientist for his revolutionary work in agronomy and water engineering. However, Craig is in fact being used by his stony boss, Loomis (Donald Pleasence), as an expendable decoy, while ambitious—and in the latter case sadistic—new recruits Benson (Sue Lloyd) and Royce (Derren Nesbitt) carry out the actual mission. When Craig realizes this, he manages, despite hostile opposition from Benson and Royce, and amid KGB efforts to liquidate the scientist before the West can make use of him, to take matters into his own hands and gain from the situation; in other words, he secures Kaplan, sells him to Loomis for £100,000 and then jets off to self-imposed retirement.

Scripted by James Mitchell from his own 1969 novel *The Innocent Bystanders* (the fourth and last in a series of John Craig adventures all written under Mitchell's pseudonym James Munro), the film suffers somewhat from unnecessary confusion in the plotting and as a result is only ever intermittently gripping. Setting the film apart from others of its ilk are a couple of instances of jarring brutality, one of which involves a particularly barbarous act of torture on the part of aforementioned new recruit Royce, played in suitably menacing style by Nesbitt, about whom *Films and Filming* (December 1972) rightly said "no one can portray sadistic ruthlessness more effectively." Also starring are Geraldine Chaplin, as an innocent (or is she?) young woman instrumental in Craig's search for Kaplan (as well as in curing him of his impotence), and Dana

Andrews as a U.S. intelligence chief whose exchanges with Loomis provide some amusing moments. Pleasence would later play a different and more famous Loomis—namely Dr. Sam Loomis—in the classic *Halloween* horror movie franchise beginning in 1978.

A seldom-seen fish-out-of-water thriller, ***Yellow Dog*** (1973) was the only feature film directed by British photographer Terence Donovan. A Japanese secret agent, Kimura (Jiro Tamiya), flies from Tokyo to London on a complicated mission to prevent a scientist's notes (pertaining to a synthetic fuel formula of interest to the Japanese) from getting into the wrong hands. His resulting adventure involves two Scotland Yard Special Branch operatives (Robert Hardy and Joseph O'Conor), as well as Della (Carolyn Seymour), an agent for a spy organization in whose "wrong" hands the notes eventually do end up, albeit—thanks to Kimura—only temporarily. The *Monthly Film Bulletin* (October 1973) found the film, which it called "a jokey espionage thriller," to be "needlessly incoherent."

Adapted by Walter Hill from Desmond Bagley's 1971 novel *The Freedom Trap*, ***The Mackintosh Man*** (1973) concerns a British Intelligence plan to smash the "Scarperers," an organization that arranges jailbreaks and safe passage abroad for the escapees. A wider aspect of the plan, masterminded by top British Intelligence chief Mackintosh (a well-cast Harry Andrews), is to expose—as a KGB agent—the prominent Member of Parliament Sir George Wheeler (James Mason), who uses the Scarperers to arrange breakouts for convicted Soviet spies. Mackintosh's scheme entails planting an undercover agent (Paul Newman)—under the alias Joseph

The Mackintosh Man (1973) features a neat cameo from Nigel Patrick (right), pictured with the film's star, Paul Newman.

Rearden—in prison so that he can arrange to be sprung by the Scarperers and thus position himself to get the goods on the organization. An escape is duly arranged, with the Scarperers concurrently liberating—at Wheeler's behest—a communist spy named Slade (Ian Bannen). The two men are taken to a safe house in rural Ireland, from where Rearden is forced to make a daring escape after his cover gets blown, this an unfortunate consequence of an expedient move on the part of Mackintosh in his strategy to expose Wheeler.

Newman mixes well with his British co-stars, but there's a distinct lack of chemistry between him and French actress Dominique Sanda, who plays it all icy cool and ambiguous as Mackintosh's daughter-cum-secretary, known as "Mrs. Smith." The inimitable Mason plays master villain Wheeler in typically urbane fashion, and special mention should be made of Nigel Patrick's great cameo as the Scarperers' fixer inside the prison. Malta is the setting for a tense climactic confrontation involving Wheeler, Slade, Rearden and Mrs. Smith, the latter by now having a personal score to settle with Wheeler after he causes her father's death. There's a fittingly drab color palette, some good action sequences (punctuated with occasional sudden bursts of violence) and a catchy, if a little overused, *Third Man*-style theme tune; but overall the film is an unremarkable effort from director John Huston.

Assassin (1973) is a slow-moving and downbeat existential tale with a solid performance by Ian Hendry. The ever-excellent character actor plays an assassin hired by MI5 to liquidate John Stacy (Frank Windsor), a supposed traitor in the British Air Ministry. When it emerges that Stacy is innocent, MI5 attempts to stop the assassin but are saved the trouble when he is killed in a hit-and-run incident. However, unbeknownst to them, he has been working with a back-up man who goes on to complete the job. In contrast to Edward Fox's super-cool assassin in the same year's *The Day of the Jackal*, Hendry's character is portrayed as a lonely, haunted man looking for a way out. A final revelation as to the real traitor's identity is not that surprising.

In ***The Tamarind Seed*** (1974), widowed British Home Office employee Judith Farrow (Julie Andrews) is befriended and romanced by dashing Paris-based Russian diplomat Feodor Sverdlov (Omar Sharif) while the two are vacationing in Barbados. The friendship, closely monitored by MI5 (due to their mistaken belief that the Russian is attempting to recruit Judith as a spy), continues back in Europe with Judith helping Feodor when he decides, for personal and political reasons, to defect. Events lead back to Barbados, where Soviet agents attempt to kill Feodor after his impending defection is disclosed to his superior by senior British diplomat Fergus Stephenson (Dan O'Herlihy), actually a Russian spy Feodor was planning to expose as part of an asylum deal. Director Blake Edwards' handsomely mounted romantic thriller has two pleasant lead performances, an elegant John Barry score, an uplifting if bittersweet ending and an exceptional supporting cast including a scene-stealing Sylvia Syms as Stephenson's spiteful and disillusioned wife.

> "Callan doesn't make friends—
> and all his enemies are dead!"

The fondly remembered British TV series *Callan* (1967–1972) starred Edward Woodward (later U.S. TV's *The Equalizer*) as the eponymous anti-hero, a reluctant, distinctly unglamorous and decidedly deadly agent-assassin for a murky black-ops government department known as "The Section." The movie spin-off, also called ***Callan*** (1974), was scripted by James Mitchell and is a remake of his 1967 *Armchair Theatre* TV episode "A Magnum for Schneider" from which the series sprung. Containing added elements from the TV play's 1969 novelization (also by Mitchell and known in the U.S. as *A Red File for Callan*), the story has a forcibly retired Callan (Woodward) offered the chance of reinstatement with "The Section" in return for carrying out an urgent assignment, namely the assassination of a German gunrunner named Schneider (Carl Mohner). In the course of events, the department's double-crossing boss (Eric Porter) instructs another operative, a jealous rival of Callan's named Meres (Peter Egan), to set up Callan so that he will be arrested upon Schneider's liquidation. However, in the end, the resourceful Callan manages to kill two birds with one stone by liquidating Schneider and framing Meres for the killing, before then telephoning the department to reject his reinstatement, or as he rather less politely puts it, "you can stuff it!"

Although a missed opportunity to do something new with the character, the film remains a decent enough effort with a first-class performance by Woodward and overall proficient direction by Don Sharp, who reminds us of his not undeserved status as an action maestro by throwing in a very well-staged car chase. Finally, the venture wouldn't be complete without Russell Hunter, reprising his role from the TV series as Callan's malodorous underworld contact, the appropriately named "Lonely."

Within the first few minutes of the British-Israeli co-production *The Sellout* (1975), the audience is let in on a secret joint CIA-KGB plot to systematically liquidate obsolete double agents. The latest target on the death list is Gabriel Lee (Oliver Reed), a former CIA operative who defected to the KGB. The plan to assassinate Gabriel involves luring him from Moscow to Jerusalem by way of a faked letter supposedly from his old CIA mentor Sam Lucas (Richard Widmark), now retired and running an antiques business in the city. When the assassination attempt fails, events lead to Sam reluctantly putting his old skills back to use in order to help his former protégé stay alive, this complicated by the fact that his girlfriend Deborah (Gayle Hunnicutt) is Gabriel's ex-lover. Some nice location work and a couple of well-staged action scenes cannot compensate for a muddled and largely forgettable movie which *Films and Filming* (April 1976) made no bones about calling "a horrible cinematic experience." Vladek Sheybal has fun as a sinister assassin known as The Dutchman, and there's a pivotal final twist involving Hunnicutt's character.

The British-Canadian co-production ***Russian Roulette*** (1975) concerns a plot by rogue KGB agents to assassinate the Russian Premier during his visit to Vancouver for talks that could de-escalate Cold War tensions, something these particular KGB operatives do not want. Their intention is to frame the CIA for the assassination, this to involve kidnapping and drugging one of that agency's Russian informants in Vancouver and then turning him into a human bomb to be dropped onto the Premier by helicopter. George Segal has the lead role as Tim Shaver, a Royal Canadian Mounted Police officer on suspension for misconduct who foils the plot, having become caught up in the affair as the result of some shady undercover work for Canadian Intelligence. Slow and confusing at the start, the film soon picks up pace and culminates in a breathtaking climax where our hero attempts to shoot down the helicopter from atop the roof of the Hotel Vancouver. That great British character actor Denholm Elliott plays Shaver's seedy intelligence contact and manages to steal every scene he's in.

When it came to the subject of espionage, director Lindsay Shonteff seemed most at home sending up the genre with films such as *Licensed to Kill* (1965) and *No.1 of the Secret Service* (1977). His attempt to take things completely seriously in ***Spy Story*** (1976) unfortunately resulted in what is a relentlessly boring adaptation of Len Deighton's 1974 novel of the same name. Secretly in league with the Russians, a corrupt Member of Parliament (Nicholas Parsons) is arranging the defection to England of a Soviet Rear Admiral so that the latter can act as a double agent against the British. An ultra-patriotic Pentagon strategist (Don Fellows) and a British

Intelligence chief (Michael Gwynne) are out to thwart the scheme in such a way as to suit their wider agenda, namely to sabotage negotiations (involving the Russians) into the reunification of East and West Germany. The story's main protagonist, played by Michael Petrovitch, is a British Government Strategic War Studies Centre employee used as a pawn in the nefarious scheming of all concerned. Colonel Stok, a recurring Deighton character previously portrayed so colorfully on the big screen by Oscar Homolka in two of the Michael Caine "Harry Palmer" movies, is here played by Derren Nesbitt, a good choice for the role but who unfortunately fails to make much of an impression due to insufficient screen time. Commenting on the convoluted plot, *Screen International* (July 10, 1976) suggested that one way to boost the film's sales would be to "offer prizes to those who could prove they understood it."

"Every man in love is a potential traitor."

The Human Factor (1979) stars Nicol Williamson as Maurice Castle, a dull bureaucrat in a British Secret Intelligence Service (MI6) department dealing with African security. For several years now, Castle has been leaking information to the Soviets out of gratitude to a Communist lawyer who once helped his black girlfriend—and now wife (Iman)—escape from South Africa, where she was wanted by the authorities. Derek Jacobi plays a close colleague of Castle's whom the department bosses find it expedient to liquidate upon mistakenly believing him to be the leaker, while a miscast Robert Morley is the cheerfully sinister doctor (one of said bosses) who brings about the man's death. The bleak story culminates in Castle being forced to defect to Moscow, with little chance of his wife ever being able to join him. Director Otto Preminger's final film is an occasionally compelling but mostly boring adaptation of Graham Greene's 1978 novel of the same name, lacking in dramatic punch and often resembling a mediocre television production.

Super Secret Agents

This section deals with agents who engage in a world of international intrigue, action and adventure. The super secret agent can be in full time employment by a government intelligence agency or other investigative agency, or can be an ordinary person recruited because they possess a skill or characteristic necessary to carry out a particular mission. Their exciting adventures can involve uncovering large-scale conspiracies as well as doing battle with criminal syndicates, megalomaniac masterminds and deadly assassins. They are usually devastatingly handsome or, in the case of the female super agent, stunningly beautiful. Although super secret agents frequently find themselves facing certain death at the hands of their enemies, they always coolly find a way out of the predicament, either by using their wits or a special gadget of some kind. The world of the super secret agent is one of fashion and glamour, fast cars, exotic locations, eccentric adversaries and explosive finales.

James Bond

The movie world's most famous super secret agent is British Secret Service operative James Bond 007, created by author Ian Fleming. Bond had been played by U.S. actor Barry Nelson in a CBS television production of *Casino Royale* in 1954, but it wasn't until 1962 that the character made his big-screen debut in what was the start of the longest-running film franchise to date. From 1962 until 1979 (the cut-off year in this book), James Bond was played by three actors—Sean Connery, George Lazenby and Roger Moore—in films made by Eon Productions. All these films feature the great character actor Bernard Lee as Bond's superior, known as "M," and Lois Maxwell as M's secretary, Miss Moneypenny, who enjoys a flirtatious relationship with Bond. Other recurring characters are Bond's supplier of gadgetry, "Q," played by Desmond Llewelyn, and Felix

Leiter, a CIA ally of Bond's played by various actors (including Jack Lord and David Hedison) throughout the franchise. Tough, handsome, witty, charismatic, virile, fearless and licensed to kill, James Bond is the ultimate man of the world, and it's a world he often ends up saving by foiling nefarious plots which threaten its existence. His adversaries are either independent criminal masterminds (often with their own private armies), or agents of an international crime syndicate known as SPECTRE. Bond's healthy sex drive is frequently satisfied by an array of beautiful women who have become known as "Bond girls."

THE NAME'S CONNERY, SEAN CONNERY

After toiling away for several years on television and in small film roles, a dynamic and charismatic performance in the gangster thriller *The Frightened City* (1961) made it clear that Scottish-born Sean Connery was ready for something bigger. It couldn't have gotten much bigger than landing the starring role in the first James Bond film, ***Dr. No*** (1962), which propelled the actor to international stardom. Nevertheless than magnetic in the part, Connery would star in all but one of the 1960s films, as well as the first of the 1970s adventures. Joseph Wiseman plays the titular villain (a character inspired by author Sax Rohmer's Fu Manchu), a SPECTRE operative headquartered in a nuclear-powered fortress on an island off the Jamaican coast, from where he uses radio frequency signals to interfere with U.S. missile testing at Cape Canaveral. Bond's investigation into the disappearance of a fellow agent who'd been looking into the matter puts him on Dr. No's trail, leading to an exciting adventure that culminates in the villain's lair being blown sky high in the type of spectacular climax that would become a staple of the series. Anthony Dawson appears to good effect as a geologist-cum-assassin who attempts to kill Bond with a deadly spider in the film's most suspenseful sequence; and Ursula Andress, as Bond's love interest, Honey Ryder, whose first scene is a memorable bikini-clad emergence from the sea, sets a high standard for all future Bond girls. Monty Norman provided the memorable signature theme tune that has been a mainstay of the series. *The Daily Cinema* (September 3, 1962) concluded that the film "just can't fail to make a fortune."

Having made its fortune, it wasn't long

A trade announcement for Sean Connery's second outing as James Bond 007.

before a follow-up appeared. One of the best and least ostentatious of the franchise, ***From Russia with Love*** (1963) is a tightly woven and highly suspenseful adventure that sees Connery settled nicely into the 007 role. The complex story has SPECTRE using both James Bond and beautiful Istanbul-based Russian cryptographer Tatiana (Daniela Bianchi) as pawns in a devious plot to steal a top-secret portable decoding machine, known as the Lektor, from the Russians. However, the scheme has a secondary purpose—to eliminate Bond in revenge for the death of Dr. No from the previous movie. Assigned to do this, as painfully as possible, is Donald "Red" Grant, a highly trained blond assassin played in suitably ominous fashion by a brilliantly cast Robert Shaw. The action highlight is a superbly staged bone-crunching fight between Bond and Grant in the cramped confines of an Orient Express train compartment, a sequence that looks like the inspiration for the ferocious close-quarters battle in a ship's cabin between Rod Taylor and William Smith (the latter, like Shaw, playing a blond villain) in 1970's *Darker Than Amber*. The film's other main villain is the hatchet-faced Rosa Klebb (Lotte Lenya), an evil former Soviet Intelligence officer in charge of implementing the SPECTRE plan who, in one of the series' more hair-raising moments, tries to kill Bond with a retractable poisoned blade concealed in her right shoe.

"Everything he touches turns to excitement!"

Goldfinger (1964) is one of the most memorable and celebrated Bond films for various reasons, not the least of which are the outstanding title song (brilliantly performed by Shirley Bassey) and the first appearance of 007's gadget-laden Aston Martin DB5, at the time cited as the most famous car in the world. An enigmatic megalomaniac, Auric Goldfinger (Gert Fröbe), has been busy stockpiling gold bullion while making plans to render the gold in Fort Knox worthless by contaminating it through the use of an atomic device; this would put him in the strongest position on the world's gold market. During his efforts to foil the scheme, Bond (Sean Connery) does battle with Goldfinger's Korean henchman, Oddjob (Harold Sakata), who uses his steel-rimmed bowler hat as a murder weapon, and wins the allegiance of Goldfinger's personal pilot, Pussy Galore (Honor Blackman), who remains the most provocatively named of all the Bond girls. Mike Sarne, writing for *Films and Filming* (November 1964), said, "as the story advances we are amused and excited by the solid predictability of every situation, and await it like children at a birthday party."

In ***Thunderball*** (1965), SPECTRE agent Emilio Largo (Adolfo Celi) organizes the daring theft of two atomic bombs which are subsequently hidden in an underwater cave in the Bahamas. Failure by the British government to pay a £100 million ransom (in diamonds) will result in the bombs being used to destroy a major British or U.S. city. Italian actor Celi effectively blends charm and menace in his portrayal of eye-patched villain Largo, with another Italian, Luciana Paluzzi, playing a deadly SPECTRE assassin. Raquel Welch was originally hired to play Bond girl Domino (Largo's mistress) but was released from her contract to star in *Fantastic Voyage* instead, with Claudine Auger doing just fine as her replacement. The impressive underwater sequences, including one in which Bond (Sean Connery) and his U.S. Navy allies do battle with Largo's army of frogmen, were directed by American diver and stuntman Ricou Browning, probably best remembered for his work as the Gill Man in the *Creature from the Black Lagoon* movies.

The spectacular ***You Only Live Twice*** (1967) concerns a SPECTRE plot to capture—using a specially designed rocket ship launched from a base concealed within an inactive Japanese volcano—U.S. and Russian space capsules so that both countries will blame each other and engage in mutual nuclear devastation. This will lead to the Chinese, who are in cahoots with SPECTRE, emerging as the dominant world superpower. James Bond (Sean Connery), with the support of the Japanese Secret Service and their army of highly trained ninjas, sees to it that the plot never reaches fruition, but not before many dangerous escapades including an exhilarating battle between a Bond-piloted gyrocopter (affectionately referred to as "Little Nellie" and equipped with weaponry such as heat-seeking missiles) and four SPECTRE helicopters. The inimitable Donald Pleasence plays the sinister, white-cat-stroking SPECTRE chief Blofeld, a character previously featured (although his face remained unseen) in *From Russia with Love* and *Thunderball*. In one squirm-inducing sequence, the villain feeds a female operative (Karin Dor) to his pet piranhas as punishment for her failure to kill 007. The massive volcano base is a triumph of production design, and Roald Dahl's imaginative and eventful screenplay gives Connery plenty to do, although the actor had by now tired of the role and decided it was time to quit—at least for the time being.

George Lazenby Steps In

The man chosen to step into Connery's shoes for the sixth Bond movie, ***On Her Majesty's Secret Service*** (1969), was George Lazenby, an Australian whose previous claim to fame was appearing in Big Fry chocolate commercials, and who *Films and Filming* (February 1970) noted "doesn't have quite the right voice, nor does he parade the trappings of pseudo-sophistication with quite the same ease as his predecessor." The story has 007 tracking down SPECTRE chief Blofeld with the help of powerful international businessman and racketeer Draco (Gabriele Ferzetti), in the process falling in love with Draco's willful daughter, Tracy (Diana Rigg). This time around, Blofeld, played by the charismatic Telly Savalas (eschewing the menacing demeanor of Donald Pleasence from the previous film), is headquartered in the Swiss Alps; his latest plan is to spread a destructive bacterial agent (to be unleashed worldwide by a bevy of specially programmed young women) unless he's granted a pardon for all past crimes. The combined efforts of Bond and Draco see to it that Blofeld's base of operations is destroyed (via a spectacular helicopter attack) and his scheme foiled, although the villain himself manages to escape. Bond and Tracy go on to marry, but Blofeld's desire for revenge ensures their happiness is short-lived. Among the highlights are a superbly choreographed ski chase and Louis Armstrong's rendition of the theme song "We Have All the Time in the World." For whatever reason, the film turned out to be Lazenby's one and only Bond outing.

Sean Connery made a welcome return in ***Diamonds Are Forever*** (1971), the actor's last Bond movie for Eon Productions (he later made a comeback in the 1983 *Thunderball* remake *Never Say Never Again* for a different production company). The rather weak plot has SPECTRE chief Blofeld (played charmingly if rather unthreateningly by Charles Gray) stockpiling diamonds for use in the construction of a powerful space-borne satellite laser to be pointed at Washington, D.C., so as to hold the U.S. government to ransom. The main Bond girl, a professional smuggler named Tiffany Case, is played by Jill St. John, and also starring are Bruce Glover and Putter Smith, who prove highly entertaining as a pair of gay assassins in Blofeld's employ. A couple of more-humorous-than-exciting chase sequences see 007 put a Ford Mustang Mach 1 and, of all things, a moon buggy through their paces, and Shirley Bassey lends her magnificent vocals for the second time in the franchise (after *Goldfinger*) for what is perhaps the quintessential 007 title song.

Roger Moore Takes Over

Roger Moore's first outing as 007 sees the actor adopting a lighter, more humorous approach than Connery, with a distinctly British upper-class air. ***Live and Let Die*** (1973) pits Bond against black master villain

Kananga (Yaphet Kotto), a corrupt Caribbean Prime Minister whose plot to take over the U.S. heroin market involves adopting an alter ego identity as a Harlem racketeer named Mr. Big. The scenes with "Mr. Big" and his cronies (including Julius W. Harris as a henchman with a mechanical arm complete with deadly metal pincer hand) play heavily on the then prevalent blaxploitation craze, and this is probably the only time you'll ever hear Bond referred to as a honky! A Louisiana crocodile farm provides the cover for Kananga's heroin processing plant, and is the setting for a memorable sequence in which Bond, stranded in the middle of a crocodile pond, escapes by using the reptiles as stepping stones. This is followed by a well-staged speedboat chase and the introduction of J.W. Pepper, a larger-than-life redneck sheriff played in crowd-pleasing fashion by Clifton James. Also starring are Jane Seymour as the ethereal Solitaire, Kananga's trusted Tarot reader, who falls in love with Bond ("it's in the cards"); Geoffrey Holder as a voodoo priest helping keep locals away from Kananga's poppy fields in the Caribbean; and U.S. actor David Hedison as CIA man Felix Leiter. Incidentally, Hedison had once guest-starred in Moore's classic *The Saint* TV series, specifically the 1964 episode "Luella" in which Moore's Simon Templar pretended to be James Bond.

In ***The Man with the Golden Gun*** (1974), elite assassin Scaramanga (Christopher Lee) uses his deadly skills to obtain a new invention that converts the sun's radiation into electricity, intending to sell the device to the highest-bidding nation. James Bond (Roger Moore) traces Scaramanga to his island hideout where events lead to a deadly game of cat-and-mouse in the latter's private funhouse. Lee gives a superb performance as the witty and charming villain, whose trademark weapon is a golden gun which, for ease of smuggling, disassembles into various innocuous items including a cigarette lighter and fountain pen. Britt Ekland is charming as a beautiful but blundering agent, with the main "Bond girl" (Scaramanga's lover, that is until 007 comes along) played by Maud Adams who, just under a decade later, would get a second go-around (again with Roger Moore) as a Bond girl, namely the eponymous jewel smuggler in *Octopussy* (1983). The comical and crowd-pleasing sheriff J.W. Pepper (Clifton James) returns from the previous film, this time encountering Bond while vacationing in Bangkok,

Roger Moore brought his own special brand of magic to the James Bond role.

and the film's higher-than-usual reliance on humor prompted the *Monthly Film Bulletin* (January 1975) to report that "on the evidence of this film, it would not be too incongruous to see the Bond cycle merge seamlessly into the *Carry On* canon."

A major highlight in the Bond franchise, **The Spy Who Loved Me** (1977) was the grandest entry so far in terms of production design, special effects and locations (Egypt, Sardinia, Canada and Malta to name but a few). The story concerns megalomaniac shipping tycoon Stromberg's (Curt Jürgens) plan to create and rule over a new underwater kingdom, but not before bringing about the total destruction of terrestrial civilization as we know it. To this end, he uses a specially designed giant tanker called *Liparus* to capture British and Russian nuclear submarines, these to be used in a scheme to cause World War III and resultant global annihilation.

Roger Moore is at his Bond best here, with 007 ultimately saving the day in cooperation with a beautiful Soviet agent, Anya Amasova (Barbara Bach), and with more than a little help from the captured submarine crews who engage in a tremendous battle with Stromberg's forces in a rip-roaring climax aboard the *Liparus*. Among the master villain's more deadly employees are a seductive femme fatale helicopter pilot (Caroline Munro) and a steel-toothed giant named Jaws (Richard Kiel), the latter remaining one of the best and most popular Bond baddies of the franchise. The pre-credits sequence includes a memorable stunt where, during a ski chase, Bond hurtles off the edge of a mountain and freefalls for about 20 seconds before finally deploying a Union Jack-adorned parachute, this followed by Carly Simon's wonderful rendition of the appropriately titled theme song "Nobody Does It Better." Oh, and let's not forget 007's marvelous amphibious Lotus Esprit, probably the second-best Bond car after the Aston Martin DB5 from *Goldfinger*.

"Outer space now belongs to 007."

Moore's final Bond outing of the decade was the British-French co-production **Moonraker** (1979). Billionaire megalomaniac Hugo Drax (Michael Lonsdale), a space shuttle manufacturer, has secretly built a space station from which he intends to destroy all human life on earth (using a deadly nerve toxin derived from a rare species of Amazonian orchid) before re-colonizing the planet with a "pure" race of his own breeding. The action-packed climax sees Bond, together with CIA agent and astronaut Holly Goodhead (Lois Chiles), infiltrate the space station via space shuttle, closely followed by another shuttle carrying U.S. troops who engage in battle with Drax's forces. Well timed to cash in on the sci-fi craze following the incredible success of *Star Wars* (1977), *Moonraker* is a frequently spectacular adventure with great stunts and special effects, and was the biggest-budgeted 007 film up to that time. Humor is derived from the usual abundance of one-liners, a Venetian canal chase with a gondola-cum-hovercraft, and some borderline slapstick scenes with steel-toothed villain Jaws (Richard Kiel), who returns from the previous movie. Moore played Bond an additional three times during the next decade in *For Your Eyes Only* (1981), *Octopussy* (1983) and *A View to a Kill* (1985).

Charles Vine

The phenomenal success of the early James Bond films led to a slew of imitations, many of which augmented the humorous aspects found in the 007 franchise. In the U.S., James Coburn played the super-cool Derek Flint in *Our Man Flint* (1966) and *In Like Flint* (1967). In Europe, there were dozens of productions in what has since become known as the Eurospy genre, which frequently featured U.S. stars such as Mike "Mannix" Connors (in Italy's *Kiss the Girls and Make Them Die*) and Ray "Legs Diamond" Danton (in the French-Italian-German production *Secret Agent Super Dragon* among others). The most bizarre entry in the Eurospy genre would have to be 1967's *Operation Kid Brother* (aka *Operation Double 007* and *O.K. Connery*), which stars Sean Connery's younger brother Neil along with many actors from the Bond movies including Bernard Lee and Lois Maxwell.

"Charles Vine is only No.2...That's why he tries harder ... and loves more dangerously!"

Britain's first true Bond imitation, Charles Vine, is the hero in a trio of parodic movies produced by James Ward. Every bit the consummate superspy, the unflappable Vine is tall, dark, handsome, tough, confident, and has a keen eye for the ladies. In all three films he's played—mostly straight-faced but with tongue firmly in cheek—by Tom Adams. The first picture, **Licensed to Kill** (1965), is a low-budget effort directed and co-written by cult Canadian filmmaker Lindsay Shonteff. The story concerns Swedish scientist Henrik Jacobsen's (Karel Stepanek) involvement in a complicated scheme to extort large amounts of cash from both the British and Russians for an invention (an anti-gravity device) that is in fact non-existent. Assigned to protect Jocobsen during the man's visit to London, Vine gets caught up in the mayhem resulting from cat-and-mouse games involving factions of both the British and Russian governments (in their competing efforts to secure the supposed device) and the scientist's mysterious cohorts.

This eventful and entertaining spoof contains several Bond references (at one point, a sexual conquest of Vine's says she once met a man like him named James), most of which are designed to make fun of the fact that Vine is operating very much in 007's shadow. Nevertheless, when it comes to firearms, Vine manages to outclass Bond through his unusual weapon of choice, namely a Mauser Broomhandle pistol which he uses with ruthless efficiency. The film's main letdown is the rather poor handling of the action set pieces, the only exception being an interestingly filmed and particularly brutal fight scene between Vine and a cross-dressing assassin. The story, which also involves a double of Vine assigned by the Russians to kill and replace the agent, is often confusing, although thankfully most aspects of the plot are explained in a final dialogue between Vine and his urbane superior, Rockwell (John Arnatt). As the scientist's assistant, Veronica Hurst unfortunately has very little to do, with early suggestions of a romance with Vine remaining unfulfilled. The film was released in the U.S. as *The 2nd Best Secret Agent in the Whole Wide World*, with Herbert Chappell's original opening theme replaced by a newly recorded title song performed by Sammy Davis, Jr.

The follow-up, **Where the Bullets Fly** (1966), is a better film all around thanks to the more experienced direction of veteran John Gilling. In a hilarious pre-credits sequence, Vine, who'd battled a transvestite assassin in the previous film, indulges in a little cross-dressing himself when he and fellow agents pose as female sightseers in order to mount a surprise attack on a gang attempting to blow up the Houses of Parliament. This is followed by a catchy and very Bond-like opening song, with the film's title initially appearing as "Where the Bull Flies" so as to make absolutely clear the spoofy intentions of the enterprise. In a larger than usual role, character actor Michael Ripper (best known for his many Hammer film appearances) plays Angel, a criminal mastermind determined to get hold of a top-secret lightweight alloy known as Spurium—the main ingredient in a device being tested in prototype planes in connection with nuclear-powered flight—in order to sell it to the Russians. Having failed in an attempt to steal one of the prototypes (the British are forced to destroy the aircraft to prevent it getting into his hands), Angel later succeeds in stealing a second one after mounting an assault on an airfield. However, Vine has managed to get aboard the plane and soon puts paid to the villain's plans.

This time around, the many action

scenes are handled more proficiently, and Vine has exchanged his Mauser Broomhandle pistol for a more conventional firearm. Dawn Addams makes a very welcome appearance toward the end of the movie, playing a Women's Royal Air Force officer inevitably romanced by Vine. Other cast members include Tim Barrett as an assassin with a gun disguised as an umbrella, John Arnatt returning as Vine's boss Rockwell and Sidney James in a hilarious guest appearance as a mortuary attendant left with his hands full following a massive shootout on his premises. Commenting on the many confusions of the plot, *Variety* (November 9, 1966) said "it is difficult to sort out who's up against whom, but with so much ammunition and so many corpses biting the dust, it does not much matter."

Adams' third and final outing as Vine was in the lesser-known **Somebody's Stolen Our Russian Spy** (1967), a British-Spanish production (filmed in Spain and Portugal) made for the Swiss company Paudex Distribution and which sat on the shelf for several years after Paudex reportedly went bust. Puck Films, the production company behind *Where the Bullets Fly*, is credited on the English-language version, with Andorra Films commonly cited in connection with the Spanish version, whose original title *O.K. Yevtushenko* was inexplicably changed to *O.K. Stuchensko* upon eventual release by Filmax. The plot has Vine assigned to rescue Colonel Yevtushenko (Barta Barry), a Russian spy who, while under British protection, was kidnapped off the Spanish coast by Chinese and Albanian agents. Spanish actress Diana Lorys, providing more fire than all of Vine's government-issued exploding wristwatches put together, plays a beautiful enemy agent who switches sides and helps Vine complete his mission, which culminates in an extended chase involving a tank, a speedboat and a helicopter. Screenwriter Michael Pittock returns from the pre-

British VHS cover for the second Charles Vine adventure (Abbey Video).

vious film, as does actor Tim Barrett, this time playing the chief Albanian villain. The movie took eight years to show up in British cinemas, and anybody who'd waited that long to see it would most likely have been undeterred by *Screen International*'s (November 8, 1975) description of it as "plodding nonsense."

Charles Bind

Lindsay Shonteff, director of the first Charles Vine film, belatedly resurrected the character in **No.1 of the Secret Service** (1977), only this time calling him Charles Bind, equipping him with two .357 Combat Magnums and making him much more comical than Vine ever was. (One wonders whether Shonteff was aware that the name Charlie Bind had already been used to send up James Bond in the madcap 1964 British spy comedy *Carry On Spying*.) The story has Bind (Nicky Henson) pitting his wits against Arthur Loveday (Richard Todd), a devious millionaire toy manufacturer behind the ingeniously organized assassinations (part of a moral crusade) of two unscrupulous international financiers. Having confessed his guilt to Bind early on in the proceedings, Loveday challenges the agent to try and prevent further planned assassinations, all the while attempting to eliminate him with the help of K.R.A.S.H. (Killing, Raping, Arson, Slaughter and Hits), a murderous paramilitary group on his payroll.

This ultra-low-budget nonsense is chock-full of cartoonish violence and witless humor, with some poorly staged action sequences during which Bind displays impossible acrobatic and shooting skills. The character Rockwell (head honcho at the Secret Service) returns from the Vine films and is this time played by Geoffrey Keen, who in the same year began appearing as the Minister of Defence in the James Bond franchise. Despite the overall shoddiness of the production, all involved, including Aimi Macdonald as Bind's ditzy assistant, look as if they're having tremendous fun, and Todd fans will no doubt enjoy the actor's suavely villainous performance.

Bind returned, this time played by Gareth Hunt (fresh from TV's *The New Avengers*), in **Licensed to Love and Kill** (1979). Once again directed by Shonteff, the film has Bind up against villain Lucifer Orchid (Gary Hope), whose plan to take over the U.S. presidency involves the use of clones (including one of Bind), a human bomb, blackmail and a psychopathic mercenary named Jensen Fury (Australian actor Nick Tate, best known for TV's *Space: 1999*). Hunt is pretty wooden as Bind, and the budget looks to be even lower than the previous film. Geoffrey Keen returns as Bind's boss, but the only real surprise here is an appearance by John Arnatt (the original Rockwell from the Charles Vine movies) as a Secret Service inventor—not unlike the James Bond franchise "Q" character—responsible for some frankly ridiculous gadgets which Bind puts to equally ridiculous use. Shonteff's third and final Bind film was *Number One Gun*, a truly dire 1990 offering that had all the production values of a home movie and was never theatrically released.

The Female of the Species…

A plethora of pop art, mod attire and larger than life characters adorn the outrageously camp comedy thriller **Modesty Blaise** (1966), in which Italian actress Monica Vitti plays the beautiful and impossibly chic international adventuress and criminal mastermind of the title. The often muddled plot has Modesty persuaded out of self-imposed retirement to carry out a mission for the British Secret Service, who require her skills to ensure that a consignment of diamonds (payment by the British Government to a small sheikdom in return for an oil concession) reaches its destination safely. Someone, it seems, is out to stop the shipment, and the "someone" in question turns out to be Modesty's old nemesis Gabriel (a silver-wigged Dirk Bogarde), an effete and decadent master villain headquartered in a Sicilian island fortress and whose entourage includes a sadistic female assassin named Mrs. Fothergill (Rossella Falk). Modesty and her cockney right-hand man, Willie Garvin (Terence Stamp), are soon involved in a colorfully bizarre adventure that spans London, Amsterdam and the Mediterranean, and which sees them captured by Gabriel, who forces Willie to take part in a plan to steal the diamonds from a cargo ship.

Loosely based on a popular British newspaper comic strip of the same name (created by Peter O'Donnell in 1963), the film starts promisingly with our heroine showing signs of being a female version of Derek Flint from the same year's U.S. production *Our Man Flint*. However, it soon becomes clear that she lacks the necessary vitality and resourcefulness, and is disappointingly ineffective most of the time. She does look fabulous though, and overall the film is a visual treat thanks to inventive art direction and costume design. Director Joseph Losey was not best suited to this type of material and unfortunately goes way overboard with the zany shenanigans, but he does get a hugely entertaining performance from Bogarde, who pretty much walks away with the movie. A much-anticipated fight between Modesty and Mrs. Fothergill, the latter having earlier shown just how ruthless she is by strangling a victim with her thighs, ends up being a washout, while other negatives include Modesty's two completely unengaging romantic song duets with Willie and a poorly conceived climactic invasion of Gabriel's island by the sheikdom's ruler and his warriors. *The Daily Cinema* (May 9, 1966) hit the nail on the head, correctly noting that "as a whole it doesn't altogether swing, though it's made up of many swinging components."

The British-Hong Kong co-production ***The Golden Lady*** (1979) stars Ina Skriver (billed as Christina World) as a mercenary corporate spy named Julia Hemmingway. When the Arabic state of Kubran's oil concession is offered for sale, the interested buyers include a British tycoon named Charles Whitlock (Patrick Newell). Whitlock hires Julia to discredit the competition, which she sets about doing in ruthless fashion with her team of glamorous helpers and some sophisticated computer technology. When it transpires that Whitlock is in league with the KGB to get the Russians a foothold in Kubran, another prospective buyer—actually a CIA operative (Stephen Chase)—finally sees to it, with Julia's help, that the oil concession goes to the U.S. This rather dull enterprise, helmed by Spanish director José Ramón Larraz (whose best-known British film is 1974's *Vampyres*), is vaguely reminiscent of U.S. director Ted V. Mikels' 1973 grindhouse flick *The Doll Squad*, which as the title suggests also featured a group of shapely operatives. The soundtrack includes songs performed by diverse artists such as The Three Degrees and Charles Aznavour.

…Is Deadlier Than the Male

Hugh "Bulldog" Drummond, a patriotic crime-fighting adventurer created by author H.C. "Sapper" McNeile, and last seen on the big screen in 1951's *Calling Bulldog Drummond*, was resurrected and reimagined as a James Bond–style insurance agent in ***Deadlier Than the Male*** (1966). Richard Johnson, who'd had a tiny uncredited role in the 1951 film, is suitably suave, handsome and tough as the revamped character in a glossy adventure that also features other updated McNeile characters such as Drummond's arch-nemesis Carl Petersen. Played by the great Nigel Green, Petersen is a murderous plutocrat engaged in bumping off senior executives from certain big companies in order to gain concessions and in some cases to take advantage of a resulting drop in a company's stock value. Much of the action takes place in an Italian coastal resort, with a climactic game of cat-and-mouse between Drummond and Petersen playing out on a giant, voice-operated mechanical chess board in the villain's nearby castle headquarters.

A 1979 British–Hong Kong co-production.

Elke Sommer and Sylva Koscina add considerable spice to the proceedings, living up to the title as two of Petersen's assassins, a seductive, sadistic and frequently scantily clad double act whose trail of mayhem—involving murder by harpoon gun, time bomb, poison dart and deadly cigar etc.—helped gain the film an "X" rating upon its original British release. Also starring are U.S. TV actor Steve Carlson as Drummond's nephew (a comic relief sidekick of sorts), and one would be remiss not to mention the very good if requisitely James Bond–like title song performed by The Walker Brothers. Although now a firm favorite among fans of 007-like spy flicks, the movie wasn't terribly well received back in the day, with the *Monthly Film Bulletin* (March 1967) concluding that "the original Drummond would have found the whole thing rather distasteful." Incidentally, Green and Sommer later played similar roles in the Dean Martin "Matt Helm" movie *The Wrecking Crew* (1968).

Drummond's resurrection stretched to one more film, **Some Girls Do** (1969), in which our suave hero was once again played by Richard Johnson. As before, Drummond is pitted against master villain Carl Petersen, the latter having obviously survived what looked like his demise on the giant chessboard of the previous film, and this time played by James Villiers in the actor's typically supercilious fashion. Helped by two deadly new henchwomen (Daliah Lavi and Beba Loncar) and a small army of robotized (by way of surgically implanted artificial brains) young females, Petersen is out to sabotage the success of Britain's first supersonic airliner, the S.S.T.1., in return for £8 million from a foreign power. An eventful climax takes place in Petersen's Mediterranean island headquarters, where the vil-

Richard Johnson plays with fire in the shapely form of Elke Sommer, who's *Deadlier Than the Male* (1966).

lain attempts to destroy a prototype of the aircraft (while in mid-flight) using a long-range infrasonic weapon. Needless to say, he is thwarted by Drummond with more than a little help from one of the robotized females, "Robot No. 7," after she switches allegiances.

Lavi and Loncar's characters lack the chemistry, not to mention wickedness, of those played by Elke Sommer and Sylva Koscina in the first movie, and so the prize for best female role goes to the delightful Sydne Rome (in her film debut) as a supposedly ditzy groupie of Drummond's eventually revealed to be a quadruple-crossing Russian agent. The campy shenanigans also feature a bumbling British Embassy official (Ronnie Stevens) assigned to help Drummond, and there's a fun final twist concerning the aforementioned Robot No. 7, played charmingly by Vanessa Howard.

Other Super Secret Agents

These final three agents all coincidentally debuted in 1964 novels: Jason Love in *Passport to Oblivion* by James Leasor; Boysie Oakes in *The Liquidator* by John Gardner; and Charles Hood in *Hammerhead* by James Mayo (aka Stephen Coulter). While the characters would each go on to feature in several novels, they only appeared in one film apiece.

Jason Love

At the start of **Where the Spies Are** (1965), British Intelligence MI6 operative Rosser (Cyril Cusack) is murdered by Russian agents in Beirut. Needing to know certain vital information that Rosser had uncovered, but with no spare agents to send to Beirut, MI6 is forced to recruit an outsider, which is where Jason Love (the debonair David Niven) comes in. An English country doctor and classic car fanatic, Love is persuaded—with the promise of a much-desired vintage Cord LeBaron automobile as payment—to undertake the mission, which in the end uncovers a plot by the Russians to assassinate a Middle-Eastern prince, a move that would adversely affect British oil interests. Love's adventure comes to involve a hard-drinking fellow British agent (Nigel Davenport) and a beautiful double agent (Françoise Dorléac), while his—as he calls it—"do-it-yourself spy kit" includes gadgets such as a fountain pen capable of injecting truth serum. One or two moments of brutality jar with the otherwise mostly light-hearted proceedings.

Boysie Oakes

The Liquidator (1965) features the light-hearted adventures of the bungling Boysie Oakes. We first see Boysie (Rod Taylor) as a tank sergeant during World War II where, more by accident than design, he saves the life of British Intelligence officer Mostyn (Trevor Howard), who mistakenly believes his rescuer to be a natural born killer. Two decades later, Mostyn remembers Boysie when it becomes necessary to recruit an operative to liquidate various spies in the British Secret Service. Succumbing to the lure of a glamorous spy lifestyle (complete with luxury apartment and fancy sports car), not to mention some heavy pressure from Mostyn, Boysie soon finds himself with a license to kill, even though he's essentially a coward who, in his own words, "couldn't kill a fly." For this reason, he hires a freelance assassin (comic actor Eric Sykes on fine form) to do his dirty work for him. A series of adventures culminate in Boysie being used in a scheme by the Russians to steal a top-secret British aircraft known as "The Vulture," referred to at one point as the "hottest thing since the H-Bomb." The ever-engaging Taylor is equally adept at the action as he is in the spoofery, of which there is much; Howard is gruffly hilarious (drawing on his famous Captain Bligh performance but with a comedic slant) and, as noted by the *Monthly Film Bulletin* (October 1966), "wickedly proves how dialogue can be made to sound better than it is." Jill St. John shines as Mostyn's glamorous secretary, who is amorously pursued by Boysie as well as being involved in a big final twist.

Charles Hood

Played in suitably cool if somewhat unengaging fashion by Vince Edwards, super secret agent Charles Hood, working for British Intelligence, investigates **Hammerhead** (1968), a sadistic criminal mastermind believed to be up to something nefarious in connection with an upcoming NATO conference in Lisbon. The villain (portrayed by one of Britain's best film and TV bad guys, Peter Vaughan) is in fact planning to steal anti-missile installation secrets from the conference by replacing one of its key delegates with a double. Accompanying Charles throughout his adventure, which involves the agent posing as an art dealer (Hammerhead, we learn, is a fervent collector of pornographic art), is kooky beatnik Sue Trenton (a delightful Judy Geeson), the pair first meeting in the film's opening sequence involving an avant-garde performance art show in London. Vaughan has tremendous fun as the evildoer, whose main gimmick is being lifted onto/lowered from his helicopter by way of an old Georgian-style sedan chair, in which he finally meets his demise via harpoon at the hands of a mistreated mistress (Beverly Adams). One of the more memorable scenes sees Charles and Sue, having been captured by Hammerhead, bound up in a coffin and transported by hearse through Lisbon to their intended place of execution. Producer Irving Allen and co-screenwriter Herbert Baker both also worked on Hollywood's "Matt Helm" spy movie series.

2

Mystery and Murder

Probably the most popular type of British thriller is the mystery thriller, with the mystery usually connected to murder. Apart from the whodunits (including those classic drawing room mysteries where suspects are gathered together for a reconstruction of the crime and a final unmasking of the culprit), there are also the "why-they-dun-its" and the "how-they-dun-its," which bring up questions of motive and method. The classic motives are jealousy, revenge, gaining from an inheritance or life insurance policy, and the need to cover up some secret or other. As for method, apart from the usual stabbings, shootings, stranglings and poisonings, some of the more creative means of murder include air bubble injected into vein, poisoned arrow, bullet made from ice so as to leave no trace, manipulated killer bees and even the use of snorkeling equipment as an aid to homicide.

Among the wide variety of perpetrators to be found in this chapter are a bluebeard-type killer, a wicked stepmother, various deadly doctors, a homicidal schoolteacher and several devious husbands not to mention equally devious wives. Some of the more elaborate alibis constructed by those attempting the "perfect" murder can be found in the B movies *Operation Murder* (1956), *Rogue's Yarn* (1956) and *The Third Alibi* (1961). In many murder mystery scenarios, a protagonist will awake from a drug-induced sleep only to find themselves the victim of a clever frame-up, with a dead body nearby and a murder weapon clutched in hand. And let's not forget that most vital of ingredients—the surprising final twist; two of the best occur in *Walk a Tightrope* (1963) and *Ten Little Indians* (1965). Finally, the several "Old Dark House" mysteries on offer include *What a Carve Up* (1961), *The Horror of It All* (1964) and *The House in Nightmare Park* (1973).

1950s

In the comical B movie **Someone at the Door** (1950), journalist Ronnie (Michael Medwin) comes up with a madcap scheme for a front-page scoop. It involves staging the phony murder of his sister Sally (Yvonne Owen) and making himself appear as the prime suspect so that he can be put on trial, at which point Sally will turn up to clear him. In the meantime, Sally is to remain hidden in a secret room at their shadowy mansion. However, before the plan is in full swing, the siblings, along with Sally's fiancé (Hugh Latimer), who is helping out in the scheme, run afoul of competing criminal entities—including a bogus Scotland Yard inspector—seeking stolen jewels hidden by one of them (the criminals) in the secret room sometime in the past. There are plenty of chuckles, although one particularly nasty moment of threatened torture by one of the crooks against Sally is no laughing matter.

Double Confession (1950) sees Jim Medway (Derek Farr) returning late one night to the seaside resort of Seagate to see his estranged wife Lorna, who in his absence has been having an affair with local businessman

Charlie Durham (William Hartnell). Discovering that Lorna has committed suicide, Jim uses this as an opportunity to take revenge on Durham by tricking him into thinking she's been murdered and threatening to implicate him in the "crime." This leads to Durham's devoted and psychotic sidekick, Paynter (a characteristic performance by Peter Lorre), attempting to eliminate Jim. However, circumstances, which involve drinking himself into a stupor (Lorre is great here, although his best role as a drunk was yet to come in the comedic "The Black Cat" segment of 1962's *Tales of Terror*), see Paynter inadvertently cause both his own and Durham's downfall. Also woven into the story are the mystery of a man found dead at the foot of cliffs and a romance between Jim and a troubled young woman (Joan Hopkins) he meets on the beach. The film has a simple enough premise, but as the *Motion Picture Herald* (May 16, 1953) pointed out, "a maze of confusion surrounding the characters makes it unnecessarily complex."

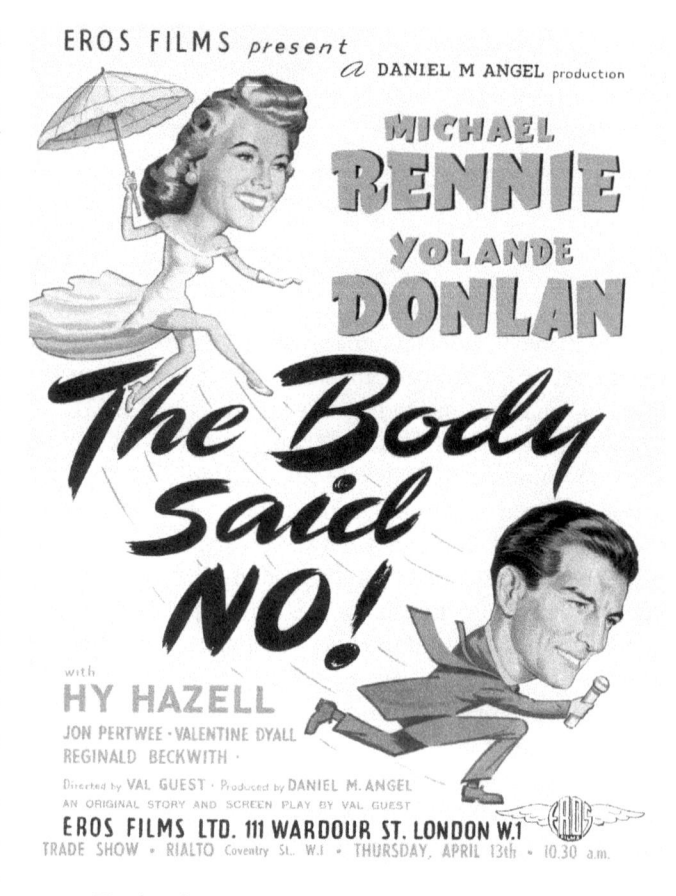

Trade advertisement for a 1950 comedy thriller.

Michael Rennie engagingly plays himself in the B-movie comedy thriller **The Body Said No!** (1950). Co-starring is a vivacious Yolande Donlan as Mikki, a scatterbrained cabaret artiste who catches unscheduled late-night television transmissions of a bearded man (Valentine Dyall) seemingly plotting to murder Rennie at London's Alexandra Palace TV studios. The rest of the story concerns Mikki's frantic attempts to convince others—her boyfriend (Canadian actor Arthur Hill), roommate (Hy Hazell), the police and Rennie himself—of the plot, until the twist ending where it's revealed that the sinister transmissions were in fact nothing more than television wavelength tests using footage from a previously filmed rehearsal for a thriller involving Rennie. Mild thrills are interspersed with some pleasant musical numbers.

"What strange mystery surrounds the beautiful Lady in Black?"

The slow-moving **Shadow of the Past** (1950), which *Today's Cinema* (May 25, 1950) called "melodramatic fare for the masses," stars Joyce Howard as a spectral figure—The Lady in Black—at the center of the story. The figure, seemingly the ghost of a woman murdered in an automobile "accident," is in reality the twin sister of the victim posing as the apparition of her dead sibling as part of a plan to draw out the killer. Terence Morgan plays an ex–Royal Air Force officer drawn into events following an encounter with the "ghost" in a deserted apartment next door to a friend's (Michael Medwin) place. Also involved in the tale is the dead woman's husband (Andrew Osborn), who has much to hide, and there's a suitably ironic ending in which the killer crashes to his death over the very same cliff where he'd sent his victim to her death.

Set against the backdrop of the 1889 Great Exhibition in Paris, the classic mystery ***So Long at the Fair*** (1950) begins with the arrival in the capital of Vicky Barton (Jean Simmons) and her brother Johnny (David Tomlinson), who book into separate rooms at the Hotel de la Licorne. The morning after a night on the town, Vicky finds that not only has her brother disappeared, but there's also no trace of the room he was staying in. With the hotel staff insisting she arrived alone, and after getting little to no help from the British Consul or the police, Vicky eventually finds an ally in dashing artist George Hathaway (Dirk Bogarde), who can verify Johnny's existence and finally helps solve the mystery. The film, beautifully presented and featuring an unusual and satisfying denouement, borrows elements from the more gruesome 1932 U.S. offering *Midnight Warning*, and was later (in 1955) reworked as a first season episode—"Into Thin Air"—of TV's *Alfred Hitchcock Presents*.

"Could she escape her tortured past?"

Co-scripted by Gerald Anstruther from his own play, ***The Third Visitor*** (1950) initially involves an investigation into the murder of foreign criminal Richard Carling (Karel Stepanek), who we later learn has faked his own death in order to escape a multitude of problems. We also learn that Carling has been operating under a false identity; his true identity is that of Otto Steiner, a brutal concentration camp commandant during World War II. Featured throughout is Sonia Dresdel as a charming and sympathetic fashion model named Steffy, who it transpires was once a prisoner at Steiner's camp (this explains a jarring opening shot of her undergoing psychological torture) and is seeking revenge. Some gothic atmosphere is provided by way of Steiner's somber London mansion (complete with secret chamber), and there's an emotional finale involving Steffy and a fellow vengeance-seeking character. Another version of the story appeared in 1952 as a fifth-season episode of the U.S. series *Kraft Television Theatre*.

Based on a 1948 BBC radio serial called *Return from Darkness*, the Hammer B movie ***Black Widow*** (1950) stars Robert Ayres as Mark Sherwin who, while driving along a country road, is tricked into stopping by a criminal who knocks him unconscious and steals his wallet and car. Mark suffers temporary insomnia and is nursed at a nearby cottage. In the meantime, the thief has crashed the car and his charred remains are mistaken for those of Mark, whose wife Christine (Christine Norden) thinks she will now inherit her husband's estate and be free to marry her lover—Mark's best friend Paul (Anthony Forwood). When Mark finally makes it home, Christine plots his murder, this being simplified by the official belief that he is already dead. An excellent noir-style plot is marred somewhat by unremarkable treatment.

In ***The Woman in Question*** (1950), the titular female under consideration is a fortune teller, Madame Astra (Jean Kent), discovered dead—strangled with a scarf—at her lodgings in a seaside town. The police interview various people, including the woman's sister (Susan Shaw) and an elderly pet store proprietor (Charles Victor), who knew her and had seen her in events that led up to the murder. In a series of flashbacks, Kent gets to play Madame Astra as a variety of personalities (ranging from a sympathetic angel to a drunken slattern) according to the way she was perceived by the various interviewees. Ultimately, the killer is exposed as the result of a crucial utterance by, of all things, a parrot! Although a little slow and lacking in suspense, the film is worth watching for Kent's skillful performance.

The quaint B movie ***She Shall Have Murder*** (1950) stars Rosamund John as Jane Hamish, a London law clerk and aspiring writer who, encouraged by her fiancé Dagobert (Derrick De Marney), begins writing a mystery novel using as characters fellow employees at her law firm. Before long, the couple find themselves in the middle of a real-life mystery upon investigating the death—in suspicious circumstances—of one of the firm's elderly clients. The amateur sleuths are faced with a number of red herrings before finally tracking down the killer. The *Monthly Film Bulletin* (December 1950) remarked that the tone of the film is one of "determined and occasionally forced gaiety."

"He planned to kill—and leave.... No Trace."

An intriguing premise is rather flatly handled in Tempean Films' first B thriller ***No Trace*** (1950). Robert Southley (Hugh Sinclair), a crime novelist and host of a BBC radio show called *The Mind of a Murderer*, uses a disguise (taking inspiration from one of his own stories) to carry out a real-life murder—that of an American (Michael Brennan) blackmailing him in connection with a robbery the two men once carried out in Philadelphia. However, things begin going wrong for Southley when he's invited by his friend, Scotland Yard's Inspector MacDougall (John Laurie), to help investigate the crime, added to which his pretty secretary, Linda (Dinah Sheridan), begins to suspect the truth, putting her in danger. Canadian actor Barry Morse also stars as an astute police sergeant.

Although there have been many television adaptations over the years, ***The Late Edwina Black*** (1950) remains the only movie version of William Dinner and William Morum's play of the same name. Set in a gloomy mansion, this atmospheric Victorian-era whodunit concerns the fatal poisoning of the titular character, the domineering and bedridden wife of schoolteacher Gregory (David Farrar). Evidence points to Edwina's companion, Elizabeth (Geraldine Fitzgerald), and Gregory, who are in love with each other, as the culprits, but there's more to the case than meets the eye. It turns out that Edwina had decided she wanted to die and had compelled her devoted housekeeper Ellen (Jean Cadell) to poison her; resentful about Elizabeth and Gregory's affair, Ellen then planted evidence to incriminate the couple.

A great lead performance by Jean Kent distinguishes this 1950 murder mystery.

Roland Culver stands out as a Scotland Yard detective who eventually unravels the truth.

Adapted from "Maigret" creator Georges Simenon's novel *Monsieur la Souris*, **Midnight Episode** (1950) stars Stanley Holloway as a down-and-out Shakespeare-quoting street performer known as "The Professor." The story sees The Professor accidentally come into possession of a murdered man's wallet, which leads to him becoming mixed up in a dangerous adventure involving a gang of forgers responsible for the killing. Some gently comic moments punctuate the fairly complex story, which benefits greatly from a colorful portrayal by Holloway, with excellent support from Leslie Dwyer as a fellow down-and-out. The novel's Paris setting has been successfully transferred to London, and the proceedings are accompanied by a pleasant theme tune by Mischa Spoliansky.

Kenneth Hyde's stage play *The Rossiters*, which had been adapted for BBC TV in 1948, was later brought to the big screen by Hammer Films under the title **The Rossiter Case** (1950). Wheelchair-bound after becoming paralyzed in a car accident, Liz Rossiter (Helen Shingler, reprising her role from the BBC version) has to contend with the fact that her husband, Peter (Clement McCallin), and scheming sister, Honor (a particularly convincing Sheila Burrell), are having an affair. Circumstances see Honor taking drastic action in so far as feigning a pregnancy in order to pressure Peter into leaving Liz. During a confrontation between the two sisters, a struggle ensues in which Liz to some extent manages to overcome her paralysis, and which involves a gun belonging to Peter; the tussle ends with Honor being shot dead. Liz subsequently stays quiet and Peter comes under suspicion, but in the end the melodramatic events conclude positively for the couple. The *Monthly Film Bulletin* (February 1951) described this creaky B movie as "artificial in presentation, and weighed down by dialogue."

In the atmospheric night-time opening scene of **The Long Dark Hall** (1950), a maniac (the gaunt Anthony Dawson, four years away from one of his most memorable roles as the would-be strangler of Grace Kelly in Hitchcock's *Dial M for Murder*) stabs a showgirl (Jill Bennett) to death in an alleyway. Nearly one year later, he murders a second showgirl, Rose Mallory (Patricia Cutts [billed as Patricia Wayne]), in her lodgings. As a result of circumstantial evidence, Arthur Groome (Rex Harrison), a married man who'd been having an affair with Rose, is tried and sentenced to death for the crime. In an evil maneuver, the maniac anonymously confesses to the police via a letter timed to arrive just after Groome's scheduled execution. However, in a stroke of luck, the execution is called off due to a temporary parliamentary suspension of the death penalty, and a clue in the letter eventually leads to the killer's capture. Lilli Palmer, Harrison's real-life wife at the time, plays his sympathetic fictional wife, and there's an extended courtroom sequence that generates one or two moments of tension.

In the B movie **Chelsea Story** (1950), unemployed journalist Mike Harvey (Henry Mollison), together with another man, Chris (Michael Ward), breaks into a house as the result of a wager offered by the shady Fletcher Gilchrist (Sydney Tafler) at the latter's party in London's Chelsea. Circumstances lead to Chris accidentally killing the homeowner, whereupon both men flee in panic, with Chris ending up badly injured and hospitalized. Fearing he will be blamed for the killing, Mike goes to ground in a Soho café and is befriended by Janice (Ingeborg Wells), a young woman who tries to help him. Mike's ensuing escapades also involve his fiancée, whose jealousy over Janice leads to her informing the police as to his whereabouts, and Gilchrist, who has attempted to distance himself from the whole affair. The film's June 5, 1951, U.S. television showing on New York's WCBS-TV (as a *Film Theater of the Air* presentation) predated its British theatrical release by several weeks.

Despite some sluggish pacing, director

Jacques Tourneur's ***Circle of Danger*** (1950) manages to hold the interest by sustaining an effective air of mystery throughout, and it benefits greatly from a likeable performance by charismatic Welsh-born Hollywood star Ray Milland as American ex-Navy man Clay Douglas. We first encounter Clay working with a salvage team off the coast of Florida, where he gains sufficient funds for a visit to England to investigate his commando brother's mysterious death during World War II. Clay's suspicion is that his sibling may have been murdered by a fellow commando from his squadron. His search for the truth takes him from London to the Scottish Highlands as he questions former members of the squadron, with the story eventually reaching a completely unexpected conclusion. Patricia Roc co-stars as a writer-illustrator of children's books involved in a blossoming romance with Clay, and Marius Goring stands out among the supporting cast as one of the ex-commandos (now a ballet master).

"He thought he was smart, but...!"

One of *The Towering Inferno* director John Guillermin's earliest efforts was the sprightly B-movie comedy thriller ***Smart Alec*** (1951). Peter Reynolds plays the titular know-it-all, Alec Albion, a young hedonist who plans and carries out (using a bullet made of ice so as to leave no trace) what he believes is a perfect murder—that of his wealthy uncle—in order to gain an inheritance. He is duly suspected, arrested and put on trial but is acquitted due to the flimsy evidence presented. Then, relying on the double jeopardy legal principle whereby a person cannot be tried twice for the same crime, he invites the police investigators from the case to a party and arrogantly confesses his guilt. However, a neat if rather contrived final twist sees him get his comeuppance. Reynolds is on fine form as the cocky Alec, and Leslie Dwyer heads the supporting cast as janitor of a London apartment block where the story mostly unfolds.

A sinister atmosphere permeates the B movie ***Home to Danger*** (1951), in which Barbara Cummings (Rona Anderson), upon her father Alfred's supposed suicide, inherits the old man's share in a business as well as the family mansion known as Greensleeves. It transpires that Alfred was murdered upon learning that his business partner had been using their office in connection with a drugs racket, whose mysterious boss soon targets Barbara for death so as to prevent her discovering the truth. Guy Rolfe (later to make a big impression stateside in the title role of William Castle's cult 1961 horror flick *Mr. Sardonicus*) plays Robert Irving, a novelist and childhood friend of Barbara's, while Alan Wheatley is cast as the suave head of a widows and orphans charity who turns out to be not so charitable after all; and Stanley Baker appears in a small early role as a feeble-minded servant who twice saves Barbara's life, the second time at the cost of his own. In the prolonged and atmospheric climax, the chief villain, while trying to escape a dragnet, gets his comeuppance in the marshland surrounding Greensleeves. An epilogue (set some time later) shows Barbara and Robert at a bookstall, where the latter's new novel, obviously inspired by preceding events and called *The Vengeance of the Marshes*, is evidently selling very well indeed.

Death of an Angel (1951) is a somber B movie revolving around the village practice of Dr. Robert Welling (Patrick Barr). Having become convinced that his lovely wife Mary (Jane Baxter) has been gradually poisoning him with arsenic, Robert switches his bedtime milk with hers, believing it to contain just a small dose. However, the drink proves fatal and Robert, suspected of murder, is forced to go on the run. The real poisoner all along is eventually revealed as an obnoxious local bank manager named Walter Grannage (Russell Waters), a regular visitor to the Welling household. A dangerous psychopath, Grannage, who we learn killed his own wife in a nasty "accident," had been slowly feeding Robert arsenic to get him out of the way with a view to having Mary all to himself. Other prominent characters include Robert's junior assistant (Raymond Young), the practice nurse (Jean Lodge) and the Wellings' young daughter (Julie Somers), the latter involved in a climactic chase which sees Grannage meet a dramatic end in an old water mill.

The entertaining B movie *Mystery Junction* (1951) boasts an unusual structure and some spirited performances. During a train journey, an elderly lady, Miss Owens (Christine Silver), gets chatting to a fellow passenger whom she has recognized as being mystery author Larry Gordon (Sydney Tafler). To illustrate his writing technique to the inquiring lady, Gordon improvises a murder story in which the two of them feature among a group of passengers stranded at a snowbound railway station. Gordon's made-up scenario is depicted as a film-within-a-film that reflects how Miss Owens imagines the story, with the other characters played by Martin Benson, Barbara Murray and John Salew to name but three. Having concluded the tale, Gordon disembarks, this immediately followed by a quaint final twist which has Miss Owens begin to see people in real life—including a newly boarded passenger and the train guard—who are the spitting image of how she'd imagined certain characters in the story. The short and sweet initial set-up segues nicely into Gordon's fictitious narrative, an atmospheric little mystery that takes up the bulk of the subsequent running time.

Tafler also stars in the rarely seen B movie *Blind Man's Bluff* (1951) and was, according to the *Kinematograph Weekly* (January 24, 1952), "easily the best player in the cast." He portrays a bookmaker mixed up with a gang of jewel thieves whose presumed leader is found hanged at a London boarding house. The police, headed by Superintendent Morley (Norman Shelley), believe it's a case of suicide, but Morley's son Roger (Anthony Pendrell), a writer working on a novel about the gang's activities, finds proof that it was in fact murder. Before the culprit is identified, Roger becomes embroiled in a dangerous adventure surrounding the gang's theft of a £5,000 diamond. Other characters include a taxi driver (John Le Mesurier), whom the victim had been blackmailing, and his daughter (Zena Marshall).

> "She had everything you could give a woman to torment a man!"

Set on the Yorkshire moors, the melodramatic and talky *Another Man's Poison* (1951) stars the legendary Bette Davis in great form as a conniving and highly strung thriller writer named Janet Frobisher. The film begins with Janet having just murdered—via poisoned alcohol—her estranged husband, who had attempted to blackmail her after showing up unexpectedly at her secluded house while on the run from a bank robbery. In no time at all, the dead man's partner-in-crime, George Bates (Davis' then real-life husband Gary Merrill), shows up looking for him. After learning the facts, George helps Janet dispose of the body and subsequently threatens to expose her crime unless she goes along with his plan (involving him posing as her husband) to remain indefinitely at the house. An ensuing state of uneasy co-dependency finally leads to Janet deciding that George too must be eliminated, and once again she uses poisoned alcohol. Anthony Steel and Emlyn Williams also star, the former as Janet's toy boy and the latter as a nosy local veterinarian involved in a deliciously ironic ending in which Janet gets her comeuppance.

The atmospheric and occasionally creepy B movie *Crow Hollow* (1951) stars Donald Houston and Natasha Parry as newlyweds Robert and Ann Armour. The story begins with Robert taking Ann to live at his ancestral home, an ominous country mansion known as Crow Hollow and inhabited by his three eccentric aunts. Before long, a close call with a deadly spider and a severe case of food poisoning convince Ann that someone is out to kill her. Things come to a head when the maid, Willow (Patricia

Left to right: Bette Davis, Gary Merrill, Anthony Steel and Barbara Murray in *Another Man's Poison* (1951).

Owens), is stabbed in the back after the killer mistakes her for Ann due to a dress she was wearing. Esma Cannon, Nora Nicholson and Susan Richmond give entertaining performances as the trio of aunts, one of whom proves to be the murderer—a dangerous psychopath whose twisted motive is revealed in the somewhat subdued climax.

The titular character in ***Mr. Denning Drives North*** (1951) is an aircraft engineer (John Mills) who accidentally kills—during a fight—a shady immigrant (Herbert Lom) his daughter was threatening to run off with. The reason Denning drives north is to dump the body in a ditch, making it appear that the man has died as the result of a hit-and-run accident. A subsequent lack of news reports suggests that the body has not been found by the authorities, and events lead to a troubled Denning confessing all to his wife (Phyllis Calvert) before being compelled to return to the ditch, only to find the body missing. The remainder of the film concerns Denning's determination to find out what happened to the corpse, this eventually leading to a situation—involving his daughter's new attorney boyfriend (Sam Wanamaker)—in which he faces being charged with willful murder. Despite the rather grim subject matter, the film manages to remain fairly light-hearted and benefits from all-around good performances.

The B movie ***Never Look Back*** (1951), which the *Monthly Film Bulletin* (May 1952) said "improves as it progresses," stars Rosamund John as Anne Maitland, a prominent lawyer who allows her caddish ex-boyfriend Guy (Guy Middleton) to stay the night—platonically—after he fights with his mistress. At some point during the night, the mistress is shot dead and Guy, having decided not to use Anne as an alibi so as to protect her reputation, gets charged with the murder. Events see Anne defending Guy in court, whereupon he is cleared when the truth about him staying at her place is revealed. However, there's a neat final twist in which Guy is found to be not innocent after all. Hugh Sinclair plays Anne's current suitor and the prosecuting attorney in the case, while the great character actors Harry H. Corbett and Peter Jeffrey make their feature film debuts in small uncredited roles.

Ralph Richardson stars as bank clerk David Preston, who arrives **Home at Seven** (1952) on what he believes to be Monday, only to be told by his wife (Margaret Leighton) that it's actually Tuesday and that he has been missing for 24 hours. David cannot account for the lost time, and the possibility arises that he is the culprit in a robbery and murder. The eventual solution to the mystery, which involves David having suffered a blackout in a pub, is reasonably satisfying and clears him of all suspicion in the crimes. Richardson also directed (his only movie credit in this capacity) this fairly pedestrian mystery, filmed in just over two weeks on a tiny budget and based on a 1950 play of the same name by *Journey's End* author R.C. Sherriff. The cast also features Jack Hawkins as a doctor friend of the Prestons.

During the course of the fun little B movie **I'm a Stranger** (1952), we learn that the deceased Alec Mackenzie, who spent his final few years in London, had disinherited all his relatives by making a new will leaving everything to his godson, George Westcott (Patric Doonan), in Calcutta. The film begins with Westcott, whom none of the remaining Mackenzie family has ever seen, arriving in London to arrange receipt of the inheritance, only to find that the new will is missing, although it's believed that Alec hid it somewhere in his gloomy old house before he died. In an attempt to prevent Westcott getting the fortune, one of the Mackenzies attempts to find and destroy the new will, leading to various complications and a surprise revelation concerning Westcott. Other characters involved in the neat plot include an actress (Greta Gynt playing herself), the vice-chairman (a splendid James Hayter) of an amateur crime investigation club, and a supercilious lawyer (Charles Lloyd Pack).

The *Monthly Film Bulletin* (September 1952) regarded **The Lost Hours** (1952) as "an undistinguished British thriller made with more than one eye on the American B picture market." Hollywood actor Mark Stevens, who the *MFB* went on to say "seems rather tired and bored throughout," plays Paul Smith, an American test pilot framed for the murder of one of his old World War II RAF colleagues, Kenneth Peters (John Harvey), after attending their squadron's annual reunion in London. Forced to go on the run, Smith attempts to prove his innocence with the help of old (not for long) flame Louise (Jean Kent). John Bentley refreshingly plays against type (though still suave as ever, mind you) as the real killer, one of the ex-RAF men who'd been double-crossed by Peters in connection with smuggling activities.

Bentley returns to his good guy persona in **Tread Softly** (1952) as novice stage producer Keith Gilbert. Desperately in need of a venue for his debut musical show, Gilbert secures a supposedly haunted theater that's been closed for years following the onstage murder of an actor there. Preparations for opening night are disrupted by strange events, including two new murders, that appear to support the "haunted" theater theory, but in the end it all turns out to be linked to an attempt—by a mysterious figure—to locate a cache of stolen emeralds that had been hidden therein some years earlier. The highlight of this fun B movie, whose thrills are somewhat diluted by the inclusion of various musical numbers, is the introduction of a neat mystery-within-a-mystery concerning a gruesome discovery in a sealed dressing room. A major part of the film centers on an attempted hostile takeover of Gilbert's show and involves a doomed actress played by American-born Frances Day.

"The 'T' killer is at large!"

Peter Lawford plays the Raffles-like society thief Nicholas Revel in ***The Hour of 13*** (1952), a remake of 1934's *The Mystery of Mr. X*. In Edwardian London, a serial killer known as "The Terror" is targeting police constables, and circumstantial evidence found at one of the crime scenes leads the police to suspect that Revel is the culprit. In order to clear himself, Revel begins his own investigation and sets out to bring "The Terror" to justice. Having discovered a pattern to the murders (the locations of the crimes form the letter "T" on a map), he is able to determine where the next attack will take place and lays a trap in which he baits the killer using a clever disguise. Dawn Addams plays a Scotland Yard Commissioner's daughter who provides romantic interest for Revel, and there's a tremendously staged climactic fight between hero and villain in a dockside warehouse.

An elusive international criminal and master of disguise known as ***The Ringer*** (1952) is out to kill the unscrupulous lawyer, Maurice Meister (Herbert Lom), who drove his sister to suicide. As a result, Meister secures police protection and turns his London mansion into a veritable fortress. The action mainly takes place in and around the mansion and involves, among others, two Scotland Yard inspectors (Norman Wooland and Charles Victor), a cockney ex-con (a humorous performance by William Hartnell) and an eccentric Scottish police surgeon (Donald Wolfit); one of these characters is in fact "The Ringer" and, before the film is over, he cleverly completes his mission and makes a spectacular getaway. Based on Edgar Wallace's popular play of the same name (a reworking of his 1925 novel *The Gaunt Stranger*), this was Guy Hamilton's directorial debut and he was blessed with a great cast.

In the B movie ***Circumstantial Evidence*** (1952), which the *Kinematograph Weekly* (October 9, 1952) said "grips from start to finish," Linda Harrison (Rona Anderson) plans to divorce her shady husband Steve (John Arnatt), who has deserted her, in order to marry young doctor Michael Carteret (Patrick Holt). Before long, Steve shows up with an associate (John Warwick) to cause trouble—involving blackmail—for Linda and Michael, only to end up murdered. Circumstantial evidence leads to Michael being arrested for the crime, but Linda eventually saves the

Peter Lawford (standing) and Roland Culver in *The Hour of 13* (1952).

day by turning amateur sleuth and tracking down the real killer. Woven into the storyline is Michael's father (Frederick Leister), an eminent judge whose son's situation influences his summing-up in a case likewise involving circumstantial evidence.

Based on E.C. Bentley's 1913 novel of the same name, *Trent's Last Case* (1952) begins with American financier Sigsbee Manderson (Orson Welles) being found shot dead in the grounds of his estate. Manderson had actually planned to commit suicide and make it appear as if his secretary Marlowe (John McCallum) had murdered him. This was to have been as an act of revenge against Marlowe, who he wrongly believed had been having an affair with his wife (Margaret Lockwood). However, not only was Manderson not murdered by Marlowe, but he also did not commit suicide as planned; the truth behind his death is ultimately explained in a twist (involving a character played by the scene-stealing Miles Malleson) that wraps things up nicely. The eponymous Trent, a reporter looking into the matter, is rather blandly played by Michael Wilding in this genteel mystery that had already been filmed twice in the 1920s and would later be made as a 1964 episode of the BBC TV series *Detective*. As was the case in *Citizen Kane* (1941), we only ever see Welles in action during flashbacks.

Set in London's Chelsea district, the well-acted B movie *The Night Won't Talk* (1952) begins creepily with a hooded figure breaking into a basement apartment and strangling an artists' model in her bed. Among the suspects is Clayton Hawkes (John Bailey), a troubled painter who had been engaged to the victim and who wastes little time rekindling an old romance with another model, Hazel (Mary Germaine). After an attempt is made (by the same hooded figure) on Hazel's life, the investigat-

A sinister hooded killer strikes in this 1952 B movie.

ing Scotland Yard detective (Ballard Berkeley) sets a trap that reveals the killer to be a jealous female who for some time has harbored a secret desire to marry Clayton and was attempting to destroy all competition. Also starring are Hy Hazell, in the key role of a famous houseboat-dwelling sculptress with a not-so-contented-as-it-seems existence as a single woman, and Elwyn Brook-Jones as the obsequious secretary of an arts establishment known as the Portrait Club.

"Millions heard him confess to murder!"

At the start of **The Voice of Merrill** (1952), a female blackmailer is shot dead in her apartment by an unseen intruder. During the investigation, the police have cause to question two authors, namely the successful and belligerent Jonathan Roach (James Robertson Justice) and the weak and rather less successful Hugh Allen (Edward Underdown). In the course of events, Jonathan's wife, Alycia (Valerie Hobson), falls in love with Hugh and, in an effort to get him some recognition, contrives (with his compliance) to pass off as his some of her husband's early unpublished works. Hugh wins acclaim when the material is broadcast—with him as narrator—as a 12-part serial on BBC radio. A key part of the film involves Jonathan, who it transpires is the murderer, initiating a revenge plan (for his wife's disloyalty) in which he cleverly rewrites the final episode so that it will incriminate Hugh—live on air—in the crime. This talky but engrossing Tempean Films B movie benefits from excellent performances and a couple of clever twists, one of them concerning a plan by Alycia to kill Jonathan with an overdose of his heart medication. Incidentally, the character name Jonathan Roach was later used as a pseudonym by Cy Endfield when he scripted *Impulse* (1954), another Tempean thriller.

In the B movie **Death Goes to School** (1952), a Scotland Yard detective (Gordon Jackson) investigates when a teacher is found dead—by strangulation—on the campus at The Abbotsham School for Girls. Barbara Murray plays a music tutor at the school whose scarf was used as the murder weapon, and it's with her help that the culprit (a fellow teacher) and their unusual motive for the crime are eventually revealed. The slow and rather talky events benefit from the atmospheric school setting in a film which the *Kinematograph Weekly* (April 30, 1953) said "holds the interest, even if it fails to chill the spine." At one point, Murray's character volunteers (as part of her alibi) the fact that she was in bed reading a thriller called *Death in Seven Hours*, which in reality is the title of the movie's source novel by Maisie Sharman (aka Stratford Davis), who also co-wrote the screenplay. The film's April 17, 1953, U.S. television showing on Los Angeles' KLAC-TV (as a *Film Playhouse* presentation) predated its British theatrical release by several weeks.

Street of Shadows (1952) turned out to be a one-shot gig, as writer and director, for respected actor Richard Vernon. Cesar Romero gives an engaging lead performance as Luigi, the charming owner of a nightclub-cum-gaming saloon who finds himself in trouble when the dead body of an ex-girlfriend (Simone Silva) turns up in his office. Circumstantial evidence leads to Luigi mistakenly believing that his new lover, an unhappily married society woman played by Kay Kendall, may be involved in the crime. The uncontested star of this atmospherically photographed B movie is character actor Victor Maddern, giving one of his most memorable performances in the key role of Luigi's frustrated club-footed assistant, nicknamed "Limpy." The at times incongruous soundtrack is made up almost exclusively of harmonica music played by Tommy Reilly.

Today's Cinema (February 12, 1953) described the B movie **Black Orchid** (1952) as "a competently made specimen of the British second-feature mystery drama." Ronald Howard stars as John Winnington, a dedicated research doctor whose much-awaited divorce from Sophie (Mary Laura Wood) leaves him free to be with his new love, namely Sophie's sister Christine (Olga Ed-

Street of Shadows (1952) is highlighted by Victor Maddern's (center) memorable performance as "Limpy," assistant to nightclub boss Luigi (Cesar Romero, left). On the right is Edward Underdown as a Scotland Yard inspector, and the police constable is played by Liam Gaffney.

wards). However, he's unable to wed Christine owing to a law that forbids marriage to an ex-wife's sister while the wife is still alive. Therefore, when Sophie dies as a consequence of poisoning (a toxic concoction causes her to become giddy and walk into the path of a truck), John is the natural suspect, and before long, he's arrested, tried and sentenced to death. The real poisoner, a married amateur horticulturist (and cultivator of the titular plant) whom Sophie had been pressuring into a romantic entanglement, is finally brought to justice thanks to some nifty joint detective work by Christine and an author friend of John's (John Bentley).

The Long Memory (1952) refers to a grudge held by Philip Davidson (John Mills) who, upon his release from prison following a twelve-year sentence for a murder he didn't commit, prepares to take revenge on three people—including former girlfriend Fay (Elizabeth Sellars)—who gave false testimony at his trial. A flashback shows the complex circumstances (involving a conspiratorial cover-up in connection with a plan to help an escaped convict leave the country) that led to Philip's incarceration. Eventually, his involvement with a refugee, Elsa (Eva Bergh), causes Philip to have second thoughts about his revenge plan, only for him to subsequently become targeted for death by the real murderer, whose identity comes as quite a surprise. Rather slow-moving, the film has some effective locations including a murky estuary on London's River Thames where Philip holes up in a deserted barge.

"She's not a pushover or a pickup ... she's more dangerous than either!"

The Hammer B movie *The Flanagan Boy* (1952) is a rather typical noir offering in which hunky Tony Wright (in his film debut) plays an up-and-coming pugilist named Johnny Flanagan. When Johnny is seduced by his Italian promoter's (Frederick Valk) scheming American wife Lorna (real-life tragic femme fatale Barbara Payton), a resulting love affair distracts him from his boxing. He ends up dumping Lorna, but she wins him back by pretending to be pregnant and later deviously maneuvers him into murdering her husband. Subsequently racked by guilt, Johnny prepares to confess to the police, only to be callously poisoned by Lorna, who then gets her comeuppance at the hands of one of Johnny's loyal trainers (Sidney James). The film's U.S. title, *Bad Blonde*, was far more apt.

Another Hammer B movie, **Spaceways** (1952) stars the rugged Howard Duff as Stephen Mitchell, an American engineer working on the British space program. When his wife Vanessa (Cecile Chevreau) and her scientist lover Philip Crenshaw (Andrew Osborn) go missing, Mitchell is suspected of having murdered them before then concealing their bodies on board a recently launched unmanned rocket designed to stay in space indefinitely. To prove his innocence, Mitchell blasts off in a second rocket to retrieve the first; by now though, we've learned that the supposedly murdered couple are in fact alive and have been hiding out in connection with Crenshaw being a spy for a foreign power. Also starring are Eva Bartok as a mathematician in love with Mitchell and who, in an effort to help him, stows away on the second rocket; and Alan Wheatley as a smug military intelligence man.

"Kill-crazy prowler strikes again!"

Murder at 3 A.M. (1952) tells of a vicious thief who always strikes at approximately 3 a.m. and stuns his victims (all wealthy society women) with a type of blow used by commandos. Dennis Price, who's the best thing about this B movie, plays a Scotland Yard detective on the case whose sister's fiancé (Philip Saville) just happens to be an ex-commando. The title refers to the fact that, following the attacks, the thief (whose violent methods end up causing two deaths) uses a boat to return inconspicuously to his riverside house, which means he only strikes on days when the river is at high tide, the highest point being at 3 a.m. A twist involving the identity of the culprit also explains how, at certain times during the story, he seemingly has the ability to be in two places at once.

Price also stars in **Noose for a Lady** (1953), a superb little B-movie whodunit that marked Wolf Rilla's (*Village of the Damned*) directing debut. The suave actor this time plays Simon Gale who, on leave from his post as a District Commissioner in Uganda, arrives in an English village to visit his cousin Margaret (Pamela Alan), only to learn that the woman has been sentenced to death (wrongfully as it happens) for her husband's murder. With only seven days until the execution, Simon wastes no time looking into the case and is helped by Margaret's pretty stepdaughter Jill (Rona Anderson). It seems the dead man had been blackmailing several of his neighbors and thus there is no shortage of suspects. Following the murder of a key witness (a poacher played by Robert Brown) who was about to disclose some crucial information, Simon sets a trap for the devious killer, leading to a very surprising reveal.

Clarendon, the country estate of mean-spirited Arnold Burgoyne (Nicholas Hannen), is the setting for the modest little B movie **Three Steps in the Dark** (1953). When Arnold is shot dead during a family gathering, the most likely suspect is his nephew—and heir to the estate—Henry (John Van Eyssen), who has a motive in that he faced being disinherited due to Arnold's disapproval of his bride-to-be (Helene Cordet). The police place everyone under house arrest and, during the investigation, an attempt is made to poison Henry. Eventually, Arnold's niece (Greta Gynt), a crime novelist, unmasks the real killer, who was next

Murder occurs at a family gathering in this 1953 supporting feature.

in line (after Henry) to inherit. Events are almost exclusively confined to Clarendon's interiors, which are crisply photographed.

"Every sultry inch of her was evil!"

As the title suggests, **Grand National Night** (1953) is set against the world of British horse racing. Moira Lister plays the glamorous and hard-drinking Babs Coates (the *Wicked Wife* of the film's U.S. title) who, after walking out on her lover Jack (Leslie Mitchell) in Liverpool, drives to her village home a few miles away and gets into an argument with her racehorse-owner husband Gerald (Nigel Patrick), physically attacking him in the process. In the ensuing struggle, Babs suddenly collapses and dies soon after. Fearing he will be wrongly blamed for murder, Gerald comes up with a clever plan so as to implicate Jack in the death. However, a tenacious detective (Michael Hordern) nevertheless becomes convinced that Gerald is a murderer and goes all out to prove it. Based on a hit stage play of the same name by Dorothy and Campbell Christie, the film features a couple of neat twists, although it suffers somewhat from an over-reliance on coincidence. Incidentally, the play was adapted twice (first in 1950 and later in 1958) for the BBC TV series *Sunday Night Theatre*.

In the intriguing and complex B movie **Meet Mr. Malcolm** (1953), missing businessman James Durant is found dead—with subsequent evidence suggesting murder—at the foot of cliffs near his country mansion. During an investigation, the police question a well-known local tramp who we later learn is a fictitious character (not dissimilar to the postman in the great 1944 Sherlock Holmes movie *The Scarlet Claw*) created by the murderer to carry out the crime, the motive being revenge in connection with Durant having once stolen a patented process from him. There's much more to the story however, including the killer's attempt to get Durant's entire fortune through the man's widow (Adrianne Allen), to whom he was once (and legally still is as it turns out) married, with the only person standing in his way being Durant's daughter (Pamela

Galloway) from a previous marriage, an aspiring actress he plans to kill under the guise of another fictitious character—this time a theatrical producer called "Mr. Malcolm." The film, aspects of whose plot hinge on an annoyingly catchy melody whistled by the killer, has some light-hearted moments, mostly involving Durant's secretary (Sarah Lawson) and her estranged mystery-writer husband (Richard Gale), who resolve their marital differences while helping out in the investigation.

A U.S. Air Force pilot, Bill Rogers (Hollywood legend Dan Duryea), arranges a *36 Hours* (1953) stopover in England to visit his estranged wife Katie (Elsy Albiin), only to end up on the run after getting framed for her murder. Seeking refuge, Bill breaks into an apartment whose occupant, a sympathetic welfare worker (Ann Gudrun), believes in his innocence and subsequently helps him bring the real killer—a supposed Customs Intelligence agent (John Chandos) Katie had unwittingly become entangled with in a blackmail racket—to justice. Duryea's strong presence lifts this otherwise routine B movie, whose cast also features Eric Pohlmann as a blackmailed diamond smuggler operating under cover of an oriental antiques business.

Flannelfoot (1953) is the nickname of a murderous jewel thief operating in England. Among those involved in efforts to catch him are two Scotland Yard detectives (Ronald Howard and Ronald Adam), an ace reporter (Jack Watling) for *The Daily Comet*, and a crime novelist (Kim Peacock). Apart from a prologue set in Berlin, where Flannelfoot had operated as a black marketeer, the action alternates between various London locations and the *Comet* owner's country mansion, where a trap is set for the thief. There's a plethora of suspects and red herrings, not to mention lots of prowling around the mansion (à la *The Bat*), before Flannelfoot's ultimate unmasking, which comes as quite a surprise. The *Monthly Film Bulletin* (November 1953) concluded that

Publicity for a 1953 Hammer Films B movie.

this B movie was "a routine thriller of no great merit."

Alex Nicol stars as an American trumpeter named James Bradley in ***Face the Music*** (1953), the first of four British B thrillers in which the sturdy Hollywood actor appeared. While visiting England to perform at the London Palladium, Bradley becomes suspected, due to circumstantial evidence, in the murder of a nightclub singer (Ann Hanslip). When he begins his own investigation, the real murderer attempts to kill him by poisoning the mouthpiece of his trumpet, but this fails to get the desired result and Bradley goes on to unmask the culprit. Nicol mimes adequately in the trumpet sequences, having been taught the technique by Kenny Baker (whose music is heard on the soundtrack), and the film also stars Geoffrey Keen in a key role as a record producer.

In the engaging B movie *The Large Rope* (1953), Tom Penney (a robust Donald Houston) returns to his English village home after serving a prison sentence for assaulting local good-time girl Amy Jordan (Vanda Godsell), who we soon learn had lied about the charge. The homecoming is met with malicious gossip and hostility, and things come to a head when Amy is murdered with circumstantial evidence pointing to Tom as the culprit. The pressure of police interrogation, plus the threat of lynch mob behavior by some of the villagers, causes Tom to go on the run. Events see him ultimately seek refuge in an old windmill, where he comes face to face with the real killer—Amy's husband Mick (Robert Brown), who was insanely jealous of his provocative wife's many dalliances—for a climactic showdown. Susan Shaw gives a pleasant performance as Tom's former girlfriend (the pair are predictably reunited at the end), and the film offers an effective depiction of rural village life.

One of the very best British comedy thrillers is *The Runaway Bus* (1953), an ingeniously conceived mystery with just the right blend of laughs and suspense, not to mention lashings of atmosphere. On the instructions of a mysterious mastermind known as the "Banker," a gang carries out a daring gold bullion robbery at London's Heathrow Airport during heavy fog. At around the same time, with the fog having rendered the airport unusable, the elderly and cantankerous Miss Beeston (Margaret Rutherford), one of many stranded travelers, demands to be transferred to another airport from where flights are leaving for Ireland. The staff duly provide a relief bus (unluckily numbered "13") and Miss Beeston is joined on the journey by a handful of other passengers as well as a stewardess (Petula Clark) assigned to look after them all. It soon emerges that the takings from the robbery—200 gold bars—are stashed in the vehicle's trunk and that one of those on board is in fact the aforementioned "Banker," although their identity is cleverly concealed until the finale. Before then, there are plenty of other surprises in store as the bus gets lost in fog and winds up in a deserted booby-trapped village that's being used for military training maneuvers.

The film marked the big-screen debuts of legendary British comic Frankie Howerd, who's on splendid form as bus number 13's hapless driver, and the lovely Belinda Lee as a delightfully ditzy young passenger obsessed with gruesomely titled thriller novels such as *The Corpse Sat Up* and *Torso for Sale*. The remaining travelers are played splendidly by George Coulouris, Toke Townley and Terence Alexander. The film did not impress *New York Daily News* movie critic Wanda Hale who, in her October 24, 1954, review of the U.S. theatrical premiere (held the previous day in the Big Apple's Trans–Lux Normandie Theatre), did not mince her words when she called it "a dud that cannot hurt anybody, but which may shake the faith of the claque of Americans who are under the misapprehension that English pictures are the only ones worth seeing." Interestingly, the film had already premiered on U.S. television 16 days earlier on *Larry Finley's Late Show*, which aired on KNXT-TV (Channel 2) in Los Angeles.

In **Solution by Phone** (1953), circumstances lead self-absorbed London actor Peter Wayne (John Witty) to murder the wife, with whom he'd had an affair, of crime novelist Richard Hanborough (Clifford Evans). Then, in order to find out how best to dispose of the body, he cunningly seeks advice from Richard by phoning him and pretending to be a writer encountering plot difficulty regarding just such a scenario. The unwitting Richard duly provides a solution, only to later become a suspect when the body is discovered. In the end, Richard's lovestruck (for him) secretary (Thea Gregory) comes up with a clever ruse—involving a diary that supposedly belonged to the dead woman—that draws a confession from Peter, leading to a chase in which he falls to his death from a theater roof. The *Monthly Film Bulletin* (March 1954) regarded this now rare B movie as "a fairly satisfactory thriller, with an ingenious denouement."

> "Hypnotic … fascinating … a lure to all who crossed her path!"

One of the best of Hammer's many B thrillers and one of the better British noir films, ***The House Across the Lake*** (1953) stars Hollywood's Alex Nicol as Mark Kendrick, an American writer in England who rents a house on the shores of Lake Windermere. Nicol's fellow Hollywoodian, Hillary Brooke, plays Carol Forrest, a neighbor across the lake who seduces Mark and then, during a boating trip, seizes an opportunity—with the infatuated Mark's complicity—to murder her husband (Sidney James). In ensuing events, Carol abandons Mark for her true love (a pianist played by Canadian actor and British B movie regular Paul Carpenter), leading to a typically melodramatic noir ending which involves Mark revealing all to the police. The two American leads (Brooke makes a great femme fatale) work well together, and the cast also includes Alan Wheatley, appearing to good effect as a detective. The script by Ken Hughes (also the film's director) was based on his own 1952 novel, *High Wray*.

Another noir-style Hammer offering, ***Murder by Proxy*** (1953) was the second of three B thrillers that Hollywood actor Dane Clark made for the company. Casey Morrow (Clark), a down-on-his-luck American, is drunk in a bar when an attractive socialite, Phyllis Brunner (Belinda Lee), offers him £500 cash in return for marrying her. The next morning, he wakes up in a strange apartment with blood on his coat, the £500 in his pocket and little memory of what happened. It transpires that during the night, Phyllis' financier father was murdered and Casey incriminated himself by handling the murder weapon. Determined to find out what exactly took place, Casey turns amateur sleuth and, having reunited with Phyllis (the particularly complex plot manages to keep one guessing as to her true motivations), discovers there'd been a scheme to swindle her father by the latter's wife (Betty Ann Davies) and a crooked lawyer (Andrew Osborn), one of whom is the murderer. Eleanor Summerfield is on marvelous form as a friendly artist and resident of the apartment in which Casey wakes up.

In director Lance Comfort's excellent ***Eight O'Clock Walk*** (1953), circumstantial evidence leads to taxi driver Tom Manning (Richard Attenborough) being arrested for the murder of a little girl. During a trial at the Old Bailey, the real killer, Horace Clifford (Maurice Denham), gives false evidence against Tom, and a guilty verdict seems inevitable. However, outside the courtroom, Tom's defense attorney (Derek Farr) notices Clifford offering a sweet—the same type as one found at the murder scene—to a child. Clifford is then recalled to the stand in an attempt to expose him as the guilty party. Denham is decidedly unsettling as the sly child murderer, and the cast also features American actress Cathy O'Donnell in a sympathetic role as Tom's supportive wife. Comfort's direction is assured, and there are a couple of memorably tense moments, including during the beginning where the killer's shadow looms over his young soon-to-be victim to the increasingly frenzied strains of composer George Melachrino's arrangement of the "Oranges and Lemons" folk song.

Another Lance Comfort offering, ***Bang! You're Dead*** (1953), is an absorbing tale set around a ramshackle British woodland

Left to right: Anthony Richmond, Veronica Hurst and Michael Medwin in *Bang! You're Dead* (1953).

community where an adventurous seven-year-old boy (Anthony Richmond) finds a loaded revolver in a deserted U.S. Army supply depot. While playing at being a highwayman, he holds up and then shoots a man dead before discarding the weapon and running away. Due to circumstantial evidence, Bob Carter (Michael Medwin), who was the victim's rival for a local woman, is suspected. Jack Warner and Derek Farr play the boy's widowed father and a detective respectively, and the sensitively handled story also involves another youngster, played by Sean Barrett, who proves crucial to the outcome. In the U.S., the film was initially shown on television under the title *Game of Danger* but as of the late 1960s was broadcast under its British title.

With a plot correctly described by the *Monthly Film Bulletin* (May 1954) as becoming "at times very nearly incomprehensible," the B movie *Johnny on the Spot* (1954) stars Hugh McDermott as freelance mining engineer Johnny Breakes, who returns to England to clear his name after serving three years in a South American jail on trumped-up charges. Making his way to the seaside villa of the wealthy financier responsible for his incarceration, he arrives to find the man's dead body along with that of a young woman. Circumstances lead to Johnny investigating the deaths in what turns out to be a complicated mystery involving, among others, a prominent colleague (Ronald Leigh-Hunt) of the dead man, and a mysterious blind pianist.

Affable Canadian actor Paul Carpenter, who played a pal of Johnny's in the previous film, also appears in the character-driven B movie *The Stranger Came Home* (1954).

The confusing plot revolves around businessman Philip Vickers (William Sylvester) who, having for some time been missing and presumed dead after going on a fishing trip to Portugal, returns to his English country estate. His wife Angie (Hollywood's Paulette Goddard) is understandably surprised, as are Job Crandall (Patrick Holt) and Bill Saul (Carpenter), two of three colleagues who had been with Vickers on the fishing trip, one of whom he correctly believes had drugged him before hitting him over the head in an attempt to kill him. Subsequent events, including the murder of one of the colleagues and a further attempt on Vickers' life, all turn out to be connected to what went down in Portugal. Unfortunately, Goddard, whose character is ultimately revealed as central to the proceedings (the villain of the piece wanted Vickers out of the way so as to have her all to himself), is sadly underused and fails to make much of an impact, leaving the always excellent Sylvester to carry the film. The source novel, *Stranger at Home*, is credited to actor George Sanders, although in reality it was ghost-written for him by Leigh Brackett.

France is the setting for the absorbing mystery ***The Green Scarf*** (1954), in which Kieron Moore gives an impressive performance as Jacques Vauthier, a man who has managed to become a successful writer despite being blind, deaf and dumb. When Jacques confesses to the murder of an American man on board an ocean liner on which he and his wife Solange (Ann Todd) had been traveling, his defense is taken up by the elderly, eccentric and quite brilliant lawyer, Deliot (a colorful performance by a heavily bearded, almost unrecognizable Michael Redgrave). Much of the story unfolds in the courtroom, where it's revealed that Jacques, who communicates via tactile signing, has confessed in order to protect Solange, believing her to be the culprit in connection with her having had an affair with the victim. Flashbacks concerning Jacques' upbringing (future British sitcom star Richard O'Sullivan plays Jacques in his youth) provide some moving moments, and there's a last-minute unmasking of the real killer—one of the ship's stewards (Michael Medwin)—whose wife, like Solange, had been a lover of the dead man.

The B movie ***Profile*** (1954), described by *Today's Cinema* (August 19, 1954) as being a "soundly made British thriller" with a "tortuous plot line," revolves around the creation of a family-oriented magazine called *Profile*, the brainchild of publisher Aubrey Holland (Stuart Lindsell). Kathleen Byron revels in her role as Aubrey's ruthless and bitchy second wife Margot, whose advances are rejected by the publication's editor, Peter (the ever-suave John Bentley), and who later becomes jealous of his interest in Aubrey's daughter from a previous marriage (Thea Gregory). Following Aubrey's death by heart attack, Peter becomes wrongly suspected of having embezzled the man, with evidence that could clear him held back by Margot—the as-yet undisclosed brains behind the embezzlement—unless Peter succumbs to her advances. Margot is subsequently murdered by her secret partner in the embezzlement, whose identity is revealed in a climax involving an exciting chase around a printing press.

"Why throw away your whole future ... for a girl you've known only 24 hours?"

A solid example of a British film noir, the B movie ***Impulse*** (1954) stars Hollywood character actor Arthur Kennedy as Alan Curtis, a married real estate agent living a routine existence in a Suffolk village. However, his life takes an unexpected turn when he offers assistance to a nightclub singer, Lila (Constance Smith), after her car breaks down. Said assistance extends to Alan not only helping Lila avoid the unwanted attentions of two men claiming to be police officers, but also driving her to London where he ends up staying the night at her place. Before long, he is mixed up in Lila and an accomplice's plan to double-cross the nightclub's boss in connection with stolen diamonds. During his ill-advised adventure, which includes a further encounter with the aforementioned "police officers" (actually the club boss' goons), Alan proves to be surprisingly tough and resourceful. Hedy Lamarr lookalike Smith is a more-than-capable femme fatale, while Joy Shelton provides contrasting feminine appeal as Alan's forgiving—luckily for him when he finally returns home—wife.

Miss Tulip Stays the Night (1954) is a quaint and breezy B movie starring Patrick Holt as thriller writer Andrew Dax who, with his wife Kate (Diana Dors), becomes involved in a real-life "thriller" while staying at a rented country cottage. After giving shelter for the night to Miss Tulip (Cicely Courtneidge), an elderly kook whose car has apparently broken down during a storm, the couple wakes to find the woman has been shot dead with a revolver she herself had left in Andrew's care. Eventually, after some amateur sleuthing, and having himself come under suspicion, Andrew solves the mystery, a complicated affair—satisfactorily explained in the film's final few moments—involving Miss Tulip's disgraced twin sister and a substantial inheritance. Holt and Dors are delightful, and the film also stars Courtneidge's real-life husband, Jack Hulbert, as a trying police constable.

Set in the English coastal town of Hastings and including some pleasant location work (including a climactic chase on Hastings Pier), the B movie **Shadow of a Man** (1954) revolves around the murder of Paul Bryant (Bill Nagy). Although he died of heart failure, this is found to have been deliberately caused by the injection of an air bubble into a vein via hypodermic needle. Amiable Canadian actor Paul Carpenter, complete with a narrative voice-over to give a noir flavor to the otherwise non-noir proceedings, plays a writer and wartime friend of Bryant's looking into the case, which involves Bryant's widow, Linda (Rona Anderson), and two of her friends (Ronald Leigh-Hunt and Jane Griffiths). The killer, who wanted Bryant out of the way so as to get close to Linda, is finally caught thanks to a clue involving his being a diabetic, hence the hypodermic needle.

The enchanting Anderson also stars in **The Flaw** (1954), an enjoyable B movie in which she plays Monica Crewson, beneficiary of a £500,000 fortune, who marries the not-so-well-off racing driver Paul Oliveri (John Bentley). Oliveri is soon revealed to be a nasty piece of work (a nice change from Bentley's usual good-guy persona) with not only a mistress on the side but also an evil plan to kill Monica in an engineered accident, having already tricked her into making a will in his favor. When Monica's attorney and long-time admirer, John Millway (Donald Houston), gets wise to Oliveri's scheming, the latter plots his demise, creating a clever alibi before spiking his drink with a deadly Amazonian poison and telling him—as he begins weakening—that he will dispose of his body at sea. However, there's a great final twist that leads to Oliveri getting a well-deserved comeuppance.

The Glass Cage (1954) refers to the locked enclosure in which Henri Sapolio (Eric Pohlmann)—the "World's Champion Starving Man"—will attempt to break his fasting record by not eating for 70 days, all for the sake of public entertainment. Organizing the event is London-based carnival showman Pel Pelham (John Ireland). This Hammer B movie gets off to a good start with an effective depiction of low-rent carnival life and its many interesting characters, but it soon becomes a complicated mess involving creepy theatrical agent Stanton (Geoffrey Keen), who murders a woman (Sapolio's neighbor) and then has to tie up loose ends which include poisoning Sapolio (by now in his cage) because the latter may be able to identify him. Sidney James and Sydney Tafler play, respectively, a bookmaker and a blackmailing Circus and Carnival Owner's League agent, both with connections to Stanton that are never made clear, lending weight to an observation by *Today's Cinema*

From left: Ferdy Mayne, Eric Pohlmann, John Ireland and Nora Gordon admire an impressively tattooed Valerie Vernon in *The Glass Cage* (1954).

(July 15, 1955) that the film "shows evidence of some fairly ruthless cutting."

Under the title *The Glass Tomb*, the picture had extensive—possibly the most extensive for a Hammer B movie—U.S. theatrical distribution from mid–1955 through 1956. As late as January of 1966, having already had a solid television presence for the previous 10 years, it made a surprising theatrical reappearance on a triple bill (at the Capitol Theatre, Brownsville, Texas) with *The Return of Mr. Moto* (1965) and *Tarzan the Magnificent* (1960).

Sydney Chaplin (son of Charlie) has the lead role in the B movie ***Confession*** (1954), a moderately gripping if rather drawn-out tale with faint echoes of Hitchcock's *I Confess* (1953). Mike Nelson (Chaplin) returns to England from America with the takings from a robbery, having double-crossed an accomplice (Patrick Allen) who soon turns up demanding his share of the loot. Alan (Peter Hammond), the devoutly Catholic boyfriend of Mike's sister (Audrey Dalton), witnesses a resultant struggle between the two men and ends up killing the accomplice in an effort to protect Mike, who dissuades him from going to the police lest they begin looking into his own affairs. In ensuing events, the guilt-ridden Alan confesses to a priest (John Welsh), only to then be shot dead by Mike, with the priest unable to help Scotland Yard with their enquiries due to the Seal of the Confessional. However, Mike ultimately gets his comeuppance after being cleverly baited—in a ruse involving the priest—by the investigating detective (John Bentley).

"Murder? She never knew when, where or how it would happen..."

American director Albert S. Rogell's final film was the B movie ***Before I Wake*** (1955). A young woman, April Haddon

(Rogell's fellow American Mona Freeman), returns to England from California upon the supposedly accidental death of her wealthy father. For the first time, she meets her strict and manipulative stepmother Florence (Jean Kent), who'd been nurse to April's real mother until the latter's untimely death. April begins to suspect—correctly—that both her parents were murdered by Florence, and she's soon in fear for her own life as, with her out of the way, Florence would gain control of the whole family estate. Kent is suitably sinister as the wicked stepmother, who is finally apprehended, following two attempts on April's life, through a stroke of luck involving a handsome local doctor (Maxwell Reed).

Under the title *Shadow of Fear*, the film had an amazing four years (from mid–1956 to late 1959) of theatrical distribution in the U.S., playing as support to dozens of features. It's most apt pairing was undoubtedly with 1957's *How to Murder a Rich Uncle*, another British-made relative-in-mortal-danger thriller, for a two-day run (June 28–29, 1959) at the 231 Drive-In Theatre in Huntsville, Alabama; two years earlier, another screening in the city (this time at the Center Theatre) drew praise from *The Huntsville Times* (May 19, 1957), who called the film "one of the most exciting murder thrillers to hit the screen in a long time" and applauded Jean Kent for doing "a terrific job as one of the most dastardly female villains ever presented on the screen."

"No woman could resist his fatal charm!"

The atmospheric and expertly photographed **Cast a Dark Shadow** (1955) features Dirk Bogarde in brilliantly sinister mode as psychotic good-for-nothing Edward Bare, whose marriage to Monica (Mona Washbourne), a wealthy older woman, is purely for financial gain. When Monica arranges to change her existing will in Edward's favor, he mistakenly believes she's doing just the opposite and murders her, making it look like an accident. He then finds out that, as it stands, he only inherits some property (including the shadowy country mansion in which the couple had been living), while the woman's money is left in trust to a sister in Jamaica. It's not long before the fortune-hunting Edward, desperate for some ready cash, meets—and goes on to marry—brash well-to-do widow Freda Jeffries (Margaret Lockwood in a scene-stealing performance), only to find that she keeps a tight rein on her money. Events lead to a great twist involving another woman (Kay Walsh) whom Edward sets his greedy sights on and later tries to murder by severing the brake lines of her car. When the game's finally up, a panic-stricken Edward attempts to escape and uses the car himself—with disastrous consequences. A 1956 BBC TV movie version (in which Lockwood repeated her role) went under the title of Janet Green's original source play, *Murder Mistaken*.

You Can't Escape (1955) concerns author Peter Darwin (Robert Urquhart) who, fearing he will be accused of murder following the accidental death of his ex-lover during a struggle, secures the complicity of his fiancée Kay (Noelle Middleton) in a cover-up. The body is buried in woods, but complications ensue when a scheming reporter stumbles on the truth and attempts blackmail. Also involved is an old doctor friend (Guy Rolfe) of the victim who becomes suspected of her death through circumstantial evidence. When Kay wants to come clean, Peter, having by now murdered the reporter, tries to kill her too. Although uninspired, this gloomy B movie (set in London and the countryside) is nevertheless technically well put together and certainly worth a watch for a typically shifty performance by the great Peter Reynolds as the doomed reporter.

When Dave Nelson (Paul Carpenter), a crime fiction writer for Venture Publications' *Murder Magazine*, is framed for the real-life murder of rival fellow employee Bill Strayte (Ferdy Mayne), ***The Narrowing Circle*** (1955) of the hangman's noose threatens to close in around him. This snappily paced B movie also stars Hazel Court as an attractive colleague of Nelson's helping him track down the real killer, who commits two further murders before finally being exposed. The killings turn out to be connected with protecting a dark secret from the culprit's past in South Africa, and it's probably giving too much away to say that the excellent Russell Napier plays a character (the head of Venture Publications) with a dark secret in his past. *The Cinema* (February 1, 1956) correctly characterized Canadian star Carpenter as being "his usual burly, easy-going and wise-cracking self" in the role of Nelson.

Hardly seen since its original British release, the Danziger brothers B movie **Operation Murder** (1956) stars Tom Conway as Dr. Wayne, a surgeon whose private hospital faces financial ruin. In order to raise necessary funds, Wayne plots with his associate, Dr. Bowen (Patrick Holt), to murder his wealthy cousin for an inheritance. An alibi can be established on the basis that the two doctors, while wearing surgical masks and gowns, are indistinguishable from each other. Bowen therefore poses as Wayne during an operation while Wayne carries out the murder. However, the scheming medicos get their comeuppance in a final twist involving a small boy who wrote his name in the dust on Wayne's car when the latter was forced to stop at a service station en route to commit the murder. Conway and Holt make a fine pair of conspirators, and the film also stars Holt's real-life spouse Sandra Dorne as Dr. Wayne's extravagant wife. *The Cinema* (December 19, 1956) noted that scriptwriter (this was his debut) Brian Clemens'

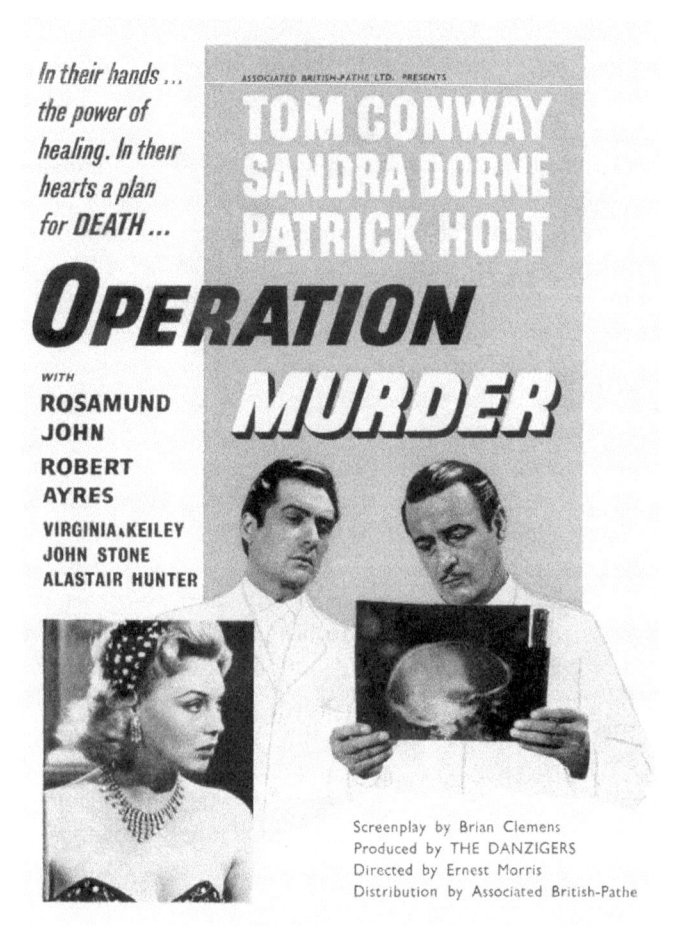

Pressbook for a rare 1956 Danziger brothers B movie.

story is "clearly and logically worked out."

Due to McCarthy blacklisting, Joseph Losey (director) and Howard Koch (screenwriter) used pseudonyms for their work on the by-the-numbers noir B movie ***The Intimate Stranger*** (1956). The always interesting Richard Basehart, a Hollywood veteran of stateside noir offerings such as *Tension* (1949) and *The House on Telegraph Hill* (1951), plays Reggie Wilson, an American former film editor who has moved to England and become a successful movie studio executive married to the boss' daughter (Faith Brook). Another Hollywood star, Mary Murphy, plays it cool as a mysterious woman plaguing Reggie with letters and a phone call indicating they've had an affair. Fearing he's being set up for blackmail, Reggie investigates and, with the help of actress and old flame Kay (Constance Cummings), eventually exposes a diabolical plot from within the studio to ruin his career. An intriguing build-up is let down by a somewhat weak denouement, although it's still an above-average production from Merton Park Studios, whose facilities double for the fictional "Commonwealth Pictures" studios depicted in the film. U.S. prints run 84 minutes.

"Life in the Casbah, at the crossroads of the Seven Seas"

In 1945, following World War II service and several subsequent months in hospital for a leg injury, American pilot Rip Reardon (Phil Carey) finally returns to his French-Moroccan plantation in **Port Afrique** (1956), only to find his wife shot dead at their villa. A coroner's verdict concludes suicide, but Rip is not convinced and begins his own investigation, putting him at loggerheads with the local police chief (Eugene Deckers on great form). During the ensuing mystery, which involves his business partner Robert (Dennis Price) and Robert's wife Diane (Rachel Gurney), Rip discovers some unsavory facts about his dead spouse, while being supported and consoled by a pretty nightclub singer (Pier Angeli) who also provides us with three alluring songs. Filmed on authentic Moroccan locations, this colorful whodunit also features Christopher Lee in a small part as an amorous artist.

Guilty? (1956) is an efficient adaptation of Michael Gilbert's novel *Death Has Deep Roots*, first published in 1951. John Justin plays an attorney, Nap Rumbold, persuaded by a French journalist friend to organize the defense of a Resistance heroine (Andrée Debar) accused of murdering an ex-lover at a London hotel. Having appointed a counselor-at-law (a great performance by Norman Wooland) to tackle the courtroom duties, Rumbold embarks on some sleuthing which leads him to the French city of Avignon and the eventual uncovering of a counterfeiting racket, one of whose London operators proves to be the real killer. Barbara Laage plays an enigmatic blonde (actually an Interpol agent) keeping tabs on Rumbold during the adventure, and the film, which also exists in a simultaneously filmed French version titled *Je plaide non coupable*, ends with an inevitable last-minute dash to the courtroom with the vital evidence.

The *Motion Picture Herald* (March 2, 1957) noted that **The High Terrace** (1956) was made with "admirable British disregard of the conventional introduction, sub-plotting and resolution in relating a murder mystery." Hollywood's Dale Robertson stars as Bill Lang, an American writer in England who wants actress Stephanie Blake (Lois Maxwell) to be the leading lady in his new play *The High Terrace*. The only problem is she's tied up with another production whose boss, impresario Otto Kellner (Eric Pohlmann), is in love with her and doesn't want to let her go. When Stephanie finds Kellner dead in his office with evidence (including the large pair of scissors protruding from his back) pointing to her as the culprit, Bill goes to great, not to mention illegal, lengths (involving moving the body and disposing of clues) to help her avoid suspicion, before then casting her in his new oeuvre. The suave Derek Bond plays an actor with a secret past involving Stephanie; during the murder hunt, he disappears so as to cast suspicion on himself in an effort to protect the real killer, who is revealed in a neat twist ending. This B movie from producers Robert S. Baker and Monty Berman seems to have been out of circulation since the 1960s, and before then its biggest claim to fame was playing as support to Hitchcock's *The Wrong Man* on a 1957 U.S. double bill.

In another B movie, **The Last Man to Hang** (1956), music critic Sir Roderick Strood (the ever suave Tom Conway) is put on trial for allegedly murdering—by sedative overdose—his wife Daphne (Elizabeth Sellars), whose neurotic and unbearably jealous behavior had driven him into the arms of another woman. With the House of Commons debating the abolition of capital punishment, the question arises (although interestingly there's no question mark in the film's title) as to whether Roderick will be the last man to hang. Following much *12 Angry Men*–style deliberation by the jury, Roderick's fate is decided, this almost immediately followed by what the *Monthly Film Bulletin* (October 1956) rightly called an "implausible surprise ending" involving the Stroods' housekeeper (Freda Jackson), who knows more than she has let on about the whole affair. Having to some extent been given away fairly early on, the "surprise" is not as surprising as it could have been but does provide a heartwarming finale to the story. Anthony Newley, Margaretta Scott and Victor Maddern stand out from among those playing the jurors.

"A midnight intruder … a scream in the night"

Set in a quaint French town called La Bandelette, ***That Woman Opposite*** (1956) is a clever but ultimately rather dull affair that suffers from too much uninteresting talk. The murder of British antiques collector Sir Maurice Lawes (Wilfrid Hyde White) throws up many suspects, including his son and heir Toby (Jack Watling), before the culprit is found to be a notorious jewel thief (William Franklyn) who feared that Lawes could identify him in connection with his fatal wounding of a gendarme during a robbery. In the second of her two low-budget 1950s British thrillers (see also *River Beat*), Hollywood star Phyllis Kirk plays Eve Atwood, a woman living opposite the Lawes residence who gets tricked by the thief (her ex-husband) into providing him with an alibi. Based on John Dickson Carr's 1942 novel *The Emperor's Snuff-Box*, the film also stars Dan O'Herlihy and Guido Lorraine as an insurance investigator and local police chief respectively, both involved in investigating the affair; the former, a real charmer, ends up with Eve, who up until then had been planning to marry Toby.

In the B movie ***Suspended Alibi*** (1956), married news editor Paul Pearson (Patrick Holt) visits his mistress (Naomi Chance) to break off their affair. In case his wife (Honor Blackman) should check up on him, Paul creates an alibi whereby he pretends to be at a friend's (Bryan Coleman) apartment. However, things get complicated when the friend is stabbed and later dies, resulting in Paul being suspected, charged and subsequently sentenced to death for the crime, which proves most convenient for the real killer. Andrew Keir plays a determined crime reporter trying to help Paul out of his predicament, and there's some fairly decent suspense during a sequence where the killer, whose identity has been revealed from the start, finds it necessary to silence the aforementioned mistress.

The above-average B movie ***Rogue's Yarn*** (1956) stars Derek Bond as John Marsden, whose wealthy wife is expected to recover from what was thought to be a fatal illness, thus depriving him of an anticipated inheritance. He therefore murders her, having constructed an ingenious alibi that puts him at sea—crossing the English Channel on his motor yacht—at the time of the death. With the killer's identity known from the outset, and a detailed depiction of his carefully constructed alibi (which entails using the yacht's autopilot), the film is almost a blueprint for the following decade's TV series *Columbo*, this being further reinforced by the introduction of an offbeat and tenacious detective (Elwyn Brooke-Jones). As Marsden's heartless mistress, who instigates the murder as well as coming up with the idea for the alibi, top-billed Nicole Maurey brings to the role what the *Kinematograph Weekly* (August 29, 1957) called a "tantalizing" quality. The title refers to a colored thread used in the manufacture (for identification purposes) of naval rope, a piece of which finally proves to be a vital clue in Marsden's undoing.

In the dramatic opening sequence to ***Lady of Vengeance*** (1956), a young woman commits suicide by jumping in front of a train. William T. Marshall (Dennis O'Keefe), a tough newspaper mogul who'd been the woman's guardian, receives from her a posthumous letter requesting revenge upon the man who drove her to take such drastic action. Anton Diffring is on great form as a smooth criminal mastermind and philatelist named Karnak, whom Marshall persuades (with the lure of a rare stamp) to devise a sadistic plan for a fitting retribution. A great twist sees Marshall ultimately turn the plan against Karnak, who is in fact the guilty party, and thus had been the object of the revenge all along. O'Keefe gives a strong performance in this melodramatic B movie whose cleverly plotted story comes to a satisfyingly ironic conclusion.

Grippingly directed by Joseph Losey, the London-based ***Time Without Pity*** (1957) begins with an effective pre-credits sequence in which wealthy megalomaniac car manufacturer and family man Robert Stanford (a somewhat over-exaggerated performance by Leo McKern) murders a young woman with whom he'd been having an affair. Circumstances see a young student (Alec McCowen) wrongly convicted and sentenced to death for the crime, whereupon his father David (Michael Redgrave), a recovering alcoholic, flies over from Canada 24 hours before the execution in a desperate attempt to prove his son's innocence. Redgrave, whose character finds himself in a situation where he has no option but to make the ultimate sacrifice in order to bring Robert to justice, has rarely been better, and there's solid support from the ever-excellent Peter Cushing—just prior to his star-making role in *The Curse of Frankenstein*—as the son's lawyer.

"Mystery in mid-Channel"

Stormy Crossing (1957) is memorable for being set against the interesting backdrop of a cross–Channel (Dover to Calais) swimming event. One of the participants,

A father visits his condemned son in prison. Michael Redgrave (foreground) and Alec McCowen in *Time Without Pity* (1957).

Kitty (Joy Webster), has been having an affair with her sponsor, smooth fashion boss Paul Seymour (Derek Bond), and threatens to tell his wife unless he files for divorce. Paul decides he has no option but to silence Kitty and does so during the swim where, with the use of a motor boat, and under cover of thick fog, he intercepts and drowns her. The event is henceforth abandoned and a verdict of accidental death is returned. The sneaky Paul later attempts to murder Kitty's fellow swimmer, Danny Parker (Sheldon Lawrence), who knows too much, but in the end he's brought to justice by Danny's brother/trainer Griff (one-time real-life marathon swimmer John Ireland) with more than a little help from the attractive manageress (Maureen Connell) of the hotel where all have been staying. Authentic locations and likeable performances by Ireland and Connell are highlights in what was production company Tempean Films' final B picture. By the time of its belated British release in the autumn of 1958, the film, under the title *Black Tide*, had already enjoyed more than a year of healthy theatrical distribution in the U.S. and was already being shown there on television.

Some neat twists and turns and a well-sustained atmosphere of mystery highlight **The Traitor** (1957), in which ex-members (including characters played by Anton Diffring and Christopher Lee) of a wartime resistance organization gather for a reunion at a large English country house. The host, Colonel Price (Donald Wolfit), announces that one of those present—although he does not yet know exactly who—had betrayed their former leader, resulting in the latter's execution by the Nazis. Before long, one of Price's agents arrives with the name of the traitor but is murdered before he can reveal it. Two Army Intelligence officers (Robert Bray and John Van Eyssen) subsequently call at the house and, during a night of intrigue and further murder, the surprising truth about the wartime betrayal is revealed.

Described in *Leonard Maltin's Movie Guide* as a "not-bad little crime drama," the Merton Park B movie **Man in the Shadow** (1957) treats us to two Hollywood stars, namely Zachary Scott and Faith Domergue. Domergue plays Barbara Peters, the owner of an antiques shop in England whose husband, Alan (John Horsley), is facing execution for a murder he did not commit. Scott plays the real murderer, John Sullivan, who has since ended up languishing in an Italian hospital due to a heart condition. Carlo Raffone (Peter Illing), the hospital barber, hears a delirious Sullivan essentially confess to the murder, whereupon he searches the man's hotel room and finds newspaper articles about the crime as well as the incriminating evidence—a bloodstained statuette—that could clear Alan. In ensuing events, Raffone travels to England and callously demands a hefty payout from Barbara in exchange for the crucial evidence; meanwhile, Sullivan, having made a recovery, checks out of hospital and follows him in an effort to retrieve the statuette. The film went straight to television in the U.S., initially broadcast under the title *Violent Stranger* but later also shown under its British title. (The reason for the U.S. name change was to avoid confusion with another *Man in the Shadow*, namely the then recently released Jack Arnold-directed crime drama [also dated 1957] starring Jeff Chandler and Orson Welles.)

*"The movie no niece or
nephew can afford to miss!"*

Based on the French play *Il faut tuer Julie* by Didier Daix, **How to Murder a Rich Uncle** (1957) is a black comedy directed by Nigel Patrick, who also stars as Sir Henry, patriarch of the Clitterburn family. Desperate for money to maintain his large decaying country estate, Henry, with the cooperation of other family members, plots to kill elderly Uncle George (a cheery Charles Coburn)—a visiting relative from America—for a $3 million fortune. However, several murder attempts backfire, each one resulting in the accidental death of one of the conspirators

John Mills (right, pictured with co-star Derek Farr) is a doctor framed for murder in *The Vicious Circle* (1957).

instead. Despite some decent performances, the film tries too hard to be funny and the repetitive nature of the story soon becomes tedious. The supporting cast includes Katie Johnson as a whimsical aunt and Anthony Newley as an inept criminologist friend of Henry's daughter (Paddy Webster).

Adapted by Francis Durbridge from his 1956 BBC TV serial *My Friend Charles*, *The Vicious Circle* (1957) is, as one would expect from the author, a devilishly complex mystery. John Mills plays Howard Latimer, an eminent London physician cleverly framed for the murder of a German actress, Frieda Veldon (Lisa Daniely), who it later transpires was a Scotland Yard Special Branch agent. The killing was in fact the work of an international criminal organization—headquartered in a Berlin café known as The Brass Candlestick (a brass candlestick was also the murder weapon)—dealing in forged passports and illegal visas. During the course of the serpentine plot, Latimer is initially used as a pawn and later becomes a willing participant in a plan by Special Branch (working on behalf of Interpol) to uncover the brains behind the racket. The excellent cast also includes Roland Culver as a Scotland Yard detective, Derek Farr as a not so good (as it turns out) friend of the physician's, and Wilfrid Hyde White as a crafty Special Branch chief. In the U.S., the film was released theatrically as *The Circle* but shown on TV under its British title.

Another physician—this time not so innocent—features in the rarely seen B movie *The Surgeon's Knife* (1957). Ambitious Welsh doctor Alexander Waring (Donald Houston) negligently, through intoxication and lack of sleep, causes a patient's death during a surgical procedure and, for the moment at least, gets away with it. Leaving town soon after, he goes on to establish a successful private practice, but is later forced to murder two senior members of his old medical staff, who knew he had been unfit to carry out the operation, when they pose a threat (in one case via blackmail) to his career. Laura

(Adrienne Corri), who'd been a nurse during the fateful procedure and is now married to Waring, herself becomes in danger when the murderous medico, revealed to have a history of mental illness, wrongly suspects that she also knows too much. In the end, as the result of a private investigation initiated by his assistant (Lyndon Brook), Waring is trapped into confessing his crimes, whereupon he commits suicide with a fatal potion previously intended for Laura. The *Kinematograph Weekly* (October 24, 1957) noted that "there are a number of tense moments, particularly in the last reel."

In the Danziger brothers B movie **Three Sundays to Live** (1957), London nightclub bandleader Frank Martin (Kieron Moore) gets arrested, tried and sentenced to death after being framed for the fatal shooting of the club's boss. Ruth Chapman (Sandra Dorne), a singer who can prove Frank's innocence, has been threatened by the killer and cannot therefore come forward; in any case, the police discount Ruth as a potential witness because she's believed (due to erroneous newspaper reporting) to have died in a train crash in America some time back. While awaiting execution (the film's title refers to a legal ruling whereby three Sundays must pass before a condemned man can be put to death), Frank manages to escape from prison and sets out to establish his innocence with the help of girlfriend Judy (a pleasant performance by Jane Griffiths) and a lawyer (Basil Dignam). Not a bad effort overall, although it does suffer somewhat from an unusually dull performance by Moore. By contrast, Ferdy Mayne shines in a one-scene appearance as an underworld figure with crucial information that leads to the killer being identified.

Another Danziger B movie, **The Depraved** (1957), is a not-bad little noir offering that successfully captures the feel of many of its American counterparts, right down to the femme fatale's house which looks like a 1950s mid-century modern California dwelling relocated to the British countryside. Dave Dillon (Robert Arden), a U.S. Army officer stationed in England, meets and falls in love with the beautiful and unhappily married Laura Wilton (Anne Heywood), and together they plan and carry out the murder—made to look like an accident—of her abusive wealthy husband, Tom (Basil Dignam). Laura claims Tom's life insurance, but instead of preparing for a future with Dave, she makes arrangements to leave the country with a secret lover while seeing to it that Dave comes under suspicion during an official investigation into the "accident." Having been confined to his Army base pending further inquiries, Dave manages to escape and takes his revenge on Laura. According to *Today's Cinema* (November 4, 1957), the film's "unoriginal theme" is "put over with clarity if not inspiration."

Circus acrobat Harry Belair (Peter Arne) gets into a violent fight with fellow acrobat Johnny (Arthur Sullivan), whose negligence has just caused the death of Harry's girlfriend during their trapeze act. A prop girl, Rosie (Barbara Archer), intervenes and kills Johnny with an axe. Harry is found holding the weapon and, with nothing left to lose, takes the blame and is jailed for 12 years. This all happens within the first five minutes of the B movie **Strangers' Meeting** (1957), which subsequently concerns Harry's escape after five years, although his exact reason for doing so—which involves Rosie—becomes very confusing due to a muddled and inconsistent script. A doctor and his wife (Conrad Phillips and Delphi Lawrence) are woven into the exacting storyline, which ends on a distinctly melodramatic note.

"Suddenly in the night ... a woman of wayward passions pays for her evil!"

A murder investigation ensues after Lucille (Ursula Howells), the cold-hearted adulterous wife of London banker Robert Ainsworth (Griffith Jones), is found strangled on Hampstead Heath in **Account Rendered** (1957). Suspects include Robert's business manager Gilbert Morgan (Carl

Bernard), whom Lucille had been blackmailing; Clive Franklin (John Van Eyssen), an artist who was infatuated with the woman; and Robert himself, who had followed her onto the heath just prior to the murder. Evidence concerning a brooch points to one of these men, but he has an alibi involving the time it would have taken to reach the crime scene. However, the police eventually discover he'd used a shortcut across railway lines, which feature in an exciting chase climax. Some fairly well-written characters highlight this efficiently directed B movie, which also stars Honor Blackman as a friend of the Ainsworths secretly in love with Robert. The film went straight to television in the U.S., initially broadcast as a first-season episode of *Kraft Mystery Theatre*.

The End of the Line (1957) was described by the *Motion Picture Herald* (August 8, 1959) as a "compactly produced and enacted suspense thriller calculated to provide a sufficient quantity of tautness for the action customer." The film's title was quite apt as far as its star Alan Baxter was concerned, the U.S. actor having more or less reached *the end of the line* in his movie career, with most of his subsequent work being for the small screen. Mike Selby (Baxter), a hard-up American playwright in England, runs into his avaricious former girlfriend Liliane (Barbara Shelley), now married to a nightclub owner (Arthur Gomez) who also deals in stolen jewelry. When Liliane persuades the gullible Mike to rob her husband's safe so that they can start a new life together, this proves to be just the beginning of a twisty plot that sees Mike framed for the husband's subsequent murder, actually committed by Liliane's true lover (Ferdy Mayne). Baxter supplies some voice-over narration to shore up the noir elements of this unremarkable B movie, which features Shelley in the type of femme fatale role she went on to perfect in 1963's *Blind Corner*.

Adapted from Edith Pargeter's (aka Ellis Peters) novella *The Assize of the Dying*, the intriguingly titled ***The Spaniard's Curse*** (1957) concerns a 15th century curse that has mortal consequences for anyone condemning an innocent person to death. Having just been sentenced to hang for the murder of actress Zoe Trevor, Guy Stevenson (Basil Dignam) addresses the court to proclaim his innocence before invoking the curse against the judge (Michael Hordern), the prosecuting attorney, the foreman of the jury and whoever the true guilty party may be. Shortly afterward, the foreman dies in a road accident, and subsequent events lead to circumstances in which the prosecuting attorney and judge are murdered by Zoe's real killer, whose ultimate confession we can assume will lead to the death penalty and thus the fulfillment of the curse, if one is to believe the whole thing was not just a coincidence. The leading characters in this so-so London-based B movie, which despite its supernatural suggestions ends up being a rather straightforward murder mystery, are the judge's crime reporter son (Tony Wright) and Zoe's half-brother (Canada's Lee Patterson), one of them not as innocent as they seem.

The unpretentious and surprisingly suspenseful B movie ***The House in the Woods*** (1957) begins with London-based writer Jeff and his wife Carol (Michael Gough and Patricia Roc) renting a secluded country cottage so that Jeff can concentrate on a new thriller novel. Little do they know that they are about to become part of a real-life thriller in which the cottage's owner, an unbalanced artist named Spencer Rowland (Ronald Howard), plans to kill them and use Carol's body in a diabolical plan to claim a legacy in connection with his late wife, whom he murdered. Luckily, an increasingly suspicious Jeff comes to realize what's afoot (there's a pivotal scene in which he finds the body of Spencer's wife buried in the woods), and the situation culminates in a tense showdown between the two men. It's good to see Gough and Howard play against type; both are great, the latter especially so as the sinister artist whose repeated playing of his favorite record—an eerily melancholic harmonica composition called "Fantasy of Lost Love" (written and played by Larry Adler)—provides the majority of the film's soundtrack. A well-thought-out script ensures the story has no loose ends.

> *"Is it madness—or is she targeted for murder?"*

In ***The Solitary Child*** (1957), James Random (Philip Friend) takes his new wife Harriet (Barbara Shelley) to live at Random End, the family estate where his first wife was murdered by shotgun blast two years earlier. James and his mixed-up teenage daughter (Julia Lockwood) have always believed each other responsible for the murder, and James had been formally charged but later acquitted of the crime. Harriet soon becomes targeted by the real killer (eventually revealed as an unbalanced female neighbor, played against type by Rona Anderson), who now wants wife number two out of the way so that she herself can marry James and reclaim Random End, which had once belonged to her family. Shelley and Lockwood shine in this solid B movie, whose cast also includes Jack Watling as a local veterinarian, and which culminates in a tense if slightly rushed climax. Although no composer credit is given, the rich Les Baxter-esque theme music is, according to some sources, stock music by Stanley Black.

Set on the French Riviera, ***The Strange Awakening*** (1957) is a rather underwhelming B movie known in the U.S. under the spicier title *Female Fiends*, and based on Patrick Quentin's 1946 novel *Puzzle for Fiends*. After seeing his wife (Monica Grey) off at the airport, writer Peter Chance (Lex Barker) drives back toward his villa. En route, he picks up a hitchhiker (Richard Molinas) who attacks him, leaves him unconscious and steals his car and wallet. Hospitalized and found to be suffering from amnesia, Peter is soon tricked by an unscrupulous doctor (Peter Dyneley), together with three relatives—the mother, sister and wife—of a certain Gordon Friend, into believing he *is* Gordon, this being part of a scheme to get their hands on an inheritance which cannot be claimed by the real Gordon as he has gone missing. It eventually transpires that the sister (Lisa Gastoni) has in fact murdered Gordon for reasons that are explained in the tense finale, while other developments in the convoluted plot include the re-emergence of the hitch-hiker, who is the key to Peter finally regaining his memory and thus also his identity.

The CinemaScope B movie ***Family Doctor*** (1958) unfolds in the English seaside resort of Frogmouth and stars Marius Goring as Henry Dysert, a much-respected local physician whose past three wives, including the vivacious Stella (Sandu Scott), all died tragic deaths. As the story progresses, it becomes clear, thanks to the investigations of a young visitor named Jethro (Hollywood's Rick Jason)—actually an American doctor who was once married to Stella and is attempting to discover the truth about her mysterious fall from cliffs—that Dysert murdered the three women. The medical malpractitioner ultimately confesses all to Jethro before then knocking him unconscious and attempting to push him from the same cliffs as he had thrown Stella. The rather leisurely paced film, which employs flashbacks to show events leading up to each of the wives' deaths, also stars Lisa Gastoni as Dysert's secretary, who's in danger of becoming wife number four.

Jason, who incidentally would go on to clock up more marriages—five in total—than our good Dr. Dysert, was in some ways ideally cast, having a particularly keen real-life interest in medicine. (The actor's curiosity for medical matters was revealed by Hedda Hopper, a devotee of his, in one of her widely syndicated "Hollywood" reports, e.g., in *The Hartford Courant*, Hartford, Connecticut [June 30, 1957].) Sandu Scott had been 1951's Miss New York City and was also a vocalist who later fronted the kilted band, Sandu Scott and Her Scotties. The film is based on a 1955 novel, *The Deeds of Dr.*

Marius Goring plays a murderous medico in this 1958 B movie.

Deadcert (aka *The Merry Widower*) by Joan Fleming.

"The most ingenious murder you'll ever see!"

Co-scripted by the great Jimmy Sangster (his first non-horror offering for Hammer Films), **The Snorkel** (1958) plays out against an attractive Italian Riviera setting and features a superbly sinister performance by Peter Van Eyck. The film opens with a detailed depiction—à la *Columbo*—of an ingenious murder: having drugged his wealthy wife in their living room, Paul Decker (Van Eyck) seals the doors and windows with tape and locks the door from the inside before turning on several gas taps in what is designed to look like a suicide; he survives inside the room by breathing fresh air with the use of the titular apparatus, before then hiding in a secret crawlspace until the "suicide" is discovered and resultant police examination concluded. The devious Decker has created a clever alibi, but this doesn't fool the dead woman's teenage daughter—Decker's stepdaughter—Candy (the talented Mandy Miller in what turned out to be her final film), who is convinced of his guilt. Much of the story involves a psychological game of cat-and-mouse between Decker and Candy, which leads to the latter almost meeting the same fate as her mother; however, happenstance sees the tables being turned on Decker in one of the best British thriller endings of the decade. A crisply photographed production, the film also stars Betta St. John and Gregoire Aslan as Candy's governess and the local police chief respectively. U.S. cinemagoers originally saw the film in a heavily edited 74-minute version.

The extremely convoluted **Hidden Homicide** (1958) begins with novelist Michael Cornforth (a rather over-theatrical Griffith Jones) being ingeniously framed for the murder of his rich cousin Martin. Ending up on the run, he attempts to clear his name and catch the real killer, namely a female impersonator named Oswald Castellan (James Kenney). Castellan, it transpires, has already murdered Martin's former wife Kathleen, a music hall performer known for her "Colorado Kate" cowgirl act, and heir to a large chunk of her ex-husband's money; he has since been masquerading as her (including performing the "Colorado Kate" act) with a view to claiming the inheritance upon killing Martin. (Sharp-eyed viewers may spot Castellan posing as Michael's housekeeper at one point during the proceedings.) This bizarre B movie, which benefits from Kenney's spirited playing, also stars Patricia Laffan (probably best remembered for her title role in the low-budget 1954 sci-fi flick *Devil Girl from Mars*) as a young woman helping Michael prove his innocence.

Links of Justice (1958) stars Sarah Lawson as Clare Mills, president of her late father's company Mills Textiles, who finds herself on trial at the Old Bailey for the premeditated murder of her husband Edgar (Jack Watling). Edgar, it emerges, had plotted with his mistress Stella (Kay Callard) to murder Clare in an elaborate scheme (involving Stella posing as Clare) that would have made it look like the latter had committed suicide by jumping overboard while traveling on a cross-Channel steamship from Dover to Calais. The plot of this very modest and coincidence-laden B movie unfolds through flashbacks during the court case, culminating in the last-minute testimony of a surprise witness that proves Clare had in fact killed her husband in self-defense.

According to *The Daily Cinema* (June 20, 1958), **The Whole Truth** (1958) has "a good pace throughout and is notable for some clever continuity." The setting is the French Riviera, where film producer Max Poulton (Stewart Granger) ends up in police custody after being cleverly framed for the murder of a tempestuous actress (Gianna Maria Canale) with whom he'd once had a brief fling. The ever-urbane George Sanders is on great form as the real murderer, Carliss, a smug character whose crafty frame-up plot entails posing as a Scotland Yard detective, and who we later learn is the dead woman's husband (he committed the murder out of frustration after being cuckolded one time too many). Carliss ultimately sets out to eliminate Max's loyal wife Carol (an understated Donna Reed) when she finds evidence—an inscribed cigarette lighter—that can prove him guilty. The story is told in flashback following Max's escape from custody to save Carol from being pushed off the deck of a mountainside villa. Based on a 1955 BBC *Sunday Night Theatre* TV play of the same name, the film is slickly directed, crisply photographed and has a neat jazz score.

In **Dublin Nightmare** (1958), Steven Lawlor (Richard Leech) takes part in a cash robbery for a terrorist organization known as "The Movement." Later, his getaway car is found crashed with a mangled body (believed to be his) and no sign of the money. In fact, Lawlor is still alive, having faked his own death (using the body of an accomplice he'd murdered) in a plot to double-cross the organization. William Sylvester shines as self-assured photographer John Kevin, an old friend of Lawlor's who gets innocently mixed up in the affair, which culminates in the organization taking a terrible revenge on Lawlor. This well-produced and atmospherically photographed B movie also stars Marla Landi as Lawlor's girlfriend, and features a haunting whistling theme by Edwin Astley that prefigures his classic theme tune for *The Saint* TV series.

Margaretta Scott plays **A Woman Possessed** (1958), namely Katherine Winthrop, a wealthy widow whose possessive desire to have her weak-willed doctor son John (Francis Matthews) all to herself is challenged when, following a stay in America, the latter returns home with a surprise fiancée, Ann (Kay Callard), in tow. As the story progresses, Katherine's jealousy over Ann, who is prone to heart seizures, causes no end of stressful situations. During one of Ann's seizures, Katherine administers the wrong pills which leave Ann at death's door; John manages to save her and then accuses his mother of attempted murder. Finally, a twist involving family servant Emma (Alison Leggatt) sees this Danziger brothers B movie come to a somewhat happy conclusion. Scott would later play another frightful mother—only worse—in the Hammer psychological thriller *Crescendo* (1969).

In another Danziger B movie, ***Moment of Indiscretion*** (1958), happily married Janet Miller (Lana Morris) witnesses the murder of a woman at an apartment block but does not subsequently come forward as this would reveal that she had been there to meet her ex-fiancé (John Stone). Even though the meeting was innocent, Janet is worried that her attorney husband John (Ronald Howard) will become jealous. However, when a handkerchief she dropped at the crime scene is traced back to her, Janet is forced to tell all and becomes the prime suspect. The remainder of the so-so story, in which characters make particularly foolish decisions, details the supportive John's attempt to trap the real killer (John Van Eyssen), whose identity is revealed to the audience quite early on.

Alec Guinness has a dual role in ***The Scapegoat*** (1958), a visually sumptuous adaptation of Daphne Du Maurier's then recent novel of the same name. While vacationing in France, mild-mannered French-speaking Englishman John Barratt (Guinness) becomes acquainted with Count Jacques De Gue (also Guinness), an impoverished aristocrat bearing an exact resemblance to him. Jacques engineers a situation that forces John to temporarily assume his identity, the idea being to use him as a scapegoat in a devious plot to murder his wife (Irene Worth), who stands between him and a fortune. Bette Davis, in what amounts to little more than a scenery-chewing cameo, plays Jacques' morphine-addicted mother, while Nicole Maurey provides romantic interest as the nobleman's mistress (although by film's end she has fallen for John). The moderately intriguing, if far-fetched, story culminates in an underwhelming showdown between the two lookalikes.

> *"Suspense—when a glamorous model meets murder!"*

Around the time he crossed the Atlantic to star in the B movie ***Model for Murder*** (1958), U.S. actor Keith Andes was more or less working exclusively in television and would soon achieve his first starring role in a regular series, the police drama *This Man Dawson* (1959–60). In what would be his only British film, the clean-cut Andes gives a rather wooden performance as David Martens, a U.S. Merchant Navy officer visiting London in connection with a family matter involving a top model (Julia Arnall). When the model is murdered after stumbling on a jewel robbery in progress at a fashion house, circumstances lead to David getting framed for the crime. Hazel Court plays an attractive fashion design assistant helping him elude the police and clear his name, while Michael Gough has by far the best role as the marvelously named Kingsley Beauchamp, a couturier who masterminded the robbery. Some incongruous comedy moments and odd incidental music don't help what the *Monthly Film Bulletin* (April 1959) called a "routine thriller" that "leans far too heavily on coincidence."

Danger Within (1959) is an entertaining wartime whodunit (in the style of *Stalag 17*) with a good mix of thrills and humor. At an Italian prisoner-of-war camp during World War II, attempts by the prisoners to escape are constantly thwarted by a mysterious traitor. Eventually, with the camp about to be handed over to the Germans, a massive escape—of nearly 400 men via a tunnel—is planned under cover of a POW performance of Shakespeare's Hamlet. The traitor tries to foil the effort but is caught just in time by members of the British Officers' Escape Committee. The escape goes ahead successfully and there's a satisfying finale in which the traitor meets his end in suitably ironic fashion. A great cast is headed by Richard

Todd (as head of the Escape Committee) and also includes Bernard Lee as an escape planner, Peter Arne as the sadistic camp commandant, and Michael Caine in a tiny, uncredited role.

Bernard Lee also features in ***Beyond This Place*** (1959), an absorbing adaptation of A.J. Cronin's 1953 novel of the same name. Paul Mathry (Van Johnson) arrives in Liverpool from America to learn more about his father, Patrick (Lee), believed to have died during World War II. He is therefore astounded to find that Patrick is not dead after all and is instead languishing in prison, having served almost 20 years of a life sentence for the alleged murder of a young woman. Convinced of his father's innocence, Paul investigates the matter and, aided in his quest for justice by both an attractive librarian (Vera Miles) and the *Liverpool Clarion* newspaper, eventually (despite attempts by certain people in high places to prevent it) secures his father's release before then going on to expose the real killer. In the role of Patrick, on whom imprisonment has taken a terrible toll, Lee proves why he was one of Britain's great character actors, and the cast also includes the multi-talented Welshman Emlyn Williams (the playwright of *Night Must Fall* fame) as a wealthy religion-obsessed shipping magnate harboring a dark secret. Cronin's novel had been previously adapted as a 1957 episode of U.S. TV's *DuPont Show of the Month*, with Farley Granger in the lead role.

The previous film's U.S. title was *Web of Evidence*, not to be confused with the Danziger brothers B movie ***Web of Suspicion*** (1959), which *The Daily Cinema* (May 22, 1959) described as an "average whodunit which will serve its purpose as a double bill attraction for less discerning audiences." Bradley Wells (Philip Friend), a popular physical training instructor at the Hayden Co-educational College, goes on the run from a bloodthirsty lynch mob when circumstantial evidence points to him as the murderer of a coed (Vivienne Lacey) found dead in the local woods. The story also involves an art teacher (Susan Beaumont) at the college who helps Bradley prove his innocence and is ultimately saved by him from the real killer—a mentally unbalanced fellow teacher of theirs. This remains one of the rarer Danziger B thrillers whose last appearance seems to have been on Canadian television circa 1973.

"He flew home ... to death and accusation!"

In the brisk and neatly scripted B movie ***Deadly Record*** (1959), airline pilot Trevor Hamilton (Lee Patterson) becomes suspect number one when his fiery playgirl wife Jenny, an ex-dancer from whom he lived a separate life, is found stabbed in the back. In an effort to prove his innocence, Trevor begins his own investigation in which he questions Jenny's former Spanish dancing partner, Ramon Casadas (Ferdy Mayne), and a doctor, Bruce Morrow (Peter Dyneley), with whom she'd been romantically involved. Believing he has discovered the killer's identity, Trevor sets a trap; however, he soon discovers that the culprit is not who he thought—instead, it's a previously unsuspected party. Patterson is at his most handsome as the resolute hero, while the two main female roles are filled by the exquisite Barbara Shelley, as an airport public relations officer helping Trevor in his sleuthing, and Jane Hylton as Dr. Morrow's secretary-receptionist. The film went straight to television in the U.S., initially broadcast as a first-season episode of *Kraft Mystery Theatre*. On the day of the broadcast (June 21, 1961), "TV Scout" previews (syndicated content carried in the TV pages of many newspapers) spoke of Patterson "looking younger and considerably less able as an actor" than he currently was in his hit stateside series *Surfside 6*.

Set in southeast England, the Eastmancolor B movie ***More Deadly Than the Male*** (1959) tells the sordid tale of visiting American Saul Coe (Jeremy White) and his infatuation with the duplicitous Estelle

Canadian actor Lee Patterson with Jane Hylton in *Deadly Record* (1959).

(Pamela Ann Davy), who encourages him to murder her wealthy husband Godfrey (John Mahoney). Saul hides the body in a deserted coastal blockhouse, and later events see Estelle murder Saul's possessive old flame (Lorraine Peters), whose body she hides with that of Godfrey's. An ensuing confrontation between Saul and Estelle leads to the latter falling to her death from cliffs, after which Saul gets his comeuppance at the hands of Godfrey's vengeful mother (Edna Doré). The film, which the *Monthly Film Bulletin* (July 1959) called an "ugly and extremely amateurish shocker," features narration (by Canadian actor Don Mason) in place of dialogue.

Director Joseph Losey's **Blind Date** (1959) is the absorbing story of a struggling young Dutch artist (an impressive Hardy Kruger) who begins an affair (shown in flashbacks) with a classy older woman calling herself Jacqueline Cousteau (French star Micheline Presle), only to become suspected when she is supposedly murdered. Welsh actor Stanley Baker, second-billed to Kruger, gets to speak freely in his native accent as an unyielding Welsh detective inspector, and there's a neat twist involving switched identities and the artist having been set up as a patsy. The well-written script touches on social class issues, with the rank-and-file detective often at odds with his upper-class colleagues, particularly the Assistant Commissioner played most convincingly by Robert Flemyng.

In the riveting courtroom suspenser **Libel** (1959), wealthy and titled Englishman Mark Loddon (Dirk Bogarde) is forced to take legal action when a Canadian World War II veteran (Paul Massie) publicly accuses him of being an impostor. The Canadian, who'd been held in a prisoner-of-war camp with Loddon, is convinced that another prisoner, a small-time actor named Frank Welney who bore a striking resemblance to Loddon, took over the latter's identity after the three men escaped from the camp. If the allegation is true, then the question remains as to what became of the real Loddon. During a resulting high-profile and twist-laden trial, the introduction of a surprise witness has repercussions that ultimately lead to the truth being revealed. Bogarde is excellent in the dual roles of Loddon (or is he?) and Welney (some inventive camera techniques are employed to show the two together in a series of effective flashbacks), while Olivia De Havilland gives a suitably emotional performance as Loddon's American wife, who comes to doubt whether the man that came back from the war was really the man she had known before. Robert Morley and Wilfrid Hyde White provide entertaining support as attorneys on opposing sides of the case.

The unassuming Danziger brothers B movie **Man Accused** (1959) is pleasantly acted and has plenty of twists and turns packed into its short running time. The ever-reliable Ronald Howard plays Bob Jensen who, as the victim of an elaborate frame-up (which includes being falsely identified as an international jewel thief and murderer), finds himself jailed for both the theft of his fiancée Kathy's (Carol Marsh) family jewels and the fatal stabbing of a supposed insurance investigator. With the help of Kathy and her butler (Kenneth Edwardes), Bob escapes from prison (in what proves to be a ludicrously easy task) and sets out to prove his innocence. Robert Dorning plays a smooth and decidedly shady (as it turns out) solicitor involved in the proceedings.

Another modest Danziger B movie is **Sentenced for Life** (1959). Fifteen years after his father John (Jack Gwillim) was sentenced to life imprisonment for selling a periscope blueprint to the Nazis, Jim (Francis Matthews), a law student, begins an investigation in an effort to clear him. John has always claimed to be innocent and suspects his business partner at the time (Basil Dignam) of involvement in the treachery. Essential to uncovering the truth is Jim's tracking down of a key witness (Nyree Dawn Porter) who mysteriously disappeared before the trial. As the convicted man, Gwillim is unconvincing mainly due to make-up man George Partleton having gone somewhat overboard in his efforts to display the effects of 15 years' incarceration, resulting in what looks like the inspiration for the ashen-faced living dead in Hammer's *Plague of the Zombies* (1966). Incidentally, Partleton would later work on several Hammer productions, three of them—*The Witches* (1966), *Frankenstein Created Woman* (1966) and *The Mummy's Shroud* (1967)—together with *Plague*'s hairstylist.

1960s

In the B movie **Danger Tomorrow** (1960), Dr. Bob Murray and his wife Ginny (Robert Urquhart and Zena Walker) move to the countryside upon Bob becoming assistant practitioner to Dr. Campbell (Rupert Davies). One of the perks of the job is free accommodation in a large gloomy house belonging to Campbell. Before long, Ginny, who has a history of extrasensory perception, has a vision involving a man named Bob violently struggling with a woman in the attic. This and other strange events lead her to believe that the "Bob" in her vision may have been a representation of her husband and that he may be out to murder her. However, the real threat is in fact from Dr. Campbell, whose middle name is Robert (thus also Bob), the vision having been a depiction of him murdering his wife—whose death was deemed a suicide—12 years earlier. A tense climax sees Campbell attempt to silence Ginny for fear that her vision will eventually lead to the truth coming out.

The creepy thriller promised by a couple of early scenes never fully materializes, but there are still one or two darkly atmospheric moments to savor thanks to some creative lighting and camerawork. The lead players are all excellent, and the supporting cast includes the always exquisite Lisa Daniely as a French doctor assisting Dr. Murray in some research. The film went straight to television in the U.S., initially broadcast as a first-season episode of *Kraft Mystery Theatre*. On the day of the broadcast (July 12, 1961), "TV Scout" previews (syndicated content carried in the TV pages of many newspapers) commented that the drama "is done with English restraint and builds up to genuine spine-tingling scenes."

"From war-torn Burma to the asphalt jungles of the big city—his revenge was the crime of the century!"

Described by the *Monthly Film Bulletin* (November 1960) as "a grisly mystery thriller," *The Hand* (1960) has the distinction of being one of the most bizarre British B movies ever made. The story begins during the Burma Campaign, although curiously, an on-screen caption reads "Burma 1946." Captain Roberts (Derek Bond) and two of his men, Brodie (Reed De Rouen) and Adams (Bryan Coleman), are captured by the Japanese. One by one, they are brought before a commander (Walter Randall) who demands to know the position and strength of their battalion. Adams and Brodie refuse to reveal the information and each has a hand cut off as punishment. We do not see what happens to Captain Roberts. Years later in London, a series of weird events—including an old drunk being paid £500 by Roberts to have one of his hands surgically removed, and the murder of Brodie—are ultimately found to be connected with the wartime incident.

The screenwriters, Ray Cooney and Tony Hilton (both usually associated with stage farces), have fashioned a fiendishly complicated original story, and it's kudos to director Henry Cass for translating it onto the screen in such a way that everything just about makes sense—if attention is paid—by the time the final credits roll. The plot basically boils down to Roberts, who it turns out had saved his hand in Burma by giving information to his captors, being subsequently pressured by Brodie to give up one of his hands as recompense. Roberts tries

Walter Randall is about to relieve Reed De Rouen of an appendage in the opening sequence of the bizarre B movie *The Hand* (1960).

to fob Brodie off with the aforementioned old drunk's amputated hand, but Brodie discovers the deception and continues the pressure, leading to Roberts murdering him. There are one or two gruesome scenes along the way, including the discovery of the elderly drunk's hand in Brodie's lodgings, and events culminate in a suitably ironic ending in which Roberts has his day of reckoning. The film, whose original 64-minute running time was cut to 60 minutes for release in some territories (including theatrical showings in its home country), became one of the most widely distributed British B thrillers in the U.S., playing there regularly (mainly on the drive-in circuit) throughout the first half of the 1960s.

There's not much to recommend in the dreary Danziger brothers B movie **Feet of Clay** (1960), which concerns a male young offender (Brian Smith) who confesses to the brutal stabbing-to-death of his well-respected probation officer Mrs. Richmond (Edith Saville). Vincent Ball stars as a lawyer convinced that there's more to the case than meets the eye, and sure enough it emerges that the youth has confessed in order to protect a female friend (Angela Douglas) whom he wrongly assumes is the culprit. As it turns out, the dead woman was not so respectable after all, having been involved in a drugs racket, one of whose members is the real killer.

The offbeat **Johnny Nobody** (1960) begins in a quiet Irish village, where atheistic Irish-American author Mulcahy (William Bendix), having aroused the ire of the locals with blasphemous remarks, stands outside the local church daring God to strike him down. Just then, a stranger (Aldo Ray) shows up and shoots him dead. Claiming to have heard a voice saying "destroy this man," the apparently amnesiac stranger—dubbed "Johnny Nobody" in the press—becomes a national sensation and faces acquittal at his subsequent trial in Dublin if it can be determined that the killing was an act of God. Scheduled to give an opinion on the matter in court, the village priest, Father Carey (Nigel Patrick, who also directed), decides to do some independent sleuthing and is soon involved in an exciting adventure in which he uncovers a diabolical and premeditated conspiracy behind the shooting. Bendix and the typically polished Patrick are the main reasons to watch this rather tall tale based on A.H.Z. Carr's "The Trial of John Nobody," first published in *Ellery Queen's Mystery Magazine* (November 1950) before being rewritten as a play in 1957.

"Don't tell your friends the ending … they won't believe it!!!"

The Technicolor Danziger brothers B movie **The Spider's Web** (1960) is a lively comedy thriller adapted from a 1954 Agatha Christie play more simply titled *Spider's Web*. An effervescent Glynis Johns plays Clarissa Hailsham-Brown, who lives in a rented country house with her diplomat husband Henry (John Justin) and the latter's 12-year-old daughter (Wendy Turner) from a previous marriage. One day, while Henry is out, Clarissa discovers the dead body of Oliver Costello (Ferdy Mayne), the shady new husband of Henry's ex-wife, in the drawing room. A resulting investigation, in which suspects include Clarissa's guardian (Jack Hulbert), the gardener (Hulbert's real-life wife Cicely Courtneidge) and a family friend (Ronald Howard), leads to a surprise conclusion involving an envelope—affixed with a valuable stamp—that had been hidden within a secret compartment in the drawing room's antique desk.

The film, which was humorously described by *The Daily Cinema* (November 11, 1960) as having "nearly as much talk as an American presidential election," went straight to television in the U.S., initially broadcast as a first-season episode of *Kraft Mystery Theatre*, and with much of said "talk" edited out; indeed, on the day of the broadcast (August 9, 1961), "TV Scout" previews (syndicated content carried in the TV pages of many newspapers) noted that the fault of the film's loose ends lay not with the author, "but with the fact that 38 minutes were cut from the story, originally released in England as a movie."

The seldom-seen B movie *The Trunk* (1960) was the directing and scripting debut of former actor Donovan Winter, whose later work as an independent filmmaker comprised a handful of sexploitation flicks (such as 1974's *Escort Girls*) and the exploitative thrillers *The Deadly Females* (1975) and *Give Us Tomorrow* (1978). An American, Stephen Dorning (Phil Carey), deviously plots to extort money from former girlfriend Lisa (Julia Arnall) as revenge for her past rejection of his offer of marriage. In cahoots with Diane (Vera Day), an ex-girlfriend of Lisa's husband (Dermot Walsh), Stephen engineers a situation whereby Lisa is tricked into thinking she has killed Diane. He thus gets her to cough up £2,000 as payment for disposal of the "body," this aspect of the con requiring Diane to spend time in an old trunk. However, in a twist ending, Diane really does wind up dead in the trunk, having been killed by a jealous ex-suitor (Peter Swanwick) in such a way as to incriminate Stephen. Speaking of the final twist, Charles Stinson, in his rather reluctant review in the *Los Angeles Times* (October 6, 1961), concluded that "it comes along after such a stretch of aimless plotting, slow direction and dishwater dull dialogue that we don't much care." The film's main U.S. theatrical exposure was as support to the superlative 1961 Hammer Films psychological thriller *Taste of Fear*, known stateside as *Scream of Fear*.

Another Technicolor B movie from the Danziger brothers (see also *The Spider's Web*), the comedy thriller ***Escort for Hire*** (1960) stars Pete Murray and Noel Trevarthen as Buzz and Steve, a pair of out-of-work actors who take up employment as professional escorts. When one of his regular clients (Jan Holden) is found murdered in circumstances that implicate him, Steve goes on the run and tries to clear his name with the help of Buzz and the escort agency's female boss (top-billed June Thorburn). The murder proves to be connected with married couple Barbara and Arthur Vickers (Mary Laura Wood and Guy Middleton) and is linked to Arthur having had an affair with the victim. Murray's attempts at comedy fall a little flat, but Peter Butterworth (later a regular in the hilarious *Carry On* film series) manages to elicit a few chuckles in his role as a Scotland Yard detective.

A further Danziger offering, ***Strip Tease Murder*** (1961) is, despite its sensational title, a mostly tame B movie set around an establishment known as the Flamingo Club. To rid himself of Rita (Ann Lynn), a singer-dancer at the club who's been blackmailing him, drug dealer Branco (Kenneth J. Warren) hires a psychopathic electronics expert (Peter Elliot) who arranges to electrocute the woman via her microphone during a performance. However, Diana (Jean Muir), a stripper at the club, ends up using the microphone and is killed instead. Not convinced with the official verdict that she died from a brain hemorrhage, Diana's husband (John Hewer), an emcee at the club, sets out to investigate. A couple of quite risqué (for the time) striptease scenes earned the film an "X" rating (unusual for a B movie) on its original British release.

One of the more memorable 1960s B movies, ***The Third Alibi*** (1961) stars Laurence Payne as composer Norman Martell, a nasty piece of work whose callous nature is revealed early on when he injures an elderly man in a hit-and-run incident. Patricia Dainton plays his wife Helen, a heart sufferer whom Norman plans to murder with the help of his lover—namely Helen's stepsister Peggy (Jane Griffiths). To be on the safe side, Norman creates three alibis which he comes to rely on when Helen turns the tables by killing Peggy and framing him for the crime. However, in the course of the surprise-laden story, the alibis collapse one by one, the third spectacularly so in an ironic twist ending involving the elderly man in the hit-and-run incident and which is hinted at in the name of the source play, *A Moment of Blindness*, by Pip and Jane Baker. Look closely for an uncredited Dudley Moore, who puts his sublime piano skills to use as accompanist to singer Cleo Laine during a rehearsal sequence. The film went straight to television in the U.S., initially broadcast as a first-season episode of *Kraft Mystery Theatre*. On the day of the broadcast (September 20, 1961), "TV Scout" previews (syndicated content carried in the TV pages of many newspapers) mentioned what they called the film's "crack story" as being "told by a fine cast of English actors with typical English understatement."

A Question of Suspense (1961) is a little-seen B movie which *The Daily Cinema* (June 26, 1961) noted "concentrates its drama on the characters and what makes them tick." Peter Reynolds plays Tellman Drew, a businessman involved in a forged bonds scam. When his chief clerk and childhood friend Frank (Norman Rodway) discovers the fraud, Drew murders him, buries the body in a lonely spot by the coast and then presents things to the police in such a way as to make it look like Frank had been behind the scam and has absconded. However, Rose Marples (Noelle Middleton), who has known both men since her youth, is not convinced and begins her own investigation, ultimately discovering the burial site and bringing about Drew's comeuppance. The featured surnames Drew and Marples bring to mind the classic literary characters Nancy Drew and Miss Marple; whether or not the film has any of the class associated with those two iconic mystery staples remains to be seen, as it has been out of circulation for decades.

"There's no place like homicide!"

Loosely adapted from Frank King's 1928 novel *The Ghoul*, the hilarious ***What a Carve-Up*** (1961) is a superbly atmospheric comedy thriller in the "Old Dark House" tradition. The house in this case is Blackshaw Towers, a creepy remote mansion on the Yorkshire Moors to where Ernie Broughton (Kenneth Connor), a nervy and timid proofreader of pulp horror novels (he also proofs what he calls "sexy ones" for which he gets paid less because the publisher assumes he will gain pleasure from them), is summoned for the reading of his late uncle Gabriel's will. Accompanied by his wisecracking best buddy and roommate Syd (Sidney James), Ernie arrives at the gloomy estate only to find that he and other relatives—an eccentric bunch including an alcoholic ex-military officer (Dennis Price) and a batty old aunt (Esma Cannon)—have in fact inherited nothing. Owing to bad weather, the assembled guests are forced to stay the night, during which a mysterious assassin begins murdering them one by one.

Connor and James (the latter delivering a succession of humorous and frequently sarcastic remarks with impeccable timing) make a fabulous double act, with their antics—including a bed-sharing scene—often bringing to mind the classic 1930 short *The Laurel-Hardy Murder Case*. There are plenty of bumps in the stormy night, as well as the usual secret passageways and revolving panels, before a final twist involving the unexpected arrival of a police inspector. Also starring are Shirley Eaton as Uncle Gabriel's nurse and Michael Gough as a sinister club-footed butler. The film was the inspiration for a 1994 satirical novel of the same name by Jonathan Coe.

The undistinguished B movie ***Two-Letter Alibi*** (1961)—or *Two Letter-Alibi* according to the title screen—was shown in the U.S. as *Death and the Sky Above*, the name of the 1953 novel on which it is based. When his estranged wife (Ursula Howells), who had refused him a divorce, is murdered, botanist and author Charles Hilary (Peter Williams) is unable to substantiate his alibi and ends up wrongfully convicted and sentenced to death for the crime. His girlfriend (Petra Davies), a television interviewer, sets out to prove his innocence with the help of a retired police commissioner (Ronald Adam) who guested on her TV show. A sequence in which Charles escapes from custody and is swiftly recaptured is unexciting and of no consequence, and the film saves its best for last with a mildly suspenseful climax involving the real killer's apprehension. The film went straight to television in the U.S., initially broadcast as a first-season episode of *Kraft Mystery Theatre*. The novel had previously been adapted as a 1955 episode of the U.S. series *Robert Montgomery Presents*.

The Lamp in Assassin Mews (1962) is a genteel Danziger brothers B movie with distant echoes of *Arsenic and Old Lace*. Francis Matthews plays young council chairman Jack Norton, whose determination to rid his street of an antique gas lamp (as part of a desire to modernize his community) attracts the murderous attentions of his staunchly traditional neighbors, elderly siblings Albert and Victoria Potts (Ian Fleming and Amy Dalby), a pair of homicidal maniacs already responsible for the deaths of several door-to-door salesmen. The ever-exquisite Lisa Daniely plays a schoolteacher who becomes romantically involved with Jack and is ultimately responsible for saving him from the aged assassins.

One of the better B movies from Butcher's Film Productions, *Serena* (1962) tells the twisty tale of an artist's (Emrys Jones) devious plot—in league with the titular mystery woman (his lover)—to murder his estranged wife so as to get hold of her recently inherited fortune. The story cleverly misdirects the audience as to certain characters' true identities, particularly in the case of a murdered woman—blasted twice in the face by a

Left to right: Honor Blackman (in portrait form), Emrys Jones, Patrick Holt and Bruce Beeby in *Serena* (1962), an above-average B movie from Butcher's Film Productions.

shotgun in the film's opening—who may or may not be the artist's wife. Top-billed Patrick Holt gives an agreeable performance as a Scotland Yard detective, and the cast also includes Honor Blackman (just prior to appearing as Cathy Gale on TV's *The Avengers*) in a crucial role. A satisfying twist rounds out what *Leonard Maltin's Movie Guide* called a "neat mystery programmer."

> "Instrument of Terror! The pounding of the afterbrain signals vengeance and death!!!!"

The British-German co-production **Vengeance** (1962) is a moody B movie adapted from—and putting a decidedly noirish mystery-thriller spin on—Curt Siodmak's classic 1942 sci-fi novel *Donovan's Brain*. When unscrupulous international financier Max Holt clinically dies following a plane crash, his still-active brain is secretly stolen by maverick scientist Dr. Corrie (Peter Van Eyck) for his radical neurological experiments, hitherto conducted using the disembodied gray matter of monkeys. The plane had in fact been deliberately blown up in order to murder Holt, whose brain is soon, via some sort of telepathy, influencing Corrie to play detective in order to track down the killer from among Holt's family and colleagues. Also starring are Anne Heywood as Holt's daughter and Bernard Lee as Corrie's assistant. The film is not bad overall, but Siodmak's story had been better served by the U.S. adaptations *The Lady and the Monster* (1944) and *Donovan's Brain* (1953).

In **Mix Me a Person** (1962), circumstantial evidence resulting from his theft of a Bentley automobile results in teenager Harry Jukes (Adam Faith) becoming the main suspect in a murder for which he is tried, found guilty and sentenced to hang. Hollywood's Anne Baxter plays Dr. Anne Dyson, a psychiatrist who develops an interest in the case and, firmly believing the youngster to be innocent, takes it upon herself to find new evidence in an effort to save him from the gallows. Through an association with the Bentley's owner, Anne eventually learns the truth about the murder (involving IRA gunrunners) which puts her in considerable danger. Teen idol Faith sings a couple of songs (including the great title number) and, in nice contrast to Baxter's more melodramatic acting style, gives a natural and quietly sympathetic performance. The movie surprisingly managed to gain an "X" rating on its original British release, which one can only imagine was due to a few candid remarks about sex.

"It should satisfy thriller addicts" was the good news reported by *The Daily Cinema* (May 17, 1963) about the promisingly titled **Night of the Prowler** (1962), an entertaining B movie whose twisty plot centers on an engineering company involved in the production of a new racing car. When one of the firm's four partners is shot dead, evidence—a threatening letter signed with the initials D.L.—suggests that the culprit is Don Lacey, a grudge-bearing former employee. The remaining three partners are company chairman Robert Langton (Patrick Holt), his estranged wife Marie (Colette Wilde) and Paul Conrad (Bill Nagy). One of the three, it turns out, is the real killer, having plotted with the company's accountant (Mark Singleton) to take control of the business by bumping off the others and scapegoating Lacey (whom the audience never sees for reasons that become clear by the end). The most atmospheric part is arguably the opening credits sequence, accompanied by a nifty jazz theme and featuring pretty much the only activity that in any way comes close to justifying the film's intriguing title.

Gimmicky American fright-film director William Castle joined forces with Hammer Film Productions for **The Old Dark House** (1962), a comedy thriller very loosely based on J.B. Priestley's 1927 novel *Benighted*, and which *The Daily Cinema* (August 24, 1966) called an "elementary spoof of the classic horror yarn." All the members of the bizarrely eccentric Femm family are heir to an ancestral fortune which an ancient will stipulates can only be claimed should their mansion, made of solid rock, be destroyed. Before long, they are being murdered one by one, with the culprit planning to blow the house to smithereens in order to lay sole claim to the fortune. Robert Morley and Fenella Fielding are great as two of the Femms (respectively, the family patriarch and a sex-starved temptress named Morgana), while Janette Scott plays the only normal (or is she?) member of the household. American comic actor Tom Poston tops the bill as a hapless car salesman forced by circumstances to stay at the mansion, and a frantic climax sees him attempt to locate and disarm a succession of time bombs planted by the killer. This Eastmancolor film's belated 1966 British release was in an edited down 77-minute version; U.S. theatergoers had gotten the full 86-minute version three years earlier, but in black and white. The opening credits feature illustrations by *The Addams Family* creator Charles Addams.

Not seen since its initial theatrical release, the B movie **Farewell Performance** (1963) concerns backstage intrigues at a variety theater where obnoxious pop star Ray Baron (David Kernan) is the star attraction. When Baron is found murdered—via cyanide-laced throat spray—in his dressing room, suspicion falls on Marlon (Alfred Burke), the handler of a chimpanzee act who'd been jealous of his wife Janice's (Delphi Lawrence) amorous interest in the pop star. In the end, it transpires that it was Janice who had laced the throat spray with the intention of poisoning Marlon; however, she'd been seen doing this by Baron's manager (Frederick Jaeger)—the actual murderer—who subsequently made sure the spray found its way into Baron's possession. Janice doesn't fare well in a climactic confrontation with the killer, the latter ultimately arrested by Scotland Yard's Chief Superintendent Raven (Derek Francis). *The Daily Cinema* (August 12, 1963) concluded their review with: "it's no great shakes as a murder mystery, but the juke-box fans might get a kick out of it." Among the attractions on offer for those "juke-box" fans are British instrumental group The Tornados.

"Only seventeen ... but no secret ... no passion ... no crime escaped her eyes!"

In the prologue to the B movie **The Eyes of Annie Jones** (1963), Geraldine Wheeler (Jean Lodge) is murdered in her country mansion by her ex-lover Lucas (Shay Gorman), a taxi driver, who buries her body in the woods nearby. Concerned with her disappearance, her aunt (Joyce Carey) gets help from Annie (Francesca Annis), a troubled 17-year-old orphan with ESP who can "find" things. A tired-looking Richard Conte plays Geraldine's obnoxious brother David, eventually revealed as having paid Lucas to carry out the murder so as to take control of the family business. Annie almost locates the body, which prompts the conspirators to attempt to move it to another location, this ultimately leading to their downfall. Based on a Henry Slesar story, this Parroch-McCallum production suffers from a surfeit of heavy characters and situations (e.g. certain moments between Annie and the sleazy David that create a creepy vibe) that make it a largely dispiriting experience.

Parroch-McCallum were also behind **Walk a Tightrope** (1963), a much better film with a great performance by Dan Duryea as an unstable deadbeat named Lutcher. Ellen (Patricia Owens), an American living in London, is devastated when her beloved husband is shot dead at their home—right in front of her—by Lutcher. To make matters worse, Lutcher acts as if Ellen had hired him to carry out the murder and tells her that he'll be in touch to claim the remainder of his fee. In ensuing events, Lutcher is trapped by the police (with Ellen's help) and is disbelieved when, in a subsequent trial, he continues to assert that he'd been hired by Ellen. A crucial twist at the story's conclusion involves a mysterious character (David Bauer) seen lurking around throughout the movie. This above-average B feature was written by the prolific Mann Rubin, who provides some disturbing insights into Lutcher's character; particularly effective in this regard is a scene where Lutcher recounts an unsettling childhood experience involving the horrific fate of some birds he'd trapped on a branch using birdlime. The plot's "bothersome loopholes" reported by the U.S. trade paper *Motion Picture Herald* (June 24, 1964) were probably due to the version under review having been shorn of nine minutes. Talented director Frank Nesbitt, whose career proved to be extremely short-lived, reteamed with Duryea for the following year's even better British thriller *Do You Know This Voice?*, again produced by Parroch-McCallum. *Walk a Tightrope* would not get a British theatrical release until 1967.

Another excellent B movie, and one of the better British noirs, **Blind Corner** (1963) benefits from good all-around performances and polished direction by Lance Comfort. Anne (Barbara Shelley), the beautiful wife of wealthy blind composer Paul Gregory (William Sylvester), has begun an affair with an artist named Ricky Seldon (Alexander Davion). In order to get hold of her husband's money, Anne persuades Ricky to agree to murder him and make it look like an accident. However, Ricky is actually just a pawn in a wider scheme by Anne and her true lover, Paul's obnoxious manager (Mark Eden), their plan being that the artist will be arrested for the eventual murder. Luckily, Paul finds out about the evil plot and manages to make an alliance with Ricky, resulting in the schemers getting their comeuppance. One of the film's many double-billings in the U.S. was with director William Castle's atmospheric psychological thriller *The Night Walker* (1964), a particularly apt pairing given that both movies featured a blind protagonist.

"The zaniest bunch of ghouls ever to haunt a house!"

Director Terence Fisher's engagingly zany B movie **The Horror of It All** (1964) stars U.S. actor-crooner Pat Boone as Jack Robinson, a London-based American salesman who pays a surprise visit to his fiancée Cynthia Marley (Erica Rogers) at her gloomy ancestral country mansion. He is soon embroiled in a mystery in which one of Cynthia's eccentric—and in one case totally insane—relatives is bumping off the others to secure a £300,000 legacy. The madcap shenanigans, which run along similar lines to Hammer/William Castle's *The Old Dark House* (1962), are highlighted by a deliciously camp performance by Dennis Price as a hammy theatrical member of the family. We're also treated to a great vampire-like character played by Andrée Melly (looking not unlike she did as one of *The Brides of Dracula*), not to mention a fun rendition—about halfway through—by Boone of the title song. Produced by Lippert Films, for whom Fisher also directed the same year's sci-fi B movie *The Earth Dies Screaming*.

Agatha Christie's famous novel, *Ten Little Indians*, originally published in 1939 as *Ten Little Niggers* (and in the U.S. as *And Then There Were None*), tells the story of a varied group of people invited to an island where a fiendish assassin begins murdering them one by one. The novel's decidedly bleak ending was later changed—by Christie herself—for the stage version, which features a relatively happier, audience-friendly outcome and has been the template for all English-language film adaptations to date.

The first British-produced version was **Ten Little Indians** (1965), a hugely enjoyable interpretation which embraces the swinging sixties era in which it was made through the inclusion of a pop star character played by real-life singer and teen idol Fabian. Produced and co-written by Harry Alan Towers, the film changes Christie's island setting to an isolated castle in the Austrian Alps, to where ten people (including the aforementioned pop star) from various walks of life are lured. Their host, a certain Mr. U.N. Owen, whom none of them has ever met, is nowhere to be seen, but he soon accuses each (via a tape recording) of having committed a past crime

Left to right: Wilfrid Hyde White, Stanley Holloway, Daliah Lavi, Shirley Eaton and Hugh O'Brian in *Ten Little Indians*, an entertaining 1965 version of Agatha Christie's classic mystery.

for which no justice was ever served. Before long, the guests are being murdered one by one, with the deaths patterned on the "Ten Little Indians" nursery rhyme. A thorough search of the place reveals that no one else is present, leading the guests to conclude that one of them must therefore be the killer. The murders continue in an atmosphere of mutual distrust, until only two of the ten—an enigmatic American (Hugh O'Brian) and a pretty English secretary (Shirley Eaton)—remain. At this point, the film presents viewers with a gimmicky one-minute "whodunit break" complete with a recap of the murders and an invitation to guess the outcome, which as it happens is one of the greatest twists in thriller history.

Things get off to a good start with a catchily scored title sequence in which the characters make their way (including via a cable car that will later feature in one of the murders) to the castle, and which effectively conveys the remoteness of the location. Also in the superb international cast are Wilfrid Hyde White, Dennis Price and the sultry Daliah Lavi, with Christopher Lee providing the tape-recorded voice of the mysterious U.N. Owen—or "unknown" if read in a certain way.

A second British version (again produced by Towers with Italian, German, French and Spanish input) appeared almost a decade later under the title ***And Then There Were None*** (1974), although to confuse matters it was released in the U.S. as *Ten Little Indians*. This time around, the setting is an abandoned palatial hotel in the Iranian desert, and the star-studded cast includes Oliver Reed, Elke Sommer, Richard Attenborough, Herbert Lom and Stéphane Audran, with

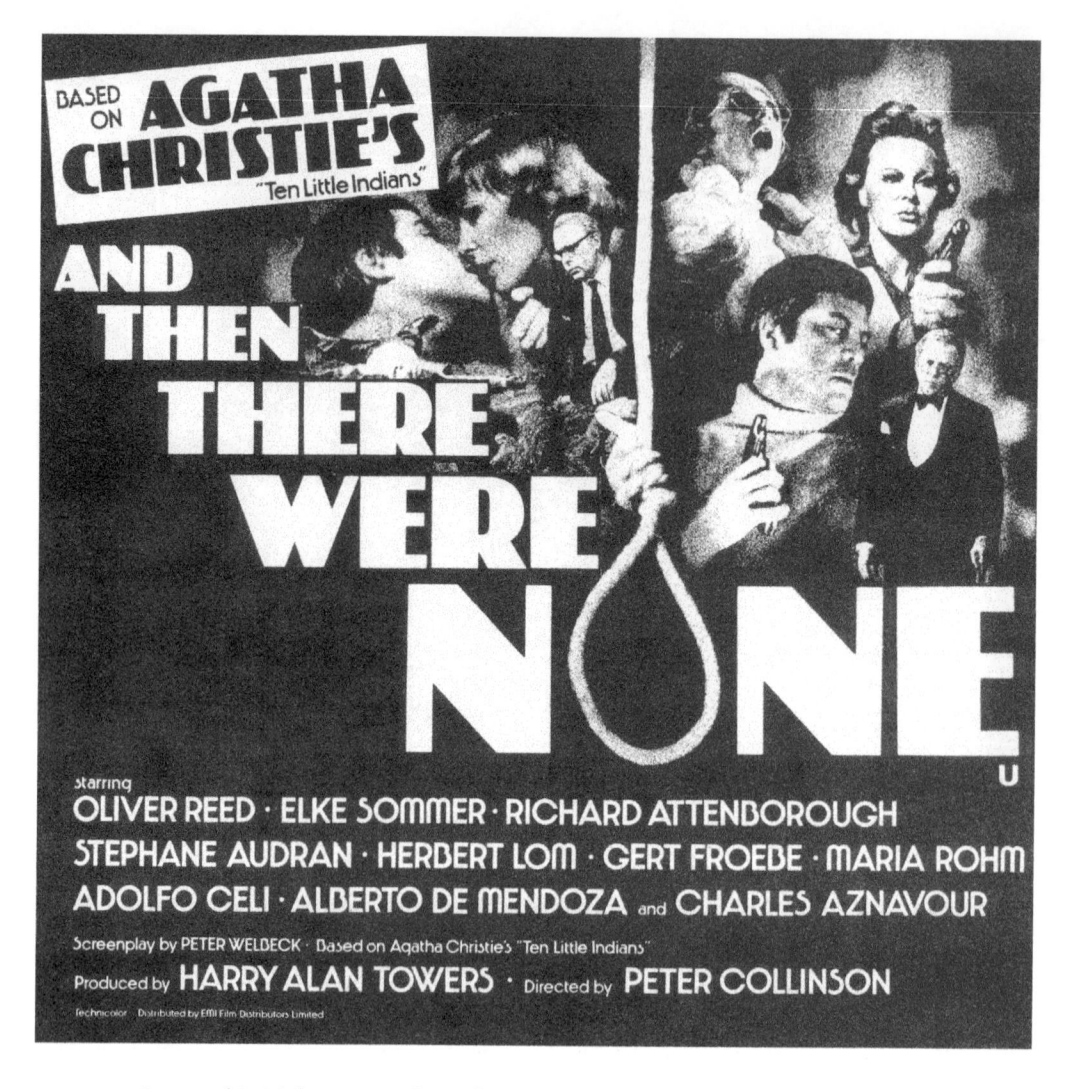

A second British version of Agatha Christie's classic *Ten Little Indians* story.

Orson Welles providing the voice of U.N. Owen. Overall, it's a monumental bore that lacks the inspiration, atmosphere and fun of its predecessor, with skilled director Peter Collinson surprisingly failing to inject anything substantially new into the proceedings. Incredibly, Towers made a third version of the story in 1989, this time even worse and with an African Safari setting.

"You're 'it' in the murder game"

The *Monthly Film Bulletin* (June 1966) described the B movie *The Murder Game* (1965) as a "competent thriller, directed without frills and with a happy disregard for coincidence." Aeronautical engineer Chris Aldrich (Trader Faulkner) marries Marie (Marla Landi), blissfully unaware that she has adopted a false identity in order to escape the clutches of first husband Steve (Ken Scott), a reprehensible American to whom she's still legally married. Steve soon shows up, gets a job as handyman on Chris' country estate and attempts to blackmail Marie; she in turn tries to kill him in a car "accident" which ends up injuring Chris instead. While recuperating at home, Chris hears a conversation between Marie and Steve that convinces him they are plotting his demise. This leads to him putting into motion a cunning plan—involving faking his own murder and pinning the blame on the pair—so as to turn the tables on them. Although they are acquitted at a resulting trial, events do finally lead to justice being served in connection with Steve's prior murder of a priest (Victor Brooks).

A highly polished production, **Bunny Lake Is Missing** (1965) stars the ethereal Carol Lynley as Ann Lake, a young American single mother recently arrived in London who reports her four-year-old daughter Bunny (whom the audience has not seen) missing. The problem is she's unable to produce any evidence that the child ever existed. Laurence Olivier gives a quietly authoritative performance as an increasingly skeptical police inspector (the fact that Ann once had an imaginary childhood playmate named "Bunny" doesn't help matters), and Keir Dullea plays the woman's possessive journalist brother, a complex character who grows in importance as the story progresses. For the most part, Otto Preminger directs compellingly and elicits generally excellent performances all around; especially effective are some rich character portrayals by notables such as Martita Hunt, Noël Coward and Finlay Currie, the latter as the proprietor of a doll repair shop where the film's most atmospheric sequence (Ann searching for a doll that could prove Bunny's existence) takes place. Also worthy of note are the superb Saul Bass-designed opening titles (strips of black paper are torn away to reveal the cast and credits beneath) and an appearance (via a TV broadcast during a pub scene) by rock group The Zombies.

A Grand Guignol backdrop and a plot involving a blood-drinking killer have often led to **Theatre of Death** (1966) being categorized as a horror movie, although the film's director Samuel Gallu defended it—within the pages of the *Kinematograph Weekly* (October 21, 1965)—as a "straight mystery thriller." Events revolve around the Paris-based Théâtre de Mort, a Grand Guignol venue whose sinister stage director, Philippe Darvas (Christopher Lee), is suspected of a series of vampire-like murders. Lelia Goldoni and Jenny Till play actresses at the theater, one of them ultimately revealed

A deadly double bill.

to be the killer whose craving for blood is explained by a gruesome secret from the past. Lee gives a forceful performance as the Svengali-like Darvas, who inexplicably disappears during the course of the story and later turns up dead, having been targeted by the killer because of his intention to exploit her in a Grand Guignol production based on her grisly history. Julian Glover has a heroic role as a police surgeon (and lover of Goldoni's character) and is involved in a spirited climax in which the blood-drinking fiend meets an unexpected and grisly demise below stage at the "Theatre of Death."

Lee also features in another venue-based offering, *Circus of Fear* (1966), a British-German Harry Alan Towers production in which he plays a mysterious hooded lion tamer. The entertaining and incident-packed story begins with an excitingly staged (on London's Tower Bridge) armored car robbery whose mastermind is connected with a circus where a large share of the stolen money is subsequently stashed. Leo Genn is great as a polite and unpretentious detective who follows clues to the circus, where a series of baffling murders occur in connection with the theft. The German edit, regarded as a *krimi* (a subgenre of German crime films usually based on Edgar Wallace stories), is known under the title *Das Rätsel des Silbernen Dreieck* (*The Mystery of the Silver Triangle*), which refers to triangular emblems on circus throwing knives used by the killer as murder weapons. Margaret Lee and Suzy Kendall attractively fill the only female roles, playing shapely circus artistes, while Klaus Kinski is suitably sinister as a crook seeking the hidden loot. Both the aforementioned German version and the original U.S. theatrical release were in black and white, with the latter running just 65 minutes under the title *Psycho-Circus*.

Montgomery Tully's late-stage B thriller *Who Killed the Cat?* (1966) turned out to be one of the prolific director's least suspenseful and most talky efforts. The film begins just after the funeral of Thomas Trellington, whose death leaves behind an illegitimate teenage daughter, Mary (Natasha Pyne), and a mean-spirited second wife named Eleanor (played in suitably nasty fashion by Vanda Godsell). Livid upon learning that she has inherited less than expected—including modest rental income from her late husband's three elderly female lodgers (Mary Merrall, Ellen Pollock and Amy Dalby)—with the bulk of the inheritance having been put in trust for Mary, the vindictive Eleanor begins making life hell for all involved; this includes raising the rents and culminates in her callous poisoning of a cat belonging to one of the elderly ladies. The three pensioners plan to poison Eleanor in revenge but then have second thoughts, only for Eleanor to be subsequently found dead—from poisoning! Conrad Phillips stars as a detective investigating the death (the case comes to a somewhat underwhelming conclusion), and also involved in the story is a jeweler played by Mervyn Johns. The 1956 stage play, *Tabitha*, on which the film is based, was co-written by Arnold Ridley of *The Ghost Train* fame.

*"Excited by the smell of fear,
they inflict their fatal stings!"*

Psycho author Robert Bloch co-wrote (with Anthony Marriott) the screenplay for ***The Deadly Bees*** (1966), a whodunit in which the titular stingers are used as a murder weapon. Vicki Robbins (Suzanna Leigh), a pop singer suffering from exhaustion, is prescribed a period of convalescence on a remote island farm run by surly beekeeper Ralph Hargrove (Guy Doleman). During her stay, the island is plagued by a series of killer bee attacks, in one case claiming the life of Hargrove's wife. The story offers two main suspects, namely Hargrove and another of the island's residents, a rival beekeeper named Manfred (Frank Finlay). One of them has developed a liquid compound that attracts the bees to their victims, and we find out who (not to mention why) in a drawn-out climax in which Vicki, about to be tainted with the liquid herself, manages to turn the tables on the culprit. Clearly influenced by Hitchcock's *The Birds*, this Amicus production features some fairly intense attack sequences and one particularly gruesome make-up effect.

Based on Belgian author Georges Simenon's 1940 novel *Les Inconnus dans la maison*, **Stranger in the House** (1967) changes the book's small French town locale to the English city of Winchester, with the story updated to suit the swinging sixties. The rather drawn-out proceedings, which get off to a jarring start with a psychedelic title sequence that seems to have been designed for another production altogether, would have been intolerable were it not for a superb performance by James Mason. As the backbone of the film, Mason dominates every scene he's in as former distinguished attorney John Sawyer, now a cynical and reclusive alcoholic as the result of his wife (Lisa Daniely) having left him years before. John's teenage daughter Angela (Geraldine Chaplin), although living with him in their shabby mansion, is a virtual stranger to her father and spends most of her time hanging out with a group of similarly aged hipsters including her Cypriot boyfriend Jo (Paul Bertoya) and cousin Desmond (Ian Ogilvy). When a new member of the group—the older and immoral Barney Teale (Bobby Darin)—is found shot dead in the mansion with evidence planted to frame Jo, John sees a chance to reclaim something of his life when Angela asks him to defend Jo in court. Events, many of which are shown in flashback, lead to a somewhat anticlimactic ending, with John solving the case (by exposing one of the group members as the killer) before it even gets to trial.

Scripted by Jack Roffey from his own play, **Hostile Witness** (1968) stars Ray Milland (who also directed) as Simon Crawford, an irascible London attorney devastated by the death of his daughter in a hit-and-run incident. Crawford is later framed for the murder of his judge friend Sir Matthew Gregory (Percy Marmont), with evidence against him including a fabricated letter (supposedly sent to him by a private detective) falsely naming Sir Matthew as the hit-and-run-driver, making it appear as if Crawford has carried out a revenge killing. Crawford ends up defending himself at his trial, during which the real killer—a member of Crawford's staff with a years-old grudge against both him and Sir Matthew—is eventually revealed. (We never, however, discover who the real hit-and-run driver was.) Milland, who'd also starred in the play on Broadway, is more animated in his performance than in his direction; Sylvia Syms provides able support as a junior lawyer, and there's a clever twist involving the killer being color-blind. Milland's next film, the U.S. TV movie *Daughter of the Mind* (1969), saw him once again playing the bereaved father of a daughter killed in a car accident.

In **The Last Shot You Hear** (1968), world-famous marriage guidance counselor and advice columnist Charles Nordeck (Hugh Marlowe in his final film role) refuses to grant his wife Anne (Patricia Haines) a divorce for fear the publicity will ruin his career. Anne and her lover, Peter (William Dysart), consequently carry out a plan to murder Charles, which entails shooting him with his own gun. However, Charles' secretary Eileen (Zena Walker), having stumbled on their scheme, begins blackmailing them by demanding that Peter, with whom she's in love, marry her in return for her silence. A major twist involves the disappearance of Charles' body following the shooting, not to mention the fact that the bullets had been replaced with blanks. Made in color but originally released in black-and-white, the film suffers from poor photography, art direction and editing, and was accurately described by *Films and Filming* (May 1970) as having "one of the most implausible, hoary plots to be dragged out in years."

1970s

"A phantasmagoria of fright."

Paranoia is the order of the day in **Fragment of Fear** (1970), masterfully directed by Richard C. Sarafian, whose next and probably best-remembered film was the cult existential road movie *Vanishing Point*. The intriguing plot begins with the death by strangulation of elderly widow Lucy Dawson (Flora Robson) while vacationing in Italy with her nephew Tim (David Hemmings at his best), an author and recovered heroin addict she had just recently been getting to know. Upon returning to England, Tim begins making enquiries into his aunt's background, and it begins to look as if the woman had been involved in nefarious activity, namely a racket whereby she nurtured (through a legitimate charity) ex-jailbirds and helped them secure high-powered jobs, only to later blackmail them about their criminal pasts. Throughout his investigation, Tim becomes the target of a sinister conspiracy (involving threatening phone calls, a mysterious warning letter that he discovers had been written on his own typewriter and an attempted frame-up involving drugs) designed to discredit his findings and make it appear as if he's suffering from paranoid delusions. A late revelation that Lucy may have been murdered by foreign agents who wished to prey on her blackmail victims for spy recruitment, leads to a shattering finale that, while somewhat inconclusive, is nevertheless perfectly suited to the surreal quality of preceding events. The film, which often feels like an Italian *giallo* thriller (Hemmings would later star in the 1975 *giallo* classic *Deep Red*), co-stars Gayle Hunnicutt as Tim's fiancée, and features an occasionally obtrusive but generally effective jazz score.

Set in early twentieth-century Paris, **Murders in the Rue Morgue** (1971) centers on a Grand Guignol theater company headed by Cesar Charron (Jason Robards), whose latest production is an adaptation of the titular Edgar Allan Poe story. Cesar's much younger wife, Madeleine (Christine Kaufmann), who has a starring role in the play, is haunted by dreams in connection with the axe murder 12 years earlier of her actress mother (Lilli Palmer in flashbacks), who'd also worked with Cesar and had unintentionally disfigured her fellow performer and lover Marot (Herbert Lom) during a live performance after somebody substituted fake acid with the real thing. Marot, subsequently thought to have committed suicide, is in fact alive and well and is busy viciously killing—with acid—past and present members of Cesar's company as part of a revenge plot in connection with his disfigurement and the aforementioned axe murder, the true culprit in both these cases ultimately revealed in a surprise twist.

Filmed in Spain, this unsatisfying blend of Poe with elements of *The Phantom of the Opera* (Lom's masked—due to the disfigurement—killer is a virtual throwback to the actor's Phantom from the 1962 Hammer Films version of Gaston Leroux's famous story) suffers from a dull script and stiff performances, with a miscast Robards looking like he'd rather be somewhere else. Originally released theatrically at 87 minutes, the film has since become available in a 98-minute director's cut.

An English coastal town is the setting for the occasionally creepy and fairly suspenseful *Ten Little Indians*-style mystery **The Flesh and Blood Show** (1972), in which several young actors and their director (Ray Brooks) gather at a dilapidated old pier theater to rehearse a play for a mysterious production company. Before long, they begin falling victim to a maniacal former thespian with an intense hatred of young actors which stems from a past incident (at the same theater) involving his actress wife's infidelity with another performer. The windswept seaside locale provides an appropriately bleak backdrop to the goings-on, while everything in the plot that needs explaining is clarified in a 3D black-and-white flashback sequence near the end. In a neat twist, one of the actors is found to have a surprising connection to the maniac and turns out to be responsible for one of the murders. Although somewhat shabbily put together by cult director Pete Walker, the film is lent some gravitas by the presence of veteran character actor Patrick Barr as a local eccentric with a dark secret. The flesh of the title is rather more plentiful than the blood, with the original British "X" rating a result of gratuitous nudity as opposed to gore, the latter kept to a minimum with murders occurring off-screen.

A classier take on thespianism and murder is the blackly comic ***Theatre of Blood*** (1973). A flashback some way into the film shows veteran Shakespearean actor Edward Lionheart (Vincent Price) making a suicide jump into London's River Thames after failing to win the 1970 London Theatre "Critics Circle" award. However, his body was never found—and with good reason, for he is in fact alive and well, having been rescued from his near watery grave by a group of meths-drinking down-and-outs. Instead of a further suicide attempt, Lionheart has turned his attentions to taking revenge on the members of said "Critics Circle" who relentlessly vilified his performances and who he feels robbed him of the much-coveted award by presenting it to a newcomer instead. Indeed, by the time the flashback occurs, he has already dispatched four of the critics in a spectacularly gruesome variety of ways based on Shakespearean death scenes. Helping him enact his vengeance are his devoted daughter (Diana Rigg) and the aforementioned down-and-outs. Eventually, the one remaining critic (Ian Hendry) faces grim consequences unless he presents Lionheart with the desired award in a mock ceremony at the actor's deserted theater hideout.

Price is nothing short of fantastic, giving full rein to his delightfully theatrical style as he carries out the often quite graphic murders in a variety of guises from Richard III to a camp hairdresser. The critics are played by a prestigious line-up of actors,

Aided by his daughter (Diana Rigg), vengeful actor Edward Lionheart (Vincent Price) prepares to mete out Shakespearean death upon one of his critics (Harry Andrews) in *Theatre of Blood* (1973).

including Dennis Price, Michael Hordern and Robert Morley (the latter suffering a particularly unpleasant culinary death involving his pet poodles), and the whole thing benefits immeasurably from some evocative and beautifully composed music by Michael J. Lewis.

The theatrical theme continues in *The House in Nightmare Park* (1973), a superb comedy thriller set in the Edwardian era. Foster Twelvetrees (legendary funnyman Frankie Howerd), a hammy one-man-show actor, accepts an invitation to perform at the gloomy Henderson mansion, unaware that he is the secret heir to a fortune in diamonds hidden somewhere on the estate. It transpires that the real reason for the invitation is that some of the family members believe he unwittingly holds a clue to the location of the gems, and are planning to get hold of it—and murder him once they do.

While being a great showcase for Howerd's wonderfully eccentric humor, the film also delivers some genuine chills, not the least of which is Twelvetrees' encounter with a meat cleaver-wielding old crone in the attic. Ray Milland, in one of his best 1970s roles, plays the Henderson patriarch, and there's a truly bizarre sequence in which he and other family members dress as human puppets to perform a routine called "Dance of the Dolls." Good attention to Edwardian period detail and a hair-raising scene in a snake house are further plusses in a story that has quite a few twists and turns before the side-splitting finale involving Twelvetrees' inadvertent destruction—before he's even had a chance to look at it—of a map pinpointing the treasure. The original British opening titles, which feature a surprisingly haunting theme by Harry Robinson, were substituted in the U.S. (where the film was initially released as *Crazy House* and later as *Night of the Laughing Dead*) with a new sequence comprising wacky haunted house animation and correspondingly goofy music.

"*...the stamp of murder!*"

Set in Windsor (in the shadow of the historic royal castle), the unexceptional **Penny Gold** (1973), as the title suggests, revolves around the world of philately. Francesca Annis plays identical twins Diane and Delphi, the latter involved in a respected stamp collecting business with their stepfather Charles (Joseph O'Conor). The convoluted story involves a devious plot by the evil Diane to assume Delphi's identity in order to use the stamp business to sell a priceless—and dishonestly acquired—Penny Gold stamp. James Booth plays a dogged detective investigating two murders carried out by Diane's lover-accomplice (Richard Heffer) as part of the scheme, and one of the film's highlights is a short but very well-executed car chase.

The ingenious if slightly far-fetched plot of *The Internecine Project* (1974) unfolds in London and concerns Professor Robert Elliot (James Coburn in an excellent if lesser-known performance), an unscrupulous American economics expert with political and big business interests who's offered a top advisory position in the U.S. Government. However, before he can take up the appointment, Elliot must eliminate four people—members of a European network he had set up to carry out industrial espionage—who could possibly compromise him in the future. To this end, he formulates a devious plan whereby each of the four is manipulated into murdering one of the others. Harry Andrews and Ian Hendry stand out as two of the victims and are subjected to the film's most vicious killings (a bathroom strangling and a hammer attack respectively), while a neat final twist is not dissimilar to that in the 1972 Charles Bronson classic *The Mechanic*.

"*Three or four drops a day can relieve the patient ... of her fortune!*"

Directed by Sidney Hayers and produced in association with Bristol-based television company HTV, **Diagnosis: Murder** (1974) is an unpretentious suspenser about a psychiatric doctor with a decidedly unhealthy bedside manner. Planning to murder his wealthy wife Julia (Dilys Hamlett) for her money, Dr. Hayward (Christopher Lee) maneuvers the police—in a scheme involving the use of faked anonymous letters—into thinking she may already be dead and her body buried in a nearby lake. The police duly drag the lake and find nothing. This leaves the way clear for Hayward, who's been keeping Julia under sedation at a farmhouse, to carry out her murder, his intention being to now really dump her body in the lake which he knows will not be searched a second time. Judy Geeson plays Hayward's secretary and lover, who becomes complicit in the plan and ultimately meets a fitting end after Julia manages to cleverly turn the tables on the conspirators. The original and mostly solid script by Philip Levene, who worked with Hayers on the same year's *Deadly Strangers*, includes a rather superfluous last-minute twist relating to a subplot concerning the cynical investigating detective (Jon Finch). While conceding that the plot was "neat enough," *CinemaTV Today* (July 12, 1975) nevertheless felt the characters had "come out of a packet of ready-mix in which all the ingredients are artificial."

The British-Canadian co-production **The Disappearance** (1977) stars Donald Sutherland as Jay Mallory, a Montreal-based assassin for a mysterious organization known as "The Office." The story charts Mallory's attempts to solve the sudden disappearance of his wife Celandine (Francine Racette), while at the same time trying to resist unyielding pressures by his paymasters to carry out a new contract in England. The film's non-linear structure employs several flashbacks that give us insights into Mallory's troubled relationship with Celandine, and we eventually find out that a man she'd been having an affair with is the very same man Mallory has been assigned to assassinate. After carrying out the contract, Mallory returns home to Montreal and finds Celandine (who has reappeared just as suddenly as she had disappeared) waiting for him with a surprising revelation about his assignment.

The slow-paced, bleak and mostly pretentious proceedings fail to engage due to unappealing main characters and a surprising lack of chemistry between real-life husband-and-wife Sutherland and Racette, while a last-minute shock ending (in connection with Mallory having decided to quit "The Office") is fairly predictable. The amazing supporting cast includes David Warner and Christopher Plummer in key roles. An alternate 81-minute version exists that restructures the narrative and replaces the original's haunting score with inferior synthesizer-led arrangements.

The last big-screen version to date of John Willard's 1922 play, **The Cat and the Canary** (1977) is a comedy thriller boasting a superb Anglo-American cast and competent scripting and direction by Radley Metzger, best known for his stylish work in the erotic film genre. On a stormy night in 1934, the six surviving relatives of deceased millionaire Cyrus West (Wilfrid Hyde White) gather at the latter's estate, Glencliff Manor, to find out which of them will inherit his fortune. In a particularly inventive sequence, Cyrus posthumously addresses his potential heirs by way of a pre-recorded home movie in which he names Annabelle (Carol Lynley) as sole beneficiary. However, he makes it clear that, should Annabelle die or be judged insane during the course of the night, then another inheritor will be named in a second film held by the estate's executor (Wendy Hiller). Before long, a supposed psychologist (Edward Fox) from a nearby asylum turns up to warn that a dangerous lunatic, with a penchant for slowly ripping apart his victims, is on the loose in the area. The maniac is soon stalking the house via secret passageways and claims two victims before a neat twist reveals him to be part of a devious plot to get hold of the inheritance.

The comedy elements, unlike those which worked so well in the classic 1939 Bob Hope version, fall rather flat in this adaptation, mostly because nobody in the cast can hold a candle to Hope. (Speaking of candles, there's actually no need for any, as what should have been the star of the film—the house itself—is generally far too brightly lit for what is essentially an "old dark house" movie.) In any case, the comedic moments jar with Metzger's introduction into the proceedings of an often unpleasant streak of sadism, including the threatened torture of Annabelle in a disturbingly depicted secret torture room. Michael Callan plays the hero among the relatives, a mostly immoral bunch that Cyrus amusingly refers to as "bastards" and "leeches."

Adapted from Kathleen Tynan's semi-fictional novel of the same name, **Agatha** (1978) concerns a true-life incident in which famed mystery writer Agatha Christie vanished for 11 days in 1926, causing a national stir. Amid much speculation, she was eventually found staying at a chic spa hotel in Yorkshire and chose to never publicly disclose the real reason for her disappearance. An elegant production with great attention to period detail, the film presents known facts while theorizing that Christie (sensitively played by Vanessa Redgrave) attempted suicide while at the hotel; the suicide theory is certainly plausible given the author's then real-life emotional distress over her husband's decision to leave her for another woman, but the way it's presented here is wholly unconvincing. Also starring are Dustin Hoffman as a fictional character (an American newsman who tracks down and falls for Christie) and Timothy Dalton as the husband.

Another female goes missing in **The Lady Vanishes** (1979), a remake of Alfred Hitchcock's classic 1938 film of the same name, which in turn had been adapted from the 1936 Ethel Lina White novel *The Wheel Spins*. Set one year after the Hitchcock version was made, the story concerns the disappearance of a British nanny (Angela Lansbury) on board a train traveling from Bavaria to England, with certain fellow passengers falsely denying (for various reasons) having ever seen her. Cybill Shepherd and Elliott Gould are engaging as two American passengers—a madcap heiress and an acerbic *Life* magazine photographer—teaming

A decent 1979 remake of an Alfred Hitchcock classic.

up to search for the woman, who they discover has been kidnapped as part of a Nazi plot to prevent her delivering to the British Foreign Office vital information (coded in the form of a melody) from her anti–Nazi German employer. Herbert Lom plays a duplicitous doctor involved in the plot (he literally keeps the kidnapped nanny under wraps on the train by disguising her as a heavily bandaged patient), while Arthur Lowe and Ian Carmichael are delightful as a pair of cricket-obsessed British passengers. Beautifully photographed on location in Austria, the movie, described by *Films and Filming* (June 1979) as "a comedy-thriller par excellence," is notable as being the last feature made by Hammer Film Productions if one doesn't count the company's resurrection in the late 2000s.

3

The Psychological and the Psychopathic

This chapter contains thrillers that are often described under the blanket term "psycho thriller" but which can in fact be split into two categories, namely the psychological thriller and, for want of a better term, the "psychopathic" thriller. While both deal with psychology and insanity, there are substantial differences to merit their consideration as separate sub-genres. Psychological thrillers often involve unscrupulous characters employing mind control, gaslighting and/or other forms of deception in order to manipulate the state of mind of others for their own evil agendas; scenarios can include scaring somebody to death or inducing someone to commit murder or suicide. These films can also include situations involving insanity by natural causes, feigned insanity and the pinning of crimes on characters suffering from mental illness. The "psychopathic" thriller usually concerns stalkers and serial killers, and can have sexual undertones with themes of voyeurism, fetishism, repression and religious fanaticism.

The Psychological

Hammer's Psychological Thrillers

From 1960 to 1972, Hammer Film Productions made a series of ten psychological thrillers. The first few, beautifully shot in black and white, were dubbed "mini Hitchcocks" by the company's managing director Sir James Carreras, who no doubt wanted them to be seen in the same light as the then recent internationally successful, not to mention similarly monochrome, Alfred Hitchcock shocker *Psycho*. While certainly Hitchcockian to some degree, the films overall are actually much more reminiscent of director Henri-Georges Clouzot's 1955 French classic *Les Diaboliques*. Clouzot's film was based on a novel by famed Gallic thriller-writing duo Boileau-Narcejac (the collective nom de plume of Pierre Boileau and Thomas Narcejac), while the driving force behind the Hammer thrillers was the great Jimmy Sangster, most of whose scripts for the series (he was involved in eight of the ten films) were adaptations of his own original stories. (Sangster had cut his teeth as a film writer on Hammer's 1956 sci-fi flick *X the Unknown* before going on to script many of their influential horror movies including the classic monster reboots *The Curse of Frankenstein*, *Dracula* and *The Mummy*.) The similarities with *Les Diaboliques* are most evident in the first two—*Taste of Fear* (1961) and *Maniac* (1962)—of Sangster's entries, not only because of their French settings, atmospheric black-and-white photography, or for that matter the presence in *Taste of Fear* of a murky and foreboding swimming pool (an obvious homage), but also because of their particularly labyrinthine plots involving the truly devious maneuverings of diabolically deceptive characters; in this latter respect, Sangster showed he could easily give the aforementioned Boileau-Narcejac a run for their money—and then some. *Taste of Fear*'s original pressbook contains a quote from the film's lead star, Susan Strasberg, which stands as a testament to Sangster's greatness:

When I started to read the script, I couldn't put it down. Here was a thriller with a brilliantly conceived and thought-out story—a thriller with new surprises, new shocks, new twists on almost every page. I promptly cabled Hammer saying I'd sue them if they didn't let me play the heroine.

Following 1972's *Fear in the Night* (his final psychological thriller for Hammer not to mention his swansong for the company), Sangster went on to work almost exclusively in American television, where his credits include the teleplay for one of the highest regarded episodes—"Horror in the Heights"—of the 1974/5 series *Kolchak: The Night Stalker*.

"A diabolical new technique in suspense!"

At 109 minutes, the first film in the series, ***The Full Treatment*** (1960), is about 20 minutes too long, and had probably fared better in its 93-minute original U.S. theatrical release version. (The picture's stateside title is the arresting *Stop Me Before I Kill!*)

Ronald Lewis plays Alan Colby, a London-based Formula One star dubbed the "Demon of the Track" but whose driving skills off the track prove less than satisfactory when, on his wedding day, he suffers major head injuries in a dreadful highway crash. Discharged following several months in hospital, Alan finds he has acquired an overly aggressive streak, including the occasional and extremely worrying compulsion to strangle his wife Denise (Diane Cilento). During a belated honeymoon in the South of France, the newlyweds meet Dr. Prade (Claude Dauphin), a psychiatrist who convinces Denise to persuade Alan to undergo treatment with him, this subsequently taking place at the doctor's Harley Street practice back in London. It's not difficult to guess that Prade is up to no good, and sure enough, he seriously abuses his position by faking evidence to make it appear as if Denise has been killed, dismembered and disposed of, all designed—having already prepared him through intense psychiatric manipulation—to make Alan believe himself responsible for the "crime." An attempt by Prade to have Alan committed results in the latter going on the run. He winds up back in the South of France, where Prade is busy cozying up to Denise (this was the diabolical doctor's plan all along), who's been led to believe that her husband is insane and incarcerated. In a final confrontation involving all three characters, the doctor's evil plot is exposed and he dies while attempting to escape on a faulty gondola lift.

Lewis and Cilento are excellent as the troubled couple who eventually wise up (after missing many obvious signals) to the devious machinations of the all-too-smooth Prade, played with just the right amount of arrogance and self-importance by top-billed Dauphin. Things get off to a great start with a brilliantly shot credits sequence detailing the aftermath of Alan's car crash, but the film gradually loses steam as a result of repetitive situations and improbable actions on the part of the main characters, and there's also the problem of some awkward foreshadowing of key events such as the gondola lift ending.

"It is imperative that you see it from the start!"

A "contrived but expertly executed mystery shocker" was how *Variety* (August 9, 1961) summarized ***Taste of Fear*** (1961), the jewel in the crown of the series, with a superlative original screenplay by Jimmy Sangster. Susan Strasberg plays a young wheelchair-bound woman named Penny Appleby who, responding to an invitation by her father, returns to the family estate on the French Riviera following an absence of 10 years. Penny is puzzled by her father's absence (he's supposedly away on business) and in the meantime gets acquainted with her stepmother Jane (Ann Todd), whom she'd never previously met. Two other main characters are a handsome live-in chauffeur (Ronald Lewis) and a seemingly sinister physician played by Hammer regular Christopher Lee. In a series of horrifying events, Penny twice sees the dead body of her father, first in the summerhouse and then in her bedroom, but cannot prove this as both times the corpse subsequently disappears. We eventually learn that there's an evil scheme afoot to drive Penny insane so as to gain control of the estate. The conspirators, who ultimately decide to kill Penny, are revealed at just over the one-hour mark, which still leaves time for several more neat twists, including a spectacular reveal that even the most seasoned thriller addicts may not see coming. All roles are well acted by an excellent cast, with the eerie atmospherics including a particularly creepy sequence involving a corpse in the depths of a stagnant swimming pool.

France, specifically the Camargue, was also the setting for what is almost certainly the most tortuously plotted film of the series, **Maniac** (1962). While visiting the area, American artist Geoff Farrell (Kerwin Mathews) is seduced by and falls in love with Eve (Nadia Gray). Eve's husband, Georges, has been locked up in an insane asylum ever since his blowtorch murder of the man (Arnold Diamond) who sexually assaulted his daughter—Eve's stepdaughter—Annette (Liliane Brousse). Eve tells Geoff that Georges will divorce her and disappear out of her life forever if they help him escape, this to involve the cooperation of a male nurse from inside the institution. Geoff agrees, and everything seemingly goes to plan. However, we later learn that Eve and a secret lover have concocted a complex scheme (in which the escape plays a major part) to murder Georges in a scenario that will leave them free of suspicion. To pull off their plan, the plotters need the remains of two corpses to be found, one of which will be Georges'. As for the other one, this is where Geoff comes in: it turns out Eve was only

Arnold Diamond and Liliane Brousse in the effective opening sequence of *Maniac* (1962).

ever interested in his body—only not in the usual sense of the expression! Geoff survives his planned fate thanks in no small part to the local police inspector (George Pastell), who comes up with a clever ruse that leads to the diabolical conspirators getting their comeuppance; but not before much unpleasantness has occurred, including a reappearance of the infamous blowtorch.

Mathews, who told the authors of the excellent *Hammer Films: An Exhaustive Filmography* (Jefferson, NC: McFarland, 1996) that he became "a blatant Francophile because of *Maniac*," makes for a handsome if none-too-bright hero, and the film also features Donald Houston in what proves a crucial role. Sangster's attempt to top *Taste of Fear* has resulted in a particularly twisty script that is forced to unfairly misdirect the audience during one of the film's key scenes. Notwithstanding, it remains a well-acted and superbly atmospheric mini-masterpiece of a British thriller.

Paranoiac (1962) stars Oliver Reed and Janette Scott as twenty-something siblings Simon and Eleanor Ashby, who've lived with their aunt Harriet (Sheila Burrell) on their large coastal family estate ever since the death—just over a decade earlier—of their parents in an airline crash. Simon is a hard-drinking playboy given to bouts of depression and violent fits of rage, while Eleanor is a sensitive soul who has never managed to get over a second family tragedy in which another sibling, her beloved 15-year-old brother Tony, supposedly (as no body was ever found) drowned himself three years after the air crash. Into their lives comes a young man (Alexander Davion) claiming, very convincingly, to be Tony, which delights Eleanor but causes unease among the others. The audience is soon let in on the fact that "Tony" is an impostor, having arranged the deception as part of an inheritance swindle plot in cahoots with the crooked son of the family attorney; and he's eventually forced to come clean to Eleanor after she panics upon developing more than just sibling affections for him. As the story progresses, the man's presence proves to be a catalyst for unraveling the horrifying truth about what really happened to the genuine Tony. Reed gives a truly riveting performance (his final descent into full-blown insanity has to be seen to be believed), and there's some great atmosphere in the family estate's dilapidated chapel, where Simon conducts strange rituals in which organ playing and a mysterious masked figure (dressed as a choir boy and wielding a meat hook) are involved. It's in the chapel that the film's one big shock moment, not to mention the grotesque *Psycho*-esque finale, occurs.

Hammer's success with the one-word titles (à la *Psycho*) of the previous two movies inevitably saw their next thriller's intended title, *Here's the Knife, Dear—Now Use It*, being dropped in favor of ***Nightmare*** (1963). Janet (Jennie Linden), a 16-year-old boarding school student, returns home to the family estate after her studies are disrupted by terrifying nightmares about her mother, who we learn was certified insane and incarcerated in an asylum after murdering her husband on Janet's 11th birthday. The traumatic incident has left Janet fearful that she may have inherited her mother's insanity. The first half of the film introduces us to several characters: Janet's firm but kindly teacher (Brenda Bruce); the girl's guardian and executor of the estate, Henry (David Knight); a woman (Moira Redmond) hired by Henry as a companion for Janet; and two long-standing family servants (George A. Cooper and Irene Richmond). Two of these initiate an evil plot (which entails engineering nightmare-like scenarios involving the ghostly figure of a woman in white) that drives Janet to commit a murder beneficial to them, the devious pair consequently gaining control of the estate after Janet is institutionalized just like her mother had been. The movie's second half is the weakest and sees the conspirators themselves become victims of a plot by those who wish to avenge Janet. John Wilcox's superbly atmospheric photography was overseen by the film's director Freddie Francis, himself a famed cinematographer, and is a highlight in what *Films and Filming* (April 1964) called "a thoroughly routine exercise."

Set in London, **Hysteria** (1964) had by far the most modern feel of the series up to that time. American actor Robert Webber, then mostly working in television (this was only his third big-screen outing since starring as "Juror 12" in *12 Angry Men* [1957]), plays an amnesiac patient—temporarily given the name Chris Smith due to having no identification—at a private hospital who claims to remember nothing about events prior to a car crash some months back. Dr. Keller (Anthony Newlands), with help from nurse Gina (Jennifer Jayne), has taken care of his physical recuperation, while his medical bills, not to mention the luxury modern penthouse apartment waiting for him upon his release, have been paid for by a mysterious benefactor revealed to be an attractive model named Denise (Lelia Goldoni). The story involves two of these latter three characters cunningly framing Chris for a murder, having already conditioned him (by way of a devious plot using tape recordings and hallucinogenic drugs) so that he'll actually believe he carried out the crime while in a state of hysteria. However, the conspirators are not as clever as they think, and Chris, with more than a little help from a disheveled but extremely proficient private detective (Maurice Denham), eventually manages to turn the tables after revealing a surprising ace up his sleeve. Overall, the film is a disappointment, with little suspense, weak characterizations (apart from the great Denham) and an unsuitable jazz soundtrack.

As well as being Hammer's first color psychological thriller, **Fanatic** (1965) is also the first British "Grande Dame Guignol" film, whose U.S. retitling as *Die! Die! My Darling!* was no doubt an attempt to cash in on that genre's *Hush ... Hush, Sweet Charlotte* (1964). The story begins with a young American woman, Patricia Carroll (Stefanie Powers), paying a courtesy visit to Mrs. Trefoile (legendary Hollywood grande dame Tallulah Bankhead), the mother (whom she'd never met) of her deceased one-time fiancé, Stephen. A dangerous religious fanatic, Mrs. Trefoile soon makes it clear that she considers Patricia eternally betrothed to Stephen and, aided and abetted by her unethical husband-and-wife staff members (a superbly cast Peter Vaughan and Yootha Joyce), keeps the woman prisoner in her large country house; there, she is subjected to starvation, beatings and daily religious readings in preparation for an eventual reunion with Stephen in heaven. The solid cast also includes Donald Sutherland, in an early role as Mrs. Trefoile's mentally disabled gardener, and Maurice Kaufmann as Patricia's new fiancé, who finally saves her from being murdered (in front of a portrait of Stephen) by the fanatic. The great Richard Matheson provides a cracking screenplay adapted from a 1961 Anne Blaisdell (aka Elizabeth Linington) novel titled *Nightmare*.

"Would you trust the nanny ... or the boy?"

Based on the novel of the same name by Evelyn Piper, **The Nanny** (1965) features a masterfully restrained performance by Bette Davis as the stoical and seemingly perfect nanny-housekeeper of husband-and-wife Bill and Virginia Fane (James Villiers and Wendy Craig). The story begins with the return home of the Fanes' precocious and bratty 10-year-old son Joey (William Dix) following two years in a special school, where he was sent after Nanny blamed him for the accidental drowning of his little sister in the bath. Joey causes embarrassment to all by being openly antagonistic toward Nanny, secretly believing it was she who'd caused his sister's death and certain that she will now attempt to silence him. A tense battle of wits (during which Virginia is poisoned in circumstances that implicate Joey) ensues between Nanny and the youngster, with the latter's aunt (Jill Bennett) ultimately proving to be the catalyst for a revelation in which the truth behind the little girl's death is laid

Bette Davis is *The Nanny* (1965).

bare. Dix gives a remarkably mature performance (a great match for the impeccable Davis) in this creepy and expertly carpentered chiller that should keep you guessing until the powerful and at once tragic and sympathetic ending.

Having survived the horrors of Mrs. Trefoile in the earlier *Fanatic*, Stefanie Powers had to contend with another matriarchal maniac in the slow-burning **Crescendo** (1969). By way of doing some research into the late composer Henry Ryman, American student Susan Roberts (Powers) visits Ryman's widow Danielle (Margaretta Scott) in the South of France and soon becomes attracted to the woman's drug-addicted wheelchair-bound son, Georges (James Olson). It eventually transpires that Danielle is counting on Susan becoming pregnant in order to produce an heir to the Ryman musical legacy. However, because Georges is impotent and has no musical talent to pass down, Danielle plans to trick Susan into sleeping with Georges' secret identical twin, Jacques (also Olson), who is both potent and musically gifted; unfortunately, he's also hopelessly insane. The film, whose small cast also includes Jane Lapotaire and Joss Ackland as two contrastingly deviant servants, lacks the overall flair of its predecessors despite a decent script co-written by Jimmy Sangster and Alfred Shaughnessy.

Sangster's next psychological thriller undertaking was a teleplay for an American TV movie (an *ABC Movie of the Week*) called *A Taste of Evil* (1971); a darker-toned reworking of both *Taste of Fear* and *Nightmare*, it features an outstanding portrayal of evil by Barbara Stanwyck and is actually far better than Sangster's next—and what turned out to be the final—entry in the Hammer series. That's not to say **Fear in the Night** (1972) is an unworthy effort, but it remains, despite the great cast and atmospheric setting, an unremarkable footnote to the series. The film begins with vulnerable (due to a recent nervous breakdown) newlywed Peggy Heller (Judy Geeson) preparing to move from London to the countryside, where her husband Robert (Ralph Bates) has supposedly been working as a teacher at an all-boys boarding school. The night before the move, Peggy is attacked from behind by a mysterious black-gloved figure with a prosthetic arm, and she's later subjected to a similar assault at the couple's new home in the school grounds. The attacks have in fact been engineered as part of a wicked plot to make Peggy believe the culprit is the school's strange (not to mention prosthetic arm-wearing) owner-headmaster, Michael (Peter Cushing), in the hope that she will eventually kill him with a conveniently provided shotgun. The only other main character is Michael's bitchy and sadistic wife Molly (Joan Collins), and while it's not difficult to guess that she and Robert are behind the plot (all about taking control of Michael's estate), it's nevertheless fun seeing how they get their comeuppance when things don't go quite according to plan. Along the way, we learn some secrets about the school and about Robert's real role there, apart from being Molly's secret lover and co-conspirator.

Sangster, who co-scripted with Michael

Syson, also produced and directed, with the story containing ideas (such as the conveniently supplied shotgun) from his aforementioned *A Taste of Evil* teleplay, as well as plot elements which he'd later revisit when writing the CBS TV movie *No Place to Hide* (1981). Hammer would return to the psychological thriller format with the episodes "Visitor from the Grave" and "The Sweet Scent of Death" from the respective series *Hammer House of Horror* (1980) and *Hammer House of Mystery and Suspense* (1984/5), the latter airing in the U.S. as *Fox Mystery Theatre*.

Other Psychological Thrillers

"A would-be frightening picture which, through inadequacy of script and handling, becomes instead comically melodramatic" is how the *Monthly Film Bulletin* (December 1950) described the rare B movie **Dark Interval** (1950). Following their honeymoon, Walter Jordan (Andrew Osborn) and his young bride Sonia (Zena Marshall) take up residence at Walter's gloomy family mansion. Unbeknownst to Sonia, the Jordan family has a history of insanity, and Walter proves to be no exception. The shock of learning the truth causes Sonia to lose a pregnancy and, in further events, the increasing disintegration of Walter's mind (not helped by banging his head in a nasty fall down the stairs) leads to paranoid delusions and violent actions that put the young woman in mortal danger. John Barry plays the hero of sorts (a close confidant of Walter's and bringer of some solace for Sonia), and John Le Mesurier is the sinister family butler who we learn had long ago promised to kill Walter should he ever become dangerously insane.

In **Night Was Our Friend** (1951), Martin Raynor (Michael Gough), thought dead following a plane crash in the Amazon, returns home to his wife Sally (Elizabeth Sellars) after nearly two years; however, some horrific experiences as the result of capture by jungle savages have left him unbalanced. His increasingly strange behavior involves wandering around the neighborhood in the dead of night and culminates in a violent attack on a local man. When it becomes necessary to have him certified, Sally takes steps to put him out of his misery with an overdose of sleeping pills. Martin stumbles on her plan but then takes the overdose anyway, with the result that Sally is accused of murder. Unfolding mostly in flashback, this somber B movie has a bittersweet ending which sees Sally free to start a new life with a doctor (Ronald Howard) she'd grown close to during Martin's absence.

A Killer Walks (1952) stars Laurence Harvey as Ned, an unbalanced young man living with his slow-witted brother Frankie (Trader Faulkner) on their grandmother's (Ethel Edwards) farm. Driven by discontent and greed, Ned schemes to get an early inheritance by stabbing grandma to death one night and making it appear as if Frankie committed the crime during one of his frequent bouts of sleepwalking. Harvey is suitably intense in the type of role he excelled at and is the main reason to watch this gloomy little B movie. The scene where Ned carries out the murder during a thunderstorm is actually pretty creepy, as is the quickly following shot of the framed Frankie lying in bed (having been drugged by Ned) with knife conveniently in hand. Susan Shaw gets top billing as an unprincipled young woman whom Ned is desperate to impress (something the inheritance would give him the means to do), and the cast also includes Laurence Naismith as a local doctor. *Today's Cinema* (September 19, 1952) called the film a "passable second-feature thriller for unsophisticated tastes."

*"All aboard the Paris Express for....
Corruption! Murder! Scandal!"*

Set in Holland and based on a 1938 novel (*L'homme qui regardait passer les trains*) by "Maigret" author Georges Simenon, **The Man Who Watched Trains Go By** (1952) stars Claude Rains as Kees Popinga, the loyal chief clerk at a respected shipping firm. When he learns that the managing director, Julius De Koster (Herbert Lom), has been embezzling the firm and is planning to let it collapse while fleeing with the cash assets to his mistress Michele (Marta Toren) in Paris, Kees (whose savings are invested in the company) attacks the man and accidentally kills him. Having lived a life totally lacking in excitement, Kees decides to keep the cash for himself and, using his dead boss' train ticket, sets off for an adventure in Paris. Once there, he contacts Michele in the hope of some romance, only to be played along by the woman, whose only interest (as was her true interest in the case of De Koster) is to part him from the cash. Rains is excellent as Kees, a growingly creepy little chap who eventually suffers a psychological meltdown (leading to dire consequences for Michele), and the cast also includes Marius Goring and Ferdy Mayne as, respectively, a French police inspector and a shady colleague of Michele's.

The low-key *Alias John Preston* (1955) was the first of what turned out to be nearly three dozen British B thrillers produced by American siblings Edward J. and Harry Lee Danziger from 1955 to 1962. The movie sustains a reasonable air of mystery throughout and marked Christopher Lee's first big role in a feature film. Lee plays the eponymous Preston, a handsome young man who takes up residence in, and soon becomes a leading citizen of, an English town named Deanbridge, only to be plagued by a series of nightmares in which he commits acts of violence including murder. Canadian actor Alexander Knox, noted by the *Monthly Film Bulletin* (August 1956) as bringing "some degree of plausibility to the proceedings," plays a psychiatrist who discovers that the events in Preston's nightmares are all-too real and that the man has a split personality (he's actually David Garrity, a military deserter and killer who's been under investigation for some time). American-born Betta St. John gets top-billing as a young woman making the mistake of leaving her boyfriend for Preston.

"Murder by remote control!"

An unremarkable B movie, ***The Hypnotist*** (1956) is not nearly as dramatic as its misleading U.S. title, *Scotland Yard Dragnet*, would suggest. While test-flying a prototype jet plane, pilot Valentine "Val" Neal (Paul Carpenter) is forced to make an emergency ejection which results in hospitalization. The incident triggers paralyzing psychosomatic pains followed by unconsciousness and mental blackouts, all connected (as we eventually learn) with a suppressed childhood trauma. Dr. Francis Pelham (Roland Culver), a retired psychiatrist and old friend of Val's fiancée Mary (Patricia Roc), takes Val on as a live-in patient at his London apartment, and is soon using hypnosis as part of the treatment. When an obnoxious female neighbor of Pelham's (later revealed to be his estranged wife, who had refused him a divorce) is found strangled, everything points to Val having committed the crime while in a hypnotic trance. However, Mary is ultimately instrumental in proving that Pelham had attempted to program Val into carrying out the murder, only for this to fail at the last minute, forcing the doctor to carry out the evil deed himself and then incriminate Val. Certain aspects of the story, including Pelham's motive (he was secretly in love with Mary and wanted rid of any obstacles), anticipate Hammer's *The Full Treatment* (1960), a much classier psychological thriller all around. A sequence where a hypnotized Val wanders aimlessly around London offers some nice views of the capital.

*"Throttling, choking terror—
that will leave you gasping for breath!"*

Proficiently directed by Robert Day and energetically acted by the great Boris Karloff, ***Grip of the Strangler*** (1957) really *does* grip. Set in London, the film begins in 1860 with a prologue in which Edward Styles, the man accused of being "The Haymarket Strangler,"

U.S. title for 1957's *Grip of the Strangler*.

is publicly hanged for the gruesome murders—via strangulation and slashing—of five young women. Twenty years later, novelist James Rankin (Karloff) attempts to clear Styles' name, correctly believing that the true culprit was an insane physician named Dr. Tennant, who subsequently disappeared without a trace. In a creepy night-time sequence, Rankin, during his quest for the truth, disinters Styles' body and within his coffin finds a knife that had been used in the killings, and which in the aforementioned prologue we'd seen somebody sneak into the casket before it was sealed. Upon handling the weapon, Rankin is transformed (through some creative facial and bodily contortions on the part of Karloff) into "The Haymarket Strangler," the film's big twist being that Rankin and the insane Dr. Tennant are in fact one and the same, the physician having until now blocked out his murderous past with a new persona. It's not long before he's back on the rampage and revisiting his old stalking ground, a seedy and boisterous music hall venue known as The Judas Hole, where he'd once killed a showgirl.

Excellent production design ensures an effective Victorian London atmosphere, and there's a clever script (co-written by Jan Read from his original story, created especially for Karloff) which, even after the big reveal, has some neat surprises in store, one of them regarding Rankin's wife (Elizabeth Allan). Karloff performs with the vigor of a man 20 years younger (he was almost 70 at the time) and skillfully evokes sympathy for his character, who it becomes clear has all along had a subconscious desire to be caught so as to put his horrific past to rest. Jean Kent plays a seasoned showgirl at The Judas Hole, while the hatchet-faced Anthony Dawson, as a police superintendent, may initially come under suspicion by viewers if only by virtue of having played both a would-be strangler in Hitchcock's *Dial M for Murder* (1954) and the brutal knifer of showgirls in the 1950 British thriller *The Long Dark Hall*.

Strangulation also occurs in **Violent Moment** (1958), in which army deserter Douglas Baines (Lyndon Brook) throttles his whorish partner Daisy (Jane Hylton) after she gives their two-year-old son up for adoption. Baines then hastily leaves their lodgings, taking with him a tumbler doll he had bought for the child. Five years later, he has become a successful businessman but has never gotten over his son; he has also developed an obsession with—to the point of becoming almost inseparable from—the tumbler doll, which his fiancée Janet (Jill Browne) tries to wean him off by keeping it at her apartment. An unusual sequence of events, involving the doll and a robbery at the apartment, lead to Baines finally being identified as Daisy's murderer. The great Sidney Hayers' directing debut is a first-class B movie with a standout performance by Brook, who manages to elicit a good deal of sympathy for his character.

*"Had they come to help him
… torment him … or to kill him?"*

Acclaimed French thriller-writing duo Boileau-Narcejac's (Pierre Boileau and Thomas Narcejac) 1953 novel *Les Visages de l'ombre* was adapted into **Faces in the Dark** (1960), and it remains the authors' only work so far to have been turned into a British feature film. Richard Hammond (John Gregson), an obnoxious wealthy electronics manufacturer, becomes permanently blinded as the result of an accidental explosion at his factory. His wife Christiane (Mai Zetterling), who was about to leave him, decides to stay and look after him; to this end she arranges some post-hospital rest and recuperation at their country home in Cornwall, and they are later joined by Richard's brother (John Ireland) and business partner (Michael Denison). Although massively hindered by his lack of sight, Richard's other senses begin to tell him that certain things inside and outside the house are not as they should be. He eventually comes to the realization that he's not at the location he thought he was (he has in fact been taken to France) and that there's a diabolical conspiracy afoot to murder him and take over his business. His desperate attempts to escape this fate lead to an unexpected and shocking (for the conspirators) conclusion. Suspense builds nicely in the later stages, but overall the film is marred by a lack of sympathetic characters. The novel was Boileau-Narcejac's second after *Celle qui n'était plus*, which had been the basis for the classic French thriller *Les Diaboliques* (1955).

*"Only the man who wrote
'Psycho' could jolt you like this!"*

The New York Times (July 1, 1961) was not impressed with Gary Cooper's final film **The Naked Edge** (1961), believing that "old Coop deserved something better to ring down the curtain on his career." The Hollywood legend plays George Radcliffe, whose witness testimony in the trial of his boss' murder condemns a co-worker to life imprisonment. A large sum of money stolen in connection with the murder is never found, and this coincides with George's apparent success on the stock market, which enables him to invest in a successful business. Six years later, a letter—written one year after the trial but delayed in connection with a mail train robbery—arrives and proves to have been a belated one-off attempt to blackmail George, accusing him of the theft and murder. This immediately instills suspicion in his wife Martha (Deborah Kerr), who starts digging into the old case in an effort to allay her fear that George may actually be guilty. Her search for the truth, which involves meeting the condemned man's wife (Diane Cilento) and the creepy letter writer (Eric Portman), leads to her being marked for death by the real killer. The spacious bathroom of the Radcliffes' palatial home is the setting for a terrifying climax in which an attempt is made to kill Martha with a straight razor.

Joseph Stefano's next screenwriting assignment after *Psycho* (1960) is a very professionally directed and photographed effort that's unfortunately saddled with unconvincing dialogue and an annoyingly exaggerated music score; however, like in *Psycho*, we get a brilliantly staged and shocking bathroom sequence, only this time focusing on a bathtub instead of a shower. Cooper's performance suffers as a result of illness during production (he died before the film's release), while the lovely Kerr dutifully goes through the motions dictated by the mechanical script, which uses too many obvious tricks to make George appear guilty.

The B movie **Stranglehold** (1962) stars the once-dubbed "King of the Bs" himself, Macdonald Carey, as Bill Morrison, an actor known for his gangster roles. However, certain unsavory traits from his screen characters have begun rubbing off on his real-life persona, resulting in all sorts of problems including estrangement from his wife (Barbara Shelley). Things come to a head when Bill mistakenly believes he's strangled a woman in his London apartment while in a drunken stupor; his supposed victim—an out-of-work foreign actress (Nadja Regin) who'd been seeking employment through him—has in fact killed herself with poison. In an effort to cover up his "crime," Bill is forced to deal with a real underworld operator, "The Dutchman" (Leonard Sachs), who arranges to get rid of the body by shipping it out of the country in a coffin. In ensuing events, the coffin is stopped by Customs and turned over to the police, although things turn out well when an autopsy establishes suicide, leaving Bill free to reclaim his life—and wife. A real rarity, the film seems to have disappeared since its last showing on U.S. TV in the early 1980s.

The Mind Benders (1962) begins with an Oxford University physiologist, Professor Sharpey (Harold Goldblatt), committing suicide while under suspicion of colluding with a foreign power. His colleague, Dr. Henry Longman (Dirk Bogarde in one of his finest performances), tries to convince a British Military Intelligence investigator (John Clements) that Sharpey was not a traitor and that any suspicious behavior was likely due to the man's altered mental state, resulting from isolation experiments involving sensory deprivation in a large water tank. In an attempt to prove this, Longman subjects himself to a test in which he spends several hours in the tank. However, the outcome of this—due to interference on the part of the investigator who for his own reasons attempts to brainwash Longman just after the test and while he's in an altered state—has a devastating Jekyll and Hyde effect on Longman that threatens to destroy his life and marriage. An intelligent and disturbing forerunner to 1980's *Altered States*, the film is superbly acted (Mary Ure is outstanding as Longman's wife), photographed and scored, but the story runs out of steam well before the satisfying, if a little unconvincing, happy ending.

*"She came back from the grave ...
to haunt his every living moment!"*

In **Catacombs** (1964), a plot to murder the wealthy and controlling Ellen Garth (Georgina Cookson) is hatched by her weak-willed husband, Raymond (Gary Merrill), in cahoots with the woman's disgruntled personal assistant, Corbett (Neil McCallum). Raymond carries out the murder and buries Ellen's body in the garden shed of their English country cottage. Corbett then puts into motion a complicated plan—necessitating another murder—to make it appear as if Ellen has died in a motoring accident while vacationing in Italy. However, Raymond, now free to continue a relationship he had already started with Ellen's niece Alice (Jane Merrow), soon becomes disturbed by eerie happenings that convince him Ellen may have returned from the grave. Eventually, the woman's apparent ghost causes him to fall to his death from a window. It turns out that the eerie occurrences and the "ghost" had in fact been engineered as part of a wider scheme, whose conspirators are revealed (and get their comeuppance) in a satisfying ending involving Ellen's astute housekeeper (Rachel Thomas). Based on the 1959 novel of the same name by Jay Bennett, this B movie is notable as being the feature directing debut of Gordon Hessler, who had previously suggested the story as a possible episode while working as a producer on TV's *The Alfred Hitchcock Hour*.

The Daily Cinema (April 29, 1964) observed that **Woman of Straw** (1964) is "spiced with passionate undercurrents" and "provocative performances," the best example of the latter being Ralph Richardson's larger-than-life portrayal as Charles Richmond, a tyrannical wheelchair-bound business tycoon. Charles' only living relative, his nephew Anthony (Sean Connery), stands to gain a measly £20,000 from the old man's will, with the rest of the £50 million fortune destined for charity. Anthony soon gets an Italian nurse, Maria (Gina Lollobrigida), to cooperate in a devious plot which involves ingratiating herself with and subsequently marrying Charles who, according to plan, changes his will in her favor. Because Maria has made all the sacrifices, Anthony apparently only wants £1 million upon Charles' death, which could be at any moment due to a medical condition. In the twisty events that follow, Charles is murdered and Maria framed in what transpires is a wider and particularly evil scheme by Anthony: the idea is that Maria will be executed, thus entitling Anthony, as the next of kin, to the entire fortune. Lollobrigida deservedly gets top billing for her strong performance as the ultimately sympathetic Maria, while Connery, in between James Bond outings *From Russia with Love* and *Goldfinger*, delivers a chilling portrayal as the nastiest character he's ever played. Shot on location in England and Majorca, the film also stars Alexander Knox as a police officer and Johnny Sekka as one of Charles' servants, the latter instrumental in Anthony's ultimate comeuppance.

Easily the best of the handful of films directed by Charles Crichton in the 1960s, **The Third Secret** (1964) is a somber and slow-burning affair that begins with the death (supposedly suicide) by gunshot of eminent psychoanalyst Dr. Leo Whitset (Peter Copley) at his London home. Alex Stedman (Stephen Boyd), an expatriate American broadcast journalist who was one of Whitset's few active patients, is particularly distraught over the death. After talking with the analyst's precocious 14-year-old daughter, Catherine (a brilliant Pamela Franklin),

A 1964 gem from director Charles Crichton.

who insists her father was murdered and that he'd been aware one of his patients (he hadn't said whom) had it in for him, Alex decides to investigate the matter. Catherine gives him details of her dad's three other active patients—an art dealer (Richard Attenborough), a secretary (Diane Cilento) and a judge (Jack Hawkins)—all of whom Alex strikes up acquaintances with in an attempt to find clues. A shocking twist, involving the discovery of a previously undisclosed patient—a schizophrenic—who proves to be the culprit, rounds out this compelling mystery, which is highlighted by some great chemistry between Boyd and Franklin.

The Black Torment (1964) is a blood-and-thunder period costume mystery set in 18th century England. Following a three-month stay in London, Sir Richard Fordyke (John Turner) returns with a new bride (Heather Sears) to his ancestral estate in Devon. During his absence, someone looking just like him, and whom some would swear *was* him, has been seen in and around the estate and is responsible for the rape and murder (depicted in the film's opening) of a local woman. Richard soon finds himself the chief suspect in the crime as well as becoming plagued by the apparent ghost of his former wife, who committed suicide (one of the film's highlights is an energetic sequence in which he's chased through woodland on horseback by the spectral figure). It's not hard to guess that there's a devious plot afoot to drive Richard insane, the perpetrators and motives of which are revealed in the exciting and violent climax of this sumptuously photographed and well-scored film. Turner gives a vigorous performance (he actually gives two performances, for Richard is found to have a crazed twin brother he never knew about), and Peter Arne is on excellent form as Richard's good (or is he?) friend and steward.

Production company Parroch-McCallum's final B thriller, **Troubled Waters** (1964), went straight to television in Britain and seemingly suffered the same fate in the U.S., where it's known under the more apt title *The Man with Two Faces*. Hollywood hunk Tab Hunter gives a creepy performance as Alex Carswell, a wild-eyed neurotic who has spent five years in a London prison for drunkenly killing a man, an incident that occurred on the same day as his son Ronnie was born. Upon his release, Alex goes home to his wife Janet (Zena Walker) and the now 5-year-old Ronnie (Andy Myers), but soon begins making their lives a living hell through psychological torment as it becomes increasingly obvious that he has all along been jealous of Ronnie's existence. (There's plenty here to suggest that the crime for which Alex was incarcerated had resulted from misdirected aggression in connection with Janet's pregnancy.) Events lead to a drunken Alex taking Ronnie out on a rowing boat in what turns into a "will he or won't he kill the boy?" finale. Michael Goodliffe has a pivotal role as Alex's business partner and close friend of Janet's, and there's some effectively bleak music by Elisabeth "12-tone Lizzie" Lutyens. In a production report for the *Kinematograph Weekly* (July 9, 1964), Derek Todd spoke of Stanley Goulder's (the film's director) belief that B movies must be "different" in order to survive; Todd concluded with "he [Goulder] and the producers deserve credit for their initiative: these 'Troubled Waters' certainly run deep."

"...almost a love story!"

A late entry in celebrated director William Wyler's career, **The Collector** (1965) tells the tale of a lonely, socially awkward and highly disturbed young man whose idea of getting to know women is extreme to say the least. Terence Stamp plays the man in question, Freddie, a butterfly collector who, after secretly stalking art student Miranda (Samantha Eggar) for some time, kidnaps her and imprisons her in a specially prepared cellar at his recently acquired (thanks to a big win on the football pools) country manor, misguidedly hoping that she will learn to love him. A psychological game of cat and mouse ensues between captor and captive as the latter desperately tries to figure a way out of her situation, with several attempts to escape or to get help failing miserably. A somewhat unpredictable denouement is followed by a chilling coda which sees Freddie on the prowl for a new victim. The two stars give great performances, although Stamp's blue-eyed good looks somewhat detract from the overall terror, and one can imagine the more perverse among female viewers wishing they were—at least to some extent—in Miranda's shoes.

Eggar also has a major role in **Return from the Ashes** (1965), set shortly after World War II. Things kick off with the return to Paris of Jewish concentration camp survivor Dr. Michele Wolf (Ingrid Thulin), heir to the collective fortune of various relatives, all of whom perished in the Holocaust. Believing Michele had also died, her good-for-nothing husband Stanislaus (Maximilian Schell), a Polish amateur chess player who never really loved her, has since shacked up with the amoral Fabienne (Samantha Eggar), Michele's stepdaughter from a previous marriage. During the course of the dramatic story, Fabienne concocts an evil scheme to murder Michele for her money, but Stanislaus ends up planning to get both women out of the way and keep all the money for himself. Thulin gives a vivid performance in this unusual, poignant and vastly underrated film, which also stars Herbert Lom (as a good guy for a change) and features a disturbing bathroom murder scene.

Director Peter Collinson's auspicious feature debut was the "home invasion" thriller **The Penthouse** (1967), in which Bruce (Terence Morgan) and his mistress Barbara (Suzy Kendall) are terrorized in their love nest (the titular apartment) by deviants Tom and Dick (Tony Beckley and Norman Rodway). Bruce is tied up and taunted while Barbara is subjected to liquor, drugs and rape, all adding up to a nightmarish scenario whose atmosphere and dialogue borrow heavily from Harold Pinter.

The splendid Martine Beswick shows up late in the proceedings as Tom and Dick's controller (aptly named Harry to complete the commonality of the trio), a part that looks like a warm-up for her "Queen of Evil" role in Oliver Stone's *Seizure* (1973), where she once again controlled two male crazies. As noted by *The Daily Cinema* (September 22, 1967), the film, which is based on a C. Scott Forbes play called *The Meter Man* (one of the deviants initially gains entry to the premises by claiming he's come to read the gas meter), "goes about its nasty business with considerable flair."

The bizarre **Mumsy, Nanny, Sonny & Girly** (1969) concerns a seriously dysfunctional fatherless household whose youngest members, teenagers Sonny and Girly (Howard Trevor and the amazing Vanessa Howard), act and dress like little schoolchildren and inveigle adult men into becoming their "playmates." Compelled to take part in childish games at the family mansion, the men soon learn that breaking the rules, which includes trying to leave, results in brutal murder. The latest playmate (Michael Bryant) manages to stay alive, regardless of the rules, by playing his own games—involving sexual manipulation—that cause certain members of the household to turn violently against each other. Ursula Howells brings a regal air to her role as the clan's ruthless matriarch, Mumsy, in this darkly grotesque comedy thriller (based on the even darker play *Happy Family* by *Almonds & Raisins* author Maisie Mosco), elements of which were echoed in later shockers such as *The Baby* (1972) and *American Gothic* (1988).

"You'll feel four hands reaching for you ... when the Gemini twins arrive!"

The offbeat and stylishly photographed **Goodbye Gemini** (1970) stars Judy Geeson and Martin Potter as young adult twins Jacki and Julian, who live in a childish game-playing world of their own in which the possessive Julian harbors incestuous desires. The film begins with the pair arriving in

Alexis Kanner faces ritualistic murder in 1970's *Goodbye Gemini*.

London, having been sent there (it's unclear from where) by their wealthy father to live in a large Chelsea town house complete with strict housekeeper. We quickly get a sense of how dangerous the twins' games can be when they get rid of said housekeeper by fixing it—via the strategic placement of their trusty teddy bear, Agamemnon—so that she "accidentally" falls down the stairs. Alexis Kanner plays Clive, a sleazy character the twins hook up with during their first few days in the swinging capital, and who later gets Julian drunk before leaving him at the mercy of two male transvestite prostitutes in order to then blackmail him with photographs of the sordid encounter. Events lead to the film's most bizarre sequence in which the twins ritualistically murder Clive with Japanese knives, all the while covered in white sheets with eyeholes in what could have been the inspiration for that creepy scene—involving a similarly garbed Michael Myers—from John Carpenter's *Halloween* (1978). The murder has profound and very different psychological effects on Julian and Jacki, who end up separated and on the run, the latter suffering from amnesia. The aimlessly plotted film, which finishes on a decidedly bleak note, was adapted from Jenni Hall's 1964 novel *Ask Agamemnon*, and also stars Michael Redgrave as a senior politician who gives shelter to the amnesiac Jacki.

The dark and slow-burning ***The Night Digger*** (1971) is ultimately too ambiguous and inconclusive to be the great thriller promised by early scenes. Patricia Neal stars as Maura, a repressed spinster completely dominated by her elderly adoptive mother Mrs. Prince (Pamela Brown). Echoing Emlyn Williams' classic *Night Must Fall*, the story (a much modified adaptation by Roald Dahl of Joy Cowley's 1967 novel *Nest in a Falling*

Tree) has a young man, Billy (Nicholas Clay), inveigle his way into the household, having persuaded Mrs. Prince to take him on as a handyman. He is in fact a sexually frustrated psychopath who has already murdered five women and buried their bodies in road construction sites. Maura eventually falls in love with Billy, but their alliance can only lead to tragedy. Cinematographer Alex Thomson achieves an appropriately moody look, which is complemented by the atmospheric music of Bernard Herrmann. In the U.S., the film was initially released theatrically and on television under the British title, and later on cable as *The Road Builder*, which had been its original working title.

Unman, Wittering and Zigo (1971) was adapted from Giles Cooper's 1958 play of the same name, which for many years was part of the English literature curriculum in British high schools. David Hemmings gives a nuanced performance as John Ebony, a conscientious teacher taking short-term employment at an all-boys boarding school, only to be tormented and intimidated—to the point where he submits to their demands (including falsifying exam papers)—by a class of precocious and unruly teenagers who may or may not have murdered their previous teacher. This undeservedly obscure film, whose title refers to the last three names on the class register, successfully sustains a palpable atmosphere of mystery and menace while building to a satisfying conclusion explaining how said previous teacher came to be found dead at the foot of cliffs. Carolyn Seymour plays Ebony's wife (one disturbing scene sees her almost gang-raped by the boys in the school squash court), while the most famous face among the students is Michael Kitchen.

> *"The hands of Jack the Ripper live again ... as his fiendish daughter kills again ... and again ... and again!"*

Hammer Film Productions' **Hands of the Ripper** (1971) is an interesting if underdeveloped slasher set in Edwardian London. Psychoanalyst Dr. Pritchard (Eric Porter) takes into his care Anna (Angharad Rees), a 17-year-old orphan he's pretty sure is the culprit in a brutal murder, and begins practicing Freudian psychoanalysis techniques on the girl. Thanks to the film's opening sequence, the audience is aware that Anna is the daughter of none other than notorious serial killer Jack the Ripper and that, as a child, she had witnessed him stab her mother to death. Now, certain circumstances, including being kissed (her demented father had given her a peck on the cheek following the stabbing), have begun sending her into a trance-like state during which she commits gruesome murders that would make her dad proud. The misguided Pritchard covers up for the crimes until he seals his own fate by kissing Anna himself.

Porter gives a solid performance as the therapist whose irresponsible decisions end up putting all around him at considerable risk from the psychotic Anna, the latter played in occasionally sympathetic but mostly terrifying fashion by Rees. The film plays with, though never commits to, the notion that the girl may actually be possessed by the spirit of her infamous father, especially during an impressively staged climax at the famous Whispering Gallery of St. Paul's Cathedral. There's some strong (even by Hammer standards) violence, particularly in a jarring scene where a ferocious Anna slashes and stabs the throat of Pritchard's maid.

> *"Say goodnight to Auntie Roo, kiddies ... it's dead time."*

Hot on the heels of their collaboration on the 1971 U.S. production *What's the Matter with Helen?*, director Curtis Harrington and star Shelley Winters teamed up to ask a further question: **Whoever Slew Auntie Roo?** (1971). Winters dominates every scene she's in as Rosie Forrest (known affectionately as "Auntie Roo"), a wealthy reclusive widow with a Christmas tradition of inviting selected children from the local orphanage

You'll have to watch it for the answer.

to celebrations at her large country mansion. However, beneath Rosie's kindly exterior lies a tormented woman given to brooding over the accidental death of her young daughter, whose skeleton she keeps in a cradle in the little girl's old bedroom. Child stars Mark Lester and Chloe Franks, both regulars in horror films and thrillers of the era, play orphan siblings Christopher and Katy, who gatecrash the latest celebrations. Rosie takes a particular shine to Katy (the girl reminds her of her dead daughter) and ends up holding her prisoner; Christopher is also imprisoned after attempting a rescue and, having got it into his head that Rosie intends to cook and eat them both (à la "Hansel and Gretel"), ultimately takes drastic measures to avoid such a fate. Harrington directs with great attention to detail and atmosphere, helped in no small measure by some stylish art direction by George Provis. One effective sequence takes place in the mansion's attic and involves masks, mechanical devices and dummies that belonged to Rosie's deceased magician husband. A subplot features Ralph Richardson as a fake medium scheming to rob Rosie of her riches.

Young Lester was also in the international (British-Spanish-Italian-German) co-production **Night Hair Child** (1971), this time playing Marcus Bezant, a precocious, creepy and deeply disturbed 12-year-old sociopath who makes Auntie Roo seem like a pussycat. During the course of the sleazy proceedings, which mostly unfold at his ineffectual father Paul's (Hardy Kruger) Spanish villa, we discover that, as well as being a pathological liar and a perverted peeping Tom, Marcus also enjoys torturing and killing animals; and, worst of all, he's secretly responsible for having caused the death (officially deemed accidental) of his mother via electrocution in a bathtub. Britt Ekland has never looked lovelier and is truly splendid in her role as Paul's new wife Elise, who enters into a battle of wills with her evil stepson, the film's most controversial scene involving her stripping for the horny lad in exchange for information about his mother's death. Elise's efforts to expose Marcus result in her being branded the crazy one, leading to a spell in a psychiatric ward. Upon her release, the boy's continued psychotic behavior prompts Elise to take drastic action against him.

Lester's performance, while not bad, lacks the menace truly needed for the role, leaving Ekland to effortlessly walk away with the film. James Kelley (*The Beast in the Cellar*) directed with input (uncredited, at least on English-speaking prints) from Italian director Andrea Bianchi, and the cast also includes Lilli Palmer and Harry Andrews in "guest-star" roles as a psychiatrist and headmaster respectively. Originally released at 89 minutes, the movie has since become available on DVD in an extended 95-minute version.

"An agonisingly slow and uninteresting thriller" was a fair description by the *Monthly Film Bulletin* (October 1972) of ***What Became of Jack and Jill?*** (1971). Actor-singer Paul Nicholas plays Johnny, a twenty-something deadbeat living at home with his grandmother (Mona Washbourne)—or "gran" as he calls her—and who's desperate to get his hands on the old woman's fortune. Helped by his equally corrupt girlfriend Jill (Vanessa Howard), Johnny plans to induce a fatal heart attack in "gran" by scaring her with a made-up scenario about a radical youth movement out to exterminate elderly people. The scheme works, but a surprise amendment in the woman's will causes tension in Johnny and Jill's relationship, ultimately leading to their downfall. Very much a product of its time, this claustrophobic and mean-spirited film is best viewed as a black comedy.

The brooding and low-key ***Endless Night*** (1972) reunites actors Hayley Mills and Hywel Bennett, as well as composer Bernard Herrmann and cinematographer Harry Waxman, from the 1968 shocker *Twisted Nerve*. Bennett plays Michael, a young working-class chauffeur whose dream is to live on an idyllic tract of land known as Gipsy's Acre in the English countryside. His dream is realized when Ellie (Mills), an American heiress he has fallen in love with and subsequently marries, buys the land and funds the construction there of an exclusively designed modern house. The couple moves into the finished property and are soon joined—to Michael's seeming annoyance—by Ellie's long-time companion Greta (Britt Ekland). The film's long build-up is permeated by a subtle sense of unease (including suggestions of a local curse), and events take a particularly sinister turn in the last half hour in which the "accidental" death of one of the three aforementioned characters is followed by a shocking twist concerning the other two. Also starring in this faithful adaptation of Agatha Christie's 1967 novel are George Sanders (in one of his last roles) as Ellie's family lawyer and Per Oscarsson as a celebrated architect.

Scripted by Anthony Shaffer from his own 1970 stage play of the same name, ***Sleuth*** (1972) is an alternately light-hearted and dark classic that turned out to be Joseph L. Mankiewicz's directorial swansong. Andrew Wyke (Laurence Olivier), a middle-aged, eccentric and games-obsessed author of mystery novels, summons the younger Milo Tindle (Michael Caine), who he knows wants to marry his wife, to his fabulous mansion in the English countryside. Once there, Milo is persuaded by Andrew to steal jewelry from the latter's safe (supposedly as part of an insurance scam that will benefit both men), this turning out to be a set-up by the vengeful Andrew, who ends up shooting Milo after making him beg for his life. Two days later, Inspector Doppler, a dogged detective, calls by to investigate Milo's disappearance. After finding incriminating evidence inside and outside the mansion, Doppler seems determined to arrest Andrew for murder, despite the man's claim that he had in fact shot Milo with a blank cartridge and that the whole thing had been a game. Plenty of twists ensue, including Milo's reappearance—alive after all—in a reveal that explains why the Inspector Doppler character was the only role ever played by one "Alec Cawthorne."

Armed with Shaffer's sublime dialogue, Olivier and Caine play off each other marvelously, while Ken Adam's production design within the mansion (where events almost exclusively unfold) inventively reflects Andrew's passion for puzzles, games and mechanical toys. *Leonard Maltin's Movie Guide* gave the film four out of four stars, whereas the awful 2007 remake (featuring Caine in the Olivier role) incurred their lowest "BOMB" rating.

Another film with stage origins is ***Night Watch*** (1973), adapted from Lucille Fletcher's 1972 play of the same name. Elizabeth Taylor is on superb form as wealthy insomniac Ellen Wheeler, who claims one night to have sighted a dead body in the window of an old

Elizabeth Taylor and Laurence Harvey in *Night Watch* (1973).

disused house opposite hers. Although the police, led by Inspector Walker (Bill Dean), find nothing, Ellen pesters them about the matter and later reports sighting another body. By this time, the inspector has decided she's a timewaster and disregards her. Eventually, before departing for some rest and recuperation at a Swiss clinic, Ellen makes it clear to both her husband (Laurence Harvey) and best friend (Billie Whitelaw) that she knows they've been having an affair; she then maneuvers them into the disused house and brutally murders them, whereupon we discover, in a great twist, the truth behind her "sightings." Along the way in this slow but creepy chiller, we learn a surprising fact about the abandoned house and are shown pivotal flashbacks concerning an earlier betrayal of Ellen by a previous husband. There are also some atmospheric rain and thunder effects, a particularly savage murder scene and Robert Lang as a suspicious neighbor.

A British-Italian co-production, ***Don't Look Now*** (1973) has much in common with Italy's many *giallo* thrillers of the era, only with an art-house makeover. Following the tragic death of their young daughter Christine in a drowning accident, John and Laura Baxter (a perfectly cast Donald Sutherland and Julie Christie) temporarily leave their English country home for Venice, where John has been employed to supervise a church restoration. While there, Laura comes into contact with elderly Englishwoman Wendy and her blind sister Heather (Clelia Matania and Hilary Mason). Heather, a clairvoyant, tells Laura that Christine is happy in the afterlife, although less reassuring is her revelation that John's life is in danger while he remains in Venice. Recognizing John as also being clairvoyant, Heather believes that he may be unaware of, or is possibly resisting, his psychic ability; second sight, she says, can be "a curse as well as a gift." Unfortunately, in John's case, it proves to be more of the former when, in the wake of many strange events, which include foreseeing his own funeral, he ends up pursuing a small figure (fleetingly glimpsed by him earlier during the proceedings and clad in a shiny red raincoat just like that worn by Christine when she drowned) who it turns out, to John's extreme detriment, is a hideous dwarf serial killer responsible for a recent string of murders in the city.

Director Nicolas Roeg's realization of Daphne Du Maurier's novella is a thought-provoking and necessarily slow-moving chiller that suffers somewhat from a surfeit of ambiguity, heavy symbolism and unnecessary red herrings. Mainly remembered for its atmospheric Venice locations, a tastefully steamy lovemaking scene and a shocking climax, the film also features a remarkably fitting soundtrack by Pino Donaggio in what was his motion picture scoring debut.

*"If stark terror were ecstasy …
living here would be sheer bliss!"*

The AIP/Amicus co-production **Madhouse** (1974) is an excellent early example of the slasher-whodunit genre; as such, it features a prologue set-up (showing a horrific past event), a variety of gruesome kills (including a pitchfork through the neck) and a big twist ending. Paul Toombes (Vincent Price), an actor famed for playing a cloaked, skull-faced character called "Dr. Death," suffers a breakdown following the unsolved decapitation murder of his fiancée during a 1960s Hollywood party. After years in retirement, Toombes agrees to resurrect the character in a British TV series, resulting in a trip to London where he is reunited with former co-star—and "Dr. Death" co-creator—Herbert Flay (Peter Cushing). However, his visit is soon blighted by a series of murders committed by a "Dr. Death"–like figure, who it turns out is someone with a long-term resentment out to destroy the actor.

Legendary horror stars Price and Cushing are great in their scenes together, and much use is made of footage from many of Price's earlier AIP films—such as *Pit and the Pendulum* and *The Raven*—standing in for scenes of the fictional "Dr. Death" movies. Robert Quarry is perfectly cast as an obnoxious producer, and Adrienne Corri plays a bitter, crazed and disfigured actress integral to the plot. Although often regarded as part of the horror genre, the film is probably best described by its director Jim Clark who, during an on-location interview, said "I don't think of it as a horror film—it's more of a murder mystery with horror overtones."

Plodding, depressing and often unintentionally funny, **Persecution** (1974) sees Hollywood legend Lana Turner play a wealthy, evil and manipulative single mother named Carrie Masters, whose hatred and ill-treatment of her young and only child, David (Mark Weavers), leads to the boy deliberately drowning mom's beloved cat Sheba by forcing its head down into a bowl of milk. Years later, a grown-up David (Ralph Bates), now the married father of a newborn child, continues to be dominated by Carrie, who has some nasty surprises in store for her son's new family. Events come to a head with David taking a terrible revenge on his mother by subjecting her to the same fate as Sheba (yes, really, he drowns her in a bowl of milk!), while along the way we learn the reason for the woman's cruelty.

The draggy proceedings, which mainly unfold in Carrie's gloomy country mansion, also feature Olga Georges-Picot as a prostitute brought in by the wicked matriarch to cause problems in David's marriage, and Trevor Howard in a "special guest appearance" as an eminent politician crucial to the story. The original screenplay, under the title "I Hate You, Cat," was co-written by American actor Robert Hutton and fourth wife Rosemary Wootten, who were unhappy with the end result due to significant changes made by the producers; in an interview conducted by Tom Weaver (published in *Science Fiction Stars and Horror Heroes* [Jefferson, NC: McFarland, 1991]), Hutton said: "I have both scripts, my original and the shooting script, and it's like day and night. What they did to it broke my heart."

The low-budget exploitationer ***Exposé*** (1975) stars Udo Kier and Linda Hayden, both magnetic performers with Hayden probably best remembered for her remarkable portrayal of a seductive teenage devil-cult leader in 1970's *Blood on Satan's Claw*. Here she plays Linda, who goes to work at a secluded country cottage as live-in typist to successful first-time novelist Paul Martin (Kier). However, it's later revealed that she has a hidden and cold-blooded agenda to completely destroy the author for reasons that are signposted in the violent hallucinations that plague Paul during the course of the film. The leisurely paced proceedings are punctuated with lashings of sex and violence (including a gratuitous rape scene in which Linda is assaulted by two local thugs whom she subsequently blasts with their own shotgun), with an abundance of nudity from both Hayden, who spends much of the time sexually pleasuring herself, and Fiona Richmond; a big name in adult entertainment at the time, Richmond plays Paul's girlfriend, whom the ruthless Linda seduces before then slashing to death in such gruesome fashion as to ensure the movie a place on the notorious "video nasties" list during that great British moral panic of the 1980s.

In another low-budgeter, ***The Lifetaker*** (1975), bored housewife Lisa (Lea Dregorn) begins a torrid affair with a younger man named Richard (Peter Duncan). When her wealthy businessman husband James (Terence Morgan) finds out, he plans a devastating revenge which involves cold-bloodedly shooting Lisa and framing Richard for the murder. Along the way, we learn about James' past as a brutal mercenary, and events culminate in a bloody showdown between husband and lover. Although there are some interesting moments, this would-be arty erotic thriller ultimately suffers by being drawn-out to the point of tediousness. The always interesting Morgan is the best thing about the film, which according to the *Monthly Film Bulletin* (September 1979) ends up becoming "an unusually repellent and reactionary study in physical violence."

"Schizophrenia ... when the left hand doesn't know who the right hand is killing!"

In cult director Pete Walker's unsettling ***Schizo*** (1976), middle-aged William Haskin (a superb Jack Watson) begins terrorizing—including stalking and making sinister phone calls—twenty-something ice-skating star Samantha Grey (Lynne Frederick) after seeing a newspaper report about her impending marriage. Haskin's campaign of terror coincides with a series of gruesome slayings, the victims all in some way connected with the young woman. In the course of events, we learn that Haskin had served a lengthy prison sentence following his conviction for viciously slashing to death the mother of the then seven-year-old Samantha; it would appear that he is now out to get Samantha too. However, a far darker truth is revealed in a chilling climactic confrontation between Haskin and Samantha. The film generates some decent suspense, and a pervading atmosphere of unease is punctuated with violent murders, including—in a nod to Italian director Dario Argento's classic spine-chiller *Deep Red* (1975)—that of a medium who may have learned too much.

Walker's next shocker was ***The Comeback*** (1977), in which U.S. actor and vocalist Jack Jones plays Nick Cooper, an American pop singer staying at Mr. and Mrs. B's (Bill Owen and Sheila Keith) country mansion while recording an album in England. Nick is soon plagued by ghostly noises and other strange occurrences, and he eventually suffers a breakdown following a gruesome incident involving the rotting head of his ex-wife (Holly Palance), who had earlier been shown—in the film's most frightening sequence—being hacked to death by a hideously masked attacker. Following psychiatric treatment, Nick returns to the mansion and is almost immediately involved in a terrifying confrontation with Mr. and Mrs.

B; the couple are revealed as having engineered the weird goings-on as part of a revenge plot against him which they now attempt to complete with the use of some particularly nasty weapons. (It turns out the deranged couple blames Nick for the death of their daughter, a pop music fan who idolized him and committed suicide upon learning of his marriage.) Jones gives a far better performance than many critics give him credit for, and was apparently chosen for the role after the director saw him in a 1977 episode—"Coffee, Tea or Cyanide?"—of Rock Hudson's *McMillan* series. The film also stars David Doyle (Bosley from *Charlie's Angels*) as a transvestite recording manager and Pamela Stephenson as his secretary (and Nick's love interest).

An amazing cast cannot save the darkly atmospheric ***Dominique*** (1978) from a clichéd screenplay which *Films and Filming* (June 1979) said "is sadly lacking in cohesion and motivation." At times reminiscent of the earlier British thriller *Catacombs* (1964), this slow and overlong film stars a rather leaden Cliff Robertson as American businessman David Ballard who, in order to inherit his wealthy wife Dominique's (Jean Simmons) fortune, drives her insane to the point where she hangs herself. Or does she? It's not long before David is haunted by Dominique's supposed ghost, which eventually drives him to his own death. A twist reveals the "ghost" as having been part of a plot against David by two other principal characters in the story, and there's also a surprising revelation about Dominique—who did die but not when and how we thought she did—and her initial involvement in said plot.

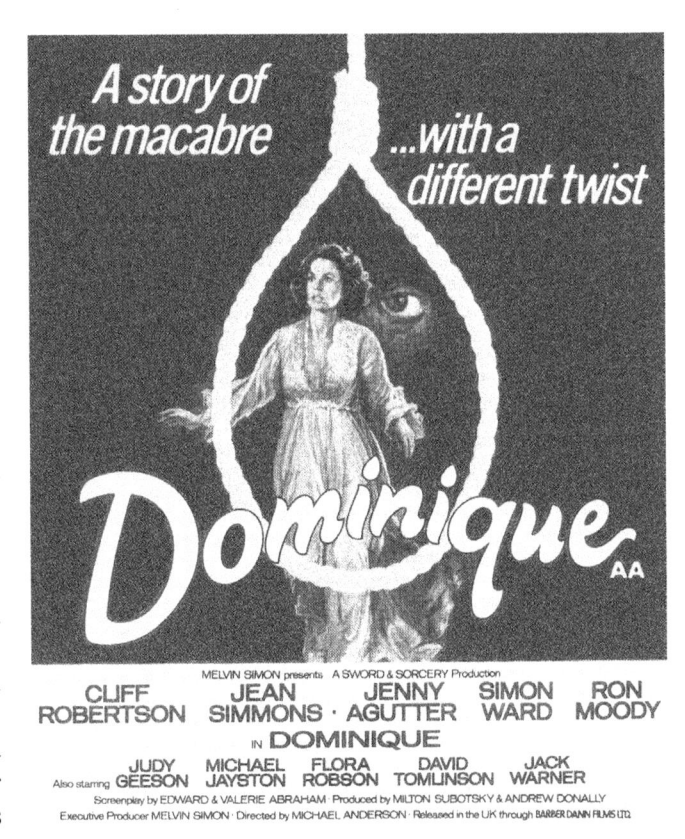

Publicity for a star-studded 1978 psychological thriller.

Absolution (1978) stars Richard Burton as Father Goddard, a strict schoolmaster-priest at a rural Catholic boys' school who is tormented and driven to murder in a devious plot hatched by a psychotic student in revenge for Goddard's unsympathetic behavior toward him. Burton is suitably intense as the persecuted padre and, in his first film acting role, comedian-musician Billy Connolly (he also plays banjo on the soundtrack) is surprisingly well cast as a nomadic hippy camping out in the local woods, where he gets fatally caught up in the student's evil scheme. There's some excellent claustrophobic atmosphere with key scenes taking place in the confessional, and the clever script (not one of the best remembered by Anthony Shaffer) includes a great twist involving one of the characters' uncanny ability to mimic voices.

The Psychopathic

"The secrets and scandals of a whole town shocked into the open ... as the nylon stocking killer runs amok!"

Oakley Park (imagine a British Peyton Place) is the setting for ***Town on Trial*** (1956), which begins with the strangling—by nylon stocking—of the local blonde bombshell. Among the suspects are the country club's philandering secretary (Derek Farr) and a young man (Alec McCowen) with a history of psychiatric problems, both of whom lusted after the woman. It would appear that the killer is acting out of a deep hatred of his own desire, and along the way we learn that his fetish is to first steal from his victims the nylon stocking which he later uses to strangle them. Top-billed John Mills is excellent as an aggressive detective, and U.S. stars Charles Coburn and Barbara Bates appear to good effect as a suspicious-acting doctor (in whose car trunk a second victim is found) and his niece. Maureen Connell, in a smallish role as the aforementioned philanderer's disillusioned wife, was rightly noted by *Films and Filming* (March 1957) as giving the best performance, which they described as "an unforced, attractive piece of work." A tense climax atop a church steeple closes out this fast-moving whodunit. The film was originally to have been called *The Nylon Web*, with Ella Raines in Bates' role.

Jack the Ripper (1958) is a decent mystery thriller loosely based on history's most famous (or infamous) series of murders. In 1888, London's Whitechapel district is plagued by the eponymous serial killer who carves his way through a succession of lower-class women while seeking out the one—a certain Mary Clarke—he believes drove his son to suicide. During an investigation, Inspector O'Neill (Eddie Byrne) is assisted by his old friend Sam Lowry (Lee Patterson), a New York policeman sent by his department to research the social repercussions of the case. Atmospherically shot in black-and-white, the film culminates with the ripper (whose identity comes as quite a surprise) being gruesomely crushed to death by an elevator after becoming trapped at the bottom of the shaft. The U.S. theatrical release featured an alternate soundtrack and a slightly altered finale with a momentary transition to color when the squashed killer's blood seeps up through the elevator floorboards. A "continental" version also exists containing alternately shot footage with nudity.

"First you're a cover girl ... then you're a corpse!"

Set in London's Soho district (for years a thriving center of the capital's sex industry), the neatly constructed B movie ***Cover Girl Killer*** (1959) stars Harry H. Corbett as a puritanical psychopath who murders cover girl models from the sexy pin-up magazine *Wow*; in his own words, he wants to "give man back his dignity, to free him from the prison of lustful images which foul his mind and his sanity." Disguised in a greasy wig, raincoat and pebble glasses (a creepy sight indeed), he pretends to work in the fashion industry in order to lure the models to their deaths, his preferred method of murder being a lethal dose of morphine administered via hypodermic needle. Spencer Teakle plays the quirky owner of both *Wow* and a nightclub where much of the story unfolds, while Felicity Young stars as one of the club's showgirls, who volunteers to act as bait in a bid to trap the killer.

The film, which has developed something of a minor cult following over the years, has the distinction of being the first to feature a serial killer systematically targeting pin-up models, a theme subsequently used in another British thriller, *The Playbirds* (1978), as well as in U.S. productions like *The Centerfold Girls* (1974), *Calendar Girl Murders* (1984) and *The Cover Girl Murders* (1993). It also happens to have been one of the most widely seen—at least theatrically—British B thrillers in the U.S., where it played (mainly on the drive-in circuit) all throughout the 1960s; this healthy stateside distribution

Felicity Young plays a showgirl baiting Harry H. Corbett's *Cover Girl Killer* (1959).

saw it support dozens of different features from *The Magnificent Seven* (1960) and *Dr. No* (1962) to *Tower of London* (1962) and *Hells Angels on Wheels* (1967). It also regularly appeared on "Adults Only" programs, the most successful being a double bill with *The Desperate Women* (1954) that managed a record-breaking 12-week run (ending January 22, 1961) at the Highway 85 Drive-In, Fayetteville, Georgia.

A gruesome murder occurs right at the start of director Vernon Sewell's modest B movie **Urge to Kill** (1960). The locale is a small English seaport town and the murder in question is that of a young woman who was strangled and severely lacerated. Although no weapon has been found, the police believe that broken glass may have been used to inflict the slash wounds. The locals begin to suspect Hughie (Terence Knapp), a mentally disabled young man cared for by his aunt (Ruth Dunning) at her boarding house, and who just happens to have recently started collecting and carrying around bits of broken glass. The real killer—revealed fairly early on as Charles Ramskill (Howard Pays), a lodger at the boarding house—capitalizes on the townsfolk's growing anger toward Hughie by framing him for his next murder. Top-billed Patrick Barr lends his reassuring presence to the proceedings as a detective who eventually outsmarts the psychopathic Ramskill. Knapp had already played Hughie in a 1959 TV version (an *Armchair Theatre* episode called "Hand in Glove" after the 1944 source play) in which Ramskill was portrayed by the great Peter Reynolds.

"Do you know what the most frightening thing in the world is…?"

Made way ahead of its time, ***Peeping Tom*** (1960) is a chilling exploration of fear and was the last great film by director Michael Powell. Carl Boehm plays Mark Lewis, a severely introverted, insecure and secretive young man who works as a movie studio focus puller by day and makes a little extra on the side taking titillating photographs of young women for under-the-counter sale at Mr. Peters' (Bartlett Mullins) newspaper shop. Mark lives in the upstairs quarters of the London house where he grew up, with the rest of the building occupied by his tenants including Helen Stephens (Anna Massey). When Helen begins making steps toward getting to know her landlord a little better, she does not yet know what the viewer knows—that the man is a psychopathic serial killer who murders women with a spike concealed in one of his camera tripod legs, while at the same time filming the grisly doings; as if this wasn't bad enough, the disturbed Mark also wants his victims to witness the intense fear on their own faces, and achieves this by attaching a mirror to the camera set-up. Mark's insanity stems back to his childhood, during which his now deceased scientist father not only filmed him while cruelly subjecting him to fear-inducing experiments but also encouraged voyeuristic tendencies in the boy. We also learn that the experiments involved the whole house being wired up with listening devices, which Mark now uses to secretly record his tenants. Mark's character begins to unravel through a tentative romance with Helen, to whom he ultimately confesses just prior to claiming his final victim—himself—as the police close in.

Photographed in gloriously garish Eastmancolor, the film opens with a disturbing pre-credits sequence that forces us to look through Mark's dreadful camera as it records his murder of a prostitute; the ensuing credits play over a repeat of the scene as watched by the sick young man in his secret viewing room. This is strong stuff indeed, and it's mercifully followed shortly after by pretty much the film's only instance of comic relief wherein an elderly customer (the inimitable Miles Malleson) buys a couple of newspapers and a collection of salacious pictures from the aforementioned Mr. Peters, who afterward comments to Mark, "he won't be doing the crossword tonight." Back in 1960, wide condemnation by horrified audiences and critics led to the film's premature withdrawal from distribution, which in turn precipitated a sharp decline in Powell's career. The original 1961 U.S. theatrical release (by Astor Pictures) was in the form of a heavily edited 86-minute version. Later in the 1960s, Bradley Marks Enterprises took up the rights and sold the film—with even more cuts—to television under the title *Face of Fear*. Whatever one's feelings about the picture's subject matter, it cannot be denied, as even *Films and Filming* (May 1960) conceded in their mostly unfavorable review, that "*Peeping Tom* is a brilliantly made film. Let there be no doubt about that."

Another Eastmancolor shocker, ***Circus of Horrors*** (1960), is a lurid offering with a plot that, according to the *Monthly Film Bulletin* (June 1960), "only a very simple-minded sadist would take seriously." Anton Diffring is on superbly villainous form as experimental plastic surgeon Dr. Rossiter who, wanted by the British authorities for disfiguring a woman in a botched operation, assumes a new identity as "Dr. Schuler" and escapes to France with his two loyal assistants (Kenneth Griffith and Jane Hylton). Circumstances see him acquire and make a success of a failing circus, under cover of which he is able to continue his surgical experiments. As the circus tours Europe, Schuler begins procuring sundry disfigured females—all criminals of one kind or another—on whose visages he performs wonders and who subsequently become the surgeon's lovers as well as performers in the circus. However, any of them wishing to leave become victims of fatal "accidents" (one of them during a knife-throwing act in the film's most famous sequence) arranged by the possessive doctor. The police eventually begin closing in, and a visit by the circus to England leads to a hectic finale involving a gorilla on the loose and a showdown between Schuler and his increasingly disgruntled assistants, with the surgeon finally getting his comeuppance at the hands of the initial botched-surgery victim. The excellent cast also includes Donald Pleasence as the circus' prior owner and Conrad Phillips as a Scotland Yard inspector.

"The shadowy terror struck only at night!"

The above-average B movie *The Impersonator* (1960) is set in an English town whose park has become the stalking ground for a mysterious prowler. When the prowler murders café owner Mrs. Lloyd (Patricia Burke), circumstantial evidence leads to Jimmy Bradford (John Crawford), a locally stationed U.S. Air Force sergeant and the last person to see the woman alive before she took a shortcut through the park, coming under suspicion. The real killer is in fact an obnoxious man who had hassled Mrs. Lloyd at the café on the night of her death. The man is later recognized by Mrs. Lloyd's young son as the female impersonator in a children's pantomime show, this leading to his eventual capture backstage. U.S. actor Crawford gives a very relaxed performance as the personable Sergeant Bradford, and the story also involves a pretty schoolteacher (Jane Griffiths) with whom he attempts to promote—in more ways than one—Anglo-American relations. John Salew delivers a suitably creepy portrayal as the murderous prowler, whose identity is revealed early on, and also worthy of note are the rousing title sequence and some atmospheric nighttime scenes in the park. Surprisingly, given

Patricia Burke is menaced by John Salew in the atmospheric B movie *The Impersonator* (1960).

how good it is, this turned out to be the final film directed by Alfred Shaughnessy, who subsequently concentrated on television work.

Quite strong stuff in its day, the Danziger brothers B movie **Return of a Stranger** (1961) is an early example by Brian Clemens of a woman-in-peril suspenser, a type of story the writer would return to in *And Soon the Darkness* (1970) and *Blind Terror* (1971), as well as in many episodes of his *Thriller* TV series (1973–76). Happily married Pamela Allen (Susan Stephen) is stalked by Homer Trent (Cyril Shaps), a vile individual who once sexually assaulted her while working as a handyman at the orphanage where she was raised, and who has recently been released from his resultant incarceration. Trent had warned Pamela never to marry (the creep wanted her all to himself) and so now tries to kill her husband John (John Ireland) by tampering with the elevator at his workplace, but this leads to the death of one of John's colleagues (Kevin Stoney) instead. Events culminate in the unbalanced stalker invading the Allen household, where the couple's young son manages to save the day with the help of John's revolver. Shaps cuts a menacing figure as Trent (we only see him from the back until the final ten minutes), but tension is all too frequently diluted by an inappropriate and at times comical music score.

The "choking" fog that paralyzed London in December 1962 was predated by the release, a couple of months earlier, of the B movie **Out of the Fog** (1962), which dealt with a different type of choking altogether. Upon his release from London's Wandsworth prison, where he was serving time for theft, surly George Mallon (David Sumner) takes up residence at a hostel for ex-cons. Before long, a maniac begins strangling blondes on a nearby common known as The Flats, with George coming under suspicion after a girlfriend he was seen arguing with becomes the latest victim. Having figured out that the murders occur on a full moon, the police send blonde female sergeant June Lock (Susan Travers) undercover to strike up a friendship with George in an effort to entrap him. In the fog-filled climax, George insists that June walk with him across The Flats; it's a full moon, and we're about to learn the surprising truth behind the killings.

Sumner is suitably edgy and ambiguous as George, who may or may not be the psychopathic blonde-fixated psychopath, and the screenplay provides us with a fair amount of insight (more than is usual for this type of movie) into his complex character, particularly in a telling scene involving his cold-hearted mother (Olga Lindo). The only downside is that, despite the promising title, there's a distinct lack of fog until the tense finale. The rest of the main cast, including John Arnatt and Jack Watson as detectives, all have adequately written characters to work with, and a catchy jazz score rounds out what the *Monthly Film Bulletin* (October 1962) called "a neat enough affair, on the whole creditably acted, and with a good pay-off." The film is known in the U.S. as *Fog for a Killer* (the name of Bruce Graeme's 1960 source novel) and seemingly went straight to television there, featuring in a 5-picture syndication package known as "Kamp Features" as of 1964.

"A killer on the loose—
and she walks into his trap!"

In **Don't Talk to Strange Men** (1962), teenager Jean (Christina Gregg) fails to heed the titular warning upon answering the ringing telephone of a public call box near a lonely bus stop. The man on the other end charms the girl and phones her at the same call box on subsequent days, before eventually persuading the infatuated youngster to meet him there one night. While waiting for the man to arrive, Jean comes to her senses, panics and leaves the scene. Meanwhile, her concerned younger sister (Janina Faye) has gone looking for her, only to end up falling into the clutches of the man, a psychopathic sex murderer who's been terrorizing the area.

This one-of-a-kind B movie gets off to a scary start with what is probably the creepiest opening sequence ever in a low-budget British thriller: eerie wind sounds, a great tracking shot plus thunder and lightning are all used to unnerving effect in the depiction of an innocent young woman accepting a ride from a curb-crawler who she soon finds out is the maniac. Chilling stuff! Equally chilling are the central telephone conversations that make for uncomfortable listening, with the man asking Jean all sorts of personal questions and deviously toying with her emotions in a foreshadowing of the dangers faced by modern day youngsters from online predators. Conrad Phillips, as a pub landlord and husband of Jean's older sister, is the eventual hero in a film whose darker moments are offset with quaint scenes of English family life. Although the killer's face is never revealed to the audience, Jean's horrified expression when she does finally catch sight of him tells us all we need to know. Faye had previously starred in another cautionary tale, 1959's *Never Take Sweets from a Stranger*, an extremely dark British drama about child molestation in a Canadian community.

Happily married and expecting their first child, Tracey and Geoff (Anne Heywood and Richard Todd) are driven to **The Very Edge** (1962) by an unhinged stalker obsessed with Tracey from her days as a glamour model. Future—and some would say definitive—Sherlock Holmes actor Jeremy Brett plays the stalker in question, a young man named Mullen who first attacks Tracey in her own home (causing her to miscarry) and then continues to plague her until he's arrested and sent to prison. With their marriage having come under considerable strain (not least because of Tracey's resultant frigidity toward Geoff) during the ordeal, the couple starts afresh by moving to a new locale; however, Mullen escapes and tracks them down, leading to a dramatic final confrontation. Brett steals the show with an intense performance, but overall the film is a workmanlike affair which *Variety* (May 8, 1963) felt "lacks the very edge of its title."

An updated adaptation of Emlyn Williams' famous 1930s play of the same name, **Night Must Fall** (1964) stars Albert Finney as Danny, a charismatic, flirtatious and boyishly playful young man who charms his way into a job as handyman at the country house of elderly, wheelchair-bound Mrs. Bramson (Mona Washbourne), and sets about seducing the woman's daughter (Susan Hampshire). However, Danny is also a dangerous psychotic responsible for the murder of a local woman, the eventual discovery of whose headless body leaves us wondering as to the contents of a leather hatbox he keeps on top of a wardrobe in his bedroom. The film looks stunning thanks to some brilliant cinematography, and tension builds nicely to a disturbing and unforgettable climax. Finney gives a mostly effective—if at times a little over the top—performance as Danny, a character who'd already been played on the big screen by Robert Montgomery in a classic 1937 U.S. adaptation, as well as in TV versions by such talents as Ronald Lewis and Neil McCallum.

"A new peak in shriek!"

Inventively directed by Freddie Francis from an original screenplay by Robert Bloch, the Amicus production **The Psychopath** (1965) was humorously described by *The Daily Cinema* (October 12, 1966) as "gruesome Grand Guignol with gore galore." In London, four men are murdered, and in each case a doll—fashioned in the likeness of the victim—is left at the crime scene. It transpires that all the victims were once members of a war crimes commission and had given false evidence leading to the conviction of a German industrialist, who subsequently committed suicide in prison. Patrick Wymark gives a solid performance as the investigating detective, and Judy Huxtable is engaging as a young woman (the daughter of one of the murdered men) who precipitates a bizarre climax at the home of the industrialist's doll-obsessed and supposedly wheelchair-bound widow, Mrs. Von Sturm (Margaret Johnston), in which the shocking truth behind the murders is revealed. The film's most memorable scene is its last, in which Mrs. Von Sturm's son (John Standing), having broken his back, is found propped up in a chair like an oversize doll, pitifully crying "mama, mama."

"A unique manhunt across the capitals of Europe ... across three decades up to today!"

The Anglo-French co-production **The Night of the Generals** (1966) begins in 1942 with the horrific slashing to death of a Polish prostitute (who was also a German agent) in Nazi-occupied Warsaw. Only after a similar murder two years later in Paris does the audience learn (although it had already become fairly obvious) that the killer is General Tanz (Peter O'Toole), one of three Wehrmacht generals who'd been suspected of the Warsaw slaying. This time, Tanz pins the crime on a young German Corporal (Tom Courtenay), who as a result is forced to go on the run. As the unhinged maniac, O'Toole is intense and never less than frightening, while in contrast, and in an effective bit of casting, his old *Lawrence of Arabia* co-star Omar Sharif plays an extremely agreeable German Military Intelligence officer with a zealous determination to solve the case. He doesn't succeed however, thanks to his sudden and shocking departure from the story, and it's not until 1965—in Hamburg—that matters come to a close: following his release from prison for other (war related) crimes, Tanz murders another prostitute before finally getting his comeuppance thanks to both an Interpol agent (Philippe Noiret), formerly a police inspector who'd helped out in the original investigation, and the aforementioned framed corporal, who makes a surprise reappearance.

The film's extended running time allows for a subplot involving the real-life July 1944 plot to kill Hitler, this to some extent diluting the power and suspense of the central murder story; however, the film just about manages to hang together and, while not nearly the classic it could have been, it's certainly far from the "dud" as referred to by *Leonard Maltin's Movie Guide*. Donald Pleasence and Charles Gray, both future Blofelds in the James Bond franchise, play the two other suspected generals, and there's a cameo by Christopher Plummer as Field Marshal Rommel.

The at once campy and grisly Joan Crawford vehicle **Berserk** (1967) sees the legendary actress playing Monica Rivers, ruthless owner and ringmaster of a circus beset by a series of horrifying murders. The victims include the loud-mouthed Matilda (Diana Dors), who gets bisected for real when her sawing-in-half act is sabotaged, and Dorando (Michael Gough), Monica's disillusioned business partner who gets a tent spike driven through his head in the film's most gruesome scene. Ty Hardin plays a high-wire artist (his act involves a bed of spikes and no safety net) who tries to muscle in on the ownership of the circus; he's the last to die before the killer is revealed in a denouement not dissimilar to that of an earlier Crawford shocker, the William Castle–directed *Strait-Jacket* (1964). Judy Geeson plays Monica's wayward daughter, and the whole enterprise is energetically directed by Jim O'Connolly. Incidentally, Dors had an almost identical death scene in the 1961 *Alfred Hitchcock Presents* episode "The Sorcerer's Apprentice."

"Enough to make even Hitchcock jump!"

At some point during its original release, the producers added a pre-credits disclaimer to **Twisted Nerve** (1968) making it clear that in no way did the film imply (as many mistakenly felt it did, thanks to some confusing scenes featuring a professor played by Russell Napier) that future siblings of Down's syndrome children are more likely to display psychotic or criminal behavior. Hywel Bennett gives a powerful performance as Martin Durnley, a cherubic 22-year-old sexually

3. The Psychological and the Psychopathic 143

Who's holding the knife? Frankie Avalon and Julian Barnes in a tense moment from the creepy *The Haunted House of Horror* (1969).

immature closet psychopath who has grown up with an extremely overprotective (in connection with her first son having been born with Down's syndrome) mother (Phyllis Calvert) and a stern stepfather (Frank Finlay) who ends up throwing him out of the house. Adopting a second persona—"Georgie"—with the mental age of an infant, the cunning Martin inveigles himself into the life of young student Susan (Hayley Mills), securing a room in her mother Joan's (Billie Whitelaw) boarding house. While there, he plans—and subsequently carries out with a pair of scissors—the murder of his stepfather, and later butchers Joan with a hatchet after becoming stressed out by her attempt to seduce him. A terrifying finale sees Susan trapped by Martin as he goes into a full-blown mental collapse.

Apart from Bennett's brilliantly disturbing performance, the film is probably most memorable for Hitchcock composer Bernard Herrmann's haunting whistling theme, a once-heard-never-forgotten melody later used by Quentin Tarantino in *Kill Bill: Vol 1* (2003) and also featuring in TV's *American Horror Story*. Bennett starred in two further British psycho thrillers: the first, *Endless Night* (1972), reunited him with Mills and the second, *Murder Elite* (1985), with Whitelaw. Barry Foster, who plays a politically incorrect lodger at the boarding house, would get his own chance at playing a maniac in the 1972 Alfred Hitchcock shocker, *Frenzy*.

Despite the title, there are no supernatural elements in ***The Haunted House of Horror*** (1969), which concerns a group of bored young trendies—including Chris (Frankie Avalon), Sheila (Jill Haworth), Gary (Mark Wynter) and Richard (Julian Barnes)—who one night (on a full moon) decide to visit an abandoned and supposedly haunted old manor house that Richard knows from his childhood. After holding a midnight séance, they split up to explore the place and, before long, Gary is hacked to death by an unseen assailant. Chris takes charge of the situation and, having come to the conclusion that someone from among the group must be the killer, determines that their best option is to dispose of the body and say nothing to the authorities. They do just that, but circumstances see them eventually return to the house (on another full moon) where the killer is revealed in a nerve-wracking climax.

Clean-cut U.S. star Avalon, a long way from the zany adventures of his various "beach" movies, mixes well with his British co-stars, but whether or not he's "the epitome of swinging London," as one character refers to him, is another matter altogether. Dennis Price has little to do as a police inspector (a role originally intended for Boris Karloff), and there's a rather tedious subplot involving a character (an obvious red herring) played by George Sewell. A Tigon/AIP co-production, the film is very well directed by Michael Armstrong, who reportedly had to endure much unwanted interference by then AIP producer/scripter/troubleshooter Louis M. "Deke" Heyward. The scenes in the house are creepily atmospheric and generate some decent suspense, and there are three (two of them particularly brutal for the time) murders by kukri knife; this type of forward-curving Gurkha machete seems to have had only one other major appearance in a psycho-thriller, namely as the head-chopping maniac's weapon of choice in 1980's *Night School* (aka *Terror Eyes*). Avalon would return to the psycho-killer genre with the now largely forgotten low-budget outing *Blood Song* (1982; aka *Dream Slayer*).

"Lurid, pedestrian and totally unconvincing" was how the *Monthly Film Bulletin* (April 1970) characterized **Night, After Night, After Night** (1969), an ultra-sleazy slasher offering from cult director Lindsay Shonteff. Jack May gives a fairly disturbing performance as Charles Lomax, a mentally unbalanced judge behind a series of vicious London murders dubbed the "Ripper Killings." Gilbert Wynne, who'd played a private detective in Shonteff's other 1969 thriller, *Clegg*, here stars as an official police detective whose wife (Linda Marlowe) becomes one of the judge's victims, and who obsessively hounds a young man (Donald Sumpter) he wrongly believes is the culprit. What could have been a sordid but biting critique of hypocrisy within the criminal justice system (our maniacal and morally crusading magistrate sees fit to hand out harsh sentences to others while himself committing diabolical atrocities) settles instead for being just sordid, not to mention unremittingly dull and boring. Although not revealed early on, it's pretty easy to guess that Lomax is the culprit, this despite the red herrings of which the most conspicuous is the judge's clerk (Terry Scully), another hypocritical moralist who frequents strip clubs and keeps a secret stash of pornography at work. Lomax's eventual full-blown mental meltdown leads to an agonizingly protracted climax in which, grotesquely disguised in women's apparel, he's chased down and killed by police. A "continental" version exists with added scenes of nudity.

*"In the world of the nightmare,
a little blood adds colour!"*

In the slow but absorbing **I Start Counting** (1969), a psychopathic killer targets teenage girls in an English town where 14-year-old Wynne (Jenny Agutter) lives with her adoptive family in a modern tower block. Through a combination of circumstances and an overactive imagination, Wynne comes to suspect that her 32-year-old adoptive brother (Bryan Marshall), on whom she has an all-consuming crush, is the murderer. The family's previous abode, a condemned cottage bordering on some creepy common land (where victims have been found), features prominently throughout, including in the climax where Wynne has a terrifying encounter with the killer after he murders her flirtatious best friend

(Clare Sutcliffe). Agutter gives a remarkable performance in this perceptive and underrated coming-of-age story, which also stars Simon Ward as a puritanical local bus conductor.

"A sun-drenched nightmare!"

Filmed on a superb French location comprising flat landscapes, long deserted roads and a few patches of woodland, the moody and masterful ***And Soon the Darkness*** (1970) achieves exactly what the filmmakers set out to do, namely to make a thriller that would terrify audiences despite events taking place in broad daylight. Co-scripted by Brian Clemens and *Doctor Who* scribe Terry Nation from their original story, the film opens with two young English nurses, Jane and Cathy (Pamela Franklin and Michele Dotrice), on a cycling vacation in rural France. Before long, the girls arrive in an area where, unbeknownst to them, a young woman had been murdered two years earlier by a depraved sex killer who's still at large. While resting by the roadside near woodland, the girls get into an argument and Jane rides off; shortly after, Cathy is attacked by an unseen assailant. Jane eventually returns to the spot, finds Cathy missing and spends the rest of the film frantically trying to locate her with the help of a supposed Sûreté detective (Sandor Eles), whose overly ambiguous behavior makes him a rather obvious red herring. The local gendarme and an English schoolmistress are among potential suspects, and a chilling finale takes place in a clearing filled with disused vehicles, where Jane finally discovers what became of Cathy before herself coming face to face with the killer.

Director Robert Fuest, who went on to helm the two Vincent Price *Dr. Phibes* movies, successfully conveys a palpable sense of dread and, as pointed out by Kathleen Carroll in her review for New York's *Daily News* (April 5, 1971), "insists upon making the French look so formidable that France should suffer another setback in tourism after this film." Adding immeasurably to the atmosphere is some particularly effective incidental music courtesy of frequent Clemens collaborator Laurie Johnson. An inferior 2010 remake changed the locale to Argentina.

"If you go down in the woods today..."

In director Sidney Hayers' lurid ***Assault*** (1970), a brutal rapist attacks teenage schoolgirls in an area of local woodland known as Devil's End (hence the U.S. title *In the Devil's Garden*). The movie plays like a British version of an Italian *giallo* thriller, complete with brutal assault sequences, black-gloved psychopath and any amount of possible suspects, the most *giallo*-like of these being the sleazy husband (Tony Beckley) of the school's headmistress. Lesley-Anne Down makes her film debut as a victim struck dumb by her ordeal, while Suzy Kendall (herself a star of the *giallo* genre, most notably in Dario Argento's directorial debut *The Bird with the Crystal Plumage* [also dated 1970]) plays an art teacher who glimpses the attacker (after he murders a girl) and then helps the police in what turns out to be a botched—almost to the detriment of her own life—plan to trap the maniac. Described by *Variety* (February 24, 1971) as a "modest, unpretentious whodunit," the film features a literally "shocking" climax in which the culprit, while trying to escape after finally being exposed, gets fried upon foolishly climbing an electricity pylon situated in the grim woodland.

Assault has a fascinating distribution history in the U.S. Hemisphere Pictures initially released it under the provocative title *Molested*, with a debut screening on March 7, 1973, at the United Artists "Penthouse" Theatre in Louisville, Kentucky. The following day, Louisville's *The Courier-Journal* carried a review (under the heading "Despite lack of publicity, 'Molested' turns out to be good British thriller") by their contributing critic Gregg Swem, who stated "the British know how to zip off low-budget mysteries filled with entertaining suspense. Certainly, they are the masters of that craft." The *Molested* title remained in use until early October 1973; after that, Hemisphere renamed it *In the Devil's Garden*, which would become the title most associated with the picture in the U.S. Throughout most of its American theatrical history (in which it played at least once as *Assault*), the film shared bills with the Belgian-Italian horror flick *The Devil's Nightmare* (1971), including in the early 1980s when both films were reissued as, respectively, *Satan's Playthings* and *Vampire Playgirls*. The movie's principal title for stateside television showings, including on the horror show "Fright Night" (broadcast on New York's WOR-TV), was *Tower of Terror*; and it had one more title up its sleeve, namely *The Creepers*, which was used for four of its many home video releases.

As if the teenage rape and murder in *Assault* wasn't horrifying enough, Hayers' next thriller, the nasty-toned **Revenge** (1971), had even younger victims. Joan Collins has top billing as Carol, the second wife of Jim Radford (James Booth), a pub landlord whose 10-year-old daughter has been brutally murdered after being abducted outside her school. Taking the law into their own hands, Jim and his twenty-something son Lee (Tom Marshall), together with the father (Ray Barrett) of another young victim, kidnap the main suspect, a grubby recluse named Seely (Kenneth Griffith) whom the police have not charged due to insufficient evidence. Lacking a properly thought-out plan of action, they bring Seely back to the pub, beat him almost to death and then keep him prisoner in the cellar. Ensuing events end up having repercussions on Jim's already dysfunctional family that boil over

Suspected child murderer Seely (Kenneth Griffith) is held prisoner and tormented by pub landlord Jim Radford (James Booth) in *Revenge* (1971).

into paranoia, hysteria and sexual tension, the latter leading to a bizarre scene in which Lee ravishes stepmother Carol in front of Seely. Lee and Carol subsequently run out on Jim, but not before Carol has let Seely escape, and in any case a newspaper report suggests the man may be innocent after all. However, there's a final shocking twist in store. Collins, Booth and Griffith are all excellent, and the claustrophobic interiors and bleak small-town surroundings are perfectly suited to the sordid goings on, with the film's Britishness emphasized through an authentic pub atmosphere and plentiful tea drinking amid traumatic situations.

Revenge, like *Assault*, has an interesting American distribution history, and is best remembered theatrically from its PG-rated 1976 release as *Terror from Under the House*. However, before that, it had played for a few months between 1973 and 1974 with an "R" rating under the title *After Jenny Died*. Predating both releases were TV showings as *Inn of the Frightened People*, which remained the film's principal television title over the years; highlights under that name included airings on the horror movie showcase "Fright Night" (on New York's WOR-TV) and presentations by horror hosts Svengoolie (on his penultimate "Screaming Yellow Theater" slot in September 1973) and Elvira (on her "Movie Macabre" show in January 1983). Under the aforementioned *Terror from Under the House* title, the film was in theaters for a good half-dozen years, appearing on double bills with a wide variety of horror/thriller fare from *The Hills Have Eyes* (1977) and *Eyes of Laura Mars* (1978) to *Don't Go in the House* (1979) and *Swamp Thing* (1982). A one-night-only (October 27, 1978) late show at The Stage Door Theatre in Sheboygan, Wisconsin, saw it paired with another British terror-under-the-house flick, *The Beast in the Cellar* (1970); *Behind the Cellar Door*, which sounds like an umbrella name for that particular double bill, was in fact yet another U.S. retitling of *Revenge*, this time for a home video release.

"Now the screen has a new definition of terror!"

Variety (October 27, 1971) called **Fright** (1971) a "well-mounted shocker" despite its "unbelievable and rather nasty story." One night, young student Amanda (Susan George) turns up at an isolated house to babysit for Mrs. Lloyd (Honor Blackman), who goes out to celebrate her divorce from husband Brian (Ian Bannen). Brian is in fact

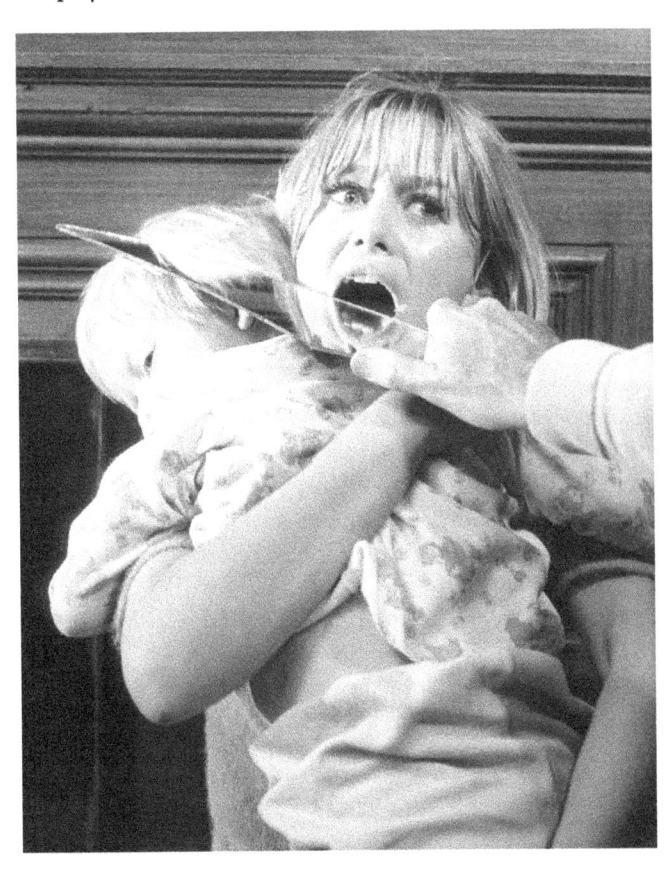

Amanda (Susan George) may never babysit again after a night of abject terror in the chilling *Fright* (1971).

a homicidal maniac and has been incarcerated in an asylum ever since attempting to kill Helen and their baby boy. The audience is soon made aware of a prowler—actually Brian, having escaped from the asylum—lurking around outside the house. Eventually, he manages to gain access to the property, whereupon Amanda is subjected to an unforgettable night of terror.

One of director Peter Collinson's more accomplished efforts, and the original babysitter-in-peril thriller, the film begins with an atmospheric credits sequence (depicting the heroine making her lonely way to the creepy house at night, and looking like the inspiration for the opening to another babysitter thriller, the semi-classic 1979 U.S. production *When a Stranger Calls*) that gets things off to a great start. George, who was at the height of her talents, is fantastic as the terrorized Amanda and shares many intense scenes with Bannen, whose portrayal of the unhinged Brian is at once terrifying and sympathetic. Also woven into the plot is Amanda's cheeky sex-starved boyfriend (Dennis Waterman), whose unexpected visit to the house leads to a particularly nasty encounter with the psychopath. The early scenes are extremely suspenseful, with Amanda becoming unnerved by strange noises and a face at the window, but the film gradually loses steam and is somewhat let down by an improbable ending. George Cole, playing the new man in Mrs. Lloyd's life, would later star with Waterman in the hit TV series *Minder*. In what looks to have been an attempt to cash in on the slasher movie craze, the film had a very brief early 1980s U.S. reissue (through Max J. Rosenberg's Dynamite Entertainment) under the title *I'm Alone and I'm Scared*, complete with vivid slasher-style poster and the tagline "Amanda will never babysit again."

"Keep your eyes on what she cannot see—the boots, the bracelet and the bodies..."

Featuring an original screenplay by Brian Clemens, the slow but frequently terrifying **Blind Terror** (1971) is a sightless-woman-in-peril chiller that gives the more famous U.S. production, *Wait Until Dark* (1967), a run for its money. Mia Farrow delivers a credible performance as Sarah, a young woman left blind as the result of a horse-riding accident. After a long spell in hospital, Sarah returns to her family—an uncle (Robin Bailey), aunt (Dorothy Alison) and cousin (Diane Grayson)—at their country estate. However, the peace and quiet is violently shattered when a psychopathic killer calls by and brutally murders the three relatives as well as fatally wounding their groundskeeper. Sarah, who'd been out with old flame Steve (Norman Eshley) while the slaughter took place, returns home to eventually, in a tense and horrifying sequence, stumble over the dead bodies, while at the same time the maniac makes his way back to the house to look for an identity bracelet he lost during the attack. Guided by the barely-alive groundskeeper, Sarah locates the bracelet and then narrowly avoids the killer's clutches, escaping on horseback to seek help.

In a welcome change from the black-gloved murderers of so many psycho-killer movies, *Blind Terror*'s maniac is shown to us via his distinctive cowboy-style boots, and it would appear that his motivation for targeting the family has to do with an incident early on where their car causes water to splash onto said footwear. We get our first glimpse of the boots in the brilliantly executed (and forceful in its suggestion that the consumption of violence has a causal link to homicidal behavior) opening credits sequence, which begins with the killer exiting a theater after having just viewed a dubious (and fictitious, it should be said) "X"-rated double bill comprising *The Convent Murders* and *Rapist Cult*; as the sequence progresses, the boots make their way past a succession of storefronts, in which we see what the killer can see, namely a bombardment of further projections of violence including sensational newspaper headlines (e.g., "Massacre of the Children"), toy guns and, in the case of a television store, multiple

TV screens showing a brutal moment from Amicus Productions' 1967 horror anthology *Torture Garden*. The handsome Eshley's character, a neighboring farm-owner, is ultimately the hero of the piece (arriving just in time to save Sarah from being drowned in a bathtub), and the story also features a group of gypsies, one of whose number becomes suspected of the crimes due to a mix-up with identity bracelets. Elmer Bernstein's exciting score lends dramatic punch to the proceedings, while the many instances of nail-biting suspense are handled admirably by director Richard Fleischer.

Eight years before playing the unhinged Curt Duncan in the U.S. suspenser *When a Stranger Calls*, Tony Beckley reached even higher levels of psychosis as puritanical serial killer Kenny Wemys in **The Fiend** (1971). Kenny's mission in life is to save the souls of sexually active young women by brutally murdering them. However, it doesn't end there, for he also makes tape recordings of his evil deeds for later consumption, which in one instance involves being surrounded by trophies in the form of undergarments taken from his victims. Kenny still lives at home with his devout mother Birdy (Ann Todd), and his problems stem from having grown up subjected to the teachings of an extreme religious sect known as "Christ's Children Evangelical Crusade." Members of the sect regularly gather at a shabby chapel in Birdy's large and gloomy London house, where a fanatical fire-and-brimstone preacher known as "The Minister" (the brilliant Patrick Magee) delivers sermons and plays recorded messages from the sect's leader in the U.S. state of Arizona. An effective opening sequence depicts one such sermon, in which a congregation member's rendition of an unashamedly catchy gospel-style ditty called "wash me in his blood" is intercut with scenes of Kenny stalking and killing a victim. There's much gratuitous nudity and crude symbolism, with the lurid proceedings reaching a spectacularly overwrought climax in which Kenny literally crucifies The Minister in revenge for causing the diabetic Birdy's death by withholding insulin according to the sect's strict stance on drugs. Also involved in the story is an investigative journalist (Suzanna Leigh) out to expose the sect.

> *"From the master of shock
> ... a shocking masterpiece!"*

Alfred Hitchcock's first British film since 1949's *Stage Fright*, **Frenzy** (1972) sees the master on top form, aided by a solid Anthony Shaffer screenplay which includes a strong vein of black humor. Jon Finch plays Richard Blaney, a down-on-his-luck former RAF pilot whose ex-wife becomes a victim in a rash of London strangulation killings dubbed the "necktie murders." The killer is revealed early on as one of Blaney's acquaintances, an outwardly charming and friendly Covent Garden fruit market dealer named Bob Rusk, played brilliantly by Barry Foster of TV's *Van Der Valk* fame. As if killing Blaney's ex-wife wasn't bad enough, Rusk goes on to murder the man's girlfriend and then engineers a frame-up that results in Blaney—already a suspect in the killings—being arrested, tried and imprisoned for the "necktie" slayings. However, Blaney soon manages to escape and sets out for revenge.

One of the highlights is a great tracking shot that begins just after we've seen Rusk enter his apartment with a soon-to-be victim: the camera, focused on the quiet hallway outside the apartment door, begins slowly backing away down a staircase, continuing to reverse along an entrance hall and finally out into the hustle-bustle of the street, leaving the viewer to imagine just what dreadful things Rusk is up to back inside. That's not to say Hitchcock shies away from showing murder—far from it in fact, for the film features a shockingly explicit rape-strangulation that ranks as one of the most intense and disturbing murder scenes ever to appear in a British thriller. Another grim but well-staged sequence takes place in the back of a truck where Rusk attempts to retrieve an incriminating tie pin from the death grip of a victim whose body he'd stashed in a sack of potatoes. Some welcome comic relief is provided in scenes of the investigating detective (Alec McCowen) discussing the case with his wife while nervously sampling her rather unsavory attempts at gourmet cooking. Ron Goodwin provides a grandiose score, and Hitchcock makes his customary cameo appearance in a crowd during the film's opening scene.

In Hammer's **Straight on Till Morning** (1972), Liverpudlian "plain Jane" Brenda (Rita Tushingham) fantasizes about marrying a Prince Charming. In an effort to make her dream come true, she moves to London, engineers a meeting with the handsome Peter (Shane Briant) and ends up moving in with him. However, far from being a Prince Charming, Peter is in fact a psychopathic serial killer compelled—by a pathological hatred of beauty—to murder attractive women. (One of the film's more upsetting scenes has him also kill his own dog after Brenda prettifies the unfortunate creature.) Due to her ordinary looks, the unwitting Brenda initially remains safe, but it's only a matter of time until she learns the truth. Sure enough, the grim goings-on reach their crescendo when Peter plays Brenda tape recordings of his murders (which, incidentally, were carried out in quite nasty fashion with a retractable-blade utility knife), this having repercussions that ultimately lead to a somewhat ambiguous ending. Briant and Tushingham fit their roles well, and overall it's stylishly shot (with some effective use of cross-cutting techniques in the earlier stages), but in the end the whole thing's too slow, bleak and morbid to fully engage. The film's title, as well as several other references during the story, is reflective of Peter's obsession with the tale of Peter Pan.

Appropriately described by the *Monthly Film Bulletin* (January 1974) as being at heart "just another sexploitation film posing as a thriller," **Scream—and Die!** (1973) was one of several British films directed by Spain's José Ramón Larraz during the 1970s. On a dark and foggy night, while driving his friend Valerie (Andrea Allan) to London, the shady Terry (Alex Leppard) stops off to rob a remote house. Valerie reluctantly becomes his accomplice and, while exploring the place, they witness a woman being slashed to death by a mysterious black-gloved figure. Valerie flees the house, eludes the pursuing killer (this is a particularly suspenseful sequence involving creepy woodland, a car salvage yard and eerie music) and eventually manages to hitchhike back to London, with Terry's fate remaining a mystery. Subsequent strange events convince Valerie, who cannot remember the exact location of the house, that the killer has tracked her down and is stalking her. A romantic entanglement with troubled artist Paul (Karl Lanchbury) helps take her mind off things—that is, until he invites her to his country house whereupon she shockingly realizes it's not the first time she's been there.

Some occasional and effective moments of moody atmosphere punctuate the sleazy goings-on, which include gratuitous nudity, incest (Paul is the secret sexual plaything of a jealously possessive aunt) and a nasty rape-murder, while the main red herring (a sinister black-gloved neighbor of Valerie's) is glaringly obvious and overplayed. Apart from as *Scream—and Die!*, the movie was originally also submitted to the British Board of Film Censors under the title *Psycho Sex Fiend*, but doesn't appear to have ever been released as such.

"...and no one escaped..."

Although often regarded as part of the grindhouse "women in prison" genre, the complex characters and issues in director Pete Walker's grim and dark shocker, **House of Whipcord** (1974), make it somewhat more than just another exploitation flick. (This clearly made no difference to U.S. distributor United Producers, who gleefully ramped up the exploitation angle by renaming the picture *Stag Model Slaughter*.) A deranged former prison governess, Mrs. Wakehurst (Barbara Markham), and a doddery blind ex-judge (Patrick Barr), run their own private and illegal correctional institution where severe punishments are doled out to those they feel have been let off too lightly by the current justice system. Penny Irving plays Ann-Marie, a young French model who, having been discharged in court with a small fine after posing nude in public, is lured to the place and imprisoned there. Unfortunately, an incident from Mrs. Wakehurst's past (involving another French girl) causes her to have a particular dislike toward Ann-Marie, who as a consequence is made to suffer accordingly.

Markham and Barr are frighteningly good as the self-appointed arbiters of their own twisted brand of justice, and there's a suavely sinister performance by Robert Tayman (Count Mitterhaus from 1971's *Vampire Circus*) as their evil offspring, who lures victims to the institution. Sheila Keith, who would go on to star in several other productions for Walker, plays a wicked authoritarian prison guard administering brutal floggings, and there's a twist involving Ann-Marie escaping and seeking help from a truck driver (Ivor Salter), only for him to unwittingly hand the dazed girl back to the institution in the belief that it's a legitimate private clinic. Many scenes were filmed at an actual gloomy old prison building in Gloucestershire.

Walker's next film, *Frightmare* (1974), tells the horrifying tale of husband and wife Dorothy and Edmund Yates (Sheila Keith and Rupert Davies), who have lived on a farm ever since their release from an asylum for the criminally insane. Dorothy had murdered and cannibalized six people, with a particular liking for their brains, while the totally devoted Edmund had been complicit in the crimes. It soon transpires that Dorothy has relapsed and has been luring new victims to the farm; and there's an added problem in that the couple's delinquent daughter, Debbie (Kim Butcher), has inherited her mother's anthropophagous tendencies. The story also involves Edmund's daughter (Deborah Fairfax) from another marriage, who tries in vain to allay Dorothy's cravings, and whose meddling psychiatrist boyfriend (Paul Greenwood) pays a visit to the farm from which he never returns.

One of Walker and screenwriter David McGillivray's most

A 1972 shocker from Hammer Film Productions.

accomplished efforts, this grim, disturbing and downbeat chiller has first-rate performances, photography and editing, not to mention a hauntingly effective score by Stanley Myers. Through its combination of cannibalism and mutilation by power tool (Dorothy puts an electric drill to horrific use on her victims), the film is Britain's answer to the same year's U.S. classic *The Texas Chain Saw Massacre* only without that movie's flamboyance and heightened Grand Guignol style.

Keith gives a truly terrifying and unsettling performance, but in the end it's Davies who takes the acting honors with a more nuanced characterization as aider and abettor Edmund. Of the film's four U.S. retitlings, the most interesting—if only for being so sensational (referring as it does to Dorothy's preferred part of the human anatomy)—is *Brainsuckers*, under which it's known to have played for one week (double-billed with early 1970s kung fu actioner *Fearless Fighters*) at the Fox Theatre, Detroit, Michigan, May–June 1976; its second most interesting retitling would have to be as *Frightmare II* (for home video in 1985), which appears to have been an attempt to distinguish it from, while at the same time cashing in on, a then recent video release of another *Frightmare* (an early 1980s U.S. flick also known as *The Horror Star*).

Produced in association with Bristol-based television company HTV, **Deadly Strangers** (1974) features an original and brilliantly crafted screenplay by Philip Levene, and is arguably director Sidney Hayers' best thriller of the 1970s. Unfolding against bleak wintry English landscapes, the exciting story opens with the escape from an asylum of a psychopathic killer whose identity is not shown. Soon after, traveling salesman Stephen Slade (Simon Ward) gives a ride to Belle Adams (Hayley Mills) after she becomes stranded following a nasty encounter with a sexually assaultive truck driver. It's easy to guess that one of the two protagonists is the escapee, but the film cleverly conceals (by way of some devious audience manipulation) exactly which of the two is the culprit until a tense climax set at an isolated fishing lodge. Along the way, there are flashbacks in which we learn about Stephen's sexual hang-ups and Belle's unfortunate past as a victim of abuse at the hands of a lecherous uncle (Peter Jeffrey).

Ward and Mills, both superb, play off each other perfectly, and there's an entertaining appearance midway through by a generously bearded Sterling Hayden in a small but pivotal role as an old eccentric who takes a liking to Belle. The film gets it right on most levels, not the least of which is Ron Goodwin's gorgeous and expertly judged soundtrack. *Films Illustrated* (April 1975) noted that "if you haven't worked it out in the opening five minutes, the chances are that the tortuous corkscrewing of the plot might still hold surprises for you." Apart from as *Deadly Strangers*, the movie was originally also submitted to the British Board of Film Censors under the title *Silhouettes*, but doesn't appear to have ever been released as such.

The Spiral Staircase (1975), a disappointing remake of the classic 1946 U.S. spine-tingler of the same name (which in turn was based on Ethel Lina White's 1933 novel *Some Must Watch*), stars Jacqueline Bisset as a young woman rendered mute from the shock of witnessing the deaths of her husband and young daughter during a fire. While staying at the large country house of her psychologist uncle, Professor Sherman (Christopher Plummer), she becomes targeted by a psychopathic serial killer who preys on those with disabilities. Copious and well-done thunderstorm effects create some good atmosphere, but this tepid and virtually suspense-free updating of the story fails to generate the sense of dread that made the earlier version so memorable, with even the titular staircase itself proving to be a big disappointment. Lensed in England and set in America, the film has an impressive supporting cast—including Mildred Dunnock and Gayle Hunnicutt as members of the Sherman household—and is at least better than the U.S.-Canadian TV movie version from 2000.

Director Pete Walker's nihilistic anti-establishment chiller **House of Mortal Sin** (1975) did not attract as much controversy on its original release as one might have expected, considering the sensational subject matter. Having just been reacquainted with her old friend—and now priest—Bernard Cutler (Norman Eshley), twenty-something Jenny Welch (Susan Penhaligon) visits him at his church to discuss her boyfriend troubles. However, Bernard's not around, and Jenny winds up in the confessional booth talking to a senior priest, Father Xavier Meldrum (Anthony Sharp). Disturbed by Meldrum's intense manner and over-zealous interest in her love life, Jenny makes a hasty retreat; but the clergyman, by now fixated with the girl, almost immediately begins stalking her, and anyone who tries to stop him is brutally eliminated.

Peter Cushing, Harry Andrews and Lee J. Cobb had all apparently been considered for the lead role, but it's difficult to imagine any of them doing a better job than Sharp; the veteran actor goes all out as the demented priest, delivering his dialogue in a manner often reminiscent of the great Basil Rathbone. (Anyone who's seen Sharp's prior guest appearances as a priest in the BBC comedy show *Steptoe and Son* should take note: there is nothing whatsoever humorous about his performance in *House of Mortal Sin*.) The psychopathic padre, who is revealed to have a history of stalking (we also learn that he blackmails confessants with secretly taped recordings of their disclosures in the confessional), includes among his weapons of destruction an incense burner and poisoned communion wafers. Oh, and let's not forget the rosary, which he uses in the particularly vicious strangling of Jenny's sister (Stephanie Beacham) for whom, incidentally, the aforementioned Bernard was about to give up the priesthood. A revelation about Meldrum's past, involving both his mother and his sinister housekeeper (the latter, sporting glasses with one lens blacked out to hide a deformed eye, played by Walker regular Sheila Keith), goes a long way to explaining his fixation with Jenny. Described by *Films and Filming* (April 1976) as a "swift, if run-of-the-mill, suspense/horror story," the movie ends with Meldrum still at large—having engineered a frame-up to absolve him of any suspicion—and Jenny still in danger.

"A murder thriller with thrilling bodies!"

Vaguely reminiscent of the 1959 B movie *Cover Girl Killer*, **The Playbirds** (1978) concerns a maniacal murderer targeting women that pose for the sex magazine *Playbirds* (a real-life men's magazine). Mary Millington, a top performer in British adult entertainment during the 1970s, stars as Scotland Yard policewoman Lucy Sheridan, who goes on an undercover mission as a decoy (a nude model) to trap the killer. While Millington (whose life was tragically cut short at age 33 in 1979) may not live up to the requirements demanded of her as an actress, her special talents as an adult entertainer are celebrated during a fun sequence in which Scotland Yard holds striptease auditions to find the most suitable candidate for the undercover police work. The cast includes many familiar faces from British films and television such as Derren Nesbitt, Windsor Davies and, best of all, Dudley Sutton as a religious fanatic. Just when it seems the killer has been caught, there's a cruel and totally unexpected twist that leads to a decidedly downbeat ending for our heroine. The London locations include the district of Soho, which was then the thriving center of the capital's sex industry.

Set in Northwest England's Lake District, **Killer's Moon** (1978) is a cheap and distasteful exploitation flick whose content pushed the British "X" rating to the limit back in the day. The story concerns four psychopathic criminals escaping from a rural cottage hospital (where they were undergoing experimental drug and dream therapy) to terrorize—in an orgy of rape, murder, and cruelty to animals—the local countryside, including attacking a group of teenage schoolgirls and their chaperones who have taken refuge at an isolated out-of-season hotel following the breakdown of their bus. Anthony Forrest and Tom Marshall play two heroic campers, and the film was written, produced and directed by Alan Birkinshaw, whose more famous sister, Fay Weldon, contributed to the dialogue.

4

Focus on Crime Solvers

Most thrillers feature crime solvers of one kind or another, and this chapter is devoted to those in which the investigators are the focal point of the story. To cope with the many different kinds of crime detectors, both professional and amateur, the chapter has been arranged in five main sections. "Official Investigators" contains films featuring state-sanctioned police officers. While these mainly deal with investigators from British institutions such as Scotland Yard, London's Thames River Police and the Manchester City Police, there are also examples featuring detectives from Egypt's Narcotics Bureau, the French Sûreté and the international Interpol organization, not to mention Dutch and Australian police forces. *Brannigan* (1975) stars the great John Wayne as a Chicago cop in London, and there's even a solver of ecological crime in a 1972 spin-off film from BBC TV's *Doomwatch*.

Under "Agatha Christie Sleuths" can be found the legendary author's two most famous characters, Miss Marple and Hercule Poirot, while "Private Eyes and Other Independent Sleuths" features many famous names including Sherlock Holmes, Bulldog Drummond, The Saint, Father Brown, Paul Temple, The Toff, Mike Hammer and Philip Marlowe. Made up mainly of B movies, the "Intrepid Reporters" section includes a multitude of brave and tenacious newsmen tackling everything from serial killers to atomic weapons smugglers. While the majority of the featured reporters are British characters (played by dashing actors such as John Bentley, Dermot Walsh and Conrad Phillips), there are also a fair few American protagonists portrayed by a variety of Hollywood stars including Larry Parks, Gene Nelson and Jeff Morrow. One actor particularly suited to this type of role was the amiable Canadian, Paul Carpenter, who it's fair to say was the quintessential player of British B-thriller reporters. Lastly, we have "Insurance Agents" investigating crimes including murder and arson.

Official Investigators

The exotically located **Cairo Road** (1950) stars Eric Portman as Colonel Youssef Bey of Egypt's Anti-Narcotics Bureau. The story has Bey and his young assistant, Lieutenant Mourad (Laurence Harvey), attempting to smash a highly efficient drugs smuggling operation run by siblings Edouardo and Rico Pavlis (Karel Stepanek and Harold Lang), with Rico proving to be a particularly slippery customer due to his use of a false identity to move in and out of Port Said. Good use of authentic locations and an occasional semi-documentary feel give the film a realistic edge, with the only weak spot being a rather feeble climax in which Mourad disguises himself as a crippled associate of the siblings in order to trap them. The diverse supporting cast includes a veritable "Who's Who" of ubiquitous British-based foreign actors such as Ferdy Mayne, Eric Pohlmann and Marne Maitland.

"They robbed.... They killed.... They paid!"

From left: Abraham Sofaer, Eric Portman and Harold Lang in *Cairo Road* (1950).

In the B movie *The Six Men* (1950), a young man known as Johnny the Kid is shot dead by Lewis (Reed De Rouen), one of his cohorts in the notorious six-strong (now only five-strong) robbery gang of the title. This prompts Scotland Yard's Superintendent Holroyd (Harold Warrender) to take a month off his general duties in order to concentrate all his efforts into bringing about the downfall of the remaining gang members. At the same time, an actress (Olga Edwardes) and a mysterious blind man known as "The Mole" are making their own efforts (involving a series of frame-ups) to bring down the criminals. By the end, three of the crooks have been arrested and the boss (Peter Bull) murdered by Lewis, who as a result is left facing the gallows; thus putting an end to "The Six Men." A final twist reveals a very surprising connection between Holroyd, the actress, "The Mole" and Johnny the Kid, as well as explaining Holroyd's fixation with the case. On the lighter side, there's a brief cameo—as herself—by comedy actress Avril Angers and some goofy humor involving Holroyd's assistant (Michael Evans).

Based on a BBC radio show of the same name, *The Adventures of P.C. 49* (1949) was a Hammer B movie starring Hugh Latimer as Archibald Berkeley-Willoughby, a police constable (the titular P.C. 49) involved in a dangerous adventure concerning truck hijackers. In Hammer's follow-up B movie, *A Case for P.C. 49* (1951), Willoughby (this time played by Brian Reece) is manipulated into being an alibi in a clever plot by a model, Della Dainton (Christine Norden), and her lover, jewel-heist mastermind Victor Palantine (Leslie Bradley), to murder a millionaire. Palantine carries out the murder but is then himself bumped off. Willoughby, helped by his resourceful fiancée (Joy Shelton), investigates the complicated events (which also involve Palantine's two criminal errand boys, played by Michael Balfour and Jack Stewart) and sees to it that all guilty parties are dealt with appropriately; in the process, he clears an ex-convict (Hammer regular Michael Ripper) who'd been framed for Palantine's murder. The *Monthly Film Bulletin* (August 1951) remarked that the film's "many moments of suspense too often end in elaborate anti-climaxes."

In the fast-moving B movie **13 East Street** (1951), tough Scotland Yard detective Gerald Fraser (Patrick Holt) goes undercover (posing as a crook) to infiltrate a notorious gang of thieves. The title refers to the East London address of the gang's headquarters, where American mastermind Larry Conn (Robert Ayres) runs the criminal activities through a legitimate haulage contracting business. During his mission, Fraser, a married man, has to contend with the amorous attentions of Larry's attractive moll Judy (Sandra Dorne), not to mention the constant threat of having his cover blown by suspicious gang member Mack (Michael Brennan), before the criminals are finally rounded up in a dockside warehouse while attempting a £50,000 fur robbery. Holt's on-screen wife is played by his real-life spouse at the time, Sonia Holm, although shortly after a divorce in 1953, the actor went on to marry his other co-star, Dorne.

The third filmed version of A.E.W. Mason's 1924 novel of the same name, **The House of the Arrow** (1953) is dominated by Oscar Homolka's excellent performance as Inspector Hanaud, the charming, humorous, incisive and ever-so-conceited Sûreté detective who describes himself as "the most clever detective in all France." A wealthy widow's death, apparently from natural causes, is eventually proved by Hanaud to be a case of murder, with the culprit having used a type of African arrow poison that leaves no trace. Yvonne Furneaux stars as the widow's niece, a suspect by virtue of being heir to her aunt's entire fortune, and the story contains plenty of red herrings while maintaining a good sense of mystery throughout.

The formulaic B movie **The Blue Parrot** (1953) stars Dermot Walsh as Bob Herrick, an American detective visiting London to study British methods of crime detection. He is soon helping Scotland Yard investigate the murder of a car-hire operator in a case centering on a Soho nightclub called The Blue Parrot. John Le Mesurier portrays the club's inscrutable boss, while Ferdy Mayne, as a decidedly shady character, gets the film's best line when warning Herrick that "asking questions around Soho is an occupation without a future." The main female cast member, Jacqueline Hill, plays an undercover policewoman (she poses as a hostess at the club) held hostage by the murderer during a climactic sequence involving a secret underground passageway running beneath the establishment.

Another Dermot Walsh B movie, **The Floating Dutchman** (1953), was described by the *Monthly Film Bulletin* (January 1954) as "a routine crime story after the American B picture style." The body of a Dutch jeweler found in London's River Thames provides vital clues in the authorities' ongoing efforts to catch an elusive criminal mastermind (Sydney Tafler) currently running a jewel theft racket from his nightclub headquarters. Walsh plays a special police agent assigned to infiltrate the racket, while Mary Germaine is a hostess at the club who gets kidnapped in a plan by the mastermind's henchman (Guy Verney) to ultimately lure the agent into a death trap. The film was shown only on television in the U.S., initially under the title *Clue from a Corpse* (although some old newspaper TV pages show it listed under its originally intended U.S. title, *The Corpse Finds a Clue*) and later under its British title.

"Diamonds on her meant trouble!"

Excellent location work highlights the unpretentious B movie **River Beat** (1953), in which John Bentley plays Inspector Dan Barker of London's Thames River Police. Top billing, however, goes to Hollywood's Phyllis

Kirk as Judy Roberts, a radio operator on a moored American freighter who helps Dan smash a diamond smuggling racket in which she has been unwittingly used as a courier. Kirk and Bentley make a likeable team, and the film features a nice blend of romance, mystery and action. Robert Ayres plays the freighter's crooked (as it turns out) captain who, in the hectic climax, holds Judy hostage and makes off in a stolen police launch with Dan in hot pursuit.

Today's Cinema (July 30, 1954) characterized the seldom-seen B movie *The Golden Link* (1954) as "solid whodunit entertainment" with "fairly watertight story construction." Andre Morell stars as Superintendent Blake, a Scotland Yard CID detective residing with his daughter Joan (Thea Gregory) in a London apartment block known as Parkside Mansions. The film opens with the estranged wife (Dorinda Stevens) of one of Blake's fellow residents, Terry Maguire (Patrick Holt), being pushed to her death down the block's stairwell. During the investigation, and as a result of evidence planted by the killer, suspicion falls on Joan, who has a potential motive in that she's in love with Terry and may not have taken too kindly to his wife refusing him a divorce. A crucial break in the case comes when the murderer makes an anonymous phone call to Scotland Yard which is traced (thanks to a song heard in the background) to a nightclub; this enables Blake, with the help of the venue's songstress (Marla Landi), to set a trap into which his quarry—one of Parkside Mansions' other residents—duly walks. Speaking of these other residents, they're a colorful bunch including a bogus major (Edward Lexy), an eccentric fortune teller (Ellen Pollock) and a trusty (or is he?) friend of the Blakes (Jack Watling).

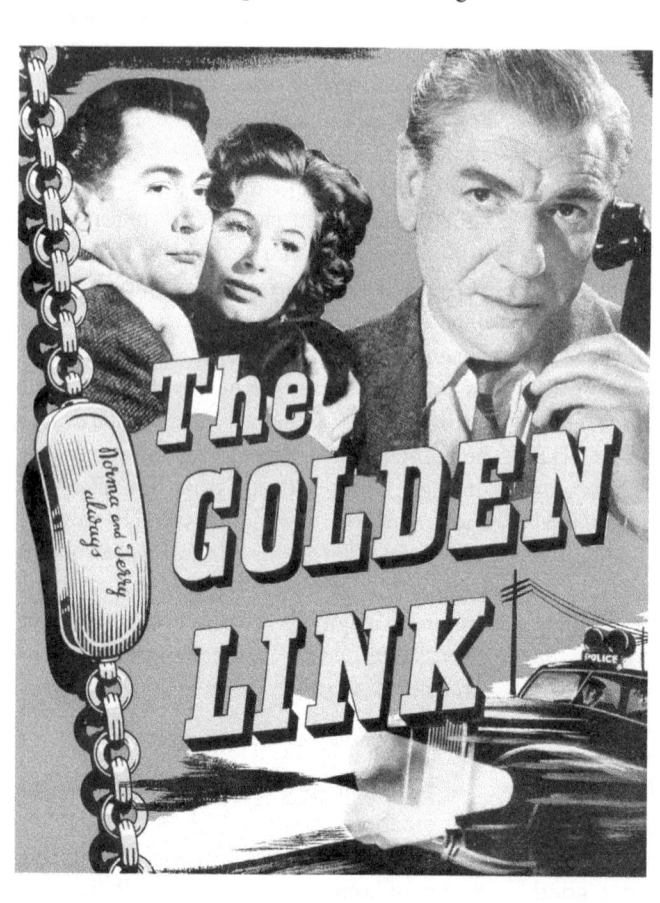

Police Dog (1955) is a quaint little B movie starring Tim Turner as Frank Mason, a police constable who takes charge of Rex, a savage Alsatian, and trains the animal to become a first-class police dog. The plot mostly concerns the search for a criminal (Cecil Brock) responsible for the death of Frank's partner, with Rex playing a crucial part in the man's eventual capture. There are some semi-documentary sequences detailing methods of police dog training, and at times the film bears much similarity to the 1960 U.S. B movie *The Police Dog Story*. Christopher Lee has a small role as a grumpy constable, while Joan Rice and Sandra Dorne, as Frank's girlfriend and the criminal's moll respectively, provide contrasting feminine appeal.

Pressbook for a 1954 B movie starring Andre Morell.

The above-average B

movie ***One Way Out*** (1955) sees Eddie Byrne on great form as John Harcourt, a soon-to-retire Scotland Yard inspector determined to bring to justice a criminal mastermind named Danvers (John Chandos). To protect himself, Danvers implicates Harcourt's daughter (Jill Adams) in a violent robbery and uses this to successfully blackmail the inspector into backing off. Later events see Harcourt, now retired, putting his family at possible risk of retribution by continuing his pursuit of the criminal, this leading to a tense climax in which he takes drastic action to ensure Danvers will serve a life sentence. The imaginative screenplay was written by Cy Endfield under the pseudonym Jonathan Roche.

"Scotland Yard's most baffling case..."

The crisply photographed and well-scored police procedural ***The Long Arm*** (1956) stars Jack Hawkins as Tom Halliday, a Scotland Yard detective investigating a baffling series of robberies in which safes are opened using tailor-made keys. The first big break in the case comes with the realization that all the safes in question had been supplied by the same manufacturer, a company called Rock Safes. It eventually transpires that the thief (Richard Leech) once worked for the company and had made copies of certain keys before faking his own death in order to avoid suspicion of the robberies he would later carry out. Hawkins manages to inject some humanity into his role despite the script's tendency to treat characters as pieces on a chess board, while the supporting cast of familiar faces includes Ursula Howells as the thief's cold-hearted wife and accomplice. The exciting finale is set at London's Royal Festival Hall, where Halliday sets a trap for the criminals.

The ultra-cheap B movie ***They Never Learn*** (1956), which the *Monthly Film Bulletin* (November 1956) remarked is "determinedly stereotyped in plot and conception," details Scotland Yard and Interpol's efforts to smash a currency counterfeiting ring operating in England and France. Adrienne Scott plays a policewoman going undercover (which involves posing as a criminal and spending three months in London's Holloway Prison) to infiltrate the British arm of the criminal enterprise, headed by Frank "Frankie" Strutton (John Blythe) and involving Frank's moll, Lil (future best-selling novelist Jackie Collins). Despite her cover getting blown, our heroine's endeavors eventually lead to the necessary arrests being made; that is, except in the case of Frank who, following a chase in London's West End, escapes justice by jumping to his death from the bell tower at Westminster Cathedral.

Reminiscent of the 1948 Dick Powell starrer *To the Ends of the Earth* and anticipating the later *French Connection* movies, the intermittently exciting ***Interpol*** (1957) concerns efforts by both the United States Federal Bureau of Narcotics and Interpol to smash an international network of drug smugglers headed by the elusive and smoothly sinister Frank McNally (Trevor Howard at his best). Victor Mature makes a solid hero as Charles Sturgis, one of the Bureau's agents whose kid sister—a fellow agent—was cold-bloodedly murdered by McNally (in the pre-credits sequence), and Anita Ekberg plays a woman in McNally's control, forced to carry out illicit dealings for the villain. The expertly shot (in CinemaScope) film begins in New York, after which there are episodes in London and various European cities before things wind up back in the Big Apple, where McNally is shot and killed by Sturgis on the docks while attempting to get away with a $3 million shipment of heroin just arrived from Athens. In a supporting role, Bonar Colleano stands out as an exiled American in Rome, a street seller and police informant crucial to the story's outcome. The picture was co-produced by Albert R. Broccoli, who employs some of the technicians (cinematographer Ted Moore and art director Syd Cain) and character actors (Eric Pohlmann, Marne Maitland and Martin Benson) who would later contribute to his James Bond franchise.

Drug kingpin Frank McNally (Trevor Howard, left) and one of his henchmen (Marne Maitland) in *Interpol* (1957).

Shot on location in the city of Liverpool, **Violent Playground** (1958) is a social conscience thriller which, according to the *Monthly Film Bulletin* (February 1958), settles for a "superficial, glib approach and a general reliance on formula." Stanley Baker plays a CID detective volunteered by his superior for temporary juvenile liaison work, through which he discovers the culprit—psychotic teenage gang leader Johnny Murphy (David McCallum giving a typically edgy early performance)—in a series of arson attacks he'd previously been investigating. Also starring are Anne Heywood as Johnny's older sister, to whom the detective grows close, and Peter Cushing as a local priest. The tense and prolonged climax involves a machine gun-wielding Johnny holding a classroom of schoolchildren hostage.

One of the better Danziger brothers B movies, ***The Great Van Robbery*** (1958) features a bright script and efficient direction that keeps things moving at a brisk pace. Caesar Smith (Denis Shaw), a rotund detective and judo expert from Scotland Yard's Interpol division, investigates when £18,000 worth of stolen banknotes (part of a £150,000 cash haul from the titular Royal Mint van heist in London) turns up in Rio de Janeiro as payment for a consignment of coffee beans. Smith flies to Rio, and subsequently follows clues—via Europe—back to London, a trail that ultimately leads to crooked importer Ralph Chase (Philip Saville), a fence who set up the coffee deal as a way of laundering some of the stolen cash. Character actor Shaw is great in a rare leading role, and the cast also features Kay Callard as the criminal's moll, Ella. In the climax set in Chase's warehouse, Ella attempts to run Smith down with a car, only for the vehicle to skid on some of the shadily obtained coffee beans (spilled during a shootout) and hit Chase instead.

*"The sensational story
of a girl who didn't belong!"*

Sapphire (1959) is a beautifully crafted combination of police procedural and racial drama, in which issues of prejudice are tackled in an honest and uncompromising way that was groundbreaking at the time. The story details an investigation by Detectives Hazard (an assured Nigel Patrick) and Learoyd (Michael Craig) into the brutal stabbing of pregnant young music student Sapphire Robbins (Yvonne Buckingham). It transpires that Sapphire was of mixed race (a white father and black mother), although she had been passing herself off as white and distancing herself from her black friends. Among those questioned by the detectives are a black petty criminal (Harry Baird), Sapphire's white boyfriend (Paul Massie), and the latter's sister (Yvonne Mitchell). The eventual unmasking of the killer reveals a truly horrific racial motive. Absorbing, thought-provoking and featuring a uniformly excellent cast, the movie was a worthy winner of the 1960 BAFTA award for best British film. Watch out for Barbara Steele in a small role as a student.

Stanley Baker stars as Inspector Martineau, a detective with the Manchester City Police in **Hell Is a City** (1959). This tense Hammer production involves the escape from prison of vicious criminal Don Starling (U.S. star John Crawford in one of his most dynamic British film roles), who sets out to retrieve the hidden spoils from a jewel robbery for which he'd originally been arrested by Martineau. In the meantime, Starling organizes another robbery in which a bookmaker's (Donald Pleasence) female clerk is killed. Eventually, after breaking into a furniture store (where the gems are hidden) and callously shooting the proprietor's deaf-mute granddaughter, Starling is captured by Martineau following a spectacularly staged rooftop chase. Along the way, we're given glimpses into the detective's troubled home life with wife Julia (Maxine Audley), while the well-photographed city of Manchester provides an excellent backdrop to the tough action.

The very modest B movie **Crossroads to Crime** (1960) remains the only theatrical feature directed by Gerry Anderson, who would go on to achieve immortality as creator of classic television shows such as *Thunderbirds* and *Space 1999*. Unable to persuade his superior that a gang of truck hijackers are operating from a roadside café, conscientious young police constable Don Ross (Anthony Oliver) embarks on his own unofficial investigation and manages to infiltrate the gang. Just when he has the evidence needed to trap the criminals, his cover gets blown and he faces certain death. However, a surprise development involving one of the gang members sees that all ends well, bringing the film to a satisfying conclusion. Ferdy Mayne plays the suave gang boss, and also caught up in the intrigues is Miriam Karlin as the café's proprietress.

Offbeat (1960) is an above-average B movie with a sterling performance by William Sylvester as Steve Layton, a cynical MI5 agent who infiltrates a criminal organization to obtain inside information for Scotland Yard. However, he soon finds himself forming genuine friendships among the crooks and slowly becomes seduced by their lifestyle—not to mention by the charms of one of their number, Ruth (Mai Zetterling). Events see Layton plan to double-cross Scotland Yard and abscond with Ruth upon obtaining his share of the proceeds from the gang's upcoming heist, which he's been tasked with planning. When his cover gets blown by the gang's Tangier fence (Joseph Furst), Layton quick-wittedly takes action toward reassuring the crooks he had no intention of betraying them; but then, rather reluctantly, he reverts back to the right side of the law when the police unexpectedly show up to make their arrests. Anthony Dawson impresses as the criminal boss, who runs his outfit with a strict but friendly code of honor, and there's a well-staged diamond robbery sequence which adds a little action to the interesting and thought-provoking story.

The comedy thriller *A Matter of WHO* (1961) stars the inimitable Terry-Thomas as eccentric World Health Organization investigator Archibald Bannister or, as he amusingly refers to himself, a "germ detective." The film concerns Bannister's attempt to trace the source of a smallpox outbreak following the arrival in London of Cooper (Cyril Wheeler), an infected American who'd been prospecting for oil in the Middle Eastern province of South Wahbar. U.S. star Alex Nicol plays Cooper's tough business partner who helps Bannister in his investigation, in the process uncovering a swindle (involving a crooked millionaire [Guy Deghy]) relating to the oil venture. The scene-stealing Terry-Thomas effortlessly handles both the comedic and more serious aspects of his role, and the film, which involves an episode in Switzerland, also stars Sonja Ziemann as Cooper's provocative wife.

The rare B movie *Enter Inspector Duval* (1961) concerns a mysterious international jewel thief dubbed "Mr. March" (due to his first robbery having occurred in that month) whose modus operandi includes challengingly leaving a perfect set of his fingerprints at the crime scenes. Anton Diffring plays the titular investigator, a French Sûreté detective who has sworn to catch "Mr. March" and whose visit to London just happens to coincide with a murder there committed by the elusive thief during a break-in (depicted in the opening sequence). Scotland Yard's Inspector Wilson (Mark Singleton) enlists Duval's help in the subsequent investigation, while at the same time "Mr. March" attempts to find a stash of diamonds swindled from him by a double-crossing contact in connection with the aforementioned break-in. The eventual revelation of the villain's identity should come as no surprise to anyone who'd been suspicious not only about that ubiquitous player of bad guys, Diffring, being cast as the supposed hero, but also about the synchronistic presence of Duval and "Mr. March" in London.

"The most baffling whodunit ever filmed...!"

The engrossing and chilling police procedural *Jigsaw* (1961) is based on Hillary Waugh's 1959 novel *Sleep Long, My Love*, but with the setting switched from the U.S. state of Connecticut to the seaside resort of Brighton in England. The film details the painstaking investigation that ensues following the horrifying discovery of a woman's dismembered body (inside a trunk) in a remote house on the cliffs. Jack Warner is on superb form as a sarcastic but kindly senior detective, with co-star Ronald Lewis (here at the height of a career that would soon taper off into a handful of lesser film

Obscure U.S. retitling for the equally obscure B movie *Enter Inspector Duval* (1961).

and television roles) providing solid support as his handsome sidekick. The excellent supporting cast includes Michael Goodliffe as a vacuum cleaner salesman under suspicion, John Le Mesurier as the victim's grief-stricken father and John Barron as an urbane estate agent. Val Guest directs with a measured pace, and there are some great twists and turns along the way to an astonishingly effective climax involving one of the three last-mentioned characters.

Another procedural, this one based on a 1961 novel, *The Nose on My Face*, by actor-author Laurence Payne, **Girl in the Headlines** (1963) concerns an investigation by Chief Inspector Birkett and Sergeant Saunders (Ian Hendry and Ronald Fraser) into the murder of a 22-year-old model. Among those questioned are the victim's estranged mother (Margaret Johnston) and a supercilious actor (James Villiers). The discovery that the victim had been a drug addict leads to the detectives smashing a cocaine smuggling racket, while the murder remains unsolved. That is until Birkett overhears an utterance at the model's funeral which leads to the shocking revelation of the killer and their motive. The great cast also includes a young Jeremy Brett as an unwitting drug courier, and good use is made of locations along the River Thames during a stake-out.

Nigel Patrick gives a seemingly effortless performance as Scotland Yard's Inspector Johnnoe in **The Informers** (1963), which in its day was awarded the good old British "X" rating for brutality. When one of Johnnoe's informers is murdered by a violent gang of robbers headed by Leon Sale (a larger than life Frank Finlay), the latter attempts to get the dogged policeman off his back by framing him for a heist. Colin Blakely has a strong role as the murdered informer's brother, who organizes a mob of toughs in a fierce revolt against the gang. Sale manages to escape the ensuing carnage, but then gets his comeuppance in a final showdown with Johnnoe. Derren Nesbitt is excellent as Sale's chief thug who, in a memorably nasty scene,

Handsome Welsh actor Ronald Lewis at the pinnacle of his career in *Jigsaw* (1961).

murders the informer by running back and forth over him with a car. Ken Annakin directs at a decent pace, and effective use is made of various London locations.

"The most famous secret agent of all is back in a new adventure!"

The B movie **The Return of Mr. Moto** (1965) was the first big-screen outing for the wily eponymous Japanese investigator since Peter Lorre ended an eight-film run as the character with *Mr. Moto Takes a Vacation* (1939). Set in contemporary London, the plot has Moto (Henry Silva) working for Interpol on a case involving a murderous crime syndicate that's planning to take over every major oil lease in the Persian Gulf so as to dominate the world's oil concerns. Having survived an attempt by the criminals to drown him, Moto pretends, with the aid of a fake newspaper report, that he has in fact perished. He then continues his investigation in disguise, eventually going on to smash the syndicate. It's nice to see Hollywood's Silva depart from his typical bad guy persona, although unfortunately he's let down by a weak script that sees Moto relying more on luck than guile. Among those supplying the villainy are Marne Maitland and Martin Wyldeck, the latter as a brutal ex-Nazi (the syndicate's hitman) ruthlessly dispatched by Moto in one of the film's more exciting sequences. Made by Lippert Films for 20th Century–Fox, the studio behind the aforementioned Peter Lorre movies.

Commissaris Van Der Valk, a Dutch detective created by British crime writer Nicolas Freeling, first appeared on the big screen in **Amsterdam Affair** (1968), an adaptation of the author's 1962 debut novel *Love in Amsterdam*. Holland's capital provides some nice locations in a lethargic story that sees Van Der Valk (rather boringly played by German actor Wolfgang Kieling) investigate the murder of a former lover of thriller writer Martin Ray (William Marlowe), the latter placed under police supervision due to circumstantial evidence pointing to him as the culprit. In a foreshadowing of true events, Marlowe's future real-life wife, Catherine Schell, here plays his on-screen wife, with whose help the detective is able to trap the real killer—a suspect who comes to light late in the proceedings. The Dutch investigator would later be definitively portrayed by Barry Foster in the British TV series *Van Der Valk*.

"A man in a hurry ... about to be stopped dead in his tracks!"

Nobody Runs Forever (1968) was adapted from *The High Commissioner*, the first of many Jon Cleary novels featuring Australian detective Scobie Malone, and which is also the film's U.S. title. Scobie, played by the great Rod Taylor, is sent to London to arrest Australian High Commissioner Sir James Quentin (Christopher Plummer) on a charge of murdering his first wife, and ends up protecting the dignitary from assassination attempts in connection with his involvement in vital peace talks. Taylor is perfect as the outspoken, rough-and-tumble yet sensitive detective, while Lilli Palmer is beautifully cast as Quentin's devoted second wife, who harbors a dark secret about spouse number one. Also starring are Daliah Lavi as a sultry femme fatale behind plans to sabotage the peace talks, Derren Nesbitt as one of the assassins and the inimitable Clive Revill as Quentin's treacherous (as it turns out) butler. A tennis match at Wimbledon is the setting for one of the assassination attempts (by way of a gun concealed in a newsreel camera), and there's a tense climax involving a time bomb. The glossy proceedings are accompanied by a beautiful soundtrack courtesy of French composer Georges Delerue.

"A remote island village.... A team of intrepid scientists.... A terrifying secret..."

A spin-off from a popular BBC TV series of the same name, **Doomwatch** (1972) focuses on crime solving of the ecological kind, the title referring to a fictional British governmental department set up to combat worldwide pollution. One of the department's scientists, Dr. Del Shaw (Ian Bannen), travels to the remote Cornish island of Balfe (also fictional) to gather wildlife samples so as to study the effects of a recent oil spill in the region. The strange behavior and general air of hostility he encounters from the island's close-knit and superstitious community is eventually found to stem from their efforts to conceal—through both shame and fear (believing it has resulted from either generations of in-breeding or some kind of divine judgment)—an outbreak of a disfiguring disease accompanied by aggressive tendencies, which in one case have led to the murder of a young girl. Shaw himself is brutally attacked by one of the afflicted before learning (with help from his Doomwatch colleagues) that the disease is in fact acromegaly, with both this and the aggression caused by the ingestion of fish contaminated by a synthetic protein (similar to pituitary growth hormone) illegally dumped in a stretch of the surrounding waters. Shaw's attempts to convince the community that they need outside medical help proves no easy task due to fierce resistance over the disruptions this will inevitably bring to their insular way of life.

This "topical, thought-provoking mystery thriller," as described by *Leonard Maltin's Movie Guide*, has some great atmosphere in the build-up scenes on the island, plus a couple of effective shock sequences involving encounters with characters heavily disfigured by the acromegaly, the devastating physical symptoms of which had hardly been seen in movies since real-life sufferer Rondo Hatton made his final appearance as "The Creeper" in 1946's *The Brute Man*. John Paul, one of several cast members reprising their roles from the TV show, plays Doomwatch head Dr. Quist, and the bleak wintry locale brightens up considerably every time Judy Geeson appears as the island's pretty schoolmistress. In the U.S., the film went straight to television in 1975 via a 13-picture (mostly Spanish horror) Avco-Embassy syndication package known as "Nightmare Theatre." For the Canadian market, *Doomwatch* was exploitatively retitled *Island of the Ghouls* and mostly shown as part of a triple bill (dubbed "The Ghoul Show") along with *Grave of the Vampire* (1972) and *Garden of the Dead* (1972).

Another fictional remote island, this time called Summerisle and situated off the Scottish coast, features in the classic **The Wicker Man** (1973). Edward Woodward gives a standout performance as Sergeant Howie, an upright police officer from the Scottish mainland who travels to Summerisle by seaplane upon receiving an anonymous letter reporting the disappearance there of a young girl. The place turns out to be populated by pagans whose behavior—including bawdy sing-alongs, fertility rituals and an attempt to seduce him by the innkeeper's provocative daughter (Britt Ekland)—soon causes the devoutly Christian Howie much consternation, this not helped by the fact that he's also seemingly being led on a wild goose chase regarding his investigation into the missing girl. Having become convinced that the youngster has been hidden in preparation for her use as a human sacrifice to ensure the islanders a successful crop yield for the year ahead, Howie sets out to save her, only to discover that it's actually he who has all along been the sacrificial target, brought to the island under false pretenses to face a terrifying encounter with the giant and fearsome effigy of the film's title.

Working from an absorbing and highly literate screenplay by the great Anthony Shaffer, director Robin Hardy has crafted a masterful shocker that builds a steady sense of unease while working its way toward a shattering and brilliantly executed climax whose effect is hard to shake off. Christopher Lee, in what was reportedly one of his favorite roles, plays the island's ruler, Lord Summerisle, from whom we learn the interesting history of the place; and the actor also lends his fine baritone singing voice to a cleverly composed soundtrack made up mainly of folk songs that integrate perfectly with the proceedings. Originally released theatrically in a truncated 87-minute version, the film has since become available in several longer versions, the most complete of which is a 102-minute director's cut. Although improving the clarity of some aspects of the plot, these longer edits can seem somewhat padded, while the much-maligned 87-minute version is actually pretty tight and tells the story adequately. Unfortunately, none of the magic of this masterpiece would rub off on the Neil LaBute-directed 2006 remake, or for that matter on Hardy's later re-imagining of the story as *The Wicker Tree* (2011).

> "You've seen the Duke in action
> … now watch him lose his temper."

The great John Wayne took his unique brand of toughness across the Atlantic for **Brannigan** (1975), in which "Duke" gives one of his most enjoyable latter-day performances. In what is the perfect companion piece to his previous year's *McQ* (both films feature unorthodox cops in the vein of Clint Eastwood's *Dirty Harry*), the Hollywood

Duke hits London.

legend plays the eponymous lawman, a Chicago police lieutenant at one point humorously described as being "slightly smaller than the Statue of Liberty" and who, at least where villains are concerned, likes to make his entrance by first breaking down the door—and then saying "knock knock!" The fairly complex plot sees Brannigan travel to London to extradite gangster Ben Larkin (John Vernon in great form), wanted back in America for tax evasion and extortion, only to find that the man has been kidnapped while under the supervision of Scotland Yard. In fact, the kidnapping had been arranged by Larkin in cahoots with his crooked attorney, Mel Fields (Mel Ferrer), as part of their plan to double-cross Larkin's U.S. associates out of a large sum of money (namely the ransom fee) before then absconding to South America. However, having survived attempts on his life by a sinister assassin (Daniel Pilon) dispatched by Mel, Brannigan ultimately puts paid to the pair's scheme after tracking them to a riverside hideout.

The film makes good use of many London locations including Tower Bridge (where an exhilarating car chase comes to a spectacular conclusion), and features a comical pub brawl which plays like a homage to the typical saloon fights that featured in many classic Wayne westerns. Richard Attenborough, as a Scotland Yard chief, has a nice rapport with Wayne (their characters' contrasting attitudes toward law enforcement provide some humorous moments), and there's a brief role for Ralph Meeker as Brannigan's boss in a Chicago-set prologue.

At the time of *Brannigan*'s original UK release, *The Sweeney*, a new breed of British cop show, had already completed its first season on television. Gritty, hard-hitting and violent, the popular ground-breaking series follows the exploits of Scotland Yard's Flying Squad, an elite detective unit tasked with investigating armed robbery and other serious violent crime in London. ("Sweeney" derives from Sweeney Todd, which is cockney rhyming slang for Flying Squad.) Two spin-off movies were made, with both John Thaw and Dennis Waterman reprising their TV roles as hard-drinking detective Jack Regan and his second-in-command George Carter.

4. Focus on Crime Solvers

The first film, simply titled *Sweeney!* (1976), is a gripping suspenser in which Regan stumbles onto a high-level conspiracy involving ruthless and obnoxious American press agent McQueen (Barry Foster in a persuasive if somewhat mannered performance). Working for multinational oil companies, McQueen has set into motion a scheme (involving murder and blackmail) to influence a government energy minister's (Ian Bannen) vote on oil prices at an important conference. McQueen has at his disposal some sadistic assassins (one of them memorably played by Michael Coles) who gleefully and none too discreetly go about the business of eliminating opposition by way of machine gun, explosives or, in the case of Regan, kidnapping him and force-feeding him alcohol before sending him out in his car, resulting in a suspension for drunk driving. The film has a more far-reaching plot than any episode of the series ever had, but may disappoint fans with its ending in which the close relationship between Regan and Carter is shattered when the latter turns squarely against Regan for causing McQueen's death by unscrupulous methods. Events are punctuated with instances of graphic violence and nudity (the film was originally awarded the good old British "X" rating), and there's a standout action sequence in which Regan and a high-class call girl (Diane Keen) are chased by the assassins.

Regan and Carter were friends again in *Sweeney 2* (1978), which bears far more resemblance to the TV show (whose fourth and final season aired the same year) than its predecessor. This time around, the Flying Squad are out to trap a gang of ruthless and well-organized expatriate British criminals living with their families in rural Malta, although they periodically return to England to carry out bank heists so as to maintain their comfortable lifestyles. Their strict code of conduct dictates, among other things, that they always steal only the equivalent of $100,000 per robbery. Overlong by about twenty minutes (thanks mainly to unnecessary plot diversions such as what turns out to be a completely fruitless trip to Malta by Regan and Carter),

A 1976 spin-off movie from a hit TV series.

the film is nevertheless engaging thanks to an interesting scenario (devised and scripted by Troy Kennedy Martin, whose brother Ian created the TV show) and stylish direction. The relationship between the two lead stars was best summed up in *Films and Filming* (July 1978): "John Thaw and Dennis Waterman as Regan and Carter work together with the precision of a finely rehearsed acrobatic team."

Agatha Christie Sleuths

Miss Marple

The early to mid–1960s saw the release of four MGM comedy thrillers featuring author Agatha Christie's famous amateur sleuth, the elderly spinster Miss Jane Marple. The wonderful Margaret Rutherford secured the starring role and turned out to be a scene-stealing sensation, lending the character a more robust, vivacious and eccentric nature than Christie's less colorful creation. Although the author had misgivings about Rutherford's performance, to the cinema-going public the great character actress *was* Miss Marple in much the same way that Basil Rathbone *was* Sherlock Holmes. Other recurring characters throughout the four films are Detective Inspector Craddock (Australian actor Charles Tingwell), who is always a few steps behind Miss Marple in the investigations, and Mr. Stringer, Marple's devoted sidekick, played by Stringer Davis (Rutherford's husband in real life). A nice touch is having Miss Marple be an avid reader of mysteries—including ones written by Agatha Christie!

The first and best of the series, **Murder She Said** (1961), is based on Christie's 1957 novel *4.50 from Paddington* (better known in the U.S. as *What Mrs. McGillicuddy Saw!*) and marks the character's first-ever big-screen appearance. During a train journey, Miss Marple sees a woman strangled to death on another train passing by, although the attacker remains hidden from view. She duly reports the incident to the police, who prove dismissive and in any case are unable to do much due to lack of evidence and no sign of a body anywhere. Miss Marple therefore begins her own investigation, soon deducing that the killer must have thrown the body from the train before later taking it onto the grounds of an estate known as Ackenthorpe Hall (coincidentally called Rutherford Hall in the novel). In order to snoop around, Marple secures a job (as a maid) at the hall and it's not long before she discovers the body in an outbuilding. After much sleuthing and interactions with various members of the Ackenthorpe family, she sets a trap—using a vital piece of evidence in the form of a compact belonging to the dead woman—that forces the killer out into the open.

Great performances, a very devious and well-concealed killer (who doesn't stop at just one murder) and an interesting motive make for a superbly entertaining mystery thriller which, although mostly light-hearted, nevertheless manages to generate some genuinely suspenseful sequences, not the least of which is Miss Marple's eventual encounter with the murderer. Standing out among Rutherford's fellow cast members are James Robertson Justice as the cantankerous family patriarch, whose verbal exchanges with Miss Marple provide some humorous and deliciously acerbic dialogue, and Arthur Kennedy in a key role as the Ackenthorpes' doctor wishing to marry into the family. Joan Hickson, who would later play Miss Marple in a BBC TV series, has a small role as a domestic worker. Used throughout all four films with some variation, Ron Goodwin's catchy theme tune is a jaunty composition perfectly tailored to Rutherford's personality.

In **Murder at the Gallop** (1963), Miss Marple treats the death of wealthy recluse Mr. Enderby (Finlay Currie in the briefest of roles) as suspicious and, while investigating, finds Enderby's sister stabbed in the back with a hatpin. Continuing her sleuthing, she books into a hotel-cum-horse-riding establishment called The Gallop, owned by Enderby's nephew (Robert Morley), and where other members of the Enderby family—as well as the dead sister's companion (Flora Robson)—are present. Eventually, Miss Marple comes up with a clever plan to draw out the murderer, whose motive involved a valuable painting. Loosely based on the 1953 novel *After the Funeral* (actually featuring Hercule Poirot and *not* Marple and which is better known in the U.S. as *Funerals are Fatal*), the movie is just as entertaining if not quite as atmospheric as its predecessor. There's a great twist, and the sequence where the killer is revealed should send a shiver up the spine.

"Misdeeds are afoot afoot the footlights!"

Another Poirot novel, 1952's *Mrs. McGinty's Dead*, is the basis for **Murder Most Foul** (1964), in which Miss Marple is the only juror to vote "not guilty" in the trial of a man accused of killing a widow. Believing there's more to the case than meets the eye, she sets about investigating the crime herself and deduces that the victim was blackmailing an actor in a repertory theater company. In order to discover the identity of the actor, who she correctly believes is the real killer, Miss Marple inveigles herself into the company (the troupe's director is played delightfully by Ron Moody), whereupon two more murders occur before she cleverly traps the culprit. The *Motion Picture Herald* (September 2, 1964) observed that the screenplay's coupling of droll humor with suspense "should delight audiences who relish their mysteries served up in a light vein."

The series sadly came to an end with **Murder Ahoy** (1964), which is the only one of the four films not based on an Agatha Christie story, instead being an original screenplay. Miss Marple joins the board of trustees at a foundation (originally established by her grandfather) that rehabilitates young offenders by training them in seamanship aboard a vintage battleship named HMS *Battledore*. Marple soon boards the vessel herself, spe-

The inimitable Margaret Rutherford as Agatha Christie's Miss Marple in *Murder Most Foul* (1964).

cifically in connection with the murder—a heart attack induced by strychnine-laced snuff—of a fellow trustee who was about to reveal something important about activities on the ship. Only after two more murders does she uncover the culprit—one of the ship's officers who'd been embezzling the foundation and killed to cover this up. Lionel Jeffries provides great support as the quirky captain of the old battleship which, incidentally, mysteriously transforms into what looks like a modern cargo steamer for the onboard sequences.

Hercule Poirot

Following the success of their Marple films, MGM turned their attention to another famous Agatha Christie creation—the impeccably attired, fastidious and mustachioed Belgian detective Hercule Poirot. Based on the author's 1936 novel *The ABC Murders*, **The Alphabet Murders** (1965) suffers from the miscasting of Tony Randall as Poirot and was correctly described by the

Tony Randall (right) as Agatha Christie's Poirot, with Robert Morley as Hastings in *The Alphabet Murders* (1965).

Monthly Film Bulletin (July 1966) as a "depressingly unfunny comedy-thriller." The story, set in London and updated to contemporary times, sees the sleuth investigating a string of murders—by poisoned dart fired from a high-velocity air pistol—whose victims have initials following the alphabet, e.g., Albert Aachen, Betty Barnard and Carmichael Clarke. Also, it's no coincidence that each killing is marked by the presence near the crime scene of an "ABC" London street guide. The most obvious suspect is a crazed alphabet-obsessed young woman (Anita Ekberg), but she later drowns (or does she?). The mystery is finally solved after Poirot deduces that only one of the victims was in fact the real target, with the other murders—and all the alphabetic shenanigans—merely a distraction.

Unfortunately, the film's director, animation legend Frank Tashlin, could not resist the temptation to treat Poirot like a cartoon character, and in the few instances where this isn't the case, the sleuth comes across as merely a second-rate Inspector Clouseau. Robert Morley fares slightly better as Hastings (though completely different from the Dr. Watson-type Hastings in Christie's stories), a portly bumbling British Secret Service man assigned to protect the detective. The best thing about the film remains a brief scene in which Poirot comes face to face with Miss Marple, played in a delightful cameo by Margaret Rutherford.

It was nine years before Poirot returned to the big screen, and it was certainly worth the wait. Made for EMI Film Distributors, **Murder on the Orient Express** (1974) boasts a star-studded cast (headed by an almost unrecognizable Albert Finney as Poirot) and sumptuous period design (Tony Walton). Apart from the distinction of having had none other than Agatha Christie herself attend the original London premiere, the epic production also reportedly joined the U.S.-made *Witness for the Prosecution* (1957) on a lonely list of just two adaptations of Christie's work which the author actually liked. Faithfully based on the 1934 novel of the same name (also known in the U.S. as *Murder in the Calais Coach*), the film details the case of a millionaire (Richard Widmark) found dead from twelve stab wounds while traveling on the Istanbul-Calais *Orient Express* train, whose other passengers just happen to include Poirot. The victim, it emerges, was a gangster who had caused five deaths, all of them resulting from his role in an American kidnapping some years before. Poirot's methodical questioning of passengers and staff reveals twelve potential suspects with motives in connection with the kidnapping case and, for those unfamiliar with the story, it isn't giving too much away to say that the murder proves to be the work of more than one person.

Finney's Poirot was perfectly described by Penelope Houston in the *Monthly Film Bulletin* (December 1974) as "a succulent *tour de force* of disguise, including a voice that seems to borrow some distant intonations from the great Sidney [*sic*] Greenstreet and a body that appears to have been strapped into its suit." Richard Rodney Bennett's superb score, which earned the film one of several Oscar nominations, beautifully conveys the glamour and romance of the luxurious passenger train which, incidentally, spends most of the time stranded in a snowdrift in Yugoslavia.

Peter Ustinov became synonymous with Poirot for a decade, starting with **Death on the Nile** (1978), based on the 1937 novel of the same name and filmed on magnificent locations in Egypt. After her fiancé Simon (Simon MacCorkindale) breaks off their engagement in order to marry beautiful American heiress Linnet Ridgeway (Lois Chiles), Jacqueline De Bellefort (Mia Farrow) pursues and plagues the honeymooning couple on a paddle-steamer cruise along the Nile. Events lead to Linnet being shot dead, whereupon a vacationing Poirot, helped by his friend Colonel Race (David Niven), takes up the investigation. After questioning passengers on the vessel, all of whom—including a writer (Angela Lansbury) and a doctor (Jack Warden)—have motives, Poirot proves that Linnet's murder was actually part of a complex scheme by Jacqueline and Simon (who never really separated) to seize her fortune without bringing suspicion upon themselves. The film, which like *Murder on the Orient Express* was made for EMI and features just as star-studded a cast, boasts some superb photography by Jack Cardiff and a beautiful and perfectly suited soundtrack by the prolific Nino Rota. Ustinov would go on to play Poirot in two more theatrical features, namely EMI's *Evil Under the Sun* (1981) and Cannon Films' *Appointment with Death* (1988), as well as in the U.S. TV movies *Thirteen at Dinner* (1985), *Dead Man's Folly* (1985) and *Murder in Three Acts* (1986).

Private Eyes and Other Independent Sleuths

Paul Temple

Created by English author Francis Durbridge, Paul Temple made his debut in a 1938 BBC radio serial and soon became a regular fixture on the airwaves. A crime fiction writer and amateur detective, Paul is aided in his investigations by his journalist wife Louise, known as "Steve" after her pen name Steve Trent. His adventures also involve the character Sir Graham Forbes, a Scotland Yard commissioner and friend of the Temples. Over the years, Paul also featured in a newspaper comic strip, several novels and a TV series, but his only big-screen appearances to date have been in four B movies made between 1946 and 1952. In the first, *Send for Paul Temple* (1946), Anthony Hulme and Joy Shelton star as the couple, who meet for the first time during an adventure involving a murderous gang of jewel thieves responsible for the death of Steve's detective brother.

John Bentley took over as Paul for the remaining three films starting with *Calling Paul Temple* (1948). In this one, Dinah Sheridan plays Steve and the story concerns a baffling series of murders in which the name "Rex" is found written at each crime scene. Sheridan returned as Steve in **Paul Temple's Triumph** (1950), based on the 1939 radio serial *News of Paul Temple*. A ruthless organization, headed by the mysterious "Z," kidnaps a scientist (Andrew Leigh) in order to get hold of his new atomic invention. Paul and Steve follow a clue (part of a map which they find clutched in the hand of the scientist's daughter after she's murdered by one of the criminals) to the New Forest, where they eventually rescue the scientist and smash the organization. There's a snappy pace and some inventive moments (one of them involving a booby-trapped corpse set up to kill our hero), although the identity of "Z" turns out to be a major disappointment.

The final film, **Paul Temple Returns** (1952), is easily the most entertaining of the four. Based on the 1942 radio serial *Paul Temple Intervenes*, the red herring-strewn plot sees Paul and Steve (the latter this time played by the demure Patricia Dainton) investigate a series of murders carried out by a devious killer known as "The Marquis." The crimes are connected to the discovery of an ancient papyrus containing details of an antidote that can counter all narcotic drugs, which therefore makes it a threat to the existence of the world's drug cartels. In an effective early role, Christopher Lee plays Sir Felix Raybourne, a sinister explorer and discoverer of the papyrus who gets cleverly framed for the murders. Sir Felix's country mansion, complete with ancient Egyptian artifacts, a statue of the God of Twilight, plus several deadly snakes, provides plenty of atmosphere, and there's a well staged climax set at Bombay Wharf on London's East India Docks (this accounting for the film's U.S. retitling as *Bombay Waterfront*). The *Kinematograph Weekly* (September 4, 1952) aptly described star John Bentley as having "an engaging and disarming way with him as Temple."

"The Toff"

Upper-class sleuth Richard Rollison, alias "The Toff," was created by prolific author John Creasey in his 1938 novel *Introducing the Toff*, the first of many to feature the character. Despite his aristocratic disposition, Rollison is equally at home in London's rough East End as he is in high society. The sleuth's only big-screen outings to date have been two 1951 B movies starring John Bentley in the title role. In both films, Rollison is assisted by his trusted valet, Jolly (Roddy Hughes), and an East End contact named Bert Ebbutt (a great part for Wally Patch), while enjoying a cordial relationship with Scotland Yard's Inspector Grice (Valentine Dyall); these three roles were all based on characters from The Toff's literary exploits.

In the first adventure, **Salute the Toff** (1951), Rollison is enlisted by Fay Gretton (Carol Marsh) in connection with the disappearance of her employer, Jimmy Draycott (Tony Britton in his first credited film role). Draycott has in fact gone into hiding after learning about a massive financial swindle, whose perpetrators want to eliminate him before he can expose them. During his efforts to locate and protect Draycott, Rollison has to contend with a variety of villains, including a sneaky knife-throwing assassin (Michael Golden) and a duplicitous crime reporter (Canadian actor Arthur Hill, future star of U.S. TV's *Owen Marshall, Counselor at Law*). The film was shown only on television in the U.S., originally under the British title and later also as *Brighthaven Express*.

In **Hammer the Toff** (1951), Rollison gets caught up in an adventure involving criminal mastermind Kennedy's (Lockwood West) attempts to steal a secret metal alloy formula from its inventor, Dr. Lancaster (Ian Fleming). Leaving a trail of murder and mayhem behind him, including the assassination of Dr. Lancaster using a briefcase fitted with a poison-filled hypodermic needle, Kennedy cleverly lays evidence so that the blame for his crimes will fall on a mysterious and benevolent Robin Hood–style crook known as "The Hammer." The inventor's niece (Patricia Dainton), who is unwittingly in possession of the formula, gets menaced—and later kidnapped—by Kennedy before the latter finally gets his comeuppance thanks to the joint efforts of Rollison and "The Hammer."

Tom "Duke" Martin

The suave Tom Conway stars as Tom "Duke" Martin in two 1955 B movies produced for RKO by Cipa Productions (Robert S. Baker and Monty Berman). A classy international detective (or as RKO's publicity dubbed him, a "Special Investigator"), Duke, not dissimilar in character to The Falcon (an earlier RKO Conway role) with a hint of The Saint thrown in, has a keen eye for the ladies as well as a nice line in sarcasm when dealing with Scotland Yard. Both films feature some often inane comic relief courtesy of Duke's trusty and somewhat dim-witted sidekick Barney, played by Michael Balfour. RKO's British marketing campaign for the second film included link-ups with then well-known clothing outlets such as Regis Shirt Company and Finesse Ties, whose customers had the opportunity to buy special "Duke Martin" products endorsed/sponsored by Conway.

The first adventure, *Barbados Quest* (1955), begins in New York, where wealthy philatelist J.D. Everleigh (Launce Maraschal)

Tom Conway (left) is special investigator Tom "Duke" Martin, pictured with sidekick Barney (Michael Balfour) in *Barbados Quest* (1955).

Trade ad for the first "Duke" Martin thriller.

hires Duke to investigate his purchase in England of a rare stamp—the Barbados Overprint—which he suspects may be a counterfeit. Duke wastes no time taking a trip over the Atlantic to get on the trail of the man, Geoffrey Blake (Brian Worth), who sold Everleigh the stamp. It turns out that Blake is the ruthless head of a forgery racket and has been passing off fake Barbados Overprints in a scam involving an original example owned by his titled aunt (Grace Arnold). Delphi Lawrence, who'd appeared with Conway in the 1953 Hammer thriller *Blood Orange*, plays a double-dealing secretary involved in the criminal activities but who ultimately helps Duke when it really counts. *Variety* (May 23, 1956) was mostly unimpressed, saying, "none of the cast can do much with the stereotype characters."

In the follow-up, ***Breakaway*** (1955), Johnny (Brian Worth from the previous film) flies from Berlin to England with some smuggled microfilm (containing a dying scientist's secret formula for combating metal fatigue) meant for his brother Michael (John Horsley), who runs a research laboratory. Shortly after, Webb (Bruce Seton), a racketeer, unsuccessfully attempts to steal the microfilm and in the process kidnaps Johnny's girlfriend (Paddy Webster). Michael, it transpires, hired Webb to secure the formula on his behalf after finding out that Johnny intended to double-cross him by selling it to a metals company. It's not long before Duke, who was on the same flight as Johnny, becomes involved in the affair, in which Webb continues to seek the formula, only now for his own nefarious purposes. This often hard-to-follow film gives prominent billing to Honor Blackman, even though her role (as the kidnapped woman's sister) ends up being of little consequence. In the U.S., *Barbados Quest*, under the title *Murder on Approval*, had quite substantial theatrical distribution, playing as support to *The Eddy Duchin Story* (1956) and Hitchcock's *The Trouble with Harry* (1954) among many others; *Breakaway* on the other hand, ended up going straight to television.

Sherlock Holmes

Undoubtedly the world's most famous fictional crime solver is Sir Arthur Conan Doyle's Sherlock Holmes, an independent Victorian-era consulting detective with ex-

Trade ad for the second and final "Duke" Martin adventure.

traordinary powers of deduction. Holmes, also a master of disguise, famously resides at 221B Baker Street and is assisted by his good friend Dr. Watson.

In the period covered by this book, three British films featuring the character could be considered thrillers with the first, ***The Hound of the Baskervilles*** (1958), being the only one based on a Doyle story. Made by Hammer Film Productions in the distinctive gothic style of their then recent hits *The Curse of Frankenstein* (1957) and *Dracula* (1958), the movie begins with a superbly executed eight-minute prologue showing the genesis of the Baskerville curse which involves the violent death—by a savage and ghostly "Hound from Hell"—of the evil Sir Hugo Baskerville (David Oxley) near the family estate on the Devonshire moors. A century or so later, at the same location, a descendant of Sir Hugo dies from heart failure, with clues suggesting he may in fact have died of fright upon seeing the legendary hound. Sherlock Holmes (Peter Cushing), aided by Dr. Watson (Andre Morell), becomes involved in saving the current Baskerville heir, Sir Henry (Christopher Lee), from a possible similar fate; in doing so he uncovers a murderous plot—which involves bringing the "Hound from Hell" legend back to life (using an all-too-real ferocious hound)—by illegitimate descendants of Sir Hugo to take control of the Baskerville estate.

A perfectly cast Cushing invests his urbane and spirited Holmes with just the right amount of priggish arrogance, while Morell as Watson remains dignified and wisely avoids (except on one occasion where he incautiously steps into a quagmire) the bungling antics of Nigel Bruce from the 1939–1946 Basil Rathbone Holmes movie series. That said, those who enjoyed Bruce's Watson will be pleased to know that the film features a similarly bungling character in the shape of a bishop-cum-entomologist played by the inimitable Miles Malleson. Terence Fisher directs at a cracking pace, and the superb production design is beautifully captured in glorious Technicolor by cinematographer Jack Asher. Cushing would later again play Holmes in the 1960s BBC TV series *Sherlock Holmes* (which included a two-part "Hound of the Baskervilles" episode) and also in the 1984 TV movie *The Masks of Death*.

"Sherlock Holmes meets Jack the Ripper!"

Sherlock Holmes met Jack the Ripper for the first time in ***A Study in Terror*** (1965), whose title combines the great detective's 1887 debut story *A Study in Scarlet* with the "terror" visited upon London just one year later by the notorious real-life serial killer. Within the first 20 minutes, three prostitutes are slain in the capital's poverty-stricken Whitechapel district, and Holmes (distinguished theatrical actor and *The X-Files'* "Well-Manicured Man" John Neville) is drawn into the investigation following receipt of an anonymous package containing a set of surgical instruments missing one item—a large scalpel which may or may not be the murder weapon. Clues eventually lead to the identification of the package's sender, a reclusive and facially disfigured former prostitute (Adrienne Corri) whose one-time marriage to a member of the aristocracy is the key to solving the case.

The aquiline-nosed Neville exudes intelligence and looks just right as Holmes, whose mental agility is matched by impressive physical abilities as evidenced in three main action scenes; these, together with some occasional campy moments, led to a bizarre U.S. publicity campaign (including the tagline "Here comes the original caped crusader!") designed to cash in on the then popular *Batman* TV series. The fog-shrouded Whitechapel streets are atmospherically depicted, as is The Angel & Crown, a bawdy pub central to the story and the setting for a fiery showdown between Holmes and the Ripper. The doomed prostitutes, although named after the real-life Ripper victims, are mostly portrayed as stereotypes and, in the case of bubbly Barbara Windsor's Annie Chapman, in comically burlesque fashion. In fact, apart from her grisly demise, Windsor's sequence, in which she offers sex to a character named Chunky, gives one an idea of what it may have been like had the British *Carry On* comedy team (of which Windsor was a regular) tackled the Ripper subject. (For the record, said team's 1964 movie *Carry On Jack* has nothing whatsoever to do with the serial killer.)

The mystery is quite nicely worked

Peter Cushing was a quintessential Sherlock Holmes in Hammer's *The Hound of the Baskervilles* (1958).

out, with many red herrings and a well-concealed killer, and Holmes' final revelation regarding his earlier detection of a vital clue will have you hitting the rewind button. The great cast also features Donald Houston as Watson (ever so slightly leaning toward the Nigel Bruce interpretation from the Basil Rathbone films), Robert Morley as Holmes' brother Mycroft, Anthony Quayle as an East End police surgeon-cum-soup kitchen operator, and last but not least, Frank Finlay, whose Inspector Lestrade looks remarkably similar to—though he's not quite as silly as—the character as played by Dennis Hoey in the aforementioned Rathbone series.

Sherlock Holmes and Jack the Ripper meet again in **Murder by Decree** (1978), a lavishly produced if rather sluggishly enacted Anglo-Canadian production that lacks the overall entertainment value of the previous film. As played by Christopher Plummer, Holmes is much too sympathetic and emotional, while not nearly as incisive as he should be. He also lacks vigilance; indeed, at one point, his inexcusable failure to sense danger results in the abduction and ultimate slaying of a victim. Watson fares somewhat better and is played knowingly and idiosyncratically by James Mason, probably the most distinguished actor to have ever been cast in the role. The plot, in which the Ripper murders are carried out by two killers in cahoots (this is given away quite early on), involves a cover-up at the highest levels of government (not to mention Freemasonry) due to the slayings having a connection with a presumptive heir to the British throne. Anthony Quayle and Frank Finlay return from *A Study in Terror* (the latter reprising his role as Inspector Lestrade), and the star-studded cast also includes Genevieve Bujold, as an asylum inmate crucial to unlocking the mystery, and David Hemmings as a radical police inspector manipulating aspects of the case for his own secret anti-establishment agenda.

Director Bob Clark, cinematographer Reginald H. Morris and editor Stan Cole had all worked on the classic Canadian slasher film *Black Christmas* (1974), whose sustained atmosphere of foreboding is sadly missing here, although that's not to say there aren't one or two moments that elicit a palpable sense of dread. The film is based on Elwyn Jones and John Lloyd's 1975 book *The Ripper File*, itself an adaptation of the same authors' six-part BBC TV docudrama *Jack the Ripper* (1973) in which it was not Holmes and Watson looking into the Ripper case, but two other fictional characters, namely detectives Barlow and Watt from the hit BBC shows *Z Cars* and *Softly, Softly*. Lastly, it's worth noting that Plummer had previously played Holmes in the 30-minute Anglo-Canadian telefilm *Silver Blaze* (1976), which originally formed part of a series called *Classics Dark and Dangerous*.

Bulldog Drummond, The Saint, Father Brown, Mike Hammer and Others

Created by author H.C. "Sapper" McNeile, Hugh "Bulldog" Drummond is a patriotic British army veteran, adventurer and crime fighter who'd been played on the big screen by a variety of actors (including Ray Milland, Ronald Colman and Tom Conway) before Walter Pidgeon landed the role in **Calling Bulldog Drummond** (1951). We first see Drummond at his country retreat, where he's busy breeding prize pigs after having retired from a life of danger and excitement. It's not long before he's visited by Scotland Yard's Inspector McIver (Charles Victor) and persuaded to help out in a case concerning a series of large-scale robberies carried out with military precision. Drummond gets busy creating a fake identity as a criminal—"Joe Crandall"—so as to infiltrate the ruthless gang behind the thefts, and he's helped no end by an attractive police sergeant (Margaret Leighton) who poses as Crandall's moll. However, they run into trouble after Drummond's cover gets blown thanks to an unwitting action on the part of his good friend and sidekick, Algy Longworth (David Tomlinson).

Pidgeon makes for a suitably robust if slightly dull Drummond, while Leighton is anything but dull, giving a positively sparkling (especially when she's in "moll" mode) performance that's one of the film's biggest draws. Robert Beatty plays a tough and charismatic gang member, who toward the end attempts to murder his cohorts (in a nasty plan involving the use of carbon monoxide) as a way of cutting them out of a £½ million haul, and Bernard Lee has a key role as a respected acquaintance of Drummond's to whom there's more than meets the eye. (Incidentally, Beatty would himself play Drummond in a 1956 British-made unsold TV pilot, *Bulldog Drummond and the Ludlow Affair*, which aired as an episode of *Douglas Fairbanks Jr. Presents*, aka *The Rheingold Theatre*.) Following a 15-year big-screen hiatus, Drummond returned in *Deadlier Than the Male* (1966), which saw the character reinvented as a James Bond–like insurance agent.

In the rare B movie **The Armchair**

Detective (1951), actor, writer and man of many other talents Ernest Dudley plays himself as host of the titular radio crime show (the film is based on Dudley's popular 1940s BBC radio show *For the Armchair Detective*). As the result of hearing one of his broadcasts, Jane (Iris Russell) calls upon Dudley to help her sister Penny (Sally Newton, daughter of Robert), a pretty singer at the Gardenia Club being harassed and threatened with blackmail by the venue's obnoxious boss Nicco (Hartley Power). Dudley soon finds himself involved in a murder investigation after Nicco is found shot dead at the club. Penny confesses to the crime, while Scotland Yard believes the man committed suicide. However, nothing is what it seems, and the truth is finally revealed when Dudley arranges a reconstruction of the crime with all concerned, including Penny's fiancé (David Oxley) and Nicco's estranged wife (Anna Korda). The *Monthly Film Bulletin* (February 1952) noted the film as being "obviously cheaply made and poorly directed."

> "Scotland Yard calls it suicide! ...
> Smith knows it's murder!"

Whispering Smith, a fictional American railroad detective, was originated in Frank H. Spearman's 1906 novel, *Whispering Smith*, the most well-known film adaptation of which is a 1948 Alan Ladd western of the same name. In the Hammer Films B movie **Whispering Smith Hits London** (1951), the character, played by the charming Richard Carlson, is reimagined as a celebrity private eye living in contemporary times. The story sees Smith arrive in London for a vacation, only to end up on a case concerning the death (supposedly a suicide but possibly murder) of a New York publisher's daughter. Before long, he uncovers a particularly nasty blackmail syndicate—involving the enigmatic Louise (Greta Gynt)—responsible for the girl's death. The enchanting Rona Anderson plays the publisher's secretary (she's the catalyst for Smith's involvement in the case) who inevitably pairs off with the lucky detective, and there's a brilliant twist regarding the Louise character. A planned sequel by Hammer never materialized, but the heroic investigator did re-emerge in a 1961 U.S. TV series, *Whispering Smith*, starring Audie Murphy.

In **Venetian Bird** (1952), private detective Edward Mercer (Richard Todd) travels to the Italian city of Venice to locate one Renzo Uccello (John Gregson) in connection with an American who wishes to reward the man for an act of bravery during World War II. Several attempts are made to prevent Mercer locating Uccello, who we learn is masquerading under a different identity. We also learn that he has been hired to—and subsequently does—assassinate a popular political figure in a plot arranged by the sinister Count Boria (Walter Rilla). Mercer ends up being framed for the assassination but escapes from police custody and sets out to clear himself, with events leading to an exhilarating climax in which he chases Uccello across the rooftops of the Piazza San Marco. The rather talky proceedings are uplifted by the beautifully shot Venice locations.

Hugo Bishop, a brilliant pipe-smoking independent sleuth, was created by British author Elleston Trevor in a series of 1950s chess-themed mystery novels, one of which, *Queen in Danger*, is the source of the B movie **Mantrap** (1952). The film depicts Bishop (Paul Henreid) as a lawyer who turns detective in order to help an escaped prisoner, Mervyn Speight (Kieron Moore), track down the real culprit behind a murder (committed in a bombed-out ruin near London's St. Paul's Cathedral) for which Speight has been wrongfully convicted. Lois Maxwell plays Speight's wife, who mistakenly believes that her husband has escaped in order to take revenge on her for becoming involved with another man (Bill Travers), while Kay Kendall steals every scene she's in as Bishop's secretary-girlfriend in a film the *Monthly Film Bulletin* (April 1953) said "has its moments of tension," but "does not succeed because it is too contrived."

Park Plaza 605 (1953) stars Tom Conway as the marvelously named private detective Norman Conquest. During a game of golf, Conquest literally scores a birdie when he knocks a carrier pigeon out of the sky. A message attached to the bird—requesting that the recipient make contact at eight o'clock that evening in room 605 at London's Park Plaza Hotel—piques Conquest's interest, and his decision to keep the appointment leads to an adventure in which he becomes embroiled in murder, intrigue and doublecross involving a seductive blonde diamond smuggler (Eva Bartok) and a wanted Nazi war criminal (Robert Adair). The debonair Conway is a little too smug for his own good in this B-movie adaptation of *Dare-Devil Conquest*, one of many Berkeley Gray novels featuring the "Norman Conquest" character. Joy Shelton plays Conquest's assistant/girlfriend, and Sidney James has fun as an exasperated—because he's always one step behind our hero—Scotland Yard detective. About two months prior to its British theatrical release (December 1953), the film had already been doing the rounds (as *Norman Conquest*) in U.S. theaters as support to fare such as *The Big Heat* (1953) and an Irwin Allen documentary called *The Sea Around Us* (1953).

"The Saint moves in! Blondes … bullets and blackmail … can't stop him!"

The Saint's Return (1953) not only saw a return to the big screen of author Leslie Charteris' debonair independent crime fighter Simon Templar (alias "The Saint") following a hiatus of over a decade, but also marked the return to the role of actor Louis Hayward, who'd played Templar in the first-ever "Saint" film, *The Saint in New York*, in 1938. The story puts the sleuth on the trail of "The Chief," the mysterious boss of a gang of London racketeers who caused the death of an old friend. Known as "The River Mob" due to their running of an illegal gambling club aboard a barge on the River Thames, the racketeers blackmail indebted clients—including Lady Carol Denbeigh (Naomi Chance)—into working for them to pay off their IOUs. Hayward's appropriately smooth performance is the best thing about this otherwise formulaic Hammer B movie, which also stars Charles Victor as Scotland Yard's Inspector Teal.

Slim Callaghan, a hard-boiled, down-at-heel and wryly witty private investigator, was created by Peter Cheyney in his 1938 novel (the first of several to feature the character) *The Urgent Hangman*, which is the basis for **Meet Mr. Callaghan** (1953). Derrick De Marney, who also co-produced, proves to be the quintessential Slim (he'd already made a success of the role on stage) in this convoluted but never boring story in which the gumshoe investigates the murder of wealthy financier August Meraulton (Robert Adair). Potential suspects are August's stepdaughter Cynthis (Harriette Johns) and four nephews, one of them Cynthis' fiancé (Peter Neil), with the motive appearing to involve a recently drawn-up will that names Cynthis as sole beneficiary. Slim proves to be a smart, tough cookie, not to mention a rude and arrogant one at times; he's also not averse to employing unscrupulous tactics (such as blackmail, accepting bribes and planting incriminating evidence) in his dealings with the suspects, one of whom he cleverly baits into admitting their guilt in a neat finale. Eric Spear's hugely popular "Meet Mister Callaghan" title tune had been published in 1952, with a recording that year by guitar legend Les Paul reaching #5 in the U.S. pop charts; the film's version of the catchy ditty is in the form of a full orchestral arrangement.

Today's Cinema (March 15, 1954) called the B movie **Double Exposure** (1954) a "businesslike blend of mystery, action and comedy." Pete Fleming (John Bentley), a debonair private eye with Beaumont's Detective Agency, becomes involved in helping a freelance photographer (Rona Anderson); the latter is in danger due to having unwittingly captured—in one of a series of snapshots she took outside an apartment block—evidence that could lead to a vicious bookmaker (Eric Berry) being identified as the culprit in a woman's murder, which up until now has been deemed a suicide. Integral to the plot is the dead woman's husband (Alexander Gauge), an advertising magnate with heavy gambling debts whose use of his wife's jewelry to pay off the bookmaker created a situation that led to the murder. Bentley is his usual likeable self as the quick-witted hero, whose badinage with the agency's boss (Garry Marsh) provides most of the humor, while the unassuming Anderson is especially fetching as the endangered heroine.

Father Brown (1954), rather unimaginatively titled *The Detective* in the U.S., is a mildly amusing comedy thriller based on G.K. Chesterton's stories featuring the titular Roman Catholic priest, an amateur sleuth dedicated to the redemption of criminals. Alec Guinness, in one of his several collaborations with director Robert Hamer (1949's *Kind Hearts and Coronets* being the highlight), plays the quirky clergyman, who determines to track down and save the soul of notorious thief and master of disguise Flambeau (Peter Finch) after the villain cleverly steals from him the priceless Cross of St. Augustine en route to a Eucharistic Congress. The whimsical story, which goes back and forth between England and France—Flambeau keeps a collection of his ill-gotten gains in a Burgundy château—also stars husky-voiced Joan Greenwood as a wealthy parishioner, whose valuable chess set Father Brown uses to bait the thief, and Bernard Lee as a Scotland Yard detective. Later appearances of the ecclesiastical sleuth include the U.S. TV movie *Sanctuary of Fear* (1979), in which Bernard Hughes plays a modern Manhattan-based version of the character, while Chesterton's stories were the inspiration for American author Ralph McInerny's "Father Dowling" novels, which in turn led to television's *Father Dowling Mysteries*.

> "Wayne Morris, private investigator—blasts the lid off London's gangster bosses!"

Jimmy Baxter (Wayne Morris), a private eye employed at a detective agency known as Anglo American Investigations, is on the trail of **The Gelignite Gang** (1955), a murderous group of safe-breakers whose elusive leader is known only as "Mr. G." Jimmy's secretary-girlfriend (Sandra Dorne) does some sleuthing of her own and stumbles on a vital clue, only to end up captured by Mr. G whose identity, when it's finally revealed, comes as quite a surprise. U.S. star Morris is his usual tough

Alec Guinness as G.K. Chesterton's priest-detective in *Father Brown* (1954).

but friendly self in this well-paced B movie that also prominently features Patrick Holt as the detective agency's boss. Among the remaining cast members are Eric Pohlmann as a nightclub owner and James Kenney as a young jeweler's assistant involved in a subplot in which he unwisely attempts to blackmail Mr. G's second-in-command (Arthur Young) in connection with the gang's theft of a diamond tiara. The film is set in London but was filmed in and around Brighton.

The B movie *Passport to Treason* (1956) is based on Manning O'Brine's 1955 novel of the same name, one of seven to feature the crime-fighting journalist character Mike O'Kelly. For whatever reason, the filmmakers decided to change O'Kelly's profession to that of a private detective. The plot sees our hero (played by rugged Canadian-born Hollywood star Rod Cameron) tangling with a neo-fascist group that caused the death of a fellow gumshoe and which operates secretly from within a legitimate organization known as the International League for World Peace. It's always nice to see Lois Maxwell in the days when she had more to do than exchange, as Miss Moneypenny, flirtatious remarks with James Bond, and here she plays an undercover MI5 agent posing as a secretary at the organization. Plenty of fisticuffs ensue, and our hero suffers being captured and drugged before escaping for a final showdown with the chief criminals at a dockside wharf in London's East End. Clifford Evans and Douglas Wilmer appear to good effect as a pair of not-so-peace-loving (as it turns out) officials at the peace league.

Described unflatteringly by the *Kinematograph Weekly* (August 20, 1959) as "a damp squib," the seldom-seen B movie *Murder at Site Three* (1958) is the last film to date to feature Sexton Blake, a popular fictional investigator dating back to 1893. Set in contemporary times, the story places Blake (Geoffrey Toone) and his assistant Tinker (Richard Burrell) in an adventure concerning "The Syndicate," a ruthless organization (traffickers in official secrets) that has managed to infiltrate a British ICBM site known as "Site Three." Blake spends the first part of the film in Paris, where international security officers gather at NATO headquarters for an emergency meeting about the syndicate; and in a nightclub called Le Petit Corniche, one of the syndicate's agents (a female cabaret artiste) is arrested after drugging an old friend of Blake's, U.S. Security man Joe Hennessey (Gordon Sterne), with what is found to be a truth serum. Later, back in England, Blake uses the same truth serum formula in a clever plan to root out the spies (John Warwick and Reed De Rouen) at "Site Three." Barbara Shelley and Jill Melford also star, the latter as Blake's secretary.

One of the most quintessentially British of British comic actors, Terry-Thomas, is on fine form in the side-splitting *Kill or Cure* (1962). The legendary funnyman plays a bungling private eye, J. Barker-Rynde, investigating the murder (by ricin-laced carrot juice) of a wealthy widow at a health clinic. During his adventure, he is aided by one of the clinic's physical training instructors (Eric Sykes) and is almost murdered himself upon finally coming face-to-face with the killer, who all along had managed to completely avoid suspicion by way of an ingenious ruse. Made by the same team behind the Margaret Rutherford Miss Marple series, the film is a superb mix of slapstick and mystery with some effective moments such as when the hand of a second murder victim (the clinic's director played by Dennis Price) emerges from a crack in the frozen surface of a swimming pool. Terry-Thomas and Sykes make a hilarious double act, and Lionel Jeffries also has some amusing moments as a Scotland Yard detective suffering one injury after another as a result of the blundering duo's antics. The main female role, namely the dead widow's secretary, is played by the attractive Moira Redmond.

The most interesting thing about the U.S.-set *The Girl Hunters* (1963) is the fact that its main protagonist, a certain two-fisted, take-no-prisoners private eye by the

Terry-Thomas (left) and Eric Sykes investigate murder at a health clinic in the comedy thriller *Kill or Cure* (1962).

name of Mike Hammer, is played by his actual creator, namely pulp novelist Mickey Spillane. While maybe not possessing the acting ability to pull off all aspects of the character, Spillane certainly has no shortcomings when it comes to the rough stuff. Said rough stuff includes a violent and tremendously staged fight with a villain known as "The Dragon" (bit-part actor and stuntman Larry Taylor's best-ever role), a battle that culminates in Hammer living up to his name by literally nailing his opponent's hand to the floor. The complex plot involves a U.S. senator's murder under orders from a gang of communist spies, who are also behind the long-ago vanishing of Hammer's beloved secretary-companion, Velda. (The detective's despair over Velda's disappearance resulted in a prolonged state of drunkenness to which he is still surrendered at film's start, although he soon sobers up to get cracking on the case.) Shirley Eaton plays the murdered senator's attractive widow, who turns out to be heavily implicated in her husband's death, and Lloyd Nolan has a small role as an FBI boss. Spillane's source novel of the same name had been published just a year earlier.

"A cop on the make ... not on the take!"

Clegg (1969), first name Harry (Gilbert Wynne), is an unscrupulous and broke private eye who, by his own admission, is "a cold-blooded killer, a lecher, a liar and a thief." When four wealthy men receive notes threatening their lives, Clegg provides his services to protect them but fails miserably at every turn as they are bumped off one by one. (There's a running gag whereby the detective keeps losing out financially due to the men not living long enough to pay their fees.) The murders turn out to be a revenge plan engineered by fashion-house owner Francis

Wildman (Gary Hope), whose father had been sent to prison (where he subsequently died) after being framed for embezzlement by the four men. A cheap and strictly tongue-in-cheek production by cult director Lindsay Shonteff, the shabby and frequently violent proceedings also feature Gilly Grant as a blonde prostitute-cum-assassin, this no doubt having had more than a little to do with one of the film's U.S. retitlings as *Harry and the Hookers*. The catchy theme music was composed by the talented Paul Ferris, best known for his beautiful soundtrack to the previous year's *Witchfinder General*.

"Contrived and unconvincing capers for uncritical adolescents and others of immature tastes" was how *Today's Cinema* (March 26, 1971) referred to the shenanigans in low-budget exploitation director Arnold Louis Miller's little-seen ***A Touch of the Other*** (1970). A young man, Delger (Kenneth Cope, probably best remembered as ghost Marty Hopkirk from the cult 1960s British TV show *Randall and Hopkirk—Deceased* [shown in the U.S. as *My Partner the Ghost*]), takes over an office in London's Soho district and sets up as a private investigator. Before long, he becomes the victim of an attempted frame-up for the murder of an acquaintance who occupied the premises before him. During his adventure, in which he has to contend with thugs in the employ of the ruthless protection racketeer (Martin Wyldeck) behind the murder, Delger is helped (in more ways than one) by two prostitute neighbors, whose presence in the film led to its retitling in the U.S. as both *The Happy Hookers* and *The House of Hookers*.

The superlative ***Gumshoe*** (1971) is a clever homage to the writings of Dashiell Hammett and Raymond Chandler, with some superbly witty dialogue and a faultless lead performance by Albert Finney. Liverpool bingo caller and aspiring comedian Eddie Ginley (Finney) fantasizes about being a Humphrey Bogart–style private detective and, without really expecting any results, runs a newspaper ad ("Ginley's The Name, Gumshoe's The Game") offering his services as such. A reply to the ad summons him to a hotel room where he collects—from a mysterious obese gentleman (à la Sydney Greenstreet)—a package containing a gun, £1,000 and a photograph of a girl. This proves to be

A superb 1971 starring role for Albert Finney.

just the start of a dangerous adventure that sees the would-be sleuth up to his neck in murder, gunrunning and a kidnap attempt. American actress Janice Rule plays the requisite femme fatale, and the well-woven plot has a neat twist involving Ginley's brother (Frank Finlay) and the latter's wife (Billie Whitelaw).

Harriet Zapper

Director Lindsay Shonteff's amateurish *Big Zapper* (1973) is a largely unfunny spoof starring Linda Marlowe as the sexy, stylish and indestructible Harriet Zapper, a London-based private eye equally adept in unarmed combat as she is with her trusty pair of .357 Magnums. The wafer-thin plot sees Zapper hired by a millionaire (Jack May) to find his missing daughter, who it turns out was the young lady we saw murdered by sadistic crime boss Kono (Shonteff regular Gary Hope) in the film's opening. Zapper is soon on Kono's trail and spends almost the entire time fending off the villain's seemingly never-ending supply of henchmen/assassins/thugs, including three specially imported Japanese samurai warriors.

The zany, sleazy and campy nonsense is laced with nudity, comic-book violence and crude humor, with sexually suggestive character names such as Rock Hard (Zapper's sex-crazed boyfriend-assistant played by Richard Monette) and Randy Horn. Marlowe looks great in her white skirt-suit (harmonizing elegantly with her white Mercedes 190SL sports car), and the eye-popping sight of her manning—legs akimbo—a tripod-mounted Vickers machine gun during the climax has no doubt contributed to the film's minor cult following. Apart from as *Big Zapper*, the movie was originally also submitted to the British Board of Film Censors under the title *The Sex Life of a Female Private Eye*, but doesn't appear to have ever been released as such.

A follow-up, *The Swordsman* (1974), sees Zapper (once again played by Marlowe) pitted against the devious Reynaud Duval (Alan Lake), who runs a fencing school at the country estate of his wealthy father, Christian (Noel Johnson). In an elaborate scheme to grab the family fortune for himself, Reynaud, who we later learn was adopted, murders Christian after forcing him to sign a false will in his sole favor. He then tells younger brother Karel (Jason Kemp), the old man's biological son and rightful heir, that he—Karel—is in fact the adopted brother and that this is why he has been excluded in the so-called will. Zapper, hired by Karel to look into the question of his parentage, ultimately puts paid to Reynaud's scheming, but not before doing battle with the villain's henchmen, not to mention his mistress—a deadly markswoman played by Edina Ronay.

This time around, Zapper has a Chinese martial arts expert as a sidekick, and the whole thing thankfully avoids the lewdness of, as well as being far less corny than, its predecessor. The story also involves Reynaud framing a master swordsman (David Robb) for the murder, and there's plenty of fencing action in which Zapper is revealed to be somewhat of a master swordsperson herself (something we didn't know from the first film). The movie was made under the working title *Blade of Vengeance* and would eventually have a home video release as *Zapper's Blade of Vengeance*.

> "Some days business is good
> ... and some days it's murder!"

Having successfully played author Raymond Chandler's private investigator Philip Marlowe in the U.S. production *Farewell My Lovely* (1975), Robert Mitchum returned to the role in director Michael Winner's *The Big Sleep* (1978). When the disabled General Sternwood (James Stewart) hires Marlowe to scare off a troublemaker in connection with his unstable daughter (Candy Clark), the case soon develops into a labyrinthine mystery that ultimately concerns an attempted blackmail plot against Sternwood by gangster Eddie Mars (Oliver Reed). Although Chandler's 1939 novel of the same name was definitively filmed by Howard Hawks in 1946, this updated version nevertheless has value and brings something new by transferring events from America to England. The director manages to steer a clear course through a complicated story and is helped no end by a stellar cast of familiar faces, with Richard Boone particularly effective as an evil hitman in Eddie's employ.

Intrepid Reporters

Mike Billings

Between 1954 and 1960, A.C.T. Films produced four light-hearted B movies featuring Mike Billings (inexplicably changed to Mike Billing in the third and fourth films), an ace reporter for the *Sunday Star* newspaper in London. Mike is played by John Bentley in the first two films and by Robin Bailey and Vincent Ball, respectively, in the third and fourth outings. Jenny Drew, Mike's ambitious colleague and romantic interest (they eventually become engaged) at the newspaper, is always looking for something more challenging than her roles as either agony aunt, society gossip columnist or fashion writer; to this end she involves herself in Mike's investigations, sometimes hindering him but more often than not providing invaluable help. Jenny was played by a different actress in each film, with Eleanor Summerfield in the first being by far the most delightful. The *Sunday Star*'s editor, Percy Simpson, was played by Charles Farrell in the first three films and finally by Michael Ripper. Mike often gets on the nerves of another recurring character, the irritable Inspector Corcoran of Scotland Yard, but generally the two have a fairly tolerable relationship.

The first and best of the series, **Final Appointment** (1954), sees Mike (John Bentley) on the trail of a devious serial killer. Three of four officers who presided at a court martial during World War II have been murdered on the same date—July 10—in successive years; the fourth officer, now a respected solicitor named Hartnell (Hubert Gregg), has begun receiving death threats. The most likely suspects are three men who were charged and incarcerated (but since released) as a result of the court martial. However, in order to avoid suspicion, one of these men (the killer) has faked his own death and is going under a false identity. The likeable Bentley displays a nice lightness of touch and is easily the best of the three actors who played the reporter, with Liam Redmond a perfect foil as Inspector Corcoran. *Today's Cinema* (September 27, 1954) picked up on the more than serviceable script, noting that the "dialogue is sharp and often witty."

Bentley returned as Mike in **Stolen Assignment** (1955), in which a wealthy woman goes missing only to later turn up murdered. Suspects include the woman's artist husband (Patrick Holt) and her aunt (Joyce Carey), the latter the main beneficiary in her niece's will. In the end, it's Jenny (Hy Hazell) who uncovers the vital clue (involving a scarf worn by the victim) that leads to the killer's apprehension. This time around, Inspector Corcoran is played by Eddie Byrne.

In the cleverly titled third film, **The Diplomatic Corpse** (1958), the titular dead body is that of a man—a diplomat from the fictional Middle Eastern country of Ergynia—found drowned in the River Thames. This puts Mike (Robin Bailey, lacking the easy charm of predecessor Bentley) on a trail that leads to the uncovering of a heroin smuggling conspiracy involving two officials within the Ergynian Embassy. During the course of the story, Jenny (Susan Shaw) gets a job as switchboard operator at the embassy in order to snoop around, only to get found out and held prisoner there. However, she is duly rescued thanks to an ingenious plan devised by Mike, and the crooked officials' fate is ultimately left in the hands of the Ergynian ambassador. Liam Redmond, having taken a break after the first film, makes a welcome return as Corcoran.

In his final adventure, **Dead Lucky** (1960), which the *Kinematograph Weekly* (June 30, 1960) said produced only "occasional laughs and thrills," Mike is played by the amiable Vincent Ball, with Betty McDowall and John Le Mesurier taking on the roles of Jenny and Inspector Corcoran. The story concerns investigations into a spate of illegal gambling parties and the murder of a notorious gambler (Brian Worth). Ball and McDowall, both Australians, also appeared together in a later British thriller, 1963's *Echo of Diana*.

Banner Headlines

The "Acid Bath Murderer" (serial killer John Haigh, convicted for killing six people from 1944 to 1949) and the "Arundel Park Murder" (the unsolved rape-strangulation of a 27-year-old woman whose body was found in a secluded area of Arundel Park in Sussex, 1948) were just two of the cases covered by Robert Chapman during his time as a reporter for London daily newspaper the *Evening News*. Chapman was also a thriller writer, and created his fictional counterpart of sorts in the shape of ace newsman Rex Banner, who featured in over half a dozen of his novels during the 1950s, four of which were made into B movies from 1954 to 1957. The character kept his full literary name in the first film, where he was played by Peter Reynolds; by the second film, he was called Paul Banner and portrayed by Canadian actor Paul Carpenter, who would remain the leading man for the rest of the series. Original publicity materials for the elusive final film, *Murder Reported*, have no mention of the Banner character and instead list Carpenter as playing Jeff Holly, who'd been a lesser character (also a reporter) played by Gaylord Cavallaro in the third film, *Behind the Headlines*. (Cavallaro is also listed in the cast of *Murder Reported*, but this time as simply "reporter.") The first three films also feature the character Maxine, initially married to Rex but demoted to a colleague with romantic aspirations after Rex became Paul.

In **The Delavine Affair** (1954), based on the 1952 novel *Winter Wears a Shroud*, Rex (Peter Reynolds) runs his own news bureau, the Banner Press Agency, and sells his stories to *The Daily Comet*. When one of his informants is murdered, Rex finds that the killing is linked to a £50,000 jewel robbery. Further investigation, which involves an isolated farmhouse where the jewels are hidden, eventually succeeds in uncovering the dangerous culprit responsible for both the homicide and the theft. Reynolds, complete with a very strange hairdo, gives a spirited performance as the resolute Rex, and there's no shortage of entertaining banter thanks to the humorous exchanges between him and wife Maxine (Honor Blackman). Gordon Jackson plays the villain, whose resemblance to Rex plays a large part in the proceedings. The film went straight to television in the U.S., showing for many years under the title *Murder Is News* with occasional broadcasts under its British title.

Based on the 1951 novel of the same name, **One Jump Ahead** (1954) sees Banner employed at *The Daily Comet*. Things get off to an atmospherically creepy start with a blonde manicurist stabbed to death in the ruins of a church. The mysterious assassin subsequently seeks to silence a schoolboy who witnessed the crime, having the youngster's school cap (dropped at the scene and with name inside) with which to identify him; however, the boy had in fact been accidentally wearing a cap belonging to a fellow pupil, the latter soon turning up dead instead. While investigating with colleague Maxine (Diane Hart), Banner has to deal with an old flame, Judy (Jill Adams), coming back into his life. In an incredible coincidence, Judy is revealed as the murderer—she'd been blackmailed by the manicurist—leading to a melodramatic noir-style climax (back in the church ruins) in which Banner leaves Judy with a gun and one bullet as an alternative to facing the police. *The Cinema* (March 9, 1955) noted that Carpenter makes "a convincingly tough and tenacious newshawk."

In **Behind the Headlines** (1956), adapted from the 1955 novel of the same name, Banner is once again (as in the first film) running his own bureau, this time called Banners Newsagency. In an echo of the previous film, a blonde blackmailer is murdered (this time in her apartment), whereupon Banner investigates together with glamorous female reporter Pam Barnes (Adrienne Corri). With the net closing in, the killer tries to trick the authorities by faking his own suicide before then luring Banner and Pam into a death trap at the latter's apartment. Hazel Court plays Maxine, here portrayed as Banner's former—but still interested—girlfriend, who thwarts Pam's attempts to seduce the ace newshound and also unwittingly saves the pair in the climax. After the killer is finally captured, Pam gets the scoop and Maxine gets Banner.

The 1953 novel *Murder for the Million* provides the basis for **Murder Reported** (1957), the final and rarest of the four films and the only one made for Columbia Pictures. The story teams our intrepid reporter with *The Daily Comet* editor's (John Laurie) daughter (Melissa Stribling) for an assignment concerning the murder, by an assassin dubbed "The Judo Killer," of a politician in connection with a shady land deal. In an attempt to cover up the murder, the killer had exhumed a body from a cemetery and replaced it with the corpse of his victim. The journalistic duo first gets on the villain's trail thanks to his failure to properly dispose of the exhumed body, which is found in a

Canadian actor Paul Carpenter was a quintessential player of intrepid British B movie reporters. This shot from *Murder Reported* (1957) sees him (pictured right) with Melissa Stribling and John Laurie.

trunk at a railway station. The film was colorfully described in Columbia's pressbook as "a top-notch thriller which involves a trunkful of murder, a townful of suspects and a screenful of screaming suspense."

Other Brave Newsmen

"Unassuming, small-scale entertainment" was how *Today's Cinema* (October 20, 1950) described the B movie **Dangerous Assignment** (1950). Joe Wilson (Lionel Murton), ace reporter for the National News Bureau, is sent to London by his New York boss to begin work on a series of crime articles. Before long, he's looking into a stolen car racket that has been making the headlines and ends up tangling with the racket's murderous mastermind Frank Mayer (Ivan Craig). Pamela Deeming plays a secretary at the News Bureau's London office who provides Wilson with not only invaluable help but also a touch of romance. Over the years, the film was shown on U.S. television as both *Dangerous Assignment* and *European Assignment*. For the definitive British thriller about stolen car rackets, see *Never Let Go* (1960).

The flagship production by Group 3 (a company set up to make low-budget films with new acting talent), **Judgment Deferred** (1952) is a remake by director John Baxter of his own 1930s movie *Doss House*. The story tells of the inventive efforts of a group of eccentrics and down-and-outs—frequenters of a social club known as The Palace (located in the crypt of a ruined church)—to clear the name of the club's manager Robert Carter (Fred Griffiths) after he's framed for drug dealing by a gang of racketeers he was about to expose. Hugh Sinclair is top-billed as a reporter for *The Daily Post* who gets involved for both personal and professional reasons, while Joan Collins, in one of her earliest roles, plays Carter's daughter.

> "A hard-hitting Yank who solved
> a London murder—American style!"

Hollywood's charming Cesar Romero stars as American magazine writer Philip Odell in the B movie **Lady in the Fog** (1952), an adaptation of the 1947 BBC radio serial *Lady in a Fog*. While stranded in London due to extreme foggy conditions, Odell helps a young woman, Heather McMara (Bernadette O'Farrell), investigate the murder of her brother, Danny (Richard Johnson), who we saw run down by a mysterious female driver during the film's prologue. It eventually emerges that Danny had been blackmailing his killer, having found out that she, in league with two cohorts, had murdered her scientist husband some years earlier so as to take control of the man's new supercharged carburetor invention. Key to the proceedings are a female nightclub owner (Lois Maxwell) and an asylum at which Odell poses as a doctor to gain some necessary information, while the excitingly staged climactic showdown takes place at a movie studio run by one of the villains (Geoffrey Keen). The film's misleading U.S. title, *Scotland Yard Inspector*, refers to a secondary character played by Campbell Singer, who provides much comic relief.

Escape by Night (1953) is a well-paced B movie in which Bonar Colleano plays Tom Buchan, a self-centered, wise-cracking and hard-drinking reporter for *The Comet* newspaper. Tom likes to make news happen rather than wait for it to happen, and to this end he helps a wanted racketeer, Gino Rossini (Sidney James sporting an Italian accent), elude the police in exchange for the villain agreeing to provide an exclusive insight into his life for publication in *The Comet*. A large part of the film sees the two men, while on the run, hiding out in a derelict theater, where they trick an adventurous local youngster (Andrew Ray) into believing they're Secret Service agents. The boy is soon bringing the pair supplies as well as delivering messages for them, in Gino's case to his nightclub-singer moll Rosetta (Simone Silva) and in Tom's case an exclusive bulletin about Gino to *The Comet*'s editor. In the meantime, Gino's cohorts, including his brother (Martin Benson), abandon him, and a close shave with the police leads the gangster to mistakenly believe that Rosetta has betrayed him. The climax sees Rosetta saved from the vengeful Gino by Tom, with a resulting struggle between the two men ending in Gino's death.

Bob Wright (Vernon Gray), a newly married reporter for *The Morning Echo* newspaper, is forced to forgo his honeymoon when assigned by his editor to catch a London-bound train, *The Gold Express* (1954), and report on £10,000 worth of recently discovered ancient gold treasure being carried on board. During the journey, on which he's accompanied by his wife (Ann Walford), Bob stumbles on a plot—engineered by Rover (Patrick Boxill)—to steal the gold, which will involve throwing it from the train to cohorts en route. Other passengers include two thriller-writing spinster sisters (May Hallatt and Ivy St. Helier), who go under the collective pseudonym Grim Buckfast, and a small boy with a water pistol who proves instrumental in foiling the robbery scheme. A subplot in this very minor but lively B movie involves a woman (Delphi Lawrence) seeking revenge against Rover for a past grievance.

In the formulaic B movie *Tiger by the Tail* (1954), American journalist John Desmond (*The Jolson Story*'s Larry Parks) is sent by his news agency—Worldwide News, Inc.—to work at their London branch. His subsequent relationship with the beautiful and enigmatic Anna Ray (Lisa Daniely) leads to a situation where she pulls a gun on him after he jealously tries to look in her diary; in a resulting struggle, Anna is accidentally shot dead and John goes on the run, keeping the diary which it transpires contains coded contact details for an international counterfeiting gang that Anna was mixed up with. In the dangerous adventure that follows, which involves the ruthless gang's attempts to get hold of the diary, John is helped by his resourceful secretary, played by Constance Smith in a nice contrast to her role in the same producers' (Tempean Films) *Impulse*. John Mair's source novel, *Never Come Back*, was later adapted as a BBC TV serial in 1990.

The *Monthly Film Bulletin* (March 1955) correctly described the B movie *Track the Man Down* (1954) as being "not so much complicated as cluttered up by the introduction of so many characters." When their getaway car crashes following a London dog track robbery, the thieves split up; one of them, Rick Lambert (George Rose), who is in possession of the stolen money, decides to keep it for himself and escape abroad. Rick temporarily leaves the loot with his girlfriend Mary (Ursula Howells) and arranges to meet her in Southampton, but circumstances lead to Mary tricking her innocent sister June (Petula Clark) into delivering the cash instead. June boards a bus to Southampton, and subsequent events see Rick commandeer the vehicle and hold the passengers hostage in a boathouse where his criminal cohorts eventually converge for a showdown. Prolific U.S. star Kent Taylor gets top-billing as Don Ford, a reporter for *The Morning Star* who gets caught up in the dangerous goings-on, having boarded the bus in an attempt to interview a temperamental actress (entertainingly played by Scottish comedy actress Renee Houston). All in all, it's a fast-moving picture with good location work and an easy-going performance by Taylor.

"What was his evil mission?"

The quaint and light-hearted B movie *The Black Rider* (1954) is set in and around the coastal area of Swanhaven and involves a gang of saboteurs smuggling atomic weapons parts into the country. As a way of scaring unwanted denizens away from their illicit activities in the ruins of a supposedly haunted castle, one of the crooks dons a monk's habit to become "The Black Rider," a ghostly figure of local legend. Jimmy Hanley plays a journalist for *The Swanhaven News* who ultimately smashes the gang with help from members—one of them a Customs officer (Edwin Richfield)—of a local motorcycle

British character actor Martin Wyldeck (center) flanked by Hollywood stars Gene Nelson and Faith Domergue in *Timeslip* (1955).

club, but not before his girlfriend (Rona Anderson) has been kidnapped by the criminals. Hanley and Anderson are pleasant leads, and Lionel Jeffries has one of his earliest screen roles as the urbane and ruthless head of the saboteurs. The familiar story is in the tradition of classic British comedy thrillers such as *Oh, Mr. Porter* (1937) and *The Ghost Train* (1941).

The fast-paced B movie ***Timeslip*** (1955) gives us two Hollywood stars for our money, namely Gene Nelson and Faith Domergue. Nelson plays Mike Delaney, a wisecracking science reporter for *View* magazine, while Domergue stars as his photographer girlfriend Jill Rabowski. The story concerns a plot by the United Tungsten Corporation of Argentina to preserve their world dominance by attempting to sabotage a British research facility's experiments—these being led by nuclear physicist Stephen Rayner (Peter Arne)—to create synthetic tungsten. A double of Rayner is installed in the facility to blow the place up, while the real scientist is shot and left for dead. However, the latter subsequently recovers in hospital (his identity initially a mystery) but not before experiencing clinical death for several seconds. At this point, the film introduces a gimmicky if rather pointless time travel angle whereby the real Rayner, through a combination of his death experience and years of exposure to radiation from research work, ends up a few seconds in the future, thus confusingly answering questions before they've been asked. Making sense of Rayner's apparent ramblings proves key to uncovering the sabotage plot, which is eventually foiled by Mike and Jill but not before Jill is kidnapped by the conspirators. This borderline sci-fi flick, which was cut by approximately 15 minutes for its original U.S. release (under the title *The Atomic Man*), stems from the same year as Nelson and Domergue's respective best known films, *Oklahoma!* and *This Island Earth*.

More sci-fi elements, not to mention another Hollywood star, namely Philadelphia-born Paul Douglas, feature in **The Gamma People** (1955). While en route to cover a music festival in Salzburg, American reporter Mike Wilson (Douglas) and British photographer (Leslie Phillips) get stranded in the small uncharted republic of Gudavia and become instrumental in freeing the place from a sinister castle-dwelling dictatorial scientist named Boronski (Walter Rilla). Boronski has been holding the population in a grip of fear and subjecting the local youngsters to gamma ray experiments that turn them into either geniuses or else soulless zombie-like creatures who carry out his evil bidding. Eva Bartok plays a young woman heavily under the dictator's influence, while Phillips, by way of his character having a keen eye for the ladies, provides a sneak peek into his future "suave lothario" comedy persona. Atmospheric art direction and a grand score augment this B movie, whose predictable climax sees Boronski's castle go up in flames.

Hour of Decision (1956) is a solid B movie in which rugged American reporter Joe Sanders (Jeff Morrow) investigates the death by poisoning of obnoxious gossip columnist Gary Bax (Anthony Dawson) at a London nightclub. Complications ensue upon Sanders discovering that his own wife Peggy (Hazel Court) was not only being threatened with blackmail by Bax, but was also the last person to be seen in the man's company, making her the likeliest suspect in the eyes of Scotland Yard's Inspector Gower (Carl Bernard). All those concerned in the case are eventually summoned to the club for a reconstruction of the crime, whereupon, in a last-minute stroke of luck, the real murderer is unmasked. According to the *Motion Picture Herald* (January 5, 1957), the film contains "the basic elements of a well-integrated suspense melodrama."

"*The candid snap that cornered a killer!*"

Described by *Today's Cinema* (January 7, 1957) as a "very honest hour's entertainment," **The Girl in the Picture** (1956) is a snappy B movie featuring an energetic performance by Donald Houston as Jon Deering, a crime reporter for London newspaper *The Evening Echo*. The story has Deering investigate the four-year-old unsolved murder of a policeman via clues, including an attractive young woman waving at a car, contained in a photograph (taken on the day of the crime) which turns up in the newspaper's competitions section. This leads to the murderer, a Kensington restaurateur named Rod Mulloy (Maurice Kaufmann), who'd been a passenger in the car at the time the photo was taken (he and the driver were criminal cohorts), being forced to cover his tracks. To this end, he kills the driver and then goes after the waving woman (Junia Crawford) just to be on the safe side (as it happens, she'd actually been gesturing only to the driver and can't identify Mulloy). The ever-reliable Patrick Holt lends his urbane presence to the proceedings as a Scotland Yard detective who, in a climax involving all concerned, pulls a brilliantly timed and unorthodox maneuver that causes Mulloy to fall to his death from a fire escape.

While appearing in *Cat on a Hot Tin Roof* on Broadway, Alex Nicol was given special leave of absence to star in **A Stranger in Town** (1957), an absorbing B movie in which the charismatic actor gives a quietly authoritative performance as U.S. reporter John Madison. While vacationing in England, Madison visits a sleepy village to look into the death (a supposed suicide but actually a murder) of a young American pianist who we soon learn was a philanderer, thief and blackmailer. Among those questioned by the reporter are a woman (Anne Paige) who'd been in love with the pianist and an ex-army officer (Charles Lloyd Pack) whom the musician had been blackmailing. The killer is finally revealed in the tense and atmospheric finale set in a remote cottage during a thunderstorm.

The fast-moving ***A Woman of Mystery*** (1957) is an engaging Danziger brothers B movie with a clear and well-thought-out script that includes much noir-style voice-over narration for the hero. Ray Savage (Dermot Walsh), a tough reporter for *Fact Magazine*, is assigned to write a feature about events leading up to the suicide of a young woman, but instead finds evidence suggesting she had in fact been murdered. It transpires that the woman had worked for an escort agency used as a front by a ruthless gang of counterfeiters, whose mysterious boss killed her after she learned too much. Hazel Court, Walsh's real-life wife at the time, plays a colleague of Ray's helping in his efforts to bring the criminals to justice.

Undercover Girl (1957) begins with the murder of a *Weekly Illustrated* crime reporter who'd been delving too deeply into a story. The man's brother-in-law, Johnny Carter (Paul Carpenter), a press photographer for the same journal, investigates and ends up tangling with Ted Austin (Bruce Seton), a vicious drug dealer and blackmailer responsible for the murder. The ever-engaging Carpenter plays it more seriously than usual, and Seton is on great form as Austin, a real nasty piece of work who addicts a young woman (Jackie Collins, long before she found fame as a best-selling author) to drugs so as to manipulate her into becoming one of his pushers. The villain's climactic slashing of the woman's face is thankfully kept off-screen but is nevertheless pretty strong stuff for a B movie of the time. The film is mainly known in the U.S. as *Assignment Redhead*, although some of its television showings went under the British title. Interestingly, *Assignment Redhead* was already the title of a 1956 British thriller which, to confuse matters even further, was itself retitled in the U.S.

Carpenter was also in the rarely seen Danziger brothers offering **Date at Midnight** (1959), this time playing Bob Dillon of the *New York Daily Universe* in a role that proved to be his swansong as a B-movie reporter. Newly arrived in England, Dillon teams up with Paula Burroughs (Jean Aubrey), a pretty photographer from the newspaper's London bureau, for a series of articles about an eminent lawyer named Sir Edward Leyton (Ralph Michael). While staying at Leyton's country home, Dillon and Paula investigate the murder of a local girl in which circumstances point to the lawyer's introverted 17-year-old adoptive nephew Tommy (John Charlesworth), who'd supposedly killed his parents as a young child, as the culprit. Harriette Johns plays Leyton's wife who, in a shocking denouement, is revealed as the killer of not only the girl but also Tommy's parents. The *Monthly Film Bulletin* (March 1960) characterized the proceedings as "theatrical, confected and cliché-ridden."

A British-Swedish co-production, ***The Man in the Middle*** (1959) stars Anthony Steel as Mike Gibson, a Stockholm-based British journalist for *The Globe News*. The light-hearted B-movie shenanigans are set mainly on the Swedish island of Gotland, where Mike helps nuclear expert Professor Christenson (Hakan Westergren) and his daughter (1958's "Miss Germany" Marlies Behrens) escape from the clutches of an international spy ring trying to force secrets from the scientist. The film, titled *Med fara för Livet* in Sweden, and whose writer-director Peter Bourne (aka Ake Bjornefeldt) appears as one of the spies, features a cameo from then world heavyweight boxing champion Ingemar Johansson, and there's a neat twist involving an old World War II buddy (Birger Malmsten) of Mike's.

Filmed on pleasant South East England locations, ***The Desperate Man*** (1960) is an unassuming B movie starring Conrad Phillips as Bill Curtis, an ace London crime reporter for the *Daily Record*. While vacationing in Sussex (although he should, as he says, "be in Wigan investigating a dismembered female," to which he adds, "but I like to see my women in one piece"), Bill meets Carol

Bourne (Jill Ireland), an ambitious local *East Sussex Times* writer investigating the disappearance of a cannonball from a mediaeval castle. Events soon lead the pair into a dangerous adventure that sees them tangle with Rance (William Hartnell), a ruthless criminal recently out of jail and seeking to retrieve £50,000 worth of stolen jewels which he hid in the castle four years earlier.

Phillips and Ireland give engaging performances and, as for the mystery of the missing cannonball, it's found within a well in the castle grounds, having been used by Rance as a weight to hold down a body (that of a man he'd murdered) beneath the water. Charles Gray, in an early film appearance, gives a typically supercilious turn as a rival reporter of Curtis' looking to get a scoop on the murder. The film went straight to television in the U.S., initially broadcast as a first-season episode of *Kraft Mystery Theatre*. On the day of the broadcast (August 23, 1961), "TV Scout" previews (syndicated content carried in the TV pages of many newspapers) informed prospective audiences that the film "starts slowly but builds to a few crackerjack scenes near the end."

Michael Winner's feature directorial debut, **Shoot to Kill** (1960), for which he also wrote the original screenplay, stars Dermot Walsh as a showbiz reporter named Mike Roberts. An unexpected event, namely his involvement in a plane crash while en route to cover a European film festival, indirectly leads Mike into a dangerous adventure that sees him tangling with communists—headed by diplomat Boris Altovich (John East)—from a place called Legaria (not the town in northern Spain but a fictional Iron Curtain country). The story, which unfolds in Geneva, also features a British security agent (Frank Hawkins) and the diplomatic correspondent (Joy Webster) from Mike's newspaper, and involves the rescue of a nuclear scientist's daughter from the communists, who'd kidnapped her in an effort to force top secret atomic weapons information from her father.

While still in Switzerland, having just finished directing a short travel film (*Swiss Holiday*) for the Swiss Tourist Office, Winner began work on this minor, and by all accounts now lost, B movie, which the *Monthly Film Bulletin* (January 1961) called a "cramped and clumsy spy thriller." However, on the third day of filming, lead actor Walsh suffered an injury and had to return to England where the picture was completed, with the illusion of still being in Geneva achieved by affixing phony Swiss registration plates (made from cardboard) to every car in sight. More about the making of the film can be found in Winner's 2004 autobiography, *Winner Takes All: A Life of Sorts*, including the surprising revelation that the film's opening plane crash scene contains actual footage of the famous air crash sequence from Alfred Hitchcock's *Foreign Correspondent* (1940).

In Winner's subsequent film, **Out of the Shadow** (1961), fearless reporter Mark Kingston (Terence Longdon) investigates the death (allegedly an accident or suicide, although Mark correctly suspects murder) of his brother Tony at Cambridge University. A dangerous adventure ensues, in which there are further murders as well as an attempt to kill Mark by tampering with his car. It all has to do with a ruthless gang (masterminded by a bogus academic) and their efforts to locate jewels that were stolen during World War II and then hidden somewhere on the university campus. Having played the hero in the previous film, Dermot Walsh is this time cast as a visiting American scholar who, let's just say, is not all he seems. Overall, it's a modestly engaging B movie with some nice location shots of Cambridge (where Winner had himself once been a student) and a likable performance by Longdon. By far the most thrilling part is a scene where Mark returns to his hotel room to find a hideously masked gun-toting character waiting for him.

The title of the rare B movie **The Fur Collar** (1962) refers to the distinguishing feature of an overcoat worn by Mike Andrews (John Bentley), a "Special Investigator" for the London Sunday newspaper *The People*. When a Danish industrialist wearing a similar coat is shot in Paris, Mike, who has just begun a short vacation in the capital, correctly suspects the bullet was meant for him and sets about investigating with the help of his friend, Inspector Legrain (Martin Benson) of the Sûreté. Through some devious trickery, Mike catches the gunman (Philip Friend); however, it transpires the latter was pressured, via threats to disfigure his girlfriend (Marie Lejeune), into carrying out the shooting on behalf of Roger Harding (Hector Ross), a vengeful ex-British Foreign Office official Mike had once helped convict on espionage charges and who is once again engaged in spy activities. At the end of what the *Monthly Film Bulletin* (June 1963) called "a soporific thriller," Harding is arrested, while the gunman, despite the crime of having shot the industrialist, is allowed to go free thanks to an unlikely twist. The movie's only U.S. exposure seems to have been through TV showings in the early 1970s; since then it's been out of circulation, including in England.

The simple but enjoyable B movie **Impact** (1963) stars Conrad Phillips (he also had a hand in the script) as crusading *Evening Record* reporter Jack Moir, whose series of underworld exposés begin posing a threat to a big-time London racketeer known as "The Duke" (George Pastell). To get Moir out of the way, the villain arranges a train robbery and frames him for the crime, resulting in the journalist receiving a two-year prison sentence. When he finally gets out, Moir puts into motion a carefully worked-out plan to clear his name; this entails "The Duke" and his cohorts being lured to a cold-storage plant and then forced at gunpoint into huge refrigerators, their only way out being to sign a document admitting to the frame-up. The film reaches a satisfying conclusion with Moir giving "The Duke" a taste of his own medicine via a revenge frame-up, which will add many more years to the villain's jail sentence. Also cast are Linda Marlowe (future star of the zany 1970s "Zapper" thrillers) as Moir's girlfriend, Anita West as the criminal kingpin's moll and John Rees as Moir's cellmate, who proves invaluable to the reporter not only inside the prison, but also later—once they're both free—on the outside.

"His life depended on the squeeze of a trigger … and the squeeze of a woman!"

Based on Morris L. West's 1957 novel *The Big Story*, **The Crooked Road** (1964) is a lackluster British-Yugoslavian co-production filmed entirely in the latter country. American investigative journalist Richard Ashley (Robert Ryan) travels to the small Balkan state of Orgagna to collect evidence—in the form of some incriminating photostats—for a story intended to cause the downfall of Orgagna's corrupt leader Vittorio (Stewart Granger). What follows is essentially a game of cat-and-mouse between the two men, with Vittorio using every dirty trick in the book (including poisoning Ashley and framing him for a murder) to prevent the story coming out. The cast also features Nadia Gray as Vittorio's wife (and Ashley's old flame) and George Coulouris as a faithful servant of Vittorio's crucial to the film's sudden and unexpected outcome.

Insurance Agents

"Was this the perfect crime?"

The most interesting thing about the otherwise routine B movie **Blood Orange** (1953) is the fact that Tom Conway plays a character named…. Tom Conway. (Was this a way of mocking the critics who so often accused the actor of basically always playing himself?) The complicated story concerns insurance agent Conway's undercover investigation into the shady dealings of a certain Mr. Mercedes (Eric Pohlmann), who pulls off a scam in which he lends £50,000 worth of his own (criminally acquired, it should be said) jewelry to a fashion house and then

Left to right: Robert Ryan, Marius Goring, Stewart Granger and Nadia Gray in *The Crooked Road* (1964).

arranges to have it stolen so as to claim insurance. Conway is soon mixed up in homicide when first a model (Delphi Lawrence), who was about to give him some vital information about the jewels, and then Mr. Mercedes, are murdered. Conway is as suave and impeccably groomed as ever, and the film also features Naomi Chance as a ruthless accomplice of Mr. Mercedes, and French actress Mila Parely (one of Beauty's shrewish sisters in 1946's *La Belle et la bête*) as the fashion house proprietress and designer of a dress named "Blood Orange."

In the Brighton-based B movie *The Straw Man* (1953), circumstantial evidence leads to the arrest and sentencing to death of Lincoln Hunter (Philip Saville) for the murder of an ex-girlfriend. A life insurance policy means that Lincoln's wife, Ruth (Lana Morris), stands to collect £20,000 upon his execution. Jeff Howard (Clifford Evans), an agent for the insurers, investigates, hiring local private detective Mal Ferris (Dermot Walsh) to help with some routine enquiries. A midway twist reveals that Mal, in league with Ruth, carried out the murder to frame Lincoln and grab the payout. Mal commits another murder to cover his tracks before Howard closes in, leading to a melodramatic finale in which Ruth shoots her partner-in-crime in a futile effort to save her own skin. The film, made by the same team behind the spy thriller *The Night of the Full Moon* (also 1953), is rather blandly directed; however, a good plot, not to mention the rare occurrence of Morris and Walsh playing villains, make it worthwhile. In the U.S., both *The Straw Man* and *The Night of the Full Moon* were included in an Associated Artists Productions 55-film TV distribution package and were first broadcast in 1955. Neither appears to have had a U.S. theatrical release.

The *Monthly Film Bulletin* (July 1954) noted the fast-moving B picture *The Scar-*

let Web (1953) as being a "formula detective story, made with modest competence." Griffith Jones is on spirited form as Jake Winter, an investigator for the Imperial Insurance firm in London. The straightforward story begins with a series of circumstances (arising as a result of a stint in prison, where he'd been engaged in an undercover assignment) that lead to Jake being framed by a blonde femme fatale (the usually dark-haired Zena Marshall) for her murder of a woman. The blonde, we learn, is in cahoots with the dead woman's husband (Robert Perceval), who stands to gain a £50,000 life insurance payout. Forced to go on the run, Jake tries to prove his innocence with the help of Susan Honeywell (Hazel Court), his initially frosty (although she soon warms to him) new boss at the insurance company. A brisk climax has Susan captured by the conspirators and almost gassed to death in a country cottage. The best part is a hilarious scene in which Jake frightens the husband's sour-faced secretary (Molly Raynor), who thinks he's really a killer, into revealing some vital information.

In the leaden, not to mention laden (with coincidences, that is) B movie ***Devil's Point*** (1954), Donald Houston plays a resolute agent for a company responsible for insuring shipments of valuable cortisone, which are being regularly stolen by a gang of smugglers headed by Daller (Edwin Richfield). Hollywood's Richard Arlen (in one of two B thrillers he made back-to-back for Charles Deane Productions) has the lead role as an independent cargo-boat operator (the film's title refers to a London wharf where he moors his vessel) sought by the gang after accidentally coming into possession of a small box of the cortisone from one of their hauls. During the course of the story, we learn that the criminals have two operatives at the insurance company, one of them a senior figure providing the gang with inside information regarding the shipments. Arlen is pretty dull throughout, except when he's in the presence of the anything-but-dull Greta Gynt, who plays his barmaid girlfriend.

Dermot Walsh heads the cast of the middling B movie ***The Hideout*** (1956) as insurance investigator Steve Curry who, through a mix-up with his luggage at a hotel, comes into possession of a case full of cash. A label inside the case leads him to its rightful owner, fur dealer Robert Grant (Ronald Howard), who intends to use the cash as payment for an illegal consignment of Persian lamb skins (already in his possession) which he has yet to discover are riddled with anthrax. Events see Steve becoming embroiled in a dangerous adventure in which the furs are stolen, Robert is murdered and the money goes missing. Prolific character actor Sam Kydd has a key role as an ex-criminal (although not so "ex" as it turns out) friend of Steve's, and also featuring are Rona Anderson as Robert's sister (and romantic interest for Steve) and Howard Lang as a ship's captain who smuggled the skins into the country in the first place. What could have been an exciting story about the potential threat of an anthrax outbreak instead is nothing more than a routine crime thriller whose convolutions culminate in a moderately eventful finale in which the diseased lamb skins are destroyed in a fiery truck crash. The film went straight to television in the U.S., initially broadcast as a first-season episode of *Kraft Mystery Theatre*. On the day of the broadcast (July 19, 1961), "TV Scout" previews (syndicated content carried in the TV pages of many newspapers) had this to say: "[the film] proves that the British, masters of suspense though they are, have their off days, too. Your TV Scout found *The Hideout* a complicated, confusing, corny bit of business."

The stylish ***Fortune Is a Woman*** (1957) stars Jack Hawkins as Oliver Branwell, an insurance assessor for Abercrombie & Son (fittingly played by real-life father and son Malcolm and Geoffrey Keen). When Branwell discovers that a swindle (involving a mansion fire and forged paintings) has been perpetrated against his company, he says nothing. The reason he stays quiet is in order to protect Sarah Moreton (Arlene Dahl), an old flame he mistakenly believes is implicated, and whose husband Tracey (Dennis Price)—the fraudster—died mysteriously while implementing the scam. After rekindling their old romance, Sarah and Oliver marry, but their happiness is short-lived when they come under suspicion of having originated the fraud and of possibly having murdered Tracey. The film, based on Winston Graham's 1952 novel of the same name, is an above-average mystery with fine performances, a superbly executed fire sequence and an elaborate plot (which also involves the couple being plagued by a blackmailer) that winds its way to a surprising and satisfying conclusion.

"They dealt in dreams—and murder!"

One of the first British films to deal with mind control techniques was **Escapement** (1957), a lukewarm adaptation by Charles Eric Maine of his own 1956 page-turning novel of the same name (aka *The Man Who Couldn't Sleep*). The story concerns an exclusive clinic in the south of France where benevolent therapist Phillip Maxwell (Meredith Edwards) treats clients (who are placed in morgue-like drawers) with a self-invented soothing electronic hypnosis method involving specially produced tape-recorded movies. However, the clinic's megalomaniac owner, Paul Zakon (Peter Illing), has been secretly manipulating the technology in an attempt to take over the minds of (so as to access their wealth for his own evil ends) selected patients, some of whom go on to suffer unintended fatal side effects. In the film's opening sequence, we see one such patient, famous Hollywood movie star Clark Denver (John McCarthy), suffer these side effects while driving in the French countryside, leading to a devastating crash. Jeff Keenan (sturdy Canadian-born Rod Cameron), an American insurance agent assigned to investigate Denver's demise, uncovers the sinister goings-on; then, with help from Maxwell, whose wife/assistant (Kay Callard) has by now been callously murdered on Zakon's orders, he finally puts an end to the nefarious activity, with Zakon getting a taste of his own medicine before the clinic goes up in flames.

This interesting B movie, complete with weird dream sequences and electronic sound effects, also stars American actress Mary Murphy as an old flame of Keenan's innocently involved (both professionally and personally) with Zakon, and Carl Jaffe as an ex-Nazi crony of Zakon's. Prolific director Montgomery Tully handles the material efficiently, if unremarkably.

Tully also directed (working from Michael Winner's first feature-length screenplay) the brisk London-set B movie **Man with a Gun** (1958). Canadian star Lee Patterson plays Mike Davies, a British Apex Insurance Company agent whose investigation into a nightclub fire leads to him tangling with a vicious gang that's attempting to take over the business interests—specifically another venue called the Stardust Club (where events mostly unfold)—of the burnt-out property's owner, Harry Drayson (John Le Mesurier). Also featured are Rona Anderson as Drayson's niece (and Mike's soon-to-be love interest), Scottish-born pop singer Glen Mason, appropriately cast as a crooner at the Stardust, and Bill Nagy as the latter's manager who turns out to be a wolf in sheep's clothing.

Butcher's Film Productions' final B thriller, **Smokescreen** (1964), also turned out to be their most entertaining. This is mainly due to a scene-stealing performance by Peter Vaughan as "Ropey" Roper, a bowler-hatted, penny-pinching (it turns out he has good reason for being so) insurance man with a habit of claiming non-existent expenses. When a car crashes over a cliff in Brighton, the body of the supposed driver, a man called Dexter, is nowhere to be found and is presumed to have been swept out to sea. Roper investigates and initially comes to the conclusion that Dexter has faked his own death as part of a scheme—possibly

PETER VAUGHAN · JOHN CARSON *in* **SMOKESCREEN** Cert. U
YVONNE ROMAIN · GERALD FLOOD
Produced by: JOHN I. PHILLIPS Written and Directed by: JIM O'CONNOLLY Associate Producer: RONALD LILES

Peter Vaughan (center) as insurance investigator "Ropey" Roper in *Smokescreen* (1964). Also pictured are Deryck Guyler (left) and John Carson.

involving his wife (Yvonne Romain)—to fraudulently claim an insurance payout. However, he later discovers that Dexter has in fact been murdered and his body disposed of in a disused sandpit, the killer having cre- ated the scenario of a car crash-insurance scam as a smokescreen. The neatly plotted film has the feel of a TV pilot, and indeed it would have been nice to see more of old "Ropey" in an ongoing series.

5

The Business of Crime

The old maxim "crime does not pay" is rarely heeded by criminals until it's too late. Until that point, certain types of crime pay very well indeed. The seven sections in this chapter contain films involving various forms of criminal activity that are often treated as a business, either by lone operators or larger organized groups. Under "Robbery" can be found a variety of daring heists such as bank jobs, armored car raids, mail train robberies, truck hijackings, arms raids and jewel thefts, the latter including the Crown Jewels on more than one occasion. "Gangsters" includes films depicting the world of organized crime, in which you will find ruthless British mob bosses, American hoodlums operating in England, gang rivalry and warfare, and even a cartel of London-based protection racketeers (in 1961's *The Frightened City*). The "Blackmail" section features everything from the superb Edwardian-set period piece *Footsteps in the Fog* (1955) to the more modern London surroundings of *The Strange Affair* (1968). The half-dozen or so titles under "Kidnapping" include *Séance on a Wet Afternoon* (1964), featuring a magnificent Kim Stanley performance, and a fabulous Dan Duryea B movie asking the question *Do You Know This Voice?* (1964). "Smuggling" contains films involving contraband such as artworks, diamonds, drugs and Swiss watches, while the "Counterfeiting" section deals with everything from forged currency and fake paintings to synthetically created diamonds. Finally, "Other Rackets" includes contract killings, stolen car rackets, prostitution rings and race fixing gangs.

Robbery

Having tackled *The Mystery of the Mary Celeste* back in 1935, Hammer Films returned with a similar sea-based conundrum in ***The Dark Light*** (1950). Noticing that the Thimble Rock lighthouse has gone dark, the crew of a passing yacht (actually a vessel named *Gelert* owned by the film's director Vernon Sewell) stops by to investigate and finds the place deserted. A flashback (revealing events from the previous day) shows the lighthouse keepers rescuing two men and a woman—bank robbers attempting to flee the country—from a broken down boat, and details the ensuing struggles between the two parties that led to the place becoming abandoned. This rather shoddy B movie stars future director David Greene as one of the lighthouse staff, while the criminal trio is played by Albert Lieven, Martin Benson and Katharine Blake.

In ***Scarlet Thread*** (1951), seasoned London jewel thief Marcon (Sydney Tafler) recruits Freddie (Laurence Harvey), a small-time pickpocket who saved his life, for a smash-and-grab robbery in the city of Cambridge. During the heist, Freddie fatally shoots a passer-by and the two crooks make a hurried escape, taking refuge in the grounds of St. Mark's College. Marcon, who in a surprising little twist is revealed to have once been a student at the institute, instructs Freddie (who does a mean U.S. accent) to pose as an American. Before long, the pair are befriended by the college master's classy daughter, Josephine (a magnetic

Kathleen Byron), whom Freddie immediately sets about seducing. A major development, in which it's revealed that the doomed passer-by was in fact Josephine's father, occurs before the crooks end up falling out, with the police descending on the college for a brisk finale.

Currently available TV and DVD versions (missing approximately six minutes) end abruptly with the police making their way up a staircase to nab Freddie in the college's whispering gallery, without showing his ultimate fate. By some accounts, the original 84-minute British theatrical release version has Freddie fall to his death after attempting a daring jump from a cornice outside the whispering gallery onto a sloping roof. (This is most likely true, as an earlier scene where Marcon describes this possible jump to Freddie strongly indicates that it was the filmmakers' intention to ultimately place Freddie in a situation where he would be forced to make the leap.) It's possible that the footage in question went missing as a result of the film being cut for a 1953 British reissue by Jack Phillips Film Distributors, who removed almost 15 minutes so as to make it more flexible for showing as a B feature. Harvey overacts somewhat, but Tafler has rarely been better, and there's an early role for Canadian actor Arthur Hill as a young professor and rejected suitor of Josephine's.

Described by the *Kinematograph Weekly* (March 6, 1952) as both "thrilling and human," **The Frightened Man** (1951) is an early Tempean Films B movie with good characterizations and a well-constructed story. Mr. Rosselli (Charles Victor), a widowed antique dealer, is dismayed to learn that his son Julius (Dermot Walsh) has been kicked out of Oxford University for drunken behavior. It's not long before Julius becomes involved with a gang of crooks led by Alec Stone (Martin Benson). We later learn that Rosselli has been paying for Julius' education through income from his own secret involvement in crime, specifically as a receiver of stolen goods. Events lead to Julius, who has by now married his father's lodger, Amanda (Barbara Murray), planning (with Stone) to rob Amanda's diamond merchant employer. Rosselli, having learned about the scheme and that the police are preparing a trap, arrives too late in an attempt to prevent the heist; instead, he ends up aiding in the getaway, during which Julius falls to his death from a rooftop.

"The monster of Thrackley Castle was a master jewel thief..."

Barbara Murray also features in **Hot Ice** (1952), a light-hearted B movie in which she plays Mary, the innocent adopted daughter of mysterious eccentric jewel collector Edwin Carson (Ivor Barnard). At Carson's invitation, an assortment of high-class guests, including owners of famous diamonds, arrive for a weekend at his country residence, Thrackley, a gloomy mansion complete with secret cellar, concealed switches and hidden microphones, and where the surrounding walls and gates are wired with deadly electrical current. As it happens, the motive for the invite is to rob some of the visitors by switching precious stones from items of their jewelry with imitations. One of the guests, the dashing Jim Henderson (John Justin), falls for Mary and, along with an undercover detective posing as Carson's chauffeur (Anthony Pendrell), is instrumental in exposing the plot. When the game is finally up, Carson attempts to escape and is killed by the electrical current, purposely activated by one of his henchmen (Michael Balfour) in revenge for a double-cross. *Today's Cinema* (December 5, 1952) characterized the film, which is based on Alan Melville's 1934 novel *Weekend at Thrackley*, as "an emphatically British entertainment."

One of Tempean Films' less memorable B movies, **Recoil** (1953), stars Elizabeth Sellars as Jean Talbot, a woman determined to find the man—small-time criminal Nicholas Conway (Kieron Moore)—whom she witnessed fatally injuring her jeweler father during a robbery. When she eventually tracks him down, the police cannot make an arrest due to the man having an alibi, which Jean subsequently tries to break in a plan that entails posing as a criminal and feigning a romantic interest in him. Also in the cast are Edward Underdown as Nicholas' doctor brother, who unwittingly supplies the aforementioned alibi, and Martin Benson as a racketeer and mastermind behind the robbery. The film suffers from too much padding and bland (with the exception of Nicholas) characters.

The B movie **Black 13** (1953) was referred to by the *Kinematograph Weekly* (November 12, 1953) as a "taut crime melodrama with intriguing pathological overtones." Stephen Barclay (Peter Reynolds), the wayward son of a professor, has fallen into a life of crime. In the course of the story, Stephen and two cohorts carry out a payroll robbery at his father's college, during which Stephen fatally wounds a security guard. Lana Morris and Rona Anderson feature in key roles, Morris as the professor's secretary, who loves Stephen, and whom the latter plans to murder after she uncovers evidence (an initialed lighter) that could incriminate him; and Anderson as Stephen's sister, who falls for the investigating detective (Patrick Barr) and unwittingly imparts information that ultimately helps cause her brother's downfall. Psychological repercussions associated with a past car accident are given as a reason for Stephen's criminal behavior, and it's a car crash (during an escape bid) that finally puts an end to it. The film is a remake of the 1948 Italian movie *Gioventu Perduta*.

"A million pounds in gold was a dangerous cargo!"

The decent B movie **Dangerous Cargo** (1953) features a pleasant performance by Jack Watling as Tim Matthews, a security guard at London's Metropolitan Airport where regular consignments of gold bullion are delivered. Pliny (Karel Stepanek), a notorious criminal mastermind planning to rob the airport strongroom, pressures Matthews, through a campaign of blackmail and violence, to reveal details of the bullion shipments and to cooperate in the actual heist. Matthews does finally comply, only by then it's as part of an elaborate Scotland Yard plan that successfully leads to the red-handed capture of Pliny and his mob. Ballard Berkeley, best known for his later role as the "Major" in the classic TV comedy series *Fawlty Towers*, plays the airport's chief security officer, and John Le Mesurier appears as an Italian

Trade ad for a 1953 remake of an Italian movie.

associate of Pliny's. Best of all, though, is the pretty Susan Stephen as Matthews' wife, whose unwavering support for her husband (amid all his ups and downs during the adventure) merits his description of her as "the most wonderful woman a fellow could ever have."

The atmospheric ***The Good Die Young*** (1954) benefits from an amazing Anglo-American cast headed by Laurence Harvey as unbalanced playboy Miles Ravenscourt. When his wealthy wife (Margaret Leighton) stops supporting him financially, Miles plans a mail van robbery and persuades three men, all of them down on their luck in some way, to join him. During the robbery, Miles kills a policeman and then ruthlessly turns against his partners in crime, callously murdering two of them. The surviving accomplice escapes, but Miles catches up with him for a deadly showdown at an airport. Stanley Baker, Richard Basehart and John Ireland give sensitive performances as Miles' cohorts, and the film spends considerable time setting up their back-stories before getting down to conventional thriller tactics. Harvey and Leighton became real-life husband and wife in 1957.

The sprightly B movie ***Radio Cab Murder*** (1954) stars Jimmy Hanley as Fred Martin, a London cab driver with a criminal past (as an expert safecracker) who's determined to remain on the straight and narrow. When a highly organized gang of thieves makes an underhand attempt to recruit him, the police catch on and persuade the cabbie to join the criminals as an undercover agent on their behalf. In the course of events, Fred's cover gets blown and the gang locks him in a walk-in deep freeze at their ice cream factory headquarters, leaving him to face the prospect of a quick and chilly death. However, in the fast-moving climax, Martin's fellow cab drivers rally to his rescue and help the police round up the crooks. Contrasting feminine appeal is provided by Lana Morris as Martin's girlfriend (a cab dispatcher) and Sonia Helm as a femme fatale member of the gang.

"Danger and romance intermingle when a desperate man falls in love!"

"Tough good looks and an old talent on young shoulders" was how *Today's Cinema* (November 12, 1954) described Canadian actor Lee Patterson in their review of the B movie ***The Passing Stranger*** (1954). In what was his first starring role in a motion picture, Patterson plays Chick, a homesick U.S. Army deserter in England who's been taking part in arms raids for crime boss Lloyd (Paul Whitsun-Jones) in an attempt to fund a passage back to the States. The film opens with Chick on the run following one such raid in which Lloyd's henchman (played with typical slimy menace by Harold Lang) stabbed a sentry. He takes refuge at a roadside transport café, falls in love with Jill (Diane Cilento), one of two sisters running the place, and is soon making plans to take her back with him to America. In order to pay for the trip, Chick embarks on one final job for Lloyd, who unsuccessfully tries to double-cross him in the film's most exciting episode involving the criminal kingpin going crazy with a machine gun. Duncan Lamont plays a trucker and erstwhile suitor of Jill's ultimately responsible for thwarting the couple's plans, resulting in Chick being led away by police to the strains of Ken Sykora's "East Virginia Blues"–based title song.

Patterson's fellow Canuck, Paul Carpenter, stars in ***The Hornet's Nest*** (1955), a light-hearted and zippy B movie set on London's Chelsea Embankment. The story concerns a criminal gang's attempts to retrieve £20,000 worth of stolen jewels from their hiding place on a disused river barge called The Hornet's Nest. However, their efforts are complicated when two young models, Pat and Terry (June Thorburn and Marla Landi), move aboard the vessel, having rented it for use as a houseboat. Carpenter is on great form as Bob Bartlett, a friendly local salvage dealer and jack-of-all-trades who arranges the boat rental and ultimately brings the crooks to justice, in the process falling for Pat. The gang, a rather non-threatening and incompetent trio, is headed by one Mr. Arnold (Alexander Gauge), who runs operations under cover of the charitable Society for the Reformation of Unfortunates. Christine Silver and Nora Nicholson are entertaining as two local spinsters involved in a neat little final twist regarding the jewels.

Ealing Studios' delightful *The Ladykillers* (1955) is a classic black comedy thriller in which an innocent old lady, Mrs. Wilberforce (Katie Johnson), is used by a gang of thieves in their scheme to rob £60,000 from a security van. The gang's mastermind, Professor Marcus (Alec Guinness), rents a room in Mrs. Wilberforce's London house where he and his four cohorts—they pretend to be an amateur classical string quintet rehearsing a Boccherini minuet—plan the robbery, which is subsequently carried out to perfection. However, when the old lady accidentally finds out what the crooks have been up to, they decide to bump her off but instead end up falling out among themselves, with deadly consequences. Johnson and Guinness are perfectly cast (the latter, in some mildly grotesque make-up, managing to be at once creepy and hilarious), and there's some great atmosphere in the later stages where gang members die one by one (through killing each other) and where bodies are disposed of by being dropped into the wagons of steam-spewing freight trains that pass under a bridge behind the house. A 2004 remake was unremarkable.

Another film featuring an old woman and a gang of criminals is the B movie *Find the Lady* (1956), set in a village called Crayford. By film's start, the gang in question, led by a certain Mr. Hurst (Mervyn Johns), have taken over the elderly Margaret Rees'

Left to right: Peter Sellers, Danny Green, Herbert Lom, Alec Guinness and Cecil Parker as the gang in the classic *The Ladykillers* (1955).

(Enid Lorimer) large house and are keeping the woman imprisoned in an upstairs room. The reason they have picked on Margaret's house in particular is because the basement affords access to a large complex of tunnels from which they intend to break into the underground strongroom of the local bank. However, their scheme is ultimately undone thanks to the efforts of the old lady's visiting goddaughter June (Beverly Brooks) and a local doctor (Donald Houston), who find romance in the process. Ferdy Mayne has a small role as a shady London café proprietor supplying the criminals with explosives.

*"A girl white with fear ...
on a night dark with shame!"*

In their review of the B movie *Face in the Night* (1956), *Variety* (October 8, 1958) noted that Richard Rodney Bennett's music score "turns out to be more exciting than most other aspects of the film." Jean Francis (Lisa Gastoni), the only witness to a gang's £250,000 mail van robbery in London, withholds information from the police after being tracked down by the criminals and intimidated. In subsequent events, the gang's boss, Rapson (Griffith Jones), shoots dead one of his three cohorts (for attempting a double-cross) and then falls out with the other two (Victor Maddern and Eddie Byrne) over a plan to abscond to Brazil. Vincent Ball plays a zealous journalist who falls in love with Jean and is instrumental in bringing about the gang's downfall. Rapson gets his just deserts when, during a climactic chase, he crashes to his death while attempting to drive over Tower Bridge as it's being raised.

"Nightclub crime ring ruled by queen of evil!"

Mrs. Railton (Margaret Rawlings), a deaf and blind London nightclub proprietress, is also the fence for gang boss Clem Hayes (an atypical role for Canadian actor Paul Carpenter) in the B movie *No Road Back* (1956). She manages all this with the help of her adoptive daughter (Patricia Dainton), who communicates with her by way of a hand-tapping language. During the course of the story, Clem callously shoots a security guard during a robbery; then, when his getaway driver (Alfie Bass) threatens to tell the police, Clem kills him too. Circumstances see Mrs. Railton's son John (U.S. star Skip Homeier), recently returned from studies in America, become wrongly suspected of the second murder, this leading to a tense finale in which Mrs. Railton, by now having decided to quit her criminal ways, attempts to force a confession from Clem with the help of a gun and her trusty seeing-eye dog. Sean Connery, in his first feature film role, plays a speech-impaired criminal named Spike.

The Secret Place (1956) is atmospherically set in a war-scarred London neighborhood and features a career-best performance by Belinda Lee as a kiosk salesgirl named Molly. In the well-developed story, Molly abuses her close friendship with smitten schoolboy Freddie (Michael Brooke) by manipulating him in order to gain access to his police constable father's (Geoffrey Keen) uniform, to be used by her ruthless boyfriend Gerry (Ronald Lewis) as a disguise in a jewel heist. Following the robbery, Gerry hides the jewels—unbeknownst to her—in Molly's gramophone, which she then gifts to Freddie. The boy's eventual discovery of the gems, and his decision to return them to their rightful owner, ends up putting him in considerable danger from Gerry. Brooke is terrific as Freddie, who, in the vertiginous climax, is pursued by Gerry high up on a hazardous building site.

A 10-year-old robbery, in which the £20,000 takings were never found, is at the center of the B movie *The Key Man* (1957). The loot is in fact stashed in a safety deposit box which can only be opened by two unique keys, one of them in the possession of Smithers (Philip Leaver), who'd taken part in the heist. Smithers subsequently spent seven years in prison for allegedly killing his partner-in-crime, Nick Domigo, holder of the second key. In reality, Domigo had been murdered by Haddow (Henry Vidon), a vicious criminal who took possession of the second key and is now seeking Smithers in order to relieve him of his key. A broadcaster, Lionel Hulme (Lee Patterson), becomes caught up in the dangerous goings-on when he too tries to find Smithers in an effort to recreate the old robbery for his *Crimes of the Times* radio show. Nothing special, but Canadian star Patterson is always worth watching, as is Hy Hazell, who plays Smithers' cabaret artiste wife.

Date with Disaster (1957) is an efficient little B movie with a low-key performance by U.S. star Tom Drake as Miles Harrington, owner of a used-car dealership called Highgrade Autosales. (As it happens, Drake became a real-life used-car salesman in the early 1960s to supplement his acting work.) Unbeknownst to Miles, his partner Don (Maurice Kaufmann) and sales manager Ken (Richard Shaw) team up with seasoned safe-breaker Tracy (William Hartnell) and carry out a factory heist using one of the dealership's vehicles—previously "sold" to a fictitious buyer—which they duly abandon. Circumstances surrounding the vehicle lead to the police asking questions. Don soon begins showing signs of cracking under pressure and is murdered by Ken (on Tracy's orders), who then frames Miles for the crime. Nicely woven into the story is Don's provocative girlfriend (Shirley Eaton), who'd really rather be with Miles (he's her sister's ex-husband), and whom Miles ultimately saves from the lecherous clutches of Ken after the latter tries to force her to abscond with him in the film's climax. Most unconvincing is a scene in which Tracy, a professional who supposedly never makes mistakes, gets caught as a result of accidentally pulling out of his pocket a vital piece of evidence right in front of the investigating Scotland Yard inspector (Michael Golden).

One of Lee Patterson's better B movies was *The Flying Scot* (1957), which *The Daily Cinema* (November 29, 1957) called a "gem of a thriller." The handsome Canadian actor plays the impetuous Ronnie, mastermind of a plan to rob £500,000 from the mail compartment of the Flying Scotsman express train during an overnight journey. The idea is that Ronnie and two accomplices, Phil (Alan Gifford) and Jackie (Kay Callard), will board the train as passengers, break into the mail compartment (from an adjoining compartment) and then throw the loot to another accomplice en route. The first ten minutes of the film shows the robbery carried out to perfection, with the gang jetting off to some exotic locale to enjoy their spoils. However, this turns out to be just a visualization of the plan as outlined by Ronnie to his cohorts. The real heist does not go so smoothly: Phil begins suffering the symptoms of a perforated ulcer and the plan to break into the mail compartment proves more difficult than anticipated. In the end, the gang gets their comeuppance thanks to a mischievous little boy passenger, this having been given away on the film's U.S. publicity by the tagline "A nefarious plot, foiled by an innocent child!"

Discontented with his job, marriage and life in general, travel agency clerk Bill Anderson (William Russell) seizes **The Big Chance** (1957) to run out on his wife (Penelope Bartley) and start afresh. This entails embezzling a large amount of cash from the company safe and stealing the identity—and airline ticket to Panama—of a wealthy client (Ferdy Mayne). At the airport, Bill suffers a setback when, owing to heavy fog, the flight is postponed until the next day. However, he does manage to pair up with the attractive Diana Maxwell (Adrienne Corri), who'd been waiting for the same flight; she, like Bill, has run out on her spouse, namely the wealthy Adam (Ian Colin). A series of adventures, which involve Adam's efforts to trace Diana, and which begin when the latter and Bill leave the airport looking for somewhere to stay the night, culminate in a callous attempt by Diana to grab Bill's stolen cash for herself. This minor B movie ends with Bill realizing that the life he's been trying to escape isn't so bad after all.

"The crook who became a commando!"

Ray Milland not only directed the crime/spy flick *The Safecracker* (1957) but also has the lead role as Colley Dawson, a lock expert and one of only a few people that can open any safe just by the feel of the dial and by listening to the tumblers inside the lock. The film begins in London, 1938, with Dawson working for a safe and vault manufacturer. However, it's not long before he's tempted into putting his skills to more lucrative use—as a thief—by an antique dealer-cum-fence (Barry Jones). His eventual capture leads to a 10-year jail sentence. The film jumps forward to 1941, during World War II, by which time Dawson has served two years of his sentence. In return for his freedom, he agrees to take part in a commando mission behind enemy lines; the destination is a Nazi-occupied chateau in Belgium, where his skills as a cracksman are required to open a safe for the purpose of photographing details of German secret agents operating in England.

While not one of Milland's best efforts, it's nevertheless a very competent one, and the charismatic actor-director seems to be enjoying himself, especially during an amusing sequence where Dawson has to endure some grueling mission training. Overall, the film could have done with a little more suspense, particularly in the climactic safecracking scene, and a tighter script. Oh, and be prepared for a downbeat ending, which jars somewhat with the lighter tone of preceding events. The cast also features Ernest Clark as the mission leader and Jeannette Sterke as a Belgian Resistance member. See *The Secret Door* (1963) for a similar story.

In *Three Crooked Men* (1958), a gang of thieves plan to rob a bank by accessing its vault through the wall of an adjacent general store run by a bitter disabled ex-boxer named Don Wescot (Gordon Jackson). Produced by the Danziger brothers, this B movie is lifted out of the routine thanks to a couple of fairly well-drawn characters, namely the aforementioned Wescot and a diffident bank clerk named Prinn (played by Warren Mitchell). Both men end up being held prisoner by the gang during the actual heist, and resulting circumstances lead to them becoming suspects in the crime; that is, until they ultimately clear themselves by bravely bringing the crooks to justice. Sarah Lawson gives a sympathetic performance as Wescot's wife, who's happy to see her husband a less bitter man following his ordeal, while that ubiquitous player of "British thriller" villains, Eric Pohlmann, portrays the gang's mastermind.

A nicely paced B movie that doesn't outstay its welcome, *The Bank Raiders* (1958) stars the always excellent Peter Reynolds as petty crook and would-be playboy Terry, who takes part in a bank robbery masterminded by suave crime lord Bernie Shelton (Sydney Tafler). Later, Terry is wrongly suspected by Shelton's brutish henchman (Arthur Mullard) of having squealed to the police and, during a struggle between the two, the henchman is shot dead. Terry ends up hiding out with Shelton's embittered gold-digging ex-girlfriend (Sandra Dorne), who persuades him to rob Shelton, unaware that the latter has fitted his safe with a deadly booby trap. A subplot has Shelton kidnap a young woman (Ann King) to ensure the silence of her boyfriend (Tim Ellison), a key witness in the robbery investigation.

"A stark drama filmed against the turbulent fiery background of steel"

On the run from gambling debts, Johnny (George Baker) winds up in his industrial hometown of Rawborough, where he soon hooks up with his brother Dave (Terence Morgan) in the first-class noir offering *Tread Softly Stranger* (1958). When circumstances lead Dave to rob the payroll at his workplace (a steel foundry), from where he has already been misappropriating funds,

A criminal mastermind (Eric Pohlmann) threatens store owner Don Wescot (Gordon Jackson) in the B movie *Three Crooked Men* (1958).

Johnny ends up getting caught up in the heist, during which Dave shoots dead a security guard (Joseph Tomelty). While escaping, the brothers have a brush with an aged tramp but are in luck when the man does not subsequently come forward as a witness. Diana Dors (Britain's answer to Marilyn Monroe) is at her sultry best, smoldering her way through the proceedings as femme fatale Calico, a good-time girl causing friction between the brothers and encouraging the robbery in the first place. Patrick Allen gives a persuasive performance as the dead guard's vengeful son, who suspects the brothers and sets out to bring them to justice, and there's some very atmospheric night-time photography depicting the bleak and depressing fictional town of Rawborough. A neat final twist sees Dave confess after finally being brought face-to-face with the tramp, unaware that the old man is blind and could never have identified him.

An intelligent, "French New Wave"–style noir offering from Ealing Studios, *Nowhere to Go* (1958) stars Hollywood's George Nader in one of his best roles as a heartless London-based Canadian con artist named Paul Gregory. Figuring he'll be caught but reckoning on less than five years in jail, Gregory pulls a confidence trick—with help from an accomplice, Vic Sloane (Bernard Lee)—involving rare coins. This nets him £55,000 cash which he stores in a safety deposit box for future collection. Sure enough, he's arrested but, instead of the expected short sentence, he receives a whopping 10 years, which soon prompts him to escape (a brilliantly shot sequence) with Sloane's help. An attempt by Sloane to then grab the stashed money for himself results in a dangerous game of cat-and-mouse between the two men that leaves Sloane dead and Gregory without the safety deposit key. In her first credited film role, Maggie Smith plays a young socialite who shelters Gregory on her family's Welsh estate, where the eventual arrival of the police leads to a grim end for the criminal.

The very obscure B movie **Robbery with Violence** (1958) centers on murderous criminal Peter Frayne (Ivan Craig) who, following a bank robbery, runs out on his accomplices and goes hop-picking in the Kent countryside while waiting to launder the stolen money. Events, which involve Frayne's re-acquaintance with a former flame (Sally Day) and his murder of her husband, culminate in him being cornered in an antiques shop (owned by a fence) by his accomplices, one of them shooting him in the back as the police intervene. Directed, produced, photographed and edited by Ivan Barnett (whose only other feature was a 1948 version of Edgar Allan Poe's *The Fall of the House of Usher*), the film was matter-of-factly described by *The Daily Cinema* (February 23, 1959) as a "routine supporting feature for situations where audiences will not be demanding."

Another obscure B movie is **No Safety Ahead** (1958), produced by the Danziger brothers. Lowly office clerk Clem's (James Kenney) financial problems lead to the break-up of his engagement to Jean (Susan Beaumont), after which he takes part in a bank robbery with Jean's good-for-nothing brother (Tony Doonan) and his cohorts. During the raid, the bank manager (Robert Raglan) is fatally shot by one of the crooks. Clem, having had to make his own escape when the getaway car leaves him behind, thinks about fleeing the country. However, while hiding out in a monastery, he is persuaded by a priest to give himself up, this leading to the downfall of the rest of the gang. The aforementioned gunning down of the bank manager is connected to a subplot in which one of the bank tellers (Mark Singleton), who wants the manager out of the way so as to be with the man's wife, purposely brings about a situation during the robbery that causes the fatal shooting.

The Danzigers were also behind **High Jump** (1958), a fairly plodding B movie in which a former trapeze artist, Bill Ryan (Richard Wyler), becomes involved in a jewel robbery, his acrobatic skills required to make a risky jump between two buildings. He successfully performs the jump but then goes on to scupper the heist after the plan's mastermind (Michael Peake) callously murders two security guards. Lisa Daniely, playing a femme fatale who seduces Bill into the crime, is the best thing about the film, while Leigh Madison provides contrasting feminine appeal as a pretty receptionist at a television repair shop where Bill works as a technician.

Yet another Danziger B movie is **A Woman's Temptation** (1958). In this one, young widow Betty (Patricia Driscoll) finds a load of cash under her trash can—placed there for safekeeping by thieves while being pursued by the police—and decides to keep it in order to provide better opportunities for her adolescent son Jimmy (John Pike), who has fallen in with a rough youth gang. Betty and Jimmy later face danger when the crooks (Neil Hallett and Kenneth J. Warren) attempt to reclaim the cash, but help is at hand in the shape of Betty's friend, a heroic merchant seaman played by Robert Ayres. The *Monthly Film Bulletin* (September 1959) was not impressed, describing the film as "drab and dispirited."

The impressive **Naked Fury** (1959) features some memorably atmospheric photography and probably the catchiest theme music to ever grace a British B thriller. Following a robbery, a gang of crooks—including Eddy (Reed De Rouen) and Syd (Arthur Lovegrove)—retreat to their hideout, a dilapidated warehouse. They have with them £50,000 and a female captive, Carol (Leigh Madison), who has seen too much. Syd goes home and is later arrested after killing his wife when she attempts to blackmail him. The gang suffers various other setbacks, but their fate is ultimately decided when the dilapidated warehouse unexpectedly collapses,

The mostly dreary B movie *High Jump* (1958) brightens up considerably whenever Lisa Daniely is on screen. Here she's pictured with the film's chief villain, played by Michael Peake.

killing them all, with Carol surviving to tell the tale. Kenneth Cope plays a sex-starved gang member whose constant lusting after Carol explains the movie's exploitative retitling in the U.S. as *The Pleasure Lovers*, complete with the tagline: "A film that dares to reveal the angry, compulsive hungers of the unsatisfied sex!" The climactic collapse of the warehouse is very effectively staged, with Cope's character being literally swallowed up by the floor. An originally intended 64-minute running time was reduced to 60 minutes after last-minute cuts by the film's aptly named owner at the time, Butcher's Film Distributors.

"Whispering wires trapped a killer!"

The workmanlike B movie **Wrong Number** (1959) stars the ever-excellent Peter Reynolds as Angelo, a criminal gang member who fatally wounds a security guard in a mail van robbery. During the heist, an accomplice calls out Angelo's name, this being heard by another security guard and duly reported in the newspapers. "Angelo" is now wanted for murder. At around the same time, an elderly eccentric, Miss Crystal (Olive Sloane), dials a wrong number that connects her to the gang's hideout; Maria, the criminal outfit's female member (Lisa Gastoni), answers the call with the words "Angelo darling, are you all right?" Linking the name with the news report, Miss Crystal subsequently tries to remember where she went wrong in dialing the number so that she can help the police trace the crooks' location. This stagy Merton Park production, which generates very little suspense (mainly because the old lady never ends up being in any danger from the gang), is based on a Norman Edwards radio play of the same name and had previously been filmed as a

1955 German TV movie titled *Falsch Verbunden* (*False Connection*).

Another Merton Park B feature, ***The Witness*** (1959), was described by the *Monthly Film Bulletin* (December 1959) as "unconvincing and repetitious." Following a prison sentence for robbery, Richard Brindon (Dermot Walsh) gains respectable employment at a service station and vows, to the delight of his wife May (Greta Gynt) and 10-year-old son Peter (Martin Stephens), to remain on the straight and narrow. However, before long, he agrees to join members of his old gang in a raid. Having overheard the plot, but unaware that his father has since changed his mind about taking part, Peter spies on the eventual raid and witnesses the criminals kill a policeman. The police later (and rather irresponsibly) use Peter in a plan to trap the villains, having correctly figured they'll attempt to locate and silence the boy. This elusive little film features Russell Napier in a familiar role as a Scotland Yard inspector, and *The Daily Cinema* (November 2, 1959) talked about "the extensive use of authentic London locations adding to the atmosphere."

> *"They dared to commit the crime of the century..."*

The pressbook for ***The Day They Robbed the Bank of England*** (1959) tells of how, during filming, lead star Aldo Ray spent much of his spare time at the British Museum library and at the files of Scotland Yard, studying the fine art of larceny; Ray is quoted as saying: "But only for the picture. Of course, if the movies ever decide to give me up, this knowledge might come in handy." Events are set in 1901, and Ray plays Charles Norgate, an Irish-American adventurer hired by Irish patriots (fighting for home rule) to engineer a £1 million gold bullion robbery at London's Bank of England. Norgate comes up with a daring plan to tunnel into the subterranean bullion room by way of a disused sewer running beneath the bank vaults. In an impressive early role, Peter O'Toole plays a young security officer whose suspicions are aroused during the heist (not least because the excavations end up playing havoc with gas lamps in the bank's underground corridors), with this and other complications ultimately spelling disaster for the robbers. Among those playing the patriots are Kieron Moore and Elizabeth Sellars, he a belligerent active accomplice in the heist and she a widow in a love-hate relationship with Norgate.

The Challenge (1959) stars Anthony Quayle as Jim Maxton, a widower and father of a young son named Joey (Peter Pike). Jim is tempted by beautiful criminal Billy Lacross (Jayne Mansfield) into taking part in a robbery with her four male cohorts. However, a double-cross by one of the gang members sees him wind up in prison for five years, but not before he hides the spoils in the countryside at a location known only to him. On his release, he plans to retrieve the loot to benefit Joey, but the gang kidnaps the boy and demands the money as ransom. In ensuing events, the loot is accidentally destroyed and Joey is left in the hands of a particularly sadistic gang member named Buddy (Peter Reynolds), who contrives to kill the boy by having him play "chicken" on train tracks. Mansfield doesn't register too strongly here, and was much better in her other British thriller from the same year, *Too Hot to Handle*. The score by Bill McGuffie includes a catchy opening credits jazz theme.

Moment of Danger (1960) begins with a suspenseful sequence detailing a London jewel robbery carried out by Peter Carran (Edmund Purdom) and John Bain (Trevor Howard), the latter a bitter and disillusioned locksmith looking to make enough money to go to Mexico. Following the heist, Carran not only walks out on his world-weary girlfriend Gianna (the wonderful Dorothy Dandridge in her last film) but also double-crosses John and makes his way to Spain to exchange the jewels for cash. Events see John and Gianna teaming up to pursue Carran, an adventure that takes them to Madrid, Malaga (*Malaga* was the film's U.S. title) and finally Gibraltar. A slowly developing romance between John and Gianna is sensitively handled, and there's some nice Spanish scenery en route to a satisfying conclusion.

The B movie ***Jackpot*** (1960) sees deported criminal Carl Stock (George Mikell) illegally return to England in an attempt to reclaim his hesitant wife (Betty McDowall) and to collect his share of the loot from a heist masterminded by London's so-called "King of Soho" Sam Hare (Eddie Byrne), owner of the titular nightclub. When Sam refuses to hand over the money, Carl robs the club's safe, callously killing a policeman before getting away with £6,000 and documents that, unbeknownst to him, can incriminate Sam. Carl is soon being pursued by not only the police, but also Sam, who wants to retrieve said documents, with events leading to a showdown at London's Arsenal football stadium which the *Monthly Film Bulletin* (May 1960) noted is "more resourceful than the average B-picture finale." Top-billed William Hartnell plays a Scotland Yard man, while Michael Ripper, in a more substantial role than usual, is an ex-safebreaker persuaded by Carl to help in the nightclub robbery.

> *"What is the league? ...*
> *Who are the gentlemen?"*

In the classic ***The League of Gentlemen*** (1960), a forcibly retired British Army officer (Jack Hawkins in one of his finest roles) plans a daring London bank robbery inspired by events in an American pulp novel called *The Golden Fleece*. To carry out the scheme, which is to be executed like a textbook military campaign, he enlists seven

Robbery in progress in *The League of Gentlemen* (1960).

other former officers, all of them with shady pasts and an urgent need for cash. The gang's preparations include raiding an army training camp to obtain arms for the main heist, which is subsequently carried out—using smoke bombs, gas masks and submachine guns—to perfection ... except, that is, for one small detail which ultimately leads to the gang's comeuppance. The manner in which the thieves are caught is the only let-down in an otherwise expertly crafted entertainment whose fabulous cast includes Nigel Patrick, Richard Attenborough and Bryan Forbes, the latter also responsible for the literate and witty screenplay.

Director Don Sharp, who was particularly adept when it came to thrillers, cut his teeth in the genre with the uncluttered and well-paced B movie **The Professionals** (1960). Just released from prison, notorious safecracker Phillip Bowman (William Lucas) is soon making plans to not only marry the girlfriend, Ruth (Colette Wilde), who waited patiently while he served a four-year sentence, but to also carry out a £100,000 bank heist intended to be his swansong. Together with colleague Joe Lawson (Stratford Johns) and other cohorts, the heist is meticulously planned and successfully carried out. Bowman and Ruth get married, but events, in which one of the cohorts (Charles Vance) inadvertently puts the police on the gang's trail, ensure they never get to enjoy their honeymoon. The film went straight to television in the U.S., initially broadcast as a first-season episode of *Kraft Mystery Theatre*. On the day of the broadcast (June 14, 1961), "TV Scout" previews (syndicated content carried in the TV pages of many newspapers) noted that the "British have a way with this sort of film."

The B movie **The Man Who Couldn't Walk** (1960) stars Eric Pohlmann (top-billed for a change) as "The Boss," a wheelchair-bound Consul General of a small Central American republic who is also a racketeer with headquarters in a luxury apartment above the Palermo Espresso bar in London's Soho district. Peter Reynolds plays a brash safecracker recruited into the Consul's gang who, while taking part in a series of jewel robberies designed to net over £2 million, learns that the Consul was the Chicago mobster who'd murdered his father—a New York racketeer—years earlier. He resists revenge for the sake of the Consul's stepdaughter (Pat Clavin), but the Consul nevertheless gets his comeuppance in an unexpected development involving the Palermo's manageress (Margot Van Der Burgh). The film, which the *Kinematograph Weekly* (August 11, 1960) said "packs quite a punch for its size," is extremely rare, which is strange considering it was made by the same company behind the same year's relatively easy-to-find B thriller, *The Hand*.

In the Joseph Losey-directed **The Criminal** (1960), recently released convict Johnny Bannion (a dynamic Stanley Baker) teams up with Mike Carter (Sam Wanamaker) to carry out a robbery, the proceeds of which he buries in a field. Betrayed by a jealous ex-girlfriend (Margit Saad), Bannion lands up back in jail and decides to keep the location of the hidden loot to himself. Using contacts inside the prison, Carter tries to pressure Bannion into revealing the hiding place, but when this fails, he comes up with a plan that compels Bannion to escape, intending to follow him when he eventually goes to retrieve the money. The prison sequences (Patrick Magee gives a standout supporting performance as a chief warder) and a climactic showdown between Bannion and Carter are particularly well handled, and there's a cool jazz score to round out what is justly regarded as a classic British crime thriller. The screenplay is based on an original story by Jimmy Sangster.

Piccadilly Third Stop (1960) features Terence Morgan as suave and ruthless playboy Dominic Colpoys-Owen, who teams up with elderly safecracker Colonel Whitfield (William Hartnell) and brash American Joe Preedy (John Crawford) to rob a safe at a foreign embassy in London. The plan, which

From left: John Crawford, Terence Morgan and William Hartnell en route to a heist in *Piccadilly Third Stop* (1960).

entails Dominic cold-heartedly seducing an ambassador's daughter (Yoko Tani) in order to gain some vital inside information, ultimately ends in disaster following an attempted double-cross by Preedy. Morgan is perfect as the manipulative Dominic, and the excellent cast also includes Mai Zetterling as Preedy's wife (and Dominic's lover) and Dennis Price as a shady organizer of gambling parties. The access to—and getaway from—the embassy involves the use of a tunnel at a fictitious London subway station called Belgravia.

> *"Trapped by a past they would not let him forget!"*

The routine Danziger brothers B movie ***Compelled*** (1960) stars Ronald Howard as Paul Adams, a respectable engineer who, unbeknownst to either his wife (Beth Rogan) or employers, once served time in prison. It's not long before a shady former associate, the supercilious Fenton (John Gabriel), arrives on the scene and compels him to lend his engineering skills to the construction of a tunnel to be used for a £250,000 jewel robbery, threatening to expose his past—and to physically harm his wife—if he refuses. Left with little choice, Paul complies. Eventually however, as the result of a murder (that of a man who'd muscled in on the robbery scheme) committed by Fenton's dull-witted and brutal henchman (Richard Shaw), Paul has second thoughts and determines to thwart the heist. This leads to an explosive finale in the tunnel involving a lit match and a leaking gas main.

The complicated plot of ***The Breaking Point*** (1960) concerns a plan by communist agents to take control of the small Middle

Eastern state of Lalvadore. This will involve causing economic chaos by flooding the place with forged currency, but first they must prevent the delivery there of a new legitimate currency being printed in England. To this end, they target the shiftless Eric Winlatter (Peter Reynolds) of Winlatters, a family printing company tasked with creating the new money. Through bribery and blackmail, they ensure Eric's cooperation in a scheme that entails first obtaining inside information from the company and later hijacking an armored van transporting the newly minted cash to an airport. Reynolds gives his customary excellent performance in this entertaining B movie that packs a great deal of plot into its short running time. Dermot Walsh plays a journalist caught up in events (he also gets caught up in a budding romance with Eric's neglected wife, played by Joanna Dunham) and there's a fast-moving climax involving a time bomb set to destroy the currency. Albert Elms' soundtrack prefigures his incidental music for the cult TV series *Man in a Suitcase* (1967–68). Under the title *The Great Armored Car Swindle*, the film had solid theatrical distribution in the U.S., a high point being a pairing with the classic Alan Ladd western *Shane* (1952) upon the latter's 1966 reissue.

The little-seen Danziger brothers B movie **Transatlantic** (1960) was noted by the *Monthly Film Bulletin* (September 1961) as having "one or two faint tremors of tension" while being "for the most part elementary." The story tells of an airliner—the "Southern Wind"—carrying 26 passengers and £1 million worth of diamonds that disappears during a flight from London to New York. The pilot, John Wentworth (Anthony Oliver), is initially suspected of foul play. However, it turns out that a ruthless gang had carried out a clever and decidedly evil plan that involved two of their number (Bill Nagy and Neil Hallett) commandeering the plane, securing the diamonds and then bailing out, leaving behind a time bomb which caused the plane and all those on board to perish in the Atlantic. The truth is uncovered thanks to the workings of an FBI agent (Pete Murray) and Wentworth's journalist sister (June

Pressbook cover for a rare 1960 B movie.

Thorburn). The film has hardly been seen since its original British release except for in Australia, where it had decent theatrical exposure in the mid–1960s followed by TV showings up until the late 1970s.

Energetically directed by Sidney Hayers, who makes excellent use of Newcastle upon Tyne locations, **Payroll** (1961) concerns a gang's robbery of a £100,000 factory payroll from a supposedly impenetrable armored van, this made possible thanks to inside information about the vehicle from meek wages clerk Dennis Pearson (William Lucas). During the heist (an exhilarating and brilliantly staged sequence), one of the thieves is fatally wounded and the van driver killed. The driver's widow, Jackie (Billie Whitelaw), vows revenge against the criminals and begins by sending Pearson anonymous letters designed to break his nerve. Meanwhile, a falling out among the thieves results in their psychopathic leader, Johnny Mellors (a superb Michael Craig), being the only one left alive; that is, until the exciting climax, where his attempt to abscond with the loot (following an attempted double-cross by Pearson's greedy wife [Françoise Prévost] whom he'd hooked up with) is fatally thwarted by Jackie.

The B movie **Jungle Street** (1961) stars then real-life husband and wife David McCallum and Jill Ireland: he as psychotic lowlife Terry Collins, who in the opening scene mugs and kills a defenseless 65-year-old man on a London street; and she as Sue, a stripper (the object of Terry's lust) at The Adam & Eve Club. The story sees Terry persuade an old pal—Sue's lover, Johnnie (Kenneth Cope), just out of prison after taking the rap for a crime in which both men were involved—to help him carry out a robbery at the club. Once the safe has been blown, Terry double-crosses Johnnie by knocking him unconscious and making off with all the loot before then attempting to force Sue into absconding with him. Involved throughout is a small-time hustler (Brian Weske) who blackmails Terry (in connection with the opening murder) and ultimately tips off the police as to his whereabouts. This leads to a showdown which culminates in a hysterical Terry, having by now caused the death of a second man, being led away screaming "I don't want to hang!" The film was retitled *Jungle Street Girls* in the U.S., where publicity played up its racier aspects (actually nothing more than a couple of mild striptease scenes) while amusingly claiming the whole thing was shot in "Sin-O-Rama."

*"They set a trap for each other
... from which only one could escape!"*

Information Received (1961) is a well-paced B movie which the *Monthly Film Bulletin* (September 1961) described as "disarming" by way of its "confidently contrived thrills and dashing disregard for logic." William Sylvester is his usual engaging self as independent secret agent Rick Hogan, recruited by Scotland Yard to assume the identity of an American safecracker in order to bring down two criminal masterminds. One of the masterminds, Drake (Edward Underdown), plans to steal a NATO blueprint, while the other, Vic Farlow (Walter Brown), is behind a series of prison breaks. There's also a major subplot involving Vic's wife Sabina (Sabina Sesselman), a femme fatale who murders her husband and tries to lay the blame on Rick.

While **Pit of Darkness** (1961) is not one of director Lance Comfort's best B movies, even a lesser Comfort offering is better than average. William Franklyn stars as Richard Logan, an expert safe designer discovered injured and suffering from amnesia after having been missing for some time. It turns out he'd been held prisoner by a gang of thieves who tricked him into helping carry out a robbery (involving one of his own safes) before then attempting to kill him. As he begins to regain his memory, Logan realizes he's still in danger from the criminals, but finally manages to outwit them after they try to force him, by holding his wife (Moira Redmond) hostage, to help in another robbery. Anthony Booth, almost unrecognizable behind a false nose, plays one of the thieves, while the brisk pace leaves little time to dwell on the many unconvincing situations.

The surprisingly hard-hitting B movie **Freedom to Die** (1961) begins with the escape from prison of black-hearted criminal Craig Owen (Canadian actor Paul Maxwell) while serving time for the manslaughter of one of his accomplices in a £300,000 robbery. He is soon applying pressure on Felix Gray (Bruce Seton), a wrestling promoter who masterminded the heist, in an attempt to get hold of his due share—£50,000—of the proceeds. In the course of events, the evil Craig devastates Gray's beloved and innocent adopted daughter Linda (Felicity Young) by telling her about her father's criminal activities before then blackmailing her for sex and also into handing over the keys to her father's safe. However, it's not long before circumstances see him land up back in prison. On the day of his eventual release, Craig gets a surprise comeuppance from one of the many enemies he had made on the outside. Good support is provided by Kay Callard and T.P. McKenna, she as Craig's moll and he as an associate who ends up getting framed by the pair for Craig's callous hit-and-run of a little girl during the opening escape.

Seton was also in **Ambush in Leopard Street** (1961), this time playing Nimmo, a veteran crook who teams up with fellow criminal Harry Garland (Michael Brennan) in a plan to steal £500,000 worth of diamonds being transported to a jewelry firm called Beaumonts. A key part of the plan entails Harry convincing, through persuasion and blackmail, his handsome brother-in-law Johnny (James Kenney) to woo Beaumonts' reserved secretary (Jean Harvey) in order to obtain vital inside information about the transportation details. However, Big George, a gangster Nimmo had earlier tried to interest in the robbery, plans to ambush the crooks once they have secured the diamonds. A sluggish pace and an underwhelming robbery sequence do this very low-budget B movie no favors.

"Never in the history of crime was so much taken from so many by so few"

Noted as being "a very good film indeed of its formulary type" by the *Monthly Film Bulletin* (December 1962), **A Prize of Arms** (1961) details a plan by three men—a dishonorably discharged army officer (Stanley Baker), an explosives expert (Helmut Schmid) and a mechanic (Tom Bell)—to rob the paymaster's office at a military camp during preparations for the mass deployment of troops overseas. Posing as soldiers, and using a borrowed army truck, they enter the camp, carry out the meticulously prepared heist (which involves starting a fire to create a diversion) and hide their swag of over £100,000 cash in one of the truck's wheels. However, their getaway, under cover of a truck convoy departing from the camp, is soon beset by unforeseen circumstances that lead to the trio's comeuppance in an explosive climax. Natural locations and some convincing army camp atmosphere lend an air of authenticity to the well-staged action.

The Primitives (1961) is the stage name of a group of cabaret artistes-cum–jewel thieves who carry out robberies in the cities where they perform. The main plot sees the gang pull off a daring heist in London, only to then get their comeuppance as the result of one of their number, Philip (Derek Ware), attempting to murder a journalist he mistakenly thinks poses a threat to them. Jan Holden, as an exotic dancer and the brains behind the robberies, is the star attraction of this unassuming and light-hearted B movie; light-hearted, that is, except for the part where Philip plans to kill the journalist by blowing up a plane with 100 passengers on board. According to original publicity material, there exists an extended 90-minute version with extra nightclub footage.

The workmanlike B picture **Gaolbreak** (1962) concerns a gang of thieves run by Eddie Wallis (Peter Reynolds) and his mother (Avice Landone) under cover of their family newspaper store. An upcoming heist at an auction house requires the services of Eddie's brother Ron (David Gregory), a safecracker currently in prison serving time for another robbery. A jailbreak is organized for Ron and another gang member, but a third convict who escapes with them causes complications—in connection with his girlfriend (Carol White)—that ultimately lead to the red-handed capture of the thieves at the auction house. Also starring are Andre Mikhelson as a crooked art dealer and Geoffrey Hibbert as a doctor being blackmailed by the gang for the use of his nursing home as a hideout.

One of the rarer British B thrillers, ***Night Without Pity*** (1962) stars Neil McCallum and Alan Edwards as O'Brien and Randall, two crooks whose plan to rob a factory involves first breaking into the factory-owner's house to obtain some necessary keys. After said keys have been secured, O'Brien stays behind at the house and holds the owner's wife Diana (Sarah Lawson) and young son—and later also a doctor (Patrick Newell) who arrives to treat the boy for an injury—prisoner while Randall goes off alone to carry out the robbery. In subsequent events, O'Brien forces Diana to drive him in pursuit of Randall when the latter double-crosses him, leading to a showdown at a service station. Critics weren't too impressed upon the film's belated release, with *The Daily Cinema* (May 11, 1966) calling it a "feeble-minded suspense melodrama" which "makes a promising start but fails to sustain conviction."

Described by *Variety* (January 30, 1963) as a "weak grade B crime-suspense meller," ***Cairo*** (1962) is indeed a rather feeble adaptation of the oft-filmed W.R. Burnett novel *The Asphalt Jungle*, only with a more exotic setting. A gang of crooks, led by English-

George Sanders (foreground) and Richard Johnson in MGM's *Cairo* (1962).

man Major Pickering (George Sanders), steals the Tutankhamun jewels from the Cairo Museum, but never gets to benefit from the spoils owing to a disastrous series of setbacks including an attempted double-cross by a businessman (Walter Rilla) who'd agreed to fence the gems. Then Egyptian superstar (and wife of Omar Sharif) Faten Hamama plays a singer in love with the gang's strong-arm man (a somewhat miscast Richard Johnson), and also worth a mention is the ever-reliable Eric Pohlmann as a Greek immigrant casino boss who ultimately betrays the gang to the police. The authentic locations are unimaginatively used in what amounts to a suspense-free misfire.

An original idea is efficiently put across in the B movie **Bomb in the High Street** (1963). An unexploded bomb found on a building site in a suburban high street results in the immediate vicinity being evacuated. The bomb is in fact a fake and part of a clever plan engineered by Manning (Ronald Howard), head of a gang of robbers who turn up posing as a bomb squad. While the unwitting police dutifully keep people away from the area, Manning and his crew set about their real task, namely robbing the local bank. Terry Palmer and Suzanna Leigh play runaway teenagers who sleep through the evacuation while sheltering in a half-built house nearby, and whose presence in the locality causes complications for the gang. A fake bomb scare and bogus bomb squad also featured in a later British heist thriller, *The Jokers* (1966).

The Daily Cinema (March 15, 1965) recognized the B movie **Panic** (1963) as being "quite enterprisingly plotted, but stolidly handled and not too brightly acted." Janine (Janine Gray), a young Swiss woman living in London, is unaware that her boyfriend, jazz trumpeter Johnnie (Dyson Lovell), is planning for two cohorts to steal a valuable diamond from a Hatton Garden diamond merchant for whom she works as a secretary. During the eventual heist, the merchant is shot dead and Janine knocked unconscious. She subsequently wakes up with amnesia before wandering off in a state of confusion and panic. In ensuing events, she has an unpleasant encounter with a seedy hotelier (Marne Maitland), becomes suspected in the death of Johnnie's brother (who was involved in the robbery plan and has in fact been accidentally killed by Johnnie) and is befriended by an ex-boxer, Mike (Glyn Houston), who returns to the ring as a way of raising some cash to help her. There's a surprising revelation involving the authenticity of the diamond, and circumstances ultimately lead to Janine and Mike facing danger from a jealous and crazed Johnnie.

In a faster-paced B movie, **The Hi-Jackers** (1963), truck driver Terry McKinley (the likeable Anthony Booth) is in transit when he's ambushed by a notorious gang of hijackers who steal his valuable cargo of whisky. He subsequently endeavors to track the criminals down with the help of Shirley (Jacqueline Ellis), a hitchhiker who'd been riding with him at the time of the theft. During the course of the story, Shirley gets captured by the gang but is rescued—and the crooks rounded up—after Terry forcibly obtains vital information from his sometime co-driver (Ronald Hines), who is secretly in league with the crooks. Derek Francis and Patrick Cargill are on fine form as, respectively, the chief hijacker, whose spare time is spent indulging his passion for gourmet cooking, and a supercilious police inspector.

*"The most audacious robbery of all time—
for the world's mightiest haul!"*

A "lively thriller, presented with speed and panache" was how the *Monthly Film Bulletin* (August 1965) regarded the British-German co-production **Traitor's Gate** (1964), an updating of a 1920s Edgar Wallace novel. Albert Lieven plays a character called Trayne, the mastermind behind a daring plan to steal the Crown Jewels from the Tower of London. A key part of the plot involves kidnapping one of the Tower's main security guards (Gary Raymond) and switching him with a look-alike convict (also Raymond) sprung from prison especially for the job. Margot Trooger and Klaus Kinski play two of Trayne's cohorts (she a femme fatale and he a cold-blooded assassin), and some comic relief is provided by Eddie Arent as a camera-happy German tourist who gets captured by the criminals after stumbling on and attempting to foil the plan. The German edit, known as *Das Verrätertor*, runs 87 minutes as opposed to the 80-minute original British theatrical release.

Dateline Diamonds (1965) is a late-stage B movie in which jewel thief Major Fairclough (William Lucas) blackmails successful pop music manager Lester Benson (Kenneth Cope) into aiding in a diamond robbery and the subsequent smuggling of the gems into Holland via an offshore pirate radio ship. George Mikell and Conrad Phillips play two investigators—Dutch Interpol agent Paul Verlekt and British CID detective Tom Jenkins—on Fairclough's trail, with Jenkins' teenage daughter (Anna Carteret) inadvertently spotlighting a vital clue (a photograph of a pop group in which Fairclough appears) that cracks the case. The film, which *The Daily Cinema* (December 15, 1965) said ensures "support from both thriller and pop music fans," features several songs by artists such as The Small Faces and Kiki Dee.

"The robbery of the century …
it would be a crime to miss it!"

Directed in quite lively fashion by Michael Winner, the comedy thriller **The Jokers** (1966) is a film whose vivid characters and locations perfectly capture the essence of swinging sixties London. Oliver Reed and Michael Crawford play the titular pranksters, upper-class siblings David and Michael Tremayne, who plan to rob key components of the Crown Jewels from the Tower of London as a publicity stunt to test the security precautions for the nation's most treasured possessions. A major part of the heist entails creating a fake bomb scare, with the brothers then posing as army bomb squad officers (a ploy used in the earlier British thriller *Bomb in the High Street*) to nab the jewels. The zany shenanigans later involve a double-cross by one of the brothers when it comes time to hand back the treasure.

A British-German production in the *krimi* genre, **The Trygon Factor** (1966) is an entertainingly quirky picture about a ruthless gang of thieves headed by the eccentric Livia Emberday (Cathleen Nesbitt) with the aid of her psychotic daughter Trudy (Susan Hampshire). The proceeds of their robberies are packed into pottery vessels—under cover of a convent set up in the grounds of Livia's English country estate (where female gang members pose as an order of nuns called The Sisters of Vigilance)—prior to being smuggled abroad. Stewart Granger is great as the hero of the piece, a suave Scotland Yard detective who smashes the gang following their £1 million gold bullion heist at a London bank. The heist scene is the most outlandish part of the film and features *krimi* regular Eddi Arent as a specially hired safecracker who uses a futuristic-looking multi-barreled machine gun to break into the bank vault. The film's German title is *Das Gemeimnis der Weissen Nonne*.

"Who says crime doesn't pay?
£3 million says it does!"

Inspired by the true-life British "Great Train Robbery" of 1963, director Peter Yates' **Robbery** (1967) is as lean and straightforward as its title. Stanley Baker (also the co-producer) plays a career criminal, Paul Clifton, who masterminds a London jewel robbery in order to fund a much larger criminal undertaking, namely the daring theft of over £3 million from an overnight Glasgow-London Royal Mail train. The film's highlights are a brilliantly staged car chase (Yates' expert handling of this sequence helped him secure his subsequent directing gig—the Steve McQueen actioner *Bullitt*—which featured an even better car chase) and the train heist itself; the latter, a meticulously planned operation that involves fixing railway signals in order to stop the train en route, is carried out by the robbers with military precision. A great supporting cast includes William Marlowe as Clifton's second-in-command and James Booth as a detective in charge of the eventual round-up of the criminals—that is, except for Clifton, who, with the cinema having by then practically given up on its moral stance of "crime does not pay," is allowed by the filmmakers to get away with it. A distinct lack of character development (save for some brief interaction between Clifton and his unhappy wife, played by Joanna Pettet) actually benefits the mechanical nature of the film, which *Films and Filming* (November 1967) said "deserves to gain as much prestige for its makers as The Great Train Robbery gained notoriety for the British criminal."

Regarded by *Variety* (September 11, 1968) as being "too obtuse and boring for general audiences," **Deadfall** (1968) sees jewel thief Henry Clarke (Michael Caine) join forces with the beautiful Fe Moreau (Giovanna Ralli) and her older gay husband Richard (Eric Portman) in a daring plan to rob a millionaire's fortified mansion. During preparations (involving a practice-run robbery on a more accessible property) for the job, Henry and Fe become lovers. However, a startling revelation about Fe's background and her relationship with Richard (it turns out, through a complicated set of circumstances dating back to World War II and involving the French Resistance and the Gestapo, that Richard is actually Fe's father) have a devastating effect on Henry that lead to him embarking on a disastrous (to himself) attempt to carry out the robbery alone. Set in Spain, the film is highlighted by a 23-minute heist sequence intercut with scenes of a guitar concerto performed by Catalan guitarist Renata Tarragó and conducted by its composer John Barry, who also provides the remainder of the soundtrack.

The super-trendy **Duffy** (1968) stars James Coburn as the eponymous character, an American ex–Navy man based in Tangier and probably best described as a combination of hipster, adventurer and criminal mastermind. The entertaining yarn has two half-brothers (James Fox and John Alderton) recruit the resourceful Duffy in a plan to rob their shipping magnate father (James Mason) of £1 million cash from a safe on board one of his luxury liners traveling from Tangier to Zurich. The heist itself, which also involves the bed-hopping girlfriend (Susannah York) of one of the brothers, is a fairly well-staged affair and is followed by a surprising double-cross and neat final twist. Fans of the ever-charismatic Coburn won't be disappointed, and from the moment we are introduced to the cool and free-spirited Duffy, we know, as in the words of one of the characters, that "it's gonna be a groovy little happening, man!"

"It's daylight robbery!
How do they get away with it?"

A bona fide cult classic, **The Italian Job** (1969) is a comedic caper with a decidedly patriotic slant best exemplified by the three Mini Coopers—each painted in a different color of the British Union Jack flag—used in its brilliant getaway sequence. Soon after his release from a London prison, cockney criminal Charlie Croker (Michael Caine) puts the finishing touches on a plan—inherited from an associate (Rossano Brazzi) killed by the mafia—to steal $4 million in gold bullion from a security van in Turin, Italy. A crucial part of the plan involves causing a major traffic jam by changing a computer program in the city's traffic control center, with the aforementioned Mini Coopers avoiding the resulting chaos by using a carefully planned getaway route involving sidewalks, tunnels, underpasses and even rooftops. A final escape by coach across the Alps leads to a literal cliff-hanger of an ending.

Caine is on sparkling form and has many great lines, of which "you're only supposed to blow the bloody doors off!" went on to become one of the most quoted in movie history. Also starring are madcap comedian Benny Hill as an eccentric computer boffin, Noël Coward as an imprisoned patriotic crime lord who finances the robbery plan as a matter of national pride (the British getting one over on the Italians), and Raf Vallone as a mafia don. The film's many highlights include the evocative opening sequence (featuring the beautiful "On Days Like These" performed by British crooner Matt Monro) and some superb stunt driving by the legendary Remy Julienne and his team, L'Equipe Remy Julienne. Interestingly, *Leonard Maltin's Movie Guide* awarded the forgettable 2003 remake a higher rating than the original.

David Hemmings and Samantha Eggar, both at the peak of their creative powers, deliver flawless performances in the emotionally charged romantic thriller **The Walking Stick** (1970). Eggar is the vulnerable and attractive Deborah Dainton, an antiques appraiser for an exclusive London auction house who has relied on the titular device ever since a childhood bout of polio. Hemmings is Leigh Hartley, a handsome struggling artist who persistently woos the initially reluctant Deborah until she finally falls in love with him. Before long, Deborah is cunningly manipulated by Leigh into divulging security arrangements at the auction house and, having gotten in over her head, is coerced into becoming an active accomplice in a subsequent robbery of the place by Leigh and some shady associates. Deborah's growing realization that she had been used as a pawn right from the start leads to her composing a letter confessing all to the police, but only after a final soul-searching conversation with Leigh does she decide whether or not to post it.

An adaptation of *Marnie* author Winston Graham's 1967 novel of the same name, the film was perfectly summed up by the *Monthly Film Bulletin* (June 1970) as "a knowingly detailed, beautifully acted portrayal of deceit and the failure of love." The supporting cast includes Emlyn Williams (the Welsh playwright of *Night Must Fall* fame) as the mastermind behind the robbery, and it's worth noting that Stanley Myers' delicate score includes a version of his *Cavatina* composition eight years before it became the theme tune for *The Deer Hunter*.

Stanley Baker stars in **Perfect Friday** (1970) as Mr. Graham, the reputable deputy manager of a large London bank whose dissatisfaction with his mundane life spurs him to devise a foolproof plan to rob the bank's reserve of £300,000. To help carry out the scheme, he enlists his beautiful new lover Britt (Ursula Andress), whom he met when she applied for a loan at the bank, and her eccentric, titled but penniless husband Nicholas (David Warner), whose part in the heist entails posing as a bank inspector. Britt subsequently plots with each man to double-cross the other and ends up double-crossing them both in a surprise ending. It's nice to see Baker eschew his tough-guy image in this stylish, light-hearted and witty caper, which contains a fair bit of nudity thanks to Andress frequently living up to her "undress" nickname. T.P. McKenna deserves mention for his excellent supporting role as one of Graham's bank colleagues.

"The only way out was death!"

Although justly noted by the *Monthly Film Bulletin* (November 1972) as having "insufficiently fleshed out" central characters, **The Fast Kill** (1972) nevertheless remains one of cult director Lindsay Shonteff's more accomplished films. Ruthless mastermind Max Stein (Tom Adams), helped by his attractive assistant Angelique Dumas (Susie Hampton), recruits a gang to carry out a daring diamond robbery. The heist is successful, but Stein soon puts into motion a vicious plan to double-cross his cohorts while they hide out in Jersey to await payment. Adams, who played superspy Charles Vine in Shonteff's spoofy espionage thriller *Licensed to Kill* (1965), is excellent as the cold-blooded Stein, and standing out among those playing the gang members are Michael

Stanley Baker and Ursula Andress in *Perfect Friday* (1970).

Culver as a skilled driver and Patricia Haines as a lesbian markswoman. The film, full of surprising developments and highlighted by a violent robbery sequence followed by an exhilarating getaway through narrow streets, is only slightly let down by a rather incongruous soundtrack by the Average White Band's Alan Gorrie. An alternate edit reportedly exists under the title *Hard Recoil*.

A British-Italian co-production filmed entirely on location in Italy (where it's known as *Senza Ragione*), **Redneck** (1972) is a typically crude and violent 1970s Eurocrime flick and a mediocre one at that. Child actor Mark Lester plays a British diplomat's son discovered hiding in the back of a Mercedes stolen by two thieves following their clumsy raid on a jewelry store. The criminals are played by Franco Nero and Telly Savalas, the latter's character a particularly vulgar and annoying psychotic loudmouth named Memphis. The main title theme was composed by John Cacavas, who went on to score Savalas' *Kojak* series.

Charles Grodin (complete with dryly humorous voice-over narration) stars in **11 Harrowhouse** (1974) as a small-time American diamond dealer deviously maneuvered by an eccentric tycoon (Trevor Howard) into stealing $12 billion worth of gems from the world's largest diamond exchange at the titular address in London. Helping him carry out the heist (an ingenious affair involving running a hose through a power cable duct so as to vacuum up the diamonds) are his daredevil girlfriend (Candice Bergen) and a resentful employee (James Mason) at the exchange. Although the robbery succeeds, a subsequent double-cross by the tycoon causes problems. Beware of versions without Grodin's narration, as these are decidedly flat in comparison.

"Never have so few taken so much from so many."

The First Great Train Robbery (1978) is a witty and extravagantly entertaining Victorian-era caper featuring excellent production design and cinematography. The year is 1855, and the plan is to rob a fortune in gold bars—destined as payment to British troops in the Crimean War—from two safes on board a London-Folkestone train. Sean Connery and Donald Sutherland make a great double act as chief heisters Edward Pierce and Robert Agar, who spend a substantial part of the film cleverly accessing and taking imprints of four unique keys (held in different locations) required to open the safes. Also majorly involved in the plan is Edward's lover Miriam, a lady of many disguises played fetchingly by Lesley-Anne Down. Jerry Goldsmith's score is exquisite, and the climactic robbery sequence includes some breathtaking stunt work involving Connery atop a speeding train. Michael Crichton directed and scripted from his own 1975 novel *The Great Train Robbery*, in turn based on a true incident.

"Pinky" Green (Richard Jordan), the likeable anti-hero of **A Nightingale Sang in Berkeley Square** (1979), is a London-based American "good ol' boy" (complete with bluegrass-style music to accompany his antics) and repeat offender who we first encounter being released from a spell in prison. His decision to go straight goes straight out the window when he's coerced by his old associates—ruthless criminal kingpin Ivan (David Niven) and gang—into helping rob a London bank at which he has gained respectable employment as an electrical maintenance engineer. Inspired by a real-life 1975 Mayfair bank robbery, the film is a mostly light-hearted affair with a pleasant performance by Jordan, and also features Oliver Tobias as Pinky's half-brother and Hollywood legend Gloria Grahame as their mother. The criminals are all finally caught and sentenced but, in a neat ending, Pinky cleverly manages to escape from police custody at the courthouse.

Gangsters

A beautifully photographed London provides the backdrop to **Night and the City** (1950), a superior example of a British film noir. Richard Widmark plays a doomed small-time hustler and nightclub tout named Harry Fabian, who attempts to supplant Greek racketeer Kristo (Herbert Lom) as the capital's dominant wrestling promoter. Having deviously maneuvered Kristo's father (Stanislaus Zbyszko), a former professional wrestler and now a trainer, into becoming his business partner, Fabian ends up inadvertently causing the man's death in connection with a fearsome wrestler known as "The Strangler" (Mike Mazurki in a pivotal role). This incurs Kristo's wrath, and Fabian is soon on the run with a £1,000 contract out on him. Widmark is never less than riveting, and the superb Anglo-American cast also includes Gene Tierney as Fabian's put-upon nightclub singer girlfriend, Francis L. Sullivan as the nightclub's oily boss and Googie Withers as the latter's deceitful wife. The slightly shorter U.S. cut features alternate music by Franz Waxman. Don't expect too much from the 1992 remake with Robert De Niro in the Widmark role.

"Their wheel of fortune was spun by the cold steel of an automatic!"

The Gambler and the Lady (1952) charts the misfortunes of London-based American ex-con Jim Forster, a nightclub owner and illegal gambling operator played by Hollywood's Dane Clark. An obsession with British high society leads to Jim falling in love with the upper-class Susan (Naomi Chance), but he is soon massively swindled in a venture connected with her father. Things go from bad to worse when a disgruntled former employee frames him so that he becomes targeted for death by a

Hollywood's Richard Widmark in a great 1950 British noir thriller.

gangster (Eric Pohlmann) who'd previously been planning to take over his gambling business. In the end, Jim's fate is decided by a jealous and vengeful admirer he'd earlier rejected, played in scarily convincing fashion by Kathleen Byron. The film is a perfect companion piece to the previous year's U.S. production, *Never Trust a Gambler*, in which Clark similarly played a doomed gamester.

> "She'll ensnare you with her kisses
> ... entrap you in her crimes!"

Based on Robert Westerby's more interestingly titled novel *Wide Boys Never Work*, **Soho Incident** (1955) stars Canada's Lee Patterson as Jim Bankley, a young man whose desire for easy money leads to him joining a gang of racketeers based in London's Soho district. U.S. star Faith Domergue, in what was one of a trio of British B thrillers she made during the 1950s, steals the show as femme fatal Bella, the gang boss' (Martin Benson) ruthless sister who becomes Jim's lover only to later try to kill him after he quits both her and the gang over a cold-blooded murder. Rona Anderson has a pivotal role as a good friend of Jim's whose boxer brother had been killed by one of the criminals for refusing to take a fall during a fight, and there's some atmospheric art direction by future James Bond production designer Ken Adam.

The Long Haul (1957) is a gloomy and melodramatic noir-style offering starring Victor Mature as Harry Miller, a U.S. Army man discharged from service in Germany who moves with his wife Connie (Gene Anderson) and young son to Liverpool in England. Before long, Harry has a fling with the glamorous girlfriend, Lynn (Diana Dors), of racketeer Joe Easy (a powerful performance by Patrick Allen), leading to a marital crisis during which Connie reveals that their son is not his biological child. Subsequent circumstances force Harry to embark on a fur-smuggling operation with Joe and Lynn, this leading to an impressive nine-minute sequence in which he maneuvers a truck along hazardous terrain in the Scottish Highlands, where events see Joe attempt to kill him.

Anderson gives a sympathetic performance as Connie, and the ending is appropriately bittersweet.

One of the better Danziger brothers B movies, the engaging ***On the Run*** (1957) stars Neil McCallum as Robert Wesley Edwards, a drifter—eventually revealed to be a boxer known as "Kid" Edwards—who has spent the last two years on the run from vicious mobsters seeking revenge for his refusal to take a fall during a fight. Having found shelter (and a job) at a service station owned by widower Tom Casey (William Hartnell), Edwards is encouraged by Casey's daughter Kitty (Susan Beaumont), who has fallen in love with him, to finally stop running and make a stand when the mobsters inevitably show up in the area looking for him. The film, which the *Kinematograph Weekly* (June 12, 1958) called "a workmanlike imitation of American gangster fare," features good characterizations by McCallum and Hartnell, not to mention Philip Saville as the sinister soft-spoken chief mobster.

In the Wake of a Stranger (1959) stars Tony Wright as Tom Cassidy, a sailor on shore leave in Liverpool who drunkenly stumbles across the dead body of a bookie—the victim of two murderous small-time gangsters (Harry H. Corbett and Danny Green)—but cannot subsequently remember details of the event. When the bookie's fearsome business partner (Willoughby Goddard) makes it known that he intends to avenge the murder, the gangsters attempt to pin the crime on Cassidy, with events culminating in a showdown (involving all parties) at a dangerously dilapidated house. The cast also includes Shirley Eaton as an attractive schoolteacher providing romantic interest for Cassidy. During 1960–1961, this now very obscure B movie had unusually extensive distribution in the U.S., and as a thriller had no greater honor than being partnered with *Psycho*, in one instance actually getting top billing over the classic Alfred Hitchcock shocker.

Released from prison following a 12-year sentence for a robbery involving £250,000, Sam Roscoe (Mervyn Johns) is the only one who knows where the stolen loot is hidden, and he intends to keep it that way in the B movie ***Echo of Barbara*** (1960). However, Sam's shiftless son Mike (Ronald Hines), in desperate need of money to pay off a debt to vicious London racketeer Caledonia Horsman (Paul Stassino), has other ideas and comes up with a cunning plan—involving striptease artist Paula (Maureen Connell) posing as Sam's beloved long-lost daughter Barbara—to coax the location out of the old man. In later events, Sam sets out to rescue Paula after she is taken prisoner by Caledonia in the latter's own attempt to get hold of the loot. Highlighted by Connell's spirited performance, the film, according to *The Daily Cinema* (January 13, 1961), "belts along single-mindedly to a reasonably exciting climax, even if it doesn't work up much suspense along the way."

The Gentle Trap (1960) is a lively B movie in which novice thief Johnny Ryan (Spencer Teakle) pulls off a jewel robbery and ends up on the run from London nightclub boss and racketeer Ricky Barnes (Martin Benson), who wants the gems for himself after learning about the heist from Johnny's double-crossing girlfriend (Dawn Brooks). The story also involves another nightclub boss, tough-talking Mary Weldon (Dorinda Stevens), and her sympathetic younger sister Jean (Felicity Young). Jean, with the use of a furniture truck belonging to her uncle (John Dunbar), helps Johnny escape to a safe hiding place in the countryside. Events see Mary betray the hideout to Ricky, but the racketeer is ultimately arrested after Johnny cleverly manages to frame him for the jewel theft. Teakle and Young had previously starred together in another B thriller, *Cover Girl Killer* (1959), from the same producer (Jack Parsons).

"The crossfire of gangland turns the frightened city into a mob jungle!"

An above-average example of the British gangster thriller is ***The Frightened City***

(1961), in which unscrupulous financier Waldo Zhernikov (Herbert Lom) masterminds a syndicate comprised of the six major London protection racket gangs, whose bosses include Harry Foulcher (a larger-than-life Alfred Marks) and Alf Peters (David Davies). Alf later quits and goes into competition with the syndicate, leading to his murder—upon Zhernikov's suggestion—by Foulcher. This incurs the wrath of Alf's good friend Paddy Damion (a dynamic Sean Connery), the main strong arm man of the cartel, who gets used as a pawn by the police in an unorthodox attempt to smash the organization. John Gregson plays a forthright detective, while Yvonne Romain gets the top female role as Zhernikov's mistress. Not to be confused with *Frightened City*, an alternate title for the 1950 U.S. thriller *The Killer That Stalked New York*.

In **The Painted Smile** (1961), a pair of confidence tricksters, Mark and Jo (Peter Reynolds and Liz Fraser), have incurred the wrath of a vicious club-footed gangster named Kleinie (Kenneth Griffith). Kleinie murders Mark and orders Jo to dispose of the body; she in turn blackmails a drunken student, Tom (Tony Wickert), to do the dirty work for her. Tom botches things and is soon, along with Jo, marked for death by Kleinie, who doesn't want any loose ends. Known mainly for comedies, Fraser shows that she was equally adept at handling a serious role in what is an average offering from director Lance Comfort's cluster of 1960s B movies. Griffith is suitably nasty as Kleinie, while Reynolds' role amounts to little more than a cameo, with his character being killed off within the first fifteen minutes. A young David Hemmings appears as one of Tom's friends.

In the Danziger brothers B movie **Gang War** (1961), a London slot machine racket is run amicably between two gangs, one led by Jim Alexis (David Davies) and the other by Tony Danton (Mark Singleton). Nightclub boss Doc Tobin (John Gabriel) and Chicago mobster Al Hodges (Sean Sullivan) plan to take over the racket by creating a feud between the two gangs, with the intention of having them wipe each other out. To this end, they murder Alexis' brother and make it look like the work of Danton's mob. However, the gang leaders eventually figure out what is going on, leading to a showdown with disastrous consequences for all concerned. Some romance is included by way of a blossoming relationship between a detective (Sean Kelly) and the daughter (Eira Heath) of the murder victim.

A meager one-and-a-half-star rating was all *Leonard Maltin's Movie Guide* could muster up for the now-rare B movie **A Guy Called Caesar** (1962), which it called a "sloppy account of gangsters on the loose in England." A gang of jewel thieves is presided over by the mysterious Caesar, whose orders are conveyed via a loudspeaker concealed in a statue of the famous Roman dictator, and whose identity is known only to the gang's manager, Maurice (George Moon). That ever-affable British B thriller regular, Conrad Phillips, plays a police officer who infiltrates the thieves and sets into motion a clever plan (involving a diamond robbery) to cause their downfall. As the story nears its end, tough new American gang member Tex (Philip O'Flynn) attempts to double-cross his cohorts and force Maurice's innocent adopted daughter (Maureen Toal) to abscond with him, in the process revealing some shocking facts about Caesar.

The Sicilians (1964) begins with a New York trial at which gangster Angelo Di Marco (Robert Ayres) testifies against the Mafia. Shortly after, his beloved 16-year-old son is kidnapped following a trip to Paris. Top-billed Robert Hutton (in his first British film after semi-permanently moving to England) plays Calvin Adams, an American Embassy Security man who flies to Paris to investigate, eventually learning that the boy is actually safe and with his mother Georgina (Ursula Howells)—Di Marco's ex-wife—at her nightclub La Crevette. It turns out that Georgina, who'd been

Reginald Marsh and Robert Hutton in *The Sicilians* (1964).

callously deserted by Di Marco, colluded with the Mafia and engineered the "kidnapping" as a plan to lure Di Marco into a death trap. This convoluted B movie, which ends with a surprising twist involving Georgina's new husband (Alex Scott), also stars Eric Pohlmann as a French police inspector, and features several neat cameos including Patricia Hayes as a talkative fellow passenger on Calvin's flight to Paris.

Roman Polanski's third directorial effort, ***Cul-de-Sac*** (1966), is a bleakly comic tale beautifully located on a tidal island off the northeast coast of England. Lionel Stander and Jack MacGowran play two wounded gangsters on the run who wind up on the island, where they take refuge in an isolated castle inhabited by meek oddball George (Donald Pleasence) and his seductive and provocative wife Teresa (Françoise Dorléac). The well-cast Stander is the more prominent of the two hoodlums (the other dies early on from his injuries), a gruff and obnoxious type who effectively holds George and Teresa hostage while waiting in vain to be rescued by his boss on the mainland. The film mainly focuses on the interesting dynamics between the three principal characters, and the results are offbeat, surreal and always entertaining thanks to quirky performances all around.

Strip Poker (1968) stars Sebastian Breaks as John Carter, a London advertising agency art director described in an opening voice-over (the distinguished tones of Patrick Allen) as "a misfit, having reached his prime in the days of rock and roll." Before long, Carter is fired from his job and blackmailed by a shady club boss (Derek Aylward)—via threats of being implicated in a seductive blonde's murder—into traveling to an agreed rendezvous in Brighton together with an ex-model (Virginia Wetherell). The pair initially has no idea what is required of them, but it eventually emerges that they are to be killed and their identities assumed by a deported gangster and his wife who wish to return to England (the film's U.S. title, *The Big Switch*, gave some inkling of the plot). Cult director Pete Walker's low-budget take on the 1951 U.S. film noir, *His Kind of Woman*, suffers from poor dialogue and an uncharismatic lead performance by Breaks. Veteran character actor Jack Allen has a small but key role as the mastermind (the advertising agency's boss) behind the scheme, and there's a lively climactic showdown involving the Ghost Train ride on Brighton's West Pier, not to mention a surprising twist regarding the aforementioned blonde's murder. Two versions exist: the original 68-minute British release version and an 81-minute cut (originally used for export) with added gratuitous nudity and violence.

"Caine is Carter"

In their review of the classic **Get Carter** (1971), *Films and Filming* (May 1971) were quite prescient when they said, "this film may well herald the beginning of a spate of hard-hitting thrillers." Michael Caine delivers an icy cool performance as London gangster Jack Carter, who travels to Newcastle to investigate the supposed accidental death of his brother. In fact, the man had been murdered in complex circumstances surrounding his discovery of an amateur pornographic film in which his teenage daughter had been exploited. When he learns the truth, Carter sets out for revenge on all those involved in the sordid venture, including local racketeer Cyril Kinnear (a rare acting role for famed writer John Osborne), who set up the film, and Kinnear's sunken-eyed chauffeur (Ian Hendry). Brutal, bleak and nihilistic, the film, which contains many quotable lines and an unforgettable ending, is the first true modern British gangster thriller whose influence continues to this day. A subplot has Carter pursued by two henchmen (Tony Beckley and George Sewell) because of an affair with his boss' wife (Britt Ekland in what

A key action scene from 1971's *Villain*.

is effectively a cameo role). Carter was later played by Sylvester Stallone in a poor 2000 remake (in which Caine also stars), while another version of Ted Lewis' source novel *Jack's Return Home* was the 1972 blaxploitation movie *Hit Man* starring Bernie Casey.

"Burton is The Villain"

Villain (1971) features a tour-de-force performance by Richard Burton as Vic Dakin, a psychopathic, sadistic and homosexual East End London mob boss. In his devotion toward his beloved mother, Dakin brings to mind James Cagney's Cody Jarrett in 1949's *White Heat* (Burton even occasionally employs a Cagney-like snarl), although the character was actually meant to reflect one half—Ronnie Kray—of the infamous real-life British gangster brothers the Kray Twins. The gritty, bleak and violent story revolves around Dakin organizing and implementing a daring payroll heist (a brilliantly staged sequence) and the ensuing complications that ultimately lead to his downfall. The cast also features Ian McShane as a bisexual small-time hustler and Dakin's reluctant lover ("nobody says no to Dakin"), Donald Sinden as a sleazy politician blackmailed into providing Dakin with an alibi for the heist, and Nigel Davenport on great form as a detective determined to bring the racketeer to justice. The film's screenplay was based on an adaptation (of James Barlow's 1968 novel *The Burden of Proof*) by American actor Al Lettieri, who himself played memorable villains in movies such as *The Getaway* (1972) and *Mr. Majestyk* (1974).

In ***Sitting Target*** (1972), a violent convicted hoodlum, Harry Lomart (Oliver Reed), escapes from prison to kill his wife Pat (a somewhat miscast Jill St. John) after she tells him she's pregnant by another man. In the film's big twist, Birdy (Ian McShane), a fellow convict and supposed close ally of Lomart's who has escaped with him, is found to be in league with Pat, the pregnancy having been a lie to prompt Lomart's escape as part of a plan to get hold of some loot he'd stashed away before his imprisonment. However, things don't go as planned, instead leading to disastrous consequences for all concerned. Reed gives a typically brutish performance, with McShane and Edward Woodward (the latter as a police inspector on Lomart's trail) providing solid support. Consummate character actor Freddie Jones has a small role as yet another escaped convict in a largely redundant subplot. Overall, the film is a slick production with well-handled prison sequences, an exciting climactic car chase and one particularly memorable action scene involving police motorcycles zigzagging through lines of hanging laundry.

The three Michaels—actor Michael Caine, producer Michael Klinger and director Mike Hodges—from the previous year's classic *Get Carter* reunited for ***Pulp*** (1972),

Oliver Reed as a mobster out for revenge in *Sitting Target* (1972).

an offbeat satire on the hard-boiled crime novels of writers such as Dashiell Hammett and John D. MacDonald. Caine is on great form as Mickey King, a Mediterranean-based British writer of pulp fiction hired to ghostwrite the memoirs of an egomaniacal former gangster movie star, Preston Gilbert (a suitably over-the-top Mickey Rooney), on the latter's private island. Before long, Gilbert is shot dead—and King targeted—by an assassin (Al Lettieri) working for a powerful politician, Prince Cippola (Victor Mercieca); Cippola, it turns out, wants to prevent a past incident, namely his and Gilbert's involvement in an orgy which resulted in the death of a young woman, from possibly coming to light in the memoirs. Made entirely on location in Malta, the film also stars Lizabeth Scott (in her final film) as Cippola's wife and Lionel Stander as Gilbert's public relations man. The often incoherent plot is best summed up in a line from Caine's dryly humorous voice-over narration: "this story was like some pornographic photograph—difficult to work out who was doing what and to whom."

> *"Who lit the fuse that tore Harold's world apart?"*

Considered by many to be one of the best modern British gangster thrillers, **The Long Good Friday** (1979) is a vivid and punchy production starring Bob Hoskins as Harold Shand, an ambitious and entrepreneurial London mob boss who has risen through the ranks and is about to embark on a multi-million-pound development of the capital's Docklands district. The fairly straightforward plot sees Harold's plans severely disrupted by a series of devastating attacks—including, in one of the film's most effective scenes, the blowing up of one of his prized establishments (a pub)—against him and his organization at the hands of a mysterious enemy. His desperate attempts to uncover those responsible eventually lead to a startling revelation that he is being targeted for revenge by the IRA in connection with a double-cross perpetrated against them by one of his close colleagues (this explaining the film's up-until-then confusing opening sequence). Harold's naïve belief that he can take on the IRA leads to an unforgettable ending in which he realizes—too late—that he's bitten off far more than he can chew.

Hoskins gives a powerhouse performance as the cocky Shand, and there's a great part for co-star Helen Mirren as his faithful moll. Also starring are Eddie Constantine, adroitly cast as an American Mafia executive visiting London to possibly go into partnership with Harold although ironically put off by all the violence surrounding the mobster; and, in his first feature film, Pierce Brosnan in a small but key role as an IRA assassin.

Blackmail

One of the rarer British B films, **Stranger at My Door** (1950) was noted by the *Monthly Film Bulletin* (April–May 1950) as being a "confused but quite well handled thriller." The story involves an out-of-work ex-commando (Joseph O'Connor) who descends into a life of crime that begins with a jewel robbery designed to raise funds to help a young woman (Agnes Bernelle) escape the influence of an evil blackmailer (Valentine Dyall). Some genteel comedy is introduced in a subsequent robbery where the targeted property's inhabitants (two eccentric old ladies) welcome the theft as an opportunity to claim some much-needed insurance money. Events ultimately lead to a rooftop showdown involving the ex-commando, the young woman and the blackmailer, and which ends badly for all three. Filmed and set in Ireland and originally released there under the title *At a Dublin Inn*.

In the melodramatic **Cage of Gold** (1950), Jean Simmons plays Judith, a naïve artist who dumps her boyfriend Alan (James Donald) after reuniting with Bill (David Farrar), a dashing World War II veteran whom she'd once had a schoolgirl crush on. Mar-

Ealing Studios present

**JEAN SIMMONS
DAVID FARRAR
JAMES DONALD** in

CAGE of GOLD (A)

The story of a girl threatened by her past

with **HERBERT LOM · BERNARD LEE
GLADYS HENSON**
and introducing **MADELEINE LEBEAU**

A **MICHAEL BALCON** PRODUCTION
GFD Directed by **BASIL DEARDEN**

Publicity for a melodramatic 1950 blackmail thriller.

riage follows, but the secretly shady Bill is really only interested in Judith's family money. When this proves to be non-existent, he deserts her and returns to his mistress Marie (Madeleine Lebeau) in Paris. After Bill is mistakenly reported dead in a plane crash, Judith returns to and marries Alan, only to then be blackmailed by Bill for being a bigamist. Skillfully directed and photographed, with excellent lead performances, the film is a leisurely paced affair that eventually turns into a whodunit after Bill is shot dead by a mystery assassin. The title refers to a Paris nightclub, The Cage d'Or, owned by Marie.

J. Lee Thompson's directorial debut was the B movie ***Murder Without Crime*** (1950), which he also scripted from his own stage play, a successful four-hander known as *Double Error*. When his wife (Patricia Plunkett) walks out during an argument, Stephen (Derek Farr) gets drunk at a nightclub and ends up back at his apartment with a young woman (Joan Dowling). Events lead to a violent struggle that ends with the woman apparently dead. Stephen hides the body in a piece of ottoman furniture but is soon taunted and blackmailed by his suave, verbose and hateful landlord, Matthew (Dennis Price), who seems to know what has taken place. Although somewhat overlong, overwrought and dialogue-heavy (including an occasional and annoying voiceover), the film is nevertheless worth a watch for Price's excellent performance, some inventive art direction and two great twists.

According to *Variety* (February 7, 1951), "a slow, old-fashioned style dominates" the little-seen ***Blackmailed*** (1950). When a social worker (Fay Compton) at a London hospital learns that one of the patients is being blackmailed, an ensuing confrontation with the blackmailer, Mr. Sine (James Robertson Justice), at his house results in her accidentally shooting him dead. Her decision to not report the matter is the catalyst for a chain of events that ends up having tragic consequences for another of Sine's blackmail victims, namely a young army deserter named Stephen Mundy (Dirk Bogarde). The screenplay, co-written by Roger Vadim (a frequent collaborator of the film's director Marc Allégret and who was instrumental in putting Brigitte Bardot on the map), keeps the thriller elements to a minimum while focusing on the personal circumstances of the blackmailer's various victims. Harold Huth, who'd been a leading actor from the late 1920s into the 1930s, produced, and he also has a small role as a newspaper editor.

The Last Page (1952) is notable as being the first of many B-movie collaborations between production company Hammer and U.S. producer Robert L. Lippert, as well as for featuring a screenplay by *Dial M for Murder* author Frederick Knott. Hollywood's George Brent stars as John Harman, a London bookstore manager who impulsively shares a kiss with his attractive invoice clerk, Ruby (Diana Dors, the *Man Bait* of the film's U.S. title), this being a one-off indiscretion which he immediately puts out of his mind. However, an evil ex-con, Jeff Hart (Peter Reynolds, the king of shifty young British B-movie villains), persuades Ruby to blackmail Harman over the incident in a scheme whose repercussions cause the death of Harman's invalid wife through stress. Harman's bad luck continues when Jeff accidentally kills Ruby and frames him for her death, forcing him to go on the run. Brent's fellow Hollywoodian, Marguerite Chapman, plays Harman's loyal secretary, who's secretly in love with him and helps him—at some considerable danger to herself—clear his name. The best things about this otherwise lackluster film (in which Brent looks rather uninterested throughout) are a fine early performance by Dors and the atmospheric setting of the bookstore.

"From black market to blackmail to murder!"

Described by the *Motion Picture Herald* (April 4, 1953) as "pleasantly short and uncomplicated," the B movie **Wide Boy** (1952) stars Sydney Tafler as a small-time black marketeer named Benny. At the swanky Flamingo bar in London's Haymarket, Benny steals a wallet in which he finds information enabling him to blackmail a famous surgeon, Robert Mannering (Colin Tapley). An ensuing rendezvous between the two men results in a struggle during which Benny shoots Mannering dead. While on the run, Benny plans an escape to the Continent, but this is thwarted when his girlfriend (top-billed Susan Shaw) inadvertently gives him away to the police, resulting in a dramatic showdown in which he falls from a bridge to be killed by a passing train. Tafler is superb in the type of role he was born to play, while Ronald Howard reprises his role as Inspector Carson from the previous year's *Assassin for Hire* (which also stars Tafler).

The Girl on the Pier (1953) is a little-seen B movie made on location in the seaside resort of Brighton. Joe Hammond (Campbell Singer), proprietor of the waxworks on Brighton Pier, is tracked down by Nick Lane (Australian star Ron Randell), a former accomplice of Hammond's in a robbery for which Lane took the rap. Lane attempts to blackmail Hammond and also seduces his wife Rita (Veronica Hurst), all of which leads to Hammond murdering him in a plan that involves disguising himself as one of the waxwork exhibits, namely The Laughing Clown. Charles Victor plays Robert Chubb, a vacationing Scotland Yard inspector whose young son Charlie (Anthony Valentine)—a chip off the old block when it comes to nosing around—proves instrumental in Hammond's undoing. A brisk climactic chase ends with Hammond, still dressed as the clown, plunging to his death from the pier. Young Valentine would go on to have a successful career in British film and television and was probably never better than in his role as the eponymous gentleman thief in *Raffles* (Yorkshire TV, 1975–77).

The entertaining **House of Blackmail** (1953) is distinguished by a lively pace, crisp dialogue and an enjoyable lead performance by William Sylvester. Carol (Mary Germaine), a London artist, drives to the country mansion of blackmailer Markham (Alexander Gauge) to confront him in connection with some incriminating evidence he has against her brother. En route, she gives a ride to the penniless Jimmy (Sylvester) and offers him money to help in a plan to retrieve the evidence. Events lead to the pair staying the night at the mansion, whose other occupants include an American colleague (John Arnatt) of Markham's. During the night, Markham is shot dead. Jimmy is framed for the crime, but eventually manages to clear himself by exposing the true culprit. Many aspects of this great little B movie hinge on the fact that Jimmy, whom we see reading a book called *Ten Years Behind Bars*, may or may not be a recently escaped convict who just happened to be serving a 10-year jail sentence. That old mystery fiction cliché, "the butler did it," actually proves to be the case here, with the servant in question played in humorously sinister fashion by Denis Shaw.

A much more convoluted B movie was ***A Time to Kill*** (1953), in which a chemist (John Horsley) is put under house arrest for the suspected murder of a young woman who'd been trying to coerce him into marriage. The real killer is actually a mysterious blackmailer with whom the dead woman was involved in an extortion racket and from whose clutches she was trying to break free. The plot's main characters are the chemist's ex-fiancée (Rona Anderson), whose brave attempts at sleuthing on his behalf almost get her strangled, and an eager reporter (top-billed Jack Watling) who plays a major part in the film's great final twist. There's some excellent atmosphere in a couple of twilight scenes where the blackmailer (wearing a sack over his head and looking just like the "Phantom Killer" from 1976's *The Town That Dreaded Sundown*) collects money from a victim at a lonely rendezvous.

"*Danger! Don't turn your back on....
The Limping Man.*"

The B movie ***The Limping Man*** (1953) opens with former U.S. soldier Franklyn Pryor (a pleasant performance by Lloyd Bridges) on a flight to London to see his wartime love, Pauline (Moira Lister). He arrives to find Pauline embroiled in a dangerous mystery involving a blackmailer and a limping sniper. Events lead to a confrontation between Franklyn and the blackmailer and, just as Franklyn is about to be killed … he wakes up! It turns out he had fallen asleep on the plane and was just having a bad dream. The plane lands—this time for real—and Franklyn prepares to have a lovely time with Pauline. While it may frustrate some viewers, the dream ending at least explains away all the loopholes and coincidences that were mounting up in the complex plot.

According to *Today's Cinema* (October 14, 1955), the plot of ***Stolen Time*** (1954) is "ingenious and moderately credible, but its narration is confusing." Released following a seven-year jail sentence—the result of a wrongful conviction for the murder of a blackmailing female cashier at a service station where he worked as a mechanic—French-Canadian Tony Pelassier (Hollywood's Richard Arlen) sets out to clear his name by finding the real killer. Helped by his devoted girlfriend (Constance Leigh) and a young lawyer (Vincent Ball), Tony eventually unmasks the culprit, but not before the latter has killed another blackmailer (Susan Shaw), a blonde model who had plagued him ever since witnessing the original murder.

The film is one of two London-based B thrillers (see also *Devil's Point*) starring Arlen that were made back-to-back by Charles Deane Productions. (Britisher Deane was a dramatic arts specialist with much experience in the U.S. including several seasons as director of the Watkins Glen Summer Theater in New York, for which he'd once, in 1950, booked Arlen to star in the romantic comedy, *Goodbye Again*.) Under the more intriguing title *Blonde Blackmailer*, it was one of the most, if not *the* most, distributed British B thrillers stateside, playing fairly steadily from the spring of 1958 through autumn 1964 as support to upward of 90 different features.

The B movie ***Time Is My Enemy*** (1954)

benefits from some excellent London location work and, as rightly observed by *Today's Cinema* (September 10, 1954), has an "ingenious if somewhat hard-to-follow plot." Happily married to wealthy publisher John Everton (Patrick Barr), Barbara (Renee Asherson) is shocked to learn that her suave first husband Martin (Dennis Price), thought to have died during World War II, is in fact alive and well. Now leading a life of crime, and unable to shift the jewels from a smash-and-grab robbery (depicted in the film's opening), Martin blackmails Barbara, threatening to expose her as a bigamist unless she hands over some much-needed cash. Martin is himself blackmailed (in connection with his fatal shooting of a jeweler) by his partner in the robbery (Bonar Colleano), but then kills the latter before setting into motion a cunning scheme to frame Barbara for the crime so as to muddy things up while preparing an escape abroad. Coincidentally, a detective friend (Duncan Lamont) of the Evertons is investigating the robbery case and ultimately brings about Martin's capture. The film has a final little twist up its sleeve—concerning the legality of Barbara and Martin's marriage—that brings things to a tidy close.

The character-driven B movie ***The Embezzler*** (1954) stars Charles Victor in a rare leading role as Henry Paulson, the mild-mannered 54-year-old chief teller at a London bank. Upon learning he has only two years to live due to a heart condition, Paulson, who in his own words has "led a very dull life," decides to break the monotony and inject a little adventure into his life. To this end he steals a small fortune from the bank's vault, but the first leg (a boat train to Paris) of his planned escape to Rio de Janeiro is rendered impossible due to police presence at the point of departure. Taking another train instead, he travels to the southeast coast of England and books into a hotel. There, he helps a newly married young woman, Clair (Zena Marshall), escape the clutches of her former lover, Johnson (Cyril Chamberlain), a heinous ex-con who has started blackmailing her. Victor gives a sympathetic portrayal as Paulson, whose good deed toward Clair brings him some much-needed purpose in life, even though it leads to a sad conclusion when his heart trouble kicks in during a physical tangle with Johnson. Michael Craig, in one of his first movie roles, plays Clair's doctor husband.

"When he came to her room at night ... was it to kiss or kill...?"

Set in Edwardian London, ***Footsteps in the Fog*** (1955) is a classic thriller whose distinguished cast is headed by Stewart Granger as the elegant Stephen Lowry. Lowry's maid Lily (Jean Simmons), who's in love with him and has evidence to prove that he poisoned his wealthy wife to death, uses blackmail to worm her way into his life. Feeling inescapably trapped by the situation, Lowry follows Lily out one evening with the intention of bludgeoning her to death. However, in the heavy fog, he mistakenly kills another woman instead, after which he is caught and put on trial for murder. At the hearing, Lily, even though she knows she was the intended victim, nevertheless gives false testimony that gets Lowry acquitted. The pair subsequently stay together in an uneasy state of co-dependency until Lowry falls in love with his business partner's daughter (Belinda Lee), whereupon he once again attempts to get rid of Lily, this time in a scheme—involving ingesting some poison so as to frame her for his attempted murder—that ends badly for both of them.

Granger is brilliant as the heartless and unscrupulous Lowry, while Simmons (Granger's then real-life wife) excels as the pitiable and disturbed Lily. The costume design is nothing short of sumptuous, and Wilfrid Shingleton's imaginative art direction creates some effective atmosphere, both in the detailed interiors of the Lowry mansion and the eternally foggy surrounding streets. The score, although haunting in parts, is often too sentimental in moments where a

Stewart Granger and Jean Simmons up to their necks in blackmail and murder in the classic *Footsteps in the Fog* (1955).

dark and foreboding tone would have been more fitting.

In the B movie **The Price of Silence** (1959), good-hearted ex-convict Richard Fuller (Gordon Jackson) starts life afresh by changing his name to Roger Fenton, whereupon he gains respectable employment as a real estate agent and begins a romantic relationship with an artist (June Thorburn). However, his happiness becomes threatened when one of his ex-cellmates, a slimy character appropriately known as "The Slug" (bit-part actor Sam Kydd in a more substantial role than usual), begins demanding money to stay silent about his past. Circumstances lead to a situation in which "The Slug" murders one of Fenton's clients, with Fenton becoming suspected due to circumstantial evidence. The only person that can provide him with an alibi is his boss' alluring wife (Maya Koumani), but she refuses to do so in revenge for Fenton having earlier rejected her advances. A final twist sees the alibi substantiated, and all ends well in this eventful little programmer, which benefits from engaging performances by Jackson and Thorburn.

Terence Morgan stars as the supersmooth, handsome and ruthless Augie Cortona in **The Shakedown** (1959), which *Films and Filming* (March 1960) called a "Warners-prohibition-type gangster film." Just released from prison, Augie starts up a legit modeling school-cum-photography studio. However, after hours, he hires the place out to clients who wish to produce private erotic photos and secretly films their activities for blackmail purposes. Pretty hard-hitting back in the day (it managed to obtain the good old British "X" rating), the film co-stars Hazel Court as an undercover policewoman who infiltrates Augie's set-up in a dangerous ruse that entails feigning a romance with him. An excellent supporting cast includes

Harry H. Corbett as a rival racketeer, Donald Pleasence as a photographer and John Salew as a blackmailed bank manager, the latter ultimately deciding Augie's fate—with four bullets.

Set in London's Soho district, ***Too Hot to Handle*** (1959) centers around an exotic dance club, The Pink Flamingo, run by the suave Johnny Solo (Leo Genn). The plot chiefly involves an attempt to ruin Solo—through a campaign of blackmail and threats—by his treacherous manager (Christopher Lee) in league with a rival club boss (Sheldon Lawrence). The Pink Flamingo's star attraction, Midnight Franklin, who's in love with Johnny, is played by Jayne Mansfield; the legendary actress is on absolutely sparkling form, especially during her rendition of the title song, one of several racy routines scattered throughout the movie. Various strands are woven into the main story, one of them involving a naive teenage dancer known as Ponytail (Barbara Windsor), who comes to a tragic and violent end at the hands of one of the club's financial backers, a truly sleazy and lecherous character played convincingly by Martin Boddey.

The blackmailee in the quaint B movie ***Dangerous Afternoon*** (1961) is notorious former jewel thief Irma Randall (a quietly strong Ruth Dunning), who has successfully avoided recapture following a jailbreak five years earlier. Now wheelchair-bound due to an injury sustained during the escape, Irma, under an assumed name, runs a boarding house populated by elderly female criminals who've hit hard times. The plot concerns Irma's poisoning of her blackmailer, a grudge-holding former fellow inmate (Gwenda Wilson), and how her fate becomes sealed as a result of circumstances involving a loyal friend's (versatile character actor Jerold Wells) attempt to dispose of the body. A secondary storyline involves a supposed ward of Irma's (Joanna Dunham) who's actually Irma's daughter but doesn't know it, and there are some humorous vignettes involving a light-fingered resident of the boarding house.

The Secret Partner (1961) stars Stewart Granger as John Brent, a shipping company executive being blackmailed by his seedy dentist Ralph Beldon (Norman Bird). A mysterious face-covered man persuades Beldon, with the prospect of a £15,000 payout, to help in the robbery of the shipping company's safe, this involving injecting Brent with a truth drug during his next appointment in order to extract from him the safe's combination. The robbery plan turns out to be part of a clever scheme by a certain blackmailee of Beldon's to not only profit from the theft, but also implicate Beldon in the crime so as to get him off their back. Many twists and turns, including the revelation of the face-covered man's identity, hold one's interest in the ingenious story, with Bernard Lee scoring as a chain-smoking Scotland Yard detective on the verge of retirement.

Both intelligent and—in its frank treatment of homosexuality (the practice of which was illegal in England at the time)—groundbreaking, ***Victim*** (1961) is a superlative accomplishment by the producer-director team of Michael Relph and Basil Dearden. The brilliant original screenplay tells a powerful story about a vicious blackmail ring targeting gay men, one of whom, Jack Barrett (Peter McEnery), is driven to suicide. Dirk Bogarde gives a career-best performance as prominent attorney Melville Farr, a married man who's had a couple of unconsummated gay relationships (including with Barrett) and, at the risk of his own indiscretions being exposed, determines to track down and bring the blackmailers to justice. The cast also includes Sylvia Syms, as the attorney's ultimately (after the shock of learning the truth about him) supportive wife, Dennis Price as a blackmailed actor and Derren Nesbitt at his slimy best as one of the extortionists.

In the Danziger brothers B movie ***Two Wives at One Wedding*** (1961), newlywed physician Tom (Gordon Jackson) becomes the victim of a blackmail plot by two past friends, both former French Resistance workers who'd helped him after he became wounded as a soldier during World War II. One of the plotters, Annette (Lisa Daniely), tells him that he married her in France all those years ago and then demands £10,000 in return for not exposing him as a bigamist; the other, Paul (André Maranne), a supposed witness to the supposed wedding, later duly backs up the story. Having suffered amnesia at the time, Tom is unable to deny the claim and is forced to pay up. However, a crucial recollection from the past proves that he could never have married Annette and leads to a dangerous confrontation when he attempts to recover his money from the conspirators. Set in London and using flashbacks to show events in wartime France, the story has Daniely's character gradually revealed as a sympathetic figure (a decent girl made bad by a manipulative partner-in-crime), while Tom's wife (Christina Gregg) remains suitably bemused throughout.

"Seven deadly steps that led to a hidden fortune!"

When an accountant named Jefferson dies in prison while serving a sentence for embezzling £20,000 (the whereabouts of which he never disclosed), his will leaves a set of **Seven Keys** (1962) to fellow inmate Russell (coolly played by Alan Dobie). Upon his release, Russell, having no prior knowledge of the keys, and thinking they may lead to the money, begins investigating their significance. However, instead of uncovering the loot, the keys unearth clues which reveal that Jefferson had been forced to embezzle the money in order to pay off a blackmailer (Delphi Lawrence) in connection with his son's involvement in a hit-and-run accident. During the adventure, Russell brings the blackmailer to justice and manages to clear Jefferson's name, as well as also learning why he was chosen to inherit the keys in the first place. This well-paced and neatly plotted B movie gives top-billing to Jeannie Carson as Jefferson's former secretary, who helps Russell uncover the truth.

Another B movie, **The Marked One** (1963), features a robust performance by William Lucas as Don Mason, an ex-con going straight after serving a two-year jail sentence for his part in a counterfeit currency ring. Before long, he is being pressured—including via anonymous calls and a letter to his estranged wife (Zena Walker) threatening to tell their young daughter about her father's criminal past—by a mysterious blackmailer into handing over a set of valuable engraving plates that had been used in the counterfeiting operations. After making inquiries among old acquaintances, Don, who never knew what became of the plates, eventually finds them with their original designer, this leading to a climactic confrontation with the blackmailer, who by then has kidnapped Don's daughter. The fast-paced proceedings are occasionally slowed by a subplot involving the increasingly lecherous advances toward Don's wife by the landlord (Arthur Lovegrove) of a pub where she lives and works. Prolific character actor Patrick Jordan appears to good effect as a fraud squad detective who's not all he seems.

"All of tonight's secrets will be used against them tomorrow!"

Regarded by *Films and Filming* (October 1968) as a "generally very intelligent film," **The Strange Affair** (1968) stars Michael York as Peter Strange, a naïve young police constable who gets seduced by an upper-class and underage beatnik named Frederika (Susan George). The girl's aunt and uncle, both involved in a pornography ring, secretly film and take photographs of the couple making love. In ensuing events, Pierce (Jeremy Kemp), an embittered detective, obtains the compromising photos and blackmails Peter into helping him trap a ruthless drug smuggler, this ultimately having disastrous consequences for the young policeman. York convinces in the lead, and character actor Jack Watson has one of his best roles as the drug kingpin. Told in flashback, the modern (for its time) film maintains a gritty and realistic edge throughout.

Michael York and Susan George in *The Strange Affair* (1968).

The Italo-British co-production ***Blue Movie Blackmail*** (1973) is a solid example of that particular Italian subgenre of police/action thrillers known as *poliziotteschi*, and in this case one in which most of the action takes place in London. Well photographed and groovily scored, the convoluted and violent *Yojimbo*-like story involves an unscrupulous undercover narcotics agent (chiseled Italian exploitation star Ivan Rassimov, here looking like Europe's answer to Clint Eastwood) playing two rival criminal organizations off against each other for his own million-dollar gain. The main British players are Stephanie Beacham, in a pivotal role as a call girl at a high-class Belgravia escort agency (an establishment used by one of the organizations as a front, and where clients are secretly filmed and then blackmailed into aiding in drug smuggling activities), and comedy actress Patricia Hayes as the eccentric *Bloody Mama*–style boss of the rival mob. The film's Italian title is *Si può essere più bastardi dell'ispettore Cliff?*

Kidnapping

The kidnap victim in ***Morning Call*** (1957) is George Manning, a Harley Street doctor for whom a £5,000 ransom is demanded. After the money is finally delivered (following a couple of unsuccessful attempts) by Manning's distressed wife (Greta Gynt), we learn that Manning has all along been dead, murdered by the kidnapper (Charles Farrell) whose main motive was revenge: he held the doctor responsible (although it wasn't actually his fault as it turns out) for the death of a loved one in a car accident. Also woven

On the set of *The Unstoppable Man* (1960), Cameron Mitchell tests out the flame-throwing device used in the film's dramatic climax.

into the plot of this indifferent B movie is the kidnapper's murder of a prostitute who pretended she could identify him just to get her picture in a newspaper. Australia's Ron Randell plays an American private eye trying to help Mrs. Manning, and the film's title refers to the 3 a.m. fake call-out that lures the doctor to his demise in the first place.

Prolific American actor Cameron Mitchell is *The Unstoppable Man* (1960), namely James Kennedy, a tough London-based American businessman who takes matters into his own hands after his young son Jimmy (Denis Gilmore) is kidnapped for ransom by a ruthless gang. Kennedy's efforts, together with a clue supplied by Jimmy in a letter he's allowed to write to his father, eventually lead to the pinpointing of the gang's headquarters in Hampstead, resulting in a violent showdown. Adapted from the much-anthologized story "Amateur in Violence" by Michael Gilbert, this is a crackerjack B movie in which our resourceful hero certainly lives up to the title, especially in the climax during which he effortlessly tosses an oversized gang member over a balustrade before going on to use a flame-throwing device against the gang's boss (Harry H. Corbett). Marius Goring puts in a pleasant performance as a patient Scotland Yard detective, and there's an excellent piano-based soundtrack composed and performed by the great Bill McGuffie. All in all, *The Unstoppable Man* is one of the more interesting items in star Mitchell's deep back catalog, and it's one his fans won't want to miss!

A minor masterpiece from director Lance Comfort, the B movie *Tomorrow at Ten* (1962) begins with a man, Marlow (a brilliant Robert Shaw), kidnapping a young boy (Piers Bishop) and imprisoning him in a large deserted house with a golliwog doll—

secretly containing a bomb set to go off at 10 o'clock the following morning—for company. Having decided to make his £50,000 ransom demand in person, Marlow pays a visit to the boy's father, Anthony Chester (Alec Clunes). However, events, which involve the arrival of a hard-nosed Scotland Yard detective (top-billed John Gregson), lead to Chester frenziedly attacking Marlow, who subsequently dies from a resulting head injury. This leaves the detective facing the seemingly impossible task of finding the boy before the bomb explodes. *The Daily Cinema* (May 22, 1963) justifiably called the film "one of the best examples yet of the British small budget feature."

One of the most impressive British thrillers of the 1960s, **Séance on a Wet Afternoon** (1964) stars the brilliant stage and television actress Kim Stanley in a rare big-screen appearance as Myra Savage, a disturbed medium who supposedly makes contact with the "other side" through her dead son Arthur. Frustrated by a lack of professional recognition, Myra gets her weak and devoted husband (Richard Attenborough) to kidnap a little girl as part of a devious scheme which involves subsequently contacting the parents and offering her "powers" to help locate the child, hoping this will bring good publicity. However, the plan ultimately goes awry when Myra becomes hopelessly insane and decides that the captive child would be better off on the "other side" with Arthur. Stanley's stunning performance gained her the 1964 award for best actress from the prestigious New York Film Critics Circle, as well as a nomination for the 1965 Oscars, in which she lost out to Julie Andrews. The creepy atmosphere of Myra's old mansion (where most of the drama takes place) is effectively put across thanks to some great art direction, and composer John Barry provides a textbook example of film scoring.

Dan Duryea gives one of his finest performances in **Do You Know This Voice?** (1964), the second of two B thrillers he made for Parroch-McCallum Productions (see also *Walk a Tightrope*). The legendary Hollywood bad guy plays Joe Hopta, a frustrated hospital orderly who kidnaps and then accidentally kills a young boy, dumping his body in woods. The body is soon found but Joe, unaware of this, sends his wife Anne (Gwen Watford) to a public pay phone to demand (with a disguised voice) a ransom from the child's parents. The police trace the call but arrive too late and find the Hoptas' next-door neighbor, an Italian widow named Rosa (Isa Miranda), in the phone booth instead. As it happens, Rosa was picking up some dropped coins as Anne exited the call box and so only saw the latter's feet without realizing who she was. However, she later reveals to Joe a sense that the person is local and somehow familiar, and that one day their identity will come to her. In order to prevent such an eventuality, Joe begins plotting Rosa's demise. Meanwhile, a special police bulletin with a recording of Anne's ransom call is broadcast to the public via TV, asking the question—"Do You Know This Voice?"

Set in the city of Bristol in South West England and based on Evelyn Berckman's 1960 novel of the same name, the film is immensely entertaining and well structured, benefiting from a solid screenplay by Neil McCallum (a British-based Canadian actor and one half of the aforementioned Parroch-McCallum Productions). Duryea gives a show-stealing performance as he effortlessly alternates between nice-guy-next-door and scheming psychopath, and his delivery of some great lines such as "before you know it, I'll be doing the trapdoor fandango" (referring to the fact that he'll be hanged if caught) is just priceless. Watford is also excellent as Joe's reluctantly complicit wife, and a shock ending involves the couple drinking a toast that goes horribly wrong because Joe neglected to rinse out a glass he'd used to mix some poison destined for Rosa. In a report about his visit to England for the filming, the British newspaper *The Evening Standard* (March 6, 1964) included a perfect descrip-

A toast that's about to have disastrous consequences. Dan Duryea and Gwen Watford in *Do You Know This Voice?* (1964).

tion of Duryea: "His face (in real life cheerful and reassuring) wears expressions which, though bloodcurdling, have discretion, dignity and style, as if they had been cut for him by some Savile Row tailor." The film went straight to television in Britain, and seemingly suffered the same fate in the U.S.

In their scathing review of the low-budget obscurity **Double Exposure** (1976), the *Monthly Film Bulletin* (May 1977) concluded that "given the pervasive lethargy of the enterprise, the only surprise is that the film ever made it past its pre-production stage." Anouska Hempel (cult film buffs may remember her as the whip-cracking villainess from director Russ Meyer's 1973 exploitationer *Black Snake* [aka *Sweet Suzy*]) plays Simone, the trophy wife of ruthless arms-dealing shipping magnate Howard Townsend (Alan Brown). The plot has Simone being kidnapped by a rival of Townsend's in order to blackmail her photographer lover James Compton (David Baron) into acting as go-between for some shady business with the tycoon. Her eventual rescue by Compton, with help from a computer espionage expert (Alan Hay), leads to an unexpected denouement with decidedly negative consequences for Townsend. As of the 1980s, the film's director-producer-writer William Webb and his company Westwind Productions were busy in the U.S. making other obscure low-budgeters such as the thrillers *Party Line* (1988) and *The Banker* (1989).

"They'd bust your head just for the hell of it. So think what they'd do for a million!"

Gritty, hard-hitting, occasionally exploitative and most certainly overlooked, **The Squeeze** (1977) stars Stacy Keach as Jim Naboth, an alcoholic ex-cop now on welfare and looking after his two sons by ex-wife Jill

(Carol White). Naboth becomes involved when Jill, together with her daughter by new husband Foreman (Edward Fox), is kidnapped on the orders of vicious racketeer Vic Smith (Stephen Boyd), the abduction designed to pressure Foreman into cooperating in a £1 million heist of an armored van from his own security firm. Keach is terrific as the perennially drunk Naboth, and there's a surprisingly good performance (in a rare acting role) by comedian Freddie Starr as his best buddy. Some effective London location shooting includes a superbly staged climax in Notting Hill, where Naboth cleverly turns the tables on Vic and his cohorts. Boyd is suitably menacing in what was one of his last roles, and the cast also includes David Hemmings as the chief kidnapper.

Smuggling

Loosely based on a six-episode 1949 BBC radio serial of the same name, the B movie *The Lady Craved Excitement* (1950) stars Hy Hazell as Pat, a cabaret artiste with an elevated sense of adventure. In the radio show, Pat helped bring to justice a gang of jewel thieves, whereas in the film she helps round up scammers who steal priceless paintings and smuggle them abroad. The main story involves the criminals attempting to cheat a demented artist, Peterson (Andrew Keir), out of valuable artworks, while in a subplot, Peterson's desire to create a painting of Anne Boleyn's execution (with Pat as the model) turns out to have sinister motivations. Joining Pat in her madcap adventures, which the *Monthly Film Bulletin* (September 1950) described as "suitable entertainment for the young," is a fellow cabaret artiste played by Michael Medwin.

The B movie *Blackout* (1950) suffers slightly from an uncertain performance by Maxwell Reed, who can't seem to decide whether to act like Robert Mitchum or Humphrey Bogart. On his way to a party, blind engineer Chris Pelley (Reed) accidentally ends up at the wrong house, wherein he stumbles on a dead body before being knocked unconscious by an unseen figure. Later, following a successful operation that restores his sight, and armed with a clue (a signet ring he picked up at the crime scene), he investigates the incident, leading to a dangerous adventure involving a ruthless gang of currency smugglers. The film, an early effort by producers Robert S. Baker and Monty Berman for their Tempean outfit, was remade by Butcher's Film Distributors as another B movie, *Blind Spot* (1958), with Berman returning as sole producer. This time the blind protagonist is a U.S. Army officer (Robert MacKenzie) and the criminals are diamond smugglers. American actor John Crawford plays the doctor responsible for restoring the hero's sight, and a young Michael Caine turns up late in the show as the gang's mysterious boss. Mid Century Imports, a company featured in the movie, is a reference to Baker and Berman's other production unit, Mid-Century Film Productions.

Publicized as "a film for the family," the B movie *The Second Mate* (1950) is a genteel comedy thriller starring Gordon Harker as Bill Tomkins, aging skipper of a barge on London's River Thames. Tomkins' crew is made up of first mate Paddy (Graham Moffatt) and six-year-old second mate Bobby (played with gusto by David Hannaford), whose grandfather—Tomkins' best pal—was killed by a gang of jewel thieves who use the Thames as part of a smuggling route. Unbeknownst to Paddy and Bobby, Tomkins has infiltrated the gang in an effort to bring them to justice and avenge his friend's murder. Circumstances lead to Bobby being captured by the thieves, but he manages to escape and is instrumental in saving Tomkins from certain death after the man's cover is blown. A leisurely pace and some scenic riverside locations are tranquil antidotes to the callous ruthlessness of the criminals, which is no better exemplified than when the gang boss orders Tomkins' death by time bomb, or as he nonchalantly puts it, "a time charge, same as we used on the airliner."

"A drama of the river underworld"

Highlighted by some interesting location work, **Pool of London** (1950) begins with a cargo ship, the *Dunbar*, docking for the weekend on the titular stretch of the River Thames. While ashore, one of the crew members, fast-talking petty smuggler Dan (Bonar Colleano), meets with a shady acquaintance (Max Adrian) and agrees, for £100, to take a package—which he's initially unaware contains diamonds from a robbery in which a security guard was killed—aboard the *Dunbar* for smuggling into Holland. Events see Dan persuaded by his girlfriend (Moira Lister) to keep the diamonds, which leads to him being sought by police for suspected involvement in the robbery, as well as putting him in danger from the murderous thieves. Earl Cameron puts in a superb performance as Dan's Jamaican fellow crew member Johnny, who occasionally helps Dan (for the sake of their friendship) with his smuggling activities. (A growing romance between Johnny and a white girl, played by Susan Shaw, came at a time when interracial relationships were not common in British film.) *Today's Cinema* (February 15, 1951) noted that the film "produces an inevitable anti-climax by virtue of the most thrilling sequences occurring in the middle rather than towards the end."

David Farrar stars in **Night Without Stars** (1951) as Giles Gordon, a partially sighted (due to a World War II injury) English lawyer who, while living in retirement on the French Riviera, meets and falls in love with Alix Delaisse (Nadia Gray), the attractive widow of a noted Resistance agent. Giles is soon warned off by Pierre Chaval (Gerard Landry), a self-proclaimed fiancé of Alix's who tells him about the latter's supposed involvement in shady activities. When Pierre turns up dead and Alix disappears, Giles travels to England and undergoes an operation that restores his full sight. He then returns to France to investigate, whereupon he gets drawn into a complex web of smug-

Publicity for a 1951 romantic thriller.

gling and wartime treachery in which Alix is heavily embroiled. This romantic mystery takes a while to get going and, when it finally does, becomes rather predictable and over-involved. On the plus side, the French atmosphere is superbly put across.

Based on Elleston Trevor's 1951 novel *Dead on Course*, **Wings of Danger** (1952) was Hollywood star Zachary Scott's first of three British B thrillers. The charming actor, who *Today's Cinema* (May 8, 1952) said "gives a competent, forceful performance," portrays Richard Van Ness, a cargo pilot for a small airline who becomes involved in smashing a counterfeiting and smuggling racket that surprisingly turns out to be headed by his boss (Arthur Lane). Rugged Canadian actor Robert Beatty plays Richard's friend and fellow pilot, who fakes his own death (in a supposed plane crash over the English Channel) to escape the clutches of the criminals, while Kay Kendall is the femme fatale of the racket. A Martello Tower provides an atmospheric setting for the counterfeiting operations, where phony dollars are manufactured—using ex-Nazi forging plates—prior to being smuggled by way of the airline, and there's a romantic subplot involving Richard's unwillingness (because of a susceptibility to blackouts) to commit to his girlfriend (Naomi Chance).

The fast-paced B movie **Three Steps to the Gallows** (1953) unfolds in London, where American cargo ship officer Gregor Stevens (Scott Brady) tries to save his brother Larry (played by the film's co-scripter Paul Erickson), who's been framed for a murder and faces imminent execution. The real culprit is in fact a member of a diamond smuggling gang. Gregor's efforts to uncover the truth are hampered not only by being led on a wild goose chase by a supposed friend (John Blythe) of Larry's who's really in league with the gang, but also through an attempt by the criminals to similarly frame him for another murder. U.S. star Brady performs energetically and is ably supported by fellow American Mary Castle (once groomed by Hollywood to be the second Rita Hayworth) as a nightclub singer and daughter of a key witness in the original murder. There's a neat twist involving the condemned brother's lawyer (Colin Tapley), some well-choreographed fight scenes and a lively finale at the British Industries Fair at London's Olympia.

"Malaga—where men are tough and a woman lives in constant danger!"

Filmed in Technicolor on authentic locations, **Malaga** (1954) was apparently described by star Maureen O'Hara as one of her "escapist" movies. The striking Hollywood redhead plays Joanna Dane, a U.S. government agent sent undercover to Tangier as part of an operation to smash a huge smuggling syndicate in the area. Proving to be something of a card shark, Joanna gets a job as dealer in a gambling club where her association with a dubious Frenchman (Leonard Sachs) leads to her securing the key to a safety deposit box containing damning information about the criminal operations. Macdonald Carey plays a roguish boat owner constantly making a play for Joanna and who may or may not be part of the racket, while Binnie Barnes appears as the club's worldly-wise boss who, in a final twist, is found to be running more than just the club.

Observed by the *Monthly Film Bulletin* (June 1954) as having a "somewhat haphazardly constructed" story, **Forbidden Cargo** (1954) stars Nigel Patrick as a British customs agent investigating a smuggling racket in which siblings Roger and Rita (Terence Morgan and Elizabeth Sellars) are involved. An episode in the French Riviera, in which an attempt is made to murder Kenyon by tampering with his diving equipment, provides a welcome change of scenery from the otherwise London-set proceedings, and there's a well-filmed sequence on the River Thames involving Roger's retrieval of contraband from a magnetic container attached to a ship's hull. Circumstances ultimately cause Rita to blow the whistle on the whole criminal enterprise, this leading to Roger's dramatic death (his car careers off London's Tower Bridge) while trying to escape.

"The waves of the Brain Machine spell.... STOP THIS KILLER!"

A well-paced and atmospheric B movie, ***The Brain Machine*** (1954) begins with temporary amnesiac Frank Smith (Maxwell Reed) being admitted to a London hospital. There, he's given a drug and questioned by Dr. Philippa Roberts (Elizabeth Allan) before then being tested on the titular apparatus—an electroencephalograph—whose readings indicate he has homicidal tendencies. Smith, who we later learn has double-crossed his partner, Spencer Simon (Gibb McLaughlin) in a cortisone smuggling deal, discharges himself and subsequently kidnaps Philippa for fear he may have told her too much while under the influence of the aforementioned drug. Events finally lead to the brain machine's readings being fulfilled when Smith kills Spencer in revenge for the strangulation murder of his wife at the hands of Spencer's sadistic henchman (Edwin Richfield). Involved throughout is Philippa's estranged psychiatrist husband played by Patrick Barr.

Diplomatic Passport (1954) stars Paul Carpenter as Ray Andersen, an American diplomat in London tricked into driving to Paris by jewel smugglers who hide diamonds in his embassy car, knowing the vehicle will go unchecked at customs. Once in France, he stops for gas and to check on a problem tire. The criminals turn up, attempt to retrieve the diamonds and end up stealing the car, which subsequently crashes due to said tire. Ray's wife, June (Hollywood's Marsha Hunt), travels to France believing (thanks to erroneous newspaper reporting) that her husband was in the crash, and gets kidnapped by the crooks. Ultimately, Ray is instrumental in the smugglers' capture as they make a getaway—with June as hostage—into Belgium. This strictly average affair was produced in England by Americans Gene Martel and Burt Balaban for television release in the U.S. and distribution as a B movie elsewhere.

The first of two Tempean Films B movies starring U.S. actor Alex Nicol, ***The Gilded Cage*** (1954) revolves around a conspiracy to steal a Degas painting from a London art gallery and leave a copy in its place. Nicol plays Steve Anderson, a U.S. Air Force security officer in England whose brother, indebted to one of the conspirators, is to be used as a courier to smuggle the painting to San Francisco, where a collector is ready to pay $200,000. Steve is ultimately instrumental in smashing the plot, masterminded by a murderous theatrical producer (Clifford Evans), and in the process wins the love of one of the latter's actresses (Veronica Hurst). The entertainingly told story culminates in a neat final twist regarding the art gallery's curator (John Stuart) and the switching of the paintings.

"Women.... Smugglers.... Murder in the Casbah—were his Tangier Assignment!"

The British-Spanish co-production ***Tangier Assignment*** (1954) is an ultra-cheap B movie starring Bob Simmons, an actor-stuntman who later worked on many James Bond films including stunt-doubling for Sean Connery. (Simmons' autobiography, *Nobody Does It Better*, was named after the theme song to the 1977 Bond epic *The Spy Who Loved Me*.) In what was his one and only top-billed role, he plays the romantically named Peter Valentine, an international agent assigned to round up arms smugglers in Tangier. Simmons certainly possesses some impressive physical skills; indeed, in what looks like an early display of some type of free-running, our tough hero employs some nifty moves—jumping, rolling, climbing, leapfrogging and somersaulting—during two escape sequences, not to mention at one point effortlessly tossing an adversary out of an upper-story window. Helping Valentine during his mission are a nightclub singer/undercover agent (June Powell) and a cordial Sûreté inspector

(Fernando Rey). The Spanish version, titled *Billete para Tánger*, allegedly runs 82 minutes.

Cross Channel (1954) is one of two British B movies that U.S. star Wayne Morris made for Republic Productions. In the other, *The Green Buddha* (1954), he played a charter plane pilot. Here, he's a charter boat skipper, Gary "Tex" Parker, who becomes innocently embroiled in the dangerous maneuverings (including an internal double-cross) of a gang of jewel smugglers. Amid much rough and tumble on and around the English Channel, Parker manages to find lasting love with a young French woman (Yvonne Furneaux). The *Motion Picture Herald* (November 5, 1955) remarked that "Morris' characteristically convincing nonchalance is very much in evidence here."

The rather lackluster **Contraband Spain** (1955) begins with some prolonged scene-setting voice-over narration by none other than Christopher Lee (uncredited). Richard Greene stars as FBI agent Lee Scott, who gets on the trail of a gang of criminals involved in the large-scale forgery of dollar bills and the smuggling of French watches into England. During the adventure, which was filmed on locations in Spain, France and England, he's helped by a quick-witted British customs officer (Michael Denison providing a welcome touch of humor) and falls in love with a nightclub singer (Anouk Aimée). The crooks are eventually trailed to the English port of Dover, leading to an eventful climactic chase. This Eastmancolor B movie was a co-production with Spain, where it's known as *Contrabando* (Spanish prints supposedly credit Julio Salvador as co-director).

Set in an overcast Brighton, **The Secret** (1955) begins when the body of a woman—who it transpires had recently smuggled diamonds into the country—is found at the foot of a cliff. Nick Delaney (Sam Wanamaker), a shiftless and self-serving American who knew the victim, is aware of the existence of the gems and eventually realizes they are concealed in a teddy bear belonging to the woman's unknowing young daughter Katie (the delightful Mandy Miller of *Mandy* fame). Nick's heartless conduct in securing the diamonds has repercussions that lead to Katie becoming badly injured on Brighton

Richard Greene plays an FBI agent on the trail of smugglers.

Pier, at which point the man changes his selfish ways. During the course of the sensitively handled story, we discover the exact circumstances of the mother's death, while also being treated to persuasive performances by Wanamaker and Andre Morell, the latter as a police inspector whose dour demeanor complements the dreary surroundings.

"A riot of thrills and fun!"

The comedy thriller **Johnny, You're Wanted** (1955) is a B movie spin-off of a 1953/4 six-episode TV series of the same name, with John Slater repeating his role as the lovable cockney truck driver of the title. Having picked up a young female hitchhiker, Johnny stops off at a café to make a phone call, whereupon the woman is abducted and shortly after found strangled by the roadside. In an ensuing adventure, Johnny faces danger as he gets involved in tracking down the murderer—a man the victim had been attempting to blackmail in connection with a drug smuggling racket he'd been running under cover of both a novelty joke shop (whose proprietor is played by Alfred Marks) and an astrology stage act.

Tough Canadian actor Robert Beatty stars in **Portrait of Alison** (1955) as an artist embroiled in a complex web of intrigue and murder following the suspicious death in a car crash of his journalist brother, who'd been about to expose an international gang of diamond smugglers known as the "Arlington Ring." The complex plot, which hinges on a postcard containing concealed information about the gang, is shrouded in mystery concerning the eponymous Alison (a fairly undemanding role for Hollywood's Terry Moore), who had supposedly also died in the crash only to later turn up alive and well. William Sylvester plays another of the artist's siblings (secretly a member of the gang), and there's a satisfying twist regarding the chief villain's identity. The story was adapted from Francis Durbridge's 1955 BBC TV serial of the same name.

The touching B movie **The Heart Within** (1957) was one of the earlier films to address the social tensions resulting from the large influx of West Indian immigrants into England. Earl Cameron stars as one such immigrant, Victor Conway, a London dock worker who goes on the run for fear he'll be mistakenly blamed for the shooting—by a mystery assassin—of a colleague who'd earlier provoked him in front of others. The real surprise here is a remarkably assured performance by a teenage David Hemmings as Danny Willard who, with his kindly junk-dealer grandfather (top-billed James Hayter), helps Victor elude the police. In a climax set on the docks, Victor saves Danny from the real killer, a pawnbroker (Clifford Evans) involved in smuggling drugs via cigarette packets. Cameron gives a sensitive performance, and there's some pleasant steel drum music co-composed by Edwin Astley and calypso artist Vivian Comma.

The British-Spanish B movie **Sail into Danger** (1957), known in Spain as *El Aventurero*, stars Dennis O'Keefe as Steve Ryman, American skipper of the *Medina* charter boat operating out of Barcelona. Steve's past as a smuggler catches up with him in the form of one-time criminal associate Lena (Kathleen Ryan), who blackmails him into transporting her and her gang to Tangier. The trip, unbeknownst to Steve, will entail smuggling a sacred Madonna that the gang plans to steal (by substituting it with a fake) from a cathedral. Steve's crew members on the *Medina* are hard-bitten Scotsman Monty (James Hayter) and a local boy named Angel (John Bull). The gang's murder of the boy after he witnesses the robbery leads to Steve seeking revenge, with the adventure culminating in a showdown in the mountains. *Today's Cinema* (November 8, 1957) called the film "average fare which will please less demanding audiences." Steven Pallos produced, as he had done on two of O'Keefe's earlier British thrillers, *The Fake* and *The Diamond* (both 1953).

Based on Edgar Wallace's 1920 novel *The Daffodil Mystery*, **The Devil's Daffodil**

(1961) is a British-German co-production filmed in London in simultaneous English and German-language versions, with some variations in the casts. The story concerns a series of murders—marked by daffodils present at the crime scenes—and their link to a drug-smuggling racket in which artificial daffodils are used to conceal heroin. Investigating alongside Scotland Yard are a British airport security agent (William Lucas [Joachim Fuchsberger in the German version]) and a Hong Kong detective played by Christopher Lee, whom it's nice to see as an Oriental good guy for a change in contrast to his roles as Chinese villains in *The Terror of the Tongs* (1960) and the later Fu Manchu series. Pivotal to the plot are a shady establishment, the Cosmos Club, and one of its employees, a drug-addicted ex-convict played by Colin Jeavons, although much more effectively portrayed by Klaus Kinski in the German version (*Das Geheimnis Der Gelben Narzissen*).

The Lance Comfort-directed B movie ***The Break*** (1962) is highlighted by well-handled action, a nice score and some excellent ensemble playing. The story centers on a remote Devonshire farmhouse-hotel whose shady owner, a smuggler named Judd Tredgar (Eddie Byrne), shelters escaped convict Jacko (William Lucas) while making arrangements for the man's escape abroad. Greg Parker (top-billed Tony Britton), a disillusioned writer and guest at the hotel, ends up tangling with the criminals after witnessing Jacko's murder of Tredgar's slow-witted servant, Moses (one of prolific character actor Edwin Richfield's more memorable roles). Sonia Dresdel has a pivotal part as another servant (Moses' sister), and Robert

William Lucas (left) and Eddie Byrne in *The Break* (1962).

Urquhart is on fine form as a private detective (on a divorce case concerning Parker) who meets a sticky end after stumbling on Tredgar's smuggling activities. *The Daily Cinema* (June 7, 1963) concluded that "if all second features were as entertaining as this, the top-liners would really have to look to their laurels."

Except for the presence of the classy Maureen Connell, everything about the B movie **Danger by My Side** (1962) is routine. When her detective brother is murdered by a ruthless gang of diamond smugglers, brave Lynne Marsden (Connell) determines to bring the criminals to justice and assumes a false identity to gain employment at a nightclub owned by the gang's boss, Venning (Alan Tilvern). When her cover is blown, Lynne is held prisoner on Venning's yacht, but luckily she'd been keeping in touch with a Scotland Yard inspector (Anthony Oliver) who duly comes to her rescue. Bill Nagy stars as the nightclub's sympathetic (and terminally drunk) manager, and Sonya Cordeau is a singer at the venue who gets murdered after threatening to disclose information to the police about the gang's activities.

In another B movie, *The Switch* (1963), Caroline Markham (Zena Marshall) becomes an unwitting courier for a smuggling gang when they hide Swiss watches in her car's petrol tank in France, intending to retrieve them by stealing the vehicle once she has driven back to London. However, the gang subsequently fails to retrieve the correct car, instead stealing—twice in a row—identical models of the same make, one of them belonging to John (Conrad Phillips), a cousin of Caroline's roommate. Events lead to Caroline being kidnapped by the criminals, but help is at hand thanks to a Customs officer (top-billed Anthony Steel) and a Scotland Yard inspector (Dermot Walsh), not to mention the aforementioned John, who'd earlier given Caroline a gadget—a miniature transmitter-receiver built into a ladies' powder compact—that she uses to convey her whereabouts. Caroline is certainly a lucky lady, having a trio of lionhearted (come to think of it, Walsh made the film during his run playing the lead in the TV show *Richard the Lionheart*) British leading men to look after her.

Set in Malta, **Death Is a Woman** (1965) stars Patsy Ann Noble (later to become Trisha Noble) as the beautiful and ruthless Francesca, described on U.S. posters as "a woman who violated every known commandment … and some that were unknown!" The story focuses on the puzzling murder of Malo (William Dexter)—he's found stabbed in an apartment locked from the inside with no murder weapon present—following his attempt to blackmail Francesca over her shooting of another man, all three characters having had a connection by way of their involvement in a drug smuggling racket. Apart from Noble as the callous Francesca (she even kills her lover when she has no further use for him), the film's main attractions are the Maltese locations and some nice sub-aqua photography detailing Francesca's journeys to and from an underwater cache of heroin. Mark Burns and Wanda Ventham play investigating British agents, and mystery addicts should enjoy the puzzle of Malo's murder.

Counterfeiting

Set in an Italian town called San Paolo, the B movie **I'll Get You for This** (1950) stars the legendary George Raft as Nick Cain, a visiting American gambler who gets framed for the murder of a U.S. Treasury agent. Forced to go on the run, Nick tries to clear himself with the help of a local flower seller (Charles Goldner), actually an Italian secret agent, and a shoeshine boy played by Enzo Staiola (the youngster from Vittorio de Sica's 1948 drama *Bicycle Thieves*). It turns out the murder was committed by a gang of ruthless counterfeiters that has gained possession of old German-developed engraving plates (known as the "Hitler plates") and are using

Hollywood legend George Raft as a gambler framed for murder in a 1950 B movie.

a mountainside prison as their hideout. Also caught up in the adventure, based on a 1946 James Hadley Chase novel, is a penniless artist played by Raft's fellow Hollywood star Coleen Gray.

"The real story behind the world's most startling racket!"

Appropriately accompanied by a score based on Mussorgsky's *Pictures at an Exhibition*, the B movie **The Fake** (1953) stars Hollywood's Dennis O'Keefe as Paul Mitchell, a wisecracking special investigator with his sights set on a $50,000 reward for the recovery of Da Vinci paintings stolen from exhibitions and replaced with forgeries. The film picks up with Mitchell in London, where he's hired to watch over a collection—including a Da Vinci insured for $1 million—on loan to the Tate Gallery. Hugh Williams plays a wealthy collector behind the thefts who in the end is cleverly tricked by Mitchell into admitting his guilt, while John Laurie is a doomed artist who'd been conned into creating the fakes. In her second of two British thrillers, American actress Coleen Gray plays the artist's daughter, an employee at the gallery romanced by Mitchell. According to Louella Parsons, in one of her widely syndicated "Hollywood" reports (e.g., in the *Hanford Sentinel*, Hanford, California [August 4, 1953]), O'Keefe took over directorial duties from Godfrey Grayson after the latter became ill, and ended up helming over half the film. "This so impressed Steven Pallos, the producer," said Parsons, "that he had no hesitance in turning over the directing job of *Rich is the Treasure* [his next project, based on a novel of the same name by Maurice Procter] to O'Keefe."

As it turned out, *Rich Is the Treasure* became **The Diamond** (1953), or *The Diamond Wizard* in the U.S., and again stars O'Keefe, although whether he ended up directing (as had been planned) or not remains unclear. He is certainly credited as director on U.S.

prints and publicity, whereas the prolific Montgomery Tully, whose style is very much in evidence, gets the credit on British publicity and prints. (The most likely scenario is that it was a collaborative effort, with O'Keefe unable to take credit in Britain due to trade union rules regarding foreign directors.) The story is about a gang of criminals who con scientist Dr. Miller (Paul Hardtmuth) into helping them profit from his secret formula for synthetic diamonds, which they manufacture at their castle headquarters. O'Keefe plays Joe Dennison, a U.S. Treasury agent sent to England on the trail of $1 million in stolen currency destined as payment to the gang for a batch of the fake stones. Philip Friend (he and O'Keefe have a great rapport) plays a Scotland Yard inspector, and the story also features an urbane diamond expert (Alan Wheatley), who's not all he seems, and Dr. Miller's daughter (Margaret Sheridan), who gets kidnapped by the gang to ensure her father's continued compliance after he realizes he's been exploited. Dennison and the inspector both become involved in rescuing father and daughter from the castle, where the gang's boss, after attempting to double-cross his cohorts, meets a fitting end in an explosive climax.

This efficient and entertaining B movie has the distinction of being the first British feature film made in 3D, although by all accounts it was never originally released anywhere in that format. The *New York Daily News* (July 17, 1954) does, however, list the film's premiere run at the capital's RKO Palace Theatre as "a United Artists 3-D release," so who knows for sure? What *is* known for sure is that it did get a 3D showing in 2006 at the World 3D Film Expo at the Egyptian Theatre in Hollywood.

Michael Craig gives a charismatic performance as British naval officer Larry Ellis in **House of Secrets** (1956), which *Today's Cinema* (October 22, 1956) observed is "put over with splendid gusto and speed." In an effort to infiltrate an international gang of counterfeiters, an Interpol-like agency persuades Larry to impersonate one of the criminals (almost his exact double) who, unbeknownst to his partners in crime, has died in a car crash. Larry ultimately exposes the gang's mastermind (David Kossoff), actually a high-ranking official at said agency, but not before almost being blown up on a plane (he bails out just in time) when a bomb is planted on board by the villain in a double-cross against his cohorts. The film, which unfolds in France and is superbly edited by future director Sidney Hayers, also stars Eric Pohlmann and Anton Diffring in familiar roles as two of the criminals.

The last of five British B thrillers starring Hollywood's Wayne Morris, **The Crooked Sky** (1956) sees the easy-going actor playing Mike Conlin, a U.S. Treasury agent. Conlin travels to England to investigate a proliferation of phony £1 banknotes that are found to have originated in America. The man behind the counterfeiting is London gambling club proprietor Fraser (Anton Diffring), who recruits flight radio operators from a U.S. company, Globe Link Airlines, to smuggle the fake currency into the country. When the authorities begin closing in on the crooked activity, the scene is set for a lively climax aboard a Globe Link aircraft where Fraser tries to force one of the radio operators, Bill Hastings (Sheldon Lawrence), to fly him out of the country. Morris is given very little to do in the finale owing to his character, despite being on board the plane, spending most of the time unconscious after getting shot by Fraser. The villain gets a fitting comeuppance when, after being pushed out of the plane during a fight with Bill, discovers—too late—that a parachute bag he'd previously strapped to his back has been used to hide a batch of phony notes and thus contains no parachute. The main female character, namely Bill's sister (the fiancée of a radio operator murdered by Fraser's henchmen at the film's start), is played by Morris' fellow Hollywoodian, Karin Booth.

The B movie **Action Stations** (1956) is an ultra-cheap British-Spanish co-production set in Spain and filmed on authentic locations there. Canadian star Paul Carpenter and British actor and one-time champion wrestler Joe Robinson play Bob and Pete, two amiable smugglers operating around the Mediterranean on Bob's yacht *Ventura*. Events see the pair befriend Anna (Maria Martin, billed as Mary Martin on British versions), a young woman whose engraver father has been recaptured after having escaped from the clutches of a murderous gang of counterfeiters headed by Kleivar (Ronald Leigh-Hunt). Kleivar later abducts Anna to use as leverage for her father's continued cooperation in the forging of U.S. dollars, but he doesn't count on Bob and Pete storming his mountain headquarters as they come to her rescue. Running times were 60 minutes in Spain (under the title *Pasaporte al Infierno*) and 50 minutes in UK.

"The bullet-blasting inside story of the world's biggest counterfeit ring!"

Hollywood's Zachary Scott is on chillingly villainous form as notorious racketeer Max Brant in the vigorous B movie ***The Counterfeit Plan*** (1957). The film begins with Brant, having been sentenced to death for a murder in France, cheating the guillotine when, while under police escort, he is rescued by his trusted associates and flown by private plane to England. Once there, he wastes no time in pressuring old acquaintance Louie (Mervyn Johns), a one-time master forger, to help in the initiation of a massive currency counterfeiting operation which ends up headquartered at the latter's large country mansion. However, after Max tries to force his attentions on Louie's daughter (Scott's fellow Hollywoodian Peggie Castle) and then callously murders the man's housekeeper, Louie tips off the police, leading to the downfall of the criminal empire. Also starring are Lee Patterson as Brant's right-hand man and Eric Pohlmann as a rival crook who pays a heavy price for trying to take over control of the racket. The film, whose meticulously detailed script reads like a manual on how to organize a counterfeiting operation, was edited down from 87 to 80 minutes for its U.S. theatrical release.

The briskly directed B movie ***Man from Tangier*** (1957) concerns the competing efforts of an international criminal, Armstrong (Emerton Court), and a gang of document forgers to take possession of a small equipment case—containing valuable engraving plates—that had once belonged to a master forger during World War II. Armstrong is first to get hold of the case, in Tangier, and is subsequently tracked by the gang to London. It's there that an American stunt man, Chuck Collins (one-time Warner Brothers contract player Robert Hutton), gets innocently caught up in the criminal goings-on after accidentally coming into possession of Armstrong's overcoat (having mistaken it for his own), which contains a ticket for a left-luggage locker where Armstrong has stored the case. Ultimately, a plan by chief gang member Voss (Martin Benson) to double-cross his cohorts leads to a rather underwhelming climactic shootout at an airfield. Lisa Gastoni plays the main female role, a displaced concentration camp survivor being blackmailed by Voss into helping in his double-cross plan. This was the second B movie (after the weird sci-fi horror offering *The Man Without a Body*, also dated 1957) that Hutton made in England, to where he eventually moved semi-permanently during the first half of the 1960s.

The Kinematograph Weekly (August 3, 1961) recognized the rare B movie ***Murder in Eden*** (1961) as having a "compact and exciting story" and "a catchy musical score." Following his acquisition of a famous Flemish painting, art dealer Arnold Woolf (Mark Singleton) arranges a viewing at the London gallery he runs with his wife Vicky (Yvonne Buckingham). Max Aaronson (Robert Lepler), a noted critic working on a book about fraud in the art world, detects that the painting is a fake and is shortly after murdered by a hit-and-run driver. Eventually, following a tricky investigation, Scotland Yard's Inspector Sharkey (Ray McAnally) unmasks the killer as a frustrated art restorer (Norman Rodway) who, in collusion with Vicky, had been running a lucrative art forgery racket. The story also features a Texan oil magnate played by Jack Aranson, an American-born actor notable for his later one-man stage version of *Moby Dick*.

"The golden goose is a dirty bird!"

In ***The File of the Golden Goose*** (1969), American secret agent Peter Novak (Yul Brynner) and Scotland Yard's Arthur Thompson (Edward Woodward) team up to infiltrate a large international currency counterfeiting ring (known as the "Golden Goose") responsible for the death of Novak's girlfriend (Hilary Dwyer). Sam Wanamaker's first film as director has some reasonable action and features plenty of touristy London locations, while some interesting developments include Novak at one point mistakenly believing that Thompson has sold out to the gang, and later not being able to save him (lest he give himself away) when the man's cover gets accidentally blown. Charles Gray and Graham Crowden stand out among the villains, the latter's weapon of choice being a deadly umbrella-swordstick. The *Monthly Film Bulletin* (July 1969) remarked on the film's "exceptionally uninteresting batch of fights, intrigues and sinister encounters" while neglecting to mention that it's actually a remake of the 1947 U.S. thriller *T-Men*.

Other Rackets

The very average B movie ***Assassin for Hire*** (1951) stars Sydney Tafler (complete with a stereotypical Italian accent) as Antonio Riccardi, a stamp dealer who moonlights as a contract killer, this helping fund his beloved and unsuspecting younger brother Giuseppe's (John Hewer) violin studies. Detective Inspector Carson (Ronald Howard) has long been aware of Antonio's criminality but has never been able to bring about a conviction due to the man always having a watertight alibi. In the end, Carson resorts to an unorthodox tactic whereby he tricks Antonio, after the latter carries out an assassination, into believing he has killed Giuseppe in mistake for the intended target, hoping this will cause him to crack and confess out of remorse. Howard and Tafler both give decent performances and would co-star again in the following year's *Wide Boy*, with Howard reprising his role as Carson and Tafler once again playing a criminal.

Dr. Mark Fenton, an intrepid London surgeon created by prolific crime writer Francis Durbridge, appears in two British thrillers (both based on six-part 1952 BBC TV serials), the first of which is ***The Broken Horseshoe*** (1953). Not long after being discharged from hospital following treatment by Fenton (Robert Beatty) for injuries sustained in a malicious hit-and-run incident, Charles Constance (Ferdy Mayne) turns up murdered. Fenton opens a letter given to him by Constance for safekeeping and finds inside a first-class rail ticket from London to Dover. This proves to be just the beginning of a complex mystery that sees the surgeon tangle with The Broken Horseshoe gang, a racehorse doping organization that will go to any lengths to get their hands on the ticket, which is encoded with vital secret information. Beatty makes a rugged hero, and the story also prominently involves an enigmatic female gang member played by Elizabeth Sellars.

In the follow-up, ***Operation Diplomat*** (1953), lanky actor Guy Rolfe takes over as Fenton, who this time around becomes embroiled in a dangerous adventure in which a gang attempts to smuggle—against his will—a top diplomat out of the country. Anton Diffring plays a discredited medic working with the gang, and Lisa Daniely has a sympathetic role as a nurse blackmailed by the criminals into helping them, only to be murdered when she tries to quit. The exciting story has a great final twist involving the identity of the gang's mysterious boss.

An exciting adaptation of a Francis Durbridge TV serial.

"The story behind the villas and the vice dens of the Riviera!"

The legendary Ginger Rogers plays Joan "Johnny" Victor, an American former actress, in the romantic and melodramatic ***Beautiful Stranger*** (1954). Johnny lives a life of luxury in Cannes funded by her married businessman lover Louis Galt (a solid early role for Stanley Baker), who makes most of his money by operating a highly organized racket involving the illegal production of gold sovereigns. After learning that Galt had lied to her about taking steps toward divorcing his wife, Johnny allows herself to fall in love with a dashing local ceramic artist named Pierre (played by Rogers' then real-life husband Jacques Bergerac). However, through a mix-up, Galt comes to believe that one of his shady associates, Emil (a show-stealing Herbert Lom), is Johnny's new lover, and a later fight between the two men (after Galt catches Emil attempting to rob him) ends in Galt's death. Circumstances lead to Johnny and Pierre becoming suspected in the killing, but they are ultimately cleared by Emil's dying words—heard by the police—after he is shot by one of Galt's henchmen. The *Monthly Film Bulletin* (August 1954) was not wrong in describing the film as one "whose motives become less clear the longer it continues."

The preposterous ***Delayed Action*** (1954) stars Robert Ayres as Ned Ellison, a washed-up American writer on the verge of suicide. However, circumstances lead to him making a deal with crooked financier Mark Cruden (Alan Wheatley) whereby he will delay his suicide in return for a large fee that will benefit a young daughter from whom he'd been separated by his ex-wife. The deal involves creating a fictitious persona—"Ned Collins"—for Ellison so that he can become the nominal figurehead in Cruden's shady dealings; the catch is that, should the authorities begin closing in on said shady dealings anytime within the next 18 months, then Ellison must go ahead with his suicide so that the dead "Ned Collins" will be blamed for all the criminality. Ellison eventually loses interest in the deal after writing a successful novel and falling in love, only to end up being used in an attempted double-cross against Cruden by the latter's second-in-command (Bruce Seton). A silly premise, unlikely situations and at least one ridiculous coincidence conspire to sink this B movie. Ayres was an American actor based in England.

*"They fight to the death—
and the weapons are ten-ton trucks!"*

In the gritty **Hell Drivers** (1957), directed at a cracking pace by Cy Endfield, ex-con Tom Yately (Stanley Baker) gets work as a truck driver at a ballast haulage company whose manager, Cartley (William Hartnell), demands twelve hauls per day along hazardous roads. One of the other drivers, the unbalanced Red (a powerhouse performance by Patrick McGoohan), holds the record for the most hauls in one day, and there's soon rivalry between him and Tom. Events lead to Tom discovering that Cartley and Red run a racket whereby money is claimed from head office for drivers who do not exist, and culminate in the two criminals attempting to kill him in a climactic truck chase. To contrast the action, we're given an insight into Tom's troubled family life, and added drama is provided by a complicated love triangle involving Tom, Gino (a friendly Italian driver played sympathetically by Herbert Lom) and Cartley's secretary (Peggy Cummins). An effective point-of-view title sequence allows the audience to experience the view from behind the wheel of a speeding truck.

The titular dagger in the B movie **The Long Knife** (1958) is wielded by the mysterious head of an extortion gang who, during the course of the story, finds it necessary to murder two cohorts as well as the wealthy Mrs. Cheam (Ellen Pollock), a nursing home patient who'd been targeted by the criminals. Central to the plot are a nurse (Joan Rice), who'd been innocently involved with one of the dead crooks, and Mrs. Cheam's American lawyer (Sheldon Lawrence), while a neat twist concerns the identity of the killer, who has been masquerading as a member of the opposite sex. *The Daily Cinema* (August 22, 1958) called the film an "exciting suspense thriller" with a "good surprise climax."

The at once sleazy and exciting **Passport to Shame** (1958) revolves around a London prostitution racket run by the odious and sadistic Nick Biaggi (Herbert Lom). Malou (Odile Versois), a naïve young Parisian, finds herself enslaved by the criminal after being tricked into traveling to London for a supposed legitimate job. The always excellent Eddie Constantine plays Johnny, a tough cab driver conned by Nick into a one-day marriage of convenience with Malou in order to get the latter a British passport. However, upon realizing what's in store for the girl, Nick sets out to rescue her, falling in love with her in the process and eventually smashing the racket with the help of his fellow cabbies. Legendary sex symbol Diana Dors stands out as a good-hearted hooker who ultimately sets into motion Nick's demise in revenge for his having caused the suicide of her kid sister.

Breakout (1959) is a cracking B movie starring the charismatic Lee Patterson as George Munro, a town planner who occasionally masterminds prison breaks as a sideline. Hired by a couple of fixers—one of them an old acquaintance (William Lucas)—to plan the breakout of an embezzler, Munro secures work as a van driver delivering groceries to the prison, the idea being to spring the convict by hiding him behind a false panel in the vehicle. Following some suspenseful last-minute hiccups, the breakout succeeds but, thanks to a vigilant jail guard, the alarm is raised almost immediately, this leading to the eventual capture of all the criminals. Hazel Court and Billie Whitelaw provide contrasting feminine appeal as, respectively, the embezzler's glamorous wife and Munro's more domesticated but no less attractive spouse. The film went straight to television in the U.S., initially broadcast as a first-season episode of *Kraft Mystery Theatre*.

The brutal London-based **Never Let Go** (1960) stars Richard Todd as a meek salesman who, unimpressed with efforts by the police, takes matters into his own hands when his uninsured new car is stolen. His investigations lead to him tangling with a vicious criminal named Lionel Meadows (Peter Sellers), the brains behind a racket in which vehicles are stolen, repainted in a new color and then resold. The biggest surprise of this energetically directed and atmospherically photographed movie is the casting-against-type of Sellers, whose villain must rate as one of the nastiest in a British film, if only for a scene in which, while victimizing a witness to the theft (Mervyn Johns), he callously stamps on the man's beloved pet terrapin. Todd is perfect as the ordinary man making a stand, and there's excellent support from teen pop idol Adam Faith who, as well as playing a youth in Meadows' employ, also gives a great rendition of the song "When Johnny Comes Marching Home Again" over the opening credits. Also worthy of note is Carol White in an impressive performance as Meadows' mistreated moll.

An automobile racket is also at the center of the B movie ***Kil 1*** (1962), in which dud checks are used to purchase cars that are then given new identities using license plates from wrecked vehicles at a car salvage yard. In the course of events, Ted-o (Jess Conrad), a young member of the racket, kills his boss (the salvage yard owner) in a fight and is then forced to shoot the latter's American partner before going on the run in a stolen car refitted with old plates reading KIL 1. However, he gets his comeuppance after the car is spotted by a man who recognizes the plates as those that belonged to a vehicle in which his son had crashed to his death. Ronald Howard gets top billing as a detective and adds a much needed touch of class to the proceedings. The director, Arnold Louis Miller, is best known for his work in the world of British sexploitation films, with credits including *Secrets of a Windmill Girl* (1966) and *Frustrated Wives* (1974); in the U.S., *Kil 1* was released (in 1965) under the guise of such a movie, complete with new

Warren Beatty tampers with playing card printing plates in *Kaleidoscope* (1966).

title (*The Skin Game*), added salacious footage and racy taglines such as "a tale of hot cars, cold cash and easy women!"

"The switched-on thriller!!!"

In the colorful and offbeat **Kaleidoscope** (1966), American playboy Barney Lincoln (Warren Beatty) comes up with an ingenious way of cheating at cards. He breaks into the Kaleidoscope playing card factory in Geneva, tampers with the printing plates so that cards manufactured from then on will be marked, and then makes a fortune at casinos where these cards are used. Clive Revill shines as an eccentric Scotland Yard detective who finds out what Barney is up to and uses this to blackmail him into helping bring down a Napoleon-obsessed—including wearing the legendary French general's hairstyle—drug trafficker named Dominion (Eric Porter). The idea is to ruin the villain financially by way of a poker match. An eminently glamorous Susannah York plays the detective's kooky daughter who hooks up with Barney, the couple ultimately involved in an exciting climax in which Dominion, together with his two henchmen (George Sewell and Larry Taylor), tries to kill them in the grounds of his castle. In 1968, the film was reissued (although only in Australia, it would seem) as *The Bank Breaker*, no doubt in an attempt to cash in on Beatty's intervening success as bank robber Clyde Barrow in *Bonnie and Clyde* (1967).

"The race against death!"

Surprisingly, only one feature film has so far been made from the many novels of Dick Francis, a former champion jockey who specialized in stories set in the world of professional horse racing. The film in question is **Dead Cert** (1974), adapted from the author's 1962 debut novel of the same name. When a professional jockey (Scott Antony) investigates the supposedly accidental death of his racehorse trainer friend (Ian Hogg), he finds it linked to an organization involved in race fixing, protection rackets and prostitution. This slow-moving affair also stars Julian Glover as a corrupt policeman implicated in the criminal goings-on, while some mediocre action includes a cross-country chase involving a horse and several radio cabs (the organization uses a radio cab company as a cover). Things perk up a bit in the final act where, in an attempt to murder our hero, his not-so-good (as it turns out) friend and fellow jockey (Michael Williams) tries to push him off his horse during the famous Grand National race, only to fall himself and become bloodily impaled on a railing.

The Deadly Females (1975) stars Tracy Reed as Joan, a housewife running a group of female assassins from a London antiques shop. Clients wishing to rid themselves of unfaithful or boring spouses, controlling lovers or unwanted business partners, usually make contact with Joan through her newspaper ads for "disposal" services, after which victims are liquidated in ways that resemble accidents or suicide. The film, episodic in structure and extremely dull in execution, suffers from a lack of plot, unengaging characters and an excessive running time. Those with radical feminist leanings will disapprove of some exploitative female nudity (two of the assassins use sex to lure their targets) but will rejoice in the fact that most of the victims are particularly obnoxious males. Rula Lenska, just before her big break in British TV's *Rock Follies* (1976), and best known in the U.S. for Alberto V05 hair product commercials a few years later, has a very brief role as a mysterious Italian assassin (poisoned cigarettes are her favored method of liquidation) planning a hostile takeover of Joan's operation.

6

Suspense

Although suspense, to one degree or another, is a crucial element in all good thrillers, what sets the films in this chapter apart is that they mainly focus on situations in which suspense is sustained, e.g., a race against time with only *Seven Days to Noon* (1950); a manhunt in *Tiger Bay* (1959); crooked cops pursuing an *Eyewitness* (1970); and a siege that ensures *Tomorrow Never Comes* (1977). Some of the better nail-biters include *Time Bomb* (1952), *The Night My Number Came Up* (1955), *Chase a Crooked Shadow* (1957), *SOS Pacific* (1959), *Cash on Demand* (1961), *Strongroom* (1961) and *Juggernaut* (1974).

1950s

Douglas Fairbanks, Jr., stars in **State Secret** (1950) as John Marlowe, a London-based American doctor and inventor of a new but as yet only experimental surgical procedure for portal hypertension. The plot has Marlowe invited to the European police state of Vosnia (a fictional creation for the story complete with its own equally fictitious language) to demonstrate the procedure on a patient. Once there, he finds that the operation has political motivations, with the patient none other than General Niva (Walter Rilla), the nation's prime minister, whose survival is crucial to an upcoming election. When Niva dies following the operation, it becomes necessary for those in authority to cover up the death. Marlowe, who must be silenced lest he spill the beans, is soon forced to go on the run. Filmed in Italy (Trento and the Dolomites), this exciting political chase thriller also stars Jack Hawkins as a government minister in charge of, among other things, state security, and Glynis Johns as a half-English music-hall entertainer helping Marlowe in his plight, which comes to an unexpected and satisfying conclusion.

> *"An A-bomb is loose ...*
> *in the world's largest city!"*

Some superb London location work, which the *Monthly Film Bulletin* (September 1950) said "catches the authentic atmosphere of the city," highlights **Seven Days to Noon** (1950), whose original story (a collaboration between Paul Dehn and future Hammer Films composer James Bernard) went on to win an Oscar at the 1952 Academy Awards. Professor John Willingdon (a convincing Barry Jones), a scientist working at an atomic weapons research facility, has become so unhinged by the conviction that his life's work will be put to evil use, that he absconds with a small atom bomb and threatens—via a letter to the Prime Minister—to blow up central London in seven days unless it is publicly announced that Great Britain will cease production of any further such weapons. Superintendent Folland (Andre Morell) of Scotland Yard's Special Branch takes charge of a manhunt for Willingdon but, as time runs out, an evacuation of the threatened 12-square-mile area begins. Plenty of tension ensues in this meticulously detailed production, which even throws a serial killer into the mix when the professor, having rented a room at a boarding house, is nearly caught after the houseowner (a nice turn by Joan Hickson) calls the police in the mistaken belief he is the much-publicized "Landlady Killer."

Needless to say, London survived for a follow-up, *High Treason* (1951), in which Andre Morell returns as Folland to help protect the capital from a subversive group involved in acts of sabotage. One of the revolutionaries (Kenneth Griffith) is held prisoner by his associates after attempting to quit, but escapes and manages to warn the authorities about a plan to sabotage power stations. There's a neat twist regarding the identity of the mastermind behind the subversives, not to mention a thrilling climactic battle in which the saboteurs and armed forces fight it out at London's Battersea Power Station. The cast also includes Liam Redmond and Anthony Nicholls as, respectively, a Special Branch commander (Folland's superior) and a prominent Member of Parliament.

"Crazed killer strikes!"

Vivid, haunting and exhilarating, *The Clouded Yellow* (1950) stars Trevor Howard (compelling as always) as ex-British Secret Service agent David Somers, who takes a job cataloging butterflies at the country house of husband and wife Nicholas and Jess Fenton (Barry Jones and Sonia Dresdel). Jean Simmons plays the Fentons' fragile niece, Sophie, whose parents died years before when the father supposedly shot the mother before then turning the gun on himself. When the local handyman is found murdered with incriminating evidence pointing to Sophie as the culprit, David is certain it's a frame-up and helps the young woman elude the police. Eventually, Sophie's recollection of a vital fact from the past enables David to set a trap that draws out the real killer who, as it shockingly turns out, also killed Sophie's parents. The film is superbly directed, photographed and edited, with the latter part of the story focusing mainly on a police manhunt for David and Sophie that spans the north of England, making effective use of locations including the beautiful Lake District. The climax features a brilliantly staged and edited chase around Liverpool docks, where the killer finally gets his comeuppance by falling into the path of a train.

The murdered handyman of the previous film was played by Maxwell Reed, who has a much more prominent role as *The Dark Man* (1950), a shadowy, ruthless and deadly thief. The plot involves the villain targeting a young actress, Molly (Natasha Parry), mistakenly believing that she may be able to identify him in connection with his murder of a taxi driver. There are one or two fairly tense moments (including Molly catching the Dark Man's reflection in a mirror when he creeps up behind her with strangulation in mind), but an excessively talky and improbable script dilutes the film's overall suspense potential. Reed conveys a suitable air of menace as the murderer, and Edward Underdown is quietly authoritative as a detective falling in love with Molly while trying to protect her. Events, which are set mostly in a pleasant seaside town, lead to a drawn-out final chase resulting in the killer meeting a violent end on an artillery range.

Set in Sweden, *Valley of Eagles* (1951) stars John McCallum as Nils Ahlen, a scientist whose disloyal wife (Mary Laura Wood) and assistant (Anthony Dawson) make off with vital components of his important new invention (a device for storing huge amounts of electricity as sound) in order to sell it behind the Iron Curtain. Nils ends up joining forces with a police inspector (Jack Warner) to go after the fleeing couple, who are heading across the snowy wastes of Lapland toward the border. This expertly photographed and intermittently exciting chase movie features one particularly well-staged sequence in which the pursuers face certain death from wolves, only to be dramatically rescued by a Lapp tribe whose giant trained hunting eagles fight off the predators. Nadia Gray plays a sensitive schoolmistress who joins

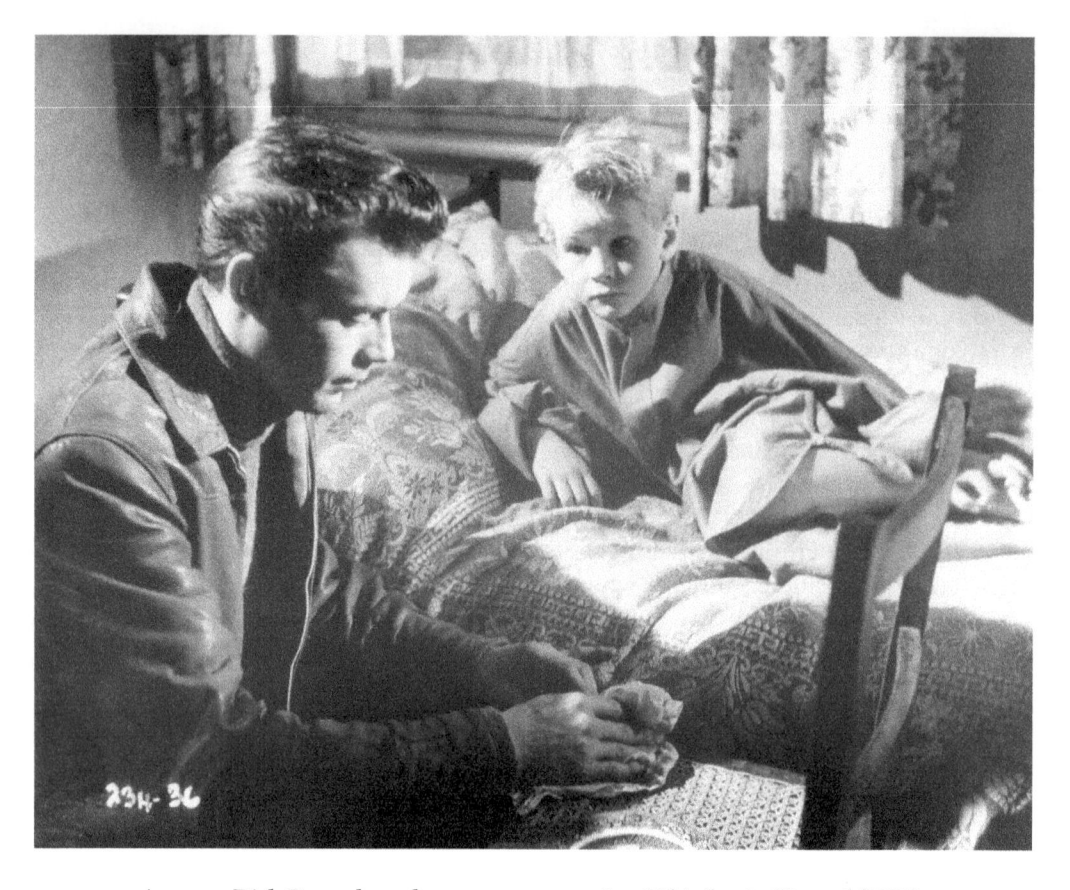

A young Dirk Bogarde and an even younger Jon Whiteley in *Hunted* (1952).

up with the pursuers and serves to remind Nils that not all women are as scheming as his wife.

Dirk Bogarde gives one of his more impressive early performances as Chris Lloyd, a young merchant seaman, in the expertly directed and fluently photographed manhunt thriller, ***Hunted*** (1952). After killing his wife's (Elizabeth Sellars) lover in a London ruin (a remnant from the Blitz), Chris goes on the run and is forced to take with him a six-year-old orphan runaway (Jon Whiteley) who witnessed him at the crime scene. As the story progresses, the youngster, Robbie, proves to have a softening effect on the initially strident Chris, with an emotional bond developing between the unlikely pair as they head north, ultimately setting sail from Scotland on a stolen fishing vessel. Their adventure ends when Robbie falls ill, leaving Chris no option but to return ashore for help, which means giving himself up to the pursuing authorities. Young Whiteley gives a very natural, unforced performance, and his great chemistry with Bogarde results in a convincing and heartwarming on-screen relationship.

In the episodic ***Emergency Call*** (1952), a little girl with leukemia urgently needs three pints of blood for a life-saving transfusion. Because of her rare blood type, it becomes a race against time to locate suitable donors. A doctor (Anthony Steel) and a Scotland Yard Inspector (Jack Warner) are involved in the search, which is complicated on many levels, such as in the case of one potential donor (Geoffrey Hibbert) proving difficult to locate after going on the run due to his past involvement in an unsolved murder. The story, which overall lacks the urgency promised by the fast-moving opening credits sequence, features real-life former world light-heavyweight boxing champion

Freddie Mills as one of the donors, namely—you guessed it—a boxer! The imperiled child is played by Jennifer Tafler, whose real-life parents, Sydney Tafler and Joy Shelton, both also star, the latter as her on-screen mother.

Much snappier (mostly due to its shorter running time) was the B-movie remake ***Emergency*** (1962), starring Glyn Houston as a forthright detective searching for blood donors when a little girl with a rare blood type is injured in a road accident. This time around, one of the potential donors is a convicted murderer facing execution (an effective turn by Patrick Jordan) who initially refuses to cooperate unless he's granted a reprieve. Zena Walker and Dermot Walsh play the girl's parents, a couple initially estranged but in the end reconciled as a result of the crisis. The *Monthly Film Bulletin* (June 1962) concluded that this version was just as "unlikely and complex" as the original.

"Will hold you wide-eyed with excitement!"

The Yellow Balloon (1952) features a remarkable performance by Andrew Ray as Frankie, a young boy whose playful stealing of a friend's balloon leads to a chase resulting in the latter's accidental death in a ruined building. The scene is witnessed by ruthless petty criminal Len Turner (an uncharacteristically menacing William Sylvester), who essentially blackmails Frankie—by scaring him with suggestions of possible police involvement in the incident—into becoming his stooge. Len ends up using Frankie as a decoy in a robbery that ends in murder, leaving the criminal no option but to silence the boy. Gilbert Taylor's photography superbly captures post-war London and is especially effective during a climactic pursuit of Frankie by Len (involving some atmospheric shots in an abandoned subway

Sandra Dorne and William Sylvester in *The Yellow Balloon* (1952).

station), a sequence which was considered intense enough to earn the film an "X" rating on its initial British release, although this was subsequently downgraded (after editing) for a prompt re-release.

Glenn Ford was one of the biggest Hollywood names to star in a British B thriller, namely ***Time Bomb*** (1952) in which he plays businessman Peter Lyncort, formerly a bomb disposal expert with the Royal Canadian Engineers. Amid marital problems, Peter is called in to help when the police correctly suspect that a saboteur has planted a time bomb on a freight train transporting naval sea mines to Portsmouth. Helped by a railroad security chief (an assured performance by Maurice Denham), he begins a search of the train (by now diverted into a siding with the surrounding area evacuated), culminating in the discovery and neutralization—just in time—of the bomb. However, tension ratchets up when the capture of the saboteur (Victor Maddern) leads to the revelation that there's a second bomb on board. Anne Vernon plays Peter's wife who, having earlier walked out on him, returns for the inevitable happy ending. Ted Tetzlaff directs competently, but the film never quite reaches the suspenseful heights of his earlier U.S. classic *The Window* (1949).

Set in Germany soon after World War II, ***Desperate Moment*** (1953) stars Dirk Bogarde as Simon Van Halder, a displaced former Dutch resistance fighter jailed for life after confessing to a murder which he knows had been committed by his friend Paul (Albert Lieven), a deserter from the German Navy. It turns out the reason Simon took the rap was because he felt there was nothing to live for after being told by Paul that his beloved girlfriend Anna (Mai Zetterling) had died. When Simon learns that Anna is in fact alive and that he'd been tricked, he escapes from prison and, with Anna's help, endeavors to clear his name by tracking down Paul, now a Berlin racketeer going under another name. Prolific German actor Lieven, probably best-remembered in Britain for the same producer's (George H. Brown) 1948 thriller *Sleeping Car to Trieste*, is always good value as a shady character, and you can't go wrong with Bogarde; that said, the incident-packed *Desperate Moment* remains, despite their presence, unconvincing and largely forgettable. The film's director, Compton Bennett, went on to take a four-year break from movie-making, and would only helm four further features, the best of which is arguably the cracking B thriller *The Flying Scot* (1957).

"I'm the guy who paid to kill ... myself!"

The entertaining and well-plotted ***Five Days*** (1954) was the last of three British B thrillers made by Dane Clark for Hammer Film Productions. The U.S. actor gives an energetic performance as businessman James Nevill who, facing financial ruin when a major deal falls through, decides to have himself killed so that his wife (Thea Gregory) can benefit from a substantial life insurance policy. To this end, he blackmails—in connection with a past murder—his old friend Paul Kirby (Paul Carpenter) into agreeing to kill him within five days. However, when his business circumstances take a turn for the better, he cannot find Kirby in order to cancel the assassination. Subsequent attempts on Nevill's life prove to have nothing to do with Kirby (he ultimately decided not to go along with the plan) and everything to do with others who want rid of Nevill and intend to make Kirby a scapegoat in his murder.

Burnt Evidence (1954) stars Duncan Lamont as Jack Taylor, a builder and decorator beset by not only financial difficulties but also a suspicion that his wife, Diana (Jane Hylton), is about to leave him for his old friend Jimmy (Donald Gray). Having decided to commit suicide, Jack prepares to shoot himself in his workshop; however, while there, he ends up getting into a fight with Jimmy instead. During the struggle, the gun goes off and a lit cigarette that Jack had been smoking causes the building to go up in flames. The charred remains of a body

(Jimmy's as it turns out) are soon discovered in the burnt-out workshop, and the rest of this dreary B movie involves the police attempting to locate Jack, who has gone on the run for fear he will be accused of deliberately causing Jimmy's death when in fact it had been an accident. All ends well after he decides to give himself up, whereupon we learn there was nothing going on between Diana and Jimmy after all.

Then British–based Australian actor John McCallum stars with real-life wife Googie Withers in **Port of Escape** (1954), a largely unconvincing hostage thriller with a London Docklands setting. In what was one of his final British films before making a permanent move—with Withers—back to Antipodean shores, McCallum plays an Australian seaman named Mitch Gillis. Bill Kerr (another Australian) plays Jeff Lloyd, Gillis' amnesiac and mentally unstable (due to a head injury) American buddy and the catalyst for all sorts of troubles including causing a situation in which Gillis winds up killing a man. Gillis and Lloyd, the latter nicknamed "Dinty Missouri" after his home state in the U.S. (to which Gillis promises to help him return for a brain operation), end up commandeering a houseboat and holding hostage the vessel's owner, Anne (Withers), who witnessed the killing, along with her sister (Wendy Danielli) and maid (Joan Hickson). Complications arising from a developing romance between Gillis and Anne lead to Lloyd going off the rails with a loaded gun, and a climactic showdown with police ensures the poor chap never makes it back to Missouri.

> "13 in a plane—Destination….
> The Unknown…"

Anyone with a fear of flying should avoid **The Night My Number Came Up** (1955), the gripping tale—scripted by *Journey's End* playwright R.C. Sherriff—of a possible impending disaster. At a dinner party in Hong Kong, a British naval commander (Michael Hordern) recounts his dream about a seemingly doomed flight involving a specific twin-engine Dakota aircraft. Through fate, three of those listening to the story end up on that very same Dakota bound for Tokyo, with key aspects of the dream—thirteen people on board, a bad storm, a broken radio and low fuel—all falling neatly into place. Top-billed Michael Redgrave brings a strong presence to his role as an RAF air marshal, but it's Alexander Knox who takes the acting honors as an increasingly nervous first-time-flying civil servant whose disregard for superstition is challenged by the apparent predestination of unfolding events. Told in a prolonged flashback and featuring some neat (for the time) special effects, the film successfully sustains tension throughout and is the type of story one could imagine would have made a classic *Twilight Zone* episode.

> "He was a man on the run
> … but his time was running out!"

"Very solid and well-made thriller entertainment" was how *Today's Cinema* (December 9, 1955) described Hollywood star Gene Nelson's second B movie for Merton Park. **Dial 999** (1955) sees the actor-dancer playing Greg Carradine, a closet philanderer and gambler who, while drunk, kills a bookmaker and lies to his wife Terry (Mona Freeman) by telling her it was self defense. Terry helps him elude the police and continues to support him even after discovering the truth about the death, as well as other unsavory facts about her no-good spouse. She is soon arranging a getaway abroad with the help of an organization that specializes in escape routes for criminals but, as a manhunt gets underway, a series of unexpected developments results in disastrous consequences for the fugitive. Nelson does a pretty good job as the aggressive and self-centered Greg, whom one character aptly describes as behaving "like a juvenile delinquent," while fellow Hollywoodian Freeman gives a nicely measured performance as the wife who, despite all her initial support, eventually gives up on her unworthy husband. Also featured are John Bentley as a detective and Michael Goodliffe as Terry's cooperative (in regard to helping Greg) brother. The film's U.S. title, *The Way Out*, was taken from Bruce Graeme's 1954 source novel.

In the harrowing ***Lost*** (1956), a baby boy is abducted after his nanny leaves him momentarily unattended in his pram outside a London drugstore. During a painstaking police investigation, Inspector Craig (an authoritative performance by David Farrar) follows clues that eventually lead to a seaside town where the abductor, a mentally unstable woman (Anna Turner), is identified. Events culminate in a tense clifftop finale in which the kidnapper threatens to jump off the cliff edge with the child, forcing Craig to risk life and limb in a daring maneuver that ends up saving the day. David Knight and Julia Arnall play the distraught parents, and film buffs will have a field day spotting the array of familiar faces (Joan Hickson, Mona Washbourne, Barbara Windsor, etc.) filling the many tiny support roles. An interesting subplot involves a couple who attempt to exploit the situation—by falsely claiming to have kidnapped the child—in an attempt to gain a ransom.

The terrific B movie ***Bond of Fear*** (1956) impresses with its skillful and extensive use of outdoor photography, managing to convey a genuine feel of danger and suspense on the open road. In the north of England, John Sewell (Dermot Walsh), his wife Mary (Jane Barrett) and kids Ann and Michael (Marilyn Baker and Anthony Pavey) set off in their Land Rover—with travel trailer in tow—toward their holiday destination in France. En route, they discover Terence Dewar (John Colicos), an armed criminal on the run for murder, hiding in the trailer. By holding Michael hostage, Dewar secures the family's help in eluding the police, who have by now set up roadblocks. An ensuing series of dangerous escapades, which include Dewar's attempt to get rid of John and take his place on a cross-channel ferry, culminates in a lively showdown between the two men at the port of Dover. Performances are good all around, especially Canadian-born Colicos in his first major role in a feature film (he'd played smaller roles in the same producers' other B thrillers *Barbados Quest*, *Breakaway* and *Passport to Treason*).

Filmed in East Africa, ***Escape in the Sun*** (1956) is an intermittently exciting Eastmancolor B movie in which, according to

Pressbook for a first-rate 1956 B movie from Tempean Films.

The Cinema (May 9, 1956), the "acting of the small cast is robust rather than profound." Obviously inspired by 1932's *The Most Dangerous Game*, the story concerns an insanely jealous millionaire, Michael O'Dell (Martin Boddey), who, during a hunting safari, notices his beautiful trophy wife Margot (Vera Fusek) and handsome hunter Jim (John Bentley) taking more than just a passing interest in each other. Crazed and vengeful, he instigates an evil plan that involves framing Jim for murder; also, and more excitingly for Michael, it involves forcing Jim and Margot to go on the run so that he can hunt them and put to the test his long-held theory that humans are the most challenging prey. Locations include the Gedi Ruins and a town on Malindi Bay, the latter the setting for a couple of surprising developments and a satisfyingly melodramatic conclusion. Director George Breakston was a former teenage actor who played Beezy in most of Mickey Rooney's *Andy Hardy* movies.

In **Eyewitness** (1956), a young woman, Lucy (Muriel Pavlow), after witnessing a robbery at a cinema, flees the scene and is knocked down by a bus. The two robbers, the dominant of whom, Wade (Donald Sinden), has killed the cinema's manager, follow an ambulance that takes the unconscious Lucy to hospital. Outside in the hospital grounds, Wade waits for an opportunity to get inside and kill the woman before she has sufficiently recovered to reveal what she witnessed. Things begin to drag a little once the hospital setting is established, and suspense comes in fits and starts, with Wade's attempts to kill Lucy being thwarted at every turn, not least by querulous elderly female patient Mrs. Hudson (Ada Reeve providing some excellent comic relief). Sinden is somewhat miscast, which is certainly not the case with Nigel Stock who, as Wade's simple and increasingly conscience-stricken accomplice, gives by far the picture's best performance. Also appearing are Belinda Lee as a nurse and Michael Craig as Lucy's husband. Over the years, the film was shown on U.S. television under the British title and also as *Peril in the Night*.

The outstanding London location work in **The Weapon** (1956) gives a great feel for post-war life in the capital with its many bomb-ravaged sites. It's in one of these sites that a young boy, Erik Jenner (Jon Whiteley), finds—hidden in brickwork—the titular item, a loaded .27 caliber German handgun with which he accidentally shoots and injures another boy before panicking and going on the run, still in possession of the firearm. A ballistics report on the shooting reveals the weapon to be the same one used in the unsolved murder 10 years earlier of a U.S. Army Officer stationed in England. It's not long before the murderer (George Cole) reads about Erik's case in the newspapers and sets out to retrieve the incriminating gun, quite willing to kill again if necessary. This workmanlike B movie features two Hollywood stars, Steve Cochran and Lizabeth Scott, he as a hard-headed U.S. Army Captain investigating the unsolved case and she as the boy's waitress mother, who has a softening influence on the captain.

In the briskly paced B movie **Booby Trap** (1956), an absent-minded professor (Tony Quinn) accidentally leaves his new invention—an explosive fountain pen fitted with a trigger device that can be activated by the sound of bells—in a taxi. His frantic attempts to retrieve the device see him come into contact with a suave criminal (Sydney Tafler) who unwittingly ends up with the explosive pen among a batch of other fountain pens which he uses as containers for smuggling drugs. Harry Fowler has the most entertaining role as a cockney wide boy, and the climax sees the pen finally exploding—to the fatal detriment of the drug smuggler—after being triggered by the chimes of Big Ben.

*"If a killer hangs—
an innocent woman must die!"*

A "very moderate British programmer" was how the *Kinematograph Weekly* (December 20, 1956) described **The Hostage**

(1956). In the South American republic of Santanio, fascist revolutionary Vorgler is due to hang for the murder of a police chief. In London, Royal Academy of Music student Rosa Gonzuelo (Mary Parker), daughter of Santanio's president, is kidnapped by pro–Vorgler activists who make it clear that she too will hang unless the president grants Vorgler a pardon. Caught up in events is Bill Trailer (Ron Randell), a wisecracking pilot who becomes instrumental in saving Rosa and bringing about the activists' downfall. Alfred Shaughnessy co-wrote the screenplay, a variation of his teleplay for the 1953 BBC TV serial *A Place of Execution*.

Toronto, Canada. One Friday evening, through an unfortunate sequence of events, six-year-old Steven (Vincent Winter) gets accidentally locked in a large vault at the bank where his father works. Due to a **Time Lock** (1957), the vault cannot be opened until after the weekend, but there is not nearly enough oxygen for the boy to survive even a quarter of that time. This film version of Arthur Hailey's likewise titled 1956 TV play (a season 10 episode of the U.S. series *Kraft Television Theatre*) is a first-class B movie that manages to sustain tension even though the outcome is never really in any doubt. Canadian star Robert Beatty is terrific as a tersely authoritative engineer and leading vault expert upon whose shoulders it falls to rescue the boy. Lee Patterson (another Canadian) and Betty McDowall are sympathetic as the boy's distressed parents, and look out for Sean Connery in a tiny role as a welder. This was the second film to come from the producer-director team of Peter Rogers and Gerald Thomas, who would go on to find lasting fame as makers of the classic *Carry On* series of comedy movies.

"Razor-edge suspense in sizzling hot thriller!"

Hollywood's Pat O'Brien, by this stage in his career a busy television performer in shows such as *Climax!*, *The United States Steel Hour* and *Lux Video Theatre*, found time to cross the Atlantic to star in director Terence Fisher's final B picture of the decade, **Kill Me Tomorrow** (1957). In it, he plays Bart Crosbie, a widowed London-based reporter whose heavy drinking costs him his job at *The Clarion* newspaper. Almost immediately afterward, he becomes in desperate need of £1,000 to fund a life-saving operation in Zürich for his young son Jimmy (Claude Kingston). When *The Clarion*'s editor (Ronald Adam) is killed in a confrontation with diamond smugglers whose activities were about to be exposed in the paper, Crosbie makes a deal with chief smuggler Heinz Webber (George Coulouris) whereby he agrees to take the rap for the killing in exchange for the much-needed £1,000. However, this only leads to complications which end up putting Jimmy's life at risk from the criminals. Lois Maxwell plays the editor's niece, who is instrumental to the story ending on a happy note. The film features the big-screen debut of British rock-and-roll star Tommy Steele.

At the Stroke of Nine (1957) stars Stephen Murray as Phillip Garrett, a concert pianist with a grudge against the *Evening Clarion*, a newspaper whose smear campaign toward his father led to the latter's suicide. Seeking revenge, Garrett kidnaps one of the paper's young reporters, Sally Bryant (Patricia Dainton), imprisons her in the cellar of his gloomy London mansion and reveals his intention to kill her in five days' time. In the meantime, he sets about sensationalizing the incident by making Sally write daily accounts about her ordeal which he sends to the newspaper for publication. The main clue that leads to Garrett's comeuppance has to do with his forthcoming performance of the (fictional) Vorslav Piano Concerto at London's Royal Festival Hall. Brian Clemens (under his pseudonym Tony O'Grady), was one of four scriptwriters involved in this rare B movie, which also stars Patrick Barr as Sally's heroic suitor (and fellow reporter) and Dermot Walsh as the newspaper's editor.

Across the Bridge (1957), based on a 1938 short story of the same name by Graham Greene, sees Rod Steiger give one of his better performances as Carl Schaffner, a British (of German origin) financier in New York who goes on the run to avoid facing charges for a $9 million embezzlement scheme. Fleeing to Mexico on a train, he encounters a character named Paul Scarff (Bill Nagy) to whom he bears a striking resemblance. Schaffner soon steals Scarff's identity (including his Mexican passport) in a plan that entails drugging the man and then throwing his body from the train; however, this doesn't work out too well when it emerges that Scarff is a wanted political killer. Events see Schaffner ending up stranded in a Mexican border town at the mercy of a corrupt and blackmailing police chief (Noel Willman), with his only friend being Dolores, a dog that belonged to Scarff and which has been tagging along with him ever since the identity switch. Bernard Lee plays a pursuing Scotland Yard detective who uses the dog in a trap that forces Schaffner to cross a bridge into U.S. territory. Greene's story was also the basis for the U.S. action comedy *Double Take* (2000).

Set during World War II, **Seven Thunders** (1957) revolves around Dave and Jim (Stephen Boyd and Tony Wright), a pair of escaped POWs temporarily hiding out in a run-down area of Marseilles. The main thriller element of the story concerns local resident Dr. Martout (James Robertson Justice), a prolific serial killer who preys on desperate refugees by promising to provide them with escape routes, only to instead poison them, steal their valuables and dispose of their bodies in quicklime. The Nazis end up razing the neighborhood, but not before Jim almost becomes a victim of the evil doctor, the latter ultimately killed in a car crash while attempting to escape with his ill-gotten gains. Our two heroes eventually make it to safety, helped no end by Lise (Anna Gaylor), an orphaned young woman who has fallen in love with Dave.

"*The picture that makes mystery history.*"

The minor classic **Chase a Crooked Shadow** (1957) opens in Barcelona with a man and woman (Richard Todd and Faith Brook) studying footage of the isolated Prescott family villa (80 miles away on the Costa Brava) and discussing its occupant, South African heiress Kimberley Prescott (Anne Baxter). Kimberley has recently returned to the place after a long convalescence following the deaths in Johannesburg of her brother (in a driving accident) and her diamond magnate father (by suicide). Late that night, Todd's character shows up at the villa and alleges to be the dead brother, whereupon an unnerved Kimberley, who cannot get him to leave, summons the local police chief, Vargas (Herbert Lom). Through evidence including a passport and driving license, the man convinces Vargas that he is in fact who he claims to be and that it was someone else who'd died in the aforementioned driving accident. Having ensconced himself in the house, the man soon brings in his friend (the woman from Barcelona) as well as a supposed butler (Alan Tilvern), and the trio implement a plan in which Kimberley is pressured to hand over a secret stash of diamonds that had mysteriously disappeared from her father's company just before he committed suicide. Eventually, Kimberley comes to believe that her life is in danger from the conspirators—now also including her beloved Uncle "Chan" Chandler (Alexander Knox)—until a terrific final twist reveals their surprising true motive.

The film, a near-perfect thriller that builds suspense slowly but steadily, features tight direction, excellent photography (with some effective expressionistic interiors), great performances by the small ensemble cast, and a soundtrack that includes Spanish guitar played by Julian Bream. The plot is a variation of the 1946 episode "Stranger in the House" from the U.S. radio show *The Whistler*, later adapted as a 1955 episode of *The Whistler* TV series. A very similar story was later told in French writer Robert Thomas' popular 1960 stage play *Piège pour un homme seul*, on which three U.S. TV movies—*Honeymoon with a Stranger* (1969),

From left: Richard Todd, Anne Baxter and Herbert Lom in the superlative *Chase a Crooked Shadow* (1957).

One of My Wives Is Missing (1976) and *Vanishing Act* (1986)—were based.

Featuring a nifty original screenplay by Brian Clemens, the B movie ***The Betrayal*** (1957) begins during World War II with five men—including Canadian pilot Michael McCall (Philip Friend)—planning an escape from a German prisoner-of-war camp. The plan is betrayed to the camp's commandant by another prisoner, resulting in a shooting ambush in which four of the men are killed and McCall permanently (it transpires) blinded; as he lies writhing in agony, McCall hears a voice he will never forget—that of the traitor as the man talks with the commandant about a deal they'd made in connection with the betrayal. Following the war, McCall, despite his blindness, becomes a successful Toronto-based perfume company executive. In 1957, while on a business trip to London, he visits an exclusive fashion house and is shocked to hear the betrayer's voice among a group of people attending a cocktail party there. Determined that justice will be done, he enlists the help of a model (American-born actress and singer Diana Decker) and begins the difficult, and very dangerous as it turns out, task of finding the man behind the voice.

Clemens reworked the story for a 1975 episode—"The Next Voice You See" (later repackaged in the U.S. as a TV movie under the title *Look Back in Darkness*)—of his British TV series *Thriller*, this time with Bradford Dillman starring as a sightless jazz pianist who, while performing at a party, hears the voice of a bank robber who blinded him years before. Unlike the film, the episode keeps the villain's identity a secret from the audience until the end, thus generating far more suspense.

Keefe Brasselle's second of two British

B thrillers was ***Death Over My Shoulder*** (1957), in which the Hollywood actor plays a widowed London-based American private detective named Jack Regan. When his five-year-old son requires experimental treatment in Vienna for a rare disease, the only way for Jack to raise the necessary £5,000 is to free up his life insurance policy by killing himself, with the boy to be left in the care of a trusted nightclub-singer friend (Brasselle's then real-life wife Arlene DeMarco). Following an unsuccessful suicide attempt, Jack pays Joe Longo (Bonar Colleano, in a role originally slated for Sam Wanamaker), boss of a protection-racket gang he'd been investigating, to put a contract out on him, only to later want it canceled after unexpectedly coming into a $25,000 legacy. However, cancellation proves impossible after Longo is killed as the result of some internal gang dispute, leaving Jack at the mercy of an unknown assassin. There's a happy ending in store for our hero, but before then he gets caught up in a dangerous escapade with his appointed executioner, a mystery blonde named Evelyn Connors (Jill Adams).

Brasselle had a big hand in the film's production and secured key investment from a pair of ambulance-chasing lawyers, Burt Pugach and Herb Weitz, with whom he formed the company Pugach-Weitz-Brasselle Productions. The picture, which employed the same director, writer and director of photography as Brasselle's earlier British thriller, *West of Suez* (1956), was intended to be the first of six collaborations between London-based Vicar Productions (run by one Nat Miller) and the Pugach-Weitz-Brasselle company; the remaining five (including titles such as *Irma Goes to London* and *I, Gangster*) never saw the light of day, no doubt due to *Death Over My Shoulder* having proved unprofitable after failing to get theatrical distribution in the U.S. and with only negligible TV exposure there. In any case, Brasselle's association with Pugach in particular was doomed, for in 1959 the latter committed what *The New York Times* would later (November 28, 1974) call "one of the most celebrated crimes of passion in New York history," which led to his spending 14 years in jail. (This at once fascinating and disturbing case is chronicled in the 2007 documentary *Crazy Love*, which contains reference to, as well as a few very short clips from, *Death Over My Shoulder*.) Brasselle would star in just one more movie, the 1972 blaxploitationer *Black Gunn*. As it stands, *Death Over My Shoulder* (originally to have been titled *Assignment for Murder* after American journalist Alyce Canfield's source story) remains the actor's rarest feature and one of the rarest British thrillers of its decade, whose last-known distribution appears to have been its couple of showings on Australian TV (Sydney's TCN Channel 9) in the early 1970s.

Canadian actor Paul Massie's first major big-screen role was as U.S. Air Corps Captain Gene Summers in the powerful ***Orders to Kill*** (1958). Set during World War II, the film begins with an account of Gene's recruitment for a mission into occupied Paris to liquidate an allied agent (Leslie French) suspected of betraying Free French agents to the Gestapo; it then goes on to examine the subsequent moral dilemma he faces when doubts creep in regarding the guilt of his intended victim. Irene Worth plays Gene's French contact, a hardened Resistance fighter who forces him to put doubts aside and follow orders (this leads to tragic consequences, although a shorter 93-minute U.S. version drastically alters the story's outcome), and also starring are Eddie Albert and James Robertson Justice as two officers in charge of Gene's mission training.

The very low-budget ***Cat and Mouse*** (1958) was produced, directed and written by famed documentary filmmaker Paul Rotha. Canadian hunk Lee Patterson casts aside his usual heroic persona to play Rod Fenner, a cold-blooded army deserter who uses unscrupulous methods, involving threats and a frame-up for a murder he himself committed, against a young woman (Ann Sears) in an effort to get her to disclose the location of diamonds stolen years ago by her now deceased father. Based on the novel of the same name by John Creasey (under his pseudonym Michael Halliday), this rather shabbily put together B movie also stars Victor Maddern as a detective and Hilton Edwards as the murder victim, a slimy blackmailer and old accomplice of the woman's father.

"She's the only wife I have so ... kill her gently!"

Marc Lawrence, one of Hollywood's most prolific players of gangsters and other assorted bad guys, brought his unique brand of screen villainy to England for the B movie **Kill Her Gently** (1958). The distinctively pockmark-faced actor gives a great performance as the sleazy Connors, one of two escaped convicts (the other is played by George Mikell) who hitch a ride with Jeff Martin (Griffith Jones). Jeff recognizes the men from a description on the radio and offers them £1,000, as well as help getting out of the country, in exchange for their cooperation in a scheme, the first part of which involves taking them back to his house and pretending to his wife Kay (Maureen Connell) that they're holding him hostage. The second part of the scheme soon becomes apparent: Jeff, it transpires, wants the two men to murder Kay, resenting her for previously institutionalizing him for a mental condition, wrongly believing she did so in order to be with another man. However, a series of unexpected circumstances, including Jeff's inability to raise the promised cash, leads to the plan spectacularly falling apart. Also mixed into the story is the Martins' live-in

When it comes to his wife, Jeff Martin (Griffith Jones, left) wants escaped convict Connors (Marc Lawrence) to *Kill Her Gently* (1958).

maid (Marianne Brauns), who gets fired by Jeff but has not yet left the premises when she gets herself into a dangerous situation with Connors. A rural night-time setting adds atmosphere to the sordid tale, whose screenplay by Paul Erickson, according to *Variety* (September 17, 1958), "is strong on dialog and weak on development."

In ***Intent to Kill*** (1958), the president of an unnamed South American republic (Herbert Lom) faces assassination attempts from a trio of killers (Peter Arne, Warren Stevens and John Crawford) while recovering from brain surgery at a Montreal hospital. The man behind the plot, the president's treacherous Canadian ambassador, is played by Carlo Justini, while top billing goes to Richard Todd as a neurosurgeon whose involvement in the proceedings leads to a tremendous climactic fight with Crawford's character. Jimmy Sangster's efficient script alternates suspenseful set pieces with some soap opera-style elements (mainly involving the neurosurgeon and his philandering wife), and the mostly fast-moving story's other characters include a detective and the hospital's chief surgeon, played respectively by Canadian actors Paul Carpenter and Alexander Knox. The film, in many respects reminiscent of the U.S. film *Crisis* (1950), is notable as being famed cinematographer Jack Cardiff's feature directing debut.

Wracked with feelings of guilt in connection with a colleague's accidental death, ***The Man Upstairs*** (1958), namely a scientist (Richard Attenborough) lodging at a boarding house, becomes increasingly stressed and suffers a mental breakdown. After attacking a neighbor (Kenneth Griffith) and then badly injuring a police sergeant (Patrick Jordan) by pushing him down the building's stairwell, he barricades himself in his room, armed with a gun. As a crowd begins to form outside, a Mental Welfare Officer (Donald Houston) and a police inspector (Bernard Lee) lock horns over how best to deal with the situation. Notable for having no music score, this superbly acted film focuses less on Attenborough's character and more on his diverse fellow lodgers, one of them—a sympathetic young mother (Dorothy Alison)—eventually coaxing him to come out quietly. In many ways, it's reminiscent of the 1939 French classic *Le Jour se lève*.

In ***The Man Inside*** (1958), quiet bookkeeper Sam Carter (Nigel Patrick) steals a $700,000 diamond, The Tyrahna Blue, from a New York jewelry firm after patiently scheming for 15 years to do so. Jack Palance gives a quirky performance (complete with strange accent) as a Texan private detective hired to retrieve the diamond, which is also sought by a mysterious blonde (Anita Ekberg) and two gangsters (Bonar Colleano and Sean Kelly). The resulting international adventure sees Carter pursued to Lisbon, Madrid and Paris before events come to a head on a train to London. Anthony Newley provides comic relief as a Spanish taxi driver, and a catchy score underpins the fairly repetitive action. There are several amusing episodes involving a golf ball in which Carter hides the diamond.

In the opening sequence of ***Innocent Meeting*** (1958), a young man, Johnny (Sean Lynch), botches an attempt to rob a convenience store and is chased back to his lodgings by police, who lay siege to the place. The circumstances leading to this tense situation are shown via a flashback in which Johnny, while on probation for another crime, falls for the well-to-do Connie (Beth Rogan) who inspires him to better himself. Connie's father gives him a job but later fires him after wrongly suspecting him of stealing a wallet. This drives Johnny back to crime (the opening sequence) in order to fund an elopement with Connie. The film, an efficient London-based Danziger brothers B movie, ends on a bittersweet note.

Despite *Films and Filming* (April 1959) asserting that John Buchan's famous 1915 source novel was "a little thin by present-day thriller standards," ***The 39 Steps*** (1958) emerges as a highly entertaining adaptation of the story and one which takes most of its cues from Alfred Hitchcock's classic 1935 version. British diplomat Richard Hannay's (Kenneth More) short association with a female MI5 agent (Faith Brook) ends with her murder, in Hannay's London apartment, by members of a spy organization she'd been investigating in connection with a plot to smuggle British ballistic missile secrets out of the country. Armed with clues, including the phrase "The 39 Steps," Hannay takes up where the agent left off and is soon caught up in a dangerous adventure that takes him to the wilds of Scotland and back again, all the while chased by the police (who suspect him of the murder) and the deadly spies. Key to the story, and featuring in the exciting climax, is a music hall performer known as Mr. Memory (James Hayter), whose amazing mental faculties are being used by the spy organization as a means of storing the missile secrets.

Distinguished by some great location work, the film wastes no time in getting down to a non-stop succession of suspenseful situations, including a thrilling escape from a train on Scotland's Forth Bridge. More makes a charming and humorous Hannay, while romantic interest comes in the shape of an attractive schoolmistress (Taina Elg) forced by circumstances to join him in the adventure.

With both the 1958 film and Hitchcock's version set during the eras in which they were made, not to mention being quite loose adaptations, it was refreshing to see a third filmed version, *The Thirty-Nine Steps* (1978), sticking more closely to the book's storyline and 1914 setting. Indeed, *Films and Filming* (November 1978) described it as "the most successful to date in conveying the novel's quiet menace and penny-dreadful plot twists." In London, mining engineer Richard Hannay (Robert Powell) becomes involved in sheltering Colonel Scudder (John Mills), a former British Intelligence operative being sought by Prussian agents wishing to stop him uncovering further details of their conspiracy to assassinate the

An entertaining remake of an Alfred Hitchcock classic.

Greek Premier during the latter's forthcoming visit to the capital. The assassination, if successful, would precipitate World War I in a manner advantageous to the Germans.

When the agents murder Scudder, Hannay attempts to complete the man's work, all the while pursued by the police (who suspect him of the crime) and the killers.

The famous "Mr. Memory" climax from both earlier versions (but not in Buchan's novel) has been replaced by an equally non–Buchan climax involving London's Big Ben where a bomb, set to be triggered by the clock's mechanism, has been planted so as to kill the Premier in the adjoining Houses of Parliament. Clearly inspired by a scene in Will Hay's 1943 comedy *My Learned Friend*, the Big Ben sequence culminates in the spectacle of Hannay hanging from one of the giant clock's hands in an effort to prevent the bomb being activated at the designated time. Powell plays a more serious Hannay than his two predecessors and would return to the role a decade later for a Thames Television series called simply *Hannay*.

The sensationally titled ***The Child and the Killer*** (1959) is set in a small English community with a U.S. Army base nearby. Mather (Ryck Rydon), a GI on the run for desertion and murder, hides out in a derelict house where he encounters seven-year-old Tommy (Richard Williams) playing in his cowboy outfit. The fugitive promises to introduce the boy to Jesse James in exchange for help. Tommy, whose mother Peggy (Patricia Driscoll) runs a general store, is soon secretly taking Mather supplies, including a gun which he steals from Peggy's friend Joe (Robert Arden), an American army officer involved in the search for the criminal. Noted by *The Daily Cinema* (February 25, 1959) as making "good use of available facilities to create an atmosphere of tension," this B movie culminates in a showdown between Joe and Mather after the criminal attempts to force Peggy to shelter him.

Richard Williams (right) and Ryck Rydon are *The Child and the Killer* (1959).

A child and a killer also feature in director J. Lee Thompson's *Tiger Bay* (1959), a stirring and moving story set around the titular locale, a rough dockland district of Cardiff in South Wales. Horst Buchholz, just prior to becoming one of *The Magnificent Seven* (1960), plays Bronislaw Korczynski, a young and overemotional Polish merchant seaman who commits a crime of passion by shooting dead the girlfriend (Yvonne Mitchell) that dumped him. Then newcomer Hayley Mills (whose father, John, gets top billing as a police detective) is nothing less than captivating as Gillie, a mischievous 11-year-old orphan who witnesses the crime and, through an unusual set of circumstances, develops a close friendship with Korczynski to the extent that she deliberately misleads the police in an effort to buy him time to escape abroad on a cargo ship. Buchholz and Mills have great chemistry, and their friendship contains many affecting moments, particularly the tear-jerking finale in which Korczynski is captured as a result of saving the girl's life. The film makes superb use of authentic locations and is expertly edited by soon-to-be director Sidney Hayers.

> "An escaped convict ... in his gunsights a shipload of dynamite and the city of Sydney! His terms—freedom or annihilation!"

Beautifully photographed in Australia, *The Siege of Pinchgut* (1959) begins immediately following the jailbreak of Matt Kirk (beefy Hollywood star Aldo Ray), who was wrongly convicted and plans to negotiate a retrial by raising public awareness for his cause. Together with three supporters—his brother Johnny (Neil McCallum) and two cohorts (Victor Maddern and Carlo Justini)—that helped him escape, Matt begins sailing out of Sydney Harbour, but boat trouble leads to the men taking refuge on the small nearby island of Pinchgut (also known as Fort Denison, a one-time strategic defense outpost), whose caretaker and family they hold hostage. A standoff soon develops whereby long-range sharpshooters besiege the island while Matt threatens to cause mass destruction by using a large and still-functional modern naval gun on the island to blow up a munitions ship (containing 1500 tons of explosives) moored off an inner-city locality of Sydney. A great opening sequence (the men escaping in an ambulance) and some superb shots of Sydney Harbour (with snipers lined up atop the famous steel arch bridge) are highlights in what was the final production by the original Ealing Studios.

The above-average B movie *Life in Danger* (1959) introduces us to a drifter (Derren Nesbitt) seeking shelter in a British village and the circumstances that lead to him ending up alone with a young girl (Julie Hopkins) in a barn. With news breaking about the escape of a child murderer from a nearby mental institution, some of the villagers, led by bloodthirsty Major Peters (Howard Marion Crawford), conclude that the drifter is the escapee and, arming themselves, prepare to take the law into their own hands. But have they got the right man? The atmosphere of a rural village literally in the grim shadow of an asylum (complete with the ominous sound of regular "escape warning" siren tests) is well put across and, although we never really doubt the drifter's innocence, Nesbitt's expertly ambiguous performance does a good job trying to convince us otherwise.

Another great B movie, *The White Trap* (1959) stars Lee Patterson in one of his finest roles as Paul Langley, a wartime hero in jail on smuggling charges for which he maintains his innocence. Desperate to be with his pregnant and ailing wife Joan (Felicity Young), Langley, who has already tried to escape twice, finally breaks free while being transferred to another prison. With police waiting at every turn, he heads for the hospital where Joan is about to give birth, helped along the way by both a wartime friend (Harold Siddons) and a sympathetic nurse (Yvette Wyatt). Michael Goodliffe is great as an astute even-tempered detective, and a tear-jerking conclusion wraps up this efficient Sidney Hayers-directed offering which *The Daily Cinema* (August 17, 1959) regarded as "almost a model of how to make best use of limited financial resources." The film went straight to television in the U.S., initially broadcast as a first-season episode of *Kraft Mystery Theatre*. On the day of the broadcast (July 26, 1961), "TV Scout" previews (syndicated content carried in the TV pages of many newspapers), referred to the fact that cuts had been made to fit the broadcast slot, saying that "in some places, it is obvious that there has been major surgery on the film but it still hangs together sufficiently."

In the tense nail-biter **Jet Storm** (1959), it emerges, during a transatlantic flight, that the deeply disturbed Ernest Tilley (Richard Attenborough) plans to detonate a bomb (which he's planted under one of the wings) and kill all those aboard in order to take revenge on just one passenger. The passenger in question is James Brock (George Rose), the man responsible for the death of Tilley's daughter in a hit-and-run incident two years earlier. Stanley Baker gives an assured performance as the plane's pilot, who desperately tries to quell the rising panic on board, while Diane Cilento plays an intuitive young woman ultimately instrumental in saving the day. The supporting cast features a veritable "Who's Who" of British film and television talent, with Patrick Allen standing out as an industrialist whose attempt to solve the crisis leads to him and two other passengers plotting to kill Brock themselves so that Tilley will have no need to blow up the aircraft, or so they believe. Among several Canadian actors on board (all based in England at the time) are Paul Carpenter, Cec Linder and Neil McCallum. (McCallum later co-formed Parroch-McCallum Productions which made five British thrillers—see Appendix I.) Attenborough convinces as Tilley, a man driven to such drastic measures through a combination of mental instability and a fundamental loss of faith in humanity. One particularly startling scene has a key character sucked right out of the plane through a broken window.

Attenborough also stars in the tremendously exhilarating **SOS Pacific** (1959) as a weasely lowlife, one of a diverse group of people who become stranded on a deserted Pacific island after their seaplane is forced to make en emergency landing. To their horror, they soon realize—by way of evidence including a lead-lined blockhouse containing camera setups and electrical timing equipment—that the island is due for an H-bomb test in a few hours' time. The charismatic Eddie Constantine is perfectly cast as a rugged ex-navy man under police escort (to face charges for smuggling) who undertakes to neutralize the bomb, a task that involves a two-mile swim to another island where the trigger mechanism is located. The excellent ensemble cast also includes John Gregson as a pilot haunted by his past and Eva Bartok as a good-time girl.

"With every step she sensed TERROR!"

In the well-written and efficiently directed B movie **Witness in the Dark** (1959), a man (Nigel Green) murders an elderly woman in an attempt to steal a valuable brooch from her apartment. Failing to find the item, the man leaves the building, but not before brushing past the victim's young blind neighbor, Jane (a convincing Patricia Dainton), on the stairs. As the only witness, Jane ends up in the newspapers, which also report on her subsequent inheritance of the brooch. Having read the report, and still desiring the precious ornament, the killer decides to pay Jane a visit. Luckily, Conrad Phillips is on hand as a likeable detective who, with the brave Jane's help, traps the killer in a fairly suspenseful finale. The film, one of the first, if not *the* first, example(s) of the blind-woman-in-peril sub-genre of thrillers (predating the Audrey Hepburn classic *Wait Until Dark* by eight years), went straight to television in the U.S., initially broadcast as a first-season episode of *Kraft Mystery Theatre*. On the day of the broadcast (August 2, 1961) "TV Scout" previews (syndicated content carried in the TV pages of

Conrad Phillips and Patricia Dainton in *Witness in the Dark* (1959).

many newspapers) mentioned that two of the film's characters (a nosy neighbor and her husband played by Madge Ryan and Stuart Saunders) had to be dubbed because "they were so English it was felt American audiences wouldn't be able to understand them."

Devil's Bait (1959) is set in a small town where Mr. Love (Dermot Kelly), a heavy-drinking pest controller of dubious experience, goes against health and safety regulations by using potassium cyanide to rid the local bakery of rats. To make matters worse, he mixes the poison in one of the shop's baking tins, subsequently neglecting to rinse out the container which is later used to make a loaf of bread for sale on the premises. A series of circumstances ultimately lead to a realization of what has happened, but by then the bread has been sold, and there follows a desperate race against time to find the lethal loaf before it can do any harm. Excellent performances—especially by Geoffrey Keen (as the baker) and Gordon Jackson (as a police detective involved in tracking down the deadly bread)—highlight this cracking little B movie.

Another B movie, the engaging ***Night Train for Inverness*** (1959), concerns ex-con Roy Lewis (Norman Wooland) who, thanks to the devious machinations of his mother-in-law, is estranged from his wife and denied access to his seven-year-old son Ted (Dennis Waterman in his first film). Roy secretly meets Ted and persuades him to go to Scotland with him, unaware that he has been diagnosed with diabetes and faces going into a coma unless he is given regular insulin injections. Meanwhile, the police, alerted by Ted's mother, frantically attempt to locate the boy before it becomes too late. Jane Hylton gives a sympathetic performance as an old girlfriend of Roy's who proves crucial to saving the day.

1960s

"The most thrilling supporting feature in years!"

Taut, vivid, fast-moving and darkly atmospheric, the exemplary B movie ***The Man in the Back Seat*** (1961) has been masterfully put together by director Vernon Sewell with crisp photography by Reginald Wyer. Derren Nesbitt (outstanding) and Keith Faulkner, both of whom also star in Sewell's other 1961 suspenser *Strongroom*, play small-time London criminals Tony and Frank, whose plan to rob a bookie (Harry Locke) at a dog track goes wrong right from the start. After knocking the bookie unconscious, the two thieves discover that the bag containing the night's takings is chained to his wrist and, unable to find the key, are forced to take the man's limp body with them as they make their getaway in the latter's own car.

The rest of the film takes place over one fatalistic night that details Tony (the more ruthless of the two) and Frank's attempts to free the bag and unburden themselves of the bookie, these tasks being constantly thwarted by various circumstances including a flat tire, running out of fuel and interference from a roadside assistance engineer (Anthony Bate). Eventually, Tony, having killed the bookie through repeated brutal beatings in an attempt to keep him unconscious, dumps the man's body on a sidewalk. When Frank threatens to run out on him, Tony manages to keep him on side by tricking him into believing that he—Frank—had actually caused the man's death while reversing the car up on said sidewalk during a turning maneuver. As the pair drive toward the north of England, an increasingly panicked Frank begins hallucinating and sees, in the rear-view mirror, the bookie sitting up in the back seat, this leading to dire consequences as he loses control of the vehicle.

The film, whose creative title sequence has the credits unfolding over the ominously empty back seat of a moving vehicle, also stars Carol White as Frank's wife in scenes set at the couple's home.

Another B movie, the fast-moving ***Crosstrap*** (1961), sees husband and wife Geoff and Sally (Gary Cockrell and Jill Adams) arrive at their rented cottage in the countryside, only to fall into the clutches of a gang of thieves—led by Duke (Laurence Payne)—who have commandeered the place while waiting for a getaway plane to take them and a haul of stolen jewels to Spain. To complicate matters further, a rival gang besieges the cottage in an attempt to get hold of the jewels, and there follows a game of cat-and-mouse between the two outfits, with Geoff and Sally caught in the middle of the ensuing mayhem. Zena Marshall is the highlight as Duke's moll, whose jealousy over her lover's lust for Sally has repercussions that lead to her thwarting the getaway plan in spectacular fashion. The *Kinematograph Weekly* (February 1, 1962) was not impressed, describing the film as "poorly scripted, overacted and indifferently directed."

Cash on Demand (1961) is a first-rate example of the British suspense thriller and one that manages to be tense and exciting without ever resorting to violence. The plot concerns a devious thief, Hepburn (Andre Morell), who convinces provincial bank manager Harry Fordyce (an impeccable Peter Cushing) that his family is being held hostage, thus compelling the man to actively cooperate in the robbery of his own bank during working hours, all the while trying not to arouse the suspicions of the staff. Set in the run-up to Christmas, the parabolic story, which features several neat twists and turns, charts the progress of the manager's character from unpopular disciplinarian at the start, to a much more sympathetic boss by the end of his ordeal. Richard Vernon plays the bank's chief clerk, who proves pivotal to the proceedings, and he and the excellent Morell reprise their roles from the

Andre Morell plays a devious thief in the tense Hammer production *Cash on Demand* (1961).

directed by Vernon Sewell, the film is a companion piece to his other suspense thriller from the same year, *The Man in the Back Seat*, and stars that film's Derren Nesbitt and Keith Faulkner as the principal robbers, only this time Nesbitt is the more compassionate of the two. The scenes in the vault are tense and claustrophobic, and be prepared for an unusually downbeat ending. James Breen, writing in the British newspaper *The Observer* (May 27, 1962), commented, "I don't say that the film goes very deep; but, in its modest way Vernon Sewell's careful direction carries it some way beyond the two-dimensional crime-and-chase pattern." In the U.S., the movie most commonly played as support to *PT 109* (1963) but also had the honor of sharing a bill with *What Ever Happened to Baby Jane?* (1962).

1960 TV play *The Gold Inside* on which the film is based, both versions also sharing the same director, Quentin Lawrence. The picture went unseen in British cinemas until 1963, and even then it was shown in a much-shortened 66-minute version.

In the simple but effective B movie, **Strongroom** (1961), three men rob a suburban bank and are forced by circumstances to leave the manager (Colin Gordon) and his secretary (Ann Lynn) locked in an airtight vault. Escaping with £30,000, the thieves plan to leave the vault keys in a location which they will anonymously disclose to the police so that the captives can be rescued before running out of oxygen. However, a series of unexpected events, including the death of one of the criminals in an accident, scupper the plan, and a situation develops in which the trapped couple face the prospect of certain death by suffocation. Efficiently

"Slowly the net closed in on another of the world's most wanted men!"

Co-written by Brian Clemens, **The Pursuers** (1962) is inspired by events surrounding the real-life trial of Adolf Eichmann, a Nazi war criminal referenced during the film. Francis Matthews plays David Nelson, a Nazi hunter on the trail of evil former concentration camp commandant Karl Borgmann (Cyril Shaps), now living in London under a new identity. During his attempts to expose Borgmann, Nelson breaks into the man's London apartment and defaces his passport to prevent him leaving the country. In the end, Borgmann gets his comeuppance in a shootout with a racketeering nightclub boss (Sheldon Lawrence) who was trying to rip him off in connection with a forged replacement passport. Shaps is first-rate as the weasely ex-commandant, and this snappy B movie also features Susan Denny as a Jewish nightclub singer whose parents perished in the villain's death camp.

The super-rare B movie ***Doomsday at Eleven*** (1962) concerns a gift-wrapped time bomb delivered to a maternity clinic and the desperate efforts of a bomb disposal man (impaired due to an injury en route to the scene) and two brave volunteers—a young police sergeant (Alan Heywood) and the clinic's Polish porter (Carl Jaffe)—to neutralize the device. The bomb is in fact the handiwork of an ex-con (Alan Edwards) seeking vengeance against a judge (Derrick De Marney), the intention being to kill the latter's wife (Jennifer Wright) who is about to undergo a caesarean section and who, along with another patient, cannot be moved when the clinic is evacuated. The film also stars Geoffrey Dunn as an evangelical hobo crucial to the story's outcome.

The exciting political chase thriller ***Guns of Darkness*** (1962) is set in the fictional revolution-torn South American republic of Tribulación, where a swift military coup on New Year's Eve leaves deposed leader President Rivera (David Opatoshu) wounded and on the run. At the height of a marital crisis, British sugar plantation manager Tom Jordan (David Niven) and his French wife Claire (Leslie Caron) become involved in helping Rivera escape to safety across the border in a dangerous adventure that strengthens the couple's marriage no end. There's a fair bit of trekking through jungle and across mountains, while the film's undisputed suspense highlight is an extended nail-biting sequence in which Tom's station wagon—with all three fugitives on board—gets stuck in quicksand. Niven is excellent, creating a believable three-dimensional character as the ordinary man caught up in extraordinary events, and he and Caron perform very well together. The great cast also includes James Robertson Justice as the plantation boss and Derek Godfrey as the republic's Minister of Justice orchestrating the manhunt for Rivera.

"Suspense and murder with a triple twist!"

Fate brings together two desperate people in the South Africa-set B picture ***Journey into Nowhere*** (1962). Ricky (Tony Wright) is a rugged gambler threatened with death unless he repays a £1,500 Mob debt within 48 hours. Maria (Sonja Ziemann) is an attractive artist who has decided to commit suicide because she's going blind and cannot afford the £2,000 needed for an operation. The improbable plot sees the two agree on a scheme based on the fact that Maria has an insurance policy with a double indemnity clause worth £2,000 should she die in an accident while using the railway. Ricky takes out a similar insurance and, having named each other as beneficiaries in their respective policies, they arrange to take a train journey together during which they will attempt to kill each other so that at least one of them will end up with the money they need. Helmut Schmid plays an odious Mob strong-arm man pressuring Ricky to pay his debt, and to whom Ricky offers £500 of the insurance payout if he will bring about Maria's death. However, this all changes when Ricky and Maria begin falling in love, with events leading to a decidedly downbeat ending. Wright performs most of his own stunt work (including clambering along the outside of a moving train carriage) in this Anglo-German co-production, which was cut to 67 minutes for its original British release.

In their review of ***Touch of Death*** (1962), *Films and Filming* (February 1963) duly acknowledged its director Lance Comfort as being one of the few "whose 'B' picture work is worth keeping an eye on." William Lucas and David Sumner play Pete and Len, two criminals who go on the run after stealing cash from the safe at a gas station. As it happens, the safe also contained poisons that have contaminated the loot, making it potentially lethal. The fugitives take refuge in a small houseboat where they hold a woman and child captive, and

Pete later uses some of the tainted cash to buy fuel, resulting in the vendor being hospitalized. This provides clues for the police, led by Inspector Maxwell (Australian actor Ray Barrett), to track the criminals down. The film features competent performances, a fast pace and good outdoor location work, but the novel storyline could have done with more fleshing out.

In the mildly intriguing B movie *Dilemma* (1962), schoolteacher Harry Barnes (Peter Halliday) arrives home to find a badly wounded man—who dies shortly thereafter—in the bathroom. Assuming that his absent wife Jean (Ingrid Hafner), who'd earlier been shown leaving the house in a panic, must be the culprit, Harry decides to cover up the death and sets about burying the body beneath the floorboards of the living room. Meanwhile, the police are in the area looking for the man in connection with drug dealing activities, and only when Jean finally returns home do we learn the shocking truth about her connection with him. Patricia Burke gives an amusing performance as the archetypal nosy neighbor, and the film generates a modicum of suspense by way of Harry's attempts to bury the body amid constant interruptions by unwanted visitors.

The above-average B movie *Calculated Risk* (1963) concerns a gang of thieves breaking into a bank vault via the adjacent wall of a derelict air-raid shelter. During the operation, they uncover an unexploded delayed-action bomb from World War II. When the final act of breaking through into the vault inadvertently activates the bomb's timing mechanism, gang leader Steve (a forceful William Lucas) is the only one to notice. However, in his eagerness to complete the robbery, he says nothing, risking his own life as well as the lives of his accomplices. The film builds up some effective suspense during the claustrophobic scenes in the air-raid shelter, and benefits from a tight script (by British character actor Edwin Richfield [his only movie screenplay]) with sharply observed working-class characters.

Another impressive B movie, *The Silent Playground* (1963) plays out against some effective south-east London locations and serves as a stark reminder about the dangers of children taking sweets from strangers. The story involves a mentally impaired young man (Roland Curram) unwittingly handing out sedatives—in the form of colored pills that resemble sweets—to children at various locales. The fallout results in multiple hospitalizations and two deaths, with events culminating in a race against time to find three unaccounted for children who are known to have accepted the "sweets." Bernard Archard as a police inspector and Ellen McIntosh as a hard-working single mother give the best performances in a movie which *Films and Filming* (June 1964) concluded "has flaws galore, but—the amazing fact remains—it works."

The three lead players and some beautifully filmed locations in southern Spain make *The Running Man* (1963) irresistible, despite it being overall one of director Carol Reed's lesser efforts. Holding a grudge against his insurance company in connection with a previous claim, Rex Black (Laurence Harvey) takes revenge by faking his own death in a gliding accident; then, under a new identity, he hides out in Malaga with his complicit wife Stella (Lee Remick) and a large payout. Alan Bates plays an insurance investigator who, having initially conducted a routine interview with Stella in connection with the claim, later turns up in Malaga—supposedly on holiday—and begins nosing around, with some ambiguous dialogue keeping us guessing as to his true motivations. A couple of nice twists keep viewer interest up, and there's a suitably ironic ending.

"*A story of passion ... in a city of fear!*"

A medical thriller-cum–soap opera, *80,000 Suspects* (1963) deals with an outbreak of smallpox in the English town of Bath. Amid marital problems, top doctor Steven Monks (Richard Johnson) finds himself at the forefront of combating the

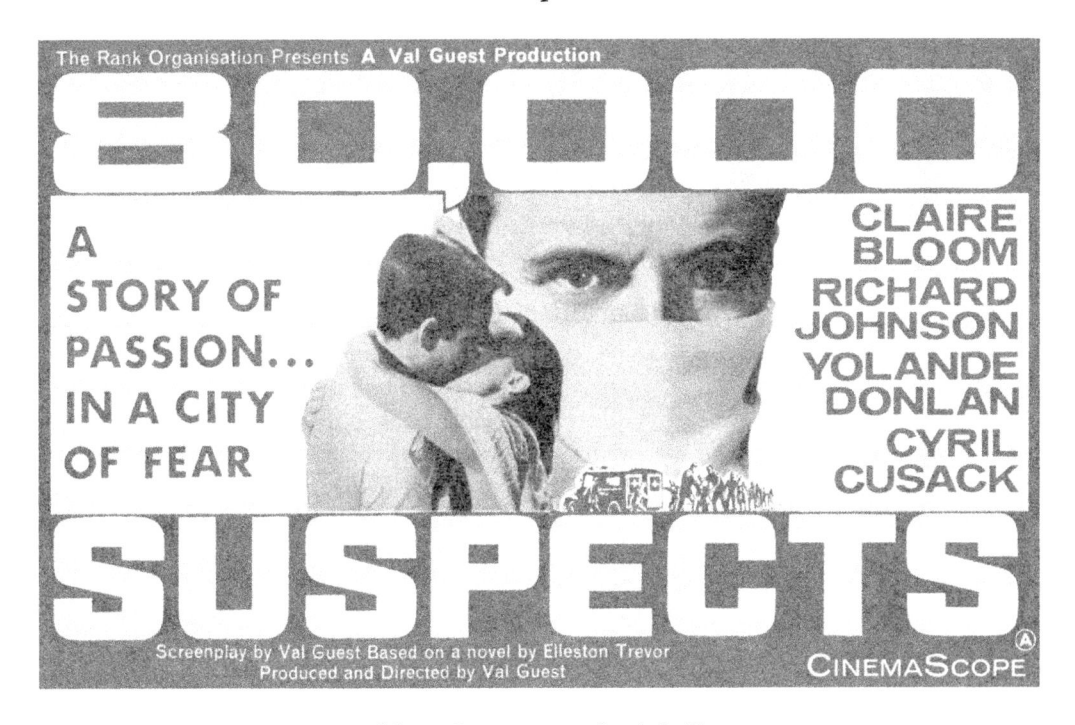

Publicity for a 1963 medical thriller.

epidemic, while his wife (Claire Bloom), a former nurse, voluntarily joins a mobile vaccination unit only to subsequently become infected herself. Featuring somewhat stereotypical characters and situations, the frequently melodramatic proceedings are efficiently directed by Val Guest, and there's some good climactic suspense involving the search for a mystery carrier of the disease. The cast also includes the always excellent Cyril Cusack as a priest who helps save the doctor's marriage.

In the Vernon Sewell-directed B movie *A Matter of Choice* (1963), a nighttime scuffle between two tipsy young men and a police officer results in the latter being pushed into a road and hit by a car. The driver, Lisa (Jeanne Moody), is a married woman traveling with her secret lover John (Anthony Steel), a diabetic. John chases the two men who, after one of them knocks him unconscious, hide his body in the garage of a nearby mews house that just happens to be Lisa's home. Lisa's husband (Ballard Berkeley) arrives and parks in front of the garage, unwittingly trapping the men inside.

At the accident scene, Lisa insists she was alone in the car, but events lead to her affair coming to light, as well as having tragic consequences for John as a result of insulin deprivation. Set over the course of a single night, this coincidence-laden morality tale (based on an original story by Sewell and actor Derren Nesbitt) takes a while to get going but is quite engaging once it does.

Set in India during World War II, *Man in the Middle* (1963) begins with an effective pre-credits sequence at a remote supply depot under joint British-U.S. command, where American Lieutenant Charles Winston (Keenan Wynn) cold-bloodedly murders a British staff sergeant. The great Robert Mitchum plays Barney Adams, a U.S. Lieutenant Colonel assigned to defend Winston in a court martial, with his superior (Barry Sullivan) making it clear that, for the sake of Anglo-American relations, his efforts must be purposely unsuccessful so that Winston will be found guilty and executed. However, Barney learns that, just after the murder, Winston was diagnosed insane and unfit for trial, and that there's a conspiracy afoot to cover this up. His eventual decision to go against the grain and see that Winston gets treated fairly proves to be an uphill struggle. France Nuyen and Trevor Howard appear in pivotal roles, she as a French-Chinese nurse who inspires Barney to do the right thing and he as a psychiatrically trained British Army Major who proves—in a dramatic courtroom finale—that Winston is indeed insane.

"A nightmare of terror and searing suspense!"

Fittingly described by *Variety* (March 3, 1965) as "routine," but with "better than routine performances," the B movie **Clash by Night** (1963) sees a criminal gang rescue their convicted boss (Tom Bowman) by hijacking a prison transport bus on which he is being transferred across the countryside. In order to delay the alarm being raised, they lock the vehicle and its occupants—the driver, a guard (a second guard is shot dead) and several other convicts—in a barn overnight. The captives are told that any attempt to escape will result in the barn, which the gang has by now doused in kerosene, and which they say will be monitored all night long, being set alight. This, plus the fact that it just happens to be Guy Fawkes Night with fireworks going off all around, not to mention one of the convicts (Peter Sallis) being an unstable pyromaniac, makes it almost a certainty that, one way or another, a fire will at some point break out. An unconvincing subplot, in which two of the convicts (Terence Longdon and Harry Fowler) temporarily escape in connection with visiting one of their wives, is the only weak spot in an otherwise well-written picture. The film's title was changed stateside to *Escape by Night* in order to avoid any possible confusion with the more famous *Clash by Night* from 1952, a Hollywood noir starring Barbara Stanwyck.

The better-than-average B movie **Stopover Forever** (1964) unfolds in the Sicilian town of Taormina, where an air stewardess is shot dead in a hotel room. Another stewardess, Susan Chambers (Ann Bell), who would have been occupying the hotel room instead had she not exchanged flight duty with the victim, becomes convinced that she was the assassin's intended target. It turns out she has good reason to be afraid, for there are three men—her married lover (Anthony Bate), a police captain (Julian Sherrier) and a pilot (Conrad Phillips)—with reasons for potentially wanting her out of the way. Increasingly paranoid, Susan ends up taking refuge with a drunken admirer, Freddie, (Bruce Boa), on his yacht; however, when circumstances convince her that he's the assassin, she kills him and scuttles the vessel. The film, noted by the *Monthly Film Bulletin* (April 1965) as being "an eminently successful experiment in raising the standard of the routine second feature," ends with a much-touted (at the time) last-minute twist which is actually not that surprising.

Made by Luckwell Productions for release by Columbia Pictures, the B movie **Delayed Flight** (1964) never saw the light of day in Britain or the U.S. but did do the rounds in Australia as support to other Columbia fare such as *Fail-Safe* and *The Long Ships*. When flight 504 lands at an airport in England, the passengers are told they must be quarantined for 24 hours due to a smallpox scare. Two of them, Lt. Col. Calvin Brampton (Hugh McDermott) and Helen Strickland (Helen Cherry), escape and head for London, he to urgently deliver some important official documents entrusted to him by a fatally shot agent (Neal Arden), and she to intercept a private letter that could spell trouble if seen by her husband. In the adventure that follows, the pair are pursued by police (for breaking quarantine) and by two sinister henchmen (one of them responsible for shooting the agent) working on behalf of an organization that wants the documents in connection with instigating an uprising in Africa. Despite some hints of romance along the way, Calvin and Helen eventually say their farewells, while the smallpox scare turns out to have been nothing more than a case of chicken pox. This proved to be producer Bill Luckwell's swansong and was the second of two B thrillers (see also *The Runaway*) he made at Bray Studios, which at that time were owned by Hammer Films.

The gripping Cold War cautionary tale **The Bedford Incident** (1965) concerns an American destroyer, the USS *Bedford*, on patrol for Russian submarines penetrating NATO territorial waters. When one such vessel is detected, the *Bedford*'s iron-willed and ultra-patriotic captain (Richard Widmark, who also co-produced) begins obsessively hunting the nuclear-armed craft in an effort to force it to surface, refusing to give up even after the sub has retreated to international waters. Mounting tensions aboard the *Bedford* have pushed the already overstressed crew to breaking point, resulting in a young officer (James MacArthur) accidentally firing a missile at the submarine, leading to a devastating retaliation. Patterned somewhat after *Moby Dick*, this British-U.S. production features a powerhouse performance by Widmark as the Captain Ahab–type semi-tyrant whose ill-judged actions ultimately bring destruction to him and his crew, while the Russian submarine stands in for the great white whale of the classic story. Sidney Poitier, in his third and final teaming with Widmark after *No Way Out* (1950) and *The Long Ships* (1964), plays a photojournalist attempting to find out what makes the captain tick; and there's excellent support from both Martin Balsam, as the ship's new chief medic, and Eric Portman as a former World War II German U-boat commander now acting for NATO as technical adviser on the *Bedford*.

"Only the killer believes him!"

A British–West German–Yugoslavian co-production, **The Boy Cried Murder** (1965) was adapted from a Cornell Woolrich story of the same name which had also formed the basis for the 1949 U.S. suspense classic *The Window*. While vacationing with his mother (Veronica Hurst) and stepfather (Phil Brown) in an Adriatic town in Montenegro, a lonely and mischievous 10-year-old boy (an impressive Frazer MacIntosh) witnesses a scene that culminates in a woman's murder. Due to his proclivity for crying wolf, the boy is disbelieved and is soon being pursued by the killer (an uncharacteristically blond Tim Barrett) who's determined to silence him. The film, nicely shot on location, has some suspenseful moments, with events culminating high up in the ruins of a fortress.

French actress Martine Carol's final movie (she died during filming) was **Hell Is Empty** (1967), produced by her fourth husband Mike Eland and which had actually been in the works since 1965. The one-time leading sex symbol plays Martine Grant who, along with her husband Robert (Robert Rietty) and other family members, ends up being held hostage at her isolated mansion in Prague by three robbers on the run from a heist in which a security guard was killed. The resulting drama—which involves heavy flirtation between Martine and gun-toting chief robber Major Morton (Anthony Steel), not to mention a developing romance between Martine's sister-in-law Catherine (Catherine Schell) and handsome younger criminal Jess (Jess Conrad)—ends in chaos as thieves fall out and police descend on the place, with Jess (the sole surviving criminal) subsequently being charged with the security guard's murder. All this is told in an extended flashback, the film beginning and ending with Jess' trial at which it's finally revealed that Morton was the actual killer. That formidable character actor James Robertson Justice has a pivotal role as a friend of the family in this British-Czechoslovakian co-production, which was cut from 109 to 90 minutes for its belated 1969 British theatrical release. Of note is the fact that most of the characters have the same first names as the actors who play them.

Taste of Excitement (1968) features a pleasant lead performance by Eva Renzi as Jane Kerrell, a young woman on a French vacation who becomes the target of mysterious assassination attempts. We later discover that these are connected to her car, a red Mini Cooper, having been randomly chosen (during a ferry crossing) by a man on the run as a hiding place for certain secret information. Set against some beautiful locations in the South of France, the film offers an exhilarating opening scene in which a white Mercedes attempts to force Jane's Mini off a mountain road. Ultimately concerning treachery within an international crime network, the complex plot has many twists and turns before an unpredictable though uninteresting climax. David Buck plays a friendly English artist helping Jane stay alive (the two stars have a nice chemistry), and other characters include an ambiguous Scotland Yard detective (expertly played by Peter Vaughan) and a sinister psychiatrist (George Pravda). One particularly nail-biting sequence involves our heroine maneuvering her car along a precipitous ledge in order to escape a second offensive by the aforementioned white Mercedes.

1970s

"Everybody saw the president shot. Only the boy saw the killer!"

Made on location in Malta, **Eyewitness** (1970) focuses on the nightmarish pursuit by two villainous motorcycle policemen (Peter Vaughan and Peter Bowles) of 11-year-old Ziggy (*Oliver*'s Mark Lester), who can identify one of them (Vaughan) as the assassin that shot dead a visiting African president during a public procession. The two cops (it transpires they're connected to the Mafia and that the intended target of the assassination had actually been a police chief sitting next to the president) spare no one—not even a little girl and a priest—in their murderous pursuit of Ziggy, whose predicament is not taken seriously by those around him due to his proclivity for telling tall tales. Direction (John Hough) and photography (David Holmes) are excellent, with some effective use of zooms, odd angles and distortions, while the cliffs, catacombs and winding streets of Malta provide effective settings for the action. Susan George (she and Hough would reteam for the 1974 U.S. cult classic *Dirty Mary, Crazy Larry*) plays Ziggy's sister, and Lionel Jeffries is on sparkling form as the boy's eccentric grandfather. According to *Films and Filming* (November 1970), the plot "is almost as full of holes as most of its numerous corpses, but that applies to most really good thrillers."

In the little-seen **Freelance** (1970), underworld thug Dean (a well-cast Alan Lake) fatally injures an old man and is then ordered by his boss (Peter Gilmore) to eliminate the only witness, a small-time con man named Robin "Mitch" Mitchell (Ian McShane). Dean makes two unsuccessful attempts to do so before Mitch turns the tables by luring his pursuer into a death trap in the countryside. This leads to the boss making Mitch the unusual offer of joining his criminal empire—as Dean's replacement. The simple and unexciting story also involves Mitch's girlfriend (Gayle Hunnicutt) and a fellow con man (Keith Barron). Upon the film's belated British theatrical release, David McGillivray, writing for the *Monthly Film Bulletin* (May 1975), accurately pointed out that the standard of acting and production were "high enough to make one wish that the talent involved had been put to more imaginative use."

"Greed takes on the sinister cloak of murder"

Despite enduring a variety of unpleasant situations, the titular heroine neither screams nor dies in **Die Screaming, Marianne** (1970), a muddled early endeavor from cult producer-director Pete Walker that just about holds together thanks to a charming performance by lead star Susan George. Surviving on her wits as well as her skills as a go-go dancer, 20-year-old free-spirited Marianne is on the run from her corrupt ex-judge father (played by Leo Genn and referred to throughout as simply "the Judge") and his black-hearted daughter from another marriage (Judy Huxtable), both of whom (for different reasons) want from her the number of a Swiss bank account. The account, to which Marianne will have access upon her 21st birthday, comes with a safety deposit box containing a large amount of money and incriminating evidence against the Judge, all stolen from him and then bequeathed to Marianne by her mother who subsequently died in mysterious circumstances. The difficult-to-follow and frankly boring plot sees our gorgeous protagonist become involved with two young Englishmen (Barry Evans and Christopher Sandford); one of them tries to help her while the other turns out to have connections with the Judge. The action begins in Spain, where Marianne narrowly escapes capture by two of the Judge's henchmen, with subsequent events taking place in England and Portugal, the latter the location of the Judge's luxurious villa where an attempt is made to extract the account information from Marianne via torture. The most memorable part of the film remains its arresting title sequence in which George go-go dances against a vivid red backdrop to some energetic music by Cyril Ornadel, who also provides a beautifully mournful melody for the theme song "Marianne."

A far more successful Susan George vehicle, and one in which she got to play opposite Hollywood superstar Dustin Hoffman, was **Straw Dogs** (1971), a vastly overrated though undeniably powerful picture directed and co-scripted by Sam Peckinpah from Gordon M. Williams' 1969 novel *The Siege of Trencher's Farm*. Hoffman and George employ their distinctive acting styles (he of the method variety and she of the instinctive) to superb effect as ill-fitting couple David Sumner (a passive American mathematician) and his British wife Amy, who have taken up temporary residence in a remote farmhouse in Cornwall near to where Amy grew up. The film spends the first eighty or so minutes slowly and effectively building to a legendary and prolonged climax in which a lynch mob of degenerate locals, headed by drunken patriarch Tom Hedden (Peter Vaughan), lay siege to the house in an attempt to get hold of village simpleton Henry Niles (David Warner), who they correctly suspect is connected with the disappearance of Hedden's provocative young daughter (Sally Thomsett). Unaware of the situation regarding the girl, David has taken Niles in after injuring him in a car accident, and makes a determined stand as the mob tries desperately to break in. The situation awakens a primal instinct in David, whose many pent-up frustrations are unleashed as he violently defends his home against the attackers by drastic means including the use of boiling oil and a deadly mantrap.

The siege sequence certainly packs a visceral punch, and it's a shame that Peckinpah lets the film down overall by the earlier inclusion of a troubling and largely unnecessary rape scene in which Amy is violated in succession by two of the degenerates, her partial consent to the first (an ex-boyfriend) remaining a point of controversy to this day, not to mention being the main reason for an almost two-decade ban on home video in the UK. Vaughan is great as usual in a typically villainous role, and the other thuggish locals are effectively cast, with Jim Norton's cackling rat-catcher a likely inspiration for the "Giggler" character in Michael Winner's cult classic *Death Wish 3* (1985). A pointless and vastly inferior remake appeared in 2011.

Based on a best-selling 1971 novel of the same name by Frederick Forsyth, **The Day of the Jackal** (1973) is a straightforward story centering on a ruthless professional killer—code-named the "Jackal" (Edward Fox in his most memorable role)—hired by the OAS (a French paramilitary underground organization) to assassinate President Charles De Gaulle. The film's main interest lies in watching the Jackal's meticulous preparation leading up to the planned assassination on Liberation Day, whereupon he disguises himself as a disabled war veteran (with a

Edward Fox in *The Day of the Jackal* (1973).

gun concealed in his crutches) in order to get past security. Michael Lonsdale plays a detective on the Jackal's trail in this slickly made British-French co-production, which manages to generate plenty of suspense despite the outcome never being in any doubt. Kenneth Ross' expert screenplay provided the basis for 1997's *The Jackal* starring Bruce Willis.

> *"One man's madness might send 1200 to the bottom of the sea— only one man can save them!"*

Juggernaut (1974) is the name used by a psychopathic explosives expert (Freddie Jones) who, having planted several large and intricate time bombs on board a transatlantic ocean liner called *The Britannic*, waits for the ship to set sail before demanding £500,000 in return for information on how to deactivate the devices. As the police attempt to trace the criminal in London, an elite bomb disposal team led by Fallon (Richard Harris) boards the vessel (whose hundreds of passengers cannot be evacuated owing to hazardous weather) in an attempt to avert a catastrophe. One particularly shocking moment involves the sudden death of a main character when one of the bombs explodes unexpectedly, and there's a neat twist on a familiar situation whereby the hero has a choice between which of two colored wires to cut in order to save the day. The great cast also includes Anthony Hopkins as a Scotland Yard man.

Harris also stars, this time as a celebrated neurosurgeon, in the entertaining and tremendously exciting British-Italian-German co-production ***The Cassandra Crossing*** (1976). After unwittingly becoming infected with a secret U.S.-developed pneumonic plague in Geneva, a fleeing terrorist boards a Transcontinental Express train bound for Stockholm and begins spreading the disease to the other 1,000 or so passengers. The authorities decide to reroute the express to a location in Poland so that the passengers can be quarantined, but not before forcing a stop-off at Nuremberg where the train is sealed off with an enclosed oxygen system and commandeered by armed medical forces. In ensuing events, the powers that be hold fast on their decision to send the train into Poland, even though they have become aware that the final part of the journey will involve traversing a disused and dangerously unsafe steel arch bridge known as the Cassandra Crossing. It is left up to a group of passengers, led by Harris' neurosurgeon and including his ex-wife (Sophia Loren) and an undercover agent (O.J. Simpson), to take back control of the train so as to avoid certain death on the perilous viaduct. Burt Lancaster excels as a sinister U.S. Army Intelligence officer, and there's some great camerawork and a very good Jerry Goldsmith score to boot.

Set in a Québec seaside resort town, the indifferent British-Canadian co-production ***Tomorrow Never Comes*** (1977) sees a situation develop whereby police lay siege to a beachside cabana. The predicament has resulted from a disturbed—partly through jealousy but mainly due to a nasty head injury sustained in a bar brawl—young man (Stephen McHattie) holding his singer-

Malcolm McDowell as evil SS officer Captain Von Berkow in *The Passage* (1978).

girlfriend (Susan George) at gunpoint after learning about her shacking up with an influential business tycoon (a rare acting role by famed playwright John Osborne). Oliver Reed plays a conscientious though disillusioned cop who has decided to quit the force, and whose last day at work is spent—amid a crowd of mostly sensation-seeking onlookers—trying to bring about a peaceful solution to the crisis. However, his superiors would rather kill the gunman, not least to avoid any potential scandal where the tycoon is concerned. The superb cast also includes Donald Pleasence in a hilarious turn as an oddball chain-smoking police doctor.

A siege also features in **Give Us Tomorrow** (1978), in which middle-class bank manager Martin Hammond's (James Kerry) family are held hostage in their home by the thuggish Ron (Derren Nesbitt) and a young accomplice (Alan Guy). Meanwhile, Hammond, under threats of harm to his family, is forced to hand over money to other members of Ron's gang at the bank. Following the robbery, in which a clerk is fatally shot, Hammond races home, only to find Ron and the accomplice still there. Ensuing events lead to police besieging the property, which ultimately doesn't go too well for the criminals. This offbeat low-budgeter favors dialogue over action, spending much time focusing on Ron's class envy toward his well-to-do captives, especially Hammond's wife played by Sylvia Syms. A liberal use of expletives, together with a gratuitous and frankly ludicrous sex scene (involving Hammond's teenage daughter and the accomplice), were the main reasons for the film's original British "X" rating.

"An ice-swept escape route in front of them. A cold-blooded killer behind them. The only way out is up!"

Set during World War II, *The Passage* (1978) stars James Mason as Professor John Bergson, a scientist in occupied France whose specialist atomic knowledge is wanted by the Nazis. A suitably rugged Anthony Quinn plays a Basque shepherd hired by the French Resistance to help Bergson and his family escape into Spain, a journey that involves a hazardous trek across the Pyrenees. The film is mainly memorable for Malcolm McDowell in an outrageously over-the-top performance as Captain Von Berkow, a sadistic SS officer relentlessly pursuing the escapees, leaving a terrifying trail of death and destruction in his wake. McDowell camps it up in a kitchen scene where, kitted out in chef's hat and apron, not to mention wielding a sharp knife, Von Berkow interrogates and tortures a Resistance agent (Michael Lonsdale), while in another scene he burns alive a gypsy (Christopher Lee) who gave shelter to the fugitives. J. Lee Thompson directs competently if unremarkably, and there's some stunning scenery to enjoy when it's not being chewed up by McDowell.

7

Merton Park's Edgar Wallace B-Movie Series

Man of Mystery

In 1960, Anglo Amalgamated Film Distributors (run by Nat Cohen and Stuart Levy) began releasing a series of B-movie thrillers based on or influenced by the works of prolific British author Edgar Wallace (1875–1932). According to an article in the British trade paper *The Daily Cinema* (January 4, 1961), "During 1960 Anglo acquired the film rights of 250 of the works of the most famous thriller writer of all time." By the time the series came to an end in 1965, an impressive total of 47 films had been made, all low in budget but high in quality. Forty-six of the films were produced by Jack Greenwood at London's Merton Park Studios, utilizing many locations in the vicinity; the remaining one, *The Malpas Mystery*, was made by Independent Artists (Julian Wintle and Leslie Parkyn) at Beaconsfield Studios. Anglo's publicity campaign for the films included material urging exhibitors to "cash in on the Edgar Wallace boom!" while proudly proclaiming "the greatest thriller stories of the century now provide brilliant film entertainment for the screens of the world." Posters included an image of the author and slogans such as "The Latest Edgar Wallace Mystery Thriller!" and "The Newest Edgar Wallace Mystery Thriller!"

One of the most memorable aspects of the series is the generic title sequence, each film opening with a bust of Edgar Wallace revolving against a smoke-filled background to the accompaniment of a particularly memorable theme tune by Michael Carr. (The final seven films also exist with alternate stand-alone title sequences.) At the start of the series, Carr's theme, known as "Man of Mystery," was a slow and haunting arrangement featuring flute, accordion and a string section but, toward the end, with the swinging sixties well under way, it had transitioned to an up-tempo version including electric guitar and percussion. A lively cover version of the theme by British instrumental rock/pop group The Shadows did very well in the charts in late 1960, but is nowhere near as evocative as the arrangements used for the films.

The world of British film and television in the 1960s was brimming with incredibly talented performers. Among the established and reliable character actors who lent their skills to the Edgar Wallace series were Bernard Lee, Ronald Howard, Geoffrey Keen, Finlay Currie, Alexander Knox, Maurice Denham, Derek Farr and Michael Gough, while the films also provided employment to fresher faces such as Barry Foster, Harry H. Corbett, John Thaw and even Michael Caine. There is no shortage of glamour thanks to such beautiful leading ladies as Hazel Court, Justine Lord and Barbara Shelley, while the alluring femme fatales on offer include Moira Redmond, Margit Saad and Rosemary Leach. There's also a wealth of talent behind the camera, with directors including Sidney Hayers, Quentin Lawrence,

Clive Donner and John Llewelyn Moxey, and writers such as Lukas Heller, Philip Mackie and Jimmy Sangster (the latter writing his two entries under the pseudonym John Sansom). The films achieve a certain stylistic consistency thanks to the input of a small pool of experienced technicians including Bert Mason and James Wilson (directors of photography), Peter Mullins (art director) and Derek Holding (editor), while incidental music throughout was almost exclusively composed by Bernard Ebbinghouse.

One year before the first Merton Park Edgar Wallace film was made, another series of Wallace-based films had begun production in Germany, with a few of them showing up on the British cinema circuit. Part of a genre known as *krimi*, with titles such as *The Fellowship of the Frog* (1959), *The Crimson Circle* (1960) and *The Green Archer* (1961), these films amplify the more sensational elements of the author's work. Highly stylized and fantastical, they often feature mysterious and flamboyant criminal masterminds, up-to-date yet at times strangely old-fashioned London settings (usually shrouded in heavy fog), creepy English country mansions and clichéd representations of Scotland Yard. They are loaded with dark gothic atmosphere and have many traditional qualities that befit the author's work. Indeed, *The Daily Cinema* (January 11, 1965), while reviewing *The Crimson Circle*, noted that "because they haven't developed their production techniques much since the Thirties, the Germans are in many ways ideally suited to filming Edgar Wallace."

In contrast, the Merton Park films are more restrained and realistic with less extravagant characters, and only a few (such as *Clue of the Twisted Candle*, *The Malpas Mystery* and *Clue of the New Pin*) could be said to include any of the more outlandish Edgar Wallace elements. (It seems that the rights held by Anglo Amalgamated were for a different, less eccentric set of Wallace stories than those held by the German producers.) Often only very loose adaptations, and with quite a few original screenplays thrown in, they play out in a distinctly modern and fashionable universe (all the films are set in the time they were made), often focusing on upper-middle-class characters. The stories, usually fairly complex with many twists and turns, involve wealthy businessmen, financiers, industrialists, investors, company directors and lawyers. In their time, the films were incredibly popular, so much so that cinemagoers reportedly often looked forward more to the Wallace B movie than to the main feature on a double bill. Such was their reputation that even John Schlesinger's 1965 film *Darling* made reference to the series in a scene where, during an audition, an actress mentions having done "a couple of Edgar Wallaces at Merton Park." The author had once again, as was the case earlier in the century, become a household name, and this continued to be so for at least two more decades thanks to subsequent British TV screenings of the films under the collective titles *Tales of Edgar Wallace* and *The Mysteries of Edgar Wallace*. The series had its first official British DVD release, as *The Edgar Wallace Mysteries*, in 2012 courtesy of Network Distributing.

U.S. Distribution

From 1964 to 1970, approximately 16 of the 47 films received sporadic theatrical distribution in the U.S. through Lester Schoenfeld (of Schoenfeld Film Distributing Corp.), playing on various double bills. Examples include *Never Back Losers* paired with *Cool Hand Luke* (1967) at the Stanley Theatre (Jersey City, New Jersey) from November–December 1967, and *The Malpas Mystery* lending its enigmatic presence to *The Shoes of the Fisherman* (1968) at New York's Selwyn Theatre in May 1969. However, the films were much better known in America from TV showings, with 34 of them—almost the complete 1960–1963 production run—included in a 39-film syndication package, the "Edgar Wallace Mystery

Package" (dating back to October 1963), in which they were edited to 53 minutes and 30 seconds to fit a one-hour time slot including commercials. (The already complex plot of *To Have and to Hold*, by far the longest film in the series at 71 minutes, was rendered almost unintelligible as a result of such drastic cutting.) Over the years, broadcasts of this package went under the generic titles *Edgar Wallace Mysteries*, *Edgar Wallace Mystery Theatre* and *Edgar Wallace Mystery Hour*, the latter no doubt an attempt to capitalize on *The Alfred Hitchcock Hour*. The remaining 13 films (*Accidental Death* and then from *Downfall* through to *Strangler's Web*) were included in a later 14-picture Avco-Embassy syndication bundle known as the "Invitation to Murder Package" and were shown unedited. (The name "Invitation to Murder" was taken from the odd film out in the package, actually a 1959 British TV thriller originally broadcast as an *Armchair Theatre* episode.)

It's worth noting that the other five titles in the 39-film TV package were *Violent Moment* (1958), *The Witness* (1959), *Urge to Kill* (1960), *Crossroads to Crime* (1960) and *The Man in the Back Seat* (1961). These had all been standalone British B thrillers distributed by Anglo Amalgamated, who at some point in the early 1960s rebranded them as "Edgar Wallace" thrillers, leading to them often being mistakenly regarded as part of the "official" Merton Park Edgar Wallace series.

The Films

The 47 films have been arranged by year of copyright, with the overall sequence in chronological order according to the dates on which they were rated by the British Board of Film Censors. A quick-reference list of the titles can be found under "Merton Park Studios' Edgar Wallace Series" in Appendix I, while Appendix III contains information on literary sources.

1960

"The Edgar Wallace series looks as though it's off to a good start!" concluded *The Daily Cinema* (September 23, 1960) in its review of **Clue of the Twisted Candle** (1960). Francis De Wolff plays devious financier Ramon Karadis, a man with many enemies who, fearing for his life, fits out his parlor with an emergency hotline to Scotland Yard. Before long, he is stabbed to death in the parlor (found locked from the inside) after apparently having just activated the hotline. The culprit has created a seemingly watertight alibi, and the key to solving the crime lies in the significance of two half-burnt candles found at the scene, one of them near the door and the other by the telephone. Top-billed Bernard Lee gives a polished performance as Superintendent Meredith, a dogged Scotland Yard detective he would play three more times during the series in *Clue of the Silver Key*, *The Share-Out* and *Who Was Maddox?*

Diamond smuggling and identity theft are the main ingredients in **The Man Who Was Nobody** (1960), which features particularly engaging performances by the two leads. A mysterious character calling himself "South Africa Smith" (burly American actor John Crawford) travels to London looking for a man known as James Tynewood. When the man turns up murdered, Smith teams up with beautiful private detective Marjorie Stedman (Hazel Court) to investigate. In the end, it transpires that the so-called Tynewood had been leading a life of crime under a false identity, and his murderer proves to be a diamond smuggler named Franz Reuter (Paul Eddington). Following Reuter's eventual capture, Smith reveals some surprising facts about his own identity and his connection to the dead man. The cast also includes Lisa Daniely in a key role.

In **Marriage of Convenience** (1960), convicted thief Larry Wilson (John Cairney) escapes from prison in order to retrieve a £20,000 stash from the robbery he was

U.S. tough guy John Crawford with English beauty Hazel Court in *The Man Who Was Nobody* (1960).

jailed for in the first place. What he doesn't know at this point is that his girlfriend and partner-in-crime Tina (Moira Redmond), who was left in charge of the stolen money, has since married John Mandle (John Van Eyssen), the detective—now retired—originally responsible for arresting Larry. Mandle, it emerges, has used the £20,000 (knowing full well where it came from) to invest in a boating business on the south coast. Needless to say, Larry isn't too happy when he learns the facts, and events lead to a climactic showdown with Mandle on the latter's yacht. The relatively straightforward plot also involves a Scotland Yard inspector (Harry H. Corbett) on Larry's trail.

Out of all the films in the series, *The Malpas Mystery* (1960) manages to convey the most in terms of authentic Edgar Wallace atmosphere. The titular character is a reclusive, mask-wearing criminal mastermind living in a shadowy London house complete with secret panels and electronically controlled doors. His presence permeates throughout the film, whose other characters include: Torrington (Geoffrey Keen), a wealthy mining magnate seeking his long-lost daughter; the daughter in question, Audrey (Maureen Swanson), just released from prison after serving time for unknowingly carrying stolen diamonds; Audrey's hedonistic stepsister Dora (Sandra Dorne), who is partly responsible for her half-sibling's incarceration; Dora's boyfriend Lacy Marshalt (Allan Cuthbertson), a slick man-about-town who comes up with a scheme, involving Dora posing as Audrey, to get hold of Torrington's riches; and a likeable Scotland Yard detective played by the likewise likeable Ronald Howard. During the course of the somewhat coincidence-laden story, we learn how all these other characters are, or become, connected with Malpas, one of them eventually revealed as actually being him. *Variety* (May 21, 1969) warned of the "very complicated plot" but reassured prospective viewers that it "can be followed if attention is paid."

1961

Clue of the New Pin (1961) stars Paul Daneman as the ruthless Rex Lander who, during the course of the film, commits two murders, the first being that of his millionaire uncle (David Horne) for an inheritance. The second victim, a blackmailer (Ramsey Brown), was in possession of information that could have threatened Rex's chances of claiming the inheritance. The police are baffled as, in each case, the body is found in a vault locked from the outside but with the only key in existence lying on a table inside. Bernard Archard plays a Scotland Yard detective, and James Villiers is on typically smooth form as an urbane television celebrity who ultimately solves the locked vault mystery. Catherine Woodville has the main female role as an actress girlfriend of Rex's who almost becomes victim number three by virtue of learning too much. Daneman gives a great performance as Rex (a part once played by John Gielgud in a 1929 film version), and the story's more old-fashioned elements blend well with the modern setting.

We discover early on in *Partners in Crime* (1961) that Frank Merril (John Van Eyssen), company director of a successful soft drinks company, is behind the murder of his business partner, having paid one of their truck drivers, Rex (Gordon Boyd), to shoot the man dead. Complications ensue when the compromising gun is stolen from Rex's truck by youths, which leads to it being identified as the murder weapon. The police are soon seeking Rex, as is Merril, who wishes to silence him. Many films in the series feature beautiful and ruthless women, and in this respect Moira Redmond does not disappoint as the murdered man's widow, who's found to be in league with Merril. Bernard Lee plays a detective, and there's an explosive finale in a car salvage yard.

In *The Fourth Square* (1961), a series of women—including Nina Stewart (Delphi Lawrence) and Sandra Martin (Natasha Parry)—all have their homes robbed of jewelry that had been given to them by wealthy playboy Tom Alvarez (Anthony Newlands). The only clues to the thefts (one of which involved the murder of a maid) are small square emblems deliberately left at the scene of each crime. Bill Lawrence (Conrad Phillips), a suave lawyer looking into the matter, deduces the significance of the emblem clues and is able to work out who the next victim will be. A trap is set, revealing the mastermind behind the crimes to be Alvarez's estranged wife (Miriam Karlin), the thefts having been an attempt to reclaim jewelry that her husband had originally bought for her but had since given away to all his various lovers (the robbery victims).

Man at the Carlton Tower (1961) begins with Rhodesian criminal Lew Daney (Nigel Green) carrying out a £100,000 jewel robbery in London, killing a policeman in the process. Shortly after, he meets with an old criminal associate, Harry Stone (Alfred Burke), and is never heard from again. Meanwhile, another Rhodesian, an ex-policeman named Tim Jordan (Lee Montague), agrees to help Scotland Yard search for Daney and the jewels. In fact, Stone has killed Daney (who tried to kill him first) and has since been looking for the gems himself, which it turns out Daney left in the safekeeping of his wife Lydia (Maxine Audley). Events lead to a climax involving Stone, Lydia and Tim in which Lydia shoots Stone in revenge for murdering her husband. The always excellent Green only appears during the first 10 minutes or so, leaving Burke, who the *Monthly Film Bulletin* (September 1961) said "gives a novel style of smooth menace to his villain," to carry the film, which he does commendably. The title refers to Tim and the plush London hotel at which he stays.

The second film in the series to feature Bernard Lee as Scotland Yard's Superintendent Meredith, *Clue of the Silver Key* (1961) sees the detective investigating the murder

Alfred Burke and Maxine Audley in *Man at the Carlton Tower* (1961).

of cantankerous moneylender Harvey Lane (Finlay Currie). The killer, who claims two other victims during the story, had found out that Lane was going blind and was taking advantage of this in a scheme (involving check fraud and masquerading under a false identity) to embezzle him, and later killed the man when he became suspicious and was about to inform the police. The silver key of the title refers to a luminous safe key belonging to Lane (luminous so that he could see it with his diminishing eyesight) which provides a vital lead in the case. Standing out among the solid cast is Patrick Cargill as Lane's not-so-faithful (as it turns out) butler. *Leonard Maltin's Movie Guide* awarded a decent two-and-a-half star rating (their highest for one of these movies) to what they called an "above-par Edgar Wallace yarn."

The Daily Cinema (December 20, 1961) observed that ***The Sinister Man*** (1961) has a "rather more international flavour than usual" for the series. The tale centers on a murdered Oxford professor and the theft of three ancient stone tablets—the Kytang Wafers (from the fictional Asian country of Kytang)—that he'd been studying. The thief-murderer proves to be one of the dead man's colleagues, paid to steal the Wafers by a Kytang ambassador who wanted them for political purposes. The film benefits from snappy direction, good cinematography and pleasant location work; and there are solid performances by John Bentley, as a trilby-wearing detective, and Patrick Allen as an American scholar up to no good. The finale takes place in a judo club, where the detective and killer fight it out.

In the low-key mystery ***Attempt to Kill*** (1961), Derek Farr gives an engagingly idiosyncratic performance as a detective investigating attempts on the life of businessman

Frank Weyman (Richard Pearson). Among the suspects are Weyman's fiancée Elisabeth (Patricia Mort), to whom Weyman has willed his estate, and Gerry Hamilton (Tony Wright), a friend of Weyman's. Gerry and Elisabeth turn out to be husband-and-wife confidence tricksters who had been swindling Weyman out of large amounts of money before attempting to kill him in a bid to grab the whole estate. They eventually get their comeuppance, but not before Gerry has murdered one of Weyman's former employees who'd been blackmailing him over the con game.

Counterfeiting and murder are the principal ingredients of **Man Detained** (1961), which the *Monthly Film Bulletin* (December 1961) described as a "taut and vivid" addition to the series. One night, small-time thief Frank Murray (an engaging performance by Michael Coles) steals £10,000 from the office of businessman Thomas Maple (Victor Platt), who is found murdered shortly after. When questioned by police, Murray admits to taking the money (which is found to be counterfeit) but denies murder. He subsequently helps the police trap the real culprit, James Helder (Paul Stassino), head of a forged currency racket in which Maple was heavily involved. Also woven into the story is an affair between Helder and his victim's widow (Ann Sears), and there's a fast-moving climax in a railway yard.

Never Back Losers (1961) was the only film in the Edgar Wallace series to be set in the world of professional horse racing, a subject the author was particularly passionate about. With a big race coming up, jockey Clive Parker (Larry Martyn) finds himself in a difficult situation: on the one hand, he faces violent consequences from a race-fixing gang (headed by a crooked bookie played by Harry Locke) unless he deliberately loses the race; on the other hand, he faces pressure from big-time gambler and racketeer "Lucky" Ben Black (Patrick Magee), who is backing Clive's horse and wants to see that it gets a fair chance. Jim Mathews (Jack Hedley), a young insurance man, gets caught up in the conflict while investigating an accident claim from another jockey who'd been victimized by the race-fixers. Magee gives a show-stealing performance as the crafty Ben who, although involved in dishonest activities, is never dishonest when it comes to gambling, which is why he always strives to "never back losers."

Michael Gough is at his creepy best as Donald Edwards, a controlling, possessive and decidedly dangerous husband in **Candidate for Murder** (1961). Insanely jealous of his wife Helene's (Erika Remberg) acting career, not to mention her friendship with a handsome lawyer (John Justin), Donald decides to eliminate her and brings in a contract killer from Germany (Hans Borsody) to do the dirty work for him. After supposedly completing his mission, the assassin secures his fee before revealing that he hasn't killed Helene after all, having correctly suspected that Donald would attempt to double-cross him. This leads to a tense climactic showdown in the countryside, where Donald has rented a cottage for the assassin to stay during his visit. One of the more violent entries in the series, the film benefits from a solid screenplay by future *The Dirty Dozen* co-scripter Lukas Heller.

The Daily Cinema (March 21, 1962) noted **Backfire!** (1961) as being "another well-made popular thriller in the Edgar Wallace series." Ben Curzon (Oliver Johnston), the elderly founder of long-established cosmetics firm Venetia, is dominated by his unscrupulous American junior partner, Mitchell Logan (Alfred Burke), who has caused the company to fall into ruin. Against Ben's wishes, Logan goes ahead with a plan to burn down the business for the insurance, this involving a professional arsonist (John Cazabon) who sets up a special device to activate the fire. When a cleaning lady stumbles on the device, Logan murders her and lets her body burn in the subsequent blaze. He also later finds it necessary to silence Ben (making it look as if the man committed suicide) before finally getting his comeuppance thanks to the efforts of Ben's daughter, Shirley (Suzanne Neve), and an insurance investigator named Jack Bryce (Noel Trevarthen). Zena Marshall is on great form as Logan's beautiful, bitchy and equally unprincipled wife.

1962

The refreshingly simple *Flat Two* (1962) revolves around the murder, in his own home (the titular apartment), of wealthy gambling club proprietor Emil Louba (David Bauer). Architect Frank Leamington (Jack Watling), as a result of circumstantial evidence—involving his having broken into the apartment to retrieve some IOUs in connection with his fiancée (Ann Bell)—is arrested for the crime and put on trial at the Old Bailey. Two other men were at Louba's apartment around the time of his death, one of them an eminent barrister (John Le Mesurier) who ends up defending Frank and securing his acquittal. During the trial, certain information is disclosed that only the real killer could have known, which leads to Scotland Yard's Inspector Trainer (Bernard Archard) catching his man in a surprising conclusion.

The Share-Out (1962) concerns a racket—run by the ruthless Colonel Calderwood (Alexander Knox) with three others including Diana Marsh (Moira Redmond)—involving a property company to which victims are blackmailed into selling their real estate at knock-down prices. The properties are then sold for profit which is converted into diamonds to be at some point shared out between the criminals. Scotland Yard's Superintendent Meredith (Bernard Lee's third time playing the character during the series) is determined to smash the racket, and to this end he persuades a mercenary private investigator, Mike Stafford (William Russell), to infiltrate the gang. As events unfold, a growing atmosphere of distrust among the crooks results in three of their deaths, these ultimately found to have been engineered by Mike and the remaining gang member in a plot to secure the diamonds for themselves.

A suitably charming Ivan Desny stars in *Number Six* (1962) as Charles Valentine, a man suspected of conning various wealthy women out of their fortunes before murdering them, and who always has a watertight alibi. The title refers to the code name of an undercover operative (their identity initially kept secret from the audience) assigned by Scotland Yard's Detective Superintendent Hallett (Michael Goodliffe) to keep tabs on Valentine. During the course of the story, Valentine makes the acquaintance of his next intended victim, a rich heiress named Nadia Leiven (Nadja Regin), and takes on an assistant (Brian Bedford); one of these two characters turns out to be "Number Six," and is revealed in the climax where Valentine finally gets his comeuppance.

The *Monthly Film Bulletin* (September 1962) was unimpressed with *Time to Remember* (1962), calling it "an inept and sometimes incoherent addition to the Edgar Wallace series." When a large house goes on sale in London, Mrs. Johnson (Genine Graham), the widow of a burglar (David Lodge), determines to buy the place in order to retrieve a fortune in jewels that were stolen from there, and then hidden there—or to be more precise, dropped down the chimney—by her husband before he suffered a fatal fall from the rooftop during the getaway. Jack Burgess (Harry H. Corbett), a small-time real estate agent, discovers what Mrs. Johnson is up to and decides to look for the gems himself, finding them in a sealed-up fireplace at the bottom of said chimney. While still in the house, he is attacked by a mysterious intruder (actually a French cohort of the dead thief who is also looking for the jewels) and ends up killing the man and concealing his body in the selfsame fireplace. A surprising development involving Mrs. Johnson leads to the discovery of the body and Jack's arrest. Top-billed Yvonne Monlaur plays a femme fatale (the French cohort's lover), and there's an atmospheric wintry setting with some well-shot scenes (including the opening in which Lodge does his own dangerous-looking stunt work) taking place atop the snowy roof of the principal house.

Barry Foster, the future necktie murderer of Alfred Hitchcock's *Frenzy* (1972), was on the right side of the law, at least initially, as a young police constable in the effective noir offering, **Playback** (1962). The constable in question is Dave Hollis, whose hopes of promotion go out the window when he meets and becomes romantically entangled with the glamorous Lisa Shillack (Margit Saad). Lisa soon introduces him to the urbane Ralph Monk's (Nigel Green) gambling club, where he falls into heavy debt, and subsequently maneuvers him into agreeing to murder her wealthy husband (George Pravda) for an insurance policy. The pair create a seemingly watertight alibi, and Hollis carries out the killing; however, he will soon discover that he's been played for a patsy by Lisa who, in cahoots with her true lover (the aforementioned Ralph), has cleverly engineered things so that he will be suspected and then charged for the crime with no links back to her. The story unfolds as one long flashback that ends where it began, namely in a courtroom where Hollis is sentenced to death for murder, which by now also includes that of Lisa in revenge for her evil scheming. Saad, suitably cool and provocative as the femme fatale, and Foster, investing his character with a good deal of intensity, play off each other nicely in what *Films and Filming* (November 1962) rightly noted as being "a neat, uncluttered film, smoothly directed by Quentin Lawrence,

Barry Foster gets played for a patsy by Margit Saad's femme fatale in *Playback* (1962).

who knows the value of keeping scenes short and succinct."

Locker Sixty-Nine (1962) is an intricate tale concerning John Griffiths (Paul Daneman) and Bennett Sanders (Edward Underdown), partners in an export company that once sent canned food as aid to flood victims in South America. As it happens, Sanders secretly knew that the food had become spoiled, and many of the recipients subsequently died of food poisoning. No charges were ever brought against the company, but Griffiths put a file of incriminating evidence in a safety deposit box (the titular locker) and has used this in order to have a hold over Sanders ever since. The main plot has Sanders attempting, via a cunning plan involving faking his own death and using a private detective (Walter Brown) as a pawn, to get hold of the evidence and break free of Griffiths' control. The solid cast also includes Eddie Byrne as an ace reporter named Simon York, and John Carson as a South American with a grudge against Sanders in connection with the food poisoning having caused death in his family. While the story sounds simple enough, the way it unfolds is devilishly complex.

A provincial policeman, Inspector Sparrow (Glyn Houston), begins his own independent investigation—hence the title ***Solo for Sparrow*** (1962)—after being sidelined by his superior (Allan Cuthbertson) in favor of London's Scotland Yard. The investigation in question concerns a jewelry store robbery in which an elderly female employee was killed; the perpetrators are a ruthless gang of thieves headed by one "Pin" Norman (Michael Coles). Anthony Newlands and Nadja Regin play the jewelry store owner and his femme fatale wife (both of whom are up to their necks in the crime, she being the actual mastermind behind the heist) in this exciting and well-filmed entry, which plays somewhat like a TV series pilot for the Sparrow character. Things conclude with a fierce gunfight at a deserted farm where Sparrow was being held prisoner by Norman and his cronies, one of whose number—an Irishman—provides Michael Caine with a small role.

Albert Lieven stars in ***Death Trap*** (1962) as Paul Heindrik, a criminal stockbroker who murders a grudge-holding former employee, Ross Williams (John Meillon), after the latter attempts to blackmail him in connection with the suspicious suicide (actually foul play on the part of Heindrik) of a young woman named Moira. Heindrik's secretary Jean (Barbara Shelley), a friend of Ross, had uncovered the evidence that enabled the blackmail in the first place, and becomes marked for death by her boss after witnessing the murder. Also woven into the convoluted storyline (at one point even one of the characters says "it is a little involved") are Moira's sister Carol (Mercy Haystead), whose nosing around puts her in danger, and Heindrik's stepson Derek (Kenneth Cope), who is ultimately instrumental in bringing an end to his stepfather's villainy.

In their review of ***The £20,000 Kiss*** (1962), the *Kinematograph Weekly* (February

Michael Coles as "Pin" Norman in *Solo for Sparrow* (1962).

28, 1963) gave fair warning that "the plot demands concentration." Michael Goodliffe plays a distinguished lawyer and Member of Parliament who becomes the victim of a blackmail racket involving his neighbors across the hall, namely aristocratic husband-and-wife Leo and Maxine Hagen (Anthony Newlands and Dawn Addams), and their maid Paula (Mia Karam), although Maxine's role in the affair is not revealed until the end. At a certain point, the convoluted story develops into a whodunit that centers on the murders of Leo and the maid, and which comes to a satisfying conclusion when the killer is unmasked thanks to a Scotland Yard inspector's (Alfred Burke) bluff concerning the murder weapon—one of a pair of antique dueling pistols (fitted with a silencer) belonging to Leo.

The great Maurice Denham stars in *The Set-Up* (1962) as a wealthy businessman, Theo Gaunt, who murders his wife so that he can be with his lover Nicole (Maria Corvin). One of Gaunt's associates, Ray Underwood (Anthony Bate), provides him with an alibi, and the two men cleverly frame an ex-convict (Brian Peck) for the crime. It later transpires that Underwood and Nicole are actually in league to blackmail Gaunt over the murder to the tune of £25,000. John Carson (he and Bate also appeared together in the later series entry *Act of Murder*) is especially good as a detective who brings the conspirators to justice by way of a clever trick.

In *Incident at Midnight* (1962), three criminals, one of them injured, turn up at an all-night London pharmacy after stealing a consignment of heroin, which they've deposited in a subway station locker. The heroin is destined for former Nazi Erik Leichner (a reliably sinister Anton Diffring), whose wife (Sylva Langova) is due to arrive at the dispensary to collect the key to the locker in return for a key to another locker containing payment for the drugs. However, an undercover operation (involving police officers posing as customers at the pharmacy) is underway, resulting in the eventual downfall of all the crooks. Martin Miller gives a sympathetic performance as a drug-addicted ex-surgeon forced to operate on the injured criminal, while William Sylvester, despite being second-billed, has just a tiny role as an American investigator for the New York Narcotics Bureau.

On the Run (1962) sees Frank Stewart (Emrys Jones) and Dave Hughes (Philip Locke) jailed for the theft of valuable bearer bonds, which they hid for safekeeping before being arrested. Wally Lucas (Kevin Stoney), a crooked bookmaker behind the robbery, makes a deal to split the bonds fifty-fifty with Hughes, who will disclose their location upon his release. To make sure Frank does not get in the way of their arrangement, Lucas has concocted a scheme that prompts Frank to escape, the idea being to fix it so that he will be rearrested immediately and have his sentence extended. However, Frank, for whom we gain sympathy after learning he'd been blackmailed into taking part in the robbery in the first place, manages to avoid being apprehended, and events culminate in a showdown between him and Lucas in a sewer where the bonds are hidden. As played by Jones, Frank is a pretty dull hero, while the busy plot is often confusing thanks to key points being explained in fleeting dialogue.

A forceful Nigel Davenport stars as Dino Steffano, a ruthless tycoon on bail awaiting trial for large-scale embezzlement in *Return to Sender* (1962). In an attempt to extricate himself from his predicament, Dino hires underworld "fixer" Mike Cochrane (William Russell) to discredit the renowned barrister (Geoffrey Keen) due to prosecute him; he also comes up with a scheme to get rid of his secret partner in the embezzlement, surprisingly revealed as the barrister's daughter, Beth (Jennifer Daniel). The plan is to kill Beth, frame Mike for her murder and then liquidate him too in an engineered "accident." The initially straightforward plot soon escalates into a series of confounding twists and turns (also involving Dino's wife, played by Yvonne Romain) that just about make sense if one pays careful attention.

1963

Described by *The Daily Cinema* (July 5, 1963) as a "trim, taut and thoroughly absorbing yarn," **Ricochet** (1963) sees lawyer Alan Phipps (Richard Leech) plot the downfall of both his wealthy wife Yvonne (Maxine Audley) and her ex-lover, ice-skating instructor John Brodie (Alex Scott). This entails embroiling the pair in a scenario (a devilishly complicated affair involving blackmail and a gun supposedly containing blanks) designed to manipulate Yvonne into shooting John dead, which will result in her incarceration, thereby killing two birds with one stone. Everything goes according to plan, but Alan is soon plagued by the sinister Dexter (an outstanding Dudley Foster), an associate of John's who has damning evidence against him and ultimately causes his undoing. The Phipps' snow-encircled house and an ice-skating rink are the main settings in this above-average offering.

The Double (1963) is a twisty tale of treachery and identity theft that involves John Cleeve (Basil Henson) and Derreck Alwyn (Alan MacNaughtan), formerly business partners in Nairobi who bear a striking similarity to one another. As the plot unfolds, it transpires that John, after learning that Derreck was due to inherit a fortune in England, drugged him and left him for dead; he then assumed his identity in order to claim the inheritance himself. However, Derreck survived and, suffering from amnesia and partial paralysis as a result of the drugging, has begun a slow recuperation with the help of two sisters (played by Jeannette Sterke and Jane Griffiths). The film is set in the English seaside town of Brighton, where events reach a satisfying conclusion following a climactic showdown between the two men.

An interesting plot is the main draw in the otherwise undistinguished **The Rivals** (1963). The kidnappers of a Swedish industrialist's (Jack Gwillim) daughter package up some of the girl's personal effects with a note demanding a £75,000 ransom upon further instructions. The package is left momentarily unattended in a car which is then stolen by small-time crooks Steve and Eddy (Brian Smith and Howard Greene). Upon reading the note and realizing they've stumbled on a kidnapping, Steve and Eddy attempt to claim the ransom for themselves; meanwhile, the real abductors do everything in their power to track the two men down, leading to trouble for all concerned. The film benefits from some good pacing, but the story runs out of steam well before the climax.

To Have and to Hold (1963) features a typically labyrinthine script by Jimmy Sangster (under his pseudonym John Sansom) which echoes U.S. noir classics such as *Double Indemnity* (1944), while also giving a nod to Hitchcock's *Vertigo* (1958). Womanizing police sergeant Henry Fraser (Australian actor Ray Barrett) begins falling for Claudia (Katharine Blake), a supposedly married woman claiming to have received a death threat from an ex-boyfriend. Soon after, the woman is found murdered, her face battered beyond recognition. Later, while conducting his own private investigation into the murder, Henry comes across a woman identical to Claudia who initially claims to be Claudia's twin sister but eventually confesses to actually being Claudia. She also confesses that she'd conspired with her lover George (Nigel Stock) to murder George's wife (the real victim) in a devilishly complicated scheme that entailed temporarily posing as the latter. Claudia takes Henry as her new lover and then cleverly manipulates him into a plot to murder George; however, things are not what they seem, and Henry will soon discover that treachery has no bounds when it comes to Claudia.

The complex story, which plays out in flashback from Henry's point of view, ties itself up in knots it can not always undo, but it's an entertaining yarn nevertheless. Blake

Ray Barrett and Katharine Blake in *To Have and to Hold* (1963), a particularly twisty British noir scripted by the great Jimmy Sangster.

makes an excellent femme fatale, and Barrett invests a great deal of intensity in his role as the hugely gullible (as it turns out) cop.

The extremely involved plot of ***The Partner*** (1963) just about makes sense, but only under very close scrutiny. Movie studio boss Wayne Douglas (Guy Doleman) attempts to avoid paying tax on some film rights via a scheme, organized by his accountant, involving passing £300,000 through the Swiss bank account of his leading lady Lin Siyan (Yoko Tani). It later becomes apparent that Lin is attempting to keep the money, although she is in fact acting under the influence of a mysterious figure who, during the course of events, murders the accountant (who'd had his own designs on the loot). Mark Eden is on good form in a key role as a private detective hired by Wayne's wife to keep tabs on her husband (she wrongly suspects he's having an affair with Lin), while Anthony Booth plays Wayne's beatnik brother-in-law, yet another character mixed up in the convolutions.

One of the more interesting films in the series is ***Accidental Death*** (1963), which unfolds in and around the large country house of wealthy Englishman Colonel Paxton (Richard Vernon). Paxton, we learn, is guardian to Henriette (Jacqueline Ellis), a young French woman whose parents were shot by the Gestapo during World War II. A prowler caught on the premises one night turns out to be Paul Lanson (John Carson), an ex-Resistance man who knows Paxton from World War II (the colonel was a liaison officer to the Resistance). Paul informs Paxton that he has come to kill him, accusing him of betraying various Resistance families, including Henriette's, to the Gestapo. Paxton denies the allegations, and a game of cat-and-mouse soon ensues between the two men. Suspense builds steadily in this entertaining and well-acted entry, but the climax, which involves an electrified swimming pool set up by one of the men as a death trap, leaves things unresolved.

In the spirited ***Five to One*** (1963), John Thaw plays a small-time crook who, together with two accomplices including his girlfriend (Ingrid Hafner), puts into motion an ingenious plan to steal £12,000 from a crooked bookmaker (Lee Montague). A major setback necessitates that the thieves break into a safe at the bookie's home instead of at his office as planned, and they are finally caught thanks to a rather incredible coincidence involving an insurance company employee they'd earlier blackmailed in order to get vital information for their scheme. Thaw is excellent in his first credited film role, and the superb character actor Jack Watson brings some interesting touches to his part as a pipe-smoking police inspector.

The above-average ***Downfall*** (1963), which *The Daily Cinema* (March 6, 1964) called an "adroit, if rather grisly, crime yarn," stars Maurice Denham (superb as always) as a top criminal lawyer named Sir Harold Crossley. The film begins with Crossley securing the acquittal of Martin Somers (T.P. McKenna), a womanizing driving instructor who'd been accused of shooting dead another man's wife. However, Crossley, secretly believing, as do others, that Somers is actually guilty, subsequently uses him as a pawn in a scheme to murder his—Crossley's—own wife (Nadja Regin); this entails hiring Somers as a chauffeur and giving him access to a loaded gun in the hope that history will repeat itself. In ensuing events, we learn the truth about Somers' guilt/innocence, and fate sees to it that things do not go according to Crossley's wicked plan. McKenna gives a cleverly ambiguous performance, and there's plenty of initial suspense, but the ingenious story peters out somewhat toward the end.

1964

Canadian actor Cec Linder plays a racketeer named Joe Armstrong in ***The Verdict*** (1964). The film begins with Joe, having been deported from the United States, relocating to London where he then finds himself facing imminent prosecution for a murder he'd committed there 24 years previously. Before being arrested for the crime, he makes arrangements with his friend and fixer, Larry Mason (a typically assertive Nigel Davenport), to rig the jury so as to ensure a "not guilty" verdict. However, when he sees an opportunity to abscond with £50,000 of Joe's money, Larry pulls a double-cross and steers the jury to a guilty verdict instead. In a final twist, Larry gets his comeuppance while attempting to leave the country with both the cash and Joe's opportunistic secretary (Zena Marshall). Paul Stassino plays to type as a London gang boss and the originally intended recipient of Joe's £50,000 as a blackmail payoff in connection with the jury-fixing plot.

We Shall See (1964) is not so much a whodunit as a when-will-they-do-it. Wealthy Alva Collins (impeccably played by Faith Brook) is an incurable sociopath who makes life hell for all those around her, including her airline pilot husband (Maurice Kaufmann), her brother (Alex McIntosh) and the gardener (Alec Mango), the latter a beekeeper whose bees she loathes. It emerges that Alva had once suffered an extreme reaction to a bee sting, and a similar incident could now prove fatal. As the story progresses, it seems inevitable that someone will attempt to murder Alva; and sure enough, right near the end of the film, a mysterious figure introduces a swarm of bees into her room at a hotel chalet. Alva is subsequently found dead, but not—as it transpires in a twist ending—as a result of the bees.

Bernard Lee played Scotland Yard's Superintendent Meredith for the fourth and last time during the series in ***Who***

Was Maddox? (1964), whose plot, as observed by *Films and Filming* (September 1964), becomes "a little muddled as it thickens." When publishing company boss Alec Campbell (an all-too-brief appearance by Finlay Currie) is murdered, evidence points to one of the company directors, Jack Heath (Jack Watling), as the culprit. However, Jack is in fact the victim of an elaborate frame-up, and a complex investigation by Meredith eventually reveals the true killer to be one of Jack's colleagues, a jealous rival Campbell had planned to sidestep in favor of Jack for chairmanship of the firm. The titular Maddox is a blackmailing newspaper columnist (played by Richard Gale) who proves key to solving the case.

Face of a Stranger (1964) is easily the best of director John Llewellyn Moxey's six films in the series and features a neat script by Jimmy Sangster (writing under his pseudonym John Sansom). When convict Vince Howard (an intense performance by Jeremy Kemp) is released from prison ahead of his cellmate John (Philip Locke) owing to the latter's sentence being extended at the last minute, he agrees to visit John's blind wife Mary (Rosemary Leach) to tell her about the delay. When she seemingly mistakes him for John, Vince, whose own wife (Jean Marsh) has left him for another man, takes the opportunity to pose as John and begins living with Mary in her country cottage. Eventually, he carries out a plan to get hold of some stolen loot that John had stashed away, which involves murdering John upon his release. However, Mary (who we learn has been aware of Vince's deception all along) and her secret lover (Bernard Archard) had also planned to get hold of the money, and are soon plotting Vince's demise. This leads to a bleakly violent climax in which things end up very badly for all concerned. Apart from the great directing and scripting, this superior effort also features the most inventive cinematography of the series, with effective use of hand-held camera techniques that give a vérité feel to certain sequences.

The masterpiece of the series, *Act of Murder* (1964), is a bizarre, engrossing, atmospheric and stylishly made psychological suspenser which the *Monthly Film Bulletin* (February 1965) called "an uncommonly intelligent little thriller." Ralph Longman (Anthony Bate) and his wife Anne (Justine Lord) are tricked into temporarily leaving their country home by thieves in a holiday home-swap scam. As the thieves begin to remove the Longmans' valuable antiques, they are interrupted by Anne's former lover Tim (John Carson) when he returns to collect a suitcase he'd left behind during a visit. Upon realizing they've been scammed, Ralph and Anne race back home expecting to have been robbed, only to find everything seemingly the same way as they'd left it; except, that is, for their animals (including chickens and Anne's beloved Pekinese dog) and plants, which they soon discover have been viciously destroyed. At this point it has been made fairly clear to the audience that Tim, who's obsessed with Anne and willing to do anything to have her back in his life, is the culprit, having carried out the atrocities (after his interruption of the robbery) with the intention of making Anne so unnerved in her own house that she will move to London and consequently get back together with him. His wicked scheme works, but Ralph eventually realizes what has happened and sets out for revenge, with tragic consequences. The three principal characters, all superbly acted (with Bate giving one of his best-ever performances), are involved in the powerful and creatively filmed climax in a London alleyway. The film is the undisputed highlight in American-born Lewis Davidson's fairly sparse screenwriting career, which included one other feature film, namely the Hammer thriller *Hands of the Ripper* (1971), and episodic television in both Britain (including one of the best *The Saint* episodes, "The Bunco Artists") and the U.S. (e.g., *The Alfred Hitchcock Hour*).

Edward De Souza is Michael Blake, a handsome and opportunistic pilot in *The*

Anthony Bate and Justine Lord in the tense final moments of *Act of Murder* (1964).

Main Chance (1964). Through clever manipulation, Blake ensures he gets hired by criminal mastermind Potter (Gregoire Aslan) to fly a package into England using Potter's own private plane. This is all part of a plan by Blake, in cahoots with a gang of small-time crooks, to steal the package, which he knows contains diamonds. Blake actually ends up going one step further by double-crossing the gang and making off with the package alone, using the plane for his getaway. However, Potter, in preparation for such an eventuality, has rigged the aircraft with explosives which can be detonated by remote control. A final twist, involving Potter's attractive secretary (Tracy Reed), ensures that Blake survives the mastermind's attempt to blow up the plane mid-flight.

Set in the Channel Islands, ***Never Mention Murder*** (1964) benefits from a great performance by the inimitable Dudley Foster, noted by *Films and Filming* (May 1965) as bringing "a welcome degree of chilling credibility" to his role. Foster plays Philip Teasdale, a top heart surgeon who comes up with a devious plan to murder his wife's (Maxine Audley) lover, hotel cabaret performer Tony Sorbo (Michael Coles). The vengeful Philip spikes Tony's anti-smoking pills, causing a mild heart attack that ensures the man is admitted to hospital. He then arranges to perform surgery, having decided that Tony will not survive the operation. Also starring are Brian Haines as a shady private detective (hired by Philip to check on his wife) who, to his own detriment, tries to blackmail the surgeon, and Pauline Yates as Tony's wife (also his partner in the cabaret act). The Channel Islands setting was later again used by the film's screenwriter, Robert Banks

Stewart, for his TV detective show creation, *Bergerac* (1981–1991).

1965

The *Monthly Film Bulletin* (July 1965) remarked that, in some respects, ***Game for Three Losers*** (1965) is "a good example of Merton Park's efforts to raise the conventional crime-drama second feature above the level of dreary routine." Having had a little too much to drink, prominent and happily married politician Robert Hilary (Michael Gough) commits a one-off indiscretion when he is unable to resist an impulse to kiss his secretary, Frances (Toby Robins). Frances tells her boyfriend Oliver (Mark Eden) who, seeing an opportunity, uses her in a scheme to blackmail Robert. In the end, Robert involves the police, leading to a major trial at the Old Bailey that ends badly for all concerned. This entry was from a story by another Edgar, namely Edgar Lustgarten, a crime specialist and broadcaster who hosted the many short features that comprised Merton Park's *Scotland Yard* and *The Scales of Justice* series. Gough, Eden and Robins all perform well as the three losers of the title.

Dead Man's Chest (1965) sees young journalists David (John Thaw) and Johnnie (John Meillon) put into motion an elaborate murder hoax intended to expose the weaknesses of circumstantial evidence. The plan, designed to make it appear as if David has murdered Johnnie, entails the latter being locked in a wooden chest which is placed in the back of David's car. In ensuing events, David becomes a little concerned when Johnnie fails to respond to him from within the sealed chest and, almost immediately afterward, the car—with the chest still on board—is stolen for use as a getaway vehicle in a bank heist. The thieves dump the chest (unopened and still with no sound coming from within) in an out-of-the-way spot in their hideout, and from here on, the film twists and turns its way toward a satisfying if somewhat silly conclusion with a surprising revelation regarding Johnnie's fate. The supporting cast is highlighted by Graham Crowden as an eccentric sensation-seeking newspaper editor.

Change Partners (1965) is a sordid little tale of an affair between Anna (Zena Walker) and her husband's business partner Ricky (Basil Henson). At Anna's instigation, the adulterous couple plan and then carry out the murder of their respective spouses (Anthony Dawson and Jane Barrett) in what seems like the perfect crime. Joe Trent (Kenneth Cope), a young opportunist who has been spying on the lovers at their secret meeting place, begins blackmailing them and becomes their next target, killed in an arranged car "accident." Walker stands out from the excellent cast as the evil and manipulative Anna, while the central murder scene, in which the doomed spouses are locked in a garage and overcome by exhaust fumes, is effectively staged. Pamela Ann Davy plays Joe's girlfriend, who ultimately brings about the murderous pair's downfall.

All good things come to an end, and the Edgar Wallace series did so in fine fashion with the atmospheric and enjoyably complex ***Strangler's Web*** (1965). The film begins with the strangulation murder in a London park of former showgirl Norma Brent (Patricia Burke in her second role as a park murder victim following 1960's *The Impersonator*), with circumstantial evidence pointing to her lover, John Vichelski (Michael Balfour), as the culprit. However, investigations—mostly carried out by an alcoholic lawyer (John Stratton) working on Vichelski's behalf—eventually lead to Jackson Delacorte (Griffith Jones), a one-time matinee idol and now disfigured recluse who had a tangled past with Norma, becoming the likeliest suspect. The story comes to a neat and satisfying conclusion with a twist involving a young woman (Pauline Munro) in Delacorte's care.

8

Action/Adventure

Towers of London

Prolific London-born producer-writer Harry Alan Towers (1920–2009) had his first successes in radio, including the early 1950s show *The Lives of Harry Lime*, in which Orson Welles repeated his role from the classic 1949 film *The Third Man*. Towers also worked on television shows such as *The Scarlet Pimpernel* (1956) and *Dial 999* (1958–1959) and was founder of the punningly named production company Towers of London. Following his involvement in a real-life "adventure" in the early 1960s (including allegations against him for vice and spy activities), Towers went on to specialize in fictional adventures of the cinematic kind in what turned out to be an extensive subsequent movie career. Among his best-remembered action/adventure-oriented thriller productions are those that fall within the time period covered by this book (beginning with 1963's *Death Drums Along the River*), most of which he also scripted under the pseudonym Peter Welbeck. Most, if not all, of the films were made in association with German companies such as Constantin Film, hence the presence of German actors including Towers' own wife Maria Rohm, and Towers also frequently employed Hollywood stars to ensure healthy distribution stateside.

Inspector Sanders

Towers' feature film debut, the excitingly titled if not so excitingly executed **Death Drums Along the River** (1963), is a contemporary-set story loosely inspired by author Edgar Wallace's 1911 anthology *Sanders of the River*. Richard Todd plays Sanders, a police inspector stationed in the fictional British West African colony of Gondra (the film was actually shot in South Africa), who becomes involved in a case of diamond smuggling and murder linked to a clinic owned by Dr. Schneider (Walter Rilla). Schneider has been hiding the existence of a diamond mine on the property so as to avoid exploitation by prospectors, making use of it only to fund his research. However, Schneider's assistant, Dr. Weiss (Albert Lieven), has secretly discovered the mine and has been freely helping himself to the diamonds, smuggling them for profit and killing when necessary to protect his new-found interest.

The excessively complicated plot is no doubt a result of too many cooks spoiling the broth, as in there were four screenwriters involved (one of them Nicolas Roeg); this does no favors to the overall end product which, despite the exotic location, is a mostly listless affair that chugs along to a moderately exciting climax in which the villainous Weiss has a fatal encounter with a crocodile. Although the *Monthly Film Bulletin* (April 1966) felt that Todd was "sorely miscast as Sanders," the stalwart actor's presence is nevertheless the most memorable aspect of the movie, with Marianne Koch as a female doctor (and romantic interest for our hero) running a close second. Not so memorable are Robert Arden as an American journalist and Jeremy Lloyd as Sanders' sidekick. Part-financed in Germany, the film seems to have been more popular there than anywhere else, most likely owing to that country's deep fan base for anything Edgar Wallace.

In the follow-up, ***Coast of Skeletons*** (1964), Sanders returns to England after losing his job as a result of Gondra gaining independence. Before long, he is hired by an insurance company and sent back to Africa (this time on the southwest coast) in connection with a claim concerning diamond-dredging activities. This leads to his involvement in the search for a fortune in gold bullion—the proceeds of a train robbery—that is known to have been on board a merchant ship that was sunk somewhere along the southwest coast during World War II. The two main competing parties in the search are a ruthless Texas-born tycoon (Dale Robertson) and the German ex–U-boat captain (Heinz Drache) responsible for sinking the ship in the first place, the latter having teamed up with one of the original train robbers. Sanders eventually locates the wrecked vessel on the barren Skeleton Coast, where it has been left high and dry due to the receding tide; and it's there that all interested parties end up for a lively finale in which much tension and double-crossing leads to the gold being destroyed in an explosion. As in the previous film, Marianne Koch provides romantic interest for Sanders, only in a different role, and Sanders' resourceful sidekick is this time played by Derek Nimmo. Some excellent location photography is a highlight.

Fu Manchu

Chinese criminal mastermind Dr. Fu Manchu, a "yellow peril" pulp fantasy character created by author Sax Rohmer in the early 1900s, has been the influence for many other arch-villains including Dr. No from the James Bond universe. Christopher Lee's portrayal of a Chinese evildoer in the 1960 thriller *The Terror of the Tongs* made him a natural choice to play Fu Manchu, and he did so in five adventure thrillers produced and written by Harry Alan Towers from 1965 to 1968. The actor is mostly successful in the role (especially in the first three outings), using his imposing stature and commanding baritone voice (with only the slightest hints of a Chinese accent) to great effect in personifying the inherently cold, calculating evil of the character. Throughout the films, Fu comes up with nefarious schemes for world domination, aided by his devoted and equally wicked daughter Lin Tang (Tsai Chin) plus a seemingly endless supply of henchmen. His main adversary, Scotland Yard's Nayland Smith (played by three different actors over the five films), aptly describes Fu as both "brilliant" and "the most evil and dangerous man in the world." Dr. Petrie, acted by Howard Marion Crawford in all the films, is Smith's sidekick, and at times the two characters are not dissimilar to Sherlock Holmes and Dr. Watson. (In fact, Douglas Wilmer, who featured as Smith in the second and third films, would portray Holmes in 1975's *The Adventure of Sherlock Holmes' Smarter Brother*; and Crawford had been a very good Dr. Watson, to Ronald Howard's Holmes, in the 1950s U.S. TV series *Sherlock Holmes*.)

The first and most entertaining of the franchise is ***The Face of Fu Manchu*** (1965), which the *Monthly Film Bulletin* (November 1965) called "a first-class thriller." The pre-credits sequence shows Nayland Smith (Nigel Green) witnessing Fu Manchu's execution in China, although the criminal is in fact still alive and well (it turns out he'd hypnotized an actor to be beheaded in his place). Now headquartered in London in a tunnel beneath the River Thames, Fu forces a top biochemist (Walter Rilla) to develop a deadly poison distilled from the seeds of a rare Tibetan flower known as the Black Hill poppy. As a demonstration of his power, and as a prelude to conquering the world, he uses the poison to wipe out the entire population of an English village. Smith's determined pursuit of Fu ultimately leads to a monastery in Tibet, where he destroys (or does he?) the

Christopher Lee as Sax Rohmer's formidable Chinese crime lord in *The Face of Fu Manchu* (1965).

villain by way of a clever—not to mention highly explosive—trap.

This cracking yarn features a wonderfully atmospheric 1920s period setting courtesy of Frank White's imaginative art direction, with kudos also to the costume and wardrobe department supervised by Dorothy Edwards. Director Don Sharp, who shot the film in Ireland, keeps events moving at a fast pace and demonstrates his particular flair for action scenes with an exciting chase in which some vintage cars perform splendidly. Green is simply fantastic as Smith, giving a robust performance in a role the commanding actor was born to play; and also in the cast are Germany's Karin Dor and Joachim Fuchsberger, the former as the biochemist's daughter and the latter his brave assistant, who proves invaluable to Smith's efforts to put paid to the evil mastermind. At the end, Fu, supposedly destroyed, fades in onscreen as we hear him intone (as he would in all the subsequent films) that the world shall hear from him again.

True to his word, the criminal mastermind returned in *The Brides of Fu Manchu* (1966). This time, from his headquarters in a North African temple (complete with deadly snake pit), Fu Manchu has been organizing the international kidnappings of women with one thing in common: they are all related to leading industrialists and scientists whom Fu can consequently force into helping advance his plan for global domination. Said plan involves a powerful directed-energy sonic beam weapon whose destructive ability the villain demonstrates to the world by vaporizing a passenger ship. Eventually, Nayland Smith (Douglas Wilmer), with the help of the Foreign Legion, invades the temple headquarters; the kidnapped women are rescued and the place is blown sky-high after Fu causes the sonic weapon to overload in his desperate effort to destroy an arms conference in London. Don Sharp returns as director for a more convoluted affair that's still mightily entertaining if never quite managing to match the excitement of the first film; sadly, Nigel Green does not return as Smith, which is not to say that his replacement, Wilmer, doesn't give a decent performance, but rather he lacks the presence and vitality of his predecessor. German actor Heinz Drache has a pivotal role as the fiancé of one of the kidnapped women.

Filmed in Hong Kong and Ireland, *The Vengeance of Fu Manchu* (1967) is weaker in plot and atmosphere compared to the first two productions. Fu Manchu's latest scheme, from his ancestral palace in Northern China, entails creating doubles of the world's top police chiefs and having them, under hypnosis, commit murders for which they'll be tried and sentenced to death; the idea is to forever discredit the reputations of the real men, themselves to be abducted and then killed by Fu elsewhere. It's no surprise to learn that first on Fu's list is Nayland Smith (once again played by Douglas Wilmer), who is duly kidnapped and transported to China for a terrible fate to be meted out at exactly the moment his double is executed in London—for the murder of Smith's maid. The story also involves Fu agreeing to lead a worldwide criminal empire at the request of various powerful crime lords from Europe, the U.S. and the Orient. Thanks, to a heroic FBI man (Noel Trevarthen), the real Smith is saved and, needless to say, Fu's evil plans are thwarted. The cast also includes Maria Rohm as a nightclub singer caught up in the proceedings.

The last two films, both international co-productions directed by prolific Spanish exploitation maestro Jess Franco, are cheap and uninspired efforts. *The Blood of Fu Manchu* (1968) was made on location in Spain and Brazil and finds the evil genius headquartered in an ancient lost city deep in the South American jungle. Having kidnapped ten beautiful women, Fu turns them into carriers of a deadly snake venom before sending them forth on worldwide missions to transmit the poison (via kissing) to his enemies. His first target is, predictably, Nayland Smith, played rather blandly by Richard Greene who takes over the role from here on. The wicked Fu also plans to wipe out the population of London with a poisonous cloud. Other characters in this mostly tedious yarn are Smith's South American agent (Götz George), a missionary (Maria Rohm) and a larger-than-life bandit (Ricardo Palacios) looking and acting like a character from a bad spaghetti western. Shirley Eaton's cameo as one of Fu Manchu's operatives appears to be unused footage from a different movie.

In *The Castle of Fu Manchu* (1968), the villain forces a dying scientist (Gustavo Re) to help develop a weapon that can instantly freeze large expanses of water. Having demonstrated his might to the world by sinking a passenger liner (using the weapon to create an iceberg for the vessel to collide with), Fu threatens further destruction unless the governments of the world declare subservience to him. The plot also involves Fu arranging a heart transplant—entailing the kidnapping of a cardiac surgeon (Gunther Stoll)—to keep the scientist alive. Set near the Bosphorus (Fu is this time headquartered in an Anatolian castle) and filmed on location in Istanbul and Spain, the film makes use of footage from other productions including earlier franchise entry *The Brides of Fu Manchu* and, for the ship-sinking sequence, tinted extracts from the black-and-white *Titanic* movie *A Night to Remember* (1958). Greene's performance as Nayland Smith is an improvement from the previous entry, but unfortunately neither he nor Christopher Lee can rescue the film, which secured its place in "bad movie" history by being featured in the cult comedy series *Mystery Science Theater 3000*.

More Towering Achievements

The busy Towers produced six other colorful British action-adventure thrillers during the 1960s, all featuring American leading stars and exotic locations. It's off to South Africa first for **Victim Five** (1964), in which a Cape Town copper magnate, Wexler (Walter Rilla), fears he's being targeted for death. As it happens, he had once murdered an engineer to get hold of the man's copper mining plans, and someone is now seeking revenge against him as well as others that helped cover up the crime. Tarzan returns to Africa, or rather, former "Ape Man" star Lex Barker plays a New York private detective summoned to Cape Town by Wexler to track down the avenger, only to have several attempts made on his own life in the process. Highlights are the stunning authentic locations (including a subterranean cave complex, and all beautifully captured by Nicolas Roeg's cinematography) and a hilarious performance by Ronald Fraser as a lustful police inspector. Danish actress Ann Smyrner plays Wexler's secretary, who hooks up romantically with Barker's handsome laconic hero.

Traveling about 1,500 miles northeast of *Victim Five*'s locale will get you to **Mozambique** (1964), the main setting for a far

U.S. publicity for producer Harry Alan Towers' 1964 Cape Town adventure *Victim Five* (1964).

an investigation regarding a murdered attorney and some mysterious bank accounts linked to a certain Colonel Valdez. Webster arrives to find that Valdez has just died from a supposed over-consumption of alcohol, although it's later revealed he had been poisoned with arsenic. Before long, he becomes embroiled in a power struggle (over Valdez's complicated business affairs) between Ilona (Hildegard Knef) and Da Silva (Martin Benson), Valdez's widow and right-hand man respectively, one of whom administered the arsenic. Smuggling, sex slavery, a dwarf assassin (whose stature enables him to blend in with a group of children so as to remain incognito during his murder of the aforementioned attorney) and a pretty nightclub singer are all included in the eventful plot, which features a spectacularly filmed climax at Victoria Falls. Cochran, who sadly died before the film's U.S. release, gives a nice relaxed performance, and there's a beautiful theme tune by Johnny Douglas. *The Daily Cinema* (August 4, 1965) concluded that, although overlong, the film "should hold the interest of all but the most blasé audiences."

The crew of a transatlantic airliner has ***24 Hours to Kill*** (1965) after their plane is forced to make an unscheduled landing in Beirut due to engine trouble. The purser, Jones (Mickey Rooney), becomes visibly nervous at being in the capital, and before long some shady individuals attempt to abduct him. It transpires that he had once worked for a murderous gold-smuggling

more convoluted story. The film begins in Lisbon, where a down-on-his-luck pilot, Brad Webster (Steve Cochran), is blackmailed by police chief Commarro (Paul Hubschmid) into accepting a job in the Portuguese province of Mozambique; in fact, Commarro plans to use him as a pawn in syndicate there, double-crossing them to the tune of £40,000, and they are now seeking revenge. Lex Barker, in his second and last film for Towers, plays the plane's captain who, with the rest of the crew, becomes involved in helping Jones avoid capture. Walter Slezak plays the syndicate boss in this rather unexciting adventure, which was originally shown in British cinemas in an edited down 83-minute version.

"A dispiritingly unoriginal enterprise that quite defeats the many talented people it involves" was how *Films and Filming* (August 1966) unflatteringly described **Our Man in Marrakesh** (1966). Among a group of visitors to the titular Moroccan city are two Englishmen (Wilfrid Hyde White and John Le Mesurier), a hapless American (Tony Randall) and a beautiful brunette (Senta Berger). One of them is secretly a courier who, acting on behalf of the Chinese, has a $2 million check for local racketeer Narim Casimir (Herbert Lom) as payment for the latter's part in a plot to influence the outcome of certain votes at an imminent United Nations assembly. The American soon becomes caught up in a dangerous adventure as a result of helping the brunette—actually a secret agent investigating the shady deal—after Casimir attempts to frame her for a murder. Legendary comedian and character actor Terry-Thomas, guest-starring as an Eton-educated sheik, is the highlight in this busy yarn, which also stars Klaus Kinski as Casimir's henchman and features a neat reveal regarding the courier's identity.

The titular **Five Golden Dragons** (1967), described by one character as "five of the most evil men the world has ever known," run a secret syndicate that controls the world's illicit gold market. The story is set in Hong Kong, where the dragons—so secretive they don't even know each other's identities—have arranged a meeting to dissolve their organization. The funny and ever-affable Bob Cummings (in what turned out to be his last big-screen role) stars as a hapless, happy-go-lucky playboy who gets innocently embroiled in a dangerous adventure surrounding the meeting. The largely incoherent plot also involves a duplicitous nightclub singer (a stunning Margaret Lee) and a Shakespeare-quoting British police commissioner (Rupert Davies). An estimable quartet of guest stars—Dan Duryea, Brian Donlevy, Christopher Lee and George Raft—appear briefly as four of the dragons, and there's a neat twist regarding the identity of the fifth. Good use is made of the colorful Hong Kong locations, and the handful of nightclub scenes are highlighted by Japanese star Yukari Ito's pleasant rendition of a pop ballad. The film's original British release was in the form of a heavily edited 70-minute version.

Having had considerable success with Sax Rohmer's Fu Manchu character, Towers turned to another of the author's creations—a Fu-type female known as **Sumuru** (1967). Shirley Eaton (usually blonde but here given a brunette makeover) proves a great casting choice as the beautiful sadistic villainess who, from her island headquarters in Hong Kong, is busy with plans for global domination. These include deploying a multitude of female agents who inveigle themselves into the lives of some of the world's most influential men with a view to controlling them. Americans Frankie Avalon and George Nader (the latter saddled with an abundance of unfunny one-liners) star as wealthy playboy Tommy Carter and his CIA buddy Nick West, whom we first see vacationing in Italy. The two men soon get on Sumuru's trail as the result of Nick reluctantly becoming entangled in a British Intelligence investigation concerning the female mastermind's plot to assassinate the president (Klaus Kinski) of a small Asian country. The adventure takes the two men (a minor twist has Tommy revealed as a British agent) to Hong Kong, where Sumuru captures Nick and blackmails him (in connection with a murder she'd framed him for in Italy) into helping bring about the assassination.

This campy hokum, which involves the

use by Sumuru and her minions of guns loaded with special bullets that turn men into statues, has the dubious distinction (in company with Towers' *The Castle of Fu Manchu*) of having been mocked in an episode of the cult comedy series *Mystery Science Theater 3000*. The alluring evildoer escapes the climactic destruction of her island fortress and would return, again played by Eaton, in Towers' 1969 Spanish/German/U.S. sequel *The Girl from Rio* (aka *Rio 70*). Towers was also majorly involved in a 2002 reboot, again titled *Sumuru*, which features the character (played by Alexandra Kamp) in a futuristic setting.

Alistair MacLean

Scottish-born Alistair MacLean (1922–1987) was a best-selling popular fiction novelist specializing in war, adventure and action stories, many of which were adapted for the big screen. Of the British-produced MacLean films, only six met the criteria for inclusion in this book; all are titled after their respective novels, with the first three also scripted by MacLean.

The war-espionage epic **Where Eagles Dare** (1968) is a perennial favorite among action-adventure fans, while also including plenty to satisfy devotees of complex spy thrillers. During World War II, MI6's top agent, Major Smith (Richard Burton), leads a seven-man team, including Lieutenant Schaffer (Clint Eastwood) of the American Ranger Division, on a mission to ostensibly rescue an important General from the headquarters of the German Secret Service in a Bavarian mountaintop fortress known as the "Castle of Eagles." Early on in the mission, two of the men are mysteriously murdered, while another three are captured and taken to the castle. This leaves only Smith and Schaffer, who go on to penetrate the fortress, whereupon we learn the real reason (so far known only to Smith) for the assignment: Smith is to pull off an ingenious deception to trick the resident Nazis and the three captured men—the latter actually German spies in league with their "captors" and who'd been attempting to sabotage (hence the two murdered men) what they'd been led to believe was the real mission—into revealing members of a German spy network in Britain, including the Nazis' top agent there.

A universally acclaimed classic of its kind, the film is a pure escapist war fantasy that's memorable for so many reasons, not the least of which are the stirring soundtrack by Ron Goodwin, some spectacular action set pieces (including a breathtaking fight between Smith and two of the spies atop a cable car during an eventual escape from the castle), a superbly sustained atmosphere courtesy of art director Peter Mullins, and Major Smith's legendary radio broadcast signal "Broadsword calling Danny Boy." Burton and Eastwood are terrific together, and there's a good role for Mary Ure as a close fellow agent of Smith's who provides invaluable help from inside the castle. The Nazi villainy is left in the more than capable hands of Derren Nesbitt, Anton Diffring and Ferdy Mayne (Nesbitt being particularly memorable as a slimy Gestapo officer), while other crucial roles are expertly filled by Patrick Wymark and Ingrid Pitt. MacLean wrote the novel and screenplay simultaneously.

When Eight Bells Toll (1970), based on MacLean's 1966 novel, is the author's only story set in his native Scotland. Filmed on stunning Western Highland locations, the plot concerns a ruthless gang involved in hijacking and sinking gold bullion-carrying ships, the contents of which are transferred to their base of operations, namely a castle high up on the cliffs of a small coastal island. The island's locals are aware of the nefarious activities, but the gang has ensured their silence by holding some of them hostage in the castle dungeon. Anthony Hopkins plays one of two investigating secret service agents (the other, played by Corin Redgrave, comes to a sticky end fairly early on) who eventually penetrates the castle and frees the hostages, with the gang being wiped out in an exciting gun battle. Accurately described by *Today's Cinema* (March 19, 1971) as "more second-rate James Bond than first-rate MacLean," the film also features Robert Morley in a humorous turn as a secret service chief, Ferdy Mayne as the gang's leader, Nathalie Delon as an enigmatic femme fatale and Derek Bond as a crooked shipping insurance underwriter.

Much more interesting is the vigorous **Puppet on a Chain** (1970), based on MacLean's 1969 novel and concerning a murderous Amsterdam drugs smuggling ring responsible for large quantities of heroin entering the United States. Swedish star Sven-Bertil Taube is well cast as Paul Sherman, a cool and ruthless American agent sent to the Dutch capital to smash the organization, which uses Bibles and souvenir puppets as containers to distribute the heroin. Also well cast is Polish actor Vladek Sheybal as one of the outfit's chief villains, a flamboyant and deadly character with a predilection for using chains to kill and hang his victims; one of these, a fellow agent of Sherman's, is played by Barbara Parkins in an all-too-brief role. The Amsterdam locations are used effectively, especially during an exhilarating and now legendary speedboat chase, and the proceedings are accompanied by a funky score courtesy of Italian composer Piero Piccioni. An eerie touch has murder victims' deaths being prefigured by puppets fashioned in their image, and there's a strong final twist involving a Dutch police inspector (Patrick Allen) and his supposedly mentally disabled niece.

> *"In the right hands, fear is the deadliest weapon of all"*

Filmed on location in Louisiana, **Fear Is the Key** (1972) stars Barry Newman in a tour-de-force performance as underwater salvage expert John Talbot. A large part of the story involves Talbot's clever infiltration

The legendary speedboat chase from the Amsterdam-set *Puppet on a Chain* (1970).

of a ruthless criminal organization responsible for downing a Dakota aircraft over the Gulf of Mexico, and who are planning to retrieve its cargo of $85 million in gold bars, emeralds and uncut diamonds. Talbot is in fact seeking justice for his wife, young son and brother, all of whom were on board the doomed Dakota. He finally succeeds during a claustrophobic and nail-biting climax in which he uses a submersible to take the criminal mastermind (John Vernon) and his creepy cohort (Ben Kingsley in his movie debut) to the wrecked plane on the Gulf floor, whereupon he cuts off the air supply until they are forced to confess. An excellent adaptation of MacLean's 1961 novel, the film features a lengthy car chase no doubt intended to capitalize on Newman's memorable automobile antics from the previous year's *Vanishing Point*, and also stars Suzy Kendall as a shady millionaire oilman's daughter used by Talbot in his infiltration scheme.

Based on MacLean's 1970 novel, **Caravan to Vaccarès** (1974) is set in Provence, France, and was described by *CinemaTV Today* (August 10, 1974) as "escapist excitement for the not-too-critical." An American adventurer, Neil Bowman (David Birney), is hired by the wealthy Duc de Croytor (Michael Lonsdale) to provide safe passage to New York for a mysterious Hungarian (Michael Bryant) later revealed to be a scientist with a secret formula destined for the United Nations. Marcel Bozzuffi, memorable as an assassin in *The French Connection* (1971), here plays a friend of de Croytor's who turns out to be the criminal mastermind behind various attempts (by his gang of murderous horsemen) to get hold of the scientist so as to access the formula for his own gain. Also starring are Charlotte Rampling as an English photographer getting caught up in the adventure after hitching a ride with Bowman, and French flamenco guitarist Manitas De Plata in a small but semi-key role (his one and only acting venture) as a doomed gypsy. Action highlights include a helicopter attack and a deadly encounter between Bowman and a bull in the mastermind's private bullring.

One of the least enjoyable MacLean adaptations (this time from a 1971 novel) is **Bear Island** (1979), in which the titular location—a real-life remote and barren Arctic isle—is depicted as having been the site of a German U-boat base during World War II. A star-studded cast, among them Donald Sutherland, Vanessa Redgrave, Richard Widmark and Christopher Lee, play participants (all with something to hide) in a United Nations scientific expedition to the island. Right from the outset, the expedition becomes plagued by murderous goings-on in connection with certain members of the group seeking a hidden cache of Nazi-plundered gold bullion for their own various purposes. A chase involving snow vehicles and murder by deliberately caused avalanche are among the very few excitements on offer in this slow and often confusing British-Canadian co-production filmed on striking locations in Alaska and British Columbia (and not on the real Bear Island itself). There's a good twist regarding one of the party being revealed as a neo–Nazi mastermind (codenamed "Zelda"), while the most memorable sequence involves the discovery of an old German U-boat, complete with the skeletal remains of its crew, in which the gold is hidden.

Other Action/Adventure Thrillers

"The torment of a man's split mind"

Fairly hard-hitting for its time, the melodramatic revenge-themed B movie **Cloudburst** (1951) was the first Hammer production to feature an American lead star, namely Robert Preston. The charismatic actor plays John Graham, an ex-commando and now Foreign Office cryptanalyst determined to avenge himself on two criminals (Sheila Burrell and Harold Lang) after they kill his pregnant wife Carol (Elizabeth Sellars) in a callous hit-and-run while fleeing from a robbery. The story involves the grief-stricken Graham tracking down and meting out savage justice on the villains using his car to run them down in the same manner as Carol had been. Preston is impressive in an emotionally charged performance, and the dependable Colin Tapley is on hand as a Scotland Yard inspector officially hunting down the villains and ultimately forced to go after vigilante Graham too.

Tapley also features (this time on the wrong side of the law as an unscrupulous doctor) in the eventful B movie *The Steel Key* (1952). The title refers to the name of a top-secret metal-hardening process worked on by two scientists, one situated in America and the other, Professor Newman (Esmond Knight), in England. The mysterious murder of the U.S.-based scientist is followed by the elaborate kidnapping of Newman—in an attempt to extract the formula from him—by a criminal organization headed by Dr. Crabtree (Tapley). Terence Morgan has the lead role as Johnny O'Flynne, a dashing and irrepressible "Saint"-style adventurer who tangles with the criminals in his own efforts to obtain the formula for reasons that are only hinted at in the particularly convoluted plot. Newman manages to escape, and all concerned end up in a confrontation aboard his yacht on the South Coast of England. Dianne Foster plays Newman's wife (actually a femme fatale in league with the kidnappers), whose death in mysterious circumstances is explained in a neat twist (involving Newman) which also clears up the mystery of the U.S.-based scientist's death.

In *The Gentle Gunman* (1952), John Mills and Dirk Bogarde play sibling IRA members Terence and Matt Sullivan. While in London as part of a cell engaged in blowing up subway stations, Terence renounces violence and quits the movement, only to be mistakenly suspected by Matt of informing on the group after two of their number are captured by police. As a gesture to prove his innocence, Terence plans and carries out a daring rescue of the captives from a Belfast jail, after which Matt aligns with him by also quitting the cause. This staunchly pro–British picture is well-acted by the two leads and also features a typically forceful Robert Beatty as an IRA chief. Some quaint comic relief comes courtesy of Joseph Tomelty and Gilbert Harding as a friendly Irish doctor and pompous Englishman respectively, who argue animatedly about British-Irish relations over amicable games of chess.

"Adventure at its boldest…. Bogart at his best!"

The last of several collaborations by director John Huston (who also co-scripted with Truman Capote) and star Humphrey Bogart, *Beat the Devil* (1953) is a real oddity that has achieved a certain cult status over the years. Plot-wise, it's unsatisfying and somewhat of a shambles, but there are enough offbeat characters and dryly humorous dialogue to keep up the interest. The story begins at an Italian port where various people are awaiting transport by steamship to Africa. Among them are four criminals (two of them played by Robert Morley and Peter Lorre) involved in an underhand uranium deal; a British would-be aristocrat Harry Chelm and his wife Gwendolen (Edward Underdown and Jennifer Jones); and Billy Dannreuther (a tired-looking Bogart), a roguish independent operator hired by the criminals to broker the uranium deal through a connection in British East Africa. The meandering narrative has Gwendolen falling for Dannreuther, while her proclivity for telling tall tales compromises her husband's safety (as regards the criminals) during the voyage. Also mixed into the proceedings are Dannreuther's alluring wife (Gina Lollobrigida, giving hands down the best performance) and a Scotland Yard detective (Bernard Lee) who ultimately nabs the crooks in connection with a murder in London. To some extent, the *Kinematograph Weekly* (November 26, 1953) was correct in saying that the film "really needs to be seen more than once before its wit can be fully appreciated."

Set in the English coastal town of Shoreham, **Dangerous Voyage** (1953) concerns a small unidentified sailing boat found drifting at sea by local brother and sister John and Joan Drew (Vincent Ball and Naomi Chance) while out cruising in their yacht, the *Gelert* (which features substantially in the story and actually belonged to the film's director Vernon Sewell). Hollywood's William Lundigan gives a nicely laid-back performance as a vacationing American thriller writer teaming up with the siblings to investigate the mystery vessel, hoping to get some inspiration for a new book. The three are soon entangled in a dangerous adventure surrounding the theft from a research laboratory of a sample of uranium derivative, which had been hidden by the thieves in the vessel's masthead. This enjoyable B movie features pleasant authentic locations (including in France, to where the investigating trio makes an excursion), and there's a brisk climactic sea chase culminating in a mini atomic explosion. The British pressbook told of how a real-life adventure unfolded when, while setting up the final shot, a drum filled with gelignite and dynamite broke free and began drifting back to shore; only through the efforts of Lundigan and director Sewell was the "mine" secured and a shattering beachside explosion averted.

Hammond Innes' 1949 novel *The White South* (also known in the U.S. as *The Survivors*) is the basis for **Hell Below Zero** (1953), in which Judie Nordahl (Joan Tetzel) travels to the Antarctic to investigate the death of her father, a partner in a whaling company. Alan Ladd, then still fresh in cinemagoers' minds from his performance in *Shane*, plays laconic adventurer Duncan Craig, who discovers that Judie's father was murdered by her old flame Erik (a dynamic Stanley Baker) as part of a plot to grab the old man's fortune. Erik's attempt to silence Craig leads

Ad for a 1954 chase thriller.

to plenty of exciting action starting with his ramming an icebreaker into the whale-catching vessel (called *Southern Truce* after a real-life whaler) on which Craig is serving as first mate; this is soon followed by a chase across frozen wasteland and a climactic battle in which the two men fight to the death with ice axes. Jill Bennett shines in her role as the *Southern Truce*'s captain, and viewers should be warned that the film contains graphic scenes depicting the capture and flensing of whales.

Filmed on location in Rhodesia but also relying heavily on stock footage and back-projection effects, **Duel in the Jungle** (1954) stars Dana Andrews as Scott Walters, an ace insurance investigator on the trail of a ruthless diamond merchant (David Farrar) he correctly suspects has faked his own death in Africa as part of a $2 million swindle. Jeanne Crain plays the merchant's fiancée, who becomes innocently caught up in the affair and inevitably falls for the heroic Scott. Things get off to a slow start, but the film soon gathers pace and culminates in an exciting 20-minute cat-and-mouse game between the two men highlighted by a couple of canoe chases filmed in the Katombora Rapids on the Zambesi river.

The B movie *Third Party Risk* (1954) was referred to by the *Monthly Film Bulletin* (May 1955) as "a somewhat dismal production." Lloyd Bridges gives a pleasant, laid-back performance as Philip Graham, an American songwriter trying to solve the murder of his old World War II flying buddy Tony (Peter Dyneley), killed in connection with some microfilm containing the formula for a new antibiotic drug. The film begins in southern Spain, where Philip and Tony are first reunited. The action then moves to London, where the murder occurs, and finally back to Spain where the killer, a wealthy industrialist (Finlay Currie), is apprehended after being tricked by Philip (with the help of a Spanish detective played by Roger Delgado) into making a confession. Maureen Swanson plays the industrialist's innocent niece, a folk dancer who finds romance with Philip, and the action highlight is an excellently staged fight in a burning warehouse. The film is mainly known in the U.S. as *The Deadly Game*, although some TV showings there went under the title *Big Deadly Game*.

"What is the mystery that surrounds the Green Buddha?"

Following a gang's theft of a valuable ancient artifact—**The Green Buddha** (1954)—from a London exhibition, one of the criminals, Tony Scott (Wolf Frees), pulls a double-cross and secures the antique for his and a secret partner's (Arnold Marle) own gain. Gary Holden (Wayne Morris), a charter plane pilot, finds himself competing with Scott's betrayed cohorts, led by Frank Olsen (Walter Rilla), when he tries to locate the Buddha himself, hoping to claim a reward to repair his plane (damaged when Scott attempted to force Gary to fly him out of the country). This lively B movie was filmed mainly in Hastings, and trivia buffs may be amused to know that while there, star Morris became the first American to receive membership of the Hastings Winkle Club and can be found listed, among luminaries such as Sir Winston Churchill, under "Famous Winklers" on their website. Mary Germaine plays a nightclub singer mixed up in the adventure, which culminates at London's Battersea Funfair where Olsen comes to a sticky end on a roller coaster.

The fast-paced Hammer Films B movie **Break in the Circle** (1954) stars Forrest Tucker as tough smuggler-adventurer Skip Morgan, captain of the high-powered cabin cruiser *Bonaventure*. An international financier, Baron Keller (Marius Goring), offers Morgan £2,000 in exchange for smuggling into England a man who has escaped from behind the Iron Curtain and become stranded in Hamburg without passport or papers. During the mission, Morgan finds that the man, actually a scientist and inventor of a valuable fuel formula, is being held by enemy agents intending to take him back

Forrest Tucker heads the cast as a rugged adventurer in the Hammer production *Break in the Circle* (1954).

into Soviet territory. Following many dangerous escapades, Morgan gets the scientist safely to England and, having realized that Keller wants to benefit from the formula, ups his price to £100,000. This leads to a tense showdown aboard the *Bonaventure*. Tucker makes a likeable hero, and the adventure also prominently involves an undercover Scotland Yard operative (Eva Bartok) and Morgan's sidekick (Reginald Beckwith). The film's original U.S. release was in a black-and-white 69-minute version.

A Prize of Gold (1955) stars Richard Widmark as Joe Lawrence, a U.S. Air Force sergeant stationed in Berlin's British sector. The first 30 minutes or so are taken up with Joe meeting and falling in love with Maria (Mai Zetterling), who oversees an orphanage within the ruins of the city and whose dream is to one day provide a new life for the children in Brazil. Then, in an effort to help Maria fund her dream, he gets mixed up in a plot to steal a consignment of recently discovered Nazi gold being flown to England via C-47 military transport aircraft. The first part of the plan, the hijacking of the C-47, is successful, but is soon followed by a series of setbacks beginning with the unintended destruction of the plane, and involving the psychopathic actions of one of Joe's accomplices, a flashy ex-RAF pilot played in show-stealing fashion by Nigel Patrick. The great cast also includes Donald Wolfit, as a former criminal reluctantly coming out of retirement to arrange the planned conversion of the gold into cash, and Eric Pohlmann as a sleazy businessman with the means to make Maria's dream come true but for a price she may be unwilling to pay. Widmark mentions the film while guest-starring as himself in the 1955 *I Love Lucy* episode, "The Tour."

Murder, mystery and romance combine in ***Beyond Mombasa*** (1956), which sees Matt Campbell (Hungarian-born Hollywood star Cornel Wilde) arriving in East Africa to join his brother George in connection with the latter's discovery of a possible uranium mine. Almost immediately, he is approached by Ralph Hoyt (Leo Genn), a soft-spoken missionary who informs him that George has been murdered by the "Leopard Men," a recently resurrected religious cult known for their violent opposition to white settlers. Ralph and his anthropologist niece (Donna Reed), as well as two of George's colleagues

(Christopher Lee and Ron Randell) and some native helpers, join Matt in an expedition to locate the mine. They eventually reach their destination, but not before being subjected to murderous attacks by the Leopard Men, about whose resurrection we learn the surprising truth in a fairly satisfying twist ending. Wilde is well cast as Matt, and his playful romantic advances toward Reed's standoffish anthropologist provide some light-hearted moments amid the mayhem. The authentic East African locations include the Gedi Ruins, which also feature in *Escape in the Sun*, another British thriller from the same year.

In the eventful B movie **Assignment Redhead** (1956), a gang of criminals led by Dumetrius (Ronald Adam) arrives in London on the trail of $12 million in counterfeit Nazi banknotes. Bit-part actor Alex Gallier has the most interesting (and substantially larger than usual) part as Max Rubenstein, an ex-informer for the Gestapo found to be in possession of the phony dollars. Rubenstein and Dumetrius agree to split the loot but then attempt to double-cross each other with disastrous consequences for Rubenstein. The low budget was nevertheless enough to pay for two U.S. stars, namely Richard Denning as an intelligence officer on the gang's trail and Carole Mathews as a doomed singer in the pay of Dumetrius. In the U.S., the film was distributed as *Million Dollar Manhunt*, while the *Assignment Redhead* title became the alternate name for another British thriller, 1957's *Undercover Girl*.

> "Power-packed suspense in the most dangerous car race in the world."

Warren Ingram (James Robertson Justice), a business tycoon and owner of a British racing team, has hired an adventurer named O'Donovan (Stanley Baker) to negotiate the acquisition of a new fuel intake design, whose blueprints are kept in a car manufacturing plant in Florence. However, things go horribly wrong when O'Donovan, having decided to break into the plant and steal the blueprints, kills a security guard and several policemen in the process and is forced to go on the run. This all happens within the first ten minutes of **Checkpoint** (1956), the remainder of which involves a scheme by Ingram to smuggle O'Donovan out of Italy by tricking one of his racing drivers (top-billed Anthony Steel) into using the fugitive as a co-driver in the Florence-Locarno race. Motor sport enthusiasts will delight in the authentic race footage involving a variety of classic cars and some beautiful Italian scenery.

Jack Havoc (a memorably menacing performance by Tony Wright) is the **Tiger in the Smoke** (1956), a psychopathic convict and ex-World War II commando who, under cover of a thick London fog, escapes from prison determined to find a letter—written by his now-deceased wartime commander—which reveals the hiding place of a priceless ancient treasure. Havoc doesn't actually make an appearance until over halfway through, and in the meantime the focus is mainly on Muriel Pavlow as the dead commander's widow and intended beneficiary of the treasure (although not if Havoc has anything to do with it), and Donald Sinden as her fiancé, to whom the letter has been bequeathed for reasons explained in the convoluted plot. Also involved are a group of shady street musicians (revealed as war veterans with ties to Havoc) who have their own designs on the loot. The three principal characters feature in the climax set in a French chateau, where the search for the treasure comes to a surprising conclusion. The film, whose highlight is a brilliantly filmed moment where Havoc jumps from a window and disappears into thick fog, and whose most disturbing moment is when the psychopath stabs a clergyman (Laurence Naismith) in the back, is based on Margery Allingham's 1952 novel *The Tiger in the Smoke*, which the *Monthly Film Bulletin* (January 1957) rightly referred to as "enjoyably confused."

A routine B movie from Butcher's Film

Productions, ***You Pay Your Money*** (1956) centers around wealthy financier Steve Mordaunt (Ivan Samson) and his extracurricular activity, namely the smuggling of rare and valuable books. Unbeknownst to him, his latest consignment of tomes includes two volumes of ancient Arabic prophecies sought by the League of the Friends of Arabia, a subversive organization led by the sinister Delal (Ferdy Mayne); in their hands, the prophecies could set the whole of the Middle East aflame by bringing about a jihad. Hugh McDermott is top-billed as Mordaunt's assistant, Bob Westlake, who tangles with the subversives after they kidnap his wife (Honor Blackman) during an attempt to steal the prophecies. Jane Hylton plays a friend of Mordaunt's in cahoots with the League, and the action is highlighted by a superbly staged fight scene between Westlake and a thug played by tough bit-part player and stuntman Larry Taylor.

"Dynamite for hire!!!"

In the first of his two British B thrillers, ***West of Suez*** (1956), *The Eddie Cantor Story*'s Keefe Brasselle plays Brett Manders, a mercenary explosives expert first introduced to us fighting an oil-well fire in the Middle East. He is subsequently hired by an organization of arms traffickers and saboteurs, headed by Langford (Karel Stepanek), to assassinate peace-loving Arab leader Ibrahim Sayed (Alex Gallier) during the latter's visit to London. The plan is to lay dynamite under a specific road over which Sayed's car will pass. The film, which *Today's Cinema* (February 5, 1957) called "a highly proficient piece of thriller entertainment," also stars Kay Callard as Brett's girlfriend, whose eventual intervention saves Sayed's life (at the cost of her own), and Harry Fowler as Brett's accomplice. A climactic clash between Langford and Brett (involving a gun and a grenade) decides both men's fate. Tom Weaver's book, *The Horror Hits of Richard Gordon* (Albany, GA: BearManor Media, 2011), reveals that Brasselle was all set to direct the picture, but the British trade union would not grant him a permit to do so. (Brasselle's name does, however, appear as director on U.S. publicity and supposedly also in the credits of U.S. versions of the film.) The book also reveals that, due to budget limitations, the film's opening oil-well fire sequence is actually footage from the U.S. movie *Wildcat* (1942) starring Richard Arlen.

Action of the Tiger (1957) stars Van Johnson as Carson, the wisecracking Athens-based skipper of a cabin cruiser who, apart from dealing in contraband, is also in the business of rescuing and repatriating Greek child hostages from Communist Albania. As the result of persuasion (including an offer of $10,000) by a young French woman (Martine Carol), Carson becomes involved in a plan to rescue a political prisoner (the woman's brother) from Albania, this leading to some dangerous confrontations with the Albanian secret police. The affable Johnson isn't as bad as many reviews have suggested, and the film, nicely shot in Cinemascope, also stars Herbert Lom as a bandit gang leader, while Sean Connery, later to play James Bond for the same director (Terence Young), appears in a small role as Carson's lusty first mate.

The thrilling and brilliantly staged ***Floods of Fear*** (1958) is set in northern Nevada, USA but was filmed in England's Pinewood Studios. When the Humboldt River bursts its banks, the resulting violent floods cause two convicts, Donovan and Peebles (Howard Keel and Cyril Cusack), their guard (Harry H. Corbett) and the attractive Elizabeth (Anne Heywood), to become stranded in the latter's partly submerged home. Donovan, actually an innocent man, soon begins building a raft in a plan to exact revenge on the man—his business partner Murphy (John Crawford)—who framed him for murder. A series of adventures, in which Elizabeth faces danger at the hands of the psychopathic Peebles (he wants his wicked way with her), and during which she and Donovan fall in love, lead to Donovan's

Anne Heywood watches as Howard Keel and Cyril Cusack duke it out in *Floods of Fear* (1958).

innocence being finally proven, but not before an exciting showdown with Murphy. Keel gives a muscular performance, and Heywood, thanks to the make-up department, always looks great despite all the dirty flood water. Both the editing and special effects are exemplary.

"A fortune in diamonds wrested from Hitler's invading armies."

A tough British Intelligence officer (Tony Britton) and two Dutch diamond experts (Peter Finch and Alexander Knox) embark on a dangerous mission in the World War II-set **Operation Amsterdam** (1959). Their task is to secure the titular city's large stocks of industrial diamonds and transport them out of the country so as to prevent them from falling into the hands of the imminently invading Nazis. With less than 24 hours to complete their mission, the team is forced to blow open a time-locked bank vault where many of the valuable stones have been stored. Superb location work and some well-choreographed action (including a fierce gun battle against Fifth Columnists) distinguish this fast-moving adventure, which also involves Dutch Resistance fighters and an employee (Eva Bartok) from the country's War Ministry.

Whirlpool (1959) stars iconic French actress and chanson singer Juliette Greco as Lora, a young beer hall waitress in Cologne, Germany, who for some time has been under the evil influence of a black marketeer named Herman (William Sylvester). Before long, Herman embroils Lora in cold-blooded murder and the two are forced to go on the run. They split up and agree to meet up in Amsterdam. However, Lora double-crosses Herman and heads for Strasbourg instead after persuading the charismatic captain, Rolph (O.W. Fischer), of a river barge to give her a ride. A romance gradually develops between Lora and Rolph, the latter ultimately helping the police in a plan to trap the pursuing Herman. The leisurely paced proceedings, which unfold against authentic Rhineland locations as well as in front of some decidedly poor back projection scenery, also feature Marius Goring and Muriel Pavlow as two of Rolph's crew members, namely a Dutchman and his frustrated (because she'd rather be with Rolph) wife.

The House of the Seven Hawks (1959), which the *Kinematograph Weekly* (November 19, 1959) charged with having "nearly as much talk as action," stars Hollywood legend Robert Taylor as charter boat skipper John Nordley. The intrigue begins when a Dutchman (Gerard Heinz) dies, apparently from natural causes, while being transported by Nordley to Holland. It's later revealed that the man had in fact been murdered and was a police inspector working undercover to recover a cache of diamonds; the gems had been looted—in a plan involving Nazi officer Captain Rohner (Eric Pohlmann)—from a bank in The Hague at the end of World War II and then lost after a boat carrying them was attacked by Dutch partisans. Nordley is soon embroiled in a dangerous adventure involving Rohner, who wants to retrieve the loot from its supposed resting place at the bottom of a river, and the murdered policeman's attractive daughter (Nicole Maurey). A surprising reveal regarding the diamonds occurs at a location known as the "House of the Seven Hawks" on said river.

Set in 1820s India, Hammer's **The Stranglers of Bombay** (1959) is loosely based on true events concerning the Kali-worshipping Thuggee (or Thug) cult, whose reign of terror (they robbed and murdered travelers before burying them in mass graves) purportedly claimed over two million victims. Guy Rolfe gives a rugged and commanding performance as a brave British East India Company officer who, as a result of his superiors' refusal to take the Thuggee problem seriously, hands in his resignation and goes after the cult on his own. The film, which would make a great double bill with Hammer's other historical thriller *The Terror of the Tongs* (1960), is masterfully directed by Terence Fisher and was quite strong stuff in its day. Allan Cuthbertson is perfect as a pompous and arrogant official, and George Pastell piles on the menace as the cult's high priest. The Thuggees were also the subject of a later British thriller, *The Deceivers* (1988).

The prologue to **The Treasure of San Teresa** (1959) is set during World War II: OSS agent Larry Brennan (Eddie Constantine), on behalf of a doomed Nazi general in league with the Allies, delivers a package to a Czechoslovakian convent wherein it is buried for safekeeping. Years later, circumstances see Larry team up with Rudi Siebert (Marius Goring) and Hedi Von Hartmann (Dawn Addams)—he a Hamburg lawyer and former aide of the general's and she the general's daughter—for a mission behind the Iron Curtain to retrieve the package, which we learn contains the Von Hartmann family jewels. However, the convent has since been turned into a People's Police barracks, and only after a daring break-in does the mission succeed. In ensuing events, Rudi double-crosses his partners and makes off with the treasure only to be then killed by a gang (there's a neat twist regarding their leader) that takes possession of the gems. A lively finale involves Larry attempting to reclaim the jewels aboard a speeding train. Released theatrically in the U.S. as *Hot Money Girl* but shown on TV there under its British title.

Originally conceived by producers Hammer as a TV series pilot, **Visa to Canton** (1960) has little to recommend it except perhaps the Technicolor photography, which initially went unseen in the U.S. due to a black-and-white-only theatrical release there. Don Benton (Richard Basehart), an American ex-fighter pilot and now boss of a Hong Kong travel agency, has been more or less adopted by a family whose matriarch, Mao Tai Tai (Athene Seyler), sheltered him during World War II. The story sees Benton embark on a mission to Canton with the aim of obtaining evidence that will clear Mao Tai Tai's grandson, who has been arrested on suspicion of colluding with the Communist Chinese. Also mixed up in the adventure are an alluring U.S. Intelligence operative (Lisa Gastoni) and a Russian Communist agent (Eric Pohlmann).

Hammer's other Oriental offering from the same year, the gruesomely entertaining *The Terror of the Tongs* (1960), is reminiscent of—and would make a great double-bill pairing with—the company's earlier historical shocker *The Stranglers of Bombay* (1959). Jimmy Sangster's original screenplay sets the story in Hong Kong, 1910, and concerns the Red Dragon Tong, a ruthless organization whose nefarious activities involve opium running, white slavery and protection rackets. Christopher Lee, in what looks like a dry run for his later Fu Manchu role, plays evil chief villain Chung King, while the hero of the piece is Jackson Sale (Geoffrey Toone), a merchant ship's captain seeking revenge after his daughter is murdered by the criminals. The grisly goings-on include stabbings, finger choppings and hatchet murders, but the most chilling moment comes when Jackson, captured by the Tong and about to undergo a particularly nasty form of torture, is asked by Chung King, "have you ever had your bones scraped, Captain?" Other key players include Marne Maitland as the leader of an underground anti–Tong movement and Yvonne Monlaur as a beautiful Tong slave who risks her life to help Jackson. Like *Visa to Canton*, the film was shot in color but had a black-and-white U.S. theatrical release.

Films and Filming (October 1963) correctly described the B movie *The Bay of Saint Michel* (1963) as "familiar stuff maybe, but quite well done all the same." Three British World War II veterans (Ronald Howard, Rona Anderson and Trader Faulkner) are summoned by their former American C.O. (a sinister-looking Keenan Wynn) to join him in a seafaring mission dubbed "Operation Mermaid." Supposedly set up by U.S. Naval Intelligence, the mission entails gathering the missing pieces of an old map that holds the location to $10 million worth of jewels, art treasures and gold bullion that was looted in occupied France and hidden by a now-deceased Gestapo officer. As it happens, one of the four adventurers is a traitor who had taken part in the looting and is planning to double-cross his comrades once the treasure is unearthed. Events lead to a dramatic climax on Mont Saint-Michel in Normandy, where the loot is found in a sealed vault within the island's medieval abbey. Pivotal to the story is a French female agent (Mai Zetterling) working for NATO Intelligence to expose the traitor, and she has very personal reasons for wanting to do so. The film, made in association with studios in Athens, was edited down to 73 minutes for its original British release.

A not dissimilar B movie, **Shadow of Treason** (1963), concerns a fortune in loot originally destined as payment to a group of traitors to the Allied cause during World War II, and which wound up hidden within a cavernous mountain—known as Lola Laquina—in East Africa by a now-deceased German Intelligence officer. An opening on-screen caption tells us "it started in Trieste," which is where we learn that Tina (Anita West), daughter of the aforementioned intelligence officer and proprietress of the Orso Bruno nightclub, has inherited a document containing a map pertaining to the hidden loot. This leads to the mounting of an expedition to Lola Laquina involving Tina and four others, namely the rugged Steve (John Bentley in his final film role), whom Tina has hired as a bodyguard following attempts on her life in connection with the document; two of the aforementioned traitors (John Gabriel and Ferdy Mayne), one of them wishing to destroy evidence of his guilt which is hidden with the loot; and the daughter (Egyptian star Faten Hamama) of another of the traitors. Plenty of danger and intrigue ensue in this entertaining British-Yugoslavian

Faten Hamama and John Bentley in *Shadow of Treason* (1963).

co-production directed by George Breakston, who collaborated with lead star Bentley several times including on another British thriller, *Escape in the Sun* (1956). The film was shortened to 77 minutes for its original British theatrical release, making the already confusing plot even more so.

> *"The fun begins when they take their cloak and daggers off!"*

Masquerade (1964) stars Jack Hawkins as Colonel Drexel, a cloak-and-dagger expert assigned by the British Government to protect—from possible assassination—a Middle Eastern prince (Christopher Witty) in connection with the renewal of certain British oil concessions. To assist him in the mission (which entails hiding the prince in a safe house in Spain), Drexel hires his old World War II comrade David Frazer, played by a laid-back Cliff Robertson. However, there's more to the story than meets the eye, for Drexel has a hidden agenda to abduct the prince and claim a ransom for his own gain.

It's interesting to hear Hawkins exchange dialogue with the similarly voiced Charles Gray (playing a government official), who would later dub for Hawkins after the latter lost his voice due to throat cancer. The attractive Marisa Mell plays one of Drexel's crooked associates, while the well-staged climax involves Frazer's dramatic rescue of Drexel and the prince from a collapsing rope bridge.

The setting for ***The High Bright Sun*** (1965) is late 1950s Cyprus, during the Greek Cypriot insurgency that led to the island gaining independence from the British. While staying with an old doctor friend (Joseph Furst) of her father's, Juno (Susan Strasberg), a visiting American student of Cypriot origin, discovers that her host is harboring a wanted guerrilla leader, Skyros (Gregoire Aslan), but doesn't let on that she knows. Partly because of her political neutrality, and partly through a sense of loyalty toward the doctor, Juno decides to not report the matter to her friend (and soon-to-be lover) Major

McGuire (Dirk Bogarde), a jaded British Intelligence officer. An impeccably groomed George Chakiris plays a fanatical young insurgent who's certain that Juno knows about Skyros and mistakenly believes that she plans to spill the beans, this leading to him organizing attempts—including a fierce assault on McGuire's apartment after she takes refuge there—on the young woman's life. Denholm Elliott has a fabulous supporting role as a world-weary but highly resourceful associate of McGuire's who proves invaluable in the latter's efforts to keep Juno safe.

The colorful locations in *Maroc 7* (1966) fail to compensate for a muddled script and unexciting direction. Louise Henderson (Cyd Charisse), editor of a fashion magazine and also an international jewel smuggler, arranges a photoshoot in Morocco as an excuse to locate an ancient and virtually priceless medallion, which she plans to smuggle out of the country. The ensuing adventure has many twists and turns as Louise finds she's not alone in the hunt for the treasure. Topping the bill is Gene Barry in a typically wooden performance as an undercover police agent inveigling himself into Louise's entourage in order to trap her, and the film also stars Leslie Phillips (who additionally co-produced) as one of Louise's accomplices (a murderous photographer) in a welcome departure from his usual comedy persona.

In *The Syndicate* (1967), set in Kenya, four prospectors—a taciturn American pilot (William Sylvester), an arrogant German (Christian Doermer), a belligerent alcoholic (Robert Urquhart) and the latter's bored wife (June Ritchie)—attempt to find a supposedly uranium-rich site in an area marked by a distinctive grouping of trees. One of the four is in fact a traitor intent on sabotaging the project on behalf of a gang, led by Dr. Singh (John Bennett), that plan to eventually take over the site. The unimaginatively used Kenyan locations, repetitive situations, dull and often confused script (the traitor's actions ultimately don't make any sense), not to mention a terrible performance by Doermer, make this almost unwatchable. The film was probably just as tedious in the heavily edited 63-minute version used for its original British theatrical release.

Set in Spain, *Fathom* (1967) features Raquel Welch at her most delightful as the eponymous heroine, Fathom Harvill, a frequently bikini-clad competitive skydiver referred to in publicity as "the world's most

Raquel Welch at her most charming and beautiful as the titular skydiver *Fathom* (1967).

uncovered undercover agent" and a "skydiving darling built for action!" The plot revolves around the Fire Dragon, a priceless figurine from the Ming dynasty that was stolen from a Peking museum and has remained lost ever since a plane on which it was being transported crashed into the Mediterranean. The man responsible for the theft (Ronald Fraser) tricks Fathom (by making her believe she's carrying out a mission for NATO Intelligence) into helping recover the figurine, which leads our heroine into a series of amusing escapades that also involve a charming detective (Anthony Franciosa), hired by the Chinese to return the ancient artifact to its rightful home, and an eccentric Armenian yacht-owning millionaire (Clive Revill) with his own designs on the antique. The fun antics are occasionally campy, although not as much as one might expect considering the director's previous film had been the ultra-campy TV series spin-off, *Batman* (1966).

> "The most exciting adventure on Earth is under it!"

In the goofy but undeniably entertaining **Battle Beneath the Earth** (1967), a rogue Chinese general (Martin Benson) and his private army are busy implementing a plan (which will involve the atomic destruction of strategic military and civilian locations) to take over the United States by way of three deep tunnel complexes created with powerful laser boring machines. Kerwin Mathews is suitably heroic as a military commander leading the resistance with the aid of a young geologist (Viviane Ventura) and an old scientist friend (Peter Arne), the latter initially disbelieved—not to mention deemed insane—after stumbling on the plot. (A neat pre-credits sequence shows the scientist with his ear plastered to a Las Vegas sidewalk declaring, "they're crawling under us I tell you, just like ants.") The adventure, which the *Monthly Film Bulletin* (February 1969) referred to as "schoolboy comic-strip capers," culminates in a mushroom cloud finale as the enemy's crucial sub–Pacific supply tunnel is destroyed by one of their own atomic devices.

Based on Wilbur Smith's 1965 novel *Dark of the Sun* (the film's U.S. title), **The Mercenaries** (1967) is a crackerjack Anglo-American production set during a time of political turmoil in the Congo. Rod Taylor, in a role he was born to play, stars as Captain Bruce Curry, a tough-as-nails mercenary leading a mission to rescue stranded civilians from Port Reprieve, an isolated town under threat from approaching rebel Simbas. However, a more pressing aspect of the mission, at least as far as concerns the Congolese president (he needs the funding), is to retrieve $50 million worth of diamonds from a vault in the town's bank. Upon reaching the town, it's discovered that the vault is time-locked and cannot be opened for three hours, resulting in serious trouble when the Simbas show up.

Taylor is reunited with his *Time Machine* co-star Yvette Mimieux, who plays the token female character (the survivor of a Simba attack picked up by the mercenaries en route) in an otherwise male-dominated film. Apart from Taylor, those males include Jim Brown, as Curry's idealistic USC-educated Congolese sidekick, and Peter Carsten as a loathsome psychopathic ex-Nazi deemed vital to the mission but who ends up causing all sorts of mayhem, including a murderous attempt to grab the diamonds for himself. Much of the action features a specially equipped steam train on which the soldiers of fortune travel; one terrifying moment comes when the train's final carriage becomes detached and begins rolling downhill, sending its occupants (mostly made up of rescued townspeople) into the hands of bloodthirsty Simbas. Curry and the ex-Nazi feature in two well-choreographed and brutal fight scenes, one of which memorably involves a chainsaw.

A Twist of Sand (1968) concerns an expedition to South West Africa's Skeleton Coast to retrieve a cache of diamonds hidden there by a now-deceased geologist. Those involved include smuggler Geoffrey Peace (Richard Johnson), an ex-naval officer familiar with the Skeleton Coast through having carried out a grim mission there during World War II; Harry Riker (Jeremy Kemp), a wartime colleague of Geoffrey's who learned about the existence of the diamonds from the geologist; the geologist's widow (Honor Blackman), who knows the exact location (within the wreckage of an old galleon) of the gems; and a violent imbecilic German (Peter Vaughan) with a surprising connection to Geoffrey's wartime mission. Riker's ultimate attempt to double-cross the others leads to deadly chaos in this unexciting Harry Alan Towers–style yarn whose characters never quite come alive.

"Unshakable!"

Charles Salt and Chris Pepper, amusingly referred to as the "middle-aged cruet couple" by *Films and Filming* (January 1969), are the trendy owners of the swanky "Salt and Pepper" nightclub in London's Soho district. Played by Sammy Davis, Jr., and Peter Lawford respectively, the likeable pair feature in two swinging sixties comedy thrillers. In the first, **Salt & Pepper** (1968), information from the diary of an agent found murdered in their club leads to Salt and Pepper stumbling on and ultimately foiling a plot by Colonel Woodstock (John Le Mesurier), leader of a revolutionary group, to overthrow the British Government and install his own puppet regime. Davis and Lawford look like they're having fun in this enjoyably zany but instantly forgettable piece of fluff. A running gag involves a bumbling police inspector (Michael Bates) repeatedly falling victim to explosive devices intended by the villains to dispatch our heroes.

More condiment capers followed in **One More Time** (1969), which the *Monthly Film Bulletin* (January 1971) called a "turgid sequel." This time around, the story has Pepper impersonate his titled identical twin brother Sydney (also played by Lawford) after the latter, working as an agent for Interpol, is murdered by a gang of jewel smugglers he'd double-crossed out of a haul of diamonds. The majority of this painfully unfunny adventure sees Salt and Pepper caught up in intrigue at the Pepper family estate—"Pepperworth Castle"—in Scotland, where the smugglers, believing they killed the wrong brother, attempt to correct the mistake and retrieve their diamonds. The movie, which features a brief and out-of-left-field scene in which Peter Cushing and Christopher Lee cameo as their most famous characters (namely Baron Frankenstein and Count Dracula), is notable as being the only feature film directed by comic legend Jerry Lewis in which he himself doesn't appear.

"Experts in the dying art"

Set in 1906, **The Assassination Bureau Limited** (1968) is a colorful romp with Oliver Reed starring as Ivan Dragomiloff, chairman of the titular organization—comprising a secret international group of aristocratic assassins—which he inherited from his father. Dragomiloff has become somewhat disillusioned with the bureau, which was originally set up to correct injustices but has since become less moral and more commercially motivated. An ambitious reporter, Sonya Winter (Diana Rigg), having uncovered the existence of the murderous organization, and determined to bring about its downfall, takes the unusual step of commissioning Dragomiloff to put a contract out on himself, figuring that killing him will "kill" the bureau. Dragomiloff surprisingly agrees, seeing this as a chance to clean house. At a meeting, he accuses the bureau's assassins of lacking idealism and being no more than common murderers; after explaining to them that he is to be their latest target, he warns that if they don't kill him first, then he will kill them, thus enabling the bureau to start afresh with its original moral intent. This leads to a zany cat-and-mouse game between Dragomiloff and the assassins that spans various European locations, and during which Dragomiloff and Sonya fall in love.

Reed and Rigg were at the height of their careers and have great chemistry, and Telly Savalas is on excellent form as one of the assassins, Lord Bostwick, a newspaper magnate and political megalomaniac with designs on the bureau for his own ends. Events culminate in a hectic climax involving Bostwick's attempt to kill (by dropping a bomb from a Zeppelin) various crowned heads of Europe gathered at a peace conference. The source novel of the same name had been started by Jack London in 1910 and was finally completed by Robert L. Fish in 1963.

Set in Ireland, **The Violent Enemy** (1969) is a rather dull IRA thriller based on a Jack Higgins novel of the same name (aka *A Candle for the Dead* under Higgins' pseudonym Hugh Marlowe). Ed Begley plays a fanatical old-time IRA boss who engineers the escape of a former collaborator, explosives expert Sean Rogan (Tom Bell), from a British jail and then blackmails the now peace-loving man into masterminding the bombing of an electronics factory in an effort to keep the Republican cause alive. In an unexpected development, two particularly unpleasant British criminals (Jon Laurimore and Michael Standing), whose job is to carry out the actual bombing, are found to have their own hidden agenda to rob the factory's payroll in the process. Susan Hampshire (complete with unconvincing Irish accent) plays a pretty patriot mixed up in the proceedings. Not bad overall, but nothing special.

Set mostly in London, **Crossplot** (1969) begins at daybreak on a deserted Westminster Bridge—deserted, that is, except for a young Englishman, Sebastian (Tim Preece), and his friend Marla Kougash (Claudie Lange), a Hungarian model. Before long, mysterious assassins turn up looking to kill the couple, who they believe (correctly in the case of Sebastian) have learned too much about a certain conspiracy. Marla gets away in a passing car full of revelers after being handed a newspaper by Sebastian, who is presently murdered by the assassins. The "cross" in *Crossplot* refers to said newspaper's crossword puzzle in which Sebastian has filled in two words—nothing to do with the actual crossword—intended to convey details about the conspiracy to a key member (a reluctant aristocrat played by Alexis Kanner) of a pacifist group known as the Marchers for Peace. The "plot" in *Crossplot* refers to the conspiracy in question, namely a plot by a shadowy and powerful anarchist organization to assassinate a visiting African statesman during a royal event in London's Hyde Park. The plotters subsequently use Gary Fenn (Roger Moore), an advertising executive, as a pawn in their efforts to track down Marla, but he ends up protecting her and eventually deduces the significance of the two puzzle words, leading to the assassination being foiled in the nick of time.

Bernard Lee and Martha Hyer play the chief plotters, the latter a TV producer (Marla's aunt as it happens) under whose setup the assassination is to be carried out by way of a high-powered gun concealed in a television camera. The Westminster Bridge opening sequence is brilliantly executed and one which the mostly light-hearted film subsequently never quite manages to live up to. As far as action goes, the highlight is a chase involving a vintage car and a helicopter, although this, like several other parts of the movie, is marred by some truly awful back projection effects. This was Moore's return to the big screen following many years as TV's *The Saint*, and was produced by that series' Robert S. Baker; in fact, the story is reminiscent of the type of material found in many episodes of *The Saint*, not to mention Moore and Baker's later series, *The Persuaders!*, and is no more or less entertaining. In other words, it's great fun and essential viewing for fans of the great Roger Moore.

In their review of cult director Pete Walker's low-budget **Man of Violence** (1969), the *Monthly Film Bulletin* (July 1970) duly noted that "the general level of the acting matches the inanity of the script." The convoluted story concerns property tycoon Bryant's (Derek Francis) plan to smuggle £30 million of gold bullion into England from a Middle Eastern state that he helped overthrow through arms sales. Grayson (Maurice Kaufmann), a protection racketeer and former partner of Bryant's, learns about the gold and intends to grab it for himself. Caught up in the dangerous intrigues is Moon (Michael Latimer), a cynical freelance crook who has been employed by each man to act against the other. Also in the cast are Luan Peters as Moon's love interest (a key character in the proceedings) and Derek Aylward as a supposed representative of Bryant's but actually an unscrupulous undercover MI5 agent whose actions lead to a particularly bleak and downbeat conclusion. Apart from as *Man of Violence*, the movie was originally also submitted to the British Board of Film Censors under the title *The Sex Racketeers*, but doesn't appear to have ever been released as such.

A tough but unengaging revenge thriller, ***The Last Grenade*** (1969) sees British mercenary Harry Grigsby (Stanley Baker) on the trail of Kip Thompson (Alex Cord, hamming it up outrageously), a psychopathic fellow soldier of fortune who ruthlessly double-crossed him during a mission in the Congo. Most of the action takes place in Hong Kong, where Thompson is busy leading Chinese Red Guards in cross-border terrorist activities, and where Grigsby decides to give up his vendetta after falling in love with the wife, Katherine (Honor Blackman), of a Hong-Kong based British general (Richard Attenborough). However, in a jarring development, Thompson forces Grigsby's hand by causing Katherine's death, leading to a final confrontation in which the film's title is explained. Andrew Keir and Julian Glover play two of Grigsby's loyal aides, and the several action set pieces are well handled, none more so than the explosive pre-credits sequence where the double-crossing Thompson commits the atrocity (a single-handed wiping out of most of Grigsby's battalion with a machine gun) that fueled the vendetta in the first place.

While not quite the "ultimate exercise in controlled terror" promised by the film's publicity, ***The Black Windmill*** (1974) is nevertheless an engaging and frequently tense offering from legendary director Don Siegel. The complex plot involves a British Intelligence agent, John Tarrant (Michael Caine), who becomes a pawn in a scheme to get hold of £500,000 worth of uncut diamonds being held by his department. Masterminded by a senior government official (Joseph O'Conor) in league with a gang of gunrunners (headed by John Vernon at his menacing best), the scheme entails first kidnapping Tarrant's young son (holding him captive in the titular edifice near Brighton) and then manipulating Tarrant into stealing the diamonds to use as ransom. Some good action, which includes the son's climactic rescue from the windmill, is punctuated by Roy Budd's exciting score, while the excellent cast also includes Janet Suzman as Tarrant's estranged wife and a mustachioed Donald Pleasence as his fastidious and dispassionate boss.

"Everything they touch turns to pure excitement!"

Co-scripted by Wilbur Smith from his own 1970 novel *Gold Mine*, ***Gold*** (1974) begins with a stirring title song that sets the tone for an exhilarating yarn in which a consortium of international businessmen conspires to flood the Sonderditch gold mine in South Africa (at the potential cost of many lives) so as to manipulate the price of the precious metal to their own financial advantage. One of the conspirators is Sonderditch executive Manfred Steyner (Bradford Dillman), married to the granddaughter (Susannah York) of the mine's owner-chairman (Ray Milland). Roger Moore, in between his first two James Bond outings, heads the cast as a heroic mining manager used as a pawn by Manfred to bring about the disaster, but who instead ends up saving the day. A romance between Moore and York's characters does nothing but slow down the film, which is at its best during some gritty, claustrophobic and superbly staged scenes in the mine. Milland has one of his more entertaining 1970s roles as the gruff magnate, but it's Dillman who steals the show with a terrific performance as the obsessive (due to a pathological fear of germs) and ruthless Manfred; in one of the more memorable sequences, he is brutally murdered by being run down with his own Rolls Royce driven by a particularly disgruntled accomplice (Tony Beckley).

Filmed on authentic French locations, The Franco-British co-production *The Marseille Contract* (1974) proved to be the last feature film directed by veteran Robert Parrish. Steve Ventura (Anthony Quinn), a senior narcotics agent in charge of a U.S. DEA bureau in Paris, becomes targeted for death by Marseille-based drug kingpin Jacques Brizard (James Mason), whose racket he has been trying to bust. In a desperate and unorthodox move, Steve takes $50,000 from a secret DEA fund and pays a professional hit man (Michael Caine) to bring down Brizard once and for all. Despite the presence of three heavyweight stars, the film remains a dull and by-the-numbers affair that aspires to *The French Connection* and is not unlike dozens of early 1970s thrillers in the Euro-crime genre. Highlights are a chase in the Paris subway (that concludes in the cavernous Gare D'Orsay building) and a nifty sequence in which two cars engage in a playful dance-like race to

A great cast was assembled for this 1974 British-French co-production.

the strains of a waltz by composer Roy Budd. Among the French cast members is Maurice Ronet as a double-dealing cop who attempts to cheat Brizard in connection with a shipment of morphine base.

Another co-production, this time between Britain and Germany, *The Odessa File* (1974) is a first-rate adaptation of Frederick Forsyth's best-selling novel with an engaging lead performance by Jon Voight. In Hamburg, 1963, journalist Peter Miller (Voight) resolves to track down Eduard Roschmann (Maximilian Schell), an ex-SS concentration camp commandant who disappeared after World War II and was responsible for the murder of Miller's father, a distinguished German officer. By infiltrating Odessa, an organization whose activities include supplying former SS officers with new identities, Miller secures vital intelligence regarding his quarry, this leading to an exciting climactic showdown between the two men. An impressive supporting cast includes Peter Jeffrey as an Israeli Intelligence chief (in a subplot concerning Odessa's development of missile technology for Egypt to use against Israel), while a thrilling highlight is an attempt on Miller's life by an Odessa assassin in the Hamburg metro.

Set in Scandinavia, the tortuously plotted **Ransom** (1974) begins with the kidnapping of a British ambassador by terrorists led by Martin Shepherd (John Quentin). Shortly after, a passenger plane is hijacked by Ray Petrie (Ian McShane), whose actions make it appear that he's in league with Shepherd and that he has secured the airliner for the terrorist's getaway. Sean Connery plays Nils Tahlvik, the head of Norwegian Security who has to deal with both the kidnapping and the hijacking, the latter turning out to be part of a plan by British Intelligence to trap Shepherd. However, Tahlvik has not been made aware of the plan, and his subsequent actions threaten the entire operation. Not even the excellent Connery and McShane can save what *Leonard Maltin's Movie Guide* rightly called a "muddled thriller."

Filmed in Kenya but set in South Africa, **The Wilby Conspiracy** (1974) is essentially an apartheid-era road movie. The story begins in Cape Town, where black revolutionary Shack Twala (Sidney Poitier), having just been released from 10 years imprisonment on Robben Island, goes on the run with the English boyfriend (Michael Caine) of his Afrikaner attorney (Prunella Gee) following a situation in which the two men are forced to beat up a pair of thuggish cops. The fugitives head to Johannesburg, from where Shack hopes to retrieve £750,000 in uncut diamonds (hidden before his imprisonment) and deliver them to Botswana where they will be used by the Nelson Mandela–like Wilby Xaba (Joseph De Graf) to fund an anti-apartheid movement known as the Black Congress. Poitier and Caine have great chemistry, with their initially uneasy alliance providing some amusingly sarcastic dialogue. However, it's Nicol Williamson who steals the acting honors as a pursuing Bureau of State Security officer with a hidden agenda concerning Wilby. Rutger Hauer has a small but pivotal role as the attorney's soon-to-be ex-husband, and there are a couple of surprising twists involving the diamonds.

Fans of Stuart Whitman, particularly when it comes to the ruggedly handsome actor's 1970s work, should not be disappointed by his performance as the eponymous Washington-funded contract killer, **Shatter** (1974). The film begins with Shatter carrying out a "hit" in Africa and then arriving in Hong Kong to collect his fee. However, it transpires that he'd been tricked into the assassination by a crime syndicate headed by Hans Leber (Anton Diffring); the victim was a puppet dictator who'd been supplying the syndicate with opium in return for arms. Leber has no intention of paying Shatter and instead orders some murderous attacks against the man in an attempt to retrieve a list (containing addresses of laboratories where the opium is processed) that he'd secured during the assignment. Like the same year's *The Legend of the 7 Golden Vampires*, this was a co-production by Hammer Films and the Hong Kong–based Shaw Brothers designed to cash in on the martial arts craze of the early 1970s; to this end, there are several well-choreographed fight scenes that mostly involve a character named Tai Pah (Ti Lung) who becomes Shatter's bodyguard. Whitman is perfect as the tough, world-weary assassin, and Peter Cushing (in his final film for Hammer) has a "guest star" role as an unscrupulous British security agent.

> *"When they did this to Hennessy, they signed a death sentence for the nation!"*

The somewhat mechanical and uninvolving **Hennessy** (1975) begins in Northern

Ireland's capital of Belfast in 1972, against a backdrop of heightened civil unrest. The title refers to pacifistic Irishman Niall Hennessy (Rod Steiger), an explosives and demolitions expert who once served with the British in the North African campaign during World War II. However, his pacifism goes out the window after his wife and daughter are killed by reckless gunfire from a British soldier during a typical Belfast street riot. To get back at the British, Hennessy travels to London, where he prepares to assassinate Queen Elizabeth by way of a suicide bombing during a ceremonial speech to be delivered by the monarch at the Houses of Parliament (the film's working title was *To Kill a Queen*). Steiger is reunited with his former *No Way to Treat a Lady* co-star, Lee Remick, who plays a London-based IRA widow providing Hennessy with shelter, while Richard Johnson (he also supplied the original story) portrays a belligerent Scotland Yard Special Branch officer. A major plot strand involves the efforts of Tobin (Eric Porter), an IRA head honcho and old friend of Hennessy's, to thwart the latter's plan, which if successful would result in irreparable damage to the IRA's cause. Real news footage of the Queen, which was not intended for use in a fictional context, was nevertheless incorporated into the movie, leading the filmmakers to add an opening disclaimer making it clear that the Royal Family took no part in the making of the picture.

The British-German co-production *Inside Out* (1975) is an enjoyable caper which, as noted by *Variety* (October 8, 1975), "doesn't take itself too seriously, and in fact plays for laughs as much as suspense." A former U.S. Army major (Telly Savalas), his ex-con pal (Robert Culp) and a one-time German prisoner-of-war camp commandant (James Mason) are the main players in a plan to locate a fortune in gold bars hidden by the Nazis in 1944. The first part of the operation entails extracting a convicted Nazi war criminal (the only person to know the exact location of the gold) from a high-security West Berlin prison; the second part sees the men on a mission to retrieve the booty from East Germany, this becoming fraught with problems beginning with their discovery that an apartment block has since been built over the hiding place. The three leads seem to be enjoying themselves here, with Savalas in particularly good form, and there are plenty of twists and turns en route to a

Publicity for an entertaining 1975 British-German co-production.

satisfying conclusion. The cast also features Aldo Ray in one of his better 1970s performances as the gang's inside man (a U.S. Master Sergeant) at the aforementioned prison. Over the years, the film was shown on U.S. TV under the titles *Inside Out*, *Hitler's Gold* and *The Golden Heist*.

> *"An outrageous band of modern day knights call it honor.... The police call it murder!"*

"The Knights of Avalon," a chivalric society originally founded to preserve the customs of the Middle Ages, has been taken over by Sir Giles Marley (Donald Pleasence) and is now being used as a vehicle for meting out vigilante justice (via ritual execution using medieval weapons) upon criminals the judicial system has failed to punish. Such is the premise of **Trial by Combat** (1975), a daftly entertaining and barely remembered film in which Peter Cushing puts in a brief pre-credits appearance as the society's founding father, Sir Edward Gifford, who is murdered by the Knights after stumbling upon their illegal activities. Involved in bringing down the corrupted organization are an eccentric former police commissioner (John Mills), Gifford's son (David Birney) and an architectural student (Barbara Hershey). A more fitting title for the film was the amusing *Dirty Knights' Work*, which was used for its principal U.S. release.

Mills also features in **The "Human" Factor** (1975), a violent revenge movie hot on the heels of the previous year's *Death Wish*. Made on location in Italy, the film stars George Kennedy as John Kinsdale, an American NATO official in Naples who resolves to find the terrorists that murdered his family. A helpful colleague (Mills) and some advanced computer technology play a part in the identification of chief terrorist Hamshari (Frank Avianca), whose plan is to periodically murder American families until his political demands are met. Later events see Hamshari and his cronies seize a NATO supply store and hold the customers hostage, but it's not long before Kinsdale turns up to mete out brutal justice. The film, capably directed by Edward Dmytryk (it was his last full-length feature), benefits greatly from Kennedy's strong presence.

Director John Sturges' final film was the star-studded World War II thriller **The Eagle Has Landed** (1976), an adaptation of Jack Higgins' 1975 novel of the same name. Set in 1943, the simple and well-handled plot involves a crack squad of German paratroopers—led by Steiner (Michael Caine)—sent into England to kidnap Winston Churchill from a quiet coastal village through which he is scheduled to pass. Posing as allied Polish soldiers on training maneuvers, the paratroopers' cover soon gets blown and they end up in conflict with U.S. Army Rangers stationed nearby. Donald Sutherland gives a heavily stereotyped performance as a roguish Irish adventurer in league with the Germans, and the film wastes valuable time on his unconvincing romance with a local girl played by Jenny Agutter. Larry Hagman is great as a blundering gung-ho American colonel who meets a memorably sticky end at the hands of an evil enemy sleeper agent (Jean Marsh), and there's a neat twist ending in which Steiner shoots Churchill dead—or does he?

An interesting international cast features in **One Away** (1976), the third and final collaboration (see also *Deadly Strangers* and *Diagnosis: Murder*) between director Sidney Hayers and producer Peter Miller through the latter's Silhouette Film Productions. Filmed in South Africa in association with South African business entrepreneur Tony Factor, the straightforward story concerns the escape of convicted gypsy Tam Bass (Patrick Mower) from a hard-labor prison camp, whereupon a prearranged plan to get him out of the country is put into motion. The scheme involves Tam's two brothers, Ruben and Pete (Bradford Dillman and Dean Stockwell), and female fixer Elsa (Elke Sommer), and entails lots of motorbike riding in efforts to avoid the pursuing authorities. The motorcycle scenes are well handled, with real-life biking enthusiast Stockwell appearing to be the only cast member to do at least some of his own stunt riding, while top-billed Dillman looks like he's having a lot of fun as by far the film's most colorful character. There's a slight subplot involving Tam's capricious wife (Roberta Durrant), and events lead to a somewhat unexpected ending amid a full-on manhunt across the veldt. Talking to Peter Noble in *Screen International* (February 14, 1976), producer Miller extolled the virtues of filming in South Africa, saying he'd "never had a more easy or enjoyable location."

Suggested by the book *Coup d'État: A Practical Handbook*, by political scientist Edward N. Luttwak, the British-Canadian co-production **Power Play** (1978) gives a fascinating insight into the planning and ultimate execution of a military coup. The setting is an unnamed totalitarian republic, and key players in the overthrow are portrayed by David Hemmings, Barry Morse and Peter O'Toole, the latter as an enigmatic tank commander, Colonel Zeller, central to the satisfyingly bleak twist ending. Overall, the film is not as gripping as it might have been, this partly due to flat characterizations with the exception of Donald Pleasence who, as the head of Secret Police, displays none of his familiar quirky traits and is all the more chilling for it. Filmed in Germany and Toronto.

"The dogs of war ... the best damn mercenaries in the business!"

A British-Swiss enterprise expertly produced by Euan Lloyd, **The Wild Geese** (1978) is a rattling good yarn in which a hardened mercenary, Allen Faulkner (Richard Burton), is hired to spearhead the rescue in Africa of a deposed, imprisoned Nelson Mandela–like head of state (Winston Ntshona). The mission is being financed from London by smooth multimillionaire merchant banker Sir Edward Matheson (Stewart Granger) and is tied in with protecting some of his African copper mining concessions. Faulkner and just over four dozen other specially chosen mercenaries, the cream of which are skilled pilot Shawn Fynn (Roger Moore), expert planner Rafer Janders (Richard Harris) and ex-South African Defence Force officer Pieter Coetzee (Hardy Kruger), complete the rescue with relative ease. However, at the last minute, when the mission no longer has any value to him, Sir Edward—anticipating a similar move by Charles Napier's Marshall Murdock in *Rambo: First Blood Part II* (1985)—calls off a planned extraction flight, leaving the mercenaries stranded and at the mercy of bloodthirsty Simba troops. Eventually, after suffering many casualties, the team makes it to safety. Three months later, Faulkner visits the treacherous Sir Edward to exact revenge.

Magnificently entertaining, this slam-bang combat thriller has achieved classic status not only through the suspenseful and superbly staged action scenes, but also for the character development afforded the main mercenaries portrayed by the illustrious quartet of Burton, Moore, Harris and Kruger. The first three in particular have a great repartee, and having got to know them so well makes it all the more affecting when Harris' character finds himself in a similar predicament to Frank Sinatra's Colonel Ryan in the climax of *Von Ryan's Express* (1965), except here it involves trying to reach the safety of a departing aircraft instead of a train. Many of the other (mostly aging) mercenaries are played by a variety of familiar British character actors such as Kenneth Griffith, Ronald Fraser, Percy Herbert and Jack Watson, the latter standing out as a drill-sergeant whipping the men into shape. There's a rousing score by Roy Budd, and the film's opening and closing credits feature a soulful rendition by Joan Armatrading of the evocative theme song "Flight of the Wild Geese." In the sequel of sorts, *Wild Geese II* (1985), Edward Fox plays Faulkner's brother in a story about mercenaries hired to spring Rudolf Hess from Berlin's Spandau Prison.

Adapted from Ira Levin's 1976 novel of

the same name, the Anglo-American blockbuster *The Boys from Brazil* (1978) is an exciting if far-fetched tale in which even one of the characters asks "who would believe such a preposterous story?" It's about the discovery in contemporary times of an in-progress neo–Nazi plot, masterminded by notorious South American–based former SS physician Josef Mengele (Gregory Peck), in which surrogate mothers have been artificially inseminated using preserved DNA from Adolf Hitler; the resulting baby Hitler clones are now being brought up in similar circumstances to that of the Führer in the hope that one of them will become the future leader of a Fourth Reich. During the course of events, we learn the reason for the fantastical scheme's reliance on the assassinations of 94 sexagenarian male civil servants in various locations across the world. Laurence Olivier was Oscar-nominated for his role as Lieberman, an aging Nazi hunter who ultimately foils the plot, and he and Peck (the two only appear in one sequence together, namely a memorable climactic showdown involving some deadly Dobermans) are both great if a little campy at times.

The Riddle of the Sands (1978) is the only big-screen adaptation to date of Erskine Childers' 1903 novel of the same name. Set in 1901, the leisurely proceedings unfold around the northwest coast of Germany, where talented English yachtsman Arthur Davies (a nicely cast Simon MacCorkindale) is busy charting the waters surrounding the Frisian Islands. Correctly suspecting that another yacht's captain, a supposed German named Dollmann (Alan Badel), is in fact a British traitor in league with the German government in some nefarious activity, Davies summons an old acquaintance, London-based Foreign Office official Charles Carruthers (top-billed Michael York), to help him investigate. Following many adventures, they uncover a German plot to militarily invade England via undefended waters on the east coast. The film has a great sense of place, and there are some nice touches of humor involving Carruthers being out of his comfort zone on Davies' small yacht—a far cry from his posh London residence complete with manservant! York is reunited with his *Logan's Run* co-star Jenny Agutter, who has a quiet role as the traitor's innocent daughter.

In the Michael Winner–directed **Firepower** (1979), former mafia operative Jerry Fanon (James Coburn) undertakes a special assignment for the U.S. government that entails bringing to justice an elusive crooked business magnate named Carl Stegner. The mission, during which Fanon mounts an assault on Stegner's Caribbean stronghold (a well-staged and memorable sequence involving a bulldozer), is initially complicated by the fact that nobody except those closest to the mysterious tycoon can identify him. Lots of explosions and chases punctuate the extremely convoluted plot, and there's a great twist involving Stegner's supposed private physician played by Anthony Franciosa. The ever-glamorous Sophia Loren gets top billing as Adele, an ex-lover of Fanon's and widow of a man murdered on Stegner's orders; initially it seems she's out to avenge her husband's death, but nothing ends up being quite what it seems when it comes to Adele. Also appearing are Eli Wallach, in a humorous turn as Fanon's erstwhile mafia boss, O.J. Simpson as Fanon's sidekick, and Victor Mature, who pops up for an ever-so-brief cameo in the film's closing scene.

"In every war there are those who kill … and those who make a killing!"

The Rhodesian Bush War provides the backdrop to **Game for Vultures** (1979), a middling political thriller made at the tail end of that conflict. Richard Harris heads the cast as David Swansey, a Rhodesian patriot and international sanctions buster involved in an illegal deal to supply the embargoed Rhodesian government with American helicopters being auctioned at a military base in West Germany. Richard Roundtree co-stars as a guerrilla fighter who ends up on a mission to sabotage the helicopters, which have

Roger Moore as the eccentric Rufus Excalibur ffolkes in *North Sea Hijack* (1979).

been shipped dismantled from Europe to an airfield in South West Africa from where they are due to be flown into Rhodesia on several Dakota aircraft. Other key characters are a business tycoon (Ray Milland), whose multi-billion dollar conglomerate is used to facilitate the deal, and a journalist (Sweden's Sven-Bertil Taube) attempting to expose Swansey's illicit activities. Joan Collins' role as Swansey's glamorous girlfriend is of little consequence in a film that, while no great shakes, certainly didn't deserve the dreaded "BOMB" rating from *Leonard Maltin's Movie Guide*.

North Sea Hijack (1979) sees Roger Moore play against type as the gruff Rufus Excalibur ffolkes, a cat-loving, chauvinistic eccentric who runs his own private counter-terrorist army (the "ffolkes ffusiliers") on a remote Scottish island. He is called into action when Lou Kramer (Anthony Perkins), heading a ruthless gang of hijackers, threatens to detonate previously planted explosives on a British North Sea oil production platform (named *Jennifer*) and drilling rig (named *Ruth*) unless the government pays a £25 million ransom. Although somewhat lacking overall in the action department, the film does manages to deliver an exciting climax where ffolkes and his men storm a supply ship (named *Esther*) on which the hijackers have been operating. Also starring are James Mason as a top naval officer and Michael Parks as Kramer's second-in-command. In the film's amusing final scene, feline fan ffolkes, who disapproves of medals and the like, is rewarded for services to his country with three white kittens, appropriately named *Esther*, *Ruth* and *Jennifer*.

Filmography

Abbreviations: Col = Color; B&W = Black and White; min = minutes; D = Director; P = Producer; Sc = Screenplay; Ph = Photography; M = Music; ABT = Alternate British Title.

1. **Absolution** (1978) Bulldog Productions Col 95 min D: Anthony Page P: Danny O'Donovan and Elliott Kastner Sc: Anthony Shaffer Ph: John Coquillon M: Stanley Myers Ca: Richard Burton, Dominic Guard, Dai Bradley, Andrew Keir, Billy Connolly, Willoughby Gray, Hilda Fenemore

2. **Accidental Death** (1963) Merton Park B&W 57 min D: Geoffrey Nethercott P: Jack Greenwood Sc: Arthur La Bern Ph: James Wilson M: Bernard Ebbinghouse Ca: John Carson, Jacqueline Ellis, Derrick Sherwin, Richard Vernon, Jean Lodge, Gerald Case, Jacqueline Lacey

3. **Account Rendered** (1957) Major Productions B&W 61 min D: Peter Graham Scott P: John Temple-Smith Sc: Barbara S. Harper Ph: Walter J. Harvey Ca: Griffith Jones, Ursula Howells, Honor Blackman, Ewen Solon, Robert Raikes, John Van Eyssen, Philip Gilbert

The Accursed see **The Traitor**

4. **Across the Bridge** (1957) Independent Film Producers B&W 103 min D: Ken Annakin P: John Stafford Sc: Guy Elmes and Denis Freeman Ph: Reginald Wyer M: James Bernard Ca: Rod Steiger, David Knight, Noel Willman, Marla Landi, Bernard Lee, Bill Nagy, Eric Pohlmann, Faith Brook

5. **Act of Murder** (1964) Merton Park B&W 62 min D: Alan Bridges P: Jack Greenwood Sc: Lewis Davidson Ph: James Wilson M: Bernard Ebbinghouse Ca: John Carson, Anthony Bate, Justine Lord, Duncan Lewis, Richard Burrell, Dandy Nichols, Michael Brennan

6. **Action of the Tiger** (1957) Claridge Film Productions Col 93 min D: Terence Young P: Kenneth Harper Sc: Robert Carson Ph: Desmond Dickinson M: Humphrey Searle Ca: Van Johnson, Martine Carol, Herbert Lom, Gustavo Rocco, José Nieto, Helen Haye, Anthony Dawson, Sean Connery

7. **Action Stations** (1956) E.J. Fancey Productions/Aqua Productions B&W 60 min D: Cecil H. Williamson P: E.J. Fancey Sc: Ted Leversuch Ph: Hal Morey M: Jackie Brown Ca: Paul Carpenter, Maria Martín, Joe Robinson, Ronald Leigh-Hunt, Douglas Robinson, Colin Cleminson, Jack Taylor

After Jenny Died see **Revenge**
Against All Odds see **The Blood of Fu Manchu**

8. **Agatha** (1978) Sweetwall Productions/First Artists Production Co./Casablanca Filmworks Col 105 min D: Michael Apted P: Jarvis Astaire and Gavrik Losey Sc: Kathleen Tynan and Arthur Hopcraft Ph: Vittorio Storaro M: Johnny Mandel Ca: Dustin Hoffman, Vanessa Redgrave, Timothy Dalton, Helen Morse, Tony Britton, Timothy West, Celia Gregory

Agent 8¾ see **Hot Enough for June**

9. **Alias John Preston** (1955) The Danzigers B&W 67 min D: David MacDonald P: Sid Stone Sc: Paul Tabori Ph: Jack Cox M: Edwin Astley and Albert Elms Ca: Betta St. John, Alexander Knox, Christopher Lee, Peter Grant, Sandra Dorne, Patrick Holt, John Longden

10. **The Alphabet Murders** (1965) MGM B&W 90 min D: Frank Tashlin P: Lawrence P. Bachmann Sc: David Pursall and Jack Seddon Ph: Desmond Dickinson M: Ron Goodwin Ca: Tony Randall, Anita Ekberg, Robert Morley, Maurice Denham, Guy Rolfe, Sheila Allen, Julian Glover

11. **Ambush in Leopard Street** (1961) Bill and Michael Luckwell Ltd. B&W 60 min D: J. Henry Piperno P: Bill Luckwell and Jock MacGregor Sc: Bernard Spicer and Ahmed Faroughy Ph: Stephen Dade M: Wilfred Burns Ca: James Kenney, Michael Brennan, Jean Harvey, Norman Rodway, Bruce Seton, Pauline Delany, Charles Mitchell

12. **Amsterdam Affair** (1968) Trio Films/Group W Films Col 91 min *D:* Gerry O'Hara *P:* George Willoughby *Sc:* Edmund Ward *Ph:* Gerry Fisher *M:* John Scott *Ca:* William Marlowe, Wolfgang Kieling, Catherine Schell, Pamela Ann Davy, Josef Dubin-Behrmann, Guy Deghy, Peter Burton

13. **And Soon the Darkness** (1970) Associated British Productions Col 99 min *D:* Robert Fuest *P:* Albert Fennell and Brian Clemens *Sc:* Brian Clemens and Terry Nation *Ph:* Ian Wilson *M:* Laurie Johnson *Ca:* Pamela Franklin, Michele Dotrice, Sandor Eles, John Nettleton, Clare Kelly, Hana-Maria Pravda, John Franklyn

14. **And Then There Were None** (1974) Filibuster Films Col 98 min *U.S. Title:* Ten Little Indians *D:* Peter Collinson *P:* Harry Alan Towers *Sc:* Harry Alan Towers (billed as Peter Welbeck) *Ph:* Fernando Arribas *M:* Bruno Nicolai *Ca:* Oliver Reed, Elke Sommer, Richard Attenborough, Stéphane Audran, Charles Aznavour, Gert Fröbe, Herbert Lom, Maria Rohm, Adolfo Celi, Alberto De Mendoza

15. **Another Man's Poison** (1951) Daniel Angel Films (in association with Dougfair Corp. [U.S.]) B&W 90 min *D:* Irving Rapper *P:* Daniel M. Angel *Sc:* Val Guest *Ph:* Robert Krasker *M:* John Greenwood (U.S. version features music by Paul Sawtell) *Ca:* Bette Davis, Gary Merrill, Emlyn Williams, Anthony Steel, Barbara Murray, Reginald Beckwith, Edna Morris

Anything for Love *see* **11 Harrowhouse**

16. **The Armchair Detective** (1951) Meridian Films B&W 60 min *D:* Brendan J. Stafford *P:* Derek Elphinstone *Sc:* Ernest Dudley and Derek Elphinstone *Ph:* Gordon Lang *M:* John Hollingsworth *Ca:* Ernest Dudley, Hartley Power, Derek Elphinstone, Sally Newton, Iris Russell, David Oxley, David Jenkins

17. **Assassin** (1973) The Pemini Organisation Col 83 min *D:* Peter Crane *P:* Peter Crane and Michael Sloan *Sc:* Michael Sloan *Ph:* Brian Jonson *M:* Zack Laurence *Ca:* Ian Hendry, Edward Judd, Frank Windsor, Ray Brooks, John Hart Dyke, Verna Harvey, Mike Pratt

The Assassin *see* **Venetian Bird**

18. **Assassin for Hire** (1951) Merton Park B&W 67 min *D:* Michael McCarthy *P:* Julian Wintle *Sc:* Rex Rienits *Ph:* Robert Lapresle *M:* Ronald Emanuel *Ca:* Sydney Tafler, Ronald Howard, John Hewer, Katharine Blake, June Rodney, Martin Benson, Sam Kydd

19. **The Assassination Bureau Limited** (1968) Heathfield Films/Paramount Pictures Corporation Col 110 min *D:* Basil Dearden *P:* Michael Relph *Sc:* Michael Relph *Ph:* Geoffrey Unsworth *M:* Ron Grainer *Ca:* Oliver Reed, Diana Rigg, Telly Savalas, Curt Jürgens, Philippe Noiret, Warren Mitchell, Beryl Reid, Clive Revill

20. **Assault** (1970) Peter Rogers Productions Col 91 min *U.S. Titles:* In the Devil's Garden; Molested (original theatrical release title); Satan's Playthings (1980s theatrical reissue); Tower of Terror (TV only); The Creepers (video—see Appendix V) *D:* Sidney Hayers *P:* George H. Brown *Sc:* John Kruse *Ph:* Ken Hodges *M:* Eric Rogers *Ca:* Suzy Kendall, Frank Finlay, James Laurenson, Lesley-Anne Down, Freddie Jones, Tony Beckley, Allan Cuthbertson, Anthony Ainley, Patrick Jordan

Assault Force *see* **North Sea Hijack**

21. **Assignment K** (1967) Mazurka Productions/Gildor Films Col 97 min *D:* Val Guest *P:* Maurice Foster and Ben Arbeid *Sc:* Val Guest, Bill Strutton and Maurice Foster *Ph:* Ken Hodges *M:* Basil Kirchin *Ca:* Stephen Boyd, Camilla Sparv, Michael Redgrave, Leo McKern, Robert Hoffmann, Jeremy Kemp, Jane Merrow, Vivi Bach, Geoffrey Bayldon

22. **Assignment Redhead** (1956) Butcher's Film Productions (in association with Amalgamated Productions [U.S.]) B&W 79 min *U.S. Title:* Million Dollar Manhunt *D:* Maclean Rogers *P:* W.G. Chalmers *Sc:* Maclean Rogers *Ph:* Ernest Palmer *M:* Wilfred Burns *Ca:* Richard Denning, Carole Mathews, Ronald Adam, Danny Green, Brian Worth, Jan Holden, Alex Gallier

Assignment Redhead *see* **Undercover Girl**

23. **At the Stroke of Nine** (1957) Tower Productions B&W 72 min *D:* Lance Comfort *P:* Harry Booth, Michael Deeley and Jon Penington *Sc:* Brian Clemens (billed as Tony O'Grady), Harry Booth, Jon Penington and Michael Deeley *Ph:* Gerald Gibbs *M:* Edwin Astley *Ca:* Patricia Dainton, Stephen Murray, Patrick Barr, Dermot Walsh, Clifford Evans, Leonard White, Marianne Stone

The Atomic Man *see* **Timeslip**

24. **Attempt to Kill** (1961) Merton Park B&W 57 min *D:* Royston Morley *P:* Jack Greenwood *Sc:* Richard Harris *Ph:* Bert Mason *M:* Bernard Ebbinghouse *Ca:* Derek Farr, Tony Wright, Richard Pearson, Freda Jackson, Patricia Mort, J.G. Devlin, Clifford Earl

Avenging Spirit *see* **Dominique**

25. **Backfire!** (1961) Merton Park B&W 59 min *D:* Paul Almond *P:* Jack Greenwood *Sc:* Robert Banks Stewart *Ph:* Bert Mason *M:* Bernard Ebbinghouse *Ca:* Alfred Burke, Zena Marshall, Oliver Johnston, Noel Trevarthen, Suzanne Neve, Derek Francis, John Cazabon

Bad Blonde *see* The Flanagan Boy

Baffled! (1972)—See Appendix VI

Bang, Bang, You're Dead *see* Our Man in Marrakesh

26. **Bang! You're Dead** (1953) Wellington Films B&W 89 min *U.S. Title:* Game of Danger (TV only) *D:* Lance Comfort *P:* Lance Comfort *Sc:* Guy Elmes and Ernest Borneman *Ph:* Brendan J. Stafford *M:* Eric Spear *Ca:* Jack Warner, Derek Farr, Veronica Hurst, Michael Medwin, Gordon Harker, Beatrice Varley, Anthony Richmond

27. **The Bank Raiders** (1958) Film Workshop B&W 60 min *D:* Maxwell Munden *P:* Geoffrey Goodhart *Sc:* Brandon Fleming *Ph:* Henry Hall *Ca:* Peter Reynolds, Sandra Dorne, Sydney Tafler, Lloyd Lamble, Rose Hill, Arthur Mullard, Tim Ellison, Ann King

28. **Barbados Quest** (1955) Cipa Productions B&W 70 min *U.S. Title:* Murder on Approval *D:* Bernard Knowles *P:* Robert S. Baker and Monty Berman *Sc:* Kenneth R. Hayles *Ph:* Monty Berman *Ca:* Tom Conway, Delphi Lawrence, Brian Worth, Michael Balfour, Campbell Cotts, John Horsley, Maureen Connell, Grace Arnold

29. **Battle Beneath the Earth** (1967) Reynolds-Vetter Productions Col 91 min *D:* Montgomery Tully *P:* Charles Reynolds *Sc:* Charles F. Vetter (billed as L.Z. Hargreaves) *Ph:* Kenneth Talbot *M:* Ken Jones *Ca:* Kerwin Mathews, Viviane Ventura, Robert Ayres, Peter Arne, Al Mulock, Martin Benson, Ed Bishop, Bill Nagy

30. **The Bay of Saint Michel** (1963) Acropolis Films/Trionyx Films B&W 80 min *U.S. Titles:* Pattern for Plunder; Operation Mermaid (TV only) *D:* John Ainsworth *P:* John Ainsworth *Sc:* Christopher Davis *Ph:* Stephen Dade *M:* Johnny Douglas *Ca:* Keenan Wynn, Mai Zetterling, Ronald Howard, Rona Anderson, Trader Faulkner, Edward Underdown, Michael Peake

31. **Bear Island** (1979) Selkirk Films/Bear Island Films Col 118 min *D:* Don Sharp *P:* Peter Snell *Sc:* David Butler and Don Sharp *Ph:* Alan Hume *M:* Robert Farnon *Ca:* Donald Sutherland, Vanessa Redgrave, Richard Widmark, Christopher Lee, Barbara Parkins, Lloyd Bridges, Lawrence Dane

The Beasts of Marseilles *see* Seven Thunders

32. **Beat the Devil** (1953) Romulus Films (Britain)/Santana Pictures (U.S.)/Dear Film (Italy) B&W 95 min *D:* John Huston *P:* John Huston *Sc:* Truman Capote and John Huston *Ph:* Oswald Morris *M:* Franco Mannino *Ca:* Humphrey Bogart, Jennifer Jones, Gina Lollobrigida, Robert Morley, Peter Lorre, Edward Underdown, Bernard Lee

33. **Beautiful Stranger** (1954) Marksman Films B&W 89 min *U.S. Title:* Twist of Fate *D:* David Miller *P:* Maxwell Setton and John R. Sloan *Sc:* Robert Westerby and Carl Nystrom *Ph:* Edward Scaife *M:* Malcolm Arnold *Ca:* Ginger Rogers, Herbert Lom, Stanley Baker, Margaret Rawlings, Eddie Byrne, Jacques Bergerac, Coral Browne, Ferdy Mayne

34. **The Bedford Incident** (1965) Bedford Productions B&W 102 min *D:* James B. Harris *P:* James B. Harris and Richard Widmark *Sc:* James Poe *Ph:* Gilbert Taylor *M:* Gerard Schurmann *Ca:* Richard Widmark, Sidney Poitier, James MacArthur, Martin Balsam, Wally Cox, Eric Portman, Gary Cockrell

35. **Before I Wake** (1955) Gibraltar Productions (in association with Roxbury Productions [U.S.]) B&W 78 min *U.S. Title:* Shadow of Fear *D:* Albert S. Rogell *P:* Charles A. Leeds *Sc:* Robert Westerby *Ph:* Jack Asher *M:* Leonard Salzedo *Ca:* Mona Freeman, Jean Kent, Maxwell Reed, Hugh Miller, Gretchen Franklin, Frederick Leister, Alexander Gauge

Behind the Cellar Door *see* Revenge

36. **Behind the Headlines** (1956) Kenilworth Film Productions B&W 67 min *D:* Charles Saunders *P:* Guido Coen *Sc:* Allan MacKinnon *Ph:* Geoffrey Faithfull *M:* Stanley Black *Ca:* Paul Carpenter, Adrienne Corri, Hazel Court, Alfie Bass, Ewen Solon, Melissa Stribling, Harry Fowler

37. **Berserk** (1967) Herman Cohen Productions Col 96 min *D:* Jim O'Connolly *P:* Herman Cohen *Sc:* Aben Kandel and Herman Cohen *Ph:* Desmond Dickinson *M:* John Scott *Ca:* Joan Crawford, Ty Hardin, Diana Dors, Michael Gough, Judy Geeson, Robert Hardy, Geoffrey Keen, Sydney Tafler

38. **The Betrayal** (1957) The Danzigers B&W 82 min *D:* Ernest Morris *P:* Edward J. Danziger and Harry Lee Danziger *Sc:* Brian Clemens and Eldon Howard *Ph:* James Wilson *M:* Leon Young *Ca:* Philip Friend, Diana Decker, Philip Saville, Peter Bathurst, Peter Burton, Ballard Berkeley, Harold Lang

Beware My Brethren *see* The Fiend

Beware of the Brethren *see* The Fiend

39. **Beyond Mombasa** (1956) Hemisphere Films (in association with Todon Productions [U.S.]) Col 90 min *D:* George Marshall *P:* Adrian D. Worker *Sc:* Richard English and Gene Levitt *Ph:* Freddie Young *M:* Humphrey Searle *Ca:* Cornel Wilde, Donna Reed, Leo Genn, Ron Randell, Christopher Lee, Dan Jackson, Clive Morton

40. **Beyond the Curtain** (1960) Martin Film Productions B&W 88 min *D:* Compton Bennett *P:* John Martin *Sc:* John Cresswell and Compton Bennett *Ph:* Eric Cross *M:* Kenneth Pakeman *Ca:* Richard Greene, Eva Bartok, Marius Goring, Lucie Mannheim, Andrée Melly, George Mikell, Denis Shaw

41. **Beyond This Place** (1959) Georgefield Productions B&W 89 min *U.S. Title:* Web of Evidence *D:* Jack Cardiff *P:* Maxwell Setton and John R. Sloan *Sc:* Kenneth Taylor *Ph:* Wilkie Cooper *M:* Douglas Gamley *Ca:* Van Johnson, Vera Miles, Emlyn Williams, Bernard Lee, Jean Kent, Leo McKern, Geoffrey Keen

42. **The Big Chance** (1957) Major Productions B&W 61 min *D:* Peter Graham Scott *P:* John Temple-Smith *Sc:* Peter Graham Scott *Ph:* Walter J. Harvey *M:* Eric Spear *Ca:* Adrienne Corri, William Russell, Ian Colin, Penelope Bartley, Ferdy Mayne, John Rae, Mary Jones

Big Deadly Game *see* **Third Party Risk**
The Big Frame *see* **The Lost Hours**
The Big Scam *see* **A Nightingale Sang in Berkeley Square**

43. **The Big Sleep** (1978) The Winkast Company/ITC Col 99 min *D:* Michael Winner *P:* Elliott Kastner and Michael Winner *Sc:* Michael Winner *Ph:* Robert Paynter *M:* Jerry Fielding *Ca:* Robert Mitchum, Sarah Miles, Richard Boone, Candy Clark, Joan Collins, Edward Fox, John Mills, James Stewart, Oliver Reed, Richard Todd

The Big Switch *see* **Strip Poker**

44. **Big Zapper** (1973) Lindsay Shonteff Film Productions Col 90 min *D:* Lindsay Shonteff *P:* Lindsay Shonteff *Sc:* Hugh Brody *Ph:* John C. Taylor *M:* Colin Pearson *Ca:* Linda Marlowe, Gary Hope, Sean Hewitt, Michael O'Malley, Jack May, Richard Monette, Penny Irving

The Biggest Bank Robbery *see* **A Nightingale Sang in Berkeley Square**

45. **Billion Dollar Brain** (1967) Lowndes Productions Col 111 min *D:* Ken Russell *P:* Harry Saltzman *Sc:* John McGrath *Ph:* Billy Williams *M:* Richard Rodney Bennett *Ca:* Michael Caine, Karl Malden, Ed Begley, Oscar Homolka, Françoise Dorléac, Guy Doleman, Vladek Sheybal

The Black Curse *see* **So Long at the Fair**
The Black Glove *see* **Face the Music**

46. **Black Orchid** (1952) Kenilworth Film Productions/Mid-Century Film Productions B&W 60 min *D:* Charles Saunders *P:* Robert S. Baker and Monty Berman *Sc:* Francis Edge and John Temple-Smith *Ph:* Eric Cross *M:* John Lanchbery *Ca:* Ronald Howard, Olga Edwards, John Bentley, Mary Laura Wood, Patrick Barr, Sheila Burrell, Russell Napier

47. **The Black Rider** (1954) Balblair Productions B&W 67 min *D:* Wolf Rilla *P:* A.R. Rawlinson *Sc:* A.R. Rawlinson *Ph:* Geoffrey Faithfull *M:* Wilfred Burns *Ca:* Jimmy Hanley, Rona Anderson, Leslie Dwyer, Beatrice Varley, Lionel Jeffries, Vincent Ball, Edwin Richfield

48. **Black 13** (1953) Vandyke Picture Corporation B&W 77 min *D:* Ken Hughes *P:* Roger Proudlock *Sc:* Ken Hughes *Ph:* Gerald Gibbs *M:* Carlo Rustichelli *Ca:* Peter Reynolds, Rona Anderson, Patrick Barr, Lana Morris, Michael Balfour, John Le Mesurier, Martin Benson

Black Tide *see* **Stormy Crossing**

49. **The Black Torment** (1964) Compton-Tekli Film Productions Col 85 min *U.S. Title:* Estate of Insanity (video—see Appendix V) *D:* Robert Hartford-Davis *P:* Robert Hartford-Davis *Sc:* Donald Ford and Derek Ford *Ph:* Peter Newbrook *M:* Robert Richards *Ca:* Heather Sears, John Turner, Ann Lynn, Peter Arne, Norman Bird, Raymond Huntley, Francis De Wolff

50. **Black Widow** (1950) Hammer Film Productions B&W 62 min *D:* Vernon Sewell *P:* Anthony Hinds *Sc:* Allan MacKinnon *Ph:* Walter J. Harvey *M:* Frank Spencer *Ca:* Christine Norden, Robert Ayres, Anthony Forwood, Jennifer Jayne, John Longden, John Harvey, Reginald Dyson

51. **The Black Windmill** (1974) Universal Pictures/Zanuck-Brown Company Col 106 min *D:* Don Siegel *P:* Don Siegel *Sc:* Leigh Vance *Ph:* Ousama Rawi *M:* Roy Budd *Ca:* Michael Caine, Joseph O'Conor, Donald Pleasence, John Vernon, Janet Suzman, Delphine Seyrig, Clive Revill, Joss Ackland, Catherine Schell

52. **Blackmailed** (1950) H.H. Films B&W 85 min *D:* Marc Allégret *P:* Harold Huth *Sc:* Hugh Mills and Roger Vadim *Ph:* George Stretton *M:* John Wooldridge *Ca:* Mai Zetterling, Dirk Bogarde, Fay Compton, Robert Flemyng, Michael Gough, James Robertson Justice, Wilfrid Hyde White

53. **Blackout** (1950) Tempean Films B&W 73 min *D:* Robert S. Baker *P:* Robert S. Baker and Monty Berman *Sc:* John Gilling *Ph:* Monty Berman *M:* John Lanchbery *Ca:* Maxwell Reed, Dinah Sheridan, Eric Pohlmann, Patric Doonan, Michael Brennan, Michael Evans, Annette Simmonds

Blackout *see* **Murder by Proxy**

54. **Blind Corner** (1963) Blakeley's Films (Manchester)/Mancunian Film Corporation B&W 80 min *U.S. Title:* Man in the Dark *D:*

Lance Comfort *P:* Tom Blakeley *Sc:* James Kelly and Peter Miller *Ph:* Basil Emmott *M:* Brian Fahey (main "concerto" theme composed by Peter Hart) *Ca:* William Sylvester, Barbara Shelley, Elizabeth Shepherd, Alexander Davion, Mark Eden, Ronnie Carroll, Frank Forsyth

55. **Blind Date** (1959) Independent Artists B&W 95 min *U.S. Title:* Chance Meeting *D:* Joseph Losey *P:* David Deutsch *Sc:* Ben Barzman and Millard Lampell *Ph:* Christopher Challis *M:* Richard Rodney Bennett *Ca:* Hardy Kruger, Stanley Baker, Micheline Presle, Robert Flemyng, Gordon Jackson, John Van Eyssen, Jack MacGowran

56. **Blind Man's Bluff** (1951) Present Day Productions B&W 68 min *D:* Charles Saunders *P:* Charles Reynolds *Sc:* John Gilling *Ph:* Ted Lloyd *Ca:* Zena Marshall, Sydney Tafler, Anthony Pendrell, Russell Napier, Norman Shelley, John Le Mesurier, Anthony Doonan

57. **Blind Spot** (1958) Butcher's Film Productions B&W 71 min *D:* Peter Maxwell *P:* Monty Berman *Sc:* Kenneth R. Hayles *Ph:* Arthur Graham *Ca:* Robert MacKenzie, Delphi Lawrence, Gordon Jackson, Anne Sharp, John Le Mesurier, George Pastell, John Crawford

58. **Blind Terror** (1971) Genesis Productions/Filmways Pictures Col 89 min *U.S. Title:* See No Evil *D:* Richard Fleischer *P:* Martin Ransohoff and Leslie Linder *Sc:* Brian Clemens *Ph:* Gerry Fisher *M:* Elmer Bernstein *Ca:* Mia Farrow, Robin Bailey, Dorothy Alison, Diane Grayson, Norman Eshley, Christopher Matthews, Paul Nicholas

Blonde Blackmailer *see* **Stolen Time**
Blood Fiend *see* **Theatre of Death**

59. **The Blood of Fu Manchu** (1968) Udastex Films Col 91 min *U.S. Titles:* Kiss & Kill; Against All Odds (alternate TV and video title); Kiss of Death (video—see Appendix V) *D:* Jess Franco *P:* Harry Alan Towers *Sc:* Harry Alan Towers (billed as Peter Welbeck) *Ph:* Manuel Merino *M:* Daniel White *Ca:* Christopher Lee, Götz George, Richard Greene, Howard Marion Crawford, Tsai Chin, Maria Rohm, Shirley Eaton

60. **Blood Orange** (1953) Hammer Film Productions B&W 76 min *U.S. Title:* Three Stops to Murder *D:* Terence Fisher *P:* Michael Carreras *Sc:* Jan Read *Ph:* Walter J. Harvey *M:* Ivor Slaney *Ca:* Tom Conway, Mila Parely, Naomi Chance, Eric Pohlmann, Andrew Osborn, Richard Wattis, Michael Ripper, Delphi Lawrence

61. **Blue Movie Blackmail** (1973) Clodio Cinematografica (Rome)/Italian International Film (Rome)/Monymusk Productions (London) Col 97 min *ABT:* Superbitch (video—see Appendix V; DVD) *U.S. Titles:* Mafia Junction; Superbitch (video—see Appendix V; DVD) *D:* Massimo Dallamano *P:* Fulvio Lucisano and Leonardo Pescarolo *Sc:* Massimo Dallamano and Ross MacKenzie *Ph:* Jack Hildyard *M:* Riz Ortolani *Ca:* Ivan Rassimov, Stephanie Beacham, Patricia Hayes, Ettore Manni (billed as Red Carter), Cec Linder, Luciano Catenacci, Verna Harvey

62. **The Blue Parrot** (1953) A.C.T. Films B&W 69 min *D:* John Harlow *P:* Stanley Haynes *Sc:* Allan MacKinnon *Ph:* Robert Navarro *Ca:* Dermot Walsh, Jacqueline Hill, Ballard Berkeley, Ferdy Mayne, Valerie White, John Le Mesurier, Edwin Richfield

63. **The Body Said No!** (1950) New World Pictures B&W 75 min *D:* Val Guest *P:* Daniel M. Angel *Sc:* Val Guest *Ph:* Bert Mason *Ca:* Michael Rennie, Yolande Donlan, Hy Hazell, Valentine Dyall, Jon Pertwee, Cyril Smith, Reginald Beckwith, Peter Butterworth

64. **Bomb in the High Street** (1963) Elthea Productions B&W 60 min *D:* Terry Bishop and Peter Bezencenet *P:* Theodore Zichy *Sc:* Benjamin Simcoe *Ph:* Gordon Dines *M:* Wilfred Josephs *Ca:* Ronald Howard, Terry Palmer, Suzanna Leigh, Jack Allen, Peter Gilmore, James Villiers, Geoffrey Bayldon

Bombay Waterfront *see* **Paul Temple Returns**

65. **Bond of Fear** (1956) Mid-Century Film Productions B&W 66 min *D:* Henry Cass *P:* Robert S. Baker and Monty Berman *Sc:* John Gilling *Ph:* Monty Berman *M:* Stanley Black *Ca:* Dermot Walsh, Jane Barrett, John Colicos, Jameson Clark, John Horsley, Anthony Pavey, Marilyn Baker, Alan MacNaughtan

66. **Booby Trap** (1956) Jaywell Productions B&W 72 min *D:* Henry Cass *P:* Bill Luckwell and Derek Winn *Sc:* Peter Bryan and Bill Luckwell *Ph:* James Wilson *M:* Wilfred Burns *Ca:* Sydney Tafler, Patti Morgan, Harry Fowler, Tony Quinn, John Watson, Jacques Cey, Fred McNaughton

67. **The Boy Cried Murder** (1965) Carlos Films/CCC Film/Avala Film Col 86 min *D:* George Breakston *P:* Philip N. Krasne *Sc:* Robin Estridge *Ph:* Milorad Markovic *M:* Martin Slavin *Ca:* Fraser MacIntosh, Veronica Hurst, Phil Brown, Tim Barrett, Beba Loncar, Edward Steel, Anita Sharp Bolster

68. **The Boys from Brazil** (1978) ITC Col 125 min *D:* Franklin J. Schaffner *P:* Martin Richards and Stanley O'Toole *Sc:* Heywood Gould *Ph:* Henri Decae *M:* Jerry Goldsmith *Ca:* Gregory Peck, Laurence Olivier, James Mason, Lilli

Palmer, Uta Hagen, John Dehner, John Rubinstein, Denholm Elliott, Steve Guttenberg

The Brain *see* **Vengeance**

69. **The Brain Machine** (1954) Merton Park B&W 84 min *D:* Ken Hughes *P:* Alec C. Snowden *Sc:* Ken Hughes *Ph:* Josef Ambor *M:* Richard Taylor *Ca:* Patrick Barr, Elizabeth Allan, Maxwell Reed, Vanda Godsell, Russell Napier, Edwin Richfield, Bill Nagy

Brainsuckers *see* **Frightmare**

70. **Brannigan** (1975) Wellborn Ltd. Col 111 min *D:* Douglas Hickox *P:* Jules Levy and Arthur Gardner *Sc:* Christopher Trumbo, Michael Butler, William P. McGivern and William Norton *Ph:* Gerry Fisher *M:* Dominic Frontiere *Ca:* John Wayne, Richard Attenborough, Judy Geeson, Mel Ferrer, John Vernon, James Booth, Lesley-Anne Down, Daniel Pilon

71. **The Break** (1962) Blakeley's Films (Manchester)/Mancunian Film Corporation B&W 76 min *D:* Lance Comfort *P:* Tom Blakeley *Sc:* Pip and Jane Baker *Ph:* Basil Emmott *M:* Brian Fahey *Ca:* Tony Britton, William Lucas, Eddie Byrne, Robert Urquhart, Sonia Dresdel, Edwin Richfield, Christina Gregg

72. **Break in the Circle** (1954) Hammer Film Productions Col 92 min *D:* Val Guest *P:* Michael Carreras *Sc:* Val Guest *Ph:* Walter J. Harvey *M:* Doreen Carwithen *Ca:* Forrest Tucker, Eva Bartok, Marius Goring, Reginald Beckwith, Eric Pohlmann, Arnold Marle, Marne Maitland

73. **Breakaway** (1955) Cipa Productions B&W 72 min *D:* Henry Cass *P:* Robert S. Baker and Monty Berman *Sc:* Norman Hudis *Ph:* Monty Berman *M:* Stanley Black *Ca:* Tom Conway, Michael Balfour, Honor Blackman, Brian Worth, Bruce Seton, Alexander Gauge, John Horsley

74. **The Breaking Point** (1960) Butcher's Film Productions B&W 59 min *U.S. Title:* The Great Armored Car Swindle *D:* Lance Comfort *P:* Peter Lambert *Sc:* Peter Lambert *Ph:* Basil Emmott *M:* Albert Elms *Ca:* Peter Reynolds, Dermot Walsh, Joanna Dunham, Lisa Gastoni, Brian Cobby, Jack Allen, Arnold Diamond

75. **Breakout** (1959) Independent Artists B&W 62 min *D:* Peter Graham Scott *P:* Julian Wintle and Leslie Parkyn *Sc:* Peter Barnes *Ph:* Eric Cross *Ca:* Lee Patterson, Hazel Court, William Lucas, John Paul, Terence Alexander, Billie Whitelaw, Rupert Davies

Breakout *see* **Danger Within**

76. **The Brides of Fu Manchu** (1966) Fu Manchu Films Col 91 min *D:* Don Sharp *P:* Harry Alan Towers *Sc:* Harry Alan Towers (billed as Peter Welbeck) *Ph:* Ernest Steward *M:* Bruce Montgomery *Ca:* Christopher Lee, Douglas Wilmer, Marie Versini, Heinz Drache, Howard Marion Crawford, Tsai Chin, Carole Gray

Brighthaven Express *see* **Salute the Toff**

77. **The Broken Horseshoe** (1953) Nettlefold Films B&W 79 min *D:* Martyn C. Webster *P:* Ernest G. Roy *Sc:* A.R. Rawlinson *Ph:* Gerald Gibbs *M:* Wilfred Burns *Ca:* Robert Beatty, Elizabeth Sellars, Peter Coke, Janet Butler, Hugh Kelly, Ferdy Mayne, Roger Delgado

The Bullet Machine *see* **Clegg**

78. **Bunny Lake Is Missing** (1965) Wheel Productions B&W 107 min *D:* Otto Preminger *P:* Otto Preminger *Sc:* John and Penelope Mortimer *Ph:* Denys Coop *M:* Paul Glass *Ca:* Laurence Olivier, Carol Lynley, Keir Dullea, Martita Hunt, Noël Coward, Adrienne Corri, Clive Revill, Finlay Currie

79. **Burnt Evidence** (1954) A.C.T. Films B&W 61 min *D:* Daniel Birt *P:* Ronald Kinnoch *Sc:* Ted Willis *Ph:* Jo Jago *Ca:* Jane Hylton, Duncan Lamont, Donald Gray, Meredith Edwards, Cyril Smith, Irene Handl, Hugo Schuster

80. **Cage of Gold** (1950) Ealing Studios B&W 83 min *D:* Basil Dearden *P:* Michael Balcon *Sc:* Jack Whittingham *Ph:* Douglas Slocombe *M:* Georges Auric *Ca:* Jean Simmons, David Farrar, James Donald, Madeleine Lebeau, Herbert Lom, Bernard Lee, Gladys Henson

81. **Cairo** (1962) MGM B&W 91 min *D:* Wolf Rilla *P:* Ronald Kinnoch *Sc:* Joanne Court *Ph:* Desmond Dickinson *M:* Kenneth V. Jones *Ca:* George Sanders, Richard Johnson, Faten Hamama, Eric Pohlmann, Ahmed Mazhar, John Meillon, Walter Rilla

82. **Cairo Road** (1950) The Mayflower Pictures Corporation B&W 90 min *D:* David MacDonald *P:* Aubrey Baring *Sc:* Robert Westerby *Ph:* Oswald Morris *M:* Robert Gill *Ca:* Eric Portman, Laurence Harvey, Maria Mauban, Harold Lang, Gregoire Aslan, Karel Stepanek, John Gregson, Abraham Sofaer, Ferdy Mayne, Eric Pohlmann

83. **Calculated Risk** (1963) McLeod Productions B&W 72 min *D:* Norman Harrison *P:* William McLeod *Sc:* Edwin Richfield *Ph:* William McLeod *M:* George Martin *Ca:* William Lucas, John Rutland, Dilys Watling, Shay Gorman, Terence Cooper, David Brierley, Warren Mitchell

Call Him Mr. Shatter *see* **Shatter**

84. **Callan** (1974) Magnum Films Col 106 min *ABT:* This Is Callan (video—see Appendix V) *D:* Don Sharp *P:* Derek Horne *Sc:* James Mitchell *Ph:* Ernest Steward *M:* Wilfred Josephs *Ca:* Edward Woodward, Eric Porter, Carl Mohner,

Catherine Schell, Peter Egan, Russell Hunter, Kenneth Griffith

85. **Calling Bulldog Drummond** (1951) MGM B&W 80 min *D:* Victor Saville *P:* Hayes Goetz *Sc:* Howard Emmett Rogers, Gerard Fairlie and Arthur Wimperis *Ph:* Freddie Young *M:* Rudolph G. Kopp *Ca:* Walter Pidgeon, Margaret Leighton, Robert Beatty, David Tomlinson, Peggy Evans, Charles Victor, Bernard Lee, James Hayter

86. **Candidate for Murder** (1961) Merton Park B&W 60 min *D:* David Villiers *P:* Jack Greenwood *Sc:* Lukas Heller *Ph:* Bert Mason *M:* Charles Blackwell *Ca:* Michael Gough, Erika Remberg, Hans Borsody, John Justin, Paul Whitsun-Jones, Vanda Godsell, Jerold Wells

87. **Caravan to Vaccarès** (1974) Geoff Reeve Productions/Société Nouvelle Prodis/Crowndale Holdings Col 98 min *D:* Geoffrey Reeve *P:* Geoffrey Reeve and Richard Morris-Adams *Sc:* Paul Wheeler *Ph:* Fred Tammes *M:* Stanley Myers *Ca:* David Birney, Charlotte Rampling, Michael Lonsdale, Marcel Bozzuffi, Michael Bryant, Serge Marquand, Marianne Eggerickx

88. **A Case for P.C. 49** (1951) Hammer Film Productions B&W 81 min *D:* Francis Searle *P:* Anthony Hinds *Sc:* Vernon Harris and Alan Stranks *Ph:* Walter J. Harvey *M:* Frank Spencer *Ca:* Brian Reece, Joy Shelton, Christine Norden, Leslie Bradley, Gordon McLeod, Michael Balfour, Michael Ripper

Case of the Red Monkey *see* **Little Red Monkey**

89. **Cash on Demand** (1961) Hammer Film Productions/Woodpecker Productions (Hammer subsidiary) B&W 84 min *D:* Quentin Lawrence *P:* Anthony Nelson-Keys *Sc:* David T. Chantler and Lewis Greifer *Ph:* Arthur Grant *M:* Wilfred Josephs *Ca:* Peter Cushing, Andre Morell, Richard Vernon, Barry Lowe, Norman Bird, Edith Sharpe, Charles Morgan

90. **The Cassandra Crossing** (1976) ITC/Associated General Films/International Cine Productions Col 129 min *D:* George Pan Cosmatos *P:* Carlo Ponti *Sc:* Tom Mankiewicz, Robert Katz and George Pan Cosmatos *Ph:* Ennio Guarnieri *M:* Jerry Goldsmith *Ca:* Sophia Loren, Richard Harris, Martin Sheen, O.J. Simpson, Lionel Stander, Ann Turkel, Ava Gardner, Burt Lancaster, Ingrid Thulin, Lee Strasberg

91. **Cast a Dark Shadow** (1955) Frobisher Productions B&W 83 min *D:* Lewis Gilbert *P:* Herbert Mason *Sc:* John Cresswell *Ph:* Jack Asher *M:* Antony Hopkins *Ca:* Dirk Bogarde, Margaret Lockwood, Kathleen Harrison, Kay Walsh, Robert Flemyng, Mona Washbourne, Philip Stainton

92. **The Castle of Fu Manchu** (1968) Towers of London (Films) Col 92 min *D:* Jess Franco *P:* Harry Alan Towers *Sc:* Harry Alan Towers (billed as Peter Welbeck) *Ph:* Manuel Merino *M:* Charles Camilleri *Ca:* Christopher Lee, Richard Greene, Howard Marion Crawford, Tsai Chin, Gunther Stoll, Rosalba Neri, Maria Perschy, Gustavo Re

93. **Cat and Mouse** (1958) Anvil Films B&W 79 min *D:* Paul Rotha *P:* Paul Rotha *Sc:* Paul Rotha *Ph:* Wolfgang Suschitzky *M:* Edwin Astley *Ca:* Lee Patterson, Ann Sears, Hilton Edwards, Victor Maddern, Stuart Saunders, Diana Fawcett, George Rose

Cat and Mouse (1974) *see* **Mousey**

94. **The Cat and the Canary** (1977) Grenadier Films Col 98 min *D:* Radley Metzger *P:* Richard Gordon *Sc:* Radley Metzger *Ph:* Alex Thomson *M:* Steven Cagan *Ca:* Honor Blackman, Michael Callan, Edward Fox, Wendy Hiller, Olivia Hussey, Carol Lynley, Wilfrid Hyde White, Daniel Massey, Peter McEnery

95. **Catacombs** (1964) Parroch-McCallum Productions (in association with Associated Producers, Inc. [U.S.]) B&W 90 min *U.S. Title:* The Woman Who Wouldn't Die *D:* Gordon Hessler *P:* Jack Parsons *Sc:* Dan Mainwaring *Ph:* Arthur Lavis *M:* Carlo Martelli *Ca:* Gary Merrill, Jane Merrow, Georgina Cookson, Neil McCallum, Rachel Thomas, Jack Train, Frederick Piper

96. **Catch Me a Spy** (1971) Ludgate Films (London)/Films de la Pléiade (Paris)/Capitole Films (Paris) Col 94 min *ABT:* To Catch a Spy *D:* Dick Clement *P:* Steven Pallos and Pierre Braunberger *Sc:* Dick Clement and Ian La Frenais *Ph:* Christopher Challis *M:* Claude Bolling *Ca:* Kirk Douglas, Marlène Jobert, Trevor Howard, Tom Courtenay, Patrick Mower, Bernadette Lafont, Richard Pearson

The Chairman *see* **The Most Dangerous Man in the World**

97. **The Challenge** (1959) Alexandra Productions B&W 89 min *U.S. Title:* It Takes a Thief *D:* John Gilling *P:* John Temple-Smith *Sc:* John Gilling *Ph:* Gordon Dines *M:* Bill McGuffie *Ca:* Jayne Mansfield, Anthony Quayle, Carl Mohner, Peter Reynolds, John Bennett, Dermot Walsh, Edward Judd

Chance Meeting *see* **Blind Date**

98. **Change Partners** (1965) Merton Park B&W 63 min *D:* Robert Lynn *P:* Jack Greenwood *Sc:* Donal Giltinan *Ph:* James Wilson *M:* Bernard Ebbinghouse *Ca:* Zena Walker, Kenneth Cope, Basil Henson, Anthony Dawson, Jane Barrett, Pamela Ann Davy, Peter Bathurst

99. **Chase a Crooked Shadow** (1957) Associated Dragon Films B&W 87 min *D:* Michael Anderson *P:* Douglas Fairbanks, Jr. *Sc:* David Osborn and Charles Sinclair *Ph:* Erwin Hillier *M:* Matyas Seiber *Ca:* Richard Todd, Anne Baxter, Herbert Lom, Alexander Knox, Faith Brook, Alan Tilvern, Thelma d'Aguiar

100. **Checkpoint** (1956) The Rank Organisation Film Productions Col 84 min *D:* Ralph Thomas *P:* Betty E. Box *Sc:* Robin Estridge *Ph:* Ernest Steward *M:* Bruce Montgomery *Ca:* Anthony Steel, Odile Versois, Stanley Baker, James Robertson Justice, Maurice Denham, Michael Medwin, Lee Patterson

101. **Chelsea Story** (1950) Present Day Productions B&W 65 min *D:* Charles Saunders *P:* Charles Reynolds *Sc:* John Gilling *Ph:* Ted Lloyd *M:* Arthur Wilkinson *Ca:* Henry Mollison, Sydney Tafler, Wallas Eaton, Ingeborg Wells, Lesley Osmond, Laurence Naismith, Michael Ward

102. **The Child and the Killer** (1959) The Danzigers B&W 65 min *D:* Max Varnel *P:* Edward J. Danziger and Harry Lee Danziger *Sc:* Brian Clemens and Eldon Howard *Ph:* James Wilson *Ca:* Patricia Driscoll, Robert Arden, Richard Williams, Ryck Rydon, Gordon Sterne, John McLaren, Robert Raglan

A Choice of Weapons *see* **Trial by Combat**
The Circle *see* **The Vicious Circle**

103. **Circle of Danger** (1950) Coronado Productions (England) B&W 86 min *D:* Jacques Tourneur *P:* Joan Harrison *Sc:* Philip Macdonald *Ph:* Oswald Morris (additional photography by Gilbert Taylor) *M:* Robert Farnon *Ca:* Ray Milland, Patricia Roc, Marius Goring, Hugh Sinclair, Naunton Wayne, Marjorie Fielding, Edward Rigby

104. **Circle of Deception** (1960) 20th Century–Fox Productions B&W 100 min *D:* Jack Lee *P:* Tom Morahan *Sc:* Nigel Balchin and Robert Musel *Ph:* Gordon Dines *M:* Clifton Parker *Ca:* Bradford Dillman, Suzy Parker, Harry Andrews, Robert Stephens, Paul Rogers, John Welsh, Martin Boddey

105. **Circumstantial Evidence** (1952) A.C.T. Films B&W 62 min *U.S. Title:* Evidence for Hire (TV only) *D:* Daniel Birt *P:* Phil Brandon *Sc:* Allan MacKinnon *Ph:* Brendan J. Stafford *Ca:* Rona Anderson, Patrick Holt, John Arnatt, John Warwick, Frederick Leister, Ronald Adam, June Ashley

106. **Circus of Fear** (1966) Circus Films/Constantin Film Col 91 min *U.S. Title:* Psycho-Circus *D:* John Llewellyn Moxey (Werner Jacobs credited on German prints) *P:* Harry Alan Towers *Sc:* Harry Alan Towers (billed as Peter Welbeck) *Ph:* Ernest Steward *M:* Johnny Douglas *Ca:* Christopher Lee, Leo Genn, Anthony Newlands, Heinz Drache, Eddi Arent, Klaus Kinski, Suzy Kendall, Victor Maddern

107. **Circus of Horrors** (1960) Lynx Films Col 91 min *D:* Sidney Hayers *P:* Julian Wintle and Leslie Parkyn *Sc:* George Baxt *Ph:* Douglas Slocombe *M:* Franz Reizenstein and Muir Mathieson *Ca:* Anton Diffring, Erika Remberg, Yvonne Monlaur, Donald Pleasence, Jane Hylton, Kenneth Griffith, Conrad Phillips

City After Midnight *see* **That Woman Opposite**

108. **City of Fear** (1966) Towers of London (Films) B&W 75 min *D:* Peter Bezencenet *P:* Harry Alan Towers *Sc:* Harry Alan Towers (billed as Peter Welbeck) *Ph:* Martin Curtis *M:* Johnny Douglas *Ca:* Terry Moore, Albert Lieven, Marisa Mell, Paul Maxwell, Pinkas Braun, Zsu Zsu Banki, Maria Rohm

109. **Clash by Night** (1963) Eternal Films B&W 75 min *U.S. Title:* Escape by Night *D:* Montgomery Tully *P:* Maurice J. Wilson *Sc:* Maurice J. Wilson and Montgomery Tully *Ph:* Geoffrey Faithfull *M:* John Veale *Ca:* Terence Longdon, Jennifer Jayne, Harry Fowler, Peter Sallis, Alan Wheatley, Vanda Godsell, John Arnatt

110. **Clegg** (1969) Lindsay Shontoff Film Productions Col 87 min *U.S. Titles:* The Bullet Machine; Harry and the Hookers (1975 theatrical reissue) *D:* Lindsay Shontoff *P:* Lindsay Shontoff (billed as Lewis J. Force) *Sc:* Lewis J. Hagleton *Ph:* John C. Taylor *M:* Paul Ferris *Ca:* Gilbert Wynne, Gary Hope, Gilly Grant, Norman Claridge, A.J. Brown, Michael Nightingale, Ronald Leigh-Hunt

111. **Cloak Without Dagger** (1955) Balblair Productions B&W 69 min *U.S. Title:* Operation Conspiracy *D:* Joseph Sterling *P:* A.R. Rawlinson *Sc:* A.R. Rawlinson *Ph:* Gerald Gibbs *M:* Wilfred Burns *Ca:* Philip Friend, Mary Mackenzie, Leslie Dwyer, Allan Cuthbertson, John G. Heller, Bill Nagy, Patrick Jordan

112. **Cloudburst** (1951) Hammer Film Productions (in association with Hollywood Exclusive Films [U.S.]) B&W 92 min *D:* Francis Searle *P:* Anthony Hinds and Alexander Paal *Sc:* Francis Searle and Leo Marks *Ph:* Walter J. Harvey *M:* Frank Spencer *Ca:* Robert Preston, Elizabeth Sellars, Colin Tapley, Sheila Burrell, Harold Lang, Mary Germaine, George Woodbridge

113. **The Clouded Yellow** (1950) Carillon Films B&W 96 min *D:* Ralph Thomas *P:* Betty E. Box *Sc:* Janet Green *Ph:* Geoffrey Unsworth

M: Benjamin Frankel *Ca:* Jean Simmons, Trevor Howard, Sonia Dresdel, Barry Jones, Maxwell Reed, Kenneth More, Eric Pohlmann

Clue from a Corpse *see* **The Floating Dutchman**

114. **Clue of the New Pin** (1961) Merton Park B&W 58 min *D:* Allan Davis *P:* Jack Greenwood *Sc:* Philip Mackie *Ph:* Bert Mason *M:* Ron Goodwin *Ca:* Paul Daneman, Bernard Archard, James Villiers, Catherine Woodville, Clive Morton, Wolfe Morris, Alex Gallier

115. **Clue of the Silver Key** (1961) Merton Park B&W 59 min *D:* Gerard Glaister *P:* Jack Greenwood *Sc:* Philip Mackie *Ph:* Bert Mason *M:* Bernard Ebbinghouse *Ca:* Bernard Lee, Lyndon Brook, Finlay Currie, Jennifer Daniel, Patrick Cargill, Anthony Sharp, Sam Kydd

116. **Clue of the Twisted Candle** (1960) Merton Park B&W 61 min *D:* Allan Davis *P:* Jack Greenwood *Sc:* Philip Mackie *Ph:* Brian Rhodes *M:* Francis Chagrin *Ca:* Bernard Lee, David Knight, Francis De Wolff, Colette Wilde, Christine Shaw, Stanley Morgan, Richard Vernon

117. **Coast of Skeletons** (1964) Towers of London (Films) Col 91 min *D:* Robert Lynn *P:* Harry Alan Towers *Sc:* Anthony Scott Veitch *Ph:* Stephen Dade *M:* Christopher Whelen *Ca:* Richard Todd, Dale Robertson, Heinz Drache, Marianne Koch, Elga Andersen, Derek Nimmo, George Leech

Code 7 Victim 5! *see* **Victim Five**

118. **The Collector** (1965) Columbia/The Collector Company Col 119 min *D:* William Wyler *P:* Jud Kinberg and John Kohn *Sc:* Stanley Mann and John Kohn *Ph:* Robert L. Surtees and Robert Krasker *M:* Maurice Jarre *Ca:* Terence Stamp, Samantha Eggar, Mona Washbourne, Maurice Dallimore

119. **The Comeback** (1977) Peter Walker (Heritage) Col 100 min *U.S. Title:* Encore (video—see Appendix V) *D:* Pete Walker *P:* Pete Walker *Sc:* Murray Smith *Ph:* Peter Jessop *M:* Stanley Myers *Ca:* Jack Jones, Pamela Stephenson, David Doyle, Bill Owen, Sheila Keith, Holly Palance, Richard Johnson

120. **Compelled** (1960) The Danzigers B&W 56 min *D:* Ramsey Harrington *P:* Edward J. Danziger and Harry Lee Danziger *Sc:* Mark Grantham *Ph:* James Wilson *Ca:* Ronald Howard, Beth Rogan, John Gabriel, Richard Shaw, Jack Melford, Mark Singleton, Colin Tapley

Con Man *see* **Freelance**

Concrete Jungle *see* **The Criminal**

121. **Confession** (1954) Merton Park/Anglo-Guild Productions B&W 90 min *U.S. Title:* The Deadliest Sin *D:* Ken Hughes *P:* Alec C. Snowden *Sc:* Ken Hughes *Ph:* Phil Grindrod *M:* Richard Taylor *Ca:* Sydney Chaplin, Audrey Dalton, John Bentley, Peter Hammond, John Welsh, Jefferson Clifford, Patrick Allen

The Confessional *see* **House of Mortal Sin**

The Confessional Murders *see* **House of Mortal Sin**

122. **Contraband Spain** (1955) Diadem Films/Balcázar Producciones Cinemátograficas Col 82 min *D:* Lawrence Huntington *P:* Ernest Gartside *Sc:* Lawrence Huntington *Ph:* Harry Waxman *M:* Edwin Astley *Ca:* Richard Greene, Anouk Aimée (billed as Anouk), Michael Denison, José Nieto, John Warwick, Philip Saville, Alfonso Estella

Cop-Out *see* **Stranger in the House**

123. **Count Five and Die** (1957) Zonic Productions B&W 92 min *D:* Victor Vicas *P:* Ernest Gartside *Sc:* Jack Seddon and David Pursall *Ph:* Arthur Grant *M:* John Wooldridge *Ca:* Jeffrey Hunter, Nigel Patrick, Annemarie Duringer, David Kossoff, Rolf Lefebvre, Larry Burns, Philip Bond

124. **The Counterfeit Plan** (1957) Merton Park (in association with Amalgamated Productions [U.S.]) B&W 87 min *D:* Montgomery Tully *P:* Alec C. Snowden *Sc:* James Eastwood *Ph:* Phil Grindrod *M:* Richard Taylor *Ca:* Zachary Scott, Peggie Castle, Mervyn Johns, Sydney Tafler, Lee Patterson, Eric Pohlmann, Robert Arden

125. **Counterspy** (1953) Merton Park B&W 69 min *U.S. Title:* Undercover Agent *D:* Vernon Sewell *P:* William H. Williams *Sc:* Guy Elmes and Gaston Lazare *Ph:* Alan T. Dinsdale *M:* Eric Spear *Ca:* Dermot Walsh, Hazel Court, Hermione Baddeley, James Vivian, Archie Duncan, Alexander Gauge, Bill Travers

126. **Cover Girl Killer** (1959) Parroch Films B&W 61 min *D:* Terry Bishop *P:* Jack Parsons *Sc:* Terry Bishop *Ph:* Gerald Gibbs *M:* William Davies *Ca:* Harry H. Corbett, Felicity Young, Spencer Teakle, Victor Brooks, Bernadette Milnes, Christina Gregg, Charles Lloyd Pack

Cover-Up *see* **Frightmare**

Crazy House *see* **The House in Nightmare Park**

The Creepers *see* **Assault**

127. **Crescendo** (1969) Hammer Film Productions/Seven Arts Col 95 min *D:* Alan Gibson *P:* Michael Carreras *Sc:* Jimmy Sangster and Alfred Shaughnessy *Ph:* Paul Beeson *M:* Malcolm Williamson *Ca:* Stefanie Powers, James Olson, Margaretta Scott, Jane Lapotaire, Joss Ackland, Kirsten Betts

128. **The Criminal** (1960) Merton Park B&W

97 min *U.S. Title:* Concrete Jungle *D:* Joseph Losey *P:* Jack Greenwood *Sc:* Alun Owen *Ph:* Robert Krasker *M:* John Dankworth *Ca:* Stanley Baker, Sam Wanamaker, Margit Saad, Patrick Magee, Noel Willman, Gregoire Aslan, Jill Bennett, Nigel Green, Rupert Davies, Patrick Wymark

129. **The Crooked Road** (1964) Argo Film Productions/Seven Arts/Triglav Films/Trident Films B&W 94 mins *D:* Don Chaffey *P:* David Henley *Sc:* Joy Garrison and Don Chaffey *Ph:* Stephen Dade *M:* Bojan Adamic *Ca:* Robert Ryan, Stewart Granger, Nadia Gray, Catherine Woodville, Marius Goring, George Coulouris, Robert Rietty

130. **The Crooked Sky** (1956) Luckwin Productions (in association with Amalgamated Productions [U.S.]) B&W 77 min *D:* Henry Cass *P:* Derek Winn and Henry Cass *Sc:* Norman Hudis *Ph:* Phil Grindrod *M:* Wilfred Burns *Ca:* Wayne Morris, Karin Booth, Anton Diffring, Bruce Seton, Sheldon Lawrence, Collette Barthrop, Richard Shaw

131. **Cross Channel** (1954) Republic Productions (Great Britain) B&W 61 min *D:* R.G. Springsteen *P:* William N. Boyle *Sc:* Rex Rienits *Ph:* Basil Emmott *M:* Lambert Williamson *Ca:* Wayne Morris, Yvonne Furneaux, Arnold Marle, Patrick Allen, Charles Laurence, Peter Sinclair, Carl Jaffe

132. **Crossplot** (1969) Tribune Productions/Television Reporters International Col 96 min *D:* Alvin Rakoff *P:* Robert S. Baker *Sc:* Leigh Vance *Ph:* Brendan J. Stafford *M:* Stanley Black *Ca:* Roger Moore, Martha Hyer, Claudie Lange, Alexis Kanner, Francis Matthews, Bernard Lee, Derek Francis, Ursula Howells

133. **Crossroads to Crime** (1960) A.P. Films B&W 57 min *D:* Gerry Anderson *P:* Gerry Anderson *Sc:* Alun Falconer *Ph:* John Read *M:* Barry Gray *Ca:* Anthony Oliver, Patricia Heneghan, Miriam Karlin, George Murcell, Ferdy Mayne, David Graham, Victor Maddern

134. **Crosstrap** (1961) Avon Films/Newbery-Clyne Associates B&W 62 min *D:* Robert Hartford-Davis *P:* George Mills *Sc:* Phillip Wrestler *Ph:* Eric Cross *M:* Steve Race *Ca:* Laurence Payne, Jill Adams, Zena Marshall, Gary Cockrell, Bill Nagy, Robert Cawdron, Larry Taylor

Cross-Up *see* **Tiger by the Tail**

135. **Crow Hollow** (1951) Merton Park B&W 69 min *D:* Michael McCarthy *P:* William H. Williams *Sc:* Vivian Milroy *Ph:* Robert Lapresle *M:* De Wolfe *Ca:* Donald Houston, Natasha Parry, Patricia Owens, Esma Cannon, Nora Nicholson, Melissa Stribling, Susan Richmond

136. **Cul-de-Sac** (1966) Compton-Tekli Film Productions B&W 111 min *D:* Roman Polanski *P:* Gene Gutowski *Sc:* Roman Polanski and Gerard Brach *Ph:* Gilbert Taylor *M:* Krzysztof Komeda *Ca:* Donald Pleasence, Françoise Dorléac, Lionel Stander, Jack MacGowran, William Franklyn, Robert Dorning, Renee Houston

137. **A Dandy in Aspic** (1968) Columbia British Productions Col 107 min *D:* Anthony Mann *P:* Anthony Mann *Sc:* Derek Marlowe *Ph:* Christopher Challis *M:* Quincy Jones *Ca:* Laurence Harvey, Tom Courtenay, Mia Farrow, Harry Andrews, Peter Cook, Lionel Stander, Barbara Murray, Per Oscarsson

138. **Danger by My Side** (1962) Butcher's Film Productions B&W 63 min *D:* Charles Saunders *P:* John I. Phillips *Sc:* Ronald Liles and Aubrey Cash *Ph:* Walter J. Harvey *M:* Martin Slavin *Ca:* Anthony Oliver, Maureen Connell, Alan Tilvern, Bill Nagy, Sonya Cordeau, Brandon Brady, Alex Gallier

139. **Danger Route** (1967) Amicus Productions Col 92 min *D:* Seth Holt *P:* Max J. Rosenberg and Milton Subotsky *Sc:* Meade Roberts *Ph:* Harry Waxman *M:* John Mayer *Ca:* Richard Johnson, Carol Lynley, Barbara Bouchet, Sylvia Syms, Harry Andrews, Sam Wanamaker, Gordon Jackson, Diana Dors, Maurice Denham

140. **Danger Tomorrow** (1960) Parroch Films/Coronado Productions (England) B&W 61 min *D:* Terry Bishop *P:* Jack Parsons *Sc:* Guy Deghy *Ph:* Ken Hodges *M:* David Lee *Ca:* Zena Walker, Robert Urquhart, Lisa Daniely, Rupert Davies, Annabel Maule, Russell Waters, Charles Houston

141. **Danger Within** (1959) Colin Lesslie Productions B&W 101 min *U.S. Title:* Breakout *D:* Don Chaffey *P:* Colin Lesslie *Sc:* Bryan Forbes and Frank Harvey *Ph:* Arthur Grant *M:* Francis Chagrin *Ca:* Richard Todd, Bernard Lee, Michael Wilding, Richard Attenborough, Dennis Price, Donald Houston, William Franklyn, Peter Arne

142. **Dangerous Afternoon** (1961) Theatrecraft Limited B&W 62 min *D:* Charles Saunders *P:* Guido Coen *Sc:* Brandon Fleming *Ph:* Geoffrey Faithfull *M:* Norman Percival *Ca:* Ruth Dunning, Nora Nicholson, Joanna Dunham, Howard Pays, Gladys Henson, Ian Colin, Jerold Wells, Gwenda Wilson

143. **Dangerous Assignment** (1950) Target Films B&W 58 min *U.S. Title:* European Assignment *D:* Ben R. Hart *P:* Miriam Crowdy *Sc:* Chick Messina *Ph:* Ben R. Hart *Ca:* Lionel Murton, Pamela Deeming, Ivan Craig, Bill Hodge, Edward Evans, Macdonald Parke, Michael Hogarth

144. **Dangerous Cargo** (1953) A.C.T. Films B&W 60 min *D:* John Harlow *P:* Stanley Haynes *Sc:* Stanley Haynes *Ph:* Lionel Banes *Ca:* Susan Stephen, Jack Watling, Karel Stepanek, Richard Pearson, Terence Alexander, John Le Mesurier, Ballard Berkeley

Dangerous Impact *see* **Impact**

145. **Dangerous Voyage** (1953) Merton Park B&W 72 min *U.S. Title:* Terror Ship *D:* Vernon Sewell *P:* William H. Williams *Sc:* Julian Ward *Ph:* Josef Ambor *M:* Allan Gray *Ca:* William Lundigan, Naomi Chance, Vincent Ball, Jean Lodge, Kenneth Henry, Richard Stewart, John Warwick

146. **Dark Interval** (1950) Present Day Productions B&W 60 min *D:* Charles Saunders *P:* Charles Reynolds *Sc:* John Gilling *Ph:* Ted Lloyd *M:* William Cox-Ife *Ca:* Zena Marshall, Andrew Osborn, John Barry, John Le Mesurier, Mona Washbourne, Wallas Eaton, Charmian Innes

147. **The Dark Light** (1950) Hammer Film Productions B&W 67 min *D:* Vernon Sewell *P:* Michael Carreras *Sc:* Vernon Sewell *Ph:* Moray Grant *M:* Frank Spencer *Ca:* Albert Lieven, David Greene, Norman MacOwan, Martin Benson, Jack Stewart, Katharine Blake, Joan Carol

148. **The Dark Man** (1950) Independent Artists B&W 91 min *D:* Jeffrey Dell *P:* Julian Wintle *Sc:* Jeffrey Dell *Ph:* Eric Cross *M:* Hubert Clifford *Ca:* Edward Underdown, Maxwell Reed, Natasha Parry, William Hartnell, Barbara Murray, Robert Long, Cyril Smith

149. **Date at Midnight** (1959) The Danzigers B&W 56 min *D:* Godfrey Grayson *P:* Edward J. Danziger and Harry Lee Danziger *Sc:* Mark Grantham *Ph:* James Wilson *M:* Tony Crombie *Ca:* Paul Carpenter, Jean Aubrey, Harriette Johns, Ralph Michael, John Charlesworth, Philip Ray, Howard Lang

A Date with Death *see* **The High Bright Sun**

150. **Date with Disaster** (1957) Fortress Film Productions B&W 61 min *D:* Charles Saunders *P:* Guido Coen *Sc:* Brock Williams *Ph:* Brendan J. Stafford *M:* Reg Owen and Anthony Spurgin *Ca:* Tom Drake, William Hartnell, Shirley Eaton, Maurice Kaufmann, Michael Golden, Richard Shaw, Charles Brodie

151. **Dateline Diamonds** (1965) Viscount Films B&W 70 min *D:* Jeremy Summers *P:* Harry Benn *Sc:* Tudor Gates *Ph:* Stephen Dade *M:* Johnny Douglas *Ca:* William Lucas, Kenneth Cope, George Mikell, Conrad Phillips, Patsy Rowlands, Burnell Tucker, Vanda Godsell

152. **The Day of the Jackal** (1973) Warwick Film Productions/Universal Productions France Col 142 min *D:* Fred Zinnemann *P:* John Woolf *Sc:* Kenneth Ross *Ph:* Jean Tournier *M:* Georges Delerue *Ca:* Edward Fox, Michael Lonsdale, Alan Badel, Eric Porter, Jean Martin, Cyril Cusack, Delphine Seyrig, Donald Sinden

153. **The Day They Robbed the Bank of England** (1959) Summit Film Productions B&W 85 min *D:* John Guillermin *P:* Jules Buck *Sc:* Howard Clewes *Ph:* Georges Perinal *M:* Edwin Astley *Ca:* Aldo Ray, Elizabeth Sellars, Peter O'Toole, Hugh Griffith, Kieron Moore, John Le Mesurier, Andrew Keir

Dead by Morning *see* **Miss Tulip Stays the Night**

154. **Dead Cert** (1974) Woodfall Limited Col 99 min *D:* Tony Richardson *P:* Neil Hartley *Sc:* Tony Richardson and John Oaksey *Ph:* Freddie Cooper *M:* John Addison *Ca:* Scott Antony, Judi Dench, Michael Williams, Nina Thomas, Mark Dignam, Julian Glover, Bill Fraser

155. **Dead Lucky** (1960) A.C.T. Films B&W 64 min *D:* Montgomery Tully *P:* Robert Dunbar *Sc:* Sidney Nelson and Maurice Harrison *Ph:* Peter Hennessy *M:* William Davies *Ca:* Vincent Ball, Betty McDowall, John Le Mesurier, Alfred Burke, Michael Ripper, Sam Kydd, Brian Worth

156. **Dead Man's Chest** (1965) Merton Park B&W 59 min *D:* Patrick Dromgoole *P:* Jack Greenwood *Sc:* Donal Giltinan *Ph:* James Wilson *M:* Bernard Ebbinghouse *Ca:* John Thaw, Ann Firbank, John Meillon, John Collin, Peter Bowles, John Abineri, Graham Crowden

157. **Dead Man's Evidence** (1962) Bayford Films/R.C.H. B&W 67 min *D:* Francis Searle *P:* Francis Searle *Sc:* Arthur La Bern *Ph:* Ken Hodges *M:* Ken Thorne *Ca:* Conrad Phillips, Jane Griffiths, Veronica Hurst, Ryck Rydon, Godfrey Quigley, Bruce Seton, Harry Webster

158. **Deadfall** (1968) Salamander Film Productions Col 120 min *D:* Bryan Forbes *P:* Paul Monash *Sc:* Bryan Forbes *Ph:* Gerry Turpin *M:* John Barry *Ca:* Michael Caine, Giovanna Ralli, Eric Portman, Nanette Newman, David Buck, Leonard Rossiter, Vladek Sheybal

159. **Deadlier Than the Male** (1966) Santor Film Productions Col 98 min *D:* Ralph Thomas *P:* Betty E. Box *Sc:* Jimmy Sangster, David Osborn and Liz Charles-Williams *Ph:* Ernest Steward *M:* Malcolm Lockyer *Ca:* Richard Johnson, Elke Sommer, Sylva Koscina, Nigel Green, Suzanna Leigh, Steve Carlson, Virginia North

The Deadliest Sin *see* **Confession**

160. **The Deadly Affair** (1966) Sidney Lumet Film Productions Col 107 min *D:* Sidney Lumet *P:* Sidney Lumet *Sc:* Paul Dehn *Ph:* Freddie

Young *M:* Quincy Jones *Ca:* James Mason, Maximilian Schell, Harriet Andersson, Harry Andrews, Simone Signoret, Kenneth Haigh, Roy Kinnear, Robert Flemyng

161. **The Deadly Bees** (1966) Amicus Productions Col 83 min *D:* Freddie Francis *P:* Max J. Rosenberg and Milton Subotsky *Sc:* Robert Bloch and Anthony Marriott *Ph:* John Wilcox *M:* Wilfred Josephs *Ca:* Suzanna Leigh, Frank Finlay, Guy Doleman, Catherine Finn, John Harvey, Michael Ripper, Katy Wild

162. **The Deadly Females** (1975) Donwin Productions Col 105 min *D:* Donovan Winter *P:* Donovan Winter *Sc:* Donovan Winter *Ph:* Austin Parkinson *Ca:* Tracy Reed, Bernard Holley, Scott Fredericks, Heather Chasen, Jean Harrington, Roy Purcell, Rula Lenska

The Deadly Game *see* **Third Party Risk**

163. **Deadly Nightshade** (1952) Kenilworth Film Productions/Mid-Century Film Productions B&W 61 min *D:* John Gilling *P:* Robert S. Baker and Monty Berman *Sc:* Lawrence Huntington *Ph:* Monty Berman *M:* John Lanchbery *Ca:* Emrys Jones, Zena Marshall, John Horsley, Joan Hickson, Hector Ross, George Pastell, Marne Maitland

164. **Deadly Record** (1959) Independent Artists B&W 59 min *D:* Lawrence Huntington *P:* Vivian A. Cox *Sc:* Vivian A. Cox and Lawrence Huntington *Ph:* Eric Cross *M:* Neville McGrah *Ca:* Lee Patterson, Barbara Shelley, Peter Dyneley, Jane Hylton, Geoffrey Keen, Ferdy Mayne, George Pastell

165. **Deadly Strangers** (1974) Silhouette Film Productions/HTV Col 93 min *D:* Sidney Hayers *P:* Peter Miller *Sc:* Philip Levene *Ph:* Graham Edgar *M:* Ron Goodwin *Ca:* Hayley Mills, Simon Ward, Sterling Hayden, Ken Hutchison, Peter Jeffrey, Hubert Tucker, Nina Francis

Death and the Sky Above *see* **Two-Letter Alibi**

166. **Death Drums Along the River** (1963) Big Ben Films/Hallam Productions Col 83 min *U.S. Title:* Sanders (TV only) *D:* Lawrence Huntington *P:* Harry Alan Towers *Sc:* Harry Alan Towers, Nicolas Roeg, Kevin Kavanagh and Lawrence Huntington *Ph:* Bob Huke *M:* Sidney Torch *Ca:* Richard Todd, Marianne Koch, Albert Lieven, Vivi Bach, Walter Rilla, Jeremy Lloyd, Robert Arden

167. **Death Goes to School** (1952) Independent Artists B&W 65 min *D:* Stephen Clarkson *P:* Victor Hanbury *Sc:* Maisie Sharman and Stephen Clarkson *Ph:* Eric Cross *M:* De Wolfe *Ca:* Barbara Murray, Gordon Jackson, Pamela Alan, Jane Aird, Beatrice Varley, Ann Butchart, Jeanne Matto

168. **Death Is a Woman** (1965) Associated British Pathé Col 81 min *U.S. Titles:* Love Is a Woman; Sex Is a Woman (briefly used alternate theatrical release title) *D:* Frederic Goode *P:* Harry Field *Sc:* Wally Bosco *Ph:* Bill Jordan *M:* Joan Shakespeare *Ca:* Mark Burns, Patsy Ann Noble, Shaun Curry, Wanda Ventham, Terence De Marney, Caron Gardner, William Dexter

169. **Death of an Angel** (1951) Hammer Film Productions B&W 64 min *D:* Charles Saunders *P:* Anthony Hinds *Sc:* Reginald Long *Ph:* Walter J. Harvey *M:* Frank Spencer *Ca:* Jane Baxter, Patrick Barr, Jean Lodge, Raymond Young, Russell Waters, Russell Napier, Julie Somers

170. **Death on the Nile** (1978) Mersham Productions Col 140 min *D:* John Guillermin *P:* John Brabourne and Richard Goodwin *Sc:* Anthony Shaffer *Ph:* Jack Cardiff *M:* Nino Rota *Ca:* Peter Ustinov, Lois Chiles, Bette Davis, Mia Farrow, Olivia Hussey, George Kennedy, Simon MacCorkindale, David Niven, Maggie Smith

171. **Death Over My Shoulder** (1957) Vicar Productions (in association with Pugach-Weitz-Brasselle Productions [U.S.]) B&W 89 min *D:* Arthur Crabtree *P:* Frank Bevis *Sc:* Norman Hudis *Ph:* Walter J. Harvey *M:* Douglas Gamley *Ca:* Keefe Brasselle, Bonar Colleano, Jill Adams, Arlene De Marco, Charles Farrell, Al Mulock, Sonia Dresdel

172. **Death Trap** (1962) Merton Park B&W 57 min *D:* John Llewellyn Moxey *P:* Jack Greenwood *Sc:* John Roddick *Ph:* Bert Mason *M:* Bernard Ebbinghouse *Ca:* Albert Lieven, Barbara Shelley, John Meillon, Mercy Haystead, Kenneth Cope, Leslie Sands, Barry Linehan

173. **The Delavine Affair** (1954) Croydon-Passmore Productions B&W 65 min *U.S. Title:* Murder Is News (TV only) *D:* Douglas Peirce *P:* Henry Passmore *Sc:* George Fisher *Ph:* Jonah Jones *Ca:* Peter Reynolds, Honor Blackman, Gordon Jackson, Valerie Vernon, Michael Balfour, Peter Neil, Peter Swanwick

174. **Delayed Action** (1954) Kenilworth Film Productions/Mid-Century Film Productions B&W 60 min *D:* John Harlow *P:* Robert S. Baker and Monty Berman *Sc:* Geoffrey Orme *Ph:* Gerald Gibbs *M:* John Lanchbery *Ca:* Robert Ayres, June Thorburn, Alan Wheatley, Michael Kelly, Bruce Seton, Michael Balfour, John Horsley

175. **Delayed Flight** (1964) Luckwell Productions B&W 62 min *D:* Tony Young *P:* Bill Luckwell and David Vigo *Sc:* Dail Ambler *Ph:* Walter J. Harvey *M:* Wilfred Burns *Ca:* Helen

Cherry, Hugh McDermott, Paul Williamson, Neal Arden, John Watson, Totti Truman Taylor, Patrick Jordan

176. **The Depraved** (1957) The Danzigers B&W 71 min *D:* Paul Dickson *P:* Edward J. Danziger and Harry Lee Danziger *Sc:* Brian Clemens and Edith Dell *Ph:* James Wilson *M:* Albert Elms *Ca:* Anne Heywood, Robert Arden, Carroll Levis, Basil Dignam, Denis Shaw, Robert Ayres, Gary Thorne

177. **The Desperate Man** (1960) Merton Park B&W 57 min *D:* Peter Maxwell *P:* Jack Greenwood *Sc:* James Eastwood *Ph:* Gerald Moss *M:* James Stevens *Ca:* William Hartnell, Conrad Phillips, Jill Ireland, Charles Gray, Peter Swanwick, Arthur Gomez, Patricia Burke

178. **Desperate Moment** (1953) Fanfare Films/British Film Makers B&W 88 min *D:* Compton Bennett *P:* George H. Brown *Sc:* Patrick Kirwan and George H. Brown *Ph:* C. Pennington-Richards *M:* Ronald Binge *Ca:* Dirk Bogarde, Mai Zetterling, Philip Friend, Albert Lieven, Theodore Bikel, Simone Silva, Ferdy Mayne

The Destructors *see* **The Marseille Contract**
The Detective *see* **Father Brown**

179. **The Devil's Agent** (1962) Emmet Dalton Productions (London)/Eichberg Film (Munich)/Bavaria Filmkunst (Munich)/CCC Film (Berlin) B&W 96 min *D:* John Paddy Carstairs *P:* Emmet Dalton *Sc:* Robert Westerby *Ph:* Gerald Gibbs *M:* Philip Green *Ca:* Peter Van Eyck, Marianne Koch, Macdonald Carey, Christopher Lee, Billie Whitelaw, Albert Lieven, Marius Goring, Helen Cherry, Eric Pohlmann

180. **Devil's Bait** (1959) Independent Artists B&W 58 min *D:* Peter Graham Scott *P:* Julian Wintle and Leslie Parkyn *Sc:* Peter Johnston and Diana K. Watson *Ph:* Michael Reed *M:* William Alwyn *Ca:* Geoffrey Keen, Jane Hylton, Gordon Jackson, Dermot Kelly, Shirley Lawrence, Eileen Moore, Rupert Davies

181. **The Devil's Daffodil** (1961) Omnia Pictures/Rialto Film Preben Philipsen B&W 86 min *D:* Akos Rathony *P:* Steven Pallos and Donald Taylor *Sc:* Basil Dawson and Donald Taylor *Ph:* Desmond Dickinson *M:* Keith Papworth *Ca:* William Lucas, Penelope Horner, Christopher Lee, Ingrid Van Bergen, Albert Lieven, Marius Goring, Colin Jeavons

Devil's Harbor *see* **Devil's Point**

182. **Devil's Point** (1954) Charles Deane Productions B&W 65 min *U.S. Title:* Devil's Harbor *D:* Montgomery Tully *P:* Charles Deane *Sc:* Charles Deane *Ph:* Geoffrey Faithfull *Ca:* Richard Arlen, Greta Gynt, Donald Houston, Mary Germaine, Edwin Richfield, Michael Balfour, Vincent Ball

183. **Diagnosis: Murder** (1974) Silhouette Film Productions/HTV Col 90 min *D:* Sidney Hayers *P:* Peter Miller *Sc:* Philip Levene *Ph:* Bob Edwards *M:* Laurie Johnson *Ca:* Jon Finch, Judy Geeson, Christopher Lee, Tony Beckley, Dilys Hamlett, Jane Merrow, Colin Jeavons

184. **Dial 999** (1955) Merton Park/Anglo-Guild Productions (in association with Todon Productions [U.S.]) B&W 86 min *U.S. Title:* The Way Out *D:* Montgomery Tully *P:* Alec C. Snowden *Sc:* Montgomery Tully *Ph:* Phil Grindrod *M:* Richard Taylor *Ca:* Gene Nelson, Mona Freeman, John Bentley, Michael Goodliffe, Sydney Tafler, Charles Victor, Paula Byrne

185. **The Diamond** (1953) Gibraltar Films B&W 83 min *U.S. Title:* The Diamond Wizard *D:* Montgomery Tully (Dennis O'Keefe credited on U.S. prints) *P:* Steven Pallos *Sc:* John C. Higgins *Ph:* Gordon Lang *M:* Matyas Seiber *Ca:* Dennis O'Keefe, Margaret Sheridan, Philip Friend, Alan Wheatley, Paul Hardtmuth, Colin Tapley, Hugh Morton

The Diamond Wizard *see* **The Diamond**

186. **Diamonds Are Forever** (1971) Eon Productions Col 119 min *D:* Guy Hamilton *P:* Albert R. Broccoli and Harry Saltzman *Sc:* Richard Maibaum and Tom Mankiewicz *Ph:* Ted Moore *M:* John Barry *Ca:* Sean Connery, Jill St. John, Charles Gray, Lana Wood, Jimmy Dean, Bruce Cabot, Joseph Furst, Putter Smith, Bruce Glover, Bernard Lee, Lois Maxwell

Die! Die! My Darling! *see* **Fanatic**

187. **Die Screaming, Marianne** (1970) Pete Walker Film Productions Col 104 min *D:* Pete Walker *P:* Pete Walker *Sc:* Murray Smith *Ph:* Norman Langley *M:* Cyril Ornadel *Ca:* Susan George, Barry Evans, Leo Genn, Christopher Sandford, Judy Huxtable, Kenneth Hendel, Anthony Sharp

188. **Dilemma** (1962) A.C.T. Films B&W 64 min *D:* Peter Maxwell *P:* Ted Lloyd *Sc:* Peter Maxwell *Ph:* Gerald Moss *M:* William Davies *Ca:* Peter Halliday, Ingrid Hafner, Patricia Burke, Patrick Jordan, Joan Heath, Robert Deane, Barbara Lott

189. **The Diplomatic Corpse** (1958) A.C.T. Films B&W 65 min *D:* Montgomery Tully *P:* Francis Searle *Sc:* Sidney Nelson and Maurice Harrison *Ph:* Phil Grindrod *Ca:* Robin Bailey, Susan Shaw, Liam Redmond, Harry Fowler, Maya Koumani, Andre Mikhelson, Bill Shine

190. **Diplomatic Passport** (1954) Rich & Rich/Princess Pictures B&W 66 min *D:* Gene

Martel *P:* Gene Martel and Burt Balaban *Sc:* Paul Tabori *Ph:* James Wilson *M:* Eric Spear *Ca:* Paul Carpenter, Marsha Hunt, Henry Oscar, Honor Blackman, Marne Maitland, John MacLaren, Arnold Diamond

Dirty Knights' Work *see* **Trial by Combat**

191. **The Disappearance** (1977) Trofar Ltd./Tiberius Film Productions/National Film Trustee Company Col 102 min *D:* Stuart Cooper *P:* David Hemmings *Sc:* Paul Mayersberg *Ph:* John Alcott *M:* Robert Farnon *Ca:* Donald Sutherland, Francine Racette, David Hemmings, John Hurt, David Warner, Virginia McKenna, Christopher Plummer

192. **Do You Know This Voice?** (1964) Parroch-McCallum Productions (in association with Lippert Incorporated [U.S.]) B&W 80 min *D:* Frank Nesbitt *P:* Jack Parsons *Sc:* Neil McCallum *Ph:* Arthur Lavis *M:* Carlo Martelli *Ca:* Dan Duryea, Isa Miranda, Gwen Watford, Peter Madden, Barry Warren, Alan Edwards, Jean Aubrey

193. **Dr. No** (1962) Eon Productions Col 105 min *D:* Terence Young *P:* Harry Saltzman and Albert R. Broccoli *Sc:* Richard Maibaum, Johanna Harwood and Berkely Mather *Ph:* Ted Moore *M:* Monty Norman *Ca:* Sean Connery, Ursula Andress, Joseph Wiseman, Jack Lord, Anthony Dawson, John Kitzmiller, Zena Marshall, Bernard Lee, Lois Maxwell

194. **Dominique** (1978) Sword and Sorcery Productions/Grand Prize Productions Col 100 min *U.S. Titles:* Dominique Is Dead; Avenging Spirit (video—see Appendix V) *D:* Michael Anderson *P:* Milton Subotsky and Andrew Donally *Sc:* Edward Abraham and Valerie Abraham *Ph:* Ted Moore *M:* David Whitaker *Ca:* Cliff Robertson, Jean Simmons, Jenny Agutter, Simon Ward, Ron Moody, Judy Geeson, Michael Jayston, Flora Robson, David Tomlinson, Jack Warner

Dominique Is Dead *see* **Dominique**

195. **Don't Look Now** (1973) Casey Productions (London)/Eldorado Films (Rome)/D.L.N. Ventures Partnership Col 110 min *D:* Nicolas Roeg *P:* Peter Katz *Sc:* Allan Scott and Chris Bryant *Ph:* Anthony Richmond *M:* Pino Donaggio *Ca:* Julie Christie, Donald Sutherland, Hilary Mason, Massimo Serato, Clelia Matania, Renato Scarpa, Giorgio Trestini

196. **Don't Talk to Strange Men** (1962) Derick Williams Productions B&W 65 min *D:* Pat Jackson *P:* Derick Williams *Sc:* Gwen Cherrell *Ph:* Stephen Dade *Ca:* Christina Gregg, Janina Faye, Cyril Raymond, Gillian Lind, Conrad Phillips, Dandy Nichols, Gwen Nelson

197. **Doomsday at Eleven** (1962) Parroch Films B&W 56 min *D:* Theodore Zichy *P:* Jack Parsons *Sc:* Paul Tabori and Gordon Wellesley *Ph:* Ken Hodges *M:* Wilfred Josephs *Ca:* Carl Jaffe, Alan Heywood, Stanley Morgan, Derrick De Marney, Jennifer Wright, Delia Corrie, Geoffrey Dunn

198. **Doomwatch** (1972) Tigon British Film Productions Col 92 min *D:* Peter Sasdy *P:* Tony Tenser *Sc:* Clive Exton *Ph:* Kenneth Talbot *M:* John Scott *Ca:* Ian Bannen, Judy Geeson, George Sanders, John Paul, Simon Oates, Norman Bird, Geoffrey Keen, Percy Herbert

199. **The Double** (1963) Merton Park B&W 56 min *D:* Lionel Harris *P:* Jack Greenwood *Sc:* Lindsay Galloway and John Roddick *Ph:* James Wilson *M:* Bernard Ebbinghouse *Ca:* Jeannette Sterke, Alan MacNaughtan, Robert Brown, Jane Griffiths, Basil Henson, Anne Lawson, Diane Clare

200. **Double Confession** (1950) Harry Reynolds Productions B&W 86 min *D:* Ken Annakin *P:* Harry Reynolds *Sc:* William Templeton *Ph:* Geoffrey Unsworth *M:* Benjamin Frankel *Ca:* Derek Farr, Joan Hopkins, Peter Lorre, William Hartnell, Naunton Wayne, Ronald Howard, Kathleen Harrison

201. **Double Exposure** (1954) Kenilworth Film Productions/Mid-Century Film Productions B&W 63 min *D:* John Gilling *P:* Robert S. Baker and Monty Berman *Sc:* John Gilling *Ph:* Monty Berman *M:* John Lanchbery *Ca:* John Bentley, Rona Anderson, Garry Marsh, Alexander Gauge, Ingeborg Wells, Ryck Rydon, John Horsley

202. **Double Exposure** (1976) Westwind Productions Col 81 min *D:* William Webb *P:* William Webb *Sc:* William Webb *Ph:* Alan Pudney *Ca:* Anouska Hempel, David Baron, Alan Brown, Robert Russell, Julia Vidler, Dean Harris, Alan Hay

203. **The Double Man** (1967) Albion Film Distributors Col 105 min *D:* Franklin J. Schaffner *P:* Hal E. Chester *Sc:* Frank Tarloff and Alfred Hayes *Ph:* Denys Coop *M:* Ernie Freeman *Ca:* Yul Brynner, Britt Ekland, Clive Revill, Anton Diffring, Moira Lister, Lloyd Nolan, Julia Arnall, George Mikell

204. **Doublecross** (1955) Beaconsfield Films/Group 3 B&W 71 min *D:* Anthony Squire *P:* Donald Taylor *Sc:* Anthony Squire and Kem Bennett *Ph:* Kenneth Talbot *M:* Edward Williams *Ca:* Donald Houston, Fay Compton, William Hartnell, Delphi Lawrence, Anton Diffring, Allan Cuthbertson, Kenneth Cope

205. **Downfall** (1963) Merton Park B&W 58 min *D:* John Llewellyn Moxey *P:* Jack Greenwood *Sc:* Robert Banks Stewart *Ph:* James Wilson *M:* Bernard Ebbinghouse *Ca:* Maurice Denham, Nadja Regin, T.P. McKenna, Peter Barkworth, Ellen McIntosh, Iris Russell, Victor Brooks

Dressed for Death *see* **Straight on Till Morning**

206. **Dublin Nightmare** (1958) Penington-Eady Productions B&W 64 min *D:* John Pomeroy *P:* Jon Penington *Sc:* John Tully *Ph:* Eric Cross *M:* Edwin Astley *Ca:* William Sylvester, Marla Landi, Richard Leech, Harry Hutchinson, William Sherwood, Jack Cunningham, Gerald Lawson

207. **Duel in the Jungle** (1954) Associated British Picture Corporation/Marcel Hellman Productions (in association with Moulin Productions [U.S.]) Col 102 min *D:* George Marshall *P:* Marcel Hellman *Sc:* Sam Marx and T.J. Morrison *Ph:* Erwin Hillier *M:* Mischa Spoliansky *Ca:* Dana Andrews, Jeanne Crain, David Farrar, Patrick Barr, George Coulouris, Charles Goldner, Wilfrid Hyde White

208. **Duffy** (1968) Columbia British Productions Col 101 min *D:* Robert Parrish *P:* Martin Manulis *Sc:* Donald Cammell and Harry Joe Brown, Jr. *Ph:* Otto Heller *M:* Ernie Freeman *Ca:* James Coburn, James Mason, James Fox, Susannah York, John Alderton, Guy Deghy, Carl Duering, Marne Maitland

The Dynamiters *see* **The Gelignite Gang**
Dynasty of Fear *see* **Fear in the Night**

209. **The Eagle Has Landed** (1976) ITC/Associated General Films Col 135 min *D:* John Sturges *P:* Jack Wiener and David Niven, Jr. *Sc:* Tom Mankiewicz *Ph:* Anthony Richmond *M:* Lalo Schifrin *Ca:* Michael Caine, Donald Sutherland, Robert Duvall, Jenny Agutter, Donald Pleasence, Jean Marsh, Larry Hagman, Anthony Quayle, Judy Geeson, John Standing, Sven-Bertil Taube, Treat Williams

210. **Echo of Barbara** (1960) Independent Artists B&W 58 min *D:* Sidney Hayers *P:* Julian Wintle and Leslie Parkyn *Sc:* John Kruse *Ph:* Michael Reed *M:* David Lee *Ca:* Mervyn Johns, Maureen Connell, Paul Stassino, Ronald Hines, Tom Bell, Brian Peck, Eddie Leslie

211. **Echo of Diana** (1963) Butcher's Film Productions B&W 61 min *D:* Ernest Morris *P:* John I. Phillips and Ronald Liles *Sc:* Reginald Hearne *Ph:* Walter J. Harvey *M:* Martin Slavin *Ca:* Vincent Ball, Betty McDowall, Geoffrey Toone, Clare Owen, Peter Illing, Michael Balfour, Dermot Walsh

212. **Eight O'Clock Walk** (1953) British Aviation Pictures B&W 87 min *D:* Lance Comfort *P:* George King *Sc:* Katherine Strueby and Guy Morgan *Ph:* Brendan J. Stafford *M:* George Melachrino *Ca:* Richard Attenborough, Cathy O'Donnell, Derek Farr, Ian Hunter, Maurice Denham, Bruce Seton, Harry Welchman

213. **80,000 Suspects** (1963) The Rank Organisation Film Productions B&W 113 min *D:* Val Guest *P:* Val Guest *Sc:* Val Guest *Ph:* Arthur Grant *M:* Stanley Black *Ca:* Claire Bloom, Richard Johnson, Yolande Donlan, Cyril Cusack, Michael Goodliffe, Mervyn Johns, Kay Walsh

The Electronic Monster *see* **Escapement**

214. **11 Harrowhouse** (1974) Harrowhouse Productions Col 95 min *U.S. Titles:* Anything for Love (TV only); Fast Fortune (video—see Appendix V) *D:* Aram Avakian *P:* Elliott Kastner *Sc:* Jeffrey Bloom *Ph:* Arthur Ibbetson *M:* Michael J. Lewis *Ca:* Charles Grodin, Candice Bergen, James Mason, Trevor Howard, John Gielgud, Helen Cherry, Peter Vaughan

215. **Embassy** (1972) Weaver Productions/The Hemdale Group/Triad Col 90 min *U.S. Title:* Target: Embassy (video—see Appendix V) *D:* Gordon Hessler *P:* Mel Ferrer *Sc:* William Fairchild *Ph:* Raoul Coutard *M:* Jonathan Hodge *Ca:* Richard Roundtree, Chuck Connors, Marie-José Nat, Ray Milland, Broderick Crawford, Max Von Sydow, David Bauer

216. **The Embezzler** (1954) Kenilworth Film Productions/Mid-Century Film Productions B&W 61 min *D:* John Gilling *P:* Robert S. Baker and Monty Berman *Sc:* John Gilling *Ph:* Jonah Jones *M:* John Lanchbery *Ca:* Charles Victor, Zena Marshall, Cyril Chamberlain, Leslie Weston, Avice Landone, Peggy Mount, Michael Craig

217. **Emergency** (1962) Butcher's Film Productions B&W 63 min *D:* Francis Searle *P:* Francis Searle *Sc:* Don Nicholl and Jim O'Connolly *Ph:* Ken Hodges *M:* John Veale *Ca:* Glyn Houston, Zena Walker, Dermot Walsh, Colin Tapley, Garard Green, Anthony Dawes, Patrick Jordan

218. **Emergency Call** (1952) Nettlefold Films B&W 90 min *U.S. Title:* Hundred Hour Hunt *D:* Lewis Gilbert *P:* Ernest G. Roy *Sc:* Vernon Harris and Lewis Gilbert *Ph:* Wilkie Cooper *M:* Wilfred Burns *Ca:* Jack Warner, Anthony Steel, Joy Shelton, Freddie Mills, Sidney James, Earl Cameron, Eric Pohlmann, Sydney Tafler

Encore *see* **The Comeback**

219. **The End of the Line** (1957) Fortress Film Productions B&W 65 min *D:* Charles Saunders *P:* Guido Coen *Sc:* Paul Erickson *Ph:* Walter

J. Harvey *M:* Edwin Astley *Ca:* Alan Baxter, Barbara Shelley, Ferdy Mayne, Jennifer Jayne, Arthur Gomez, Geoffrey Hibbert, Jack Melford

220. **Endless Night** (1972) British Lion Films/EMI Film Productions/National Film Trustee Company Col 99 min *D:* Sidney Gilliat *P:* Leslie Gilliat *Sc:* Sidney Gilliat *Ph:* Harry Waxman *M:* Bernard Herrmann *Ca:* Hayley Mills, Hywel Bennett, Britt Ekland, George Sanders, Per Oscarsson, Peter Bowles, Lois Maxwell

221. **Enter Inspector Duval** (1961) Bill and Michael Luckwell Ltd. B&W 64 min *U.S. Title:* Inspector Duval (little-known retitling by distributor Keith T. Smith [Modern Sound Pictures, Inc.]) *D:* Max Varnel *P:* Bill Luckwell and Jock MacGregor *Sc:* J. Henry Piperno *Ph:* Stephen Dade *M:* Wilfred Burns *Ca:* Anton Diffring, Diane Hart, Mark Singleton, Charles Mitchell, Aiden Grennell, Susan Hallinan, Charles Roberts

222. **Escape by Night** (1953) Tempean Films B&W 79 min *D:* John Gilling *P:* Robert S. Baker and Monty Berman *Sc:* John Gilling *Ph:* Monty Berman *M:* Stanley Black *Ca:* Bonar Colleano, Andrew Ray, Sidney James, Simone Silva, Ted Ray, Patrick Barr, Martin Benson

Escape by Night *see* **Clash by Night**

Escape from the Iron Curtain *see* **Flight from Vienna**

223. **Escape in the Sun** (1956) Phoenix Productions Col 86 min *D:* George Breakston *P:* George Breakston and John R. Carter *Sc:* George Breakston *Ph:* George Breakston *M:* Philip Green *Ca:* John Bentley, Vera Fusek, Martin Boddey, Alan Tarlton, Derek L.L. John, James Fuggel

224. **Escape Route** (1952) Banner Pictures (in association with Lippert Pictures [U.S.]) B&W 79 min *U.S. Title:* I'll Get You *D:* Seymour Friedman and Peter Graham Scott *P:* Ronald Kinnoch *Sc:* John Baines *Ph:* Eric Cross *M:* Hans May *Ca:* George Raft, Sally Gray, Clifford Evans, Reginald Tate, Patricia Laffan, Frederick Piper, John Warwick

225. **Escapement** (1957) Merton Park (in association with Amalgamated Productions [U.S.]) B&W 77 min *U.S. Title:* The Electronic Monster *D:* Montgomery Tully (dream sequences directed by David Paltenghi) *P:* Alec C. Snowden *Sc:* Charles Eric Maine *Ph:* Bert Mason (dream sequences photographed by Teddy Catford) *M:* Richard Taylor (electronic music by Soundrama) *Ca:* Rod Cameron, Mary Murphy, Meredith Edwards, Peter Illing, Kay Callard, Carl Jaffe, Carl Duering

226. **Escort for Hire** (1960) The Danzigers Col 66 min *D:* Godfrey Grayson *P:* Edward J. Danziger and Harry Lee Danziger *Sc:* Mark Grantham *Ph:* James Wilson *Ca:* June Thorburn, Pete Murray, Noel Trevarthen, Jan Holden, Peter Butterworth, Guy Middleton, Mary Laura Wood

Estate of Insanity *see* **The Black Torment**

European Assignment *see* **Dangerous Assignment**

Evidence for Hire *see* **Circumstantial Evidence**

227. **The Executioner** (1970) Ameran Films Col 111 min *D:* Sam Wanamaker *P:* Charles H. Schneer *Sc:* Jack Pulman *Ph:* Denys Coop *M:* Ron Goodwin *Ca:* George Peppard, Joan Collins, Judy Geeson, Oscar Homolka, Charles Gray, Nigel Patrick, George Baker, Keith Michell, Peter Dyneley

228. **Exposé** (1975) Norfolk International Pictures Col 82 min *U.S. Titles:* The House on Straw Hill; Trauma *D:* James Kenelm Clarke *P:* Brian Smedley-Aston *Sc:* James Kenelm Clarke *Ph:* Dennis Lewiston *M:* Steve Gray *Ca:* Udo Kier, Linda Hayden, Fiona Richmond, Patsy Smart, Karl Howman, Vic Armstrong

229. **The Eyes of Annie Jones** (1963) Parroch-McCallum Productions (in association with Associated Producers, Inc. [U.S.]) B&W 71 min *D:* Reginald Le Borg *P:* Jack Parsons *Sc:* Louis Vittes *Ph:* Peter Hennessy *M:* Buxton Orr *Ca:* Richard Conte, Francesca Annis, Joyce Carey, Myrtle Reed, Shay Gorman, Victor Brooks, Jean Lodge

230. **Eyewitness** (1956) The Rank Organisation Film Productions B&W 82 min *U.S. Title:* Peril in the Night (TV only) *D:* Muriel Box *P:* Sydney Box *Sc:* Janet Green *Ph:* Reginald Wyer *M:* Bruce Montgomery *Ca:* Donald Sinden, Muriel Pavlow, Belinda Lee, Michael Craig, Nigel Stock, Susan Beaumont, David Knight

231. **Eyewitness** (1970) Associated British Picture Corporation/Irving Allen Limited Col 91 min *U.S. Title:* Sudden Terror *D:* John Hough *P:* Paul Maslansky *Sc:* Ronald Harwood *Ph:* David Holmes *M:* Fairfield Parlour *Ca:* Mark Lester, Lionel Jeffries, Susan George, Jeremy Kemp, Peter Vaughan, Peter Bowles, Betty Marsden, Tony Bonner, Joseph Furst

232. **Face in the Night** (1956) Gibraltar Productions B&W 78 min *U.S. Title:* Menace in the Night *D:* Lance Comfort *P:* Charles A. Leeds *Sc:* Norman Hudis *Ph:* Arthur Graham *M:* Richard Rodney Bennett *Ca:* Griffith Jones, Lisa Gastoni, Vincent Ball, Eddie Byrne, Victor Maddern, Clifford Evans, Leonard Sachs

233. **Face of a Stranger** (1964) Merton Park

B&W 56 min *D:* John Llewellyn Moxey *P:* Jack Greenwood *Sc:* Jimmy Sangster (billed as John Sansom) *Ph:* James Wilson *M:* Bernard Ebbinghouse *Ca:* Jeremy Kemp, Bernard Archard, Rosemary Leach, Philip Locke, Elizabeth Begley, Jean Marsh, Ronald Leigh-Hunt

Face of Fear *see* **Peeping Tom**

234. **The Face of Fu Manchu** (1965) Hallam Productions Col 94 min *D:* Don Sharp *P:* Harry Alan Towers *Sc:* Harry Alan Towers (billed as Peter Welbeck) *Ph:* Ernest Steward *M:* Christopher Whelen *Ca:* Christopher Lee, Nigel Green, Joachim Fuchsberger, Karin Dor, James Robertson Justice, Howard Marion Crawford, Tsai Chin

235. **Face the Music** (1953) Hammer Film Productions (in association with Lippert Pictures [U.S.]) B&W 84 min *U.S. Title:* The Black Glove *D:* Terence Fisher *P:* Michael Carreras *Sc:* Ernest Borneman *Ph:* Walter J. Harvey *M:* Ivor Slaney and Kenny Baker *Ca:* Alex Nicol, Eleanor Summerfield, John Salew, Paul Carpenter, Geoffrey Keen, Ann Hanslip, Fred Johnson

236. **Faces in the Dark** (1960) Penington-Eady Productions B&W 85 min *D:* David Eady *P:* Jon Penington *Sc:* Ephraim Kogan and John Tully *Ph:* Ken Hodges *M:* Mikis Theodorakis *Ca:* John Gregson, Mai Zetterling, John Ireland, Michael Denison, Tony Wright, Nanette Newman, Valerie Taylor

Factor One *see* **The Trygon Factor**

237. **The Fake** (1953) Pax Films B&W 81 min *D:* Godfrey Grayson *P:* Steven Pallos *Sc:* Patrick Kirwan *Ph:* Cedric Williams *M:* Matyas Seiber *Ca:* Dennis O'Keefe, Coleen Gray, Hugh Williams, Guy Middleton, John Laurie, Eliot Makeham, Gerald Case

238. **Family Doctor** (1958) Templar Productions B&W 85 min *U.S. Titles:* Rx Murder; Rx for Murder *D:* Derek Twist *P:* John Gossage *Sc:* Derek Twist *Ph:* Arthur Grant *M:* John Wooldridge *Ca:* Rick Jason, Marius Goring, Lisa Gastoni, Sandu Scott, Mary Merrall, Vida Hope, Helen Shingler

239. **Fanatic** (1965) Hammer Film Productions/Seven Arts Col 96 min *U.S. Title:* Die! Die! My Darling! *D:* Silvio Narizzano *P:* Anthony Hinds *Sc:* Richard Matheson *Ph:* Arthur Ibbetson *M:* Wilfred Josephs *Ca:* Tallulah Bankhead, Stefanie Powers, Peter Vaughan, Maurice Kaufmann, Yootha Joyce, Donald Sutherland, Gwendolyn Watts

240. **Farewell Performance** (1963) Sevenay Productions B&W 73 min *D:* Robert Tronson *P:* Jim O'Connolly *Sc:* Aileen Burke and Leone Stuart *Ph:* Michael Reed *M:* Joe Meek *Ca:* Delphi Lawrence, David Kernan, Frederick Jaeger, Derek Francis, Alfred Burke, John Kelland, Toni Gilpin

Fast Fortune *see* **11 Harrowhouse**

241. **The Fast Kill** (1972) Lindsay Shonteff Film Productions Col 88 min *D:* Lindsay Shonteff *P:* Lindsay Shonteff *Sc:* Martin Gilman *Ph:* Michael Davis *M:* Alan Gorrie *Ca:* Tom Adams, Susie Hampton, Michael Culver, Peter Halliday, Patricia Haines, Ray Chiarella, Clive Endersby

242. **Father Brown** (1954) Facet Productions B&W 91 min *U.S. Title:* The Detective *D:* Robert Hamer *P:* Paul F. Moss *Sc:* Thelma Schnee and Robert Hamer *Ph:* Harry Waxman *M:* Georges Auric *Ca:* Alec Guinness, Joan Greenwood, Peter Finch, Cecil Parker, Bernard Lee, Sidney James, Marne Maitland

243. **Fathom** (1967) 20th Century–Fox Productions Col 99 min *D:* Leslie H. Martinson *P:* John Kohn *Sc:* Lorenzo Semple, Jr. *Ph:* Douglas Slocombe *M:* John Dankworth *Ca:* Anthony Franciosa, Raquel Welch, Ronald Fraser, Greta Chi, Richard Briers, Tom Adams, Clive Revill

244. **Fear in the Night** (1972) Hammer Film Productions Col 94 min *U.S. Titles:* Dynasty of Fear (video—see Appendix V); Honeymoon of Fear (video—see Appendix V) *D:* Jimmy Sangster *P:* Jimmy Sangster *Sc:* Jimmy Sangster and Michael Syson *Ph:* Arthur Grant *M:* John McCabe *Ca:* Judy Geeson, Joan Collins, Ralph Bates, Peter Cushing, James Cossins, Gillian Lind, Brian Grellis

245. **Fear Is the Key** (1972) K.L.K. Productions Col 108 min *D:* Michael Tuchner *P:* Alan Ladd, Jr., and Jay Kanter *Sc:* Robert Carrington *Ph:* Alex Thomson *M:* Roy Budd *Ca:* Barry Newman, Suzy Kendall, John Vernon, Dolph Sweet, Ben Kingsley, Ray McAnally, Tony Anholt

246. **Feet of Clay** (1960) The Danzigers B&W 55 min *D:* Frank Marshall *P:* Edward J. Danziger and Harry Lee Danziger *Sc:* Mark Grantham *Ph:* James Wilson *M:* Bill Le Sage *Ca:* Vincent Ball, Wendy Williams, Hilda Fenemore, Robert Cawdron, Brian Smith, Angela Douglas, Alan Browning

Female Fiends *see* **The Strange Awakening**

ffolkes *see* **North Sea Hijack**

247. **The Fiend** (1971) World Arts Media Col 90 min *U.S. Titles:* Beware My Brethren; Beware of the Brethren *D:* Robert Hartford-Davis *P:* Robert Hartford-Davis *Sc:* Brian Comport *Ph:* Desmond Dickinson *M:* Tony Osborne and Richard Kerr *Ca:* Ann Todd, Patrick Magee, Tony Beckley, Madeline Hinde, Suzanna Leigh, Ronald Allen, Percy Herbert

The Fighting Wildcats *see* West of Suez

248. **The File of the Golden Goose** (1969) Theme Pictures/Caralan Productions/Dador Productions Col 109 min *D:* Sam Wanamaker *P:* David E. Rose *Sc:* John C. Higgins and James B. Gordon *Ph:* Ken Hodges *M:* Harry Robinson *Ca:* Yul Brynner, Charles Gray, Edward Woodward, John Barrie, Adrienne Corri, Bernard Archard, Karel Stepanek, Graham Crowden

249. **Final Appointment** (1954) A.C.T. Films/Unit Productions B&W 69 min *D:* Terence Fisher *P:* Francis Searle *Sc:* Kenneth R. Hayles *Ph:* Jonah Jones *Ca:* John Bentley, Eleanor Summerfield, Hubert Gregg, Liam Redmond, Jean Lodge, Sam Kydd, Meredith Edwards

250. **Find the Lady** (1956) Major Productions B&W 56 min *D:* Charles Saunders *P:* John Temple-Smith *Sc:* Kenneth R. Hayles *Ph:* Brendan J. Stafford *M:* Ray Terry *Ca:* Donald Houston, Mervyn Johns, Beverly Brooks, Maurice Kaufmann, Kay Callard, Edwin Richfield, Ferdy Mayne, Enid Lorimer

Finger of Guilt *see* **The Intimate Stranger**
Fire Over Africa *see* **Malaga**
The Firechasers (1970)—See Appendix VI

251. **Firepower** (1979) Michael Winner Limited/ITC Col 104 min *D:* Michael Winner *P:* Michael Winner *Sc:* Gerald Wilson *Ph:* Robert Paynter and Dick Kratina *M:* Gato Barbieri *Ca:* Sophia Loren, James Coburn, O.J. Simpson, Eli Wallach, Anthony Franciosa, George Grizzard, Vincent Gardenia, Victor Mature

252. **The First Great Train Robbery** (1978) Starling Productions Col 110 min *U.S. Title:* The Great Train Robbery *D:* Michael Crichton *P:* John Foreman *Sc:* Michael Crichton *Ph:* Geoffrey Unsworth *M:* Jerry Goldsmith *Ca:* Sean Connery, Donald Sutherland, Lesley-Anne Down, Alan Webb, Malcolm Terris, Robert Lang, Michael Elphick

Five Angels on Murder *see* **The Woman in Question**

253. **Five Days** (1954) Hammer Film Productions (in association with Lippert Pictures [U.S.]) B&W 72 min *U.S. Title:* Paid to Kill *D:* Montgomery Tully *P:* Anthony Hinds *Sc:* Paul Tabori *Ph:* Walter J. Harvey *M:* Ivor Slaney *Ca:* Dane Clark, Paul Carpenter, Thea Gregory, Cecile Chevreau, Anthony Forwood, Howard Marion Crawford, Avis Scott

254. **Five Golden Dragons** (1967) Blansfilm Limited Col 104 min *D:* Jeremy Summers *P:* Harry Alan Towers *Sc:* Harry Alan Towers (billed as Peter Welbeck) *Ph:* John Von Kotze *M:* Malcolm Lockyer *Ca:* Bob Cummings, Margaret Lee, Rupert Davies, Maria Perschy, Klaus Kinski, Maria Rohm, Sieghardt Rupp

255. **Five to One** (1963) Merton Park B&W 56 min *D:* Gordon Flemyng *P:* Jack Greenwood *Sc:* Roger Marshall *Ph:* James Wilson *M:* Bernard Ebbinghouse *Ca:* Lee Montague, Ingrid Hafner, John Thaw, Brian McDermott, Ewan Roberts, Heller Toren, Jack Watson

256. **The Flanagan Boy** (1952) Hammer Film Productions (in association with Lippert Pictures [U.S.]) B&W 81 min *U.S. Title:* Bad Blonde *D:* Reginald Le Borg *P:* Anthony Hinds *Sc:* Guy Elmes *Ph:* Walter J. Harvey *M:* Ivor Slaney *Ca:* Barbara Payton, Frederick Valk, John Slater, Sidney James, Tony Wright, Marie Burke, George Woodbridge

257. **Flannelfoot** (1953) E.J. Fancey Productions B&W 74 min *D:* Maclean Rogers *P:* E.J. Fancey *Sc:* Carl Heck *Ph:* Geoffrey Faithfull *Ca:* Ronald Howard, Mary Germaine, Jack Watling, Ronald Adam, Gene Anderson, Edwin Richfield, Ronald Leigh-Hunt

258. **Flat Two** (1962) Merton Park B&W 60 min *D:* Alan Cooke *P:* Jack Greenwood *Sc:* Lindsay Galloway *Ph:* Bert Mason *M:* Bernard Ebbinghouse *Ca:* John Le Mesurier, Jack Watling, Bernard Archard, Barry Keegan, Ann Bell, Campbell Singer, Charles Lloyd Pack, David Bauer

259. **The Flaw** (1954) Cybex Film Productions B&W 61 min *D:* Terence Fisher *P:* Geoffrey Goodhart and Brandon Fleming *Sc:* Brandon Fleming *Ph:* Cedric Williams *Ca:* John Bentley, Donald Houston, Rona Anderson, Doris Yorke, Tonia Bern, Andrew Leigh, Cecilia Cavendish

260. **The Flesh and Blood Show** (1972) Peter Walker (Heritage) Col 96 min *D:* Pete Walker *P:* Pete Walker *Sc:* Alfred Shaughnessy *Ph:* Peter Jessop *M:* Cyril Ornadel *Ca:* Ray Brooks, Jenny Hanley, Luan Peters, Judy Matheson, Candace Glendenning, Robin Askwith, Patrick Barr

261. **Flight from Vienna** (1955) E.J. Fancey Productions B&W 58 min *U.S. Title:* Escape from the Iron Curtain *D:* Denis Kavanagh *P:* E.J. Fancey *Sc:* Denis Kavanagh *Ph:* Hal Morey *Ca:* Theodore Bikel, John Bentley, Adrienne Scott, Donald Gray, Carina Helm, Geoffrey Wilmer, George Roderick

262. **The Floating Dutchman** (1953) Merton Park B&W 76 min *U.S. Title:* Clue from a Corpse (TV only) *D:* Vernon Sewell *P:* William H. Williams *Sc:* Vernon Sewell *Ph:* Josef Ambor *M:* Eric Spear *Ca:* Dermot Walsh, Sydney Tafler, Mary Germaine, Guy Verney, Hugh Morton, James Raglan, Arnold Marle

263. **Floods of Fear** (1958) The Rank Organisation Film Productions B&W 84 min *D:* Charles Crichton *P:* Sydney Box *Sc:* Charles Crichton *Ph:* Christopher Challis *M:* Alan Rawsthorne *Ca:* Howard Keel, Anne Heywood, Cyril Cusack, Harry H. Corbett, John Crawford, Eddie Byrne, John Phillips

264. **The Flying Scot** (1957) Insignia Films B&W 69 min *U.S. Title:* Mailbag Robbery *D:* Compton Bennett *P:* Compton Bennett *Sc:* Norman Hudis *Ph:* Peter Hennessy *M:* Stanley Black *Ca:* Lee Patterson, Kay Callard, Alan Gifford, Jeremy Bodkin, Kerry Jordan, Mark Baker, Gerald Case

Fog for a Killer *see* **Out of the Fog**

265. **Footsteps in the Fog** (1955) Film Locations Col 90 min *D:* Arthur Lubin *P:* Maxwell Setton and Mike J. Frankovich *Sc:* Dorothy Reid and Lenore Coffee *Ph:* Christopher Challis *M:* Benjamin Frankel *Ca:* Stewart Granger, Jean Simmons, Bill Travers, Finlay Currie, Ronald Squire, Belinda Lee, William Hartnell

266. **Forbidden Cargo** (1954) London Independent Producers B&W 85 min *D:* Harold French *P:* Sydney Box *Sc:* Sydney Box *Ph:* C. Pennington-Richards *M:* Lambert Williamson *Ca:* Nigel Patrick, Elizabeth Sellars, Terence Morgan, Greta Gynt, Joyce Grenfell, Theodore Bikel, Eric Pohlmann

267. **Fortune Is a Woman** (1957) John Harvel Productions B&W 95 min *U.S. Title:* She Played with Fire *D:* Sidney Gilliat *P:* Frank Launder and Sidney Gilliat *Sc:* Sidney Gilliat and Frank Launder *Ph:* Gerald Gibbs *M:* William Alwyn *Ca:* Jack Hawkins, Arlene Dahl, Dennis Price, Violet Farebrother, Malcolm Keen, Geoffrey Keen, Patrick Holt

48 Hours to Live *see* **The Man in the Middle**

Four Desperate Men *see* **The Siege of Pinchgut**

268. **The Fourth Square** (1961) Merton Park B&W 57 min *D:* Allan Davis *P:* Jack Greenwood *Sc:* James Eastwood *Ph:* Gerald Moss *M:* James Stevens *Ca:* Conrad Phillips, Natasha Parry, Delphi Lawrence, Paul Daneman, Miriam Karlin, Jacqueline Jones, Anthony Newlands

269. **Fragment of Fear** (1970) Columbia British Productions Col 95 min *D:* Richard C. Sarafian *P:* John R. Sloan *Sc:* Paul Dehn *Ph:* Oswald Morris *M:* Johnny Harris *Ca:* David Hemmings, Gayle Hunnicutt, Wilfrid Hyde White, Flora Robson, Adolfo Celi, Roland Culver, Daniel Massey, Mona Washbourne

270. **Freedom to Die** (1961) Bayford Films B&W 61 min *D:* Francis Searle *P:* Charles A. Leeds *Sc:* Arthur La Bern *Ph:* Ken Hodges *M:* John Veale *Ca:* Paul Maxwell, Felicity Young, Bruce Seton, Kay Callard, T.P. McKenna, Laurie Leigh, Charlie Byrne

271. **Freelance** (1970) Freelance Films Col 81 min *U.S. Title:* Con Man (video—see Appendix V) *D:* Francis Megahy *P:* Francis Megahy *Sc:* Bernie Cooper and Francis Megahy *Ph:* Norman Langley *M:* Basil Kirchin *Ca:* Ian McShane, Gayle Hunnicutt, Keith Barron, Alan Lake, Peter Gilmore, Charles Hyatt, Luan Peters

272. **Frenzy** (1972) Universal Pictures Col 116 min *D:* Alfred Hitchcock *P:* Alfred Hitchcock *Sc:* Anthony Shaffer *Ph:* Gilbert Taylor *M:* Ron Goodwin *Ca:* Jon Finch, Alec McCowen, Barry Foster, Billie Whitelaw, Anna Massey, Barbara Leigh-Hunt, Bernard Cribbins

273. **Fright** (1971) Fantale Films Col 87 min *U.S. Titles:* Night Legs; I'm Alone and I'm Scared (early 1980s theatrical reissue) *D:* Peter Collinson *P:* Harry Fine and Michael Style *Sc:* Tudor Gates *Ph:* Ian Wilson *M:* Harry Robinson *Ca:* Susan George, Honor Blackman, Ian Bannen, John Gregson, George Cole, Dennis Waterman, Maurice Kaufmann, Michael Brennan

274. **The Frightened City** (1961) Zodiac Productions B&W 98 min *D:* John Lemont *P:* John Lemont and Leigh Vance *Sc:* Leigh Vance *Ph:* Desmond Dickinson *M:* Norrie Paramor *Ca:* Herbert Lom, John Gregson, Sean Connery, Alfred Marks, Yvonne Romain, David Davies, Olive McFarland

275. **The Frightened Man** (1951) Tempean Films B&W 69 min *D:* John Gilling *P:* Robert S. Baker and Monty Berman *Sc:* John Gilling *Ph:* Monty Berman *M:* John Lanchbery *Ca:* Dermot Walsh, Charles Victor, Barbara Murray, John Blythe, Martin Benson, Annette Simmonds, Ballard Berkeley

276. **Frightmare** (1974) Peter Walker (Heritage) Col 86 min *U.S. Titles:* Brainsuckers (briefly used 1976 theatrical release title); Once Upon a Frightmare (video—see Appendix V); Frightmare II (video—see Appendix V); Cover-Up (early to mid–1990s TV title) *D:* Pete Walker *P:* Pete Walker *Sc:* David McGillivray *Ph:* Peter Jessop *M:* Stanley Myers *Ca:* Rupert Davies, Sheila Keith, Deborah Fairfax, Paul Greenwood, Kim Butcher, Gerald Flood, Leo Genn

Frightmare II *see* **Frightmare**

277. **From Russia with Love** (1963) Eon Productions Col 116 min *D:* Terence Young *P:* Harry Saltzman and Albert R. Broccoli *Sc:* Richard Maibaum *Ph:* Ted Moore *M:* John Barry *Ca:* Sean

Connery, Daniela Bianchi, Pedro Armendariz, Lotte Lenya, Robert Shaw, Walter Gotell, Vladek Sheybal, Martine Beswick, Francis De Wolff, George Pastell, Bernard Lee, Lois Maxwell

278. **The Full Treatment** (1960) Hammer Film Productions/Falcon Films (Hammer subsidiary)/Hilary Productions B&W 109 min U.S. Title: Stop Me Before I Kill! *D:* Val Guest *P:* Val Guest *Sc:* Val Guest and Ronald Scott Thorn *Ph:* Gilbert Taylor *M:* Stanley Black *Ca:* Claude Dauphin, Diane Cilento, Ronald Lewis, Françoise Rosay, Bernard Braden, Barbara Chilcott, Katya Douglas

279. **Funeral in Berlin** (1966) Lowndes Productions Col 102 min *D:* Guy Hamilton *P:* Charles Kasher *Sc:* Evan Jones *Ph:* Otto Heller *M:* Konrad Elfers *Ca:* Michael Caine, Eva Renzi, Paul Hubschmid, Oscar Homolka, Guy Doleman, Hugh Burden, Rachel Gurney

280. **The Fur Collar** (1962) Albatross Productions B&W 71 min *D:* Lawrence Huntington *P:* Lawrence Huntington *Sc:* Lawrence Huntington *Ph:* S.D. Onions *M:* John Fox *Ca:* John Bentley, Martin Benson, Philip Friend, Nadja Regin, Balbina, Hector Ross, Gordon Sterne

281. **The Gambler and the Lady** (1952) Hammer Film Productions (in association with Lippert Pictures [U.S.]) B&W 74 min *D:* Sam Newfield and Patrick Jenkins *P:* Anthony Hinds *Sc:* Uncredited (reportedly written by Sam Newfield) *Ph:* Walter J. Harvey *M:* Ivor Slaney *Ca:* Dane Clark, Kathleen Byron, Naomi Chance, Meredith Edwards, Eric Pohlmann, Jane Griffiths, Martin Benson

282. **Game for Three Losers** (1965) Merton Park B&W 56 min *D:* Gerry O'Hara *P:* Jack Greenwood *Sc:* Roger Marshall *Ph:* James Wilson *M:* Bernard Ebbinghouse *Ca:* Michael Gough, Mark Eden, Toby Robins, Rachel Gurney, Allan Cuthbertson, Al Mulock, Roger Hammond

283. **Game for Vultures** (1979) Pyramid Films Col 113 min *D:* James Fargo *P:* Hazel Adair *Sc:* Phillip Baird *Ph:* Alex Thomson *M:* Jon Field and Tony Duhig *Ca:* Richard Harris, Richard Roundtree, Joan Collins, Ray Milland, Sven-Bertil Taube, Denholm Elliott, Ken Gampu

Game of Danger *see* **Bang! You're Dead**

284. **The Gamma People** (1955) Warwick Film Productions B&W 78 min *D:* John Gilling *P:* John Gossage *Sc:* John Gilling and John Gossage *Ph:* Ted Moore *M:* George Melachrino *Ca:* Paul Douglas, Eva Bartok, Leslie Phillips, Walter Rilla, Philip Leaver, Martin Miller, Michael Carridia

285. **Gang War** (1961) The Danzigers B&W 65 min *D:* Frank Marshall *P:* Brian Langslow *Sc:* Mark Grantham *Ph:* Stephen Dade *M:* Bill Le Sage *Ca:* Sean Kelly, Eira Heath, David Davies, Sean Sullivan, John Gabriel, Mark Singleton, Eric Dodson

286. **Gaolbreak** (1962) Butcher's Film Productions B&W 61 min U.S. Title: Jailbreak (TV only) *D:* Francis Searle *P:* Francis Searle and Ronald Liles *Sc:* A.R. Rawlinson *Ph:* Ken Hodges *M:* Johnny Gregory *Ca:* Peter Reynolds, Avice Landone, David Kernan, Carol White, John Blythe, David Gregory, Robert Desmond

287. **The Gelignite Gang** (1955) Cybex Film Productions B&W 76 min U.S. Title: The Dynamiters *D:* Francis Searle *P:* Geoffrey Goodhart and Brandon Fleming *Sc:* Brandon Fleming *Ph:* Cedric Williams *Ca:* Wayne Morris, James Kenney, Patrick Holt, Sandra Dorne, Arthur Young, Eric Pohlmann, Lloyd Lamble

288. **The Gentle Gunman** (1952) Ealing Studios B&W 86 min *D:* Basil Dearden *P:* Michael Relph *Sc:* Roger MacDougall *Ph:* Gordon Dines *M:* John Greenwood *Ca:* John Mills, Dirk Bogarde, Robert Beatty, Elizabeth Sellars, Barbara Mullen, Eddie Byrne, Liam Redmond

289. **The Gentle Trap** (1960) Butcher's Film Productions B&W 59 min *D:* Charles Saunders *P:* Jack Parsons *Sc:* Brock Williams *Ph:* Ken Hodges *M:* William Davies *Ca:* Spencer Teakle, Felicity Young, Martin Benson, Dorinda Stevens, Dawn Brooks, Alan Edwards, Hugh Latimer

290. **Get Carter** (1971) MGM Col 112 min *D:* Mike Hodges *P:* Michael Klinger *Sc:* Mike Hodges *Ph:* Wolfgang Suschitzky *M:* Roy Budd *Ca:* Michael Caine, Britt Ekland, John Osborne, Ian Hendry, Bryan Mosley, Geraldine Moffatt, Glynn Edwards, Tony Beckley, George Sewell

291. **The Gilded Cage** (1954) Tempean Films B&W 77 min *D:* John Gilling *P:* Robert S. Baker and Monty Berman *Sc:* Brock Williams *Ph:* Monty Berman *M:* Stanley Black *Ca:* Alex Nicol, Veronica Hurst, Clifford Evans, Ursula Howells, Elwyn Brook-Jones, John Stuart, Trevor Reid

292. **The Girl Hunters** (1963) Present Day Productions/Fellane Productions B&W 100 min *D:* Roy Rowland *P:* Robert Fellows and Charles Reynolds *Sc:* Mickey Spillane, Roy Rowland and Robert Fellows *Ph:* Kenneth Talbot *M:* Philip Green *Ca:* Mickey Spillane, Shirley Eaton, Lloyd Nolan, Hy Gardner, Scott Peters, Bill Nagy, Larry Taylor, Murray Kash

293. **Girl in the Headlines** (1963) Viewfinder Film Productions B&W 93 min U.S. Title: The Model Murder Case *D:* Michael Truman *P:* John Davis *Sc:* Vivienne Knight and Patrick Camp-

bell *Ph:* Stanley Pavey *M:* John Addison *Ca:* Ian Hendry, Ronald Fraser, Margaret Johnston, Natasha Parry, Jeremy Brett, Kieron Moore, James Villiers

294. **The Girl in the Picture** (1956) Cresswell Productions B&W 61 min *D:* Don Chaffey *P:* Ted Lloyd *Sc:* Paul Ryder *Ph:* Ian Struthers *Ca:* Donald Houston, Patrick Holt, Maurice Kaufmann, Junia Crawford, Paddy Joyce, John Miller, Tom Chatto

295. **The Girl on the Pier** (1953) Major Productions B&W 65 min *D:* Lance Comfort *P:* John Temple-Smith *Sc:* Guy Morgan *Ph:* William McLeod *M:* Ray Terry *Ca:* Veronica Hurst, Ron Randell, Charles Victor, Marjorie Rhodes, Campbell Singer, Brian Roper, Anthony Valentine

Girly *see* **Mumsy, Nanny, Sonny & Girly**

Gitanos—Escape from Apartheid *see* **One Away**

296. **Give Us Tomorrow** (1978) Donwin Productions Col 94 min *D:* Donovan Winter *P:* Donovan Winter *Sc:* Donovan Winter *Ph:* Austin Parkinson *M:* John Fox *Ca:* Sylvia Syms, Derren Nesbitt, James Kerry, Donna Evans, Matthew Haslett, Alan Guy, Victor Brooks

297. **The Glass Cage** (1954) Hammer Film Productions (in association with Lippert Pictures [U.S.]) B&W 59 min *U.S. Title:* The Glass Tomb *D:* Montgomery Tully *P:* Anthony Hinds *Sc:* Richard Landau *Ph:* Walter J. Harvey *M:* Leonard Salzedo *Ca:* John Ireland, Honor Blackman, Geoffrey Keen, Eric Pohlmann, Sidney James, Liam Redmond, Sydney Tafler, Valerie Vernon, Ferdy Mayne

The Glass Tomb *see* **The Glass Cage**

298. **Gold** (1974) Avton Film Productions Col 124 min *U.S. Title:* The Great Gold Conspiracy (alternate 1975 theatrical release title in certain territories only) *D:* Peter Hunt *P:* Michael Klinger *Sc:* Wilbur Smith and Stanley Price *Ph:* Ousama Rawi *M:* Elmer Bernstein *Ca:* Roger Moore, Susannah York, Ray Milland, Bradford Dillman, John Gielgud, Tony Beckley, Simon Sabela

299. **The Gold Express** (1954) Gaumont-British Picture Corporation B&W 58 min *D:* Guy Fergusson *P:* Frank Wells *Sc:* Jackson Budd *Ph:* Frank North *M:* Jack Beaver *Ca:* Vernon Gray, Ann Walford, Ivy St. Helier, May Hallatt, Patrick Boxill, Delphi Lawrence, Jill Melford

The Golden Heist *see* **Inside Out**

300. **The Golden Lady** (1979) Elcotglade Ltd./Dawnstar Ltd./Continental Film Distributors (Hong Kong) Col 94 min *D:* José Ramón Larraz *P:* Keith Cavele and Paul Cowan *Sc:* Joshua Sinclair *Ph:* David Griffiths *M:* Georges Garvarentz *Ca:* Ina Skriver (billed as Christina World), June Chadwick, Suzanne Danielle, Anika Pavel, Stephen Chase, Edward De Souza, Patrick Newell

301. **The Golden Link** (1954) Parkside Film Productions B&W 83 min *D:* Charles Saunders *P:* Guido Coen *Sc:* Allan MacKinnon *Ph:* Harry Waxman *M:* Eric Spear *Ca:* Andre Morell, Thea Gregory, Patrick Holt, Jack Watling, Marla Landi, Arnold Bell, Alexander Gauge, Dorinda Stevens, Edward Lexy, Ellen Pollock

302. **Goldfinger** (1964) Eon Productions Col 109 min *D:* Guy Hamilton *P:* Harry Saltzman and Albert R. Broccoli *Sc:* Richard Maibaum and Paul Dehn *Ph:* Ted Moore *M:* John Barry *Ca:* Sean Connery, Honor Blackman, Gert Fröbe, Shirley Eaton, Tania Mallet, Harold Sakata, Martin Benson, Cec Linder, Bill Nagy, Bernard Lee, Lois Maxwell

303. **The Good Die Young** (1954) Romulus Films/Remus Films B&W 98 min *D:* Lewis Gilbert *P:* Jack Clayton *Sc:* Vernon Harris and Lewis Gilbert *Ph:* Jack Asher *M:* Georges Auric *Ca:* Laurence Harvey, Gloria Grahame, Richard Basehart, Joan Collins, John Ireland, Stanley Baker, Margaret Leighton, Lee Patterson

304. **Goodbye Gemini** (1970) Cinerama Inc. Col 89 min *U.S. Title:* Twinsanity (video—see Appendix V) *D:* Alan Gibson *P:* Peter Snell *Sc:* Edmund Ward *Ph:* Geoffrey Unsworth *M:* Christopher Gunning *Ca:* Judy Geeson, Martin Potter, Michael Redgrave, Alexis Kanner, Marian Diamond, Freddie Jones, Peter Jeffrey

305. **Grand National Night** (1953) Talisman Films B&W 80 min *U.S. Title:* Wicked Wife *D:* Bob McNaught *P:* Phil C. Samuel *Sc:* Uncredited (reportedly written by Bob McNaught and Val Valentine) *Ph:* Jack Asher *M:* John Greenwood *Ca:* Nigel Patrick, Moira Lister, Beatrice Campbell, Betty Ann Davies, Michael Hordern, Noel Purcell, Leslie Mitchell

The Graveyard *see* **Persecution**

The Great Armored Car Swindle *see* **The Breaking Point**

The Great Gold Conspiracy *see* **Gold**

The Great Manhunt *see* **State Secret**

The Great Train Robbery *see* **The First Great Train Robbery**

306. **The Great Van Robbery** (1958) The Danzigers B&W 70 min *D:* Max Varnel *P:* Edward J. Danziger and Harry Lee Danziger *Sc:* Brian Clemens and Eldon Howard *Ph:* James Wilson *Ca:* Denis Shaw, Kay Callard, Tony Quinn, Philip Saville, Vera Fusek, Tony Doonan, Bob Simmons

307. **The Green Buddha** (1954) Republic Productions (Great Britain) B&W 62 min *D:* John Lemont *P:* William N. Boyle *Sc:* Paul Erickson *Ph:* Basil Emmott *M:* Lambert Williamson *Ca:* Wayne Morris, Mary Germaine, Walter Rilla, Mary Merrall, Arnold Marle, Lloyd Lamble, Kenneth Griffith

308. **The Green Scarf** (1954) B&A Productions B&W 96 min *D:* George More O'Ferrall *P:* Bertram Ostrer and Albert Fennell *Sc:* Gordon Wellesley *Ph:* Jack Hildyard *M:* Brian Easdale *Ca:* Michael Redgrave, Leo Genn, Ann Todd, Kieron Moore, Jane Griffiths, Michael Medwin, Richard O'Sullivan

309. **Grip of the Strangler** (1957) Producers Associates/Amalgamated Productions/M.L.C. Productions B&W 79 min *U.S. Title:* The Haunted Strangler *D:* Robert Day *P:* John Croydon *Sc:* John Croydon (billed as John C. Cooper) and Jan Read *Ph:* Lionel Banes *M:* Buxton Orr *Ca:* Boris Karloff, Jean Kent, Elizabeth Allan, Anthony Dawson, Vera Day, Tim Turner, Diane Aubrey

310. **Guilty?** (1956) Gibraltar Productions B&W 93 min *D:* Edmond T. Gréville *P:* Charles A. Leeds *Sc:* Maurice J. Wilson *Ph:* Stanley Pavey *M:* Bruce Montgomery *Ca:* John Justin, Barbara Laage, Donald Wolfit, Stephen Murray, Norman Wooland, Andrée Debar, Sydney Tafler

311. **Gumshoe** (1971) Memorial Enterprises Col 84 min *D:* Stephen Frears *P:* Michael Medwin *Sc:* Neville Smith *Ph:* Chris Menges *M:* Andrew Lloyd Webber *Ca:* Albert Finney, Billie Whitelaw, Frank Finlay, Janice Rule, Carolyn Seymour, Fulton Mackay, George Innes

312. **Guns of Darkness** (1962) Cavalcade Films B&W 102 min *D:* Anthony Asquith *P:* Thomas Clyde *Sc:* John Mortimer *Ph:* Robert Krasker *M:* Benjamin Frankel *Ca:* Leslie Caron, David Niven, James Robertson Justice, David Opatoshu, Eleanor Summerfield, Ian Hunter, Derek Godfrey, Sandor Eles

313. **A Guy Called Caesar** (1962) Bill and Michael Luckwell Ltd. B&W 62 min *D:* Frank Marshall *P:* Bill Luckwell and Umesh Mallik *Sc:* Umesh Mallik and Tom Burdon *Ph:* Stephen Dade *M:* Wilfred Burns *Ca:* Conrad Phillips, George Moon, Philip O'Flynn, Maureen Toal, Desmond Perry, Peter Maycock, Elizabeth Padget

314. **Hammer the Toff** (1951) Nettlefold Films B&W 71 min *D:* Maclean Rogers *P:* Ernest G. Roy *Sc:* Uncredited *Ph:* Geoffrey Faithfull *M:* Wilfred Burns *Ca:* John Bentley, Patricia Dainton, Valentine Dyall, John Robinson, Roddy Hughes, Wally Patch, Katharine Blake

315. **Hammerhead** (1968) Irving Allen Limited Col 99 min *D:* David Miller *P:* Irving Allen *Sc:* William Bast and Herbert Baker *Ph:* Kenneth Talbot and Wilkie Cooper *M:* David Whitaker *Ca:* Vince Edwards, Judy Geeson, Peter Vaughan, Diana Dors, Michael Bates, Beverly Adams, Patrick Cargill, Patrick Holt

316. **The Hand** (1960) Bill and Michael Luckwell Ltd. B&W 64 min *D:* Henry Cass *P:* Bill Luckwell *Sc:* Ray Cooney and Tony Hilton *Ph:* Walter J. Harvey *M:* Wilfred Burns *Ca:* Derek Bond, Ronald Leigh-Hunt, Reed De Rouen, Ray Cooney, Bryan Coleman, Walter Randall, Tony Hilton

317. **Hands of the Ripper** (1971) Hammer Film Productions Col 85 min *D:* Peter Sasdy *P:* Aida Young *Sc:* Lewis Davidson *Ph:* Kenneth Talbot *M:* Christopher Gunning *Ca:* Eric Porter, Jane Merrow, Derek Godfrey, Angharad Rees, Marjorie Rhodes, Keith Bell, Margaret Rawlings, Dora Bryan

The Happy Hookers *see* **A Touch of the Other**

Harry and the Hookers *see* **Clegg**

318. **The Haunted House of Horror** (1969) Tigon British Film Productions/American International Pictures Col 92 min *U.S. Title:* Horror House *D:* Michael Armstrong *P:* Tony Tenser *Sc:* Michael Armstrong *Ph:* Jack Atchelor *M:* Reg Tilsley *Ca:* Frankie Avalon, Jill Haworth, Dennis Price, Mark Wynter, Julian Barnes, Richard O'Sullivan, George Sewell, Gina Warwick, Robin Stewart

The Haunted Strangler *see* **Grip of the Strangler**

He Kills Night After Night After Night *see* **Night, After Night, After Night**

319. **The Heart Within** (1957) Penington-Eady Productions B&W 62 min *D:* David Eady *P:* Jon Penington *Sc:* Geoffrey Orme *Ph:* Ernest Palmer *M:* Vivian Comma and Edwin Astley *Ca:* James Hayter, Clifford Evans, Earl Cameron, David Hemmings, Betty Cooper, Dan Jackson, Jack Stewart

Heat Wave *see* **The House Across the Lake**

320. **Hell Below Zero** (1953) Warwick Film Productions Col 90 min *D:* Mark Robson *P:* Irving Allen and Albert R. Broccoli *Sc:* Alec Coppel and Max Trell *Ph:* John Wilcox *M:* Clifton Parker *Ca:* Alan Ladd, Joan Tetzel, Basil Sydney, Stanley Baker, Joseph Tomelty, Niall MacGinnis, Jill Bennett

321. **Hell Drivers** (1957) The Rank Organisation Film Productions /Aqua Films B&W 108 min *D:* Cy Endfield *P:* S. Benjamin Fisz *Sc:* John

Kruse and Cy Endfield *Ph:* Geoffrey Unsworth *M:* Hubert Clifford *Ca:* Stanley Baker, Herbert Lom, Peggy Cummins, Patrick McGoohan, William Hartnell, Wilfrid Lawson, Sidney James, David McCallum, Sean Connery

322. **Hell Is a City** (1959) Hammer Film Productions/Associated British Picture Corporation B&W 98 min *D:* Val Guest *P:* Michael Carreras *Sc:* Val Guest *Ph:* Arthur Grant *M:* Stanley Black *Ca:* Stanley Baker, John Crawford, Donald Pleasence, Maxine Audley, Billie Whitelaw, Joseph Tomelty, George A. Cooper

323. **Hell Is Empty** (1967) The Dominion Film Establishment Col 109 min *D:* John Ainsworth *P:* Mike Eland *Sc:* John Ainsworth *Ph:* Jan Stallich and Sasa Hunka *M:* Georges Garvarentz *Ca:* Martine Carol, Anthony Steel, Shirley Anne Field, James Robertson Justice, Jess Conrad, Robert Rietty, Carl Mohner

324. **Hennessy** (1975) American International Pictures/Hennessy Film Productions/Marseilles Enterprises Col 104 min *D:* Don Sharp *P:* Peter Snell *Sc:* John Gay *Ph:* Ernest Steward *M:* John Scott *Ca:* Rod Steiger, Lee Remick, Richard Johnson, Trevor Howard, Eric Porter, Peter Egan, Stanley Lebor

Her Majesty's Top Gun *see* **No.1 of the Secret Service**

325. **Hidden Homicide** (1958) Bill and Michael Luckwell Ltd. B&W 72 min *D:* Tony Young *P:* Bill Luckwell and Derek Winn *Sc:* Bill Luckwell and Tony Young *Ph:* Ernest Palmer *M:* Otto Ferrari *Ca:* Griffith Jones, Patricia Laffan, James Kenney, Bruce Seton, Maya Koumani, Robert Raglan, Richard Shaw

326. **Hide and Seek** (1963) Spectrum Films B&W 90 min *D:* Cy Endfield *P:* Hal E. Chester *Sc:* David Stone *Ph:* Gilbert Taylor *M:* Muir Mathieson and Gary Hughes *Ca:* Ian Carmichael, Janet Munro, Hugh Griffith, Curt Jürgens, Kieron Moore, George Pravda, Edward Chapman

327. **The Hideout** (1956) Major Productions B&W 57 min *D:* Peter Graham Scott *P:* John Temple-Smith *Sc:* Kenneth R. Hayles *Ph:* Brendan J. Stafford *M:* Ray Terry *Ca:* Dermot Walsh, Rona Anderson, Ronald Howard, Sam Kydd, Howard Lang, Edwin Richfield, Arnold Diamond

328. **The High Bright Sun** (1965) The Rank Organisation Film Productions Col 114 min *U.S. Titles:* McGuire, Go Home!; A Date with Death (video—see Appendix V) *D:* Ralph Thomas *P:* Betty E. Box *Sc:* Ian Stuart Black *Ph:* Ernest Steward *M:* Angelo Lavagnino *Ca:* Dirk Bogarde, George Chakiris, Susan Strasberg, Denholm Elliott, Gregoire Aslan, Joseph Furst, George Pastell

The High Commissioner *see* **Nobody Runs Forever**

329. **High Jump** (1958) The Danzigers B&W 66 min *D:* Godfrey Grayson *P:* Edward J. Danziger and Harry Lee Danziger *Sc:* Brian Clemens and Eldon Howard *Ph:* James Wilson *Ca:* Richard Wyler (aka Richard Stapley), Lisa Daniely, Leigh Madison, Michael Peake, Arnold Bell, Nora Gordon, Robert Raglan

330. **The High Terrace** (1956) Cipa Productions B&W 82 min *D:* Henry Cass *P:* Robert S. Baker *Sc:* Alfred Shaughnessy and Norman Hudis *Ph:* Eric Cross *M:* Stanley Black *Ca:* Dale Robertson, Lois Maxwell, Derek Bond, Eric Pohlmann, Mary Laura Wood, Lionel Jeffries, Jameson Clark

331. **High Treason** (1951) Conqueror Films B&W 93 min *D:* Roy Boulting *P:* Paul Soskin *Sc:* Frank Harvey and Roy Boulting *Ph:* Gilbert Taylor *M:* John Addison *Ca:* Liam Redmond, Andre Morell, Anthony Bushell, Kenneth Griffith, Patric Doonan, Joan Hickson, Geoffrey Keen

332. **Highly Dangerous** (1950) Two Cities Films B&W 88 min *D:* Roy Ward Baker *P:* Antony Darnborough *Sc:* Eric Ambler *Ph:* Reginald Wyer *M:* Richard Addinsell *Ca:* Margaret Lockwood, Dane Clark, Marius Goring, Naunton Wayne, Wilfrid Hyde White, Michael Hordern, Eric Pohlmann, Anton Diffring

333. **Highway to Battle** (1960) The Danzigers B&W 70 min *D:* Ernest Morris *P:* Edward J. Danziger and Harry Lee Danziger *Sc:* Brian Clemens and Eldon Howard *Ph:* Stephen Dade *M:* Bill Le Sage *Ca:* Gerard Heinz, Margaret Tyzack, Ferdy Mayne, Dawn Beret, Peter Reynolds, Vincent Ball, George Mikell

334. **The Hi-Jackers** (1963) Butcher's Film Productions B&W 69 min *D:* Jim O'Connolly *P:* John I. Phillips *Sc:* Jim O'Connolly *Ph:* Walter J. Harvey *M:* Johnny Douglas *Ca:* Anthony Booth, Jacqueline Ellis, Derek Francis, Patrick Cargill, Glynn Edwards, David Gregory, Harold Goodwin, Ronald Hines

Hitler's Gold *see* **Inside Out**

335. **Home at Seven** (1952) London Film Productions/British Lion Production Assets B&W 86 min *U.S. Title:* Murder on Monday *D:* Ralph Richardson *P:* Maurice Cowan *Sc:* Anatole De Grunwald *Ph:* Jack Hildyard and Edward Scaife *M:* Malcolm Arnold *Ca:* Ralph Richardson, Margaret Leighton, Jack Hawkins, Campbell Singer, Frederick Piper, Diana Beaumont, Meriel Forbes

336. **Home to Danger** (1951) New World

Productions B&W 66 min *D:* Terence Fisher *P:* Lance Comfort *Sc:* Francis Edge and John Temple-Smith *Ph:* Reginald Wyer *M:* Malcolm Arnold *Ca:* Guy Rolfe, Rona Anderson, Francis Lister, Alan Wheatley, Bruce Belfrage, Stanley Baker, Peter Jones

Honeymoon of Fear *see* **Fear in the Night**

337. **The Hornet's Nest** (1955) Kenilworth Film Productions B&W 64 min *D:* Charles Saunders *P:* Guido Coen *Sc:* Allan MacKinnon *Ph:* Harry Waxman *M:* Edwin Astley *Ca:* Paul Carpenter, June Thorburn, Marla Landi, Alexander Gauge, Charles Farrell, Christine Silver, Nora Nicholson

Horror House *see* **The Haunted House of Horror**

338. **The Horror of It All** (1964) Lippert Films/Associated Producers Inc. B&W 75 min *D:* Terence Fisher *P:* Robert L. Lippert (executive producer) *Sc:* Ray Russell *Ph:* Arthur Lavis *M:* Douglas Gamley *Ca:* Pat Boone, Erica Rogers, Dennis Price, Andrée Melly, Valentine Dyall, Jack Bligh, Erik Chitty

339. **The Hostage** (1956) Westridge Films/Douglas Fairbanks Ltd. B&W 80 min *D:* Harold Huth *P:* Thomas Clyde *Sc:* Guy Morgan and Alfred Shaughnessy *Ph:* Brendan J. Stafford *M:* Bretton Byrd *Ca:* Ron Randell, Mary Parker, John Bailey, Carl Jaffe, Anne Blake, Margaret Diamond, Victor Brooks

340. **Hostile Witness** (1968) Caralan Productions/Dador Productions Col 101 min *D:* Ray Milland *P:* David E. Rose *Sc:* Jack Roffey *Ph:* Gerald Gibbs *M:* Wilfred Josephs *Ca:* Ray Milland, Sylvia Syms, Raymond Huntley, Felix Aylmer, Geoffrey Lumsden, Norman Barrs, Ronald Leigh-Hunt

341. **Hot Enough for June** (1964) The Rank Organisation Film Productions Col 98 min *U.S. Title:* Agent 8¾ *D:* Ralph Thomas *P:* Betty E. Box *Sc:* Lukas Heller *Ph:* Ernest Steward *M:* Angelo Lavagnino *Ca:* Dirk Bogarde, Sylva Koscina, Robert Morley, Leo McKern, Roger Delgado, John Le Mesurier, Richard Vernon, Derek Nimmo, Eric Pohlmann

342. **Hot Ice** (1952) Present Day Productions/S.W.H. (Piccadilly) Productions B&W 85 min *D:* Kenneth Hume *P:* Charles Reynolds *Sc:* Kenneth Hume *Ph:* Ted Lloyd *M:* Ivor Slaney *Ca:* John Justin, Barbara Murray, Ivor Barnard, John Penrose, Michael Balfour, Gabrielle Brune, Anthony Pendrell

Hot Money Girl *see* **The Treasure of San Teresa**

343. **The Hound of the Baskervilles** (1958) Hammer Film Productions Col 86 min *D:* Terence Fisher *P:* Anthony Hinds *Sc:* Peter Bryan *Ph:* Jack Asher *M:* James Bernard *Ca:* Peter Cushing, Andre Morell, Christopher Lee, Marla Landi, David Oxley, Francis De Wolff, Miles Malleson, John Le Mesurier

344. **Hour of Decision** (1956) Tempean Films B&W 81 min *D:* C. Pennington Richards *P:* Monty Berman *Sc:* Norman Hudis *Ph:* Stanley Pavey *M:* Stanley Black *Ca:* Jeff Morrow, Hazel Court, Lionel Jeffries, Anthony Dawson, Mary Laura Wood, Carl Bernard, Vanda Godsell

345. **The Hour of 13** (1952) MGM B&W 78 min *D:* Harold French *P:* Hayes Goetz *Sc:* Leon Gordon and Howard Emmett Rogers *Ph:* Guy Green *M:* John Addison *Ca:* Peter Lawford, Dawn Addams, Roland Culver, Derek Bond, Leslie Dwyer, Michael Hordern, Colin Gordon

346. **The House Across the Lake** (1953) Hammer Film Productions (in association with Lippert Pictures [U.S.]) B&W 68 min *U.S. Title:* Heat Wave *D:* Ken Hughes *P:* Anthony Hinds *Sc:* Ken Hughes *Ph:* Walter J. Harvey *M:* Ivor Slaney *Ca:* Alex Nicol, Hillary Brooke, Sidney James, Susan Stephen, Paul Carpenter, Alan Wheatley, Peter Illing

A House in Nightmare Park *see* **The House in Nightmare Park**

347. **The House in Nightmare Park** (1973) Associated London Films/Extonation Productions Col 95 min *U.S. Titles:* Crazy House (original theatrical release title); Night of the Laughing Dead (theatrical reissue title, also used for TV and video); A House in Nightmare Park (video—see Appendix V) *D:* Peter Sykes *P:* Clive Exton and Terry Nation *Sc:* Clive Exton and Terry Nation *Ph:* Ian Wilson *M:* Harry Robinson *Ca:* Frankie Howerd, Ray Milland, Hugh Burden, Kenneth Griffith, John Bennett, Rosalie Crutchley, Ruth Dunning

348. **The House in the Woods** (1957) Film Workshop B&W 62 min *D:* Maxwell Munden *P:* Geoffrey Goodhart *Sc:* Maxwell Munden *Ph:* Edwin Catford *M:* Larry Adler *Ca:* Michael Gough, Patricia Roc, Ronald Howard, Andrea Troubridge, Bill Shine, Nora Hammond, Tim Ellison

349. **House of Blackmail** (1953) A.C.T. Films B&W 72 min *D:* Maurice Elvey *P:* Phil Brandon *Sc:* Allan MacKinnon *Ph:* Phil Grindrod *Ca:* William Sylvester, Mary Germaine, Alexander Gauge, John Arnatt, Denis Shaw, Ingeborg Wells, Hugo Schuster

The House of Hookers *see* **A Touch of the Other**

350. **House of Mortal Sin** (1975) Peter Walker (Heritage) Col 104 min *ABT:* The Confessional Murders (video—see Appendix V) *U.S. Title:* The Confessional *D:* Pete Walker *P:* Pete Walker *Sc:* David McGillivray *Ph:* Peter Jessop *M:* Stanley Myers *Ca:* Anthony Sharp, Susan Penhaligon, Stephanie Beacham, Norman Eshley, Sheila Keith, Hilda Barry, Mervyn Johns

351. **House of Secrets** (1956) The Rank Organisation Film Productions Col 97 min *U.S. Title:* Triple Deception *D:* Guy Green *P:* Vivian A. Cox *Sc:* Robert Buckner and Bryan Forbes *Ph:* Harry Waxman *M:* Hubert Clifford *Ca:* Michael Craig, Julia Arnall, Brenda De Banzie, Barbara Bates, David Kossoff, Geoffrey Keen, Anton Diffring, Eric Pohlmann

352. **The House of the Arrow** (1953) Associated British Picture Corporation B&W 73 min *D:* Michael Anderson *P:* Vaughan N. Dean *Sc:* Edward Dryhurst *Ph:* Erwin Hillier *M:* Gerald Crossman *Ca:* Oscar Homolka, Yvonne Furneaux, Robert Urquhart, Anthony Nicholls, Josephine Griffin, Pierre Lefevre, Andrea Lea

353. **The House of the Seven Hawks** (1959) Coronado Productions (England) B&W 92 min *D:* Richard Thorpe *P:* David E. Rose *Sc:* Jo Eisinger *Ph:* Edward Scaife *M:* Clifton Parker *Ca:* Robert Taylor, Nicole Maurey, Linda Christian, Donald Wolfit, David Kossoff, Gerard Heinz, Eric Pohlmann

354. **House of Whipcord** (1974) Peter Walker (Heritage) Col 101 min *U.S. Titles:* Stag Model Slaughter (1975 theatrical reissue); The Photographer's Models (second 1975 theatrical reissue) *D:* Pete Walker *P:* Pete Walker *Sc:* David McGillivray *Ph:* Peter Jessop *M:* Stanley Myers *Ca:* Barbara Markham, Patrick Barr, Ray Brooks, Ann Michelle, Penny Irving, Sheila Keith, Dorothy Gordon

The House on Straw Hill *see* **Exposé**

The House That Vanished *see* **Scream—and Die!**

355. **How to Murder a Rich Uncle** (1957) Warwick Film Productions B&W 79 min *D:* Nigel Patrick *P:* John Paxton *Sc:* John Paxton *Ph:* Ted Moore *M:* Kenneth V. Jones *Ca:* Charles Coburn, Nigel Patrick, Wendy Hiller, Anthony Newley, Athene Seyler, Kenneth Fortescue, Katie Johnson

356. **The "Human" Factor** (1975) Eton Film Productions Establishment Col 96 min *D:* Edward Dmytryk *P:* Frank Avianca *Sc:* Peter Powell and Thomas Hunter *Ph:* Ousama Rawi *M:* Ennio Morricone *Ca:* George Kennedy, John Mills, Raf Vallone, Arthur Franz, Rita Tushingham, Frank Avianca, Barry Sullivan

357. **The Human Factor** (1979) Sigma Productions Col 114 min *D:* Otto Preminger *P:* Otto Preminger *Sc:* Tom Stoppard *Ph:* Mike Molloy *M:* Richard Logan and Gary Logan *Ca:* Nicol Williamson, Richard Attenborough, Joop Doderer, John Gielgud, Derek Jacobi, Robert Morley, Ann Todd, Iman

Hundred Hour Hunt *see* **Emergency Call**

358. **Hunted** (1952) Independent Artists/British Film Makers B&W 84 min *U.S. Title:* The Stranger in Between *D:* Charles Crichton *P:* Julian Wintle *Sc:* Jack Whittingham *Ph:* Eric Cross *M:* Hubert Clifford *Ca:* Dirk Bogarde, Kay Walsh, Elizabeth Sellars, Geoffrey Keen, Frederick Piper, Jane Aird, Julian Somers, Jon Whiteley

359. **The Hypnotist** (1956) Merton Park/Anglo-Guild Productions B&W 88 min *U.S. Title:* Scotland Yard Dragnet *D:* Montgomery Tully *P:* Alec C. Snowden *Sc:* Montgomery Tully *Ph:* Phil Grindrod *M:* Trevor Duncan *Ca:* Roland Culver, Patricia Roc, Paul Carpenter, William Hartnell, Kay Callard, Ellen Pollock, Gordon Needham

360. **Hysteria** (1964) Hammer Film Productions B&W 85 min *D:* Freddie Francis *P:* Jimmy Sangster *Sc:* Jimmy Sangster *Ph:* John Wilcox *M:* Don Banks *Ca:* Robert Webber, Anthony Newlands, Jennifer Jayne, Maurice Denham, Lelia Goldoni, Peter Woodthorpe, Sue Lloyd

361. **I Start Counting** (1969) Triumvirate Productions Col 105 min *D:* David Greene *P:* David Greene *Sc:* Richard Harris *Ph:* Alex Thomson *M:* Basil Kirchin *Ca:* Jenny Agutter, Bryan Marshall, Clare Sutcliffe, Simon Ward, Gregory Phillips, Lana Morris, Madge Ryan

I'll Get You *see* **Escape Route**

362. **I'll Get You for This** (1950) Romulus Films/Kaydor Productions B&W 83 min *U.S. Title:* Lucky Nick Cain *D:* Joseph M. Newman *P:* Joseph Kaufman *Sc:* George Callahan and William Rose *Ph:* Otto Heller *M:* Walter Goehr *Ca:* George Raft, Coleen Gray, Enzo Staiola, Charles Goldner, Walter Rilla, Martin Benson, Peter Illing

363. **I'm a Stranger** (1952) Corsair Productions B&W 60 min *D:* Brock Williams *P:* Harold Richmond *Sc:* Brock Williams *Ph:* Gordon Lang *M:* Jack Beaver *Ca:* Greta Gynt, James Hayter, Hector Ross, Patric Doonan, Jean Cadell, Charles Lloyd Pack, Fulton Mackay

I'm Alone and I'm Scared *see* **Fright**

364. **Impact** (1963) Butcher's Film Productions B&W 62 min *U.S. Title:* Dangerous Impact (little-known retitling by distributor Keith T. Smith [Modern Sound Pictures, Inc.]) *D:* Peter

Maxwell *P:* John I. Phillips *Sc:* Conrad Phillips and Peter Maxwell *Ph:* Gerald Moss *M:* Johnny Gregory *Ca:* Conrad Phillips, George Pastell, Ballard Berkeley, Linda Marlowe, Richard Klee, Anita West, John Rees

365. **The Impersonator** (1960) Herald Film Productions/Eyeline Films B&W 64 min *D:* Alfred Shaughnessy *P:* Anthony Perry *Sc:* Alfred Shaughnessy and Kenneth Cavander *Ph:* John Coquillon *M:* De Wolfe *Ca:* John Crawford, Jane Griffiths, Patricia Burke, John Salew, John Dare, John Arnatt, Frank Thornton

366. **Impulse** (1954) Tempean Films B&W 80 min *D:* Cy Endfield (billed as Charles De Lautour) *P:* Robert S. Baker and Monty Berman *Sc:* Cy Endfield (billed as Jonathan Roach) and Lawrence Huntington *Ph:* Jonah Jones *M:* Stanley Black *Ca:* Arthur Kennedy, Constance Smith, Joy Shelton, Jack Allen, James Carney, Cameron Hall, John Horsley

In Saigon, Some May Live *see* **Some May Live**

In the Devil's Garden *see* **Assault**

367. **In the Wake of a Stranger** (1959) Crescent Films B&W 64 min *D:* David Eady *P:* Jon Penington *Sc:* John Tully *Ph:* Eric Cross *M:* Edwin Astley *Ca:* Tony Wright, Shirley Eaton, Danny Green, Harry H. Corbett, Willoughby Goddard, Tom Bowman, Vanda Godsell

368. **Incident at Midnight** (1962) Merton Park B&W 56 min *D:* Norman Harrison *P:* Jack Greenwood *Sc:* Arthur La Bern *Ph:* James Wilson *M:* Bernard Ebbinghouse *Ca:* Anton Diffring, William Sylvester, Justine Lord, Martin Miller, Tony Garnett, Philip Locke, Sylva Langova

369. **Information Received** (1961) United Co-Productions B&W 77 min *D:* Robert Lynn *P:* John Clein and George Maynard *Sc:* Paul Ryder *Ph:* Nicolas Roeg *M:* Martin Slavin *Ca:* Sabina Sesselman, William Sylvester, Hermione Baddeley, Edward Underdown, Walter Brown, Robert Raglan, Frank Hawkins

370. **The Informers** (1963) The Rank Organisation Film Productions B&W 105 min *U.S. Title:* Underworld Informers *D:* Ken Annakin *P:* William MacQuitty *Sc:* Alun Falconer *Ph:* Reginald Wyer *M:* Clifton Parker *Ca:* Nigel Patrick, Margaret Whiting, Catherine Woodville, Colin Blakely, Derren Nesbitt, Harry Andrews, Michael Coles

Inn of the Frightened People *see* **Revenge**

371. **Innocent Bystanders** (1972) Sagittarius Productions Col 111 min *D:* Peter Collinson *P:* George H. Brown *Sc:* James Mitchell *Ph:* Brian Probyn *M:* John Keating *Ca:* Stanley Baker, Geraldine Chaplin, Donald Pleasence, Dana Andrews, Sue Lloyd, Derren Nesbitt, Ferdy Mayne, Vladek Sheybal, Warren Mitchell, Cec Linder

372. **Innocent Meeting** (1958) The Danzigers B&W 62 min *D:* Godfrey Grayson *P:* Edward J. Danziger and Harry Lee Danziger *Sc:* Brian Clemens and Eldon Howard *Ph:* James Wilson *M:* Albert Elms, Edwin Astley and Leon Young *Ca:* Sean Lynch, Beth Rogan, Raymond Huntley, Ian Fleming, Howard Lang, Arnold Bell, Denis Shaw

373. **Inside Out** (1975) Kettledrum Films/Maclean & Co. Col 97 min *U.S. Titles:* Hitler's Gold (TV only); The Golden Heist (TV only) *D:* Peter Duffell *P:* Judd Bernard *Sc:* Judd Bernard and Stephen Schneck *Ph:* John Coquillon *M:* Konrad Elfers *Ca:* Telly Savalas, Robert Culp, James Mason, Aldo Ray, Günter Meisner, Adrian Hoven, Wolfgang Lukschy

Inspector Duval *see* **Enter Inspector Duval**

374. **Intent to Kill** (1958) Zonic Productions B&W 89 min *D:* Jack Cardiff *P:* Adrian D. Worker *Sc:* Jimmy Sangster *Ph:* Desmond Dickinson *M:* Kenneth V. Jones *Ca:* Richard Todd, Betsy Drake, Herbert Lom, Carlo Justini, Paul Carpenter, Alexander Knox, Lisa Gastoni, John Crawford

375. **The Internecine Project** (1974) Lion International/Hemisphere Productions/Maclean & Co./Domfil Associates Col 89 min *D:* Ken Hughes *P:* Barry Levinson and Andrew Donally *Sc:* Barry Levinson and Jonathan Lynn *Ph:* Geoffrey Unsworth *M:* Roy Budd *Ca:* James Coburn, Lee Grant, Harry Andrews, Ian Hendry, Michael Jayston, Christiane Kruger, Keenan Wynn, Terence Alexander, Julian Glover

376. **Interpol** (1957) Warwick Film Productions B&W 92 min *U.S. Title:* Pickup Alley *D:* John Gilling *P:* Irving Allen and Albert R. Broccoli *Sc:* John Paxton *Ph:* Ted Moore *M:* Richard Rodney Bennett *Ca:* Victor Mature, Anita Ekberg, Trevor Howard, Bonar Colleano, Andre Morell, Martin Benson, Peter Illing

377. **The Intimate Stranger** (1956) Merton Park/Anglo-Guild Productions (in association with Todon Productions [U.S.]) B&W 95 min *U.S. Title:* Finger of Guilt *D:* Joseph Losey (billed as Joseph Walton on British prints and Alec C. Snowden on U.S. prints) *P:* Alec C. Snowden *Sc:* Howard Koch (billed as Peter Howard) *Ph:* Gerald Gibbs *M:* Trevor Duncan *Ca:* Richard Basehart, Mary Murphy, Constance Cummings, Roger Livesey, Faith Brook, Mervyn Johns, Basil Dignam

378. **The Ipcress File** (1965) Lowndes Pro-

ductions Col 109 min *D:* Sidney J. Furie *P:* Harry Saltzman *Sc:* Bill Canaway and James Doran *Ph:* Otto Heller *M:* John Barry *Ca:* Michael Caine, Nigel Green, Guy Doleman, Sue Lloyd, Gordon Jackson, Aubrey Richards, Thomas Baptiste

It Takes a Thief *see* **The Challenge**

379. **The Italian Job** (1969) Oakhurst Productions Col 100 min *D:* Peter Collinson *P:* Michael Deeley *Sc:* Troy Kennedy Martin *Ph:* Douglas Slocombe *M:* Quincy Jones *Ca:* Michael Caine, Noël Coward, Benny Hill, Raf Vallone, Tony Beckley, Rossano Brazzi, Maggie Blye, John Le Mesurier

380. **Jack the Ripper** (1958) Mid-Century Film Productions B&W 85 min *D:* Robert S. Baker *P:* Robert S. Baker and Monty Berman *Sc:* Jimmy Sangster *Ph:* Monty Berman *M:* Stanley Black *Ca:* Lee Patterson, Eddie Byrne, Betty McDowall, Ewen Solon, John Le Mesurier, George Rose, Denis Shaw

381. **Jackpot** (1960) Eternal Films B&W 71 min *D:* Montgomery Tully *P:* Maurice J. Wilson *Sc:* Montgomery Tully and Maurice J. Wilson *Ph:* Walter J. Harvey *M:* Don Banks *Ca:* William Hartnell, Betty McDowall, Eddie Byrne, George Mikell, Michael Ripper, Victor Brooks, Ivan Craig

Jailbreak *see* **Gaolbreak**

382. **Jet Storm** (1959) Pendennis Productions B&W 99 min *D:* Cy Endfield *P:* Steven Pallos *Sc:* Cy Endfield and Sigmund Miller *Ph:* Jack Hildyard *M:* Thomas Rajna *Ca:* Richard Attenborough, Stanley Baker, Diane Cilento, Elizabeth Sellars, Mai Zetterling, Patrick Allen, Paul Carpenter, Cec Linder, Peter Illing, Neil McCallum

383. **Jigsaw** (1961) Figaro Films B&W 108 min *D:* Val Guest *P:* Val Guest *Sc:* Val Guest *Ph:* Arthur Grant *Ca:* Jack Warner, Ronald Lewis, Yolande Donlan, Michael Goodliffe, John Le Mesurier, Moira Redmond, Ray Barrett, John Barron

384. **Johnny Nobody** (1960) Viceroy Films B&W 88 min *D:* Nigel Patrick *P:* John R. Sloan *Sc:* Patrick Kirwan *Ph:* Ted Moore *M:* Ron Goodwin *Ca:* Nigel Patrick, Yvonne Mitchell, Aldo Ray, William Bendix, Cyril Cusack, Niall MacGinnis, Eddie Byrne

385. **Johnny on the Spot** (1954) E.J. Fancey Productions B&W 72 min *D:* Maclean Rogers *P:* E.J. Fancey *Sc:* Maclean Rogers *Ph:* Geoffrey Faithfull *Ca:* Hugh McDermott, Elspet Gray, Paul Carpenter, Jean Lodge, Ronald Adam, Valentine Dyall, Ronald Leigh-Hunt

386. **Johnny, You're Wanted** (1955) Merton Park B&W 71 min *D:* Vernon Sewell *P:* George Maynard *Sc:* Michael Leighton and Frank Driscoll *Ph:* Basil Emmott *M:* Robert Sharples *Ca:* John Slater, Alfred Marks, Christine Halward, Garry Marsh, Joan Rhodes, Jack Stewart, Frank Thornton

387. **The Jokers** (1966) Adastra Film Productions/Gildor Films/Scimitar Films Col 94 min *D:* Michael Winner *P:* Ben Arbeid and Maurice Foster *Sc:* Dick Clement and Ian La Frenais *Ph:* Ken Hodges *M:* Johnny Pearson *Ca:* Michael Crawford, Oliver Reed, Harry Andrews, James Donald, Daniel Massey, Gabriella Licudi, Michael Hordern, Frank Finlay

388. **Journey into Nowhere** (1962) Avon Films/Scully Productions B&W 75 min *U.S. Titles:* Journey to Nowhere; Murder by Agreement *D:* Denis Scully *P:* Bruce Yorke *Sc:* Peter Myers *Ph:* Vaclav Vich *M:* Ivor Slaney *Ca:* Sonja Ziemann, Tony Wright, Helmut Schmid, Don Barrigo

Journey to Nowhere *see* **Journey into Nowhere**

389. **Judgment Deferred** (1952) Group 3 B&W 88 min *D:* John Baxter *P:* John Baxter *Sc:* Geoffrey Orme, Barbara K. Emary and Walter Meade *Ph:* Arthur Grant *M:* Kennedy Russell *Ca:* Hugh Sinclair, Helen Shingler, Abraham Sofaer, Leslie Dwyer, Joan Collins, Harry Locke, Martin Benson

390. **Juggernaut** (1974) United Artists/David V. Picker Productions/Richard Alan Simmons Productions Col 110 min *ABT:* Terror on the Britannic (DVD title) *U.S. Title:* Terror on the Britannic (1975 theatrical reissue) *D:* Richard Lester *P:* Richard Alan Simmons (billed as Richard De Koker) *Sc:* Richard Alan Simmons (billed as Richard De Koker) *Ph:* Gerry Fisher *M:* Ken Thorne *Ca:* Richard Harris, Omar Sharif, David Hemmings, Anthony Hopkins, Ian Holm, Shirley Knight, Roy Kinnear, Freddie Jones, Cyril Cusack, Jack Watson

391. **Jungle Street** (1961) Theatrecraft Limited B&W 82 min *U.S. Title:* Jungle Street Girls *D:* Charles Saunders *P:* Guido Coen *Sc:* Alexander Doré *Ph:* Walter J. Harvey *M:* Harold Geller *Ca:* David McCallum, Kenneth Cope, Jill Ireland, Brian Weske, Vanda Hudson, Martin Sterndale, Howard Pays

Jungle Street Girls *see* **Jungle Street**

392. **Kaleidoscope** (1966) Winkast Film Productions Col 103 min *D:* Jack Smight *P:* Elliott Kastner *Sc:* Robert Carrington and Jane-Howard Carrington *Ph:* Christopher Challis *M:* Stanley Myers *Ca:* Warren Beatty, Susannah York, Clive Revill, Eric Porter, Murray Melvin, George

Sewell, Stanley Meadows, John Junkin, Larry Taylor

Kenya—Country of Treasure *see* **The Syndicate**

393. **The Key Man** (1957) Merton Park B&W 63 min *D:* Montgomery Tully *P:* Alec C. Snowden *Sc:* J. MacLaren-Ross *Ph:* Phil Grindrod *Ca:* Lee Patterson, Hy Hazell, Colin Gordon, Philip Leaver, Paula Byrne, George Margo, Henry Vidon

394. **Kil 1** (1962) Searchlight Films B&W 61 min *U.S. Title:* The Skin Game *D:* Arnold Louis Miller *P:* Stanley A. Long and Arnold Louis Miller *Sc:* Bob Kesten *Ph:* Stanley A. Long *M:* De Wolfe *Ca:* Ronald Howard, Jess Conrad, Melody O'Brian, Peter Gray, David Graham, Peter Hager, Larry Taylor

395. **Kill Her Gently** (1958) Fortress Film Productions B&W 73 min *D:* Charles Saunders *P:* Guido Coen *Sc:* Paul Erickson *Ph:* Walter J. Harvey *M:* Edwin Astley *Ca:* Griffith Jones, Maureen Connell, Marc Lawrence, George Mikell, Frank Hawkins, Patrick Connor, John Gayford

396. **Kill Me Tomorrow** (1957) Delta Films (in association with Amalgamated Productions [U.S.]) B&W 81 min *D:* Terence Fisher *P:* Francis Searle *Sc:* Robert Falconer and Manning O'Brine *Ph:* Geoffrey Faithfull *M:* Temple Abady *Ca:* Pat O'Brien, Lois Maxwell, George Coulouris, Wensley Pithey, Freddie Mills, Ronald Adam, Robert Brown

397. **Kill or Cure** (1962) MGM B&W 87 min *D:* George Pollock *P:* George H. Brown *Sc:* David Pursall and Jack Seddon *Ph:* Geoffrey Faithfull *M:* Ron Goodwin *Ca:* Terry-Thomas, Eric Sykes, Dennis Price, Lionel Jeffries, Moira Redmond, Katya Douglas, Derren Nesbitt, Ronnie Barker

398. **A Killer Walks** (1952) Leontine Entertainments B&W 57 min *D:* Ronald Drake *P:* Ronald Drake *Sc:* Ronald Drake *Ph:* Jack Asher and Phil Grindrod *M:* Eric Spear *Ca:* Susan Shaw, Laurence Harvey, Trader Faulkner, Laurence Naismith, Sheila Shand Gibbs, Ethel Edwards, Valentine Dunn

399. **Killer's Moon** (1978) Rothernorth Limited Col 90 min *D:* Alan Birkinshaw *P:* Alan Birkinshaw and Gordon Keymer *Sc:* Alan Birkinshaw *Ph:* Arthur Lavis *M:* John Shakespeare and Derek Warne *Ca:* Anthony Forrest, Tom Marshall, Nigel Gregory, Jane Hayden, Alison Elliott, Georgina Kean, David Jackson

Kiss & Kill *see* **The Blood of Fu Manchu**
Kiss of Death *see* **The Blood of Fu Manchu**

400. **The Lady Craved Excitement** (1950) Hammer Film Productions B&W 70 min *D:* Francis Searle *P:* Anthony Hinds *Sc:* John Gilling, Edward J. Mason and Francis Searle *Ph:* Walter J. Harvey *M:* Frank Spencer *Ca:* Hy Hazell, Michael Medwin, Sidney James, Andrew Keir, Thelma Grigg, Danny Green, John Longden

401. **Lady in the Fog** (1952) Hammer Film Productions (in association with Lippert Pictures [U.S.]) B&W 83 min *U.S. Title:* Scotland Yard Inspector *D:* Sam Newfield *P:* Anthony Hinds *Sc:* Orville H. Hampton *Ph:* Walter J. Harvey *M:* Ivor Slaney *Ca:* Cesar Romero, Lois Maxwell, Bernadette O'Farrell, Geoffrey Keen, Campbell Singer, Mary Mackenzie, Lloyd Lamble, Richard Johnson

402. **Lady of Vengeance** (1956) Rich & Rich/Princess Production Corporation B&W 74 min *D:* Burt Balaban *P:* Burt Balaban and Bernard Donnenfeld *Sc:* Irve Tunick *Ph:* Ian Struthers *M:* Phil Cardew *Ca:* Dennis O'Keefe, Ann Sears, Patrick Barr, Anton Diffring, Vernon Greeves, Eileen Elton, Frederick Schiller

403. **The Lady Vanishes** (1979) Hammer Film Productions/Rank Film Productions Col 97 min *D:* Anthony Page *P:* Tom Sachs *Sc:* George Axelrod *Ph:* Douglas Slocombe *M:* Richard Hartley *Ca:* Elliott Gould, Cybill Shepherd, Angela Lansbury, Herbert Lom, Arthur Lowe, Ian Carmichael, Gerald Harper, Vladek Sheybal

404. **The Ladykillers** (1955) Ealing Studios Col 97 min *D:* Alexander Mackendrick *P:* Michael Balcon *Sc:* William Rose *Ph:* Otto Heller *M:* Tristram Cary *Ca:* Alec Guinness, Cecil Parker, Herbert Lom, Peter Sellers, Danny Green, Jack Warner, Katie Johnson, Frankie Howerd

405. **The Lamp in Assassin Mews** (1962) The Danzigers B&W 65 min *D:* Godfrey Grayson *P:* Brian Taylor *Sc:* Mark Grantham (billed as M.M. McCormack) *Ph:* Lionel Baines *M:* Bill Le Sage *Ca:* Francis Matthews, Lisa Daniely, Ian Fleming, Amy Dalby, Ann Sears, Anne Lawson, Derek Tansley

406. **The Large Rope** (1953) Insignia Films B&W 75 min *D:* Wolf Rilla *P:* Victor Hanbury *Sc:* Ted Willis *Ph:* Geoffrey Faithfull *M:* Ronald Binge *Ca:* Donald Houston, Susan Shaw, Robert Brown, Vanda Godsell, Leonard White, Margaret Anderson, Richard Warner

407. **The Last Grenade** (1969) Lockmore Ltd./Josef Shaftel Productions Col 93 min *D:* Gordon Flemyng *P:* Josef Shaftel *Sc:* Kenneth Ware *Ph:* Alan Hume *M:* John Dankworth *Ca:* Stanley Baker, Alex Cord, Honor Blackman, Richard Attenborough, Rafer Johnson, Andrew Keir, Julian Glover, John Thaw

408. **The Last Man to Hang** (1956) A.C.T. Films/Warwick Film Productions B&W 75 min *D:* Terence Fisher *P:* John Gossage *Sc:* Ivor Montagu and Max Trell *Ph:* Desmond Dickinson *M:* John Wooldridge *Ca:* Tom Conway, Elizabeth Sellars, Eunice Gayson, Freda Jackson, Raymond Huntley, Victor Maddern, Margaretta Scott, Anthony Newley

409. **The Last Page** (1952) Hammer Film Productions (in association with Lippert Pictures [U.S.]) B&W 84 min *U.S. Title:* Man Bait *D:* Terence Fisher *P:* Anthony Hinds *Sc:* Frederick Knott *Ph:* Walter J. Harvey *M:* Frank Spencer *Ca:* George Brent, Marguerite Chapman, Raymond Huntley, Peter Reynolds, Diana Dors, Eleanor Summerfield, Conrad Phillips

410. **The Last Shot You Hear** (1968) Lippert Films Col 91 min *D:* Gordon Hessler *P:* Jack Parsons *Sc:* Tim Shields *Ph:* David Holmes *M:* Bert Shefter *Ca:* Hugh Marlowe, Zena Walker, Patricia Haines, William Dysart, Thorley Walters, Joan Young, John Nettleton

411. **The Late Edwina Black** (1950) Elvey-Gartside Productions B&W 78 min *U.S. Title:* Obsessed *D:* Maurice Elvey *P:* Ernest Gartside *Sc:* Charles Frank and David Evans *Ph:* Stephen Dade *M:* Allan Gray *Ca:* David Farrar, Geraldine Fitzgerald, Roland Culver, Jean Cadell, Mary Merrall, Harcourt Williams, Charles Heslop

412. **The League of Gentlemen** (1960) A.F.M. (Allied Film Makers) Productions B&W 114 min *D:* Basil Dearden *P:* Michael Relph *Sc:* Bryan Forbes *Ph:* Arthur Ibbetson *M:* Philip Green *Ca:* Jack Hawkins, Nigel Patrick, Roger Livesey, Richard Attenborough, Bryan Forbes, Kieron Moore, Melissa Stribling, Terence Alexander, Norman Bird, Robert Coote

413. **Libel** (1959) MGM/Anatole De Grunwald Ltd. B&W 100 min *D:* Anthony Asquith *P:* Anatole De Grunwald *Sc:* Anatole De Grunwald and Karl Tunberg *Ph:* Robert Krasker *M:* Benjamin Frankel *Ca:* Olivia De Havilland, Dirk Bogarde, Paul Massie, Robert Morley, Wilfrid Hyde White, Anthony Dawson, Richard Wattis

414. **Licensed to Kill** (1965) Alistair Film Productions Col 97 min *U.S. Title:* The 2nd Best Secret Agent in the Whole Wide World *D:* Lindsay Shonteff *P:* James Ward *Sc:* Howard Griffiths and Lindsay Shonteff *Ph:* Terry Maher *M:* Herbert Chappell *Ca:* Tom Adams, Karel Stepanek, Veronica Hurst, Peter Bull, John Arnatt, Francis De Wolff, George Pastell

415. **Licensed to Love and Kill** (1979) Lindsay Shonteff Film Productions Col 94 min *U.S. Title:* The Man from S.E.X. *D:* Lindsay Shonteff *P:* Elizabeth Gray *Sc:* Jeremy Lee Francis *Ph:* Bill Paterson *M:* Simon Bell *Ca:* Gareth Hunt, Nick Tate, Fiona Curzon, Gary Hope, Geoffrey Keen, Jay Benedict, John Arnatt

416. **Life in Danger** (1959) Parroch Films B&W 63 min *D:* Terry Bishop *P:* Jack Parsons *Sc:* Malcolm Hulke and Eric Paice *Ph:* Peter Hennessy *M:* William Davies *Ca:* Derren Nesbitt, Julie Hopkins, Howard Marion Crawford, Victor Brooks, Jack Allen, Christopher Witty, Carmel McSharry

417. **The Lifetaker** (1975) Onyx Films/National Film Trustee Company Col 103 min *D:* Michael Papas *P:* Michael Papas *Sc:* Michael Papas *Ph:* Peter Jessop *M:* Nicos Mamangakis *Ca:* Terence Morgan, Lea Dregorn, Peter Duncan, Dimitris Andreas, Leon Silver, Paul Beech, Anna Mottram

418. **The Limbo Line** (1968) Trio Films/Group W Films Col 99 min *D:* Samuel Gallu *P:* Frank Bevis *Sc:* Donald James *Ph:* John Wilcox *M:* Johnnie Spence *Ca:* Craig Stevens, Kate O'Mara, Moira Redmond, Vladek Sheybal, Robert Urquhart, Yolande Turner, Eugene Deckers, Ferdy Mayne, Norman Bird

419. **The Limping Man** (1953) Banner Pictures B&W 74 min *D:* Cy Endfield (billed as Charles De Lautour) *P:* Donald Ginsberg *Sc:* Ian Stuart Black and Reginald Long *Ph:* Jonah Jones *M:* Arthur Wilkinson *Ca:* Lloyd Bridges, Moira Lister, Helene Cordet, Leslie Phillips, Irissa Cooper, Alan Wheatley, Tom Gill

420. **Links of Justice** (1958) The Danzigers B&W 68 min *D:* Max Varnel *P:* Edward J. Danziger and Harry Lee Danziger *Sc:* Brian Clemens and Eldon Howard *Ph:* James Wilson *M:* Albert Elms, Edwin Astley and Leon Young *Ca:* Jack Watling, Sarah Lawson, Robert Raikes, Denis Shaw, Kay Callard, Michael Kelly, Jacques Cey

421. **The Liquidator** (1965) MGM Col 104 min *D:* Jack Cardiff *P:* Jon Penington *Sc:* Peter Yeldham *Ph:* Edward Scaife *M:* Lalo Schifrin *Ca:* Rod Taylor, Trevor Howard, Jill St. John, Wilfrid Hyde White, David Tomlinson, Akim Tamiroff, Gabriella Licudi, Eric Sykes, John Le Mesurier

422. **Little Red Monkey** (1954) Merton Park (in association with Todon Productions [U.S.]) B&W 74 min *U.S. Title:* Case of the Red Monkey *D:* Ken Hughes *P:* Alec C. Snowden *Sc:* James Eastwood and Ken Hughes *Ph:* Josef Ambor *M:* Trevor Duncan *Ca:* Richard Conte, Rona Anderson, Russell Napier, Colin Gordon, Arnold Marle, Sylva Langova, Donald Bisset

423. **Live and Let Die** (1973) Eon Productions Col 121 min *D:* Guy Hamilton *P:* Harry Saltzman

and Albert R. Broccoli *Sc:* Tom Mankiewicz *Ph:* Ted Moore *M:* George Martin *Ca:* Roger Moore, Yaphet Kotto, Jane Seymour, Clifton James, Julius W. Harris, David Hedison, Gloria Hendry, Bernard Lee, Lois Maxwell

424. **Locker Sixty-Nine** (1962) Merton Park B&W 56 min *D:* Norman Harrison *P:* Jack Greenwood *Sc:* Richard Harris *Ph:* Bert Mason *M:* Bernard Ebbinghouse *Ca:* Eddie Byrne, Paul Daneman, Walter Brown, Edward Underdown, Clarissa Stolz, John Carson, Edwin Richfield

425. **The Long Arm** (1956) Ealing Studios B&W 96 min *U.S. Title:* The Third Key *D:* Charles Frend *P:* Tom Morahan *Sc:* Janet Green and Robert Barr *Ph:* Gordon Dines *M:* Gerard Schurmann *Ca:* Jack Hawkins, John Stratton, Dorothy Alison, Geoffrey Keen, Ursula Howells, Sydney Tafler, Richard Leech, Ian Bannen

426. **The Long Dark Hall** (1950) Five Ocean Films/Cusick International Films B&W 86 min *D:* Anthony Bushell and Reginald Beck *P:* Peter Cusick *Sc:* Nunnally Johnson *Ph:* Wilkie Cooper *M:* Benjamin Frankel *Ca:* Rex Harrison, Lilli Palmer, Denis O'Dea, Raymond Huntley, Anthony Bushell, Michael Medwin, Anthony Dawson, Eric Pohlmann

427. **The Long Good Friday** (1979) Black Lion Films/Calendar Productions Col 114 min *D:* John MacKenzie *P:* Barry Hanson *Sc:* Barrie Keeffe *Ph:* Phil Meheux *M:* Francis Monkman *Ca:* Bob Hoskins, Helen Mirren, Dave King, Bryan Marshall, Derek Thompson, Eddie Constantine, Brian Hall

428. **The Long Haul** (1957) Marksman Films (in association with Todon Productions [U.S.]) B&W 100 min *D:* Ken Hughes *P:* Maxwell Setton *Sc:* Ken Hughes *Ph:* Basil Emmott *M:* Trevor Duncan *Ca:* Victor Mature, Diana Dors, Patrick Allen, Gene Anderson, Peter Reynolds, Liam Redmond, Michael Wade

429. **The Long Knife** (1958) Merton Park B&W 57 min *D:* Montgomery Tully *P:* Jack Greenwood *Sc:* Ian Stuart Black *Ph:* John Wiles *M:* Richard Taylor *Ca:* Joan Rice, Sheldon Lawrence, Dorothy Brewster, Ellen Pollock, Victor Brooks, Alan Keith, Arthur Gomez

430. **The Long Memory** (1952) Europa Films/British Film Makers B&W 96 min *D:* Robert Hamer *P:* Hugh Stewart *Sc:* Robert Hamer and Frank Harvey *Ph:* Harry Waxman *M:* William Alwyn *Ca:* John Mills, John McCallum, Elizabeth Sellars, Eva Bergh, Geoffrey Keen, John Chandos, Harold Lang

431. **The Long Shadow** (1961) Argo Film Productions B&W 64 min *D:* Peter Maxwell *P:* John Pellatt *Sc:* Manning O'Brine *Ph:* Norman Warwick *M:* Bill McGuffie *Ca:* John Crawford, Susan Hampshire, Bill Nagy, Humphrey Lestocq, Willoughby Goddard, Anne Castaldini, Larry Taylor

432. **The Looking Glass War** (1969) Columbia British Productions/Frankovich Productions Col 107 min *D:* Frank R. Pierson *P:* John Box *Sc:* Frank R. Pierson *Ph:* Austin Dempster *M:* Wally Stott *Ca:* Christopher Jones, Pia Degermark, Ralph Richardson, Anthony Hopkins, Paul Rogers, Susan George, Anna Massey, Robert Urquhart, Ray McAnally, Maxine Audley

433. **Lost** (1956) The Rank Organisation Film Productions Col 89 min *U.S. Title:* Tears for Simon *D:* Guy Green *P:* Vivian A. Cox *Sc:* Janet Green *Ph:* Harry Waxman *M:* Benjamin Frankel *Ca:* David Farrar, David Knight, Julia Arnall, Anthony Oliver, Thora Hird, Eleanor Summerfield, Meredith Edwards, William Lucas

434. **The Lost Hours** (1952) Tempean Films (in association with Royal Productions [U.S.]) B&W 72 min *U.S. Title:* The Big Frame *D:* David MacDonald *P:* Robert S. Baker and Monty Berman *Sc:* John Gilling and Steve Fisher *Ph:* Monty Berman *M:* William Hill-Bowen *Ca:* Mark Stevens, Jean Kent, Garry Marsh, John Bentley, Dianne Foster, John Harvey, John Horsley

Love Is a Woman *see* **Death Is a Woman**
Lucky Nick Cain *see* **I'll Get You for This**

435. **The Mackintosh Man** (1973) Newman-Foreman Company/Warner Bros. Productions Col 99 min *D:* John Huston *P:* John Foreman *Sc:* Walter Hill *Ph:* Oswald Morris *M:* Maurice Jarre *Ca:* Paul Newman, Dominique Sanda, James Mason, Harry Andrews, Ian Bannen, Michael Hordern, Nigel Patrick, Peter Vaughan, Roland Culver, Jenny Runacre

Madame Sin (1971)—See Appendix VI

436. **Madhouse** (1974) Amicus Productions/American International Productions (England) Col 92 min *D:* Jim Clark *P:* Max J. Rosenberg and Milton Subotsky *Sc:* Greg Morrison and Ken Levison *Ph:* Ray Parslow *M:* Douglas Gamley *Ca:* Vincent Price, Peter Cushing, Robert Quarry, Adrienne Corri, Natasha Pyne, Linda Hayden, Jenny Lee Wright, Peter Halliday

Mafia Junction *see* **Blue Movie Blackmail**
Mailbag Robbery *see* **The Flying Scot**

437. **The Main Chance** (1964) Merton Park B&W 61 min *D:* John Knight *P:* Jack Greenwood *Sc:* Richard Harris *Ph:* James Wilson *M:* Bernard Ebbinghouse *Ca:* Gregoire Aslan, Tracy Reed, Edward De Souza, Stanley Meadows, Jack Smethurst, Bernard Stone, Will Stampe

438. **Malaga** (1954) Film Locations Col 84

min *U.S. Title:* Fire Over Africa *D:* Richard Sale *P:* Mike J. Frankovich *Sc:* Robert Westerby *Ph:* Christopher Challis *M:* Benjamin Frankel *Ca:* Maureen O'Hara, Macdonald Carey, Binnie Barnes, Guy Middleton, Hugh McDermott, Leonard Sachs, Ferdy Mayne

Malaga *see* **Moment of Danger**

439. **The Malpas Mystery** (1960) Independent Artists B&W 59 min *D:* Sidney Hayers *P:* Julian Wintle and Leslie Parkyn *Sc:* Paul Tabori and Gordon Wellesley *Ph:* Michael Reed *M:* Elisabeth Lutyens *Ca:* Maureen Swanson, Allan Cuthbertson, Geoffrey Keen, Sandra Dorne, Ronald Howard, Catherine Feller, Richard Shaw

440. **Man Accused** (1959) The Danzigers B&W 58 min *D:* Montgomery Tully *P:* Edward J. Danziger and Harry Lee Danziger *Sc:* Mark Grantham *Ph:* James Wilson *Ca:* Ronald Howard, Carol Marsh, Ian Fleming, Catharina Ferraz, Robert Dorning, Stuart Saunders, Brian Nissen

441. **Man at the Carlton Tower** (1961) Merton Park B&W 57 min *D:* Robert Tronson *P:* Jack Greenwood *Sc:* Philip Mackie *Ph:* Bert Mason *M:* Ron Goodwin *Ca:* Maxine Audley, Lee Montague, Allan Cuthbertson, Terence Alexander, Alfred Burke, Nigel Green, Nyree Dawn Porter

Man Bait *see* **The Last Page**

442. **The Man Between** (1953) London Film Productions/British Lion Production Assets B&W 101 min *D:* Carol Reed *P:* Carol Reed *Sc:* Harry Kurnitz *Ph:* Desmond Dickinson *M:* John Addison *Ca:* James Mason, Claire Bloom, Hildegard Knef, Geoffrey Toone, Aribert Waescher, Ernst Schroeder, Hilde Sessak

443. **Man Detained** (1961) Merton Park B&W 59 min *D:* Robert Tronson *P:* Jack Greenwood *Sc:* Richard Harris *Ph:* Bert Mason *M:* Bernard Ebbinghouse *Ca:* Bernard Archard, Elvi Hale, Paul Stassino, Michael Coles, Ann Sears, Victor Platt, Patrick Jordan

The Man from S.E.X. *see* **Licensed to Love and Kill**

444. **Man from Tangier** (1957) Butcher's Film Productions B&W 67 min *U.S. Title:* Thunder Over Tangier *D:* Lance Comfort *P:* W.G. Chalmers *Sc:* Manning O'Brine *Ph:* Geoffrey Faithfull *M:* Wilfred Burns *Ca:* Robert Hutton, Lisa Gastoni, Martin Benson, Derek Sydney, Jack Allen, Leonard Sachs, Michael Balfour

Man in Hiding *see* **Mantrap**

445. **The Man in the Back Seat** (1961) Independent Artists B&W 57 min *D:* Vernon Sewell *P:* Julian Wintle and Leslie Parkyn *Sc:* Malcolm Hulke and Eric Paice *Ph:* Reginald Wyer *M:* Stanley Black *Ca:* Derren Nesbitt, Keith Faulkner, Carol White, Harry Locke, Anthony Bate, Roy Purcell, Harold Siddons

Man in the Dark *see* **Blind Corner**

446. **The Man in the Middle** (1959) A.B. Frejafilm B&W 86 min *U.S. Title:* 48 Hours to Live *D:* Peter Bourne *P:* Edward Rubin *Sc:* Peter Bourne *Ph:* Bengt Lindstrom *M:* Harry Arnold *Ca:* Anthony Steel, Marlies Behrens, Lewis Charles, Ina Anders, Birger Malmsten, Hakan Westergren, Rusty Rutledge

447. **Man in the Middle** (1963) Pennebaker Ltd./Belmont Productions B&W 94 min *D:* Guy Hamilton *P:* Walter Seltzer *Sc:* Keith Waterhouse and Willis Hall *Ph:* Wilkie Cooper *M:* Lionel Bart (theme) and John Barry *Ca:* Robert Mitchum, France Nuyen, Barry Sullivan, Trevor Howard, Keenan Wynn, Sam Wanamaker, Alexander Knox, Michael Goodliffe

448. **The Man in the Road** (1955) Gibraltar Productions B&W 84 min *D:* Lance Comfort *P:* Charles A. Leeds *Sc:* Guy Morgan *Ph:* Stanley Pavey *M:* Bruce Campbell *Ca:* Derek Farr, Ella Raines, Donald Wolfit, Lisa Daniely, Karel Stepanek, Cyril Cusack, Russell Napier

449. **Man in the Shadow** (1957) Merton Park (in association with Amalgamated Productions [U.S.]) B&W 85 min *U.S. Title:* Violent Stranger (TV only) *D:* Montgomery Tully *P:* Alec C. Snowden *Sc:* Maisie Sharman (billed as Stratford Davis) *Ph:* Phil Grindrod *M:* Trevor Duncan *Ca:* Zachary Scott, Faith Domergue, Peter Illing, Faith Brook, Kay Callard, Gordon Jackson, John Horsley

450. **The Man Inside** (1958) Warwick Film Productions B&W 97 min *D:* John Gilling *P:* Irving Allen and Albert R. Broccoli *Sc:* John Gilling and David Shaw *Ph:* Ted Moore *M:* Richard Rodney Bennett *Ca:* Jack Palance, Anita Ekberg, Nigel Patrick, Bonar Colleano, Anthony Newley, Sidney James, Eric Pohlmann

451. **Man of Violence** (1969) Pete Walker Film Productions Col 107 min *ABT:* Moon (originally a working title, but appears on the title screen of print used for BFI DVD release) *D:* Pete Walker *P:* Pete Walker *Sc:* Brian Comport and Pete Walker *Ph:* Norman Langley *M:* Cyril Ornadel *Ca:* Michael Latimer, Luan Peters, Derek Aylward, Maurice Kaufmann, Derek Francis, Virginia Wetherell, Patrick Jordan

452. **The Man Outside** (1967) Trio Films/Group W Films Col 98 min *D:* Samuel Gallu *P:* William Gell *Sc:* Samuel Gallu *Ph:* Gilbert Taylor *M:* Richard Arnell *Ca:* Van Heflin, Peter Vaughan, Heidelinde Weis, Pinkas Braun, Charles Gray, Paul Maxwell, Ronnie Barker, Linda Marlowe, Bill Nagy

453. **The Man Upstairs** (1958) A.C.T. Films B&W 88 min *D:* Don Chaffey *P:* Robert Dunbar *Sc:* Alun Falconer *Ph:* Gerald Gibbs *Ca:* Richard Attenborough, Bernard Lee, Dorothy Alison, Donald Houston, Virginia Maskell, Maureen Connell, Kenneth Griffith

454. **The Man Who Couldn't Walk** (1960) Bill and Michael Luckwell Ltd. B&W 63 min *D:* Henry Cass *P:* Jock MacGregor and Umesh Mallik *Sc:* Umesh Mallik *Ph:* Walter J. Harvey *M:* Wilfred Burns *Ca:* Eric Pohlmann, Peter Reynolds, Pat Clavin, Reed De Rouen, Bernadette Milnes, Richard Shaw, Martin Cass

455. **The Man Who Finally Died** (1962) White Cross Productions B&W 100 min *D:* Quentin Lawrence *P:* Norman Williams *Sc:* Lewis Greifer and Louis Marks *Ph:* Stephen Dade *M:* Philip Green *Ca:* Stanley Baker, Peter Cushing, Mai Zetterling, Eric Portman, Niall MacGinnis, Nigel Green, Alfred Burke

456. **The Man Who Never Was** (1955) Sumar Film Productions Col 103 min *D:* Ronald Neame *P:* Andre Hakim *Sc:* Nigel Balchin *Ph:* Oswald Morris *M:* Alan Rawsthorne *Ca:* Clifton Webb, Gloria Grahame, Robert Flemyng, Josephine Griffin, Stephen Boyd, Laurence Naismith, Andre Morell

457. **The Man Who Was Nobody** (1960) Merton Park B&W 61 min *D:* Montgomery Tully *P:* Jack Greenwood *Sc:* James Eastwood *Ph:* Brian Rhodes *M:* Francis Chagrin *Ca:* Hazel Court, John Crawford, Lisa Daniely, Paul Eddington, Robert Dorning, Kevin Stoney, Jack Watson

458. **The Man Who Watched Trains Go By** (1952) Raymond Stross Productions/Josef Shaftel Productions Col 80 min *U.S. Title:* The Paris Express *D:* Harold French *P:* Raymond Stross *Sc:* Harold French *Ph:* Otto Heller *M:* Benjamin Frankel *Ca:* Claude Rains, Marta Toren, Michael Nightingale, Felix Aylmer, Herbert Lom, Anouk Aimée, Marius Goring, Ferdy Mayne

459. **The Man Who Wouldn't Talk** (1957) Everest Pictures B&W 97 min *D:* Herbert Wilcox *P:* Herbert Wilcox *Sc:* Edgar Lustgarten *Ph:* Gordon Dines *M:* Stanley Black *Ca:* Anna Neagle, Anthony Quayle, Zsa Zsa Gabor, Katherine Kath, Dora Bryan, Patrick Allen, Hugh McDermott

460. **Man with a Gun** (1958) Merton Park B&W 60 min *D:* Montgomery Tully *P:* Jack Greenwood *Sc:* Michael Winner *Ph:* John Wiles *M:* Ron Goodwin *Ca:* Lee Patterson, Rona Anderson, John Le Mesurier, Bill Nagy, Marne Maitland, Cyril Chamberlain, Harold Lang

461. **The Man with the Golden Gun** (1974) Eon Productions Col 125 min *D:* Guy Hamilton *P:* Albert R. Broccoli and Harry Saltzman *Sc:* Richard Maibaum and Tom Mankiewicz *Ph:* Ted Moore and Oswald Morris *M:* John Barry *Ca:* Roger Moore, Christopher Lee, Britt Ekland, Maud Adams, Herve Villechaize, Clifton James, Marc Lawrence, Marne Maitland, Michael Goodliffe, Bernard Lee, Lois Maxwell

The Man with Two Faces *see* **Troubled Waters**

462. **Maniac** (1962) Hammer Film Productions B&W 86 min *U.S. Title:* The Maniac *D:* Michael Carreras *P:* Jimmy Sangster *Sc:* Jimmy Sangster *Ph:* Wilkie Cooper *M:* Stanley Black *Ca:* Kerwin Mathews, Nadia Gray, Donald Houston, Liliane Brousse, Norman Bird, George Pastell, Arnold Diamond

The Maniac *see* **Maniac**

463. **Mantrap** (1952) Hammer Film Productions (in association with Lippert Pictures [U.S.]) B&W 79 min *U.S. Title:* Man in Hiding *D:* Terence Fisher *P:* Michael Carreras and Alexander Paal *Sc:* Paul Tabori and Terence Fisher *Ph:* Reginald Wyer *M:* Doreen Carwithen *Ca:* Paul Henreid, Lois Maxwell, Kieron Moore, Hugh Sinclair, Kay Kendall, Anthony Forwood, Lloyd Lamble

464. **Mark of the Phoenix** (1957) Butcher's Film Productions B&W 64 min *D:* Maclean Rogers *P:* W.G. Chalmers *Sc:* Norman Hudis *Ph:* Geoffrey Faithfull *M:* Wilfred Burns *Ca:* Julia Arnall, Sheldon Lawrence, Anton Diffring, Eric Pohlmann, George Margo, Michael Peake, Martin Miller

465. **The Marked One** (1963) Planet Film Productions B&W 65 min *D:* Francis Searle *P:* Tom Blakeley *Sc:* Paul Erickson *Ph:* Frank Kingston *M:* Bernie Fenton (in association with Frank Patten) *Ca:* William Lucas, Zena Walker, Patrick Jordan, Laurie Leigh, David Gregory, Arthur Lovegrove, Edward Ogden

466. **Maroc 7** (1966) Cyclone Films Col 91 min *D:* Gerry O'Hara *P:* John Gale and Leslie Phillips *Sc:* David Osborn *Ph:* Kenneth Talbot *M:* Kenneth V. Jones *Ca:* Gene Barry, Elsa Martinelli, Cyd Charisse, Leslie Phillips, Denholm Elliott, Alexandra Stewart, Eric Barker, Angela Douglas

467. **Marriage of Convenience** (1960) Merton Park B&W 58 min *D:* Clive Donner *P:* Jack Greenwood *Sc:* Robert Banks Stewart *Ph:* Brian Rhodes *M:* Francis Chagrin *Ca:* Harry H. Corbett, John Cairney, John Van Eyssen, Jennifer Daniel, Moira Redmond, Russell Waters, Trevor Maskell

468. **The Marseille Contract** (1974) Kettledrum Films (London)/P.E.C.F. (Paris) Col 90 min *U.S. Title:* The Destructors *D:* Robert Parrish *P:* Judd Bernard *Sc:* Judd Bernard *Ph:* Douglas Slocombe *M:* Roy Budd *Ca:* Michael Caine, Anthony Quinn, James Mason, Maurice Ronet, Alexandra Stewart, Maureen Kerwin, Marcel Bozzuffi, Catherine Rouvel

469. **Masquerade** (1964) Novus Films Col 102 min *D:* Basil Dearden *P:* Michael Relph *Sc:* Michael Relph and William Goldman *Ph:* Otto Heller *M:* Philip Green *Ca:* Cliff Robertson, Jack Hawkins, Marisa Mell, Christopher Witty, Bill Fraser, Tutte Lemkow, John Le Mesurier, Charles Gray, Michel Piccoli

470. **The Master Plan** (1954) Gibraltar Productions B&W 78 min *D:* Cy Endfield (billed as Hugh Raker) *P:* Charles A. Leeds *Sc:* Cy Endfield (billed as Hugh Raker) *Ph:* Jonah Jones *M:* De Wolfe *Ca:* Wayne Morris, Tilda Thamar, Norman Wooland, Mary Mackenzie, Arnold Bell, Marjorie Stewart, Frederick Schrecker

471. **Master Spy** (1962) Eternal Films B&W 74 min *D:* Montgomery Tully *P:* Maurice J. Wilson *Sc:* Maurice J. Wilson and Montgomery Tully *Ph:* Geoffrey Faithfull *M:* Ken Thorne *Ca:* Stephen Murray, June Thorburn, Alan Wheatley, John Carson, John Bown, Ernest Clark, Marne Maitland

472. **A Matter of Choice** (1963) Holmwood Productions B&W 79 min *D:* Vernon Sewell *P:* George Maynard *Sc:* Paul Ryder *Ph:* Arthur Lavis *M:* Robert Sharples *Ca:* Anthony Steel, Jeanne Moody, Ballard Berkeley, Malcolm Gerard, Michael Davis, Penny Morrell, Lisa Peake

473. **A Matter of WHO** (1961) Foray Films B&W 92 min *D:* Don Chaffey *P:* Walter Shenson and Milton Holmes *Sc:* Milton Holmes *Ph:* Erwin Hillier *M:* Edwin Astley *Ca:* Terry-Thomas, Sonja Ziemann, Alex Nicol, Guy Deghy, Clive Morton, Richard Briers, Martin Benson

The Mayfair Bank Caper *see* **A Nightingale Sang in Berkeley Square**

McGuire, Go Home! *see* **The High Bright Sun**

474. **Meet Mr. Callaghan** (1953) Pinnacle Productions B&W 88 min *D:* Charles Saunders *P:* Derrick De Marney and Guido Coen *Sc:* Brock Williams *Ph:* Harry Waxman *M:* Eric Spear *Ca:* Derrick De Marney, Harriette Johns, Peter Neil, Adrienne Corri, Larry Burns, Trevor Reid, John Longden

475. **Meet Mr. Malcolm** (1953) Corsair Productions B&W 65 min *D:* Daniel Birt *P:* Theo Lageard *Sc:* Brock Williams *Ph:* Hone Glendinning *M:* Frank Chacksfield *Ca:* Adrianne Allen, Sarah Lawson, Richard Gale, Meredith Edwards, Duncan Lamont, John Horsley, Pamela Galloway

Menace in the Night *see* **Face in the Night**

476. **The Mercenaries** (1967) MGM Col 100 min *U.S. Title:* Dark of the Sun *D:* Jack Cardiff *P:* George Englund *Sc:* Ranald MacDougall (billed as Quentin Werty) and Adrian Spies *Ph:* Edward Scaife *M:* Jacques Loussier *Ca:* Rod Taylor, Yvette Mimieux, Jim Brown, Peter Carsten, Andre Morell, Calvin Lockhart, Guy Deghy, Kenneth More

477. **Midnight Episode** (1950) Triangle Film Productions B&W 78 min *D:* Gordon Parry *P:* Theo Lageard *Sc:* Paul Vincent Carroll, David Evans and William Templeton *Ph:* Hone Glendinning *M:* Mischa Spoliansky *Ca:* Stanley Holloway, Leslie Dwyer, Reginald Tate, Meredith Edwards, Natasha Parry, Wilfrid Hyde White, Joy Shelton

Million Dollar Manhunt *see* **Assignment Redhead**

The Million Eyes of Sumuru *see* **Sumuru**

478. **The Mind Benders** (1962) Novus Films B&W 113 min *D:* Basil Dearden *P:* Michael Relph *Sc:* James Kennaway *Ph:* Denys Coop *M:* Georges Auric *Ca:* Dirk Bogarde, Mary Ure, John Clements, Michael Bryant, Wendy Craig, Harold Goldblatt, Geoffrey Keen

479. **Miss Tulip Stays the Night** (1954) Jaywell Productions B&W 68 min *U.S. Title:* Dead by Morning (TV only) *D:* Leslie Arliss *P:* John O. Douglas *Sc:* John O. Douglas *Ph:* Kenneth Talbot *M:* De Wolfe *Ca:* Diana Dors, Patrick Holt, Jack Hulbert, Cicely Courtneidge, A.E. Matthews, Joss Ambler, Brian Oulton

480. **Mr. Denning Drives North** (1951) London Film Productions/British Lion Production Assets B&W 93 min *D:* Anthony Kimmins *P:* Anthony Kimmins and Stephen Mitchell *Sc:* Alec Coppel *Ph:* John Wilcox *M:* Benjamin Frankel *Ca:* John Mills, Phyllis Calvert, Sam Wanamaker, Herbert Lom, Eileen Moore, Bernard Lee, Wilfrid Hyde White

Mister Jerico (1969)—See Appendix VI

Mr. Shatter *see* **Shatter**

481. **Mix Me a Person** (1962) Wessex Film Features B&W 116 min *D:* Leslie Norman *P:* Sergei Nolbandov *Sc:* Ian Dalrymple *Ph:* Ted Moore *M:* John Barry *Ca:* Anne Baxter, Adam Faith, Donald Sinden, Walter Brown, Topsy Jane, Jack MacGowran, Anthony Booth

482. **Model for Murder** (1958) Parroch Films/British Lion Films (in association with Ludwig H. Gerber Productions [U.S.]) B&W 73 min *D:*

Terry Bishop *P:* Robert Dunbar *Sc:* Terry Bishop and Robert Dunbar *Ph:* Peter Hennessy *M:* William Davies *Ca:* Keith Andes, Hazel Court, Michael Gough, Julia Arnall, Patricia Jessel, Jean Aubrey, Edwin Richfield

The Model Murder Case *see* **Girl in the Headlines**

483. **Modesty Blaise** (1966) Modesty Blaise Limited Col 119 min *D:* Joseph Losey *P:* Joseph Janni *Sc:* Evan Jones *Ph:* Jack Hildyard *M:* John Dankworth *Ca:* Monica Vitti, Terence Stamp, Dirk Bogarde, Harry Andrews, Clive Revill, Alexander Knox, Michael Craig, Rossella Falk

Molested *see* **Assault**

484. **Moment of Danger** (1960) Cavalcade Films B&W 97 min *U.S. Title:* Malaga *D:* Laslo Benedek *P:* Thomas Clyde *Sc:* David Osborn and Donald Ogden Stewart *Ph:* Desmond Dickinson *M:* Matyas Seiber *Ca:* Trevor Howard, Dorothy Dandridge, Edmund Purdom, Michael Hordern, Paul Stassino, John Bailey, Alfred Burke

485. **Moment of Indiscretion** (1958) The Danzigers B&W 72 min *D:* Max Varnel *P:* Edward J. Danziger and Harry Lee Danziger *Sc:* Brian Clemens and Eldon Howard *Ph:* James Wilson *M:* Albert Elms, Edwin Astley and Leon Young *Ca:* Lana Morris, Ronald Howard, John Van Eyssen, Denis Shaw, Ann Lynn, John Witty, John Stone

Moon *see* **Man of Violence**

486. **Moonraker** (1979) Eon Productions/Les Productions Artistes Associés Col 126 min *D:* Lewis Gilbert *P:* Albert R. Broccoli *Sc:* Christopher Wood *Ph:* Jean Tournier *M:* John Barry *Ca:* Roger Moore, Lois Chiles, Michael Lonsdale, Richard Kiel, Corinne Clery, Emily Bolton, Geoffrey Keen, Bernard Lee, Lois Maxwell

487. **More Deadly Than the Male** (1959) U.N.A. Productions Col 60 min *D:* Robert Bucknell *P:* Robert Bucknell *Sc:* Robert Bucknell *Ph:* Robert Bucknell *M:* Louis Nordish *Ca:* Jeremy White, Pamela Ann Davy, Edna Doré, Lorraine Peters, John Mahoney

488. **Morning Call** (1957) Winwell Productions B&W 75 min *U.S. Title:* Strange Case of Dr. Manning *D:* Arthur Crabtree *P:* Derek Winn (Alfred Strauss on U.S. prints) *Sc:* Paul Tabori and Bill Luckwell *Ph:* Walter J. Harvey *M:* Wilfred Burns *Ca:* Ron Randell, Greta Gynt, Bruce Seton, Charles Farrell, Virginia Keiley, Garard Green, Wally Patch

489. **The Most Dangerous Man in the World** (1969) 20th Century–Fox Productions Col 99 min *U.S. Title:* The Chairman *D:* J. Lee Thompson *P:* Mort Abrahams *Sc:* Ben Maddow *Ph:* John Wilcox *M:* Jerry Goldsmith *Ca:* Gregory Peck, Anne Heywood, Arthur Hill, Alan Dobie, Keye Luke, Conrad Yama, Francisca Tu

Mousey (1974)—See Appendix VI

490. **Mozambique** (1964) Towers of London (Films) Col 97 min *D:* Robert Lynn *P:* Harry Alan Towers *Sc:* Peter Yeldham *Ph:* Martin Curtis *M:* Johnny Douglas *Ca:* Steve Cochran, Hildegard Knef, Paul Hubschmid, Vivi Bach, Martin Benson, Dietmar Schönherr, George Leech

491. **Mumsy, Nanny, Sonny & Girly** (1969) Fitzroy-Francis Films/Brigitte Films Col 102 min *U.S. Title:* Girly *D:* Freddie Francis *P:* Ronald J. Kahn *Sc:* Brian Comport *Ph:* David Muir *M:* Bernard Ebbinghouse *Ca:* Michael Bryant, Ursula Howells, Pat Heywood, Howard Trevor, Vanessa Howard, Imogen Hassall, Michael Ripper

492. **Murder Ahoy** (1964) MGM B&W 93 min *D:* George Pollock *P:* Lawrence P. Bachmann *Sc:* David Pursall and Jack Seddon *Ph:* Desmond Dickinson *M:* Ron Goodwin *Ca:* Margaret Rutherford, Lionel Jeffries, Charles Tingwell, William Mervyn, Joan Benham, Nicholas Parsons, Francis Matthews

493. **Murder at Site Three** (1958) Francis Searle Productions B&W 68 min *D:* Francis Searle *P:* Charles A. Leeds *Sc:* Manning O'Brine *Ph:* Bert Mason *M:* Don Banks *Ca:* Geoffrey Toone, Barbara Shelley, Jill Melford, John Warwick, Richard Burrell, Reed De Rouen, Harry Towb

494. **Murder at the Gallop** (1963) MGM B&W 81 min *D:* George Pollock *P:* George H. Brown *Sc:* James P. Cavanagh *Ph:* Arthur Ibbetson *M:* Ron Goodwin *Ca:* Margaret Rutherford, Robert Morley, Flora Robson, Charles Tingwell, Katya Douglas, Robert Urquhart, James Villiers

495. **Murder at 3 A.M.** (1952) David Henley, Partners & Co. B&W 61 min *D:* Francis Searle *P:* John Ainsworth *Sc:* John Ainsworth *Ph:* S.D. Onions *M:* Eric Spear *Ca:* Dennis Price, Peggy Evans, Greta Mayaro, Rex Garner, Arnold Bell, Philip Saville, Leonard Sharp

Murder by Agreement *see* **Journey into Nowhere**

496. **Murder by Decree** (1978) Saucy Jack Inc./Highlight Theatrical Production Corporation/Murder by Decree Productions Col 124 min *D:* Bob Clark *P:* René Dupont and Bob Clark *Sc:* John Hopkins *Ph:* Reginald H. Morris *M:* Carl Zittrer and Paul Zaza *Ca:* Christopher Plummer, James Mason, David Hemmings, Susan Clark, Anthony Quayle, John Gielgud, Frank Finlay, Donald Sutherland, Genevieve Bujold

497. **Murder by Proxy** (1953) Hammer Film

Productions (in association with Lippert Pictures [U.S.]) B&W 87 min *U.S. Title:* Blackout *D:* Terence Fisher *P:* Michael Carreras *Sc:* Richard Landau *Ph:* Walter J. Harvey *M:* Ivor Slaney *Ca:* Dane Clark, Belinda Lee, Betty Ann Davies, Eleanor Summerfield, Andrew Osborn, Harold Lang, Jill Melford

Murder Can Be Deadly *see* **The Painted Smile**

498. **The Murder Game** (1965) Lippert Films B&W 76 min *D:* Sidney Salkow *P:* Robert L. Lippert and Jack Parsons *Sc:* Harry Spalding *Ph:* Geoffrey Faithfull *M:* Carlo Martelli *Ca:* Ken Scott, Marla Landi, Trader Faulkner, Conrad Phillips, Gerald Sim, Duncan Lamont, Rosamund Greenwood, Victor Brooks

499. **Murder in Eden** (1961) Luckwell Productions B&W 64 min *D:* Max Varnel *P:* Bill Luckwell and Jock MacGregor *Sc:* H.E. Burdon *Ph:* Walter J. Harvey *M:* Wilfred Burns *Ca:* Ray McAnally, Catherine Feller, Yvonne Buckingham, Norman Rodway, Mark Singleton, Jack Aranson, Angela Douglas

Murder Is News *see* **The Delavine Affair**

500. **Murder Most Foul** (1964) MGM B&W 90 min *D:* George Pollock *P:* Ben Arbeid *Sc:* David Pursall and Jack Seddon *Ph:* Desmond Dickinson *M:* Ron Goodwin *Ca:* Margaret Rutherford, Ron Moody, Charles Tingwell, Andrew Cruickshank, Megs Jenkins, Ralph Michael, James Bolam

Murder on Approval *see* **Barbados Quest**

Murder on Monday *see* **Home at Seven**

Murder on the Campus *see* **Out of the Shadow**

501. **Murder on the Orient Express** (1974) G.W. Films Col 131 min *D:* Sidney Lumet *P:* John Brabourne and Richard Goodwin *Sc:* Paul Dehn *Ph:* Geoffrey Unsworth *M:* Richard Rodney Bennett *Ca:* Albert Finney, Lauren Bacall, Ingrid Bergman, Jacqueline Bisset, Sean Connery, Anthony Perkins, Richard Widmark, John Gielgud, Jean-Pierre Cassel, Martin Balsam, Michael York, Wendy Hiller, Vanessa Redgrave, Rachel Roberts

502. **Murder Reported** (1957) Fortress Film Productions B&W 58 min *D:* Charles Saunders *P:* Guido Coen *Sc:* Doreen Montgomery *Ph:* Brendan J. Stafford *M:* Reg Owen *Ca:* Paul Carpenter, Melissa Stribling, John Laurie, Peter Swanwick, Patrick Holt, Maurice Durant, Georgia Brown

503. **Murder She Said** (1961) MGM B&W 86 min *D:* George Pollock *P:* George H. Brown *Sc:* David Pursall and Jack Seddon *Ph:* Geoffrey Faithfull *M:* Ron Goodwin *Ca:* Margaret Rutherford, Arthur Kennedy, Muriel Pavlow, James Robertson Justice, Charles Tingwell, Thorley Walters, Conrad Phillips, Ronald Howard

Murder Will Out *see* **The Voice of Merrill**

504. **Murder Without Crime** (1950) Associated British Picture Corporation B&W 76 min *D:* J. Lee Thompson *P:* Victor Skutezky *Sc:* J. Lee Thompson *Ph:* William McLeod *M:* Philip Green *Ca:* Dennis Price, Derek Farr, Patricia Plunkett, Joan Dowling

505. **Murders in the Rue Morgue** (1971) American International Productions (England) Col 87 min *D:* Gordon Hessler *P:* Louis M. Heyward *Sc:* Christopher Wicking and Henry Slesar *Ph:* Manuel Berenguer *M:* Waldo De Los Rios *Ca:* Jason Robards, Herbert Lom, Christine Kaufmann, Adolfo Celi, Maria Perschy, Lilli Palmer, Peter Arne

Mystery at Tiger Bay *see* **Tiger Bay**

506. **Mystery Junction** (1951) Merton Park B&W 67 min *D:* Michael McCarthy *P:* William H. Williams *Sc:* Michael McCarthy *Ph:* Robert Lapresle *M:* Michael Sarsfield *Ca:* Sydney Tafler, Barbara Murray, Patricia Owens, Martin Benson, Christine Silver, Philip Dale, John Salew

507. **The Naked Edge** (1961) Pennebaker-Baroda Productions/Jason Inc./Monica Corp./Monmouth Inc./Bentley Productions B&W 99 min *D:* Michael Anderson *P:* Walter Seltzer and George Glass *Sc:* Joseph Stefano *Ph:* Erwin Hillier *M:* William Alwyn *Ca:* Gary Cooper, Deborah Kerr, Eric Portman, Diane Cilento, Hermione Gingold, Peter Cushing, Michael Wilding, Ronald Howard

508. **Naked Fury** (1959) Coenda Films B&W 60 min *U.S. Title:* The Pleasure Lovers *D:* Charles Saunders *P:* Guido Coen *Sc:* Brock Williams *Ph:* Walter J. Harvey *M:* Edwin Astley *Ca:* Reed De Rouen, Kenneth Cope, Leigh Madison, Arthur Lovegrove, Alexander Field, Tommy Eytle, Ann Lynn

509. **The Naked Runner** (1967) Artanis Productions Col 102 min *D:* Sidney J. Furie *P:* Brad Dexter *Sc:* Stanley Mann *Ph:* Otto Heller *M:* Harry Sukman *Ca:* Frank Sinatra, Peter Vaughan, Derren Nesbitt, Nadia Gray, Toby Robins, Inger Stratton, Edward Fox

510. **The Nanny** (1965) Hammer Film Productions/Seven Arts B&W 93 min *D:* Seth Holt *P:* Jimmy Sangster *Sc:* Jimmy Sangster *Ph:* Harry Waxman *M:* Richard Rodney Bennett *Ca:* Bette Davis, Wendy Craig, Jill Bennett, James Villiers, William Dix, Pamela Franklin, Jack Watling

511. **The Narrowing Circle** (1955) Fortress

Film Productions B&W 66 min *D:* Charles Saunders *P:* Frank Bevis *Sc:* Doreen Montgomery *Ph:* Jonah Jones *M:* Reg Owen *Ca:* Paul Carpenter, Hazel Court, Russell Napier, Ferdy Mayne, Trevor Reid, June Ashley, Alan Robinson

512. **The Net** (1953) Two Cities Films B&W 86 min *U.S. Title:* Project M-7 *D:* Anthony Asquith *P:* Antony Darnborough *Sc:* William Fairchild *Ph:* Desmond Dickinson (aerial photography by Stanley Grant) *M:* Benjamin Frankel *Ca:* Phyllis Calvert, James Donald, Robert Beatty, Herbert Lom, Muriel Pavlow, Noel Willman, Walter Fitzgerald

513. **Never Back Losers** (1961) Merton Park B&W 61 min *D:* Robert Tronson *P:* Jack Greenwood *Sc:* Lukas Heller *Ph:* Bert Mason *M:* Bernard Ebbinghouse *Ca:* Jack Hedley, Jacqueline Ellis, Patrick Magee, Richard Warner, Derek Francis, Austin Trevor, Harry Locke

514. **Never Let Go** (1960) Independent Artists B&W 91 min *D:* John Guillermin *P:* Peter De Sarigny *Sc:* Alun Falconer *Ph:* Christopher Challis *M:* John Barry *Ca:* Richard Todd, Peter Sellers, Elizabeth Sellars, Adam Faith, Carol White, Mervyn Johns, Noel Willman

515. **Never Look Back** (1951) Hammer Film Productions B&W 73 min *D:* Francis Searle *P:* Michael Carreras *Sc:* John Hunter, Guy Morgan and Francis Searle *Ph:* Reginald Wyer *M:* Temple Abady *Ca:* Rosamund John, Hugh Sinclair, Guy Middleton, Henry Edwards, Terence Longdon, John Warwick, Brenda De Banzie

516. **Never Mention Murder** (1964) Merton Park B&W 56 min *D:* John Nelson Burton *P:* Jack Greenwood *Sc:* Robert Banks Stewart *Ph:* James Wilson *M:* Bernard Ebbinghouse *Ca:* Maxine Audley, Dudley Foster, Michael Coles, Pauline Yates, Brian Haines, Peter Butterworth, Philip Stone

517. **Night, After Night, After Night** (1969) Dudley Birch Films Col 88 min *U.S. Titles:* He Kills Night After Night After Night (video—see Appendix V); Night Slasher (video—see Appendix V) *D:* Lindsay Shonteff (billed as Lewis J. Force) *P:* James Mellor *Sc:* Dail Ambler *Ph:* Douglas Hill *M:* Douglas Gamley *Ca:* Jack May, Justine Lord, Gilbert Wynne, Linda Marlowe, Terry Scully, Donald Sumpter, Peter Forbes-Robertson

518. **Night and the City** (1950) 20th Century-Fox Productions B&W 100 min *D:* Jules Dassin *P:* Samuel G. Engel *Sc:* Jo Eisinger *Ph:* Max Greene *M:* Benjamin Frankel *Ca:* Richard Widmark, Gene Tierney, Googie Withers, Hugh Marlowe, Francis L. Sullivan, Herbert Lom, Mike Mazurki

Night Child *see* **Night Hair Child**

519. **The Night Digger** (1971) Yongestreet Productions/Tacitus Productions Col 110 min *U.S. Title:* The Road Builder *D:* Alastair Reid *P:* Alan D. Courtney and Norman S. Powell *Sc:* Roald Dahl *Ph:* Alex Thomson *M:* Bernard Herrmann *Ca:* Patricia Neal, Pamela Brown, Nicholas Clay, Jean Anderson, Graham Crowden, Sebastian Breaks, Brigit Forsyth

520. **Night Hair Child** (1971) Leander Films/Leisure-Media Inc. Col 89 min *ABT:* Night Child *U.S. Title:* What the Peeper Saw *D:* James Kelly *P:* Graham Harris *Sc:* Trevor Preston *Ph:* Harry Waxman and Luis Cuadrado *M:* Stelvio Cipriani *Ca:* Mark Lester, Britt Ekland, Hardy Kruger, Lilli Palmer, Harry Andrews, Conchita Montez, Collette Jack

Night Legs *see* **Fright**

521. **Night Must Fall** (1964) MGM B&W 101 min *D:* Karel Reisz *P:* Albert Finney and Karel Reisz *Sc:* Clive Exton *Ph:* Freddie Francis *M:* Ron Grainer *Ca:* Albert Finney, Mona Washbourne, Susan Hampshire, Sheila Hancock, Michael Medwin, Joe Gladwin, Martin Wyldeck

522. **The Night My Number Came Up** (1955) Ealing Studios B&W 94 min *D:* Leslie Norman *P:* Michael Balcon *Sc:* R.C. Sherriff *Ph:* Lionel Banes *M:* Malcolm Arnold *Ca:* Michael Redgrave, Sheila Sim, Alexander Knox, Denholm Elliott, Ursula Jeans, Ralph Truman, Michael Hordern, Nigel Stock

523. **The Night of the Full Moon** (1953) Hedgerley Films B&W 67 min *D:* Donald Taylor *P:* Donald Taylor *Sc:* Donald Taylor and Carl Koch *Ph:* Gerald Gibbs *M:* De Wolfe *Ca:* Dermot Walsh, Kathleen Byron, Philip Saville, Anthony Ireland, Tim Turner, Everley Gregg, George Merritt, George Woodbridge

524. **The Night of the Generals** (1966) Horizon Pictures (G.B.)/Filmsonor S.A. Col 147 min *D:* Anatole Litvak *P:* Sam Spiegel *Sc:* Joseph Kessel and Paul Dehn *Ph:* Henri Decae *M:* Maurice Jarre *Ca:* Peter O'Toole, Omar Sharif, Tom Courtenay, Donald Pleasence, Joanna Pettet, Philippe Noiret, Charles Gray, Coral Browne, John Gregson, Nigel Stock, Patrick Allen, Christopher Plummer

Night of the Laughing Dead *see* **The House in Nightmare Park**

525. **Night of the Prowler** (1962) Butcher's Film Productions B&W 60 min *D:* Francis Searle *P:* John I. Phillips *Sc:* Paul Erickson *Ph:* Walter J. Harvey *M:* Johnny Gregory *Ca:* Patrick Holt, Colette Wilde, Bill Nagy, John Horsley, Benny Lee, Marianne Stone, Mark Singleton

Night Slasher *see* **Night, After Night, After Night**

526. **Night Train for Inverness** (1959) The Danzigers B&W 68 min *D:* Ernest Morris *P:* Edward J. Danziger and Harry Lee Danziger *Sc:* Mark Grantham *Ph:* James Wilson *Ca:* Norman Wooland, Jane Hylton, Dennis Waterman, Silvia Francis, Irene Arnold, Valentine Dyall, Howard Lang

527. **Night Train to Paris** (1964) Lippert Films B&W 64 min *D:* Robert Douglas *P:* Robert L. Lippert and Jack Parsons *Sc:* Harry Spalding (billed as Henry Cross) *Ph:* Arthur Lavis *M:* Kenny Graham *Ca:* Leslie Nielsen, Alizia Gur, Eric Pohlmann, Dorinda Stevens, Edina Ronay, Cyril Raymond, Hugh Latimer

528. **Night Was Our Friend** (1951) A.C.T. Films B&W 62 min *D:* Michael Anderson *P:* Gordon Parry *Sc:* Michael Pertwee *Ph:* Gerald Gibbs *Ca:* Michael Gough, Elizabeth Sellars, Ronald Howard, Marie Ney, Edward Lexy, Nora Gordon, John Salew

529. **Night Watch** (1973) Brut Productions/Night Watch Films Col 98 min *D:* Brian G. Hutton *P:* Martin Poll, George W. George and Barnard Straus *Sc:* Tony Williamson *Ph:* Billy Williams *M:* John Cameron *Ca:* Elizabeth Taylor, Laurence Harvey, Billie Whitelaw, Robert Lang, Tony Britton, Bill Dean, Michael Danvers-Walker

530. **Night Without Pity** (1962) Parroch Films B&W 57 min *D:* Theodore Zichy *P:* Jack Parsons *Sc:* Aubrey Cash *Ph:* Ken Hodges *M:* Wilfred Josephs *Ca:* Sarah Lawson, Neil McCallum, Alan Edwards, Dorinda Stevens, Michael Browning, Patrick Newell, Beatrice Varley

531. **Night Without Stars** (1951) Europa Films B&W 86 min *D:* Anthony Pelissier *P:* Hugh Stewart *Sc:* Winston Graham *Ph:* Guy Green *M:* William Alwyn *Ca:* David Farrar, Nadia Gray, Maurice Teynac, June Clyde, Gerard Landry, Gilles Quéant, Clive Morton

532. **The Night Won't Talk** (1952) Corsair Productions B&W 61 min *D:* Daniel Birt *P:* Harold Richmond *Sc:* Brock Williams *Ph:* Brendan J. Stafford *M:* Gilbert Vinter *Ca:* Hy Hazell, John Bailey, Mary Germaine, Ballard Berkeley, Elwyn Brook-Jones, Duncan Lamont, Sarah Lawson

533. **A Nightingale Sang in Berkeley Square** (1979) S. Benjamin Fisz Productions (Nightingale) Col 110 min *ABT:* The Biggest Bank Robbery (TV only) *U.S. Titles:* The Mayfair Bank Caper (video—see Appendix V); The Big Scam (video—see Appendix V) *D:* Ralph Thomas *P:* S. Benjamin Fisz *Sc:* Guy Elmes *Ph:* John Coquillon *M:* Stanley Myers *Ca:* Richard Jordan, Oliver Tobias, David Niven, Elke Sommer, Gloria Grahame, Richard Johnson, Michael Angelis

534. **Nightmare** (1963) Hammer Film Productions B&W 82 min *D:* Freddie Francis *P:* Jimmy Sangster *Sc:* Jimmy Sangster *Ph:* John Wilcox *M:* Don Banks *Ca:* David Knight, Moira Redmond, Jennie Linden, Brenda Bruce, George A. Cooper, Irene Richmond, John Welsh

No Place Like Homicide *see* **What a Carve-Up**

535. **No Road Back** (1956) Gibraltar Productions B&W 83 min *D:* Montgomery Tully *P:* Steven Pallos *Sc:* Charles A. Leeds and Montgomery Tully *Ph:* Lionel Banes *M:* John Veale *Ca:* Skip Homeier, Paul Carpenter, Patricia Dainton, Norman Wooland, Margaret Rawlings, Eleanor Summerfield, Alfie Bass

536. **No Safety Ahead** (1959) The Danzigers B&W 68 min *D:* Max Varnel *P:* Edward J. Danziger and Harry Lee Danziger *Sc:* Robert Hirst *Ph:* James Wilson *M:* Jack Gerber *Ca:* James Kenney, Susan Beaumont, Denis Shaw, Gordon Needham, Tony Doonan, John Charlesworth, Brian Weske, Mark Singleton

537. **No Trace** (1950) Tempean Films B&W 76 min *D:* John Gilling *P:* Robert S. Baker and Monty Berman *Sc:* John Gilling *Ph:* Monty Berman *M:* John Lanchbery *Ca:* Hugh Sinclair, Dinah Sheridan, John Laurie, Dora Bryan, Barry Morse, Beatrice Varley, Michael Brennan

538. **Nobody Runs Forever** (1968) The Rank Organisation Film Productions/Selmur Productions Col 101 min *U.S. Title:* The High Commissioner *D:* Ralph Thomas *P:* Betty E. Box *Sc:* Wilfred Greatorex *Ph:* Ernest Steward *M:* Georges Delerue *Ca:* Rod Taylor, Christopher Plummer, Lilli Palmer, Camilla Sparv, Daliah Lavi, Clive Revill, Calvin Lockhart, Derren Nesbitt

539. **Noose for a Lady** (1953) Insignia Films B&W 73 min *D:* Wolf Rilla *P:* Victor Hanbury *Sc:* Rex Rienits *Ph:* Walter J. Harvey *M:* De Wolfe *Ca:* Dennis Price, Rona Anderson, Ronald Howard, Melissa Stribling, Pamela Alan, Charles Lloyd Pack, Colin Tapley

Norman Conquest *see* **Park Plaza 605**

540. **North Sea Hijack** (1979) Cinema Seven Productions Col 100 min *U.S. Titles:* ffolkes; Assault Force (TV only) *D:* Andrew V. McLaglen *P:* Elliott Kastner *Sc:* Jack Davies *Ph:* Tony Imi *M:* Michael J. Lewis *Ca:* Roger Moore, James Mason, Anthony Perkins, Michael Parks, David Hedison, Jack Watson, George Baker, Faith Brook

541. **Nowhere to Go** (1958) Ealing Films B&W 97 min *D:* Seth Holt *P:* Michael Balcon *Sc:* Seth Holt and Kenneth Tynan *Ph:* Paul Beeson *M:* Dizzy Reece *Ca:* George Nader, Maggie Smith, Bernard Lee, Geoffrey Keen, Bessie Love, Andrée Melly, Howard Marion Crawford

542. **No.1 of the Secret Service** (1977) Lindsay Shonteff Film Productions Col 93 min *ABT:* Her Majesty's Top Gun (video—see Appendix V) *U.S. Title:* Number One of the Secret Service *D:* Lindsay Shonteff *P:* Elizabeth Gray *Sc:* Howard Craig *Ph:* Ivan Strasburg *M:* Leonard Young *Ca:* Nicky Henson, Richard Todd, Aimi Macdonald, Geoffrey Keen, Dudley Sutton, Sue Lloyd, Jon Pertwee

Number One of the Secret Service *see* **No.1 of the Secret Service**

543. **Number Six** (1962) Merton Park B&W 59 min *D:* Robert Tronson *P:* Jack Greenwood *Sc:* Philip Mackie *Ph:* Bert Mason *M:* Bernard Ebbinghouse *Ca:* Ivan Desny, Nadja Regin, Michael Goodliffe, Brian Bedford, Joyce Blair, Leonard Sachs, Maxwell Shaw

Obsessed *see* **The Late Edwina Black**

544. **The Odessa File** (1974) Domino Productions (London)/Oceanic Filmproduction (Munich) Col 129 min *D:* Ronald Neame *P:* John Woolf and John R. Sloan *Sc:* Kenneth Ross and George Markstein *Ph:* Oswald Morris *M:* Andrew Lloyd Webber *Ca:* Jon Voight, Maximilian Schell, Maria Schell, Mary Tamm, Derek Jacobi, Peter Jeffrey, Klaus Lowitsch

545. **Offbeat** (1960) Northiam Films B&W 72 min *D:* Cliff Owen *P:* M. Smedley-Aston *Sc:* Peter Barnes *Ph:* Geoffrey Faithfull *M:* Ken Jones *Ca:* William Sylvester, Mai Zetterling, John Meillon, Anthony Dawson, Neil McCarthy, Harry Baird, Victor Brooks, Joseph Furst

546. **The Old Dark House** (1962) Hammer Film Productions Col 86 min *D:* William Castle *P:* William Castle *Sc:* Robert Dillon *Ph:* Arthur Grant *M:* Benjamin Frankel *Ca:* Tom Poston, Robert Morley, Janette Scott, Joyce Grenfell, Mervyn Johns, Fenella Fielding, Peter Bull

547. **On Her Majesty's Secret Service** (1969) Eon Productions Col 140 min *D:* Peter Hunt *P:* Harry Saltzman and Albert R. Broccoli *Sc:* Richard Maibaum *Ph:* Michael Reed *M:* John Barry *Ca:* George Lazenby, Diana Rigg, Telly Savalas, Gabriele Ferzetti, Ilse Steppat, Catherine Schell, George Baker, Joanna Lumley, Bernard Lee, Lois Maxwell

548. **On the Run** (1957) The Danzigers B&W 70 min *D:* Ernest Morris *P:* Edward J. Danziger and Harry Lee Danziger *Sc:* Brian Clemens and Eldon Howard *Ph:* James Wilson *M:* Albert Elms *Ca:* Neil McCallum, Susan Beaumont, William Hartnell, Gordon Tanner, Philip Saville, Gilbert Winfield, Hal Osmond

549. **On the Run** (1962) Merton Park B&W 59 min *D:* Robert Tronson *P:* Jack Greenwood *Sc:* Richard Harris *Ph:* James Wilson *M:* Bernard Ebbinghouse *Ca:* Emrys Jones, Sarah Lawson, Patrick Barr, Delphi Lawrence, Kevin Stoney, Richard Warner, Brian Haines

Once Upon a Frightmare *see* **Frightmare**

550. **One Away** (1976) Silhouette Film Productions Col 99 min *ABT:* Gitanos—Escape from Apartheid (video—see Appendix V) *D:* Sidney Hayers *P:* Peter Miller *Sc:* Allan Prior *Ph:* Graham Edgar *M:* Ron Grainer *Ca:* Bradford Dillman, Elke Sommer, Dean Stockwell, Patrick Mower, Ian Yule, Erica Rogers, Roberta Durrant

551. **One Jump Ahead** (1954) Kenilworth Film Productions/Fortress Film Productions B&W 66 min *D:* Charles Saunders *P:* Guido Coen *Sc:* Doreen Montgomery *Ph:* Brendan J. Stafford *M:* Edwin Astley *Ca:* Paul Carpenter, Diane Hart, Jill Adams, Arnold Bell, Mary Jones, Peter Sinclair, Charles Lamb

552. **One More Time** (1969) Chrislaw Trace-Mark Productions Col 93 min *D:* Jerry Lewis *P:* Milton Ebbins *Sc:* Michael Pertwee *Ph:* Ernest Steward *M:* Les Reed *Ca:* Sammy Davis, Jr., Peter Lawford, Maggie Wright, Leslie Sands, John Wood, Dudley Sutton, Allan Cuthbertson

553. **One Way Out** (1955) Major Productions B&W 61 min *D:* Francis Searle *P:* John Temple-Smith *Sc:* Cy Endfield (billed as Jonathan Roche) *Ph:* Walter J. Harvey *Ca:* Jill Adams, Eddie Byrne, Lyndon Brook, John Chandos, Olive Milbourne, Arthur Howard, Arthur Lowe

554. **Operation Amsterdam** (1959) The Rank Organisation Film Productions B&W 104 min *D:* Michael McCarthy *P:* Maurice Cowan *Sc:* Michael McCarthy and John Eldridge *Ph:* Reginald Wyer *M:* Philip Green *Ca:* Peter Finch, Eva Bartok, Tony Britton, Alexander Knox, Malcolm Keen, Alfred Burke, John Horsley

Operation Conspiracy *see* **Cloak Without Dagger**

555. **Operation Diplomat** (1953) Nettlefold Films B&W 70 min *D:* John Guillermin *P:* Ernest G. Roy *Sc:* A.R. Rawlinson and John Guillermin *Ph:* Gerald Gibbs *M:* Wilfred Burns *Ca:* Guy Rolfe, Lisa Daniely, Patricia Dainton, Sydney Tafler, Brian Worth, Anton Diffring, Ballard Berkeley

Operation Mermaid *see* **The Bay of Saint Michel**

556. **Operation Murder** (1956) The Danzigers B&W 66 min *D:* Ernest Morris *P:* Edward J. Danziger and Harry Lee Danziger *Sc:* Brian Clemens *Ph:* James Wilson *M:* Edwin Astley *Ca:* Tom Conway, Patrick Holt, Sandra Dorne, John Stone, Virginia Keiley, Rosamund John, Robert Ayres

Operation Overthrow *see* **Power Play**

557. **Orders to Kill** (1958) Lynx Films B&W 112 min *D:* Anthony Asquith *P:* Anthony Havelock-Allan *Sc:* Paul Dehn *Ph:* Desmond Dickinson *M:* Benjamin Frankel *Ca:* Eddie Albert, Paul Massie, Lillian Gish, James Robertson Justice, Irene Worth, Leslie French, John Crawford

558. **Otley** (1968) Highroad Productions/Bruce Cohn Curtis Films Col 91 min *D:* Dick Clement *P:* Bruce Cohn Curtis *Sc:* Ian La Frenais and Dick Clement *Ph:* Austin Dempster *M:* Stanley Myers *Ca:* Tom Courtenay, Romy Schneider, Alan Badel, James Villiers, Leonard Rossiter, James Bolam, Fiona Lewis

559. **Our Man in Havana** (1959) Kingsmead Productions B&W 111 min *D:* Carol Reed *P:* Carol Reed *Sc:* Graham Greene *Ph:* Oswald Morris *M:* Hermanos Deniz Cuban Rhythm Band *Ca:* Alec Guinness, Burl Ives, Maureen O'Hara, Ernie Kovacs, Noël Coward, Ralph Richardson, Jo Morrow

560. **Our Man in Marrakesh** (1966) Marrakesh Films Col 94 min *U.S. Title:* Bang, Bang, You're Dead *D:* Don Sharp *P:* Harry Alan Towers *Sc:* Peter Yeldham *Ph:* Michael Reed *M:* Malcolm Lockyer *Ca:* Tony Randall, Senta Berger, Herbert Lom, Wilfrid Hyde White, Terry-Thomas, Gregoire Aslan, John Le Mesurier, Klaus Kinski

561. **Out of the Fog** (1962) Eternal Films B&W 69 min *U.S. Title:* Fog for a Killer (TV only) *D:* Montgomery Tully *P:* Maurice J. Wilson *Sc:* Maurice J. Wilson and Montgomery Tully *Ph:* Walter J. Harvey *M:* Ken Thorne *Ca:* David Sumner, Susan Travers, James Hayter, John Arnatt, Jack Watson, Renee Houston, Michael Ripper

562. **Out of the Shadow** (1961) Border Film Productions B&W 61 min *U.S. Title:* Murder on the Campus *D:* Michael Winner *P:* Olive Negus-Fancey *Sc:* Michael Winner *Ph:* Richard Bayley *M:* Jackie Brown and Cy Payne *Ca:* Terence Longdon, Donald Gray, Dermot Walsh, Diane Clare, Robertson Hare, Felicity Young, Mark Eden

Paid to Kill *see* **Five Days**

563. **The Painted Smile** (1961) Blakeley's Films (Manchester)/Mancunian Film Corporation B&W 60 min *U.S. Title:* Murder Can Be Deadly *D:* Lance Comfort *P:* Tom Blakeley *Sc:* Pip and Jane Baker *Ph:* Basil Emmott *M:* Martin Slavin *Ca:* Liz Fraser, Kenneth Griffith, Tony Wickert, Ray Smith, Nanette Newman, David Hemmings, Grazina Frame, Peter Reynolds

564. **Panic** (1963) Ingram Films B&W 69 min *D:* John Gilling *P:* Guido Coen *Sc:* John Gilling *Ph:* Geoffrey Faithfull *M:* Sydney John Kay *Ca:* Janine Gray, Glyn Houston, Dyson Lovell, Duncan Lamont, Stanley Meadows, Brian Weske, Charles Houston, Marne Maitland

565. **Paranoiac** (1962) Hammer Film Productions B&W 80 min *D:* Freddie Francis *P:* Anthony Hinds *Sc:* Jimmy Sangster *Ph:* Arthur Grant *M:* Elisabeth Lutyens *Ca:* Janette Scott, Oliver Reed, Sheila Burrell, Maurice Denham, Alexander Davion, Liliane Brousse, Harold Lang

The Paris Express *see* **The Man Who Watched Trains Go By**

566. **Park Plaza 605** (1953) B & A Productions B&W 75 min *U.S. Title:* Norman Conquest *D:* Bernard Knowles *P:* Bertram Ostrer and Albert Fennell *Sc:* Bertram Ostrer, Albert Fennell and Bernard Knowles *Ph:* Eric Cross *M:* Philip Green *Ca:* Tom Conway, Eva Bartok, Joy Shelton, Sidney James, Richard Wattis, Carl Jaffe, Frederick Schiller

567. **The Partner** (1963) Merton Park B&W 58 min *D:* Gerard Glaister *P:* Jack Greenwood *Sc:* John Roddick *Ph:* James Wilson *M:* Bernard Ebbinghouse *Ca:* Yoko Tani, Guy Doleman, Ewan Roberts, Mark Eden, Anthony Booth, Helen Lindsay, Noel Johnson

568. **Partners in Crime** (1961) Merton Park B&W 54 min *D:* Peter Duffell *P:* Jack Greenwood *Sc:* Robert Banks Stewart *Ph:* Bert Mason *M:* Ron Goodwin *Ca:* Bernard Lee, John Van Eyssen, Moira Redmond, Stanley Morgan, Gordon Boyd, Mark Singleton, Victor Platt

569. **The Passage** (1978) Hemdale Leisure Corp./Passage Films/Monday Films Col 98 min *D:* J. Lee Thompson *P:* John Quested *Sc:* Bruce Nicolaysen *Ph:* Michael Reed *M:* Michael J. Lewis *Ca:* Anthony Quinn, James Mason, Malcolm McDowell, Patricia Neal, Kay Lenz, Paul Clemens, Christopher Lee

570. **The Passing Stranger** (1954) Harlequin Productions B&W 68 min *D:* John Arnold *P:* Anthony Simmons and Ian Gibson-Smith *Sc:* Anthony Simmons and John Arnold *Ph:* Walter Lassally *M:* Ken Sykora *Ca:* Lee Patterson, Diane Cilento, Duncan Lamont, Olive Gregg, Liam Redmond, Harold Lang, Cameron Hall

Passport to China *see* **Visa to Canton**

571. **Passport to Shame** (1958) United Co-Productions B&W 91 min *U.S. Title:* Room 43 *D:* Alvin Rakoff *P:* John Clein *Sc:* Patrick Alexander *Ph:* Jack Asher *M:* Ken Jones *Ca:* Odile Versois, Herbert Lom, Diana Dors, Eddie Constantine, Brenda De Banzie, Robert Brown, Elwyn Brook-Jones

572. **Passport to Treason** (1956) Mid-Century Film Productions B&W 81 min *D:* Robert S. Baker *P:* Robert S. Baker and Monty Berman *Sc:* Kenneth R. Hayles and Norman Hudis *Ph:* Monty Berman *M:* Stanley Black *Ca:* Rod Cameron, Lois Maxwell, Clifford Evans, Peter Illing, Douglas Wilmer, Marianne Stone, Ballard Berkeley

Pattern for Plunder *see* **The Bay of Saint Michel**

573. **Paul Temple Returns** (1952) Nettlefold Films B&W 71 min *U.S. Title:* Bombay Waterfront *D:* Maclean Rogers *P:* Ernest G. Roy *Sc:* Uncredited *Ph:* Geoffrey Faithfull *M:* Wilfred Burns *Ca:* John Bentley, Patricia Dainton, Peter Gawthorne, Grey Blake, Valentine Dyall, Robert Urquhart, Christopher Lee

574. **Paul Temple's Triumph** (1950) Nettlefold Films B&W 80 min *D:* Maclean Rogers *P:* Ernest G. Roy *Sc:* A.R. Rawlinson *Ph:* Brendan J. Stafford *M:* Stanley Black *Ca:* John Bentley, Dinah Sheridan, Jack Livesey, Beatrice Varley, Barbara Couper, Hugh Dempster, Bruce Seton

575. **Payroll** (1961) Lynx Films B&W 105 min *D:* Sidney Hayers *P:* Norman Priggen *Sc:* George Baxt *Ph:* Ernest Steward *M:* Reg Owen *Ca:* Michael Craig, Françoise Prévost, Billie Whitelaw, William Lucas, Kenneth Griffith, Tom Bell, Edward Cast

576. **Peeping Tom** (1960) Michael Powell (Theatre) Col 109 min *U.S. Title:* Face of Fear (TV only) *D:* Michael Powell *P:* Michael Powell *Sc:* Leo Marks *Ph:* Otto Heller *M:* Brian Easdale *Ca:* Carl Boehm, Moira Shearer, Anna Massey, Maxine Audley, Brenda Bruce, Miles Malleson, Esmond Knight, Michael Goodliffe, Jack Watson

577. **Penny Gold** (1973) Fanfare Films Col 90 min *D:* Jack Cardiff *P:* George H. Brown *Sc:* David Osborn and Liz Charles-Williams *Ph:* Ken Hodges *M:* John Scott *Ca:* James Booth, Francesca Annis, Nicky Henson, Joss Ackland, Richard Heffer, Joseph O'Conor, Una Stubbs

578. **The Penthouse** (1967) Tahiti Films Col 96 min *D:* Peter Collinson *P:* Harry Fine *Sc:* Peter Collinson *Ph:* Arthur Lavis *M:* John Hawksworth *Ca:* Terence Morgan, Suzy Kendall, Martine Beswick, Norman Rodway, Tony Beckley

579. **Perfect Friday** (1970) Sunnymede Film Productions Col 95 min *D:* Peter Hall *P:* Jack Smith *Sc:* Anthony Greville-Bell and C. Scott Forbes *Ph:* Alan Hume *M:* John Dankworth *Ca:* Ursula Andress, Stanley Baker, David Warner, Patience Collier, T.P. McKenna, David Waller, Joan Benham

Peril in the Night *see* **Eyewitness**

580. **Persecution** (1974) Tyburn Film Productions Col 96 min *U.S. Titles:* Sheba (briefly used original theatrical release title); The Terror of Sheba (1975 theatrical re-release); The Graveyard (video—see Appendix V) *D:* Don Chaffey *P:* Kevin Francis *Sc:* Robert Hutton and Rosemary Wootten *Ph:* Kenneth Talbot *M:* Paul Ferris *Ca:* Lana Turner, Ralph Bates, Olga Georges-Picot, Suzan Farmer, Patrick Allen, Catherine Brandon, Shelagh Fraser, Trevor Howard

The Photographer's Models *see* **House of Whipcord**

581. **Piccadilly Third Stop** (1960) Ethiro Productions B&W 90 min *D:* Wolf Rilla *P:* Norman Williams *Sc:* Leigh Vance *Ph:* Ernest Steward *M:* Philip Green *Ca:* Terence Morgan, Yoko Tani, Mai Zetterling, William Hartnell, John Crawford, Ann Lynn, Dennis Price

Pickup Alley *see* **Interpol**

582. **Pit of Darkness** (1961) Butcher's Film Productions B&W 76 min *D:* Lance Comfort *P:* Lance Comfort *Sc:* Lance Comfort *Ph:* Basil Emmott *M:* Martin Slavin *Ca:* William Franklyn, Moira Redmond, Bruno Barnabe, Leonard Sachs, Nigel Green, Bruce Beeby, Humphrey Lestocq, Anthony Booth

583. **Playback** (1962) Merton Park B&W 62 min *D:* Quentin Lawrence *P:* Jack Greenwood *Sc:* Robert Banks Stewart *Ph:* Bert Mason *M:* Bernard Ebbinghouse *Ca:* Margit Saad, Barry Foster, Victor Platt, Dinsdale Landen, George Pravda, Nigel Green, Jerold Wells

584. **The Playbirds** (1978) Roldvale Limited Col 94 min *ABT:* Secrets of a Playgirl (video—see Appendix V) *D:* Willy Roe *P:* Willy Roe *Sc:* Bud Tobin and Robin O'Connor *Ph:* Douglas Hill *M:* David Whitaker *Ca:* Mary Millington, Glynn Edwards, Gavin Campbell, Alan Lake, Windsor Davies, Derren Nesbitt, Dudley Sutton

Playgirl After Dark *see* **Too Hot to Handle**
The Pleasure Lovers *see* **Naked Fury**

585. **Police Dog** (1955) Westridge Films/Douglas Fairbanks Ltd. B&W 72 min *D:* Derek Twist *P:* Harold Huth *Sc:* Derek Twist *Ph:* Cedric Williams *M:* Bretton Byrd *Ca:* Joan Rice, Tim Turner, Sandra Dorne, James Gilbert, Nora Gordon, Charles Victor, John Le Mesurier

586. **Pool of London** (1950) Ealing Studios

B&W 86 min *D:* Basil Dearden *P:* Michael Balcon *Sc:* Jack Whittingham and John Eldridge *Ph:* Gordon Dines *M:* John Addison *Ca:* Bonar Colleano, Susan Shaw, Renee Asherson, Earl Cameron, Moira Lister, Max Adrian, Joan Dowling

587. **Port Afrique** (1956) Coronado Productions (England) Col 92 min *D:* Rudolph Maté *P:* John R. Sloan *Sc:* Frank Partos and John Cresswell *Ph:* Wilkie Cooper *M:* Malcolm Arnold *Ca:* Pier Angeli, Phil Carey, Dennis Price, Eugene Deckers, James Hayter, Rachel Gurney, Anthony Newley

588. **Port of Escape** (1954) Wellington Films B&W 75 min *D:* Tony Young *P:* Lance Comfort *Sc:* Barbara S. Harper, Tony Young and Abby Mann *Ph:* Phil Grindrod *M:* Bretton Byrd *Ca:* Googie Withers, John McCallum, Bill Kerr, Joan Hickson, Wendy Danielli, Hugh Pryse, Alexander Gauge

589. **Portrait of Alison** (1955) Insignia Films (in association with Todon Productions [U.S.]) B&W 84 min *U.S. Title:* Postmark for Danger *D:* Guy Green *P:* Frank Godwin *Sc:* Ken Hughes and Guy Green *Ph:* Wilkie Cooper *M:* John Veale *Ca:* Robert Beatty, Terry Moore, William Sylvester, Josephine Griffin, Geoffrey Keen, Allan Cuthbertson, William Lucas

Postmark for Danger *see* **Portrait of Alison**

590. **Power Play** (1978) Magnum International Productions/Cowry Film Productions Col 102 min *U.S. Titles:* State of Shock (TV only); Operation Overthrow (video—see Appendix V) *D:* Martyn Burke *P:* Christopher Dalton *Sc:* Martyn Burke *Ph:* Ousama Rawi *M:* Ken Thorne *Ca:* Peter O'Toole, David Hemmings, Donald Pleasence, Barry Morse, Jon Granik, Marcella Saint-Amant, Chuck Shamata

591. **The Price of Silence** (1959) Eternal Films B&W 73 min *D:* Montgomery Tully *P:* Maurice J. Wilson *Sc:* Maurice J. Wilson *Ph:* Geoffrey Faithfull *M:* Don Banks *Ca:* Gordon Jackson, June Thorburn, Maya Koumani, Terence Alexander, Mary Clare, Victor Brooks, Joan Heal

592. **The Primitives** (1961) Border Film Productions B&W 70 min *D:* Alfred Travers *P:* Olive Negus-Fancey *Sc:* Moris Farhi and Alfred Travers *Ph:* Michael Reed *M:* Edmundo Ros *Ca:* Jan Holden, Bill Edwards, Rio Fanning, George Mikell, Terence Fallon, Derek Ware, Peter Hughes

593. **A Prize of Arms** (1961) Inter-State Films B&W 105 min *D:* Cliff Owen *P:* George Maynard *Sc:* Paul Ryder *Ph:* Gilbert Taylor and Gerald Gibbs *M:* Robert Sharples *Ca:* Stanley Baker, Helmut Schmid, Tom Bell, Tom Adams, Anthony Bate, Jack May, Patrick Magee

594. **A Prize of Gold** (1955) Warwick Film Productions Col 100 min *D:* Mark Robson *P:* Phil C. Samuel *Sc:* Robert Buckner and John Paxton *Ph:* Ted Moore *M:* Malcolm Arnold *Ca:* Richard Widmark, Mai Zetterling, Nigel Patrick, George Cole, Donald Wolfit, Joseph Tomelty, Eric Pohlmann

595. **The Professionals** (1960) Independent Artists B&W 61 min *D:* Don Sharp *P:* Norman Priggen *Sc:* Peter Barnes *Ph:* Michael Reed *M:* William Alwyn *Ca:* William Lucas, Andrew Faulds, Colette Wilde, Stratford Johns, Edward Cast, Charles Vance, Jack May

596. **Profile** (1954) Major Productions B&W 66 min *D:* Francis Searle *P:* John Temple-Smith *Sc:* John Gilling *Ph:* Brendan J. Stafford *Ca:* John Bentley, Kathleen Byron, Thea Gregory, Stuart Lindsell, Ivan Craig, Lloyd Lamble, Garard Green

Project M-7 *see* **The Net**

Psycho-Circus *see* **Circus of Fear**

597. **The Psychopath** (1965) Amicus Productions Col 83 min *D:* Freddie Francis *P:* Max J. Rosenberg and Milton Subotsky *Sc:* Robert Bloch *Ph:* John Wilcox *M:* Elisabeth Lutyens *Ca:* Patrick Wymark, Margaret Johnston, Alexander Knox, John Standing, Judy Huxtable, Don Borisenko, Thorley Walters

598. **Pulp** (1972) Three Michaels Film Productions Col 95 min *D:* Mike Hodges *P:* Michael Klinger *Sc:* Mike Hodges *Ph:* Ousama Rawi *M:* George Martin *Ca:* Michael Caine, Mickey Rooney, Lionel Stander, Lizabeth Scott, Nadia Cassini, Dennis Price, Al Lettieri, Victor Mercieca

599. **Puppet on a Chain** (1970) Big City Productions Col 98 min *D:* Geoffrey Reeve (speedboat chase sequence directed by Don Sharp) *P:* Kurt Unger *Sc:* Alistair MacLean *Ph:* Jack Hildyard *M:* Piero Piccioni *Ca:* Sven-Bertil Taube, Barbara Parkins, Alexander Knox, Patrick Allen, Vladek Sheybal, Ania Marson, Penny Casdagli

600. **The Pursuers** (1962) The Danzigers B&W 63 min *D:* Godfrey Grayson *P:* Philip Elton and Ralph Goddard *Sc:* Brian Clemens and David Nicholl *Ph:* Walter J. Harvey *M:* Bill Le Sage *Ca:* Cyril Shaps, Francis Matthews, Susan Denny, Sheldon Lawrence, George Murcell, John Gabriel, Tony Doonan

601. **A Question of Suspense** (1961) Bill and Michael Luckwell Ltd. B&W 62 min *D:* Max Varnel *P:* Bill Luckwell and Jock MacGregor *Sc:* Lawrence Huntington *Ph:* Phil Grindrod *M:* Wilfred Burns *Ca:* Peter Reynolds, Noelle Middleton, Yvonne Buckingham, Norman Rodway, James Neylin, Pauline Delany, Anne Mulvey

602. **The Quiller Memorandum** (1966) Ivan Foxwell Productions Col 103 min *D:* Michael Anderson *P:* Ivan Foxwell *Sc:* Harold Pinter *Ph:* Erwin Hillier *M:* John Barry *Ca:* George Segal, Alec Guinness, Max Von Sydow, Senta Berger, George Sanders, Robert Helpmann, Robert Flemyng, Peter Carsten

603. **Radio Cab Murder** (1954) Insignia Films B&W 70 min *D:* Vernon Sewell *P:* George Maynard *Sc:* Vernon Sewell *Ph:* Geoffrey Faithfull *Ca:* Jimmy Hanley, Lana Morris, Sonia Holm, Jack Allen, Sam Kydd, Michael Mellinger, Charles Morgan, Bruce Beeby

604. **Ransom** (1974) Peter Rawley Film and Theatre Productions Col 98 min *U.S. Title:* The Terrorists *D:* Casper Wrede *P:* Peter Rawley *Sc:* Paul Wheeler *Ph:* Sven Nykvist *M:* Jerry Goldsmith *Ca:* Sean Connery, Ian McShane, Jeffry Wickham, Isabel Dean, John Quentin, Robert Harris, James Maxwell

605. **Recoil** (1953) Tempean Films B&W 79 min *D:* John Gilling *P:* Robert S. Baker and Monty Berman *Sc:* John Gilling *Ph:* Monty Berman *M:* Stanley Black *Ca:* Kieron Moore, Elizabeth Sellars, Edward Underdown, John Horsley, Robert Raglan, Ethel O'Shea, Martin Benson

606. **Redneck** (1972) Sterle Productions (London)/Compagnia Internazionale Alessandra Cinematografica (Rome) Col 87 min *D:* Silvio Narizzano *P:* Michael Lester and Silvio Narizzano *Sc:* Win Wells and Masolino D'Amico *Ph:* Giorgio Tonti *M:* Maurizio Catalano *Ca:* Franco Nero, Telly Savalas, Mark Lester, Ely Galleani, Duilio Del Prete, Maria Michi, Aldo De Carellis

607. **Return from the Ashes** (1965) Mirisch Films/Orchard Productions B&W 104 min *D:* J. Lee Thompson *P:* J. Lee Thompson *Sc:* Julius Epstein *Ph:* Christopher Challis *M:* John Dankworth *Ca:* Maximilian Schell, Samantha Eggar, Ingrid Thulin, Herbert Lom, Talitha Pol, Jacques Brunius, Vladek Sheybal

608. **Return of a Stranger** (1961) The Danzigers B&W 63 min *D:* Max Varnel *P:* Edward J. Danziger and Harry Lee Danziger *Sc:* Brian Clemens *Ph:* Walter J. Harvey *M:* Bill Le Sage *Ca:* John Ireland, Susan Stephen, Timothy Beaton, Cyril Shaps, Patrick McAlinney, Kevin Stoney, Ian Fleming

609. **The Return of Mr. Moto** (1965) Lippert Films B&W 71 min *D:* Ernest Morris *P:* Robert L. Lippert and Jack Parsons *Sc:* Fred Eggers *Ph:* Basil Emmott *M:* Douglas Gamley *Ca:* Henry Silva, Terence Longdon, Suzanne Lloyd, Marne Maitland, Stanley Morgan, Martin Wyldeck, Anthony Booth

610. **Return to Sender** (1962) Merton Park B&W 61 min *D:* Gordon Hales *P:* Jack Greenwood *Sc:* John Roddick *Ph:* James Wilson *M:* Bernard Ebbinghouse *Ca:* Nigel Davenport, Yvonne Romain, Geoffrey Keen, William Russell, Jennifer Daniel, Paul Williamson, John Horsley

611. **Revenge** (1971) Peter Rogers Productions Col 89 min *U.S. Titles:* Terror from Under the House (1976 PG-rated release title); After Jenny Died (1973 R-rated release title); Inn of the Frightened People (TV only); Behind the Cellar Door (video—see Appendix V) *D:* Sidney Hayers *P:* George H. Brown *Sc:* John Kruse *Ph:* Ken Hodges *M:* Eric Rogers *Ca:* Joan Collins, James Booth, Ray Barrett, Sinead Cusack, Kenneth Griffith, Tom Marshall, Zuleika Robson

612. **Ricochet** (1963) Merton Park B&W 64 min *D:* John Llewellyn Moxey *P:* Jack Greenwood *Sc:* Roger Marshall *Ph:* James Wilson *M:* Bernard Ebbinghouse *Ca:* Maxine Audley, Richard Leech, Alex Scott, Dudley Foster, Patrick Magee, Frederick Piper, June Murphy

613. **The Riddle of the Sands** (1978) Worldmark Films Col 102 min *D:* Tony Maylam *P:* Drummond Challis *Sc:* Tony Maylam and John Bailey *Ph:* Christopher Challis *M:* Howard Blake *Ca:* Michael York, Jenny Agutter, Simon MacCorkindale, Alan Badel, Jurgen Andersen, Michael Sheard, Hans Meyer

614. **Ring of Spies** (1963) British Lion Films B&W 90 min *U.S. Title:* Ring of Treason *D:* Robert Tronson *P:* Leslie Gilliat *Sc:* Frank Launder and Peter Barnes *Ph:* Arthur Lavis *Ca:* Bernard Lee, William Sylvester, Margaret Tyzack, David Kossoff, Nancy Nevinson, Thorley Walters, Gillian Lewis

Ring of Treason *see* **Ring of Spies**

615. **The Ringer** (1952) London Film Productions/British Lion Production Assets B&W 78 min *D:* Guy Hamilton *P:* Hugh Perceval *Sc:* Val Valentine *Ph:* Edward Scaife *M:* Malcolm Arnold *Ca:* Herbert Lom, Donald Wolfit, Mai Zetterling, Greta Gynt, William Hartnell, Norman Wooland, Denholm Elliott, Charles Victor

The Risk *see* **Suspect**

616. **The Rivals** (1963) Merton Park B&W 57 min *D:* Max Varnel *P:* Jack Greenwood *Sc:* John Roddick *Ph:* James Wilson *M:* Bernard Ebbinghouse *Ca:* Jack Gwillim, Erica Rogers, Brian Smith, Tony Garnett, Barry Linehan, Murray Hayne, Howard Greene

617. **River Beat** (1953) Insignia Films (in association with Abtcon Pictures [U.S.]) B&W 70 min *D:* Guy Green *P:* Victor Hanbury *Sc:* Rex Rienits *Ph:* Geoffrey Faithfull *M:* Hubert

Clifford *Ca:* Phyllis Kirk, John Bentley, Robert Ayres, Leonard White, Ewan Roberts, Harold Ayer, Glyn Houston

The Road Builder *see* **The Night Digger**

618. **Robbery** (1967) Oakhurst Productions Col 114 min *D:* Peter Yates *P:* Michael Deeley and Stanley Baker *Sc:* Edward Boyd, Peter Yates and George Markstein *Ph:* Douglas Slocombe *M:* John Keating *Ca:* Stanley Baker, Joanna Pettet, James Booth, Frank Finlay, Barry Foster, William Marlowe, Clinton Greyn, George Sewell, Glynn Edwards

619. **Robbery with Violence** (1958) G.I.B. Films (Hastings) B&W 67 min *D:* Ivan Barnett *P:* Ivan Barnett *Sc:* David Cumming *Ph:* Ivan Barnett *Ca:* Ivan Craig, Sally Day, Michael Golden, John Martin Lewis, John Trevor-Davis, John Law, Robert Woollard

620. **Rogue's Yarn** (1956) Cresswell Productions B&W 80 min *D:* Vernon Sewell *P:* George Maynard *Sc:* Vernon Sewell and Ernie Bradford *Ph:* Hal Morey *M:* Robert Sharples *Ca:* Nicole Maurey, Derek Bond, Elwyn Brook-Jones, Hugh Latimer, John Serret, John Salew, Joan Carol

Room 43 *see* **Passport to Shame**

621. **The Rossiter Case** (1950) Hammer Film Productions B&W 76 min *D:* Francis Searle *P:* Anthony Hinds *Sc:* Kenneth Hyde, John Hunter and Francis Searle *Ph:* Walter J. Harvey *M:* Frank Spencer *Ca:* Helen Shingler, Clement McCallin, Sheila Burrell, Frederick Leister, Ann Codrington, Henry Edwards, Dorothy Batley

622. **Rough Shoot** (1953) Raymond Stross Productions B&W 87 min *U.S. Title:* Shoot First *D:* Robert Parrish *P:* Raymond Stross *Sc:* Eric Ambler *Ph:* Stanley Pavey *M:* Hans May *Ca:* Joel McCrea, Evelyn Keyes, Herbert Lom, Marius Goring, Roland Culver, Karel Stepanek, David Hurst

623. **The Runaway** (1964) Luckwell Productions B&W 62 min *D:* Tony Young *P:* Bill Luckwell and David Vigo *Sc:* John Perceval *Ph:* Walter J. Harvey *M:* Wilfred Burns *Ca:* Greta Gynt, Alex Gallier, Paul Williamson, Michael Trubshawe, Tony Quinn, Wendy Varnals, Denis Shaw

624. **The Runaway Bus** (1953) Conquest-Guest Productions B&W 78 min *D:* Val Guest *P:* Val Guest *Sc:* Val Guest *Ph:* Stanley Pavey *M:* Ronald Binge *Ca:* Frankie Howerd, Margaret Rutherford, Petula Clark, George Coulouris, Toke Townley, Terence Alexander, Belinda Lee, Sam Kydd

625. **The Running Man** (1963) Peet Productions Col 104 min *D:* Carol Reed *P:* Carol Reed *Sc:* John Mortimer *Ph:* Robert Krasker *M:* William Alwyn (title music by Ron Grainer) *Ca:* Laurence Harvey, Lee Remick, Alan Bates, Felix Aylmer, Eleanor Summerfield, Colin Gordon, Allan Cuthbertson

626. **Russian Roulette** (1975) ITC/Bulldog Productions Col 90 min *D:* Lou Lombardo *P:* Jerry Bick *Sc:* Tom Ardies, Stanley Mann and Arnold Margolin *Ph:* Brian West *M:* Michael J. Lewis *Ca:* George Segal, Cristina Raines, Bo Brundin, Denholm Elliott, Richard Romanus, Gordon Jackson, Peter Donat, Nigel Stock

Rx for Murder *see* **Family Doctor**

Rx Murder *see* **Family Doctor**

627. **The Safecracker** (1957) Coronado Productions (England) B&W 96 min *D:* Ray Milland *P:* John R. Sloan *Sc:* Paul Monash *Ph:* Gerald Gibbs *M:* Richard Rodney Bennett *Ca:* Ray Milland, Barry Jones, Jeannette Sterke, Victor Maddern, Ernest Clark, Cyril Raymond, Melissa Stribling

628. **Sail into Danger** (1957) Patria Films B&W 72 min *D:* Kenneth Hume *P:* Steven Pallos *Sc:* Kenneth Hume *Ph:* Phil Grindrod *M:* Ivor Slaney *Ca:* Dennis O'Keefe, Kathleen Ryan, James Hayter, Ana Luisa Peluffo, Barta Barry, Felix De Pommes, John Bull

The Saint's Girl Friday *see* **The Saint's Return**

629. **The Saint's Return** (1953) Hammer Film Productions (in association with Royal Productions [U.S.]) B&W 73 min *U.S. Title:* The Saint's Girl Friday *D:* Seymour Friedman *P:* Anthony Hinds and Julian Lesser *Sc:* Allan MacKinnon *Ph:* Walter J. Harvey *M:* Ivor Slaney *Ca:* Louis Hayward, Naomi Chance, Charles Victor, Sydney Tafler, Harold Lang, Diana Dors, Jane Carr

630. **Salt & Pepper** (1968) Chris-Mark Productions Col 101 min *D:* Richard Donner *P:* Milton Ebbins *Sc:* Michael Pertwee *Ph:* Ken Higgins *M:* John Dankworth *Ca:* Sammy Davis, Jr., Peter Lawford, Michael Bates, Ilona Rodgers, John Le Mesurier, Graham Stark, Ernest Clark

631. **Salute the Toff** (1951) Nettlefold Films B&W 76 min *U.S. Title:* Brighthaven Express (TV only) *D:* Maclean Rogers *P:* Ernest G. Roy *Sc:* Uncredited *Ph:* Geoffrey Faithfull *M:* Wilfred Burns *Ca:* John Bentley, Carol Marsh, Valentine Dyall, Shelagh Fraser, June Elvin, Arthur Hill, Michael Golden, Wally Patch, Roddy Hughes

Sanders *see* **Death Drums Along the River**

632. **Sapphire** (1959) Artna Films Col 92 min *D:* Basil Dearden *P:* Michael Relph *Sc:* Janet Green *Ph:* Harry Waxman *M:* Philip Green *Ca:* Nigel Patrick, Yvonne Mitchell, Michael Craig, Paul Massie, Bernard Miles, Olga Lindo, Earl Cameron, Rupert Davies

Satan's Playthings *see* **Assault**

633. **The Scapegoat** (1958) Du Maurier-Guinness Ltd. B&W 92 min *D:* Robert Hamer *P:* Michael Balcon *Sc:* Robert Hamer *Ph:* Paul Beeson *M:* Bronislau Kaper *Ca:* Alec Guinness, Bette Davis, Nicole Maurey, Irene Worth, Pamela Brown, Annabel Bartlett, Geoffrey Keen

634. **Scarlet Thread** (1951) Nettlefold Films/International Realist B&W 85 min *D:* Lewis Gilbert *P:* Ernest G. Roy *Sc:* A.R. Rawlinson and Moie Charles *Ph:* Geoffrey Faithfull *M:* Kenneth D. Morrison *Ca:* Kathleen Byron, Laurence Harvey, Sydney Tafler, Dora Bryan, Renee Kelly, Arthur Hill, Harry Fowler

635. **The Scarlet Web** (1953) Fortress Film Productions B&W 64 min *D:* Charles Saunders *P:* Frank Bevis *Sc:* Doreen Montgomery *Ph:* Hone Glendinning *Ca:* Griffith Jones, Hazel Court, Zena Marshall, Robert Perceval, Molly Raynor, Ronnie Stevens, Stuart Douglass

636. **Schizo** (1976) Peter Walker (Heritage) Col 109 min *D:* Pete Walker *P:* Pete Walker *Sc:* David McGillivray *Ph:* Peter Jessop *M:* Stanley Myers *Ca:* Lynne Frederick, John Leyton, Stephanie Beacham, John Fraser, Jack Watson, Queenie Watts, Trisha Mortimer

Scotland Yard Dragnet *see* **The Hypnotist**

Scotland Yard Inspector *see* **Lady in the Fog**

637. **Scream—and Die!** (1973) Blackwater Film Productions Col 99 min *U.S. Title:* The House That Vanished *D:* José Ramón Larraz *P:* Diana Daubeney *Sc:* Derek Ford *Ph:* Trevor Wrenn *M:* Terry Warr *Ca:* Andrea Allan, Karl Lanchbury, Maggie Walker, Peter Forbes-Robertson, Judy Matheson, Annabella Wood, Alex Leppard

Scream of Fear *see* **Taste of Fear**

638. **Séance on a Wet Afternoon** (1964) Beaver Films B&W 121 min *D:* Bryan Forbes *P:* Richard Attenborough *Sc:* Bryan Forbes *Ph:* Gerry Turpin *M:* John Barry *Ca:* Kim Stanley, Richard Attenborough, Nanette Newman, Patrick Magee, Mark Eden, Gerald Sim, Marian Spencer

639. **Sebastian** (1967) Maccius Productions Col 100 min *D:* David Greene *P:* Herbert Brodkin and Michael Powell *Sc:* Gerald Vaughan-Hughes *Ph:* Gerry Fisher *M:* Jerry Goldsmith *Ca:* Dirk Bogarde, Susannah York, Lilli Palmer, John Gielgud, Janet Munro, Nigel Davenport, Margaret Johnston

The 2nd Best Secret Agent in the Whole Wide World *see* **Licensed to Kill**

640. **The Second Mate** (1950) Elstree Independent Films/John Baxter Productions B&W 76 min *D:* John Baxter *P:* John Baxter *Sc:* John Baxter and Barbara K. Emary *Ph:* Arthur Grant *M:* Kennedy Russell *Ca:* Gordon Harker, Graham Moffatt, David Hannaford, Byrl Walkley, Charles Sewell, Anne Blake, Charles Heslop

641. **The Secret** (1955) Golden Era Films Col 80 min *D:* Cy Endfield *P:* S. Benjamin Fisz *Sc:* Cy Endfield *Ph:* Jack Asher *M:* Phil Cardew *Ca:* Sam Wanamaker, Mandy Miller, Andre Morell, Marian Spencer, Jan Miller, Wyndham Goldie, Harold Berens

642. **The Secret Door** (1963) Dorton Productions/Fifeshire Motion Pictures Col 72 min *D:* Gilbert L. Kay *P:* Charles Baldour *Sc:* Charles Martin *Ph:* Robert Moss and Aurelio Rodriguez *M:* Tony Osborne *Ca:* Robert Hutton, Sandra Dorne, Peter Illing, George Pastell, Shirley Lawrence, Peter Allenby, Peter Elliott, Martin Benson

643. **The Secret Man** (1958) Producers Associates/Amalgamated Productions B&W 68 min *D:* Ronald Kinnoch *P:* Ronald Kinnoch *Sc:* Brian Clemens (billed as Tony O'Grady) and Ronald Kinnoch *Ph:* Geoffrey Faithfull *M:* Albert Elms *Ca:* Marshall Thompson, John Loder, Anne Aubrey, Magda Miller, John Stuart, Henry Oscar, Murray Kash

644. **The Secret Partner** (1961) MGM B&W 91 min *D:* Basil Dearden *P:* Michael Relph *Sc:* David Pursall and Jack Seddon *Ph:* Harry Waxman *M:* Philip Green *Ca:* Stewart Granger, Haya Harareet, Bernard Lee, Hugh Burden, Lee Montague, Melissa Stribling, Conrad Phillips, Norman Bird

645. **Secret People** (1951) Ealing Studios B&W 96 min *D:* Thorold Dickinson *P:* Sidney Cole *Sc:* Thorold Dickinson and Wolfgang Wilhelm *Ph:* Gordon Dines *M:* Roberto Gerhard *Ca:* Valentina Cortesa, Serge Reggiani, Audrey Hepburn, Charles Goldner, Megs Jenkins, Irene Worth, Reginald Tate

646. **The Secret Place** (1956) The Rank Organisation Film Productions B&W 98 min *D:* Clive Donner *P:* John Bryan *Sc:* Linette Perry *Ph:* Ernest Steward *M:* Clifton Parker *Ca:* Belinda Lee, Ronald Lewis, Michael Brooke, Michael Gwynn, David McCallum, Geoffrey Keen, George A. Cooper

647. **Secret Venture** (1954) Republic Productions (Great Britain) B&W 68 min *D:* R.G. Springsteen *P:* William N. Boyle *Sc:* Paul Erickson *Ph:* Basil Emmott *M:* Lambert Williamson *Ca:* Kent Taylor, Jane Hylton, Kathleen Byron, Karel Stepanek, Frederick Valk, Martin Boddey, Maurice Kaufmann

Secrets of a Playgirl *see* **The Playbirds**

See No Evil *see* **Blind Terror**

648. **The Sellout** (1975) Grandgrange Ltd./Berkey-Pathé-Humphries (Israel)/Oceanglade (London)/Amerfilm (Rome) Col 101 min *U.S. Title:* The Set-Up (video—see Appendix V) *D:* Peter Collinson *P:* Josef Shaftel *Sc:* Murray Smith and Jud Kinberg *Ph:* Arthur Ibbetson *M:* Mick Green and Colin Frechter *Ca:* Richard Widmark, Oliver Reed, Gayle Hunnicutt, Sam Wanamaker, Vladek Sheybal, Ori Levy, Assaf Dayan

649. **Sentenced for Life** (1959) The Danzigers B&W 64 min *D:* Max Varnel *P:* Edward J. Danziger and Harry Lee Danziger *Sc:* Mark Grantham and Eldon Howard *Ph:* S.D. Onions *Ca:* Francis Matthews, Jill Williams, Basil Dignam, Jack Gwillim, Lorraine Clewes, Mark Singleton, Nyree Dawn Porter

650. **Serena** (1962) Butcher's Film Productions B&W 62 min *D:* Peter Maxwell *P:* John I. Phillips *Sc:* Reginald Hearne and Edward Abraham *Ph:* Stephen Dade *M:* Johnny Gregory *Ca:* Patrick Holt, Emrys Jones, Honor Blackman, Bruce Beeby, John Horsley, Vi Stevens, Wally Patch

651. **The Set-Up** (1962) Merton Park B&W 57 min *D:* Gerard Glaister *P:* Jack Greenwood *Sc:* Roger Marshall *Ph:* Bert Mason *M:* Bernard Ebbinghouse *Ca:* Maurice Denham, John Carson, Maria Corvin, Brian Peck, Anthony Bate, John Arnatt, Manning Wilson

The Set-Up *see* **The Sellout**

652. **Seven Days to Noon** (1950) London Film Productions/British Lion Production Assets B&W 96 min *D:* Roy Boulting and John Boulting *P:* Roy Boulting and John Boulting *Sc:* Frank Harvey and Roy Boulting *Ph:* Gilbert Taylor *M:* John Addison *Ca:* Barry Jones, Olive Sloane, Andre Morell, Sheila Manahan, Hugh Cross, Joan Hickson, Ronald Adam

653. **Seven Keys** (1962) Independent Artists B&W 57 min *D:* Pat Jackson *P:* Julian Wintle and Leslie Parkyn *Sc:* Jack Davies and Henry Blyth *Ph:* Ernest Steward *M:* Alan Clare *Ca:* Jeannie Carson, Alan Dobie, Delphi Lawrence, Robertson Hare, Colin Gordon, John Carson, Anthony Nicholls

654. **Seven Thunders** (1957) Dial Films B&W 100 min *U.S. Title:* The Beasts of Marseilles *D:* Hugo Fregonese *P:* Daniel M. Angel *Sc:* John Baines *Ph:* Wilkie Cooper *M:* Antony Hopkins *Ca:* Stephen Boyd, James Robertson Justice, Tony Wright, Anna Gaylor, Kathleen Harrison, Eugene Deckers, Rosalie Crutchley, Anton Diffring

Sex Is a Woman *see* **Death Is a Woman**

Shadow Man *see* **Street of Shadows**

655. **Shadow of a Man** (1954) E.J. Fancey Productions B&W 70 min *D:* Michael McCarthy *P:* E.J. Fancey *Sc:* Paul Erickson *Ph:* Geoffrey Faithfull *M:* Jackie Brown *Ca:* Paul Carpenter, Rona Anderson, Jane Griffiths, Ronald Leigh-Hunt, Tony Quinn, Jack Taylor, Bill Nagy

656. **Shadow of Fear** (1963) Butcher's Film Productions B&W 60 min *U.S. Title:* Target for Terror (little-known retitling by distributor Keith T. Smith [Modern Sound Pictures, Inc.]) *D:* Ernest Morris *P:* John I. Phillips *Sc:* Ronald Liles and Jim O'Connolly *Ph:* Walter J. Harvey *M:* Martin Slavin *Ca:* Paul Maxwell, Clare Owen, Anita West, Alan Tilvern, John Arnatt, Eric Pohlmann, Reginald Marsh

Shadow of Fear *see* **Before I Wake**

657. **Shadow of the Past** (1950) Anglofilm Limited B&W 83 min *D:* Mario Zampi *P:* Mario Zampi *Sc:* Aldo De Benedetti and Ian Stuart Black *Ph:* Hone Glendinning *M:* Stanley Black *Ca:* Joyce Howard, Terence Morgan, Michael Medwin, Andrew Osborn, Wylie Watson, Ella Retford, Marie Ney

658. **Shadow of Treason** (1963) Mark III Scope Productions/Triglav Films B&W 89 min *D:* George Breakston *P:* George Breakston *Sc:* George Breakston, Howard Kent and Jane Harker *Ph:* Milan Babic *M:* Martin Slavin *Ca:* John Bentley, Faten Hamama, Anita West, John Gabriel, Ferdy Mayne, Vlado Leib

659. **The Shakedown** (1959) Ethiro Productions B&W 92 min *D:* John Lemont *P:* Norman Williams *Sc:* Leigh Vance and John Lemont *Ph:* Brendan J. Stafford *M:* Philip Green *Ca:* Terence Morgan, Hazel Court, Donald Pleasence, Bill Owen, Robert Beatty, Harry H. Corbett, Gene Anderson, John Salew

660. **The Share-Out** (1962) Merton Park B&W 61 min *D:* Gerard Glaister *P:* Jack Greenwood *Sc:* Philip Mackie *Ph:* Bert Mason *M:* Bernard Ebbinghouse *Ca:* Bernard Lee, Alexander Knox, Moira Redmond, William Russell, Richard Vernon, Richard Warner, John Gabriel

661. **Shatter** (1974) Hammer Film Productions/Shaw Brothers Col 90 min *U.S. Titles:* Call Him Mr. Shatter; Mr. Shatter (video—see Appendix V) *D:* Michael Carreras *P:* Michael Carreras and Vee King Shaw *Sc:* Don Houghton *Ph:* Brian Probyn, John Wilcox and Roy Ford *M:* David Lindup *Ca:* Stuart Whitman, Ti Lung, Lily Li, Peter Cushing, Anton Diffring, Yemi Ajibade, Liu Ya Ying

She Played with Fire *see* **Fortune Is a Woman**

662. **She Shall Have Murder** (1950) Concanen Recordings B&W 91 min *D:* Daniel Birt *P:* Derrick De Marney and Guido Coen *Sc:* Allan MacKinnon *Ph:* Robert Navarro *M:* Eric Spear *Ca:* Rosamund John, Derrick De Marney, Mary Jerrold, Felix Aylmer, Joyce Heron, Jack Allen, Harry Fowler

Sheba *see* **Persecution**

Shoot First *see* **Rough Shoot**

663. **Shoot to Kill** (1960) Border Film Productions/E.J. Fancey Productions B&W 64 min *D:* Michael Winner *P:* Olive Negus-Fancey *Sc:* Michael Winner *Ph:* Adolph Burger *M:* Cy Payne *Ca:* Dermot Walsh, Joy Webster, John East, Frank Hawkins, Zoreen Ismael, Theodore Wilhelm, Victor Beaumont

664. **The Sicilians** (1964) Butcher's Film Productions B&W 69 min *D:* Ernest Morris *P:* John I. Phillips *Sc:* Ronald Liles and Reginald Hearne *Ph:* Geoffrey Faithfull *M:* Johnny Gregory *Ca:* Robert Hutton, Reginald Marsh, Ursula Howells, Alex Scott, Susan Denny, Robert Ayres, Eric Pohlmann

665. **The Siege of Pinchgut** (1959) Ealing Films B&W 104 min *U.S. Title:* Four Desperate Men *D:* Harry Watt *P:* Michael Balcon *Sc:* Harry Watt and Jon Cleary *Ph:* Gordon Dines *M:* Kenneth V. Jones *Ca:* Aldo Ray, Heather Sears, Neil McCallum, Victor Maddern, Carlo Justini, Alan Tilvern, Barbara Mullen

666. **The Silent Playground** (1963) Focus Film Productions B&W 75 min *D:* Stanley Goulder *P:* George Mills *Sc:* Stanley Goulder *Ph:* Martin Curtis *M:* Tristram Cary *Ca:* Jean Anderson, Bernard Archard, Roland Curram, Ellen McIntosh, John Ronane, Desmond Llewelyn, Rowena Gregory

667. **The Sinister Man** (1961) Merton Park B&W 60 min *D:* Clive Donner *P:* Jack Greenwood *Sc:* Robert Banks Stewart *Ph:* Bert Mason *M:* Charles Blackwell *Ca:* John Bentley, Patrick Allen, Jacqueline Ellis, John Glyn-Jones, Brian McDermott, Gerald Andersen, Wilfrid Brambell

668. **Sitting Target** (1972) MGM/Peerford Limited Col 93 min *D:* Douglas Hickox *P:* Barry Kulick *Sc:* Alexander Jacobs *Ph:* Edward Scaife *M:* Stanley Myers *Ca:* Oliver Reed, Jill St. John, Ian McShane, Edward Woodward, Frank Finlay, Freddie Jones, Robert Beatty. Tony Beckley

669. **The Six Men** (1950) Vandyke Picture Corporation/Planet Productions B&W 65 min *D:* Michael Law *P:* Roger Proudlock *Sc:* Reed De Rouen, Richard Eastham and Michael Law *Ph:* S.D. Onions *M:* Günther Stümpf *Ca:* Harold Warrender, Olga Edwardes, Peter Bull, Michael Evans, Reed De Rouen, Ivan Craig, Edward Malin

The Skin Game *see* **Kil 1**

670. **Sleuth** (1972) Palomar Pictures International Col 139 min *D:* Joseph L. Mankiewicz *P:* Morton Gottlieb *Sc:* Anthony Shaffer *Ph:* Oswald Morris *M:* John Addison *Ca:* Laurence Olivier, Michael Caine, Alec Cawthorne, Eve Channing, John Matthews, Teddy Martin

671. **Smart Alec** (1951) Vandyke Picture Corporation B&W 58 min *D:* John Guillermin *P:* Roger Proudlock *Sc:* Alec Coppel *Ph:* Ray Elton *Ca:* Peter Reynolds, Leslie Dwyer, Edward Lexy, Kynaston Reeves, Charles Hawtrey, Mercy Haystead, David Keir

672. **Smokescreen** (1964) Butcher's Film Productions B&W 66 min *D:* Jim O'Connolly *P:* John I. Phillips *Sc:* Jim O'Connolly *Ph:* Jack Mills *M:* Johnny Gregory *Ca:* Peter Vaughan, John Carson, Yvonne Romain, Gerald Flood, Glynn Edwards, John Glyn-Jones, Sam Kydd

673. **The Snorkel** (1958) Hammer Film Productions/Clarion Films (Hammer subsidiary) B&W 90 min *D:* Guy Green *P:* Michael Carreras *Sc:* Peter Myers and Jimmy Sangster *Ph:* Jack Asher *M:* Francis Chagrin *Ca:* Peter Van Eyck, Betta St. John, Mandy Miller, Gregoire Aslan, William Franklyn, Marie Burke, Irene Prador

674. **So Long at the Fair** (1950) Gainsborough Pictures B&W 86 min *U.S. Title:* The Black Curse (1953 theatrical reissue) *D:* Terence Fisher and Antony Darnborough *P:* Betty E. Box *Sc:* Hugh Mills and Anthony Thorne *Ph:* Reginald Wyer *M:* Benjamin Frankel *Ca:* Jean Simmons, Dirk Bogarde, David Tomlinson, Honor Blackman, Cathleen Nesbitt, Felix Aylmer, Betty Warren

675. **Soho Incident** (1955) Film Locations B&W 77 min *U.S. Title:* Spin a Dark Web *D:* Vernon Sewell *P:* George Maynard *Sc:* Ian Stuart Black *Ph:* Basil Emmott *M:* Robert Sharples *Ca:* Faith Domergue, Lee Patterson, Rona Anderson, Martin Benson, Robert Arden, Joss Ambler, Peter Hammond

676. **The Solitary Child** (1957) Beaconsfield Films B&W 64 min *D:* Gerald Thomas *P:* Peter Rogers *Sc:* Robert Dunbar *Ph:* Peter Hennessy *Ca:* Philip Friend, Barbara Shelley, Sarah Lawson, Jack Watling, Rona Anderson, Julia Lockwood, Catherine Lacey

677. **Solo for Sparrow** (1962) Merton Park B&W 56 min *D:* Gordon Flemyng *P:* Jack Greenwood *Sc:* Roger Marshall *Ph:* Bert Mason *M:* Bernard Ebbinghouse *Ca:* Anthony Newlands, Glyn Houston, Nadja Regin, Michael Coles, Allan Cuthbertson, Ken Wayne, Jerry Stovin

678. **Solution by Phone** (1953) Pan Productions B&W 59 min *D:* Alfred Travers *P:* Brandon Fleming and Geoffrey Goodhart *Sc:* Brandon Fleming *Ph:* Hilton Craig *Ca:* Clifford Evans, Thea Gregory, John Witty, Georgina Cookson, Enid Hewitt, Geoffrey Goodhart, Max Brimmell

679. **Some Girls Do** (1969) Ashdown Film Productions Col 93 min *D:* Ralph Thomas *P:* Betty E. Box *Sc:* David Osborn and Liz Charles-Williams *Ph:* Ernest Steward *M:* Charles Blackwell *Ca:* Richard Johnson, Daliah Lavi, Beba Loncar, James Villiers, Vanessa Howard, Maurice Denham, Robert Morley

680. **Some May Live** (1967) Foundation Pictures Col 89 min *U.S. Title:* In Saigon, Some May Live (TV only) *D:* Vernon Sewell *P:* Clive Sharp and Peter Snell *Sc:* David T. Chantler *Ph:* Ray Parslow *M:* Cyril Ornadel *Ca:* Joseph Cotten, Martha Hyer, Peter Cushing, John Ronane, David Spenser, Alec Mango, Walter Brown

681. **Somebody's Stolen Our Russian Spy** (1967) Puck Films/Andorra Films Col 84 min *D:* José Luis Madrid *P:* James Ward *Sc:* Michael Pittock *Ph:* Raul Artigot *M:* Angel Arteaga *Ca:* Tom Adams, Tim Barrett, Diana Lorys, Barta Barry, Gene Reyes, Maria Silva, Spencer Teakle

682. **Someone at the Door** (1950) Hammer Film Productions B&W 64 min *D:* Francis Searle *P:* Anthony Hinds *Sc:* A.R. Rawlinson *Ph:* Walter J. Harvey *M:* Frank Spencer *Ca:* Yvonne Owen, Michael Medwin, Garry Marsh, Hugh Latimer, Danny Green, Campbell Singer, John Kelly

683. **SOS Pacific** (1959) Remfield Films B&W 91 min *D:* Guy Green *P:* John Nasht and Patrick Filmer-Sankey *Sc:* Robert Westerby *Ph:* Wilkie Cooper *M:* Georges Auric *Ca:* Richard Attenborough, Pier Angeli, John Gregson, Eva Bartok, Eddie Constantine, Jean Anderson, Cec Linder, Clifford Evans

684. **Spaceways** (1952) Hammer Film Productions (in association with Lippert Pictures [U.S.]) B&W 76 min *D:* Terence Fisher *P:* Michael Carreras *Sc:* Paul Tabori and Richard Landau *Ph:* Reginald Wyer *M:* Ivor Slaney *Ca:* Howard Duff, Eva Bartok, Alan Wheatley, Philip Leaver, Michael Medwin, Andrew Osborn, Cecile Chevreau

685. **The Spaniard's Curse** (1957) Wentworth Films B&W 79 min *D:* Ralph Kemplen *P:* Roger Proudlock *Sc:* Kenneth Hyde *Ph:* Arthur Grant *M:* Lambert Williamson *Ca:* Tony Wright, Lee Patterson, Michael Hordern, Susan Beaumont, Ralph Truman, Henry Oscar, Brian Oulton

686. **The Spider's Web** (1960) The Danzigers Col 89 min *D:* Godfrey Grayson *P:* Edward J. Danziger and Harry Lee Danziger *Sc:* Albert G. Miller and Eldon Howard *Ph:* James Wilson *M:* Tony Crombie *Ca:* Glynis Johns, John Justin, Jack Hulbert, Cicely Courtneidge, Ronald Howard, Peter Butterworth, Ferdy Mayne

Spin a Dark Web *see* **The Soho Incident**

687. **The Spiral Staircase** (1975) Raven Film Productions Col 89 min *D:* Peter Collinson *P:* Peter Shaw *Sc:* Allan Scott and Chris Bryant (billed collectively as Andrew Meredith) *Ph:* Ken Hodges *M:* David Lindup *Ca:* Jacqueline Bisset, Christopher Plummer, Sam Wanamaker, Mildred Dunnock, Gayle Hunnicutt, Elaine Stritch, John Ronane

688. **Spy Story** (1976) Lindsay Shonteff Film Productions Col 102 min *D:* Lindsay Shonteff *P:* Lindsay Shonteff *Sc:* Uncredited *Ph:* Les Young *M:* Roger Wootton and Andrew Hellaby *Ca:* Michael Petrovitch, Philip Latham, Don Fellows, Michael Gwynn, Nicholas Parsons, Tessa Wyatt, Derren Nesbitt

689. **The Spy Who Came in from the Cold** (1965) Salem Films B&W 112 min *D:* Martin Ritt *P:* Martin Ritt *Sc:* Paul Dehn and Guy Trosper *Ph:* Oswald Morris *M:* Sol Kaplan *Ca:* Richard Burton, Claire Bloom, Oskar Werner, Sam Wanamaker, Peter Van Eyck, Rupert Davies, Cyril Cusack, Michael Hordern, Robert Hardy, Bernard Lee

690. **The Spy Who Loved Me** (1977) Eon Productions Col 125 min *D:* Lewis Gilbert *P:* Albert R. Broccoli *Sc:* Christopher Wood and Richard Maibaum *Ph:* Claude Renoir *M:* Marvin Hamlisch *Ca:* Roger Moore, Barbara Bach, Curt Jürgens, Richard Kiel, Caroline Munro, Walter Gotell, Geoffrey Keen, Sydney Tafler, Bryan Marshall, Bernard Lee, Lois Maxwell

691. **The Squeeze** (1977) Martinat Productions Col 107 min *D:* Michael Apted *P:* Stanley O'Toole *Sc:* Leon Griffiths *Ph:* Dennis Lewiston *M:* David Hentschel *Ca:* Stacy Keach, David Hemmings, Edward Fox, Stephen Boyd, Carol White, Freddie Starr, Hilary Gasson

Stag Model Slaughter *see* **House of Whipcord**

State of Shock *see* **Power Play**

692. **State Secret** (1950) London Film Productions/British Lion Production Assets/Individual Pictures B&W 104 min *U.S. Title:* The Great Manhunt *D:* Sidney Gilliat *P:* Frank Launder and Sidney Gilliat *Sc:* Sidney Gilliat *Ph:* Robert Krasker *M:* William Alwyn *Ca:* Douglas Fairbanks, Jr., Glynis Johns, Jack Hawkins, Herbert Lom, Walter Rilla, Karel Stepanek, Carl Jaffe

693. **The Steel Key** (1952) Tempean Films

B&W 70 min *D:* Robert S. Baker *P:* Robert S. Baker and Monty Berman *Sc:* John Gilling and Roy Chanslor *Ph:* Gerald Gibbs *M:* Frank Cordell *Ca:* Terence Morgan, Joan Rice, Raymond Lovell, Dianne Foster, Hector Ross, Colin Tapley, Esmond Knight

694. **Stolen Assignment** (1955) A.C.T. Films/Unit Productions B&W 62 min *D:* Terence Fisher *P:* Francis Searle *Sc:* Kenneth R. Hayles *Ph:* Walter J. Harvey *Ca:* John Bentley, Hy Hazell, Eddie Byrne, Patrick Holt, Joyce Carey, Kay Callard, Jessica Cairns

695. **Stolen Time** (1954) Charles Deane Productions B&W 59 min *U.S. Title:* Blonde Blackmailer *D:* Charles Deane *P:* Charles Deane *Sc:* Charles Deane *Ph:* Geoffrey Faithfull *Ca:* Richard Arlen, Susan Shaw, Constance Leigh, Vincent Ball, Andrea Malandrinos, Alathea Siddons, Reginald Hearne

Stop Me Before I Kill! *see* **The Full Treatment**

696. **Stop-over Forever** (1964) Associated British Pathé B&W 59 min *D:* Frederic Goode *P:* Terry Ashwood *Sc:* David Osborn *Ph:* William Jordan *M:* Edwin Astley *Ca:* Ann Bell, Anthony Bate, Conrad Phillips, Bruce Boa, Julian Sherrier, Britta Von Krogh

697. **Stormy Crossing** (1957) Tempean Films B&W 69 min *U.S. Title:* Black Tide *D:* C. Pennington-Richards *P:* Monty Berman *Sc:* Brock Williams *Ph:* Geoffrey Faithfull *M:* Stanley Black *Ca:* John Ireland, Derek Bond, Leslie Dwyer, Maureen Connell, Sheldon Lawrence, Joy Webster, John Horsley

698. **Straight On Till Morning** (1972) Hammer Film Productions Col 96 min *U.S. Titles:* Dressed for Death (video—see Appendix V); 'Til Dawn Do We Part (video—see Appendix V) *D:* Peter Collinson *P:* Michael Carreras *Sc:* John Peacock *Ph:* Brian Probyn *M:* Roland Shaw *Ca:* Rita Tushingham, Shane Briant, Tom Bell, Annie Ross, Katya Wyeth, James Bolam, Clare Kelly

699. **The Strange Affair** (1968) Paramount Film Service Col 106 min *D:* David Greene *P:* Howard Harrison *Sc:* Stanley Mann *Ph:* Alex Thomson *M:* Basil Kirchin *Ca:* Michael York, Jeremy Kemp, Susan George, Jack Watson, Nigel Davenport, George A. Cooper, Artro Morris

700. **The Strange Awakening** (1957) Merton Park (in association with Ludwig H. Gerber Productions [U.S.]) B&W 82 min *U.S. Title:* Female Fiends *D:* Montgomery Tully *P:* Alec C. Snowden *Sc:* J. MacLaren-Ross *Ph:* Phil Grindrod *Ca:* Lex Barker, Carole Mathews, Lisa Gastoni, Nora Swinburne, Peter Dyneley, Joe Robinson, Malou Pantera

Strange Case of Dr. Manning *see* **Morning Call**

701. **Stranger at My Door** (1950) Leinster Films B&W 80 min *D:* Brendan J. Stafford and Desmond Leslie *P:* Paul King *Sc:* Desmond Leslie *Ph:* Brendan J. Stafford *M:* Leslie Bridgewater and Sir Granville Bantock *Ca:* Valentine Dyall, Joseph O'Conor, Agnes Bernelle, Maire O'Neill, Liam O'Leary, Jill Raymond, Michael Moore

702. **The Stranger Came Home** (1954) Hammer Film Productions (in association with Lippert Pictures [U.S.]) B&W 80 min *U.S. Title:* The Unholy Four *D:* Terence Fisher *P:* Michael Carreras *Sc:* Michael Carreras *Ph:* Walter J. Harvey *M:* Leonard Salzedo *Ca:* Paulette Goddard, William Sylvester, Patrick Holt, Paul Carpenter, Alvys Maben, Russell Napier, Kay Callard

The Stranger in Between *see* **Hunted**

703. **Stranger in the House** (1967) De Grunwald Productions/Selmur Productions Col 104 min *U.S. Title:* Cop-Out *D:* Pierre Rouve *P:* Dimitri De Grunwald *Sc:* Pierre Rouve *Ph:* Ken Higgins *M:* John Scott *Ca:* James Mason, Geraldine Chaplin, Bobby Darin, Paul Bertoya, Ian Ogilvy, Pippa Steel, James Hayter, Lisa Daniely

704. **A Stranger in Town** (1957) Tempean Films B&W 74 min *D:* George Pollock *P:* Sidney Roberts *Sc:* Norman Hudis and Edward Dryhurst *Ph:* Geoffrey Faithfull *M:* Stanley Black *Ca:* Alex Nicol, Anne Paige, Mary Laura Wood, Mona Washbourne, Charles Lloyd Pack, Bruce Beeby, John Horsley

705. **The Stranger's Hand** (1953) Independent Film Producers (London)/Milo Film (Rome)/Rizzoli Film (Rome) B&W 86 min *D:* Mario Soldati *P:* John Stafford and Peter Moore *Sc:* Guy Elmes and Georgio Bassani *Ph:* Enzo Serafin *M:* Nino Rota *Ca:* Trevor Howard, Alida Valli, Richard Basehart, Eduardo Ciannelli, Richard O'Sullivan, Stephen Murray, Guido Celano

706. **Strangers' Meeting** (1957) Parroch Films B&W 64 min *D:* Robert Day *P:* M. Smedley-Aston and David Gordon *Sc:* David Gordon *Ph:* Arthur Grant *M:* Albert Elms *Ca:* Peter Arne, Delphi Lawrence, Conrad Phillips, Barbara Archer, Victor Maddern, David Ritch, David Lodge

707. **Stranglehold** (1962) Argo Film Productions B&W 73 min *D:* Lawrence Huntington *P:* David Henley *Sc:* Guy Elmes and Joy Garrison *Ph:* S.D. Onions *M:* Eric Spear *Ca:* Macdonald Carey, Barbara Shelley, Philip Friend, Leonard Sachs, Mark Loegering, Nadja Regin, Susan Shaw

708. **The Stranglers of Bombay** (1959) Hammer Film Productions B&W 80 min *D:* Terence Fisher *P:* Anthony Hinds *Sc:* David Zelag Goodman *Ph:* Arthur Grant *M:* James Bernard *Ca:* Guy Rolfe, Allan Cuthbertson, Andrew Cruickshank, George Pastell, Marne Maitland, Jan Holden, Paul Stassino

709. **Strangler's Web** (1965) Merton Park B&W 55 min *D:* John Llewellyn Moxey *P:* Jack Greenwood *Sc:* George Baxt *Ph:* James Wilson *M:* Bernard Ebbinghouse *Ca:* Griffith Jones, John Stratton, Pauline Munro, Pauline Boty, Gerald Harper, Michael Balfour, Patricia Burke

710. **Straw Dogs** (1971) ABC Pictures Corp./Talent Associates Films/Amerbroco Films Col 118 min *D:* Sam Peckinpah *P:* Daniel Melnick *Sc:* David Zelag Goodman and Sam Peckinpah *Ph:* John Coquillon *M:* Jerry Fielding *Ca:* Dustin Hoffman, Susan George, Peter Vaughan, T.P. McKenna, Del Henney, Ken Hutchison, Colin Welland, Peter Arne, David Warner

711. **The Straw Man** (1953) Hedgerley Films B&W 74 min *D:* Donald Taylor *P:* Donald Taylor *Sc:* Donald Taylor *Ph:* Gerald Gibbs *M:* De Wolfe *Ca:* Dermot Walsh, Clifford Evans, Lana Morris, Amy Dalby, Josephine Stuart, Peter Williams, Philip Saville

712. **Street of Shadows** (1952) Merton Park (in association with Nassour Pictures [U.S.]) B&W 84 min *U.S. Title:* Shadow Man *D:* Richard Vernon *P:* William H. Williams *Sc:* Richard Vernon *Ph:* Phil Grindrod *M:* Eric Spear *Ca:* Cesar Romero, Kay Kendall, Edward Underdown, Victor Maddern, Simone Silva, Liam Gaffney, Bill Travers

713. **Strip Poker** (1968) Pete Walker Film Productions Col 81 min *U.S. Title:* The Big Switch *D:* Pete Walker *P:* Pete Walker *Sc:* Pete Walker *Ph:* Brian Tufano *M:* Harry South *Ca:* Sebastian Breaks, Virginia Wetherell, Erika Raffael, Jack Allen, Derek Aylward, Douglas Blackwell, Julie Shaw

714. **Strip Tease Murder** (1961) The Danzigers B&W 66 min *D:* Ernest Morris *P:* Edward J. Danziger and Harry Lee Danziger *Sc:* Paul Tabori *Ph:* James Wilson *M:* Bill Le Sage *Ca:* John Hewer, Ann Lynn, Jean Muir, Kenneth J. Warren, Carl Duering, Michael Peake, Vanda Hudson

715. **Strongroom** (1961) Theatrecraft Limited B&W 80 min *D:* Vernon Sewell *P:* Guido Coen *Sc:* Max Marquis and Richard Harris *Ph:* Basil Emmott *M:* Johnny Gregory *Ca:* Derren Nesbitt, Colin Gordon, Ann Lynn, Keith Faulkner, Morgan Sheppard, Hilda Fenemore, Diana Chesney

716. **A Study in Terror** (1965) Compton-Tekli Film Productions/Sir Nigel Films Col 95 min *D:* James Hill *P:* Henry E. Lester *Sc:* Donald Ford and Derek Ford *Ph:* Desmond Dickinson *M:* John Scott *Ca:* John Neville, Donald Houston, John Fraser, Anthony Quayle, Robert Morley, Barbara Windsor, Adrienne Corri, Frank Finlay, Cecil Parker, Peter Carsten

717. **Subterfuge** (1968) Intertel (VTR Services) Limited Col 91 min *D:* Peter Graham Scott *P:* Peter Snell *Sc:* David Whitaker *Ph:* Horst Wenzel *M:* Cyril Ornadel *Ca:* Gene Barry, Joan Collins, Richard Todd, Tom Adams, Suzanna Leigh, Michael Rennie, Marius Goring

Sudden Terror *see* **Eyewitness**

718. **Sumuru** (1967) Sumuru Films Col 95 min *U.S. Title:* The Million Eyes of Sumuru *D:* Lindsay Shonteff *P:* Harry Alan Towers *Sc:* Kevin Kavanagh *Ph:* John Von Kotze *M:* John Scott *Ca:* Shirley Eaton, George Nader, Frankie Avalon, Wilfrid Hyde White, Klaus Kinski, Salli Sachse, Maria Rohm

Superbitch *see* **Blue Movie Blackmail**

719. **The Surgeon's Knife** (1957) Gibraltar Productions B&W 84 min *D:* Gordon Parry *P:* Charles A. Leeds *Sc:* Robert Westerby *Ph:* Lionel Banes *M:* Bruce Montgomery *Ca:* Donald Houston, Adrienne Corri, Lyndon Brook, Jean Cadell, Sydney Tafler, Marie Ney, Ronald Adam

720. **Suspect** (1960) Charter Film Productions B&W 81 min *U.S. Title:* The Risk *D:* Roy Boulting and John Boulting *P:* Roy Boulting and John Boulting *Sc:* Nigel Balchin *Ph:* Max Greene *M:* Piano music by John Wilkes (playing his own arrangements of music by Chopin and Scriabin) *Ca:* Tony Britton, Virginia Maskell, Peter Cushing, Ian Bannen, Raymond Huntley, Thorley Walters, Donald Pleasence, Kenneth Griffith

721. **Suspended Alibi** (1956) A.C.T. Films B&W 65 min *D:* Alfred Shaughnessy *P:* Robert Dunbar *Sc:* Kenneth R. Hayles *Ph:* Peter Hennessy *Ca:* Patrick Holt, Honor Blackman, Valentine Dyall, Andrew Keir, Naomi Chance, Lloyd Lamble, Viola Lyel, Bryan Coleman

722. **Sweeney!** (1976) Euston Films Col 89 min *D:* David Wickes *P:* Ted Childs *Sc:* Ranald Graham *Ph:* Dusty Miller *M:* Denis King *Ca:* John Thaw, Dennis Waterman, Barry Foster, Ian Bannen, Colin Welland, Diane Keen, Michael Coles

723. **Sweeney 2** (1978) Euston Films Col 108 min *D:* Tom Clegg *P:* Ted Childs *Sc:* Troy Kennedy Martin *Ph:* Dusty Miller *M:* Tony Hatch *Ca:* John Thaw, Dennis Waterman, Ken Hutchison, Denholm Elliott, Nigel Hawthorne, Lewis Fiander, Anna Gael

724. **The Switch** (1963) Philip Ridgeway Productions B&W 69 min *D:* Peter Maxwell *P:* Philip Ridgeway *Sc:* Philip Ridgeway and Colin Fraser *Ph:* Stephen Dade *M:* Eric Spear *Ca:* Anthony Steel, Zena Marshall, Conrad Phillips, Dermot Walsh, Susan Shaw, Dawn Beret, Jerry Desmonde

725. **The Swordsman** (1974) Lindsay Shonteff Film Productions Col 91 min *ABT*: Zapper's Blade of Vengeance (video—see Appendix V) *U.S. Title*: Zapper's Blade of Vengeance (video—see Appendix V) *D:* Lindsay Shonteff *P:* Lindsay Shonteff and Elizabeth Gray *Sc:* Hugh Brody *Ph:* Les Young *M:* Colin Pearson and Roger Wootton *Ca:* Linda Marlowe, Alan Lake, Edina Ronay, Jason Kemp, Tony Then, Noel Johnson, Peter Halliday

726. **The Syndicate** (1967) Associated British Pathé Col 106 min *U.S. Title:* Kenya—Country of Treasure (TV only; later used for unofficial DVD release) *D:* Frederic Goode *P:* Harry Field *Sc:* Geoffrey Hays *Ph:* George Stevens *M:* Edwin Astley *Ca:* William Sylvester, June Ritchie, Robert Urquhart, Christian Doermer, John Bennett, John De Villiers, Bill Dixson

727. **The Tamarind Seed** (1974) Jewel Productions/Pimlico Films/Lorimar Productions/ITC Col 125 min *D:* Blake Edwards *P:* Ken Wales *Sc:* Blake Edwards *Ph:* Freddie Young *M:* John Barry *Ca:* Julie Andrews, Omar Sharif, Anthony Quayle, Dan O'Herlihy, Sylvia Syms, Oscar Homolka, Bryan Marshall

728. **Tangier Assignment** (1954) Rock Pictures/Hesperia Films B&W 64 min *D:* Ted Leversuch *P:* Cyril L. Parker *Sc:* Ted Leversuch *Ph:* Stanley Lipinski *M:* Ronnie O'Dell *Ca:* Bob Simmons, June Powell, Fernando Rey, Bill Brandon, Gustavo Re, Felix Sommerly-Gade, Angel Picazo

Target: Embassy *see* **Embassy**
Target for Terror *see* **Shadow of Fear**

729. **Taste of Excitement** (1968) Trio Films/Group W Films Col 99 min *U.S. Title:* Why Would Anyone Want to Kill a Nice Girl Like You? (also used for original British video release) *D:* Don Sharp *P:* George Willoughby *Sc:* Brian Carton and Don Sharp *Ph:* Paul Beeson *M:* Keith Mansfield *Ca:* Eva Renzi, David Buck, Peter Vaughan, Paul Hubschmid, Sophie Hardy, Kay Walsh, Francis Matthews

730. **Taste of Fear** (1961) Hammer Film Productions B&W 81 min *U.S. Title:* Scream of Fear *D:* Seth Holt *P:* Jimmy Sangster *Sc:* Jimmy Sangster *Ph:* Douglas Slocombe *M:* Clifton Parker *Ca:* Susan Strasberg, Ronald Lewis, Ann Todd, Christopher Lee, John Serret, Leonard Sachs, Anne Blake

Tears for Simon *see* **Lost**

731. **The Teckman Mystery** (1954) London Film Productions/Corona Films B&W 89 min *D:* Wendy Toye *P:* Josef Somlo *Sc:* Francis Durbridge and James Matthews *Ph:* Jack Hildyard *M:* Clifton Parker *Ca:* Margaret Leighton, John Justin, Roland Culver, Michael Medwin, Duncan Lamont, Raymond Huntley, George Coulouris

732. **Ten Little Indians** (1965) Tenlit Films B&W 91 min *D:* George Pollock *P:* Harry Alan Towers *Sc:* Harry Alan Towers (billed as Peter Welbeck) and Peter Yeldham *Ph:* Ernest Steward *M:* Malcolm Lockyer *Ca:* Hugh O'Brian, Shirley Eaton, Fabian, Leo Genn, Stanley Holloway, Wilfrid Hyde White, Daliah Lavi, Dennis Price, Marianne Hoppe, Mario Adorf

Ten Little Indians *see* **And Then There Were None**
Terror from Under the House *see* **Revenge**
The Terror of Sheba *see* **Persecution**

733. **The Terror of the Tongs** (1960) Hammer Film Productions/Merlin Film Co. (Hammer subsidiary) Col 79 min *D:* Anthony Bushell *P:* Kenneth Hyman *Sc:* Jimmy Sangster *Ph:* Arthur Grant *M:* James Bernard *Ca:* Christopher Lee, Yvonne Monlaur, Geoffrey Toone, Marne Maitland, Brian Worth, Roger Delgado, Richard Leech

Terror on a Train *see* **Time Bomb**
Terror on the Britannic *see* **Juggernaut**
Terror Ship *see* **Dangerous Voyage**
Terror Street *see* **36 Hours**
The Terrorists *see* **Ransom**

734. **That Woman Opposite** (1956) Monarch Productions B&W 83 min *U.S. Title:* City After Midnight *D:* Compton Bennett *P:* William Gell *Sc:* Compton Bennett *Ph:* Lionel Banes *M:* Stanley Black *Ca:* Phyllis Kirk, Dan O'Herlihy, Wilfrid Hyde White, Petula Clark, Jack Watling, William Franklyn, Margaret Withers

735. **Theatre of Blood** (1973) Cineman Films/Harbor Productions Col 102 min *D:* Douglas Hickox *P:* John Kohn and Stanley Mann *Sc:* Anthony Greville-Bell *Ph:* Wolfgang Suschitzky *M:* Michael J. Lewis *Ca:* Vincent Price, Diana Rigg, Ian Hendry, Harry Andrews, Coral Browne, Robert Coote, Jack Hawkins, Michael Hordern, Robert Morley, Dennis Price, Arthur Lowe, Diana Dors, Milo O'Shea, Eric Sykes

736. **Theatre of Death** (1966) Pennea Productions Col 91 min *U.S. Title:* Blood Fiend *D:* Samuel Gallu *P:* M. Smedley-Aston *Sc:* Ellis

Kadison and Roger Marshall *Ph:* Gilbert Taylor *M:* Elisabeth Lutyens *Ca:* Christopher Lee, Lelia Goldoni, Julian Glover, Jenny Till, Ivor Dean, Joseph Furst, Steve Plytas

737. **They Can't Hang Me** (1955) Vandyke Picture Corporation B&W 75 min *D:* Val Guest *P:* Roger Proudlock *Sc:* Val Guest and Val Valentine *Ph:* Stanley Pavey *Ca:* Terence Morgan, Yolande Donlan, Andre Morell, Ursula Howells, Anthony Oliver, Guido Lorraine, Basil Dignam

738. **They Never Learn** (1956) E.J. Fancey Productions B&W 47 min *D:* Denis Kavanagh and E.J. Fancey *P:* E.J. Fancey *Sc:* Denis Kavanagh and E.J. Fancey *Ph:* Hal Morey *M:* Jackie Brown *Ca:* John Blythe, Jackie Collins, Graham Stark, Adrienne Scott, Michael Partridge, Diana Chesney, John Crowhurst

739. **The Third Alibi** (1961) Eternal Films B&W 68 min *D:* Montgomery Tully *P:* Maurice J. Wilson *Sc:* Maurice J. Wilson and Montgomery Tully *Ph:* Walter J. Harvey *M:* Don Banks *Ca:* Laurence Payne, Patricia Dainton, Jane Griffiths, Edward Underdown, John Arnatt, Humphrey Lestocq, Lucy Griffiths

The Third Key *see* **The Long Arm**

740. **Third Party Risk** (1954) Hammer Film Productions (in association with Lippert Pictures [U.S.]) B&W 70 min *U.S. Titles:* The Deadly Game; Big Deadly Game (TV only) *D:* Daniel Birt *P:* Robert Dunbar *Sc:* Robert Dunbar and Daniel Birt *Ph:* Walter J. Harvey *M:* Michael Krein *Ca:* Lloyd Bridges, Finlay Currie, Maureen Swanson, Simone Silva, Ferdy Mayne, Peter Dyneley, Roger Delgado

741. **The Third Secret** (1964) Hubris Productions B&W 103 min *D:* Charles Crichton *P:* Robert L. Joseph *Sc:* Robert L. Joseph *Ph:* Douglas Slocombe *M:* Richard Arnell *Ca:* Stephen Boyd, Jack Hawkins, Richard Attenborough, Diane Cilento, Pamela Franklin, Paul Rogers, Alan Webb

742. **The Third Visitor** (1950) Elvey-Gartside Productions B&W 85 min *D:* Maurice Elvey *P:* Ernest Gartside *Sc:* Gerald Anstruther and David Evans *Ph:* Stephen Dade *M:* Leighton Lucas *Ca:* Sonia Dresdel, Guy Middleton, Hubert Gregg, Colin Gordon, Karel Stepanek, Eleanor Summerfield, John Slater

743. **13 East Street** (1951) Tempean Films B&W 72 min *D:* Robert S. Baker *P:* Robert S. Baker and Monty Berman *Sc:* John Gilling *Ph:* Monty Berman *M:* John Lanchbery *Ca:* Patrick Holt, Sandra Dorne, Sonia Holm, Robert Ayres, Dora Bryan, Michael Balfour, Michael Brennan

744. **The 39 Steps** (1958) The Rank Organisation Film Productions Col 93 min *D:* Ralph Thomas *P:* Betty E. Box *Sc:* Frank Harvey *Ph:* Ernest Steward *M:* Clifton Parker *Ca:* Kenneth More, Taina Elg, Brenda De Banzie, Barry Jones, Reginald Beckwith, Faith Brook, Michael Goodliffe, James Hayter

745. **The Thirty-Nine Steps** (1978) Rank Film Productions/Norfolk International Pictures Col 102 min *D:* Don Sharp *P:* Greg Smith *Sc:* Michael Robson *Ph:* John Coquillon *M:* Ed Welch *Ca:* Robert Powell, David Warner, Eric Porter, Karen Dotrice, John Mills, George Baker, Ronald Pickup

746. **36 Hours** (1953) Hammer Film Productions (in association with Lippert Pictures [U.S.]) B&W 80 min *U.S. Title:* Terror Street *D:* Montgomery Tully *P:* Anthony Hinds *Sc:* Steve Fisher *Ph:* Walter J. Harvey *M:* Ivor Slaney *Ca:* Dan Duryea, Elsy Albiin, John Chandos, Ann Gudrun, Eric Pohlmann, Kenneth Griffith, Jane Carr

This Is Callan *see* **Callan**

747. **Three Crooked Men** (1958) The Danzigers B&W 71 min *D:* Ernest Morris *P:* Edward J. Danziger and Harry Lee Danziger *Sc:* Brian Clemens and Eldon Howard *Ph:* James Wilson *M:* Albert Elms and Edwin Astley *Ca:* Gordon Jackson, Sarah Lawson, Eric Pohlmann, Philip Saville, Warren Mitchell, Michael Mellinger, Kenneth Edwards

748. **Three Steps in the Dark** (1953) Corsair Productions B&W 61 min *D:* Daniel Birt *P:* Harold Richmond *Sc:* Brock Williams *Ph:* Hone Glendinning *M:* Gilbert Vinter *Ca:* Greta Gynt, Hugh Sinclair, Nicholas Hannen, Sarah Lawson, John Van Eyssen, Elwyn Brook-Jones, Helene Cordet

749. **Three Steps to the Gallows** (1953) Tempean Films B&W 82 min *U.S. Title:* White Fire *D:* John Gilling *P:* Robert S. Baker and Monty Berman *Sc:* Paul Erickson and John Gilling *Ph:* Monty Berman *M:* Stanley Black *Ca:* Scott Brady, Mary Castle, John Blythe, Gabrielle Brune, Colin Tapley, Lloyd Lamble, Ferdy Mayne

Three Stops to Murder *see* **Blood Orange**

750. **Three Sundays to Live** (1957) The Danzigers B&W 71 min *D:* Ernest Morris *P:* Edward J. Danziger and Harry Lee Danziger *Sc:* Brian Clemens *Ph:* James Wilson *M:* Albert Elms and Edwin Astley *Ca:* Kieron Moore, Jane Griffiths, Basil Dignam, Sandra Dorne, Hal Ayer, John Stone, Ferdy Mayne

Thunder Over Tangier *see* **Man from Tangier**

751. **Thunderball** (1965) Eon Productions Col

130 min *D:* Terence Young *P:* Kevin McClory *Sc:* Richard Maibaum and John Hopkins *Ph:* Ted Moore *M:* John Barry *Ca:* Sean Connery, Claudine Auger, Adolfo Celi, Luciana Paluzzi, Rik Van Nutter, Martine Beswick, Guy Doleman, Paul Stassino, Roland Culver, Bernard Lee, Lois Maxwell

752. **Tiger Bay** (1959) Independent Artists B&W 105 min *U.S. Title:* Mystery at Tiger Bay (1961 theatrical reissue) *D:* J. Lee Thompson *P:* John Hawkesworth *Sc:* John Hawkesworth and Shelley Smith *Ph:* Eric Cross *M:* Laurie Johnson *Ca:* John Mills, Horst Buchholz, Hayley Mills, Yvonne Mitchell, Megs Jenkins, Anthony Dawson, Kenneth Griffith

753. **Tiger by the Tail** (1954) Tempean Films B&W 83 min *U.S. Title:* Cross-Up *D:* John Gilling *P:* Robert S. Baker and Monty Berman *Sc:* John Gilling and Willis Goldbeck *Ph:* Eric Cross *M:* Stanley Black *Ca:* Larry Parks, Constance Smith, Lisa Daniely, Cyril Chamberlain, Thora Hird, Alexander Gauge, Marie Bryant

754. **Tiger in the Smoke** (1956) The Rank Organisation Film Productions B&W 94 min *D:* Roy Ward Baker *P:* Leslie Parkyn *Sc:* Anthony Pelissier *Ph:* Geoffrey Unsworth *M:* Malcolm Arnold *Ca:* Donald Sinden, Muriel Pavlow, Tony Wright, Bernard Miles, Alec Clunes, Laurence Naismith, Christopher Rhodes

'Til Dawn Do We Part *see* **Straight on Till Morning**

755. **Time Bomb** (1952) MGM B&W 72 min *U.S. Title:* Terror on a Train *D:* Ted Tetzlaff *P:* Richard Goldstone *Sc:* Kem Bennett *Ph:* Freddie Young *M:* John Addison *Ca:* Glenn Ford, Anne Vernon, Maurice Denham, Harcourt Williams, Victor Maddern, Harold Warrender, John Horsley

756. **Time Is My Enemy** (1954) Vandyke Picture Corporation B&W 64 min *D:* Don Chaffey *P:* Roger Proudlock *Sc:* Allan MacKinnon *Ph:* Geoffrey Faithfull *Ca:* Dennis Price, Renee Asherson, Susan Shaw, Patrick Barr, Bonar Colleano, Duncan Lamont, Brenda Hogan

757. **Time Lock** (1957) Romulus Films/Beaconsfield Films B&W 73 min *D:* Gerald Thomas *P:* Peter Rogers *Sc:* Peter Rogers *Ph:* Peter Hennessy *M:* Stanley Black *Ca:* Robert Beatty, Lee Patterson, Betty McDowall, Vincent Winter, Sandra Francis, Alan Gifford, Robert Ayres

758. **A Time to Kill** (1953) Fortress Film Productions B&W 64 min *D:* Charles Saunders *P:* Fred A. Swann (supervisor) *Sc:* Doreen Montgomery *Ph:* James Wilson *M:* Frank Chacksfield *Ca:* Jack Watling, Rona Anderson, John Horsley, Russell Napier, Alastair Hunter, Mary Jones, Joan Hickson, John Le Mesurier

759. **Time to Remember** (1962) Merton Park B&W 59 min *D:* Charles Jarrott *P:* Jack Greenwood *Sc:* Arthur La Bern *Ph:* Bert Mason *M:* Bernard Ebbinghouse *Ca:* Yvonne Monlaur, Harry H. Corbett, Robert Rietty, Ernest Clark, David Lodge, Ray Barrett, Patricia Mort

760. **Time Without Pity** (1957) Harlequin Productions B&W 88 min *D:* Joseph Losey *P:* John Arnold and Anthony Simmons *Sc:* Ben Barzman *Ph:* Freddie Francis *M:* Tristram Cary *Ca:* Michael Redgrave, Ann Todd, Leo McKern, Peter Cushing, Alec McCowen, Renee Houston, Paul Daneman

761. **Timeslip** (1955) Merton Park/Anglo-Guild Productions (in association with Todon Productions [U.S.]) B&W 93 min *U.S. Title:* The Atomic Man *D:* Ken Hughes *P:* Alec C. Snowden *Sc:* Charles Eric Maine *Ph:* Alan T. Dinsdale *M:* Richard Taylor *Ca:* Gene Nelson, Faith Domergue, Joseph Tomelty, Donald Gray, Vic Perry, Peter Arne, Launce Maraschal, Martin Wyldeck

To Catch a Spy *see* **Catch Me a Spy**

762. **To Have and to Hold** (1963) Merton Park B&W 71 min *D:* Herbert Wise *P:* Jack Greenwood *Sc:* Jimmy Sangster (billed as John Sansom) *Ph:* James Wilson *M:* Bernard Ebbinghouse *Ca:* Ray Barrett, Katharine Blake, Nigel Stock, William Hartnell, Patricia Bredin, Noel Trevarthen, Richard Clarke

763. **Tomorrow at Ten** (1962) Blakeley's Films (Manchester)/Mancunian Film Corporation B&W 80 min *D:* Lance Comfort *P:* Tom Blakeley *Sc:* Peter Miller and James Kelly *Ph:* Basil Emmott *M:* Bernie Fenton *Ca:* John Gregson, Robert Shaw, Alec Clunes, Alan Wheatley, Kenneth Cope, Piers Bishop, Ernest Clark

764. **Tomorrow Never Comes** (1977) Neffbourne Ltd. (London)/Classic Film Industries (Montreal)/Montreal Trust Company Col 109 min *D:* Peter Collinson *P:* Michael Klinger and Julian Melzack *Sc:* David Pursall, Jack Seddon and Sydney Banks *Ph:* François Protat *M:* Roy Budd *Ca:* Oliver Reed, Susan George, Stephen McHattie, John Ireland, Donald Pleasence, Raymond Burr, Paul Koslo, John Osborne

765. **Too Hot to Handle** (1959) Wigmore Film Productions Col 100 min *U.S. Title:* Playgirl After Dark *D:* Terence Young *P:* C.P. Hamilton Marshall *Sc:* Herbert Kretzmer *Ph:* Otto Heller *M:* Eric Spear *Ca:* Jayne Mansfield, Leo Genn, Carl Boehm, Danik Patisson, Christopher Lee, Kai Fischer, Patrick Holt, Sheldon Lawrence, Martin Boddey, Barbara Windsor

766. **Touch of Death** (1962) Helion Film Productions B&W 58 min *D:* Lance Comfort *P:* Lewis Linzee *Sc:* Lyn Fairhurst *Ph:* Basil Emmott *M:* Johnny Douglas *Ca:* William Lucas, David Sumner, Ray Barrett, Jan Waters, Frank Coda, Geoffrey Denton, Roberta Tovey

767. **A Touch of the Other** (1970) Global Films/Queensway Productions Col 92 min *U.S. Titles:* The Happy Hookers (1973 release); The House of Hookers (1975 re-release) *D:* Arnold Louis Miller *P:* Arnold Louis Miller and Sheila Miller *Sc:* Frank Wyman *Ph:* Michael Boultbee *M:* John Hawkins *Ca:* Kenneth Cope, Shirley Anne Field, Hélène Françoise, Timothy Craven, Martin Wyldeck, Noel Davis, Paul Stassino

Tower of Terror *see* **Assault**

768. **Town on Trial** (1956) Marksman Films (in association with Todon Productions [U.S.]) B&W 96 min *D:* John Guillermin *P:* Maxwell Setton *Sc:* Robert Westerby and Ken Hughes *Ph:* Basil Emmott *M:* Tristram Cary *Ca:* John Mills, Charles Coburn, Barbara Bates, Derek Farr, Alec McCowen, Fay Compton, Geoffrey Keen, Maureen Connell

769. **Track the Man Down** (1954) Republic Productions (Great Britain) B&W 75 min *D:* R.G. Springsteen *P:* William N. Boyle *Sc:* Paul Erickson *Ph:* Basil Emmott *M:* Lambert Williamson *Ca:* Kent Taylor, Petula Clark, Renee Houston, Walter Rilla, George Rose, Mary Mackenzie, Kenneth Griffith, Ursula Howells

770. **The Traitor** (1957) Fantur Films B&W 88 min *U.S. Title:* The Accursed *D:* Michael McCarthy *P:* E.J. Fancey *Sc:* Michael McCarthy *Ph:* Bert Mason *M:* Jackie Brown *Ca:* Donald Wolfit, Robert Bray, Jane Griffiths, Anton Diffring, Oscar Quitak, John Van Eyssen, Rupert Davies, Christopher Lee

771. **The Traitors** (1962) Ello Productions B&W 69 min *D:* Robert Tronson *P:* Jim O'Connolly *Sc:* Jim O'Connolly *Ph:* Michael Reed *M:* Johnny Douglas *Ca:* Patrick Allen, Jacqueline Ellis, James Maxwell, Zena Walker, Ewan Roberts, Harold Goodwin, Reed De Rouen, Jack May

772. **Traitor's Gate** (1964) Summit Film Productions/Rialto Film Preben Philipsen B&W 87 min *D:* Freddie Francis *P:* Ted Lloyd *Sc:* Jimmy Sangster (billed as John Sansom) *Ph:* Denys Coop *M:* Peter Thomas *Ca:* Albert Lieven, Catherine Schell, Margot Trooger, Klaus Kinski, Gary Raymond, Eddi Arent, Tim Barrett, Edward Underdown

773. **Transatlantic** (1960) The Danzigers B&W 63 min *D:* Ernest Morris *P:* Edward J. Danziger and Harry Lee Danziger *Sc:* James Eastwood and Brian Clemens *Ph:* Walter J. Harvey *M:* Bill Le Sage *Ca:* Pete Murray, June Thorburn, Malou Pantera, Robert Ayres, Bill Nagy, Neil Hallett, Sheldon Lawrence

Trauma *see* **Exposé**

774. **Tread Softly** (1952) Albany Film Productions B&W 70 min *D:* David MacDonald *P:* Donald Ginsberg and Vivian A. Cox *Sc:* Gerald Verner *Ph:* Reginald Wyer *M:* Ivor Slaney *Ca:* Frances Day, Patricia Dainton, John Bentley, John Laurie, Olaf Olsen, Nora Nicholson, Robert Urquhart

775. **Tread Softly Stranger** (1958) Alderdale Films B&W 91 min *D:* Gordon Parry *P:* Denis O'Dell *Sc:* George Minter and Denis O'Dell *Ph:* Douglas Slocombe *M:* Tristram Cary *Ca:* Diana Dors, George Baker, Terence Morgan, Patrick Allen, Jane Griffiths, Joseph Tomelty, Chris Fay

776. **The Treasure of San Teresa** (1959) Beaconsfield Films B&W 81 min *U.S. Title:* Hot Money Girl *D:* Alvin Rakoff *P:* John Nasht and Patrick Filmer-Sankey *Sc:* Jack Andrews *Ph:* Wilkie Cooper *M:* Jeff Davis and Don Banks *Ca:* Eddie Constantine, Dawn Addams, Marius Goring, Christopher Lee, Nadine Tallier, Georgina Cookson, Walter Gotell

777. **Trent's Last Case** (1952) British Lion Production Assets B&W 90 min *D:* Herbert Wilcox *P:* Herbert Wilcox *Sc:* Pamela Bower *Ph:* Max Greene *M:* Anthony Collins *Ca:* Michael Wilding, Margaret Lockwood, Orson Welles, John McCallum, Miles Malleson, Hugh McDermott, Sam Kydd

778. **Trial by Combat** (1975) Combat Pictures Col 90 min *U.S. Titles:* Dirty Knights' Work; A Choice of Weapons (video—see Appendix V) *D:* Kevin Connor *P:* Fred Weintraub and Paul Heller *Sc:* Julian Bond, Steven Rossen and Mitchell Smith *Ph:* Alan Hume *M:* Frank Cordell *Ca:* John Mills, Donald Pleasence, Barbara Hershey, David Birney, Margaret Leighton, Peter Cushing, Brian Glover

779. **Triple Cross** (1966) Cineurop S.A.R.L. Col 126 min *D:* Terence Young *P:* Jacques-Paul Bertrand *Sc:* René Hardy *Ph:* Henri Alekan *M:* Georges Garvarentz *Ca:* Christopher Plummer, Romy Schneider, Yul Brynner, Trevor Howard, Gert Fröbe, Claudine Auger, Harry Meyen

Triple Deception *see* **House of Secrets**

780. **Troubled Waters** (1964) Parroch-McCallum Productions (in association with Lippert Incorporated [U.S.]) B&W 74 min *U.S. Title:* The Man with Two Faces *D:* Stanley Goulder *P:* Jack Parsons *Sc:* Al Rosen and Tudor Gates *Ph:* Arthur Lavis *M:* Elisabeth Lutyens *Ca:* Tab

Hunter, Zena Walker, Michael Goodliffe, Yvette Rees, Stanley Morgan, Andy Myers, Arnold Bell

781. **The Trunk** (1960) Donwin Productions B&W 72 min *D:* Donovan Winter *P:* Lawrence Huntington *Sc:* Donovan Winter *Ph:* Norman Warwick *M:* John Fox *Ca:* Phil Carey, Julia Arnall, Dermot Walsh, Vera Day, Peter Swanwick, John Atkinson, Betty Le Beau

782. **The Trygon Factor** (1966) Rialto Film Preben Philipsen Col 87 min *ABT:* Factor One (video—see Appendix V) *D:* Cyril Frankel *P:* Brian Taylor *Sc:* Derry Quinn and Stanley Munro *Ph:* Harry Waxman *M:* Peter Thomas *Ca:* Stewart Granger, Susan Hampshire, Robert Morley, Cathleen Nesbitt, Brigitte Horney, Sophie Hardy, James Robertson Justice

783. **24 Hours to Kill** (1965) Grixflag Films Col 94 min *D:* Peter Bezencenet *P:* Harry Alan Towers *Sc:* Peter Yeldham *Ph:* Ernest Steward *M:* Wilfred Josephs *Ca:* Mickey Rooney, Lex Barker, Walter Slezak, Michael Medwin, Helga Somerfeld, France Anglade, Wolfgang Lukschy

784. **The £20,000 Kiss** (1962) Merton Park B&W 57 min *D:* John Llewellyn Moxey *P:* Jack Greenwood *Sc:* Philip Mackie *Ph:* James Wilson *M:* Bernard Ebbinghouse *Ca:* Dawn Addams, Michael Goodliffe, Richard Thorp, Anthony Newlands, Alfred Burke, Mia Karam, Ellen McIntosh

Twinsanity *see* **Goodbye Gemini**

Twist of Fate *see* **Beautiful Stranger**

785. **A Twist of Sand** (1968) Christina Films Col 91 min *D:* Don Chaffey *P:* Fred Engel *Sc:* Marvin H. Albert *Ph:* John Wilcox *M:* Tristram Cary *Ca:* Richard Johnson, Honor Blackman, Jeremy Kemp, Peter Vaughan, Roy Dotrice, Guy Doleman, Clifford Evans

786. **Twisted Nerve** (1968) Charter Film Productions Col 118 min *D:* Roy Boulting *P:* George W. George and Frank Granat *Sc:* Leo Marks and Roy Boulting *Ph:* Harry Waxman *M:* Bernard Herrmann *Ca:* Hayley Mills, Hywel Bennett, Billie Whitelaw, Phyllis Calvert, Barry Foster, Frank Finlay, Thorley Walters

787. **The Two-Headed Spy** (1958) Sabre Films B&W 93 min *D:* Andre De Toth *P:* Bill Kirby *Sc:* Michael Wilson (billed as James O'Donnell) and Alfred Levitt *Ph:* Edward Scaife *M:* Gerard Schurmann *Ca:* Jack Hawkins, Gia Scala, Erik Schumann, Alexander Knox, Felix Aylmer, Laurence Naismith, Edward Underdown

788. **Two-Letter Alibi** (1961) Playpont Films B&W 60 min *U.S. Title:* Death and the Sky Above (TV only) *D:* Robert Lynn *P:* M. Smedley-Aston *Sc:* Roger Marshall *Ph:* Ken Hodges *M:* Wilfred Josephs *Ca:* Peter Williams, Petra Davies, Ursula Howells, Ronald Adam, Bernard Archard, Peter Howell, Stratford Johns

789. **Two Wives at One Wedding** (1961) The Danzigers B&W 66 min *D:* Montgomery Tully *P:* Edward J. Danziger and Harry Lee Danziger *Sc:* Brian Clemens and Eldon Howard *Ph:* Bert Mason *M:* Bill Le Sage *Ca:* Gordon Jackson, Christina Gregg, Lisa Daniely, André Maranne, Viola Keats, Humphrey Lestocq, Douglas Ives

Undercover Agent *see* **Counterspy**

790. **Undercover Girl** (1957) Bill and Michael Luckwell Ltd. B&W 68 min *U.S. Title:* Assignment Redhead *D:* Francis Searle *P:* Kay Luckwell *Sc:* Bernard Lewis and Bill Luckwell *Ph:* Geoffrey Faithfull *M:* Bill Trytel *Ca:* Paul Carpenter, Kay Callard, Bruce Seton, Monica Grey, Jackie Collins, Maya Koumani, Kim Parker

Underworld Informers *see* **The Informers**

The Unholy Four *see* **The Stranger Came Home**

791. **Unman, Wittering and Zigo** (1971) Mediarts (in association with David Hemmings) Col 102 min *D:* John MacKenzie *P:* Gareth Wigan *Sc:* Simon Raven *Ph:* Geoffrey Unsworth *M:* Michael J. Lewis *Ca:* David Hemmings, Douglas Wilmer, Anthony Haygarth, Carolyn Seymour, Hamilton Dyce, Barbara Lott, Donald Gee

792. **The Unstoppable Man** (1960) Argo Film Productions B&W 68 min *D:* Terry Bishop *P:* John Pellatt *Sc:* Alun Falconer and Manning O'Brine *Ph:* Arthur Grant *M:* Bill McGuffie *Ca:* Cameron Mitchell, Marius Goring, Harry H. Corbett, Lois Maxwell, Denis Gilmore, Humphrey Lestocq, Ann Sears

793. **Urge to Kill** (1960) Merton Park B&W 58 min *D:* Vernon Sewell *P:* Jack Greenwood *Sc:* James Eastwood *Ph:* John Wiles *Ca:* Patrick Barr, Howard Pays, Ruth Dunning, Terence Knapp, Anna Turner, Christopher Trace, Yvonne Buckingham, Wilfrid Brambell

794. **Valley of Eagles** (1951) Independent Sovereign Films B&W 86 min *U.S. Title:* Valley of the Eagles *D:* Terence Young *P:* Nat Bronsten *Sc:* Terence Young *Ph:* Harry Waxman *M:* Nino Rota *Ca:* Jack Warner, Nadia Gray, John McCallum, Anthony Dawson, Mary Laura Wood, Alfred Maurstad, Norman MacOwan

Valley of the Eagles *see* **Valley of Eagles**

795. **Venetian Bird** (1952) British Film Makers B&W 95 min *U.S. Title:* The Assassin *D:* Ralph Thomas *P:* Betty E. Box *Sc:* Victor Canning *Ph:* Ernest Steward *M:* Nino Rota *Ca:* Richard Todd, Eva Bartok, John Gregson, George Coulouris, Margot Grahame, John Bailey, Walter Rilla

796. **Vengeance** (1962) CCC Film/Raymond

Stross Productions B&W 83 min *U.S. Title:* The Brain *D:* Freddie Francis *P:* Raymond Stross *Sc:* Robert Banks Stewart and Philip Mackie *Ph:* Bob Huke *M:* Kenneth V. Jones *Ca:* Anne Heywood, Peter Van Eyck, Cecil Parker, Bernard Lee, Maxine Audley, Ellen Schwiers, Jeremy Spenser

797. **The Vengeance of Fu Manchu** (1967) Babasdave Films Col 89 min *D:* Jeremy Summers *P:* Harry Alan Towers *Sc:* Harry Alan Towers (billed as Peter Welbeck) *Ph:* John Von Kotze (additional photography by Stephen Dade) *M:* Malcolm Lockyer *Ca:* Christopher Lee, Tony Ferrer, Tsai Chin, Douglas Wilmer, Wolfgang Kieling, Suzanne Roquette, Peter Carsten, Howard Marion Crawford

798. **The Verdict** (1964) Merton Park B&W 56 min *D:* David Eady *P:* Jack Greenwood *Sc:* Arthur La Bern *Ph:* James Wilson *M:* Bernard Ebbinghouse *Ca:* Cec Linder, Zena Marshall, Nigel Davenport, Paul Stassino, Derek Francis, John Bryans, Derek Partridge

799. **The Very Edge** (1962) Raymond Stross Productions B&W 90 min *D:* Cyril Frankel *P:* Raymond Stross *Sc:* Elizabeth Jane Howard *Ph:* Bob Huke *M:* David Lee *Ca:* Richard Todd, Anne Heywood, Jack Hedley, Nicole Maurey, Jeremy Brett, Barbara Mullen, Maurice Denham

800. **The Vicious Circle** (1957) Romulus Films/Beaconsfield Films B&W 84 min *U.S. Title:* The Circle *D:* Gerald Thomas *P:* Peter Rogers *Sc:* Francis Durbridge *Ph:* Otto Heller *M:* Stanley Black *Ca:* John Mills, Derek Farr, Noelle Middleton, Wilfrid Hyde White, Roland Culver, Mervyn Johns, Lionel Jeffries

801. **Victim** (1961) A.F.M. (Allied Film Makers) Productions/Parkway Films B&W 100 min *D:* Basil Dearden *P:* Michael Relph *Sc:* Janet Green and John McCormick *Ph:* Otto Heller *M:* Philip Green *Ca:* Dirk Bogarde, Sylvia Syms, Dennis Price, Nigel Stock, Peter McEnery, Donald Churchill, Derren Nesbitt

802. **Victim Five** (1964) Towers of London (Films) Col 88 min *U.S. Title:* Code 7 Victim 5! *D:* Robert Lynn *P:* Harry Alan Towers *Sc:* Peter Yeldham *Ph:* Nicolas Roeg *M:* Johnny Douglas *Ca:* Lex Barker, Ronald Fraser, Ann Smyrner, Veronique Vendell, Walter Rilla, Percy Sieff, Dietmar Schönherr

803. **Villain** (1971) Atlantic United Productions Col 98 min *D:* Michael Tuchner *P:* Alan Ladd, Jr., and Jay Kanter *Sc:* Dick Clement and Ian La Frenais *Ph:* Christopher Challis *M:* Jonathan Hodge *Ca:* Richard Burton, Ian McShane, Nigel Davenport, Donald Sinden, T.P. McKenna, Joss Ackland, Fiona Lewis, Cathleen Nesbitt

804. **The Violent Enemy** (1969) Trio Films/Group W Films Col 94 min *D:* Don Sharp *P:* Wilfrid Eades *Sc:* Edmund Ward *Ph:* Alan Hume *M:* John Scott *Ca:* Tom Bell, Susan Hampshire, Ed Begley, Noel Purcell, Jon Laurimore, Michael Standing, Philip O'Flynn

805. **Violent Moment** (1958) Independent Artists B&W 61 min *D:* Sidney Hayers *P:* Bernard Coote *Sc:* Peter Barnes *Ph:* Phil Grindrod *M:* Stanley Black *Ca:* Lyndon Brook, Jane Hylton, Jill Browne, John Paul, Rupert Davies, Moira Redmond, Bruce Seton

806. **Violent Playground** (1958) The Rank Organisation Film Productions B&W 108 min *D:* Basil Dearden *P:* Michael Relph *Sc:* James Kennaway *Ph:* Reginald Wyer *M:* Philip Green *Ca:* Stanley Baker, Peter Cushing, Anne Heywood, David McCallum, John Slater, Clifford Evans, George A. Cooper

Violent Stranger *see* **Man in the Shadow**

807. **Visa to Canton** (1960) Hammer Film Productions/Swallow Productions (Hammer subsidiary) Col 75 min *U.S. Title:* Passport to China *D:* Michael Carreras *P:* Michael Carreras *Sc:* Gordon Wellesley *Ph:* Arthur Grant *M:* Edwin Astley *Ca:* Richard Basehart, Lisa Gastoni, Athene Seyler, Eric Pohlmann, Alan Gifford, Bernard Cribbins, Marne Maitland

808. **The Voice of Merrill** (1952) Tempean Films B&W 84 min *U.S. Title:* Murder Will Out *D:* John Gilling *P:* Robert S. Baker and Monty Berman *Sc:* John Gilling *Ph:* Monty Berman *M:* Frank Cordell *Ca:* Valerie Hobson, Edward Underdown, James Robertson Justice, Henry Kendall, Garry Marsh, Daniel Wherry, Sam Kydd

809. **Walk a Tightrope** (1963) Parroch-McCallum Productions (in association with Associated Producers, Inc. [U.S.]) B&W 78 min *D:* Frank Nesbitt *P:* Jack Parsons *Sc:* Mann Rubin *Ph:* Basil Emmott *M:* Buxton Orr *Ca:* Dan Duryea, Patricia Owens, Richard Leech, Neil McCallum, David Bauer, Terence Cooper, Shirley Cameron

810. **The Walking Stick** (1970) Winkast Film Productions Col 101 min *D:* Eric Till *P:* Alan Ladd, Jr. *Sc:* George Bluestone *Ph:* Arthur Ibbetson *M:* Stanley Myers *Ca:* David Hemmings, Samantha Eggar, Emlyn Williams, Phyllis Calvert, Ferdy Mayne, Dudley Sutton, Francesca Annis

The Way Out *see* **Dial 999**

811. **We Shall See** (1964) Merton Park B&W 61 min *D:* Quentin Lawrence *P:* Jack Greenwood *Sc:* Donal Giltinan *Ph:* James Wilson *M:* Bernard Ebbinghouse *Ca:* Maurice Kaufmann,

Faith Brook, Alec Mango, Alex McIntosh, Hugh Paddick, Talitha Pol, Bridget Armstrong

812. **The Weapon** (1956) Periclean Productions B&W 81 min *D:* Val Guest *P:* Hal E. Chester and Frank Bevis *Sc:* Fred Freiberger *Ph:* Reginald Wyer *M:* James Stevens *Ca:* Steve Cochran, Lizabeth Scott, Herbert Marshall, Nicole Maurey, Jon Whiteley, George Cole, Laurence Naismith

Web of Evidence *see* **Beyond This Place**

813. **Web of Suspicion** (1959) The Danzigers B&W 70 min *D:* Max Varnel *P:* Edward J. Danziger and Harry Lee Danziger *Sc:* Brian Clemens and Eldon Howard *Ph:* James Wilson *Ca:* Philip Friend, Susan Beaumont, John Martin, Peter Sinclair, Robert Raglan, Ian Fleming, Peter Elliott

814. **West of Suez** (1956) Winwell Productions (in association with Amalgamated Productions [U.S.]) B&W 73 min *U.S. Title:* The Fighting Wildcats *D:* Arthur Crabtree *P:* Kay Luckwell and Derek Winn *Sc:* Norman Hudis *Ph:* Walter J. Harvey *M:* Wilfred Burns *Ca:* Keefe Brasselle, Kay Callard, Karel Stepanek, Ursula Howells, Bruce Seton, Richard Shaw, Harry Fowler

815. **What a Carve-Up** (1961) New World Pictures B&W 88 min *U.S. Title:* No Place Like Homicide *D:* Pat Jackson *P:* Robert S. Baker and Monty Berman *Sc:* Ray Cooney and Tony Hilton *Ph:* Monty Berman *M:* Muir Mathieson *Ca:* Sidney James, Kenneth Connor, Shirley Eaton, Dennis Price, Donald Pleasence, Michael Gough, Esma Cannon

816. **What Became of Jack and Jill?** (1971) Amicus Productions/Palomar Pictures International Col 90 min *D:* Bill Bain *P:* Max J. Rosenberg and Milton Subotsky *Sc:* Roger Marshall *Ph:* Gerry Turpin *M:* Carl Davis *Ca:* Vanessa Howard, Mona Washbourne, Paul Nicholas, George A. Cooper, Peter Copley, Peter Jeffrey, Patricia Fuller

What the Peeper Saw *see* **Night Hair Child**

817. **When Eight Bells Toll** (1970) Winkast Film Productions Col 94 min *D:* Etienne Perier *P:* Elliott Kastner *Sc:* Alistair MacLean *Ph:* Arthur Ibbetson *M:* Wally Stott *Ca:* Anthony Hopkins, Nathalie Delon, Robert Morley, Jack Hawkins, Corin Redgrave, Derek Bond, Ferdy Mayne, Peter Arne

818. **Where Eagles Dare** (1968) Winkast Film Productions Col 155 min *D:* Brian G. Hutton *P:* Elliott Kastner *Sc:* Alistair MacLean *Ph:* Arthur Ibbetson *M:* Ron Goodwin *Ca:* Richard Burton, Clint Eastwood, Mary Ure, Patrick Wymark, Michael Hordern, Robert Beatty, Derren Nesbitt, Anton Diffring, Ferdy Mayne, Donald Houston, Peter Barkworth

819. **Where the Bullets Fly** (1966) Puck Films Col 90 min *D:* John Gilling *P:* James Ward *Sc:* Michael Pittock *Ph:* David Holmes *M:* Kenny Graham *Ca:* Tom Adams, Dawn Addams, Tim Barrett, Michael Ripper, Ronald Leigh-Hunt, John Arnatt, Marcus Hammond

820. **Where the Spies Are** (1965) MGM Col 113 min *D:* Val Guest *P:* Val Guest and Steven Pallos *Sc:* Wolf Mankowitz and Val Guest *Ph:* Arthur Grant *M:* Mario Nascimbene *Ca:* David Niven, Françoise Dorléac, John Le Mesurier, Cyril Cusack, Eric Pohlmann, Richard Marner, Paul Stassino

821. **Whirlpool** (1959) The Rank Organisation Film Productions Col 95 min *D:* Lewis Allen *P:* George Pitcher *Sc:* Lawrence P. Bachmann *Ph:* Geoffrey Unsworth *M:* Ron Goodwin *Ca:* Juliette Greco, O.W. Fischer, Muriel Pavlow, William Sylvester, Marius Goring, Peter Illing, Geoffrey Bayldon

822. **Whispering Smith Hits London** (1951) Hammer Film Productions (in association with Royal Productions [U.S.]) B&W 82 min *U.S. Title:* Whispering Smith vs. Scotland Yard *D:* Francis Searle *P:* Anthony Hinds and Julian Lesser *Sc:* John Gilling *Ph:* Walter J. Harvey *M:* Frank Spencer *Ca:* Richard Carlson, Greta Gynt, Herbert Lom, Rona Anderson, Alan Wheatley, Reginald Beckwith, Dora Bryan

Whispering Smith vs. Scotland Yard *see* **Whispering Smith Hits London**

White Fire *see* **Three Steps to the Gallows**

823. **The White Trap** (1959) Independent Artists B&W 58 min *D:* Sidney Hayers *P:* Julian Wintle and Leslie Parkyn *Sc:* Peter Barnes *Ph:* Eric Cross *M:* Franz Reizenstein *Ca:* Lee Patterson, Conrad Phillips, Ewen Solon, Michael Goodliffe, Jack Allen, Yvette Wyatt, Felicity Young

824. **Who Killed the Cat?** (1966) Eternal Films B&W 76 min *D:* Montgomery Tully *P:* Maurice J. Wilson *Sc:* Maurice J. Wilson and Montgomery Tully *Ph:* Geoffrey Faithfull *M:* Carlo Martelli *Ca:* Vanda Godsell, Mervyn Johns, Natasha Pyne, Mary Merrall, Ellen Pollock, Amy Dalby, Conrad Phillips

Who Slew Auntie Roo? *see* **Whoever Slew Auntie Roo?**

825. **Who Was Maddox?** (1964) Merton Park B&W 62 min *D:* Geoffrey Nethercott *P:* Jack Greenwood *Sc:* Roger Marshall *Ph:* James Wilson *M:* Bernard Ebbinghouse *Ca:* Bernard Lee, Jack Watling, Suzanne Lloyd, Finlay Currie, Richard Gale, James Bree, Dora Reisser

826. **Whoever Slew Auntie Roo?** (1971)

American International Productions (England)/The Hemdale Group Col 91 min *U.S. Title:* Who Slew Auntie Roo? *D:* Curtis Harrington *P:* Samuel Z. Arkoff and James H. Nicholson *Sc:* Robert Blees and Jimmy Sangster *Ph:* Desmond Dickinson *M:* Kenneth V. Jones *Ca:* Shelley Winters, Mark Lester, Chloe Franks, Ralph Richardson, Lionel Jeffries, Hugh Griffith, Rosalie Crutchley

827. **The Whole Truth** (1958) Romulus Films/Valiant Films B&W 85 min *D:* John Guillermin *P:* Jack Clayton *Sc:* Jonathan Latimer *Ph:* Wilkie Cooper *M:* Mischa Spoliansky *Ca:* Stewart Granger, Donna Reed, George Sanders, Gianna Maria Canale, Michael Shillo, Peter Dyneley, Hy Hazell

Why Would Anyone Want to Kill a Nice Girl Like You? *see* **Taste of Excitement**

Wicked Wife *see* **Grand National Night**

828. **The Wicker Man** (1973) British Lion Film Productions Col 87 min *D:* Robin Hardy *P:* Peter Snell *Sc:* Anthony Shaffer *Ph:* Harry Waxman *M:* Paul Giovanni *Ca:* Edward Woodward, Britt Ekland, Diane Cilento, Ingrid Pitt, Christopher Lee, Roy Boyd, Russell Waters

829. **Wide Boy** (1952) Merton Park B&W 67 min *D:* Ken Hughes *P:* William H. Williams *Sc:* Rex Rienits *Ph:* Josef Ambor *M:* Eric Spear *Ca:* Susan Shaw, Sydney Tafler, Ronald Howard, Melissa Stribling, Colin Tapley, Laidman Browne, Madeline Burgess

830. **The Wilby Conspiracy** (1974) Optimus Productions/Baum-Dantine Productions Col 105 min *D:* Ralph Nelson *P:* Martin Baum *Sc:* Rod Amateau and Harold Nebenzal *Ph:* John Coquillon *M:* Stanley Myers *Ca:* Sidney Poitier, Michael Caine, Nicol Williamson, Prunella Gee, Persis Khambatta, Saeed Jaffrey, Rutger Hauer

831. **The Wild Geese** (1978) Richmond Film Productions (West)/Varius Entertainment Trading Co. Col 134 min *D:* Andrew V. McLaglen *P:* Euan Lloyd *Sc:* Reginald Rose *Ph:* Jack Hildyard *M:* Roy Budd *Ca:* Richard Burton, Roger Moore, Stewart Granger, Richard Harris, Hardy Kruger, Jeff Corey, Barry Foster, Winston Ntshona, Jack Watson, Frank Finlay, Kenneth Griffith, Ronald Fraser, Patrick Allen, Percy Herbert

832. **Wings of Danger** (1952) Hammer Film Productions (in association with Lippert Pictures [U.S.]) B&W 73 min *D:* Terence Fisher *P:* Anthony Hinds *Sc:* John Gilling *Ph:* Walter J. Harvey *M:* Malcolm Arnold *Ca:* Zachary Scott, Robert Beatty, Naomi Chance, Kay Kendall, Colin Tapley, Arthur Lane, Diane Cilento

833. **The Witness** (1959) Merton Park B&W 58 min *D:* Geoffrey Muller *P:* Jack Greenwood *Sc:* Julian Bond *Ph:* John Wiles *M:* Ron Goodwin *Ca:* Dermot Walsh, Greta Gynt, Russell Napier, Martin Stephens, John Chandos, Derek Sydney, Hedger Wallace

834. **Witness in the Dark** (1959) Ethiro Productions B&W 62 min *D:* Wolf Rilla *P:* Norman Williams *Sc:* Leigh Vance and John Lemont *Ph:* Brendan J. Stafford *M:* Philip Green *Ca:* Patricia Dainton, Conrad Phillips, Madge Ryan, Nigel Green, Enid Lorimer, Richard O'Sullivan, Stuart Saunders

835. **The Woman in Question** (1950) Javelin Films/Vic Films B&W 88 min *U.S. Title:* Five Angels on Murder *D:* Anthony Asquith *P:* Teddy Baird *Sc:* John Cresswell *Ph:* Desmond Dickinson *M:* John Wooldridge *Ca:* Jean Kent, Dirk Bogarde, John McCallum, Susan Shaw, Hermione Baddeley, Charles Victor, Duncan MacRae

836. **A Woman of Mystery** (1957) The Danzigers B&W 71 min *D:* Ernest Morris *P:* Edward J. Danziger and Harry Lee Danziger *Sc:* Brian Clemens and Eldon Howard *Ph:* James Wilson *M:* Edwin Astley and Albert Elms *Ca:* Dermot Walsh, Hazel Court, Jennifer Jayne, Ferdy Mayne, Ernest Clark, Martin Benson, Diana Chesney

837. **Woman of Straw** (1964) Novus Films Col 117 min *D:* Basil Dearden *P:* Michael Relph *Sc:* Robert Muller and Stanley Mann *Ph:* Otto Heller *M:* Muir Mathieson (conducting the music of Beethoven, Berlioz, Mozart and Rimsky-Korsakov) and Norman Percival *Ca:* Gina Lollobrigida, Sean Connery, Ralph Richardson, Alexander Knox, Johnny Sekka, Laurence Hardy, Peter Madden

838. **A Woman Possessed** (1958) The Danzigers B&W 68 min *D:* Max Varnel *P:* Edward J. Danziger and Harry Lee Danziger *Sc:* Brian Clemens and Eldon Howard *Ph:* James Wilson *M:* Albert Elms *Ca:* Margaretta Scott, Francis Matthews, Kay Callard, Alison Leggatt, Ian Fleming, Jan Holden, Tony Thawnton, Denis Shaw, Totti Truman Taylor

The Woman Who Wouldn't Die *see* **Catacombs**

839. **A Woman's Temptation** (1958) The Danzigers B&W 60 min *D:* Godfrey Grayson *P:* Edward J. Danziger and Harry Lee Danziger *Sc:* Brian Clemens and Eldon Howard *Ph:* James Wilson *Ca:* Patricia Driscoll, Robert Ayres, John Pike, Neil Hallett, John Longden, Kenneth J. Warren, Robert Raglan

840. **Wrong Number** (1959) Merton Park B&W 60 min *D:* Vernon Sewell *P:* Jack Greenwood *Sc:* James Eastwood *Ph:* Josef Ambor *Ca:*

Peter Reynolds, Lisa Gastoni, Peter Elliott, Olive Sloane, Paul Whitsun-Jones, Barry Keegan, John Horsley

841. **The Yellow Balloon** (1952) Marble Arch Productions B&W 80 min *D:* J. Lee Thompson *P:* Victor Skutezky *Sc:* Anne Burnaby and J. Lee Thompson *Ph:* Gilbert Taylor *M:* Philip Green *Ca:* William Sylvester, Kenneth More, Kathleen Ryan, Andrew Ray, Bernard Lee, Stephen Fenemore, Marjorie Rhodes

842. **Yellow Dog** (1973) Akari Productions Col 101 min *D:* Terence Donovan *P:* Terence Donovan *Sc:* Shinobu Hashimoto *Ph:* David Watkin *M:* Ron Grainer *Ca:* Jiro Tamiya, Robert Hardy, Carolyn Seymour, Joseph O'Conor, Hilary Tindall, Jonathan Newth, Keith Drinkel

843. **You Can't Escape** (1955) Forth Films B&W 77 min *D:* Wilfrid Eades *P:* Robert Hall *Sc:* Doreen Montgomery and Robert Hall *Ph:* Norman Warwick *M:* Charles Williams *Ca:* Noelle Middleton, Guy Rolfe, Robert Urquhart, Peter Reynolds, Elizabeth Kentish, Barbara Cavan, Llewellyn Rees

844. **You Only Live Twice** (1967) Eon Productions Col 116 min *D:* Lewis Gilbert *P:* Harry Saltzman and Albert R. Broccoli *Sc:* Roald Dahl *Ph:* Freddie Young *M:* John Barry *Ca:* Sean Connery, Akiko Wakabayashi, Tetsuro Tamba, Donald Pleasence, Mie Hama, Karin Dor, Charles Gray, Alexander Knox, Robert Hutton, Diane Cilento, Bernard Lee, Lois Maxwell

845. **You Pay Your Money** (1956) Butcher's Film Productions B&W 68 min *D:* Maclean Rogers *P:* W.G. Chalmers *Sc:* Maclean Rogers *Ph:* Walter J. Harvey *M:* Wilfred Burns *Ca:* Hugh McDermott, Jane Hylton, Honor Blackman, Hugh Moxey, Ivan Samson, Ferdy Mayne, Shirley Deane

Zapper's Blade of Vengeance *see* **The Swordsman**

Appendix I: British Thrillers from Selected Production Companies

This appendix lists some notable production companies along with all their pertaining films from this book.

A.C.T. Films
(Association of Cinema Technicians)

Night Was Our Friend (1951)
Circumstantial Evidence (1952)
House of Blackmail (1953)
The Blue Parrot (1953)
Dangerous Cargo (1953)
Burnt Evidence (1954)
Final Appointment (1954)
Stolen Assignment (1955)
The Last Man to Hang (1956)
Suspended Alibi (1956)
The Diplomatic Corpse (1958)
The Man Upstairs (1958)
Dead Lucky (1960)
Dilemma (1962)

Baker and Berman
(Robert S. Baker and Monty Berman)

Films are listed under producers Baker and Berman's various companies. Their main enterprise was Tempean Films, but they also controlled Cipa Productions, Mid-Century Film Productions and New World Pictures. For a couple of years during the early 1950s, they also ran Kenilworth Film Productions, which they only used in a co-production capacity for the first five of their Mid-Century films.

Cipa Productions

Barbados Quest (1955)
Breakaway (1955)
The High Terrace (1956)

Mid-Century Film Productions

Deadly Nightshade (1952)
Black Orchid (1952)
Double Exposure (1954)
The Embezzler (1954)
Delayed Action (1954)
Passport to Treason (1956)
Bond of Fear (1956)
Jack the Ripper (1958)

New World Pictures

What a Carve-Up (1961)

Tempean Films

No Trace (1950)
Blackout (1950)
The Frightened Man (1951)
13 East Street (1951)
The Lost Hours (1952)
The Voice of Merrill (1952)
The Steel Key (1952)
Recoil (1953)
Escape by Night (1953)
Three Steps to the Gallows (1953)
The Gilded Cage (1954)
Tiger by the Tail (1954)
Impulse (1954)
Hour of Decision (1956)
A Stranger in Town (1957)
Stormy Crossing (1957)

Butcher's Film Productions
(Production arm of Butcher's Film Distributors)

Assignment Redhead (1956)
You Pay Your Money (1956)
Man from Tangier (1957)
Mark of the Phoenix (1957)
Blind Spot (1958)

The Gentle Trap (1960)
The Breaking Point (1960)
Pit of Darkness (1961)
Emergency (1962)
Gaolbreak (1962)
Serena (1962)
Danger by My Side (1962)
Night of the Prowler (1962)
Impact (1963)
Echo of Diana (1963)
Shadow of Fear (1963)
The Hi-Jackers (1963)
The Sicilians (1964)
Smokescreen (1964)

The Danzigers
(Edward J. Danziger and Harry Lee Danziger)

American-born sibling producers who ran Danziger Photoplays and Danziger Productions.

Alias John Preston (1955)
Operation Murder (1956)
Three Sundays to Live (1957)
The Depraved (1957)
The Betrayal (1957)
A Woman of Mystery (1957)
On the Run (1957)
Three Crooked Men (1958)
Links of Justice (1958)
A Woman Possessed (1958)
Moment of Indiscretion (1958)
The Great Van Robbery (1958)
Innocent Meeting (1958)
High Jump (1958)
A Woman's Temptation (1958)
The Child and the Killer (1959)
Web of Suspicion (1959)
No Safety Ahead (1959)
Man Accused (1959)
Sentenced for Life (1959)
Night Train for Inverness (1959)
Date at Midnight (1959)
Highway to Battle (1960)
Compelled (1960)
Feet of Clay (1960)
The Spider's Web (1960)
Escort for Hire (1960)
Transatlantic (1960)
Strip Tease Murder (1961)
Two Wives at One Wedding (1961)
Return of a Stranger (1961)
Gang War (1961)
The Pursuers (1962)
The Lamp in Assassin Mews (1962)

Eternal Films

The Price of Silence (1959)
Jackpot (1960)
The Third Alibi (1961)
Out of the Fog (1962)
Master Spy (1962)
Clash by Night (1963)
Who Killed the Cat? (1966)

Hammer Film Productions (aka Hammer Films)

Someone at the Door (1950)
The Lady Craved Excitement (1950)
Black Widow (1950)
The Rossiter Case (1950)
The Dark Light (1950)
Cloudburst (1951)
A Case for P.C. 49 (1951)
Death of an Angel (1951)
Whispering Smith Hits London (1951)
Never Look Back (1951)
The Last Page (1952)
Wings of Danger (1952)
Lady in the Fog (1952)
The Gambler and the Lady (1952)
Mantrap (1952)
The Flanagan Boy (1952)
Spaceways (1952)
Blood Orange (1953)
The Saint's Return (1953)
36 Hours (1953)
Face the Music (1953)
The House Across the Lake (1953)
Murder by Proxy (1953)
The Stranger Came Home (1954)
Five Days (1954)
Third Party Risk (1954)
The Glass Cage (1954)
Break in the Circle (1954)
The Snorkel (1958)
The Hound of the Baskervilles (1958)
The Stranglers of Bombay (1959)
Hell Is a City (1959)
Visa to Canton (1960)
The Full Treatment (1960)
The Terror of the Tongs (1960)
Taste of Fear (1961)
Cash on Demand (1961)
Maniac (1962)
Paranoiac (1962)
The Old Dark House (1962)
Nightmare (1963)
Hysteria (1964)

Fanatic (1965)
The Nanny (1965)
Crescendo (1969)
Hands of the Ripper (1971)
Fear in the Night (1972)
Straight on Till Morning (1972)
Shatter (1974)
The Lady Vanishes (1979)

Bill Luckwell

Films are listed under the various companies with which producer Bill Luckwell was involved, namely Jaywell Productions, Luckwin Productions, Winwell Productions, Bill and Michael Luckwell Ltd and Luckwell Productions.

Jaywell Productions

Miss Tulip Stays the Night (1954)
Booby Trap (1956)

Luckwin Productions

The Crooked Sky (1956)

Winwell Productions

West of Suez (1956)
Morning Call (1957)

Bill and Michael Luckwell Ltd.

Undercover Girl (1957)
Hidden Homicide (1958)
The Hand (1960)
The Man Who Couldn't Walk (1960)
A Question of Suspense (1961)
Enter Inspector Duval (1961)
Ambush in Leopard Street (1961)
A Guy Called Caesar (1962)

Luckwell Productions

Murder in Eden (1961)
The Runaway (1964)
Delayed Flight (1964)

Merton Park Studios

Assassin for Hire (1951)
Mystery Junction (1951)
Crow Hollow (1951)
Wide Boy (1952)
Street of Shadows (1952)
Counterspy (1953)
The Floating Dutchman (1953)
Dangerous Voyage (1953)
The Brain Machine (1954)
Little Red Monkey (1954)
Confession (1954)
Timeslip (1955)
Johnny, You're Wanted (1955)
Dial 999 (1955)
The Intimate Stranger (1956)
The Hypnotist (1956)
The Counterfeit Plan (1957)
Man in the Shadow (1957)
The Key Man (1957)
Escapement (1957)
The Strange Awakening (1957)
The Long Knife (1958)
Man with a Gun (1958)
Wrong Number (1959)
The Witness (1959)
The Desperate Man (1960)
Urge to Kill (1960)
The Criminal (1960)

Merton Park Studios' Edgar Wallace Series

As of 1963's *The Double*, copyright changes from Merton Park Studios to Merton Park Productions.

1960

Clue of the Twisted Candle*
The Man Who Was Nobody
Marriage of Convenience
The Malpas Mystery**

1961

Clue of the New Pin
Partners in Crime
The Fourth Square
Man at the Carlton Tower
Clue of the Silver Key*
The Sinister Man
Attempt to Kill
Man Detained
Never Back Losers
Candidate for Murder
Backfire!

1962

Flat Two
The Share-Out*
Number Six
Time to Remember

Playback
Locker Sixty-Nine
Solo for Sparrow
Death Trap
The £20,000 Kiss
The Set-Up
Incident at Midnight
On the Run
Return to Sender

1963

Ricochet
The Double
The Rivals
To Have and to Hold
The Partner
Accidental Death
Five to One
Downfall

1964

The Verdict
We Shall See
Who Was Maddox?*
Face of a Stranger
Act of Murder
The Main Chance
Never Mention Murder

1965

Game for Three Losers
Dead Man's Chest
Change Partners
Strangler's Web

*Featuring Bernard Lee as Scotland Yard's Superintendent Meredith.
**Produced by Independent Artists at Beaconsfield Studios.

Nettlefold Films

Paul Temple's Triumph (1950)
Scarlet Thread (1951)
Salute the Toff (1951)
Hammer the Toff (1951)
Emergency Call (1952)
Paul Temple Returns (1952)
The Broken Horseshoe (1953)
Operation Diplomat (1953)

Parroch-McCallum Productions
(Jack Parsons and Neil McCallum)

The Eyes of Annie Jones (1963)
Walk a Tightrope (1963)
Catacombs (1964)
Do You Know This Voice? (1964)
Troubled Waters (1964)

Appendix II: Hollywood Actors in British B Thrillers

This appendix highlights Hollywood actors who had main roles in black-and-white British B thrillers from 1950 through to 1966, whereupon the production of such films ceased. Each entry is headed by the name of the actor followed by the applicable films, including titles used for U.S. distribution. All actors are American-born unless otherwise mentioned. (Note: Some of the actors also appeared in non–B thrillers covered in this book.)

Keith Andes
Model for Murder (1958)

Richard Arlen
Devil's Point (1954) *U.S. Title:* Devil's Harbor
Stolen Time (1954) *U.S. Title:* Blonde Blackmailer

Lex Barker
The Strange Awakening (1957) *U.S. Title:* Female Fiends

Richard Basehart
The Intimate Stranger (1956) *U.S. Title:* Finger of Guilt
Visa to Canton (1960) *U.S. Title:* Passport to China (made in color, but originally released in the U.S. in black and white)

Alan Baxter
The End of the Line (1957)

Pat Boone
The Horror of It All (1964)

Karin Booth
The Crooked Sky (1956)

Scott Brady
Three Steps to the Gallows (1953) *U.S. Title:* White Fire

Keefe Brasselle
West of Suez (1956) *U.S. Title:* The Fighting Wildcats
Death Over My Shoulder (1957)

George Brent (Born in Ireland)
The Last Page (1952) *U.S. Title:* Man Bait

Lloyd Bridges
The Limping Man (1953)
Third Party Risk (1954) *U.S. Titles:* The Deadly Game; Big Deadly Game

Hillary Brooke
The House Across the Lake (1953) *U.S. Title:* Heat Wave

Rod Cameron (Born in Canada)
Passport to Treason (1956)
Escapement (1957) *U.S. Title:* The Electronic Monster

Macdonald Carey
Stranglehold (1962)

Phil Carey
The Trunk (1960)

Richard Carlson
Whispering Smith Hits London (1951) *U.S. Title:* Whispering Smith vs. Scotland Yard

Mary Castle
Three Steps to the Gallows (1953) *U.S. Title:* White Fire

Peggie Castle
The Counterfeit Plan (1957)

Sydney Chaplin
Confession (1954) U.S. Title: The Deadliest Sin

Marguerite Chapman
The Last Page (1952) U.S. Title: Man Bait

Dane Clark
The Gambler and the Lady (1952)
Murder by Proxy (1953) U.S. Title: Blackout
Five Days (1954) U.S. Title: Paid to Kill

Steve Cochran
The Weapon (1956)

John Colicos (Born in Canada)
Bond of Fear (1956)

Richard Conte
Little Red Monkey (1954) U.S. Title: Case of the Red Monkey
The Eyes of Annie Jones (1963)

Tom Conway (English, born in Russia)
Park Plaza 605 (1953) U.S. Title: Norman Conquest
Blood Orange (1953) U.S. Title: Three Stops to Murder
Barbados Quest (1955) U.S. Title: Murder on Approval
Breakaway (1955)
Operation Murder (1956)
The Last Man to Hang (1956)

John Crawford
Blind Spot (1958)
The Impersonator (1960)
The Man Who Was Nobody (1960)
The Long Shadow (1961)

Richard Denning
Assignment Redhead (1956) U.S. Title: Million Dollar Manhunt

Faith Domergue
Timeslip (1955) U.S. Title: The Atomic Man
Soho Incident (1955) U.S. Title: Spin a Dark Web
Man in the Shadow (1957) U.S. Title: Violent Stranger

Paul Douglas
The Gamma People (1955)

Tom Drake
Date with Disaster (1957)

Howard Duff
Spaceways (1952)

Dan Duryea
36 Hours (1953) U.S. Title: Terror Street
Walk a Tightrope (1963)
Do You Know This Voice? (1964)

Glenn Ford (Born in Canada)
Time Bomb (1952) U.S. Title: Terror on a Train

Mona Freeman
Before I Wake (1955) U.S. Title: Shadow of Fear
Dial 999 (1955) U.S. Title: The Way Out

Paulette Goddard
The Stranger Came Home (1954) U.S. Title: The Unholy Four

Coleen Gray
I'll Get You for This (1950) U.S. Title: Lucky Nick Cain
The Fake (1953)

Louis Hayward (Born in South Africa)
The Saint's Return (1953) U.S. Title: The Saint's Girl Friday

Paul Henreid (Born in Austria)
Mantrap (1952) U.S. Title: Man in Hiding

Skip Homeier
No Road Back (1956)

Marsha Hunt
Diplomatic Passport (1954)

Tab Hunter
Troubled Waters (1964) U.S. Title: The Man with Two Faces

Robert Hutton
Man from Tangier (1957) U.S. Title: Thunder Over Tangier
The Sicilians (1964)
Also in the color B movie The Secret Door (1963)

John Ireland (Born in Canada)
The Glass Cage (1954) *U.S. Title:* The Glass Tomb
Stormy Crossing (1957) *U.S. Title:* Black Tide
Return of a Stranger (1961)

Rick Jason
Family Doctor (1958) *U.S. Titles:* Rx Murder; Rx for Murder

Arthur Kennedy
Impulse (1954)

Phyllis Kirk
River Beat (1953)
That Woman Opposite (1956) *U.S. Title:* City After Midnight

Peter Lawford (Born in England)
The Hour of 13 (1952)

Marc Lawrence
Kill Her Gently (1958)

William Lundigan
Dangerous Voyage (1953) *U.S. Title:* Terror Ship

Carole Mathews
Assignment Redhead (1956) *U.S. Title:* Million Dollar Manhunt
The Strange Awakening (1957) *U.S. Title:* Female Fiends

Gary Merrill
Catacombs (1964) *U.S. Title:* The Woman Who Wouldn't Die

Cameron Mitchell
The Unstoppable Man (1960)

Terry Moore
Portrait of Alison (1955) *U.S. Title:* Postmark for Danger
City of Fear (1966)

Wayne Morris
The Master Plan (1954)
The Green Buddha (1954)
Cross Channel (1954)
The Gelignite Gang (1955) *U.S. Title:* The Dynamiters
The Crooked Sky (1956)

Jeff Morrow
Hour of Decision (1956)

Mary Murphy
The Intimate Stranger (1956) *U.S. Title:* Finger of Guilt
Escapement (1957) *U.S. Title:* The Electronic Monster

Gene Nelson
Timeslip (1955) *U.S. Title:* The Atomic Man
Dial 999 (1955) *U.S. Title:* The Way Out

Alex Nicol
Face the Music (1953) *U.S. Title:* The Black Glove
The House Across the Lake (1953) *U.S. Title:* Heat Wave
The Gilded Cage (1954)
A Stranger in Town (1957)

Leslie Nielsen (Born in Canada)
Night Train to Paris (1964)

Pat O'Brien
Kill Me Tomorrow (1957)

Dan O'Herlihy (Born in Ireland)
That Woman Opposite (1956) *U.S. Title:* City After Midnight

Dennis O'Keefe
The Fake (1953)
The Diamond (1953) *U.S. Title:* The Diamond Wizard
Lady of Vengeance (1956)
Sail into Danger (1957)

Larry Parks
Tiger by the Tail (1954) *U.S. Title:* Cross-Up

Barbara Payton
The Flanagan Boy (1952) *U.S. Title:* Bad Blonde

Walter Pidgeon (Born in Canada)
Calling Bulldog Drummond (1951)

Robert Preston
Cloudburst (1951)

George Raft
I'll Get You for This (1950) *U.S. Title:* Lucky Nick Cain
Escape Route (1952) *U.S. Title:* I'll Get You

Dale Robertson
The High Terrace (1956)

Cesar Romero
Lady in the Fog (1952) *U.S. Title:* Scotland Yard Inspector
Street of Shadows (1952) *U.S. Title:* Shadow Man

Ken Scott
The Murder Game (1965)

Lizabeth Scott
The Weapon (1956)

Zachary Scott
Wings of Danger (1952)
The Counterfeit Plan (1957)
Man in the Shadow (1957) *U.S. Title:* Violent Stranger

Margaret Sheridan
The Diamond (1953) *U.S. Title:* The Diamond Wizard

Henry Silva
The Return of Mr. Moto (1965)

Mark Stevens
The Lost Hours (1952) *U.S. Title:* The Big Frame

Kent Taylor
Track the Man Down (1954)
Secret Venture (1954)

Marshall Thompson
The Secret Man (1958)

Forrest Tucker
Break in the Circle (1954) (made in color, but originally released in the U.S. in black and white)

Richard Wyler aka Richard Stapley **(Born in Canada)**
High Jump (1958)

Keenan Wynn
The Bay of Saint Michel (1963) *U.S. Titles:* Pattern for Plunder; Operation Mermaid

Appendix III: Sources for the Edgar Wallace Series

This appendix contains a list of the films featured in Chapter 7 along with information, where applicable, regarding the Edgar Wallace stories they were adapted from or inspired by. The adaptations were often extremely loose and in many cases retained only one or two of the original character names and/or had very little resemblance to the original story. Quite a few of the films appear to have had original screenplays, and these have been noted as such. As the films themselves do not credit literary sources, the information presented herein has been compiled from the often sketchy details contained on Anglo Amalgamated Film Distributors' original double-sided press sheets (which to date are the only "official" points of reference as regards source material) and my own research.

Clue of the Twisted Candle (1960)
Adapted from the 1916 novel *The Clue of the Twisted Candle*.

The Man Who Was Nobody (1960)
Adapted from the 1927 novel of the same name (previously a magazine serial).

Marriage of Convenience (1960)
Adapted from the 1924 novel *The Three Oak Mystery*.

The Malpas Mystery (1960)
Adapted from the 1924 novel *The Face in the Night*.

Clue of the New Pin (1961)
Adapted from the 1923 novel *The Clue of the New Pin*.

Partners in Crime (1961)
Adapted from the 1918 novel *The Man Who Knew*.

The Fourth Square (1961)
Adapted from the 1929 novel *Four-Square Jane*.

Man at the Carlton Tower (1961)
Adapted from the 1931 novel *The Man at the Carlton*.

Clue of the Silver Key (1961)
Adapted from the 1930 novel *The Clue of the Silver Key* (aka *The Silver Key*).

The Sinister Man (1961)
Adapted from the 1924 novel of the same name.

Attempt to Kill (1961)
Adapted from the 1929 novel *The Lone House Mystery*.

Man Detained (1961)
Adapted from the 1916 novel *A Debt Discharged*.

Never Back Losers (1961)
Original screenplay. Inspired by Wallace's horse-racing thrillers such as the 1929 novel *The Green Ribbon*.

Candidate for Murder (1961)
Adapted from the 1927 short story "The Best Laid Plans of a Man in Love."

Backfire! (1961)
Original screenplay. Features the Wallace character—albeit much modified—Jack Bryce, the main protagonist in a series of short stories collected in the 1929 anthology *The Iron Grip*.

Flat Two (1962)
Adapted from the 1924 novel *Flat 2*.

The Share-Out (1962)

Adapted from the 1920 novel *Jack O'Judgment*.

Number Six (1962)

Adapted from the 1927 novella of the same name.

Time to Remember (1962)

Original screenplay. Inspired by the 1915 novel *The Man Who Bought London*.

Playback (1962)

Original screenplay.

Locker Sixty-Nine (1962)

Adapted partly from the 1919 short story "The Murder of Bennett Sandman," which features a locker with the number 69 and a police reporter named York Symon (the reporter in the film is named Simon York).

Solo for Sparrow (1962)

Adapted from the 1928 novel *The Gunner* (aka *Gunman's Bluff*).

Death Trap (1962)

Original screenplay.

The £20,000 Kiss (1962)

Adapted from the short story "The Twenty-Thousand-Pound Kiss" from the 1929 anthology *The Black*.

The Set-Up (1962)

Original screenplay.

Incident at Midnight (1962)

Original screenplay.

On the Run (1962)

Original screenplay.

Return to Sender (1962)

Original screenplay.

Ricochet (1963)

Original screenplay. Often mistakenly cited as being based on Wallace's 1922 novel *The Angel of Terror*.

The Double (1963)

Adapted from the 1928 novel of the same name (previously a newspaper and magazine serial).

The Rivals (1963)

Original screenplay.

To Have and to Hold (1963)

Original screenplay. Often mistakenly cited as being based on Wallace's 1918 short story "The Breaking Point."

The Partner (1963)

Original screenplay.

Accidental Death (1963)

Original screenplay.

Five to One (1963)

Original screenplay.

Downfall (1963)

Original screenplay.

The Verdict (1964)

Original screenplay.

We Shall See (1964)

Original screenplay. The film takes its title from a 1926 Wallace novel, but that's where the similarities end.

Who Was Maddox? (1964)

Original screenplay. Often mistakenly cited as being based on the 1926 short story "The Undisclosed Client."

Face of a Stranger (1964)

Original screenplay.

Act of Murder (1964)

Original screenplay.

The Main Chance (1964)

Original screenplay.

Never Mention Murder (1964)

Original screenplay.

Game for Three Losers (1965)

Adapted from a 1952 Edgar Lustgarten novel of the same name.

Dead Man's Chest (1965)

Original screenplay.

Change Partners (1965)

Original screenplay.

Strangler's Web (1965)

Original screenplay.

Appendix IV: Selected Listings

This appendix contains a selection of relevant people or subjects as headings, each of which is followed by all applicable films from the book.

Agatha Christie

Films from the world of author Agatha Christie.

The Spider's Web (1960)
Murder She Said (1961)
Murder at the Gallop (1963)
Murder Most Foul (1964)
Murder Ahoy (1964)
The Alphabet Murders (1965)
Ten Little Indians (1965)
Endless Night (1972)
And Then There Were None (1974)
Murder on the Orient Express (1974)
Death on the Nile (1978)
Agatha (1978)

Best of British Noir

Films closest in style to the American film noir genre.

Night and the City (1950)
The Flanagan Boy (1952)
Face the Music (1953)
The House Across the Lake (1953)
Murder by Proxy (1953)
Impulse (1954)
The Intimate Stranger (1956)
The Depraved (1957)
The End of the Line (1957)
Tread Softly Stranger (1958)
Nowhere to Go (1958)
Playback (1962)
To Have and to Hold (1963)
Blind Corner (1963)

"Grande Dame Guignol" Films

Subgenre, originated with *What Ever Happened to Baby Jane?* (1962), featuring older Hollywood actresses in psycho thrillers.

Fanatic (1965)
The Nanny (1965)
Berserk (1967)
Whoever Slew Auntie Roo? (1971)
Night Watch (1973)
Persecution (1974)

Jack the Ripper

Films featuring the notorious real-life serial killer.

Jack the Ripper (1958)
A Study in Terror (1965)
Hands of the Ripper (1971)
Murder by Decree (1978)

Kraft Mystery Theatre

Films (all B movies) whose initial showings in the U.S. were as first-season episodes of TV's *Kraft Mystery Theatre* in 1961. (This show is not to be confused with the *Kraft Mystery Theatre* series that ran from June to October of 1958, and which had previously been called both *Kraft Theatre* and *Kraft Television Theatre*.) The films were all edited down to approximately 54 minutes to fit a one-hour broadcast slot including commercials and were hosted by radio and TV personality Frank Gallop. They are listed here in broadcast sequence.

The Professionals (1960), aired on June 14, 1961
Deadly Record (1959), aired on June 21, 1961
Account Rendered (1957), aired on June 28, 1961
Breakout (1959), aired on July 5, 1961
Danger Tomorrow (1960), aired on July 12, 1961

The Hideout (1956), aired on July 19, 1961
The White Trap (1959), aired on July 26, 1961
Witness in the Dark (1959), aired on August 2, 1961*
The Spider's Web (1960), aired on August 9, 1961
The Desperate Man (1960), aired on August 23, 1961
The Third Alibi (1961), aired on September 20, 1961
Two-Letter Alibi (1961), aired on September 27, 1961 (as Death and the Sky Above)

*Won the 1962 "Edgar" (Mystery Writers of America Edgar Allan Poe Award) for best episode in a TV series.

"Krimi" Films

British-German productions regarded as part of Germany's *krimi* subgenre of crime films usually based on or inspired by Edgar Wallace stories.

The Devil's Daffodil (1961)
Traitor's Gate (1964)
Circus of Fear (1966)
The Trygon Factor (1966)

Larry Finley's Late Show

From July 12, 1954, until early January of 1955, pioneering American broadcast entrepreneur and radio-TV personality Larry Finley hosted *Larry Finley's Late Show*, a weekday 11:30 p.m. program that aired on KNXT-TV (Channel 2) in Los Angeles. In each show, a movie was broadcast with periodic interruptions by way of cut-ins of Finley interviewing Hollywood celebrities from his own Sunset Strip eatery ("Larry Finley's Restaurant"). Seven British thrillers from this book had their U.S. TV premieres on the show and are listed here in broadcast sequence.

The Scarlet Web (1953), aired on September 7, 1954
Recoil (1953), aired on September 9, 1954
Escape by Night (1953), aired on September 10, 1954
Meet Mr. Callaghan (1953), aired on September 14, 1954
The Runaway Bus (1953), aired on October 7, 1954
The Second Mate (1950), aired on October 11, 1954
Judgment Deferred (1952), aired on December 7, 1954

Seven in Darkness

Films in which the main protagonist is blind.

Blackout (1950)
The Betrayal (1957)
Blind Spot (1958)
Witness in the Dark (1959)
Faces in the Dark (1960)
Blind Corner (1963)
Blind Terror (1971)

Appendix V:
British and U.S. Video Retitlings

During the heyday of home video in the 1980s and 1990s, it was fairly common practice for old films to be renamed in order to maximize their marketability. This appendix concerns British and U.S. video releases of films from this book where the titles used had never previously been used for release of the films on any other medium. It should be noted that most of the films in question would also have had other British and U.S. video releases under their more commonly known titles. Each entry is headed by the original British film name followed by the video retitling(s), video label name(s) and corresponding year of release.

British Releases

Blue Movie Blackmail (1973)

Released as *Superbitch* on IVS Video (1988). The same title was subsequently used for a British DVD release of the film.

Callan (1974)

Released as *This Is Callan* on Polygram Video's "Spectrum" label (1983) and later reissued on Channel 5 Video (1986).

House of Mortal Sin (1975)

RCA/Columbia Pictures Video released the film as *The Confessional Murders* on their "Silver Series" label in 1983, and then later in the decade as part of their "Hollywood Thriller Collection."

No.1 of the Secret Service (1977)

Released (supposedly) as *Her Majesty's Top Gun* on Castle Home Video (1987). There is some doubt regarding this "release": Castle Home Video submitted the film under the *HMTG* title to the British Board of Film Censors in 1987; however, apart from online images of what appears to be a video sleeve for the release, I could find no evidence that an actual finished product ever went on the market.

One Away (1976)

Released as *Gitanos—Escape from Apartheid* on Foxtrot Vidcom (1987).

The Playbirds (1978)

Released as *Secrets of a Playgirl* on Krypton Force's "Beverly's Productions" label (1986).

The Swordsman (1974)

Released as *Zapper's Blade of Vengeance* by VFO (Video Film Organisation)/Video Network (1982).

The Trygon Factor (1966)

Released as *Factor One* by Revolution Films (undated, likely early 1990s).

U.S. Releases

Assault (1970)

Released as *The Creepers* by Saturn Productions (1985), Interglobal Home Video* (1986), Video Treasures (1987) and Genesis Home Video (1987). All four releases featured different cover art.

The Black Torment (1964)

Released as *Estate of Insanity* by VCL Communications (1984) and Interglobal Home Video* (1989).

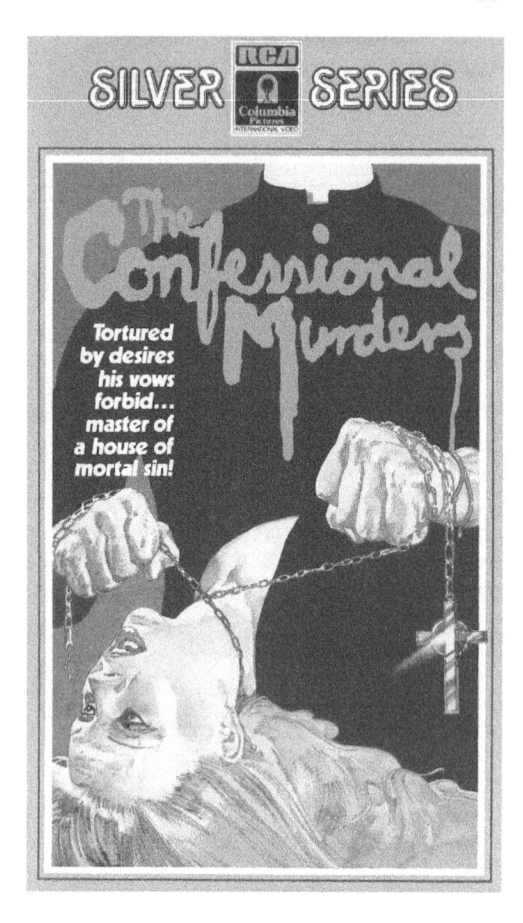

Sensational cover art and a new title for *House of Mortal Sin* on RCA/Columbia Pictures Video.

The Blood of Fu Manchu (1968)

Released as *Kiss of Death* on Bingo Video (1988), Star Classics (1989) and JTC (1992).

Blue Movie Blackmail (1973)

Released as *Superbitch* by Atlas Entertainment (1989). The same title was subsequently used for a U.S. DVD release of the film.

The Comeback (1977)

Released as *Encore* by Saturn Productions (1988). The same title was subsequently used for certain broadcasts of the film on U.S. cable/satellite TV.

Dominique (1978)

Released as *Avenging Spirit* by Impulse Productions (1989).

Alternate title for 1970's *Assault* on the Video Treasures label.

11 Harrowhouse (1974)

Released as *Fast Fortune* by MCM Entertainment (1990).

Embassy (1972)

Released as *Target: Embassy* on ACE Video/EDDE Entertainment (1994).

Fear in the Night (1972)

Released as *Dynasty of Fear* by Academy Home Entertainment (1985) and as *Honeymoon of Fear* by both Neon Video (undated, likely 1987/8) and Showcase Productions (1988).

Freelance (1970)

Released as *Con Man* on Hemdale Home Video (1992).

Fear in the Night (1972) retitled for video by Academy Home Entertainment in 1985, no doubt to capitalize on star Joan Collins' success in TV's *Dynasty* at that time.

Frightmare (1974)

Released as *Once Upon a Frightmare* on Monterey Home Video (1985) and as *Frightmare II* by Prism Entertainment (1985). Both titles were subsequently used for certain broadcasts of the film on U.S. cable/satellite TV, with *Frightmare II* also used by at least one U.S. subscription TV service.

Goodbye Gemini (1970)

Released as *Twinsanity* by Prism Entertainment (1988).

The High Bright Sun (1965)

Released as *A Date with Death* on Majestic Home Video (1989).

The House in Nightmare Park (1973)

Released as *A House in Nightmare Park* on Meteor Video (1988).

Night, After Night, After Night (1969)

Released as *He Kills Night After Night After Night* on Monterey Home Video (1985) and as *Night Slasher* on Unicorn Video (1988).

A Nightingale Sang in Berkeley Square (1979)

Released as *The Mayfair Bank Caper* by Vidamerica (1986) and as *The Big Scam* on Direct Video (1989).

Persecution (1974)

Released as *The Graveyard* by VCL Communications (1985) and Interglobal Home Video* (1987).

Power Play (1978)

Released as *Operation Overthrow* by Simitar Entertainment (1990).

Revenge (1971)

Released as *Behind the Cellar Door* by Ariel International Releasing (1987).

VCL Communications' retitling of 1974's *Persecution*.

The Sellout (1975)

Released as *The Set-Up* by Hurricane Pictures (1990).

Shatter (1974)

Released as *Mr. Shatter* by Simitar Entertainment (1993).

Straight on Till Morning (1972)

Released as *Dressed for Death* by Academy Home Entertainment (1985) and as *'Til Dawn Do We Part* by both Neon Video (undated, likely 1987/8) and Showcase Productions (undated, likely 1988).

The Swordsman (1974)

Released as *Zapper's Blade of Vengeance* by Puerto Rico Productions (1986).

Trial by Combat (1975)

Released as *A Choice of Weapons* by Paragon Video Productions (1984). The same title was originally to have been used for the film's British theatrical release.

*Interglobal Home Video (previously Interglobal Video) was actually a Canadian-based label but with huge distribution in the U.S., where they later also manufactured some of their product.

Appendix VI: British-Made U.S. TV Movies

The following five films are British-produced (or co-produced) feature-length thrillers that, although having had theatrical releases in Britain and other territories, were primarily designed for the American TV-movie market, and therefore did not qualify for coverage in the main part of the book. The reason they are included at all is because it was felt that their theatrical release history to some extent qualified them for at least some consideration. With the exception of *Mousey*, all the films were intended as try-outs for potential TV shows.

Mister Jerico (1969, ITC)

D: Sidney Hayers *Sc:* Philip Levene *Ca:* Patrick Macnee, Connie Stevens, Herbert Lom, Marty Allen, Bruce Boa. In Malta, dapper master conman Dudley Jerico (Macnee) comes up against a mysterious female rival while attempting to pull off an elaborate deception involving a shady millionaire's (Lom) prized possession—the fabulous and rare "Gemini" diamond. Originally aired in the U.S. as an *ABC Movie of the Week* on March 3, 1970.

The Firechasers (1970, ITC)

D: Sidney Hayers *Sc:* Philip Levene *Ca:* Chad Everett, Anjanette Comer, Keith Barron, Rupert Davies, James Hayter. An ace insurance investigator (Everett) is involved in tracking down a psychopathic arsonist responsible for a series of London warehouse fires, all ignited by automatic tea-makers filled with highly flammable hair lacquer. Originally aired in the U.S. as a *CBS Sunday Night Movie* on May 14, 1972.

Madame Sin (1971, Cecil Film/ITC)

D: David Greene *Sc:* Barry Oringer and David Greene *Ca:* Bette Davis, Robert Wagner, Denholm Elliott, Gordon Jackson, Catherine Schell. A former U.S. Intelligence agent (Wagner) is kidnapped while in London and taken to the Scottish island headquarters of female criminal mastermind Madame Sin (Davis), who tricks him into helping her steal a Polaris submarine. Originally aired in the U.S. as an *ABC Movie of the Weekend* on January 15, 1972.

Baffled! (1972, Arena Productions/ITC)

D: Philip Leacock *Sc:* Theodore Apstein *Ca:* Leonard Nimoy, Susan Hampshire, Rachel Roberts, Vera Miles, Ray Brooks. In America, a race driver (Nimoy) with newly developed psychic abilities teams up with a young occultic researcher (Hampshire), and together they travel to an old manor house in England to foil an evil plot against a famous actress (Miles). Originally aired in the U.S. as an *NBC Tuesday Night Movie* on January 30, 1973.

Mousey (aka *Cat and Mouse*; 1974, Associated London Films/Universal)

D: Daniel Petrie *Sc:* John Peacock *Ca:* Kirk Douglas, Jean Seberg, John Vernon, Sam Wanamaker, James Bradford. A weak, frustrated teacher (Douglas), nicknamed "Mousey" by his pupils, quits his job and begins stalking his ex-wife (Seberg) just as she's about to marry the new man in her life (Vernon). Douglas gives a creepy performance, with "Mousey" committing a couple of murders (one of them a shocking throat-slashing) en route to a "the-call-is-coming-from-inside-the-house" climax. Filmed and set in Canada. Originally aired in the U.S. as a Saturday night *ABC Suspense Movie* on March 9, 1974.

For the sake of completeness, mention should be made of another three thrillers also produced in Britain for the U.S. TV-movie market, but which had no theatrical release: *Run a Crooked Mile* (Universal, 1969), an ingenious amnesia-themed story starring Louis Jourdan as a teacher who stumbles on a conspiracy to manipulate the gold standard; and the two Jimmy Sangster-scripted (from his own novels) 1969 espionage yarns *The Spy Killer* and its sequel *Foreign Exchange*, made back-to-back by Halsan Productions for ABC and both starring Robert Horton, Jill St. John and Sebastian Cabot.

Announcement for the April 1972 London theatrical premiere of the British-produced U.S. TV movie *Madame Sin* (1971). The film had already aired stateside as an *ABC Movie of the Weekend* in January 1972.

Appendix VII: Supposed Alternate U.S. Titles

This appendix concerns titles that are commonly cited in research works and reviews as being alternate U.S. release titles for certain films in this book, and which readers may have expected to find in the Filmography, but which were not included due to my research deeming them erroneous or highly doubtful. In fact, it would appear that the titles in question were never used for any releases in any country. Each entry is headed by the actual British title, followed by notes about the supposed alternate title.

Cat and Mouse (1958)

Supposed U.S. title: *The Desperate Men*. This may have something to do with the film having once been renamed—but never released as—*The Desperate Ones*, a title which for many years was mistakenly listed as *The Desperate Men* on the British Board of Film Classification's website. In a curious coincidence, the film's star, Lee Patterson, was once mistakenly credited in a U.S. journal (the *Independent Press-Telegram* [Long Beach, California, June 6, 1965]) as the star of the 1960 British thriller *The Desperate Man*, whose title was often misprinted in other U.S. journals as *The Desperate Men*.

The Comeback (1977)

Supposed U.S. title: *The Day the Screaming Stopped*. This was in fact one of the film's working titles.

Danger by My Side (1962)

Supposed U.S. title: *Danger on My Side*. This appears to have resulted from misprints over the years in the TV pages of many U.S. journals. One such publication, *The News Leader* (Staunton, Virginia, October 1, 1972), had the film listed on one page as *Danger by My Side* and on another as *Danger on My Side*, both entries relating to the same broadcast.

The Devil's Daffodil (1961)

Supposed U.S. title: *Daffodil Killer*. No evidence could be found that this title was ever used.

Die Screaming, Marianne (1970)

Supposed U.S. title: *Die, Beautiful Marianne*. No evidence could be found that this title was ever used.

Escapement (1957)

Supposed U.S. titles: *Zex, the Electronic Fiend*; *Zex*. Both appear to have been considered as U.S. release titles. The latter title does appear on some early publicity photos, but that seems to be as far as it got.

Final Appointment (1954)

Supposed U.S. title: *Last Appointment*. No evidence could be found that this title was ever used.

The Flesh and Blood Show (1972)

Supposed U.S. title: *Asylum of the Insane*. The only known feature film with this title is a re-edited version of director Byron Mabe's 1967 horror movie *She Freak* which, like *The Flesh and Blood Show*, included a 3D sequence.

413

The Key Man (1957)

Supposed U.S. title: *Life at Stake*. This is most likely the result of a mix-up in connection with the U.S. movie *A Life at Stake* (1954), whose alternate title is *Key Man*.

Offbeat (1960)

Supposed U.S. title: *The Devil Inside*. This was in fact the film's working title.

Payroll (1961)

Supposed U.S. title: *I Promise to Pay*. This was in fact the film's working title.

Suspended Alibi (1956)

Supposed U.S. title: *Suspected Alibi*. This appears to have resulted from misprints over the years in the TV pages of many U.S. journals. One such publication, *The Tampa Tribune* (Tampa, Florida, June 23, 1963), had the film listed on one page as *Suspended Alibi* and on another as *Suspected Alibi*, both entries relating to the same broadcast.

The Treasure of San Teresa (1959)

Supposed U.S. title: *Long Distance*. This was in fact the film's working title.

Violent Moment (1958)

Supposed U.S. title: *Rebound*. No evidence could be found that this title was ever used.

Wings of Danger (1952)

Supposed U.S. title: *Dead on Course*. This was the title of Elleston Trevor's 1951 source novel and was also the film's working title.

Opposite, top left: Frightmare (1974) retitled *Brainsuckers* for a week-long run (from late May 1976) at the Fox Theatre, Detroit, Michigan. *Bottom left:* Provocative retitling for 1970's *Assault*, here making its U.S. theatrical debut (March 7, 1973) at the "Penthouse" Theatre in Louisville, Kentucky. *Top right: The Great Van Robbery* (1958), probably one of the Danziger brothers' most widely distributed (at least theatrically) B movies in the U.S., is in good company on this double bill that played at the Geneva Drive-In (Orem, Utah) in May and June 1963. *Bottom right:* The 1959 B movie *Cover Girl Killer* on one of its many "Adults Only" U.S. double bills, this one in January of 1967 at the Trail Drive-In Theatre in Glen Rock, Pennsylvania.

Appendix VIII: "Ad"dendum

This appendix contains a small collection of American newspaper ads, all of them for theater programs with interesting presentations of select films from this book.

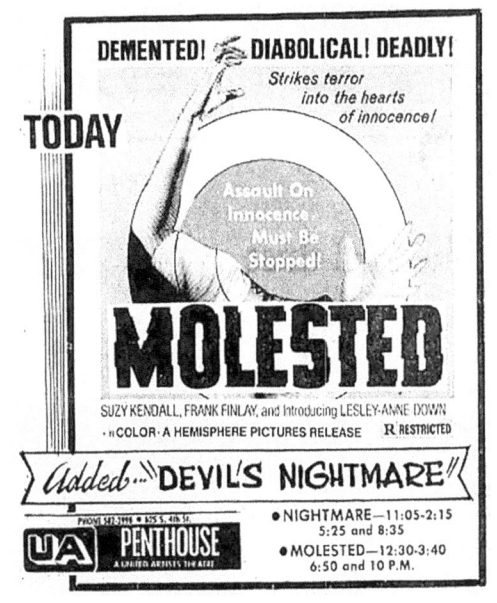

Left: The Merton Park–produced Edgar Wallace B movie *Candidate for Murder* (1961) had a couple of rare U.S. theatrical runs, including this one at the Union Drive-In (Union, New Jersey) from April to May 1968. *Right:* The Hammer B movie *The Glass Cage* (1954) under its U.S. title *The Glass Tomb*. After years away from the big screen, it turned up on this January 1966 triple bill at the Capitol Theatre in Brownsville, Texas.

The bizarre B movie *The Hand* (1960) on one of its many stateside double-bills, this one at the Grand Theatre in Huntingdon, Pennsylvania, in August of 1961. Note the misspelling in Ronald Leigh-Hunt's name.

The now rare B movie *In the Wake of a Stranger* (1959) once stood tall over a Hitchcock classic at the North End Drive-In Theatre (Eugene, Oregon) in March 1961.

Selected Bibliography

Books

Burrows, Elaine, and Janet Moat, David Sharp, Linda Wood, eds. *The British Cinema Source Book*. British Film Institute London: British Film Institute, 1995.

Chibnall, Steve. *Making Mischief—The Cult Films of Pete Walker*. Surrey, England: FAB Press, 1998.

Connors, Martin, and Jim Craddock, eds. *Videohound's Golden Movie Retriever*. Detroit: Visible Ink Press, 1992 and later editions.

Elliot, John. *Elliot's Guide to Movies on Video*. London: Boxtree, 1991 (second edition).

Gifford, Denis. *The British Film Catalogue 1895–1985*. Devon, England: David & Charles, 1986.

Gow, Gordon. *Suspense in the Cinema*. New York: Castle Books, 1968.

Hanley, Loretta, ed. *TV Feature Film Source Book*. New York: Broadcast Information Bureau, Inc., 1973-1974 edition.

Johnson, Tom, and Deborah Del Vecchio. *Hammer Films: An Exhaustive Filmography*. Jefferson, NC: McFarland, 1996.

Krafsur, Richard P., ed. *The American Film Institute Catalog of Motion Pictures, 1961–1970*. New York: R.R. Bowker Co., 1976.

Limbacher, James L. *Film Music*. Metuchen, NJ: Scarecrow, 1974.

Maltin, Leonard, ed. *Leonard Maltin's Movie Guide* (including *Leonard Maltin's Movie and Video Guide*). New York: Signet Books, 1993 and later editions.

McCarty, John. *Thrillers: Seven Decades of Classic Film Suspense*. New York: Citadel Press, 1992.

McFarlane, Brian. *An Autobiography of British Cinema*. London: Methuen Publishing, 1997.

Murphy, Robert. *Sixties British Cinema*. London: British Film Institute, 1992.

Noble, Peter, ed. *The British Film & Television Yearbook*. London: British and American Press (after 1975 became *International Film and TV Yearbook,* published by Screen International); various editions.

Pfeiffer, Lee, and Dave Worrall. *The Essential Bond*. London: Boxtree, 1998.

Rubin, Martin. *Thrillers*. Cambridge, England: Cambridge University Press, 1999.

Sova, Dawn B. *Agatha Christie A to Z: The Essential Reference to Her Life and Writings*. New York: Checkmark Books, 1996.

Vermilye, Jerry. *Bette Davis*. New York: Galahad Books, 1973.

Warren, Patricia. *British Film Studios: An Illustrated History*. London: B.T. Batsford, 1995.

Weaver, Tom. *The Horror Hits of Richard Gordon*. Albany, GA: BearManor Media, 2011.

British Periodicals

The Cinema *
Cinema TV Today *
The Daily Cinema *
Films and Filming
Films Illustrated
Kinematograph Weekly
Monthly Film Bulletin
Screen International
Today's Cinema *

*Former incarnations of *Screen International*

U.S. Periodicals

Classic Images
Films in Review
Motion Picture Herald
The New York Times
Variety

Index of Names

This index refers to film entry numbers in the Filmography.
Names in parentheses indicate alternate names under
which the listed person was sometimes billed.

Abady, Temple 396, 515
Abineri, John 156
Abraham, Edward 194, 650
Abraham, Valerie 194
Abrahams, Mort 489
Ackland, Joss 51, 127, 577, 803
Adair, Hazel 283
Adam, Ronald 22, 105, 257, 385, 396, 652, 719, 788
Adamic, Bojan 129
Adams, Beverly 315
Adams, Jill 134, 171, 551, 553
Adams, Maud 461
Adams, Tom 241, 243, 414, 593, 681, 717, 819
Addams, Dawn 345, 776, 784, 819
Addinsell, Richard 332
Addison, John 154, 293, 331, 345, 442, 586, 652, 670, 755
Adler, Larry 348
Adorf, Mario 732
Adrian, Max 586
Agutter, Jenny 194, 209, 361, 613
Aimée, Anouk (Anouk) 122, 458
Ainley, Anthony 20
Ainsworth, John 30, 323, 495
Aird, Jane 167, 358
Ajibade, Yemi 661
Alan, Pamela 167, 539
Albert, Eddie 557
Albert, Marvin H. 785
Albiin, Elsy 746
Alcott, John 191
Alderton, John 208
Alekan, Henri 779
Alexander, Patrick 571
Alexander, Terence 75, 144, 375, 412, 441, 591, 624
Alison, Dorothy 58, 425, 453
Allan, Andrea 637
Allan, Elizabeth 69, 309
Allégret, Marc 52
Allen, Adrianne 475
Allen, Irving 315, 320, 376, 450
Allen, Jack 64, 74, 366, 416, 444, 603, 662, 713, 823
Allen, Lewis 821
Allen, Patrick 121, 131, 382, 428, 459, 524, 580, 599, 667, 771, 775, 831

Allen, Ronald 247
Allen, Sheila 10
Allenby, Peter 642
Almond, Paul 25
Alwyn, William 180, 267, 430, 507, 531, 595, 625, 692
Amateau, Rod 830
Ambler, Dail 175, 517
Ambler, Eric 332, 622
Ambler, Joss 479, 675
Ambor, Josef 69, 145, 262, 422, 829, 840
Anders, Ina 446
Andersen, Elga 117
Andersen, Gerald 667
Andersen, Jurgen 613
Anderson, Gene 257, 428, 659
Anderson, Gerry 133
Anderson, Jean 519, 666, 683
Anderson, Margaret 406
Anderson, Michael 99, 194, 352, 507, 528, 602
Anderson, Rona 30, 47, 48, 105, 201, 259, 327, 336, 422, 460, 539, 655, 675, 676, 758, 822
Andersson, Harriet 160
Andes, Keith 482
Andreas, Dimitris 417
Andress, Ursula 193, 579
Andrews, Dana 207, 371
Andrews, Harry 104, 137, 139, 160, 370, 375, 387, 435, 483, 520, 735
Andrews, Jack 776
Andrews, Julie 727
Angel, Daniel M. 15, 63, 654
Angeli, Pier 587, 683
Angelis, Michael 533
Anglade, France 783
Anholt, Tony 245
Annakin, Ken 4, 200, 370
Annis, Francesca 229, 577, 810
Anouk see Aimée, Anouk
Anstruther, Gerald 742
Antony, Scott 154
Apted, Michael 8, 691
Aranson, Jack 499
Arbeid, Ben 21, 387, 500
Archard, Bernard 114, 233, 248, 258, 443, 666, 788

Archer, Barbara 706
Arden, Neal 175
Arden, Robert 102, 124, 166, 176, 675
Ardies, Tom 626
Arent, Eddi 106, 772
Arkoff, Samuel Z. 826
Arlen, Richard 182, 695
Arliss, Leslie 479
Armendariz, Pedro 277
Armstrong, Bridget 811
Armstrong, Michael 318
Armstrong, Vic 228
Arnall, Julia 203, 351, 433, 464, 482, 781
Arnatt, John 105, 109, 349, 365, 414, 415, 561, 651, 656, 739, 819
Arne, Peter 29, 49, 141, 505, 706, 710, 761, 817
Arnell, Richard 452, 741
Arnold, Grace 28
Arnold, Harry 446
Arnold, Irene 526
Arnold, John 570, 760
Arnold, Malcolm 33, 335, 336, 522, 587, 594, 615, 754, 832
Arribas, Fernando 14
Arteaga, Angel 681
Artigot, Raul 681
Asher, Jack 35, 91, 303, 305, 343, 398, 571, 641, 673
Asherson, Renee 586, 756
Ashley, June 105, 511
Ashwood, Terry 696
Askwith, Robin 260
Aslan, Gregoire 82, 128, 328, 437, 560, 673
Asquith, Anthony 312, 413, 512, 557, 835
Astaire, Jarvis 8
Astley, Edwin 9, 23, 93, 122, 153, 206, 219, 319, 337, 367, 372, 395, 420, 473, 485, 508, 551, 556, 696, 726, 747, 750, 807, 836
Atchelor, Jack 318
Atkinson, John 781
Attenborough, Richard 14, 70, 141, 212, 357, 382, 407, 412, 453, 638, 683, 741
Aubrey, Anne 643

419

Index of Names

Aubrey, Diane 309
Aubrey, Jean 149, 192, 482
Audley, Maxine 322, 432, 441, 516, 576, 612, 796
Audran, Stéphane 14
Auger, Claudine 751, 779
Auric, Georges 80, 242, 303, 478, 683
Avakian, Aram 214
Avalon, Frankie 318, 718
Avianca, Frank 356
Axelrod, George 403
Ayer, Hal 750
Ayer, Harold 617
Aylmer, Felix 340, 458, 625, 662, 674, 787
Aylward, Derek 451, 713
Ayres, Robert 29, 50, 174, 176, 556, 617, 664, 743, 757, 773, 839
Aznavour, Charles 14

Babic, Milan 658
Bacall, Lauren 501
Bach, Barbara 690
Bach, Vivi 21, 166, 490
Bachmann, Lawrence P. 10, 492, 821
Baddeley, Hermione 125, 369, 835
Badel, Alan 152, 558, 613
Bailey, John (actor) 339, 484, 532, 795
Bailey, John (screenwriter) 613
Bailey, Robin 58, 189
Bain, Bill 816
Baines, John 224, 654
Baines, Lionel 405
Baird, Harry 545
Baird, Phillip 283
Baird, Teddy 835
Baker, George 227, 540, 547, 745, 775
Baker, Herbert 315
Baker, Jane 71, 563
Baker, Kenny 235
Baker, Marilyn 65
Baker, Mark 264
Baker, Pip 71, 563
Baker, Robert S. 28, 46, 53, 65, 73, 132, 163, 174, 201, 216, 222, 275, 291, 330, 366, 380, 434, 537, 572, 605, 693, 743, 749, 753, 808, 815
Baker, Roy Ward (Roy Baker) 332, 754
Baker, Stanley 33, 55, 100, 128, 303, 320, 321, 322, 336, 371, 382, 407, 455, 579, 593, 618, 806
Balaban, Burt 190, 402
Balbina 280
Balchin, Nigel 104, 456, 720
Balcon, Michael 80, 404, 522, 541, 586, 633, 665
Baldour, Charles 642
Balfour, Michael 28, 48, 73, 88, 173, 174, 182, 211, 342, 444, 709, 743
Ball, Vincent 47, 145, 155, 182, 211, 232, 246, 333, 695
Balsam, Martin 34, 501
Banes, Lionel 144, 309, 522, 535, 719, 734
Bankhead, Tallulah 239

Banki, Zsu Zsu 108
Banks, Don 360, 381, 493, 534, 591, 739, 776
Banks, Sydney 764
Bannen, Ian 198, 273, 425, 435, 720, 722
Bantock, Sir Granville 701
Baptiste, Thomas 378
Barbieri, Gato 251
Baring, Aubrey 82
Barker, Eric 466
Barker, Lex 700, 783, 802
Barker, Ronnie 397, 452
Barkworth, Peter 205, 818
Barnabe, Bruno 582
Barnard, Ivor 342
Barnes, Binnie 438
Barnes, Julian 318
Barnes, Peter 75, 545, 595, 614, 805, 823
Barnett, Ivan 619
Baron, David 202
Barr, Patrick 23, 46, 48, 69, 169, 207, 222, 260, 354, 402, 549, 756, 793
Barr, Robert 425
Barrett, Jane 65, 98
Barrett, Ray 383, 611, 759, 762, 766
Barrett, Tim 67, 681, 772, 819
Barrie, John 248
Barrigo, Don 388
Barron, John 383
Barron, Keith 271
Barrs, Norman 340
Barry, Barta 628, 681
Barry, Gene 466, 717
Barry, Hilda 350
Barry, John (actor) 146
Barry, John (composer) 158, 186, 277, 302, 378, 447, 461, 481, 486, 514, 547, 602, 638, 727, 751, 844
Bart, Lionel 447
Barthrop, Collette 130
Bartlett, Annabel 633
Bartley, Penelope 42
Bartok, Eva 40, 72, 284, 554, 566, 683, 684, 795
Barzman, Ben 55, 760
Basehart, Richard 303, 377, 705, 807
Bass, Alfie 36, 535
Bassani, Georgio 705
Bast, William 315
Bate, Anthony 5, 445, 593, 651, 696
Bates, Alan 625
Bates, Barbara 351, 768
Bates, Michael 315, 630
Bates, Ralph 244, 580
Bathurst, Peter 38, 98
Batley, Dorothy 621
Bauer, David 215, 258, 809
Baum, Martin 830
Baxt, George 107, 575, 709
Baxter, Alan 219
Baxter, Anne 99, 481
Baxter, Jane 169
Baxter, John 389, 640
Bayldon, Geoffrey 21, 64, 821
Bayley, Richard 562
Beacham, Stephanie 61, 350, 636
Beaton, Timothy 608

Beatty, Robert 77, 85, 288, 512, 589, 659, 668, 757, 818, 832
Beatty, Warren 392
Beaumont, Diana 335
Beaumont, Susan 230, 536, 548, 685, 813
Beaumont, Victor 663
Beaver, Jack 299, 363
Beck, Reginald 426
Beckley, Tony 20, 183, 247, 290, 298, 379, 578, 668
Beckwith, Reginald 15, 63, 72, 744, 822
Bedford, Brian 543
Beeby, Bruce 582, 603, 650, 704
Beech, Paul 417
Beeson, Paul 127, 541, 633, 729
Begley, Ed 45, 804
Begley, Elizabeth 233
Behrens, Marlies 446
Belfrage, Bruce 336
Bell, Ann 258, 696
Bell, Arnold 301, 329, 372, 470, 495, 551, 780
Bell, Keith 317
Bell, Simon 415
Bell, Tom 210, 575, 593, 698, 804
Bendix, William 384
Benedek, Laslo 484
Benedict, Jay 415
Benham, Joan 492, 579
Benn, Harry 151
Bennett, Compton 40, 178, 264, 734
Bennett, Hywel 220, 786
Bennett, Jill 128, 320, 510
Bennett, John 97, 347, 726
Bennett, Kem 204, 755
Bennett, Richard Rodney 45, 55, 232, 376, 450, 501, 510, 627
Benson, Martin 18, 29, 48, 147, 222, 275, 280, 281, 289, 302, 362, 376, 389, 444, 473, 490, 506, 605, 642, 675, 836
Bentley, John 46, 121, 184, 201, 223, 249, 259, 261, 280, 314, 434, 573, 574, 596, 617, 631, 658, 667, 694, 774
Berenguer, Manuel 505
Berens, Harold 641
Beret, Dawn 333, 724
Bergen, Candice 214
Berger, Senta 560, 602
Bergerac, Jacques 33
Bergh, Eva 430
Bergman, Ingrid 501
Berkeley, Ballard 38, 62, 144, 275, 364, 472, 532, 555, 572
Berman, Monty 28, 46, 53, 57, 65, 73, 163, 174, 201, 216, 222, 275, 291, 344, 366, 380, 434, 537, 572, 605, 693, 697, 743, 749, 753, 808, 815
Bern, Tonia 259
Bernard, Carl 344
Bernard, James 4, 343, 708, 733
Bernard, Judd 373, 468
Bernelle, Agnes 701
Bernstein, Elmer 58, 298
Bertoya, Paul 703
Bertrand, Jacques-Paul 779
Beswick, Martine 277, 578, 751

Index of Names

Betts, Kirsten 127
Bevis, Frank 171, 418, 511, 635, 812
Bezencenet, Peter 64, 108, 783
Bianchi, Daniela 277
Bick, Jerry 626
Bikel, Theodore 178, 261, 266
Binge, Ronald 178, 406, 624
Bird, Norman 49, 89, 198, 412, 418, 462, 644
Birkinshaw, Alan 399
Birney, David 87, 778
Birt, Daniel 79, 105, 475, 532, 662, 740, 748
Bishop, Ed 29
Bishop, Piers 763
Bishop, Terry 64, 126, 140, 416, 482, 792
Bisset, Donald 422
Bisset, Jacqueline 501, 687
Black, Ian Stuart 328, 419, 429, 657, 675
Black, Stanley 36, 65, 73, 132, 213, 222, 264, 278, 291, 322, 330, 344, 366, 380, 445, 459, 462, 572, 574, 605, 657, 697, 704, 734, 749, 753, 757, 800, 805
Blackman, Honor 3, 73, 94, 173, 190, 273, 297, 302, 407, 650, 674, 721, 785, 845
Blackwell, Charles 86, 667, 679
Blackwell, Douglas 713
Blair, Joyce 543
Blake, Anne 339, 640, 730
Blake, Grey 573
Blake, Howard 613
Blake, Katharine 18, 147, 314, 762
Blakeley, Tom 54, 71, 465, 563, 763
Blakely, Colin 370
Blees, Robert 826
Bligh, Jack 338
Bloch, Robert 161, 597
Bloom, Claire 213, 442, 689
Bloom, Jeffrey 214
Bluestone, George 810
Blye, Maggie 379
Blyth, Henry 653
Blythe, John 275, 286, 738, 749
Boa, Bruce 696
Boddey, Martin 104, 223, 647, 765
Bodkin, Jeremy 264
Boehm, Carl 576, 765
Bogarde, Dirk 52, 91, 178, 288, 328, 341, 358, 413, 478, 483, 639, 674, 801, 835
Bogart, Humphrey 32
Bolam, James 500, 558, 698
Bolling, Claude 96
Bolster, Anita Sharp 67
Bolton, Emily 486
Bond, Derek 316, 330, 345, 620, 697, 817
Bond, Julian 778, 833
Bond, Philip 123
Bonner, Tony 231
Boone, Pat 338
Boone, Richard 43
Booth, Anthony 334, 481, 567, 582, 609
Booth, Harry 23
Booth, James 70, 577, 611, 618

Booth, Karin 130
Borisenko, Don 597
Borneman, Ernest 26, 235
Borsody, Hans 86
Bosco, Wally 168
Boty, Pauline 709
Bouchet, Barbara 139
Boultbee, Michael 767
Boulting, John 652, 720
Boulting, Roy 331, 652, 720, 786
Bourne, Peter 446
Bower, Pamela 777
Bowles, Peter 156, 220, 231
Bowman, Tom 367
Bown, John 471
Box, Betty E. 100, 113, 159, 328, 341, 538, 674, 679, 744, 795
Box, John 32
Box, Muriel 230
Box, Sydney 230, 263, 266
Boxill, Patrick 299
Boyd, Edward 618
Boyd, Gordon 568
Boyd, Roy 828
Boyd, Stephen 21, 456, 654, 691, 741
Boyle, William N. 131, 307, 647, 769
Bozzuffi, Marcel 87, 468
Brabourne, John 170, 501
Brach, Gerard 136
Braden, Bernard 278
Bradford, Ernie 620
Bradley, Dai 1
Bradley, Leslie 88
Brady, Brandon 138
Brady, Scott 749
Brambell, Wilfrid 667, 793
Brandon, Bill 728
Brandon, Catherine 580
Brandon, Phil 105, 349
Brasselle, Keefe 171, 814
Braun, Pinkas 108, 452
Braunberger, Pierre 96
Bray, Robert 770
Brazzi, Rossano 379
Breaks, Sebastian 519, 713
Breakston, George 67, 223, 658
Bredin, Patricia 762
Bree, James 825
Brennan, Michael 5, 11, 53, 273, 537, 743
Brent, George 409
Brett, Jeremy 293, 799
Brewster, Dorothy 429
Briant, Shane 698
Bridges, Alan 5
Bridges, Lloyd 31, 419, 740
Bridgewater, Leslie 701
Brierley, David 83
Briers, Richard 243, 473
Brimmell, Max 678
Britton, Tony 8, 71, 529, 554, 720
Broccoli, Albert R. 186, 193, 277, 302, 320, 376, 423, 450, 461, 486, 547, 690, 844
Brodie, Charles 150
Brodkin, Herbert 639
Brody, Hugh 44, 725
Bronsten, Nat 794
Brook, Faith 4, 99, 377, 449, 540, 744, 811

Brook, Lyndon 115, 553, 719, 805
Brook-Jones, Elwyn 291, 532, 571, 620, 748
Brooke, Hillary 346
Brooke, Michael 646
Brooks, Beverly 250
Brooks, Dawn 289
Brooks, Ray 17, 260, 354
Brooks, Victor 126, 205, 229, 296, 339, 381, 416, 429, 498, 545, 591
Brousse, Liliane 462, 565
Brown, A.J. 110
Brown, Alan 202
Brown, George H. 20, 178, 371, 397, 494, 503, 577, 611
Brown, Georgia 502
Brown, Harry Joe, Jr. 208
Brown, Jackie 7, 562, 655, 738, 770
Brown, Jim 476
Brown, Pamela 519, 633
Brown, Phil 67
Brown, Robert 199, 396, 406, 571
Brown, Walter 369, 424, 481, 680
Browne, Coral 33, 524, 735
Browne, Jill 805
Browne, Laidman 829
Browning, Alan 246
Browning, Michael 530
Bruce, Brenda 534, 576
Brundin, Bo 626
Brune, Gabrielle 342, 749
Brunius, Jacques 607
Bryan, Dora 317, 459, 537, 634, 743, 822
Bryan, John 646
Bryan, Peter 66, 343
Bryans, John 798
Bryant, Chris (Andrew Meredith) 195, 687
Bryant, Marie 753
Bryant, Michael 87, 478, 491
Brynner, Yul 203, 248, 779
Buchholz, Horst 752
Buck, David 158, 729
Buck, Jules 153
Buckingham, Yvonne 499, 601, 793
Bucknell, Robert 487
Buckner, Robert 351, 594
Budd, Jackson 299
Budd, Roy 51, 245, 290, 375, 468, 764, 831
Bujold, Genevieve 496
Bull, John 628
Bull, Peter 414, 546, 669
Burden, Hugh 279, 347, 644
Burdon, H.E. 499
Burdon, Tom 313
Burger, Adolph 663
Burgess, Madeline 829
Burke, Aileen 240
Burke, Alfred 25, 155, 240, 441, 455, 484, 554, 784
Burke, Marie 256, 673
Burke, Martyn 590
Burke, Patricia 177, 188, 365, 709
Burnaby, Anne 841
Burns, Larry 123, 474
Burns, Mark 168
Burns, Wilfred 11, 22, 47, 66, 77, 111, 130, 175, 218, 221, 313, 314, 316, 444,

454, 464, 488, 499, 555, 573, 601, 623, 631, 814, 845
Burr, Raymond 764
Burrell, Richard 5, 493
Burrell, Sheila 46, 112, 565, 621
Burton, John Nelson 516
Burton, Peter 12, 38
Burton, Richard 1, 689, 803, 818, 831
Bushell, Anthony 331, 426, 733
Butchart, Ann 167
Butcher, Kim 276
Butler, David 31
Butler, Janet 77
Butler, Michael 70
Butterworth, Peter 63, 226, 516, 686
Byrd, Bretton 339, 585, 588
Byrne, Charlie 270
Byrne, Eddie 33, 71, 232, 263, 288, 380, 381, 384, 424, 553, 694
Byrne, Paula 184, 393
Byron, Kathleen 281, 523, 596, 634, 647

Cabot, Bruce 186
Cadell, Jean 363, 411, 719
Cagan, Steven 94
Caine, Michael 45, 51, 158, 209, 279, 290, 378, 379, 468, 598, 670, 830
Cairney, John 467
Cairns, Jessica 694
Callahan, George 362
Callan, Michael 94
Callard, Kay 225, 250, 264, 270, 306, 359, 420, 449, 694, 702, 790, 814, 838
Calvert, Phyllis 480, 512, 786, 810
Cameron, Earl 218, 319, 586, 632
Cameron, John 529
Cameron, Rod 225, 572
Cameron, Shirley 809
Camilleri, Charles 92
Cammell, Donald 208
Campbell, Beatrice 305
Campbell, Bruce 448
Campbell, Gavin 584
Campbell, Patrick 293
Canale, Gianna Maria 827
Canaway, Bill 378
Canning, Victor 795
Cannon, Esma 135, 815
Capote, Truman 32
Cardew, Phil 402, 641
Cardiff, Jack 41, 170, 374, 421, 476, 577
Carey, Joyce 229, 694
Carey, Macdonald 179, 438, 707
Carey, Phil 587, 781
Cargill, Patrick 115, 315, 334
Carlson, Richard 822
Carlson, Steve 159
Carmichael, Ian 326, 403
Carney, James 366
Carol, Joan 147, 620
Carol, Martine 6, 323
Caron, Leslie 312
Carpenter, Paul 7, 36, 149, 190, 235, 253, 337, 346, 359, 374, 382, 385, 502, 511, 535, 551, 655, 702, 790
Carr, Jane 629, 746
Carreras, Michael 60, 72, 127, 147, 235, 322, 462, 463, 497, 515, 661, 673, 684, 698, 702, 807
Carridia, Michael 284
Carrington, Jane-Howard 392
Carrington, Robert 245, 392
Carroll, Paul Vincent 477
Carroll, Ronnie 54
Carson, Jeannie 653
Carson, John 2, 5, 424, 471, 651, 653, 672
Carson, Robert 6
Carstairs, John Paddy 179
Carsten, Peter 476, 602, 716, 797
Carter, John R. 223
Carter, Red *see* Manni, Ettore
Carton, Brian 729
Carwithen, Doreen 72, 463
Cary, Tristram 404, 666, 760, 768, 775, 785
Casdagli, Penny 599
Case, Gerald 2, 237, 264
Cash, Aubrey 138, 530
Cass, Henry 65, 66, 73, 130, 316, 330, 454
Cass, Martin 454
Cassel, Jean-Pierre 501
Cassini, Nadia 598
Cast, Edward 575, 595
Castaldini, Anne 431
Castle, Mary 749
Castle, Peggie 124
Castle, William 546
Catalano, Marizio 606
Catenacci, Luciano 61
Catford, Edwin (Teddy Catford) 225, 348
Cavan, Barbara 843
Cavanagh, James P. 494
Cavander, Kenneth 365
Cavele, Keith 300
Cavendish, Cecilia 259
Cawdron, Robert 134, 246
Cazabon, John 25
Celano, Guido 705
Celi, Adolfo 14, 269, 505, 751
Cey, Jacques 66, 420
Chacksfield, Frank 475, 758
Chadwick, June 300
Chaffey, Don 129, 141, 294, 453, 473, 580, 756, 785
Chagrin, Francis 116, 141, 457, 467, 673
Chakiris, George 328
Challis, Christopher 55, 96, 137, 263, 265, 392, 438, 514, 607, 613, 803
Challis, Drummond 613
Chalmers, W.G. 22, 444, 464, 845
Chamberlain, Cyril 216, 460, 753
Chance, Naomi 60, 145, 281, 629, 721, 832
Chandos, John 430, 553, 746, 833
Chanslor, Roy 693
Chantler, David T. 89, 680
Chaplin, Geraldine 371, 703
Chaplin, Sydney 121
Chapman, Edward 326
Chapman, Marguerite 409
Chappell, Herbert 414
Charisse, Cyd 466
Charles, Lewis 446
Charles, Moie 634
Charles-Williams, Liz 159, 577, 679
Charlesworth, John 149, 536
Chase, Stephen 300
Chasen, Heather 162
Chatto, Tom 294
Cherrell, Gwen 196
Cherry, Helen 175, 179, 214
Chesney, Diana 715, 738, 836
Chester, Hal E. 203, 326, 812
Chevreau, Cecile 253, 684
Chi, Greta 243
Chiarella, Ray 241
Chilcott, Barbara 278
Childs, Ted 722, 723
Chiles, Lois 170, 486
Chin, Tsai 59, 76, 92, 234, 797
Chitty, Erik 338
Christian, Linda 353
Christie, Julie 195
Churchill, Donald 801
Ciannelli, Eduardo 705
Cilento, Diane 278, 382, 507, 570, 741, 828, 832, 844
Cipriani, Stelvio 520
Clare, Alan 653
Clare, Diane 199, 562
Clare, Mary 591
Claridge, Norman 110
Clark, Bob 496
Clark, Candy 43
Clark, Dane 253, 281, 332, 497
Clark, Ernest 471, 627, 630, 759, 763, 836
Clark, Jameson 65, 330
Clark, Jim 436
Clark, Petula 624, 734, 769
Clark, Susan 496
Clarke, James Kenelm 228
Clarke, Richard 762
Clarkson, Stephen 167
Clavin, Pat 454
Clay, Nicholas 519
Clayton, Jack 303, 827
Cleary, Jon 665
Clegg, Tom 723
Clein, John 369, 571
Clemens, Brian (Tony O'Grady) 13, 23, 38, 58, 102, 176, 306, 329, 333, 372, 420, 485, 548, 556, 600, 608, 643, 747, 750, 773, 789, 813, 836, 838, 839
Clemens, Paul 569
Clement, Dick 96, 387, 558, 803
Clements, John 478
Cleminson, Colin 7
Clery, Corinne 486
Clewes, Howard 153
Clewes, Lorraine 649
Clifford, Hubert 148, 321, 351, 358, 617
Clifford, Jefferson 121
Clunes, Alec 754, 763
Clyde, June 531
Clyde, Thomas 312, 339, 484
Cobby, Brian 74
Coburn, Charles 355, 768
Coburn, James 208, 251, 375
Cochran, Steve 490, 812

Index of Names

Cockrell, Gary 34, 134
Coda, Frank 766
Codrington, Ann 621
Coen, Guido 36, 142, 150, 219, 301, 337, 391, 395, 474, 502, 508, 551, 564, 662, 715
Coffee, Lenore 265
Cohen, Herman 37
Coke, Peter 77
Cole, George 273, 594, 812
Cole, Sidney 645
Coleman, Bryan 316, 721
Coles, Michael 370, 443, 516, 677, 722
Colicos, John 65
Colin, Ian 42, 142
Colleano, Bonar 171, 222, 376, 450, 586, 756
Collier, Patience 579
Collin, John 156
Collins, Anthony 777
Collins, Jackie 738, 790
Collins, Joan 43, 227, 244, 283, 303, 389, 611, 717
Collinson, Peter 14, 273, 371, 379, 578, 648, 687, 698, 764
Comfort, Lance 23, 26, 54, 71, 74, 212, 232, 295, 336, 444, 448, 563, 582, 588, 763, 766
Comma, Vivian 319
Comport, Brian 247, 451, 491
Compton, Fay 52, 204, 768
Connell, Maureen 28, 138, 210, 395, 453, 697, 768
Connery, Sean 6, 186, 193, 252, 274, 277, 302, 321, 501, 604, 751, 837, 844
Connolly, Billy 1
Connor, Kenneth 815
Connor, Kevin 778
Connor, Patrick 395
Connors, Chuck 215
Conrad, Jess 323, 394
Constantine, Eddie 427, 571, 683, 776
Conte, Richard 229, 422
Conway, Tom 28, 60, 73, 408, 556, 566
Cook, Peter 137
Cooke, Alan 258
Cookson, Georgina 95, 678, 776
Cooney, Ray 316, 815
Coop, Denys 78, 203, 227, 478, 772
Cooper, Bernie 271
Cooper, Betty 319
Cooper, Freddie 154
Cooper, Gary 507
Cooper, George A. 322, 534, 646, 699, 806, 816
Cooper, Irissa 419
Cooper, John C. *see* Croydon, John
Cooper, Stuart 191
Cooper, Terence 83, 809
Cooper, Wilkie 41, 218, 315, 426, 447, 462, 587, 589, 654, 683, 776, 827
Coote, Bernard 805
Coote, Robert 412, 735
Cope, Kenneth 98, 151, 172, 204, 391, 508, 763, 767
Copley, Peter 816
Coppel, Alec 320, 480, 671

Coquillon, John 1, 365, 373, 533, 710, 745, 830
Corbett, Harry H. 126, 263, 367, 467, 659, 759, 792
Cord, Alex 407
Cordeau, Sonya 138
Cordell, Frank 693, 778, 808
Cordet, Helene 419, 748
Corey, Jeff 831
Corri, Adrienne 36, 42, 78, 248, 436, 474, 716, 719
Corrie, Delia 197
Cortesa, Valentina (Valentina Cortese) 645
Corvin, Maria 651
Cosmatos, George Pan 90
Cossins, James 244
Cotton, Joseph 680
Cotts, Campbell 28
Couloris, George 129, 207, 396, 624, 731, 795
Couper, Barbara 574
Court, Hazel 36, 75, 125, 344, 457, 482, 511, 635, 659, 836
Court, Joanne 81
Courtenay, Tom 96, 137, 524, 558
Courtneidge, Cicely 479, 686
Courtney, Alan D. 519
Coutard, Raoul 215
Cowan, Maurice 335, 554
Cowan, Paul 300
Coward, Noël 78, 379, 559
Cox, Jack 9
Cox, Vivian A. 164, 351, 433, 774
Cox, Wally 34
Cox-Ife, William 146
Crabtree, Arthur 171, 488, 814
Craig, Hilton 678
Craig, Howard 542
Craig, Ivan 143, 381, 596, 619, 669
Craig, Michael 216, 230, 351, 483, 575, 632
Craig, Wendy 478, 510
Crain, Jeanne 207
Crane, Peter 17
Craven, Timothy 767
Crawford, Broderick 215
Crawford, Howard Marion 59, 76, 92, 234, 253, 416, 541, 797
Crawford, Joan 37
Crawford, John 57, 263, 322, 365, 374, 431, 457, 557, 581
Crawford, Junia 294
Crawford, Michael 387
Cresswell, John 40, 91, 587, 835
Cribbins, Bernard 272, 807
Crichton, Charles 263, 358, 741
Crichton, Michael 252
Crombie, Tony 149, 686
Cross, Eric 40, 46, 75, 134, 148, 164, 167, 206, 224, 330, 358, 367, 566, 752, 753, 823
Cross, Henry *see* Spalding, Harry
Cross, Hugh 652
Crossman, Gerald 352
Crowden, Graham 156, 248, 519
Crowdy, Miriam 143
Crowhurst, John 738
Croydon, John (John C. Cooper) 309
Cruickshank, Andrew 500, 708

Crutchley, Rosalie 347, 654, 826
Cuadrado, Luis 520
Culp, Robert 373
Culver, Michael 241
Culver, Roland 269, 345, 359, 411, 435, 622, 731, 751, 800
Cumming, David 619
Cummings, Bob (Robert Cummings) 254
Cummings, Constance 377
Cummings, Robert *see* Cummings, Bob
Cummins, Peggy 321
Cunningham, Jack 206
Curram, Roland 666
Currie, Finlay 78, 115, 265, 740, 825
Curry, Shaun 168
Curtis, Bruce Cohn 558
Curtis, Martin 108, 490, 666
Curzon, Fiona 415
Cusack, Cyril 152, 213, 263, 384, 390, 448, 689, 820
Cusack, Sinead 611
Cushing, Peter 89, 244, 343, 436, 455, 507, 661, 680, 720, 760, 778, 806
Cusick, Peter 426
Cuthbertson, Allan 20, 111, 204, 282, 439, 441, 552, 589, 625, 677, 708

Dade, Stephen 11, 30, 117, 129, 151, 196, 221, 285, 313, 333, 411, 455, 650, 724, 742, 797
D'Aguiar, Thelma 99
Dahl, Arlene 267
Dahl, Roald 519, 844
Dainton, Patricia 23, 314, 535, 555, 573, 739, 774, 834
Dalby, Amy 405, 711, 824
Dale, Philip 506
Dallamano, Massimo 61
Dallimore, Maurice 118
Dalrymple, Ian 481
Dalton, Audrey 121
Dalton, Christopher 590
Dalton, Emmet 179
Dalton, Timothy 8
D'Amico, Masolino 606
Dandridge, Dorothy 484
Dane, Lawrence 31
Daneman, Paul 114, 268, 424, 760
Daniel, Jennifer 115, 467, 610
Danielle, Suzanne 300
Danielli, Wendy 588
Daniely, Lisa 140, 329, 405, 448, 457, 555, 703, 753, 789
Dankworth, John 128, 243, 407, 483, 579, 607, 630
Danvers-Walker, Michael 529
Danziger, Edward J. 38, 102, 120, 149, 176, 226, 246, 306, 329, 333, 372, 420, 440, 485, 526, 536, 548, 556, 608, 649, 686, 714, 747, 750, 773, 789, 813, 836, 838, 839
Danziger, Harry Lee 38, 102, 120, 149, 176, 226, 246, 306, 329, 333, 372, 420, 440, 485, 526, 536, 548, 556, 608, 649, 686, 714, 747, 750, 773, 789, 813, 836, 838, 839
Dare, John 365
Darin, Bobby 703

Darnborough, Antony 332, 512, 674
Dassin, Jules 518
Daubeney, Diana 637
Dauphin, Claude 278
Davenport, Nigel 610, 639, 699, 798, 803
Davidson, Lewis (L.W. Davidson, Lew Davidson) 5, 317
Davies, Betty Ann 305, 497
Davies, David 274, 285
Davies, Jack 540, 653
Davies, Petra 788
Davies, Rupert 75, 128, 140, 180, 254, 276, 632, 689, 770, 805
Davies, William 126, 155, 188, 289, 416, 482
Davies, Windsor 584
Davion, Alexander (Alex Davion) 54, 565
Davis, Allan 114, 116, 268
Davis, Bette 15, 170, 510, 633
Davis, Carl 816
Davis, Christopher 30
Davis, Jeff 776
Davis, John 293
Davis, Michael 241, 472
Davis, Noel 767
Davis, Sammy, Jr. 552, 630
Davis, Stratford *see* Sharman, Maisie
Davy, Pamela Ann (Ann Davy) 12, 98, 487
Dawes, Anthony 217
Dawson, Anthony 6, 98, 193, 309, 344, 413, 426, 545, 752, 794
Dawson, Basil 181
Day, Frances 774
Day, Robert 309, 706
Day, Sally 619
Day, Vera 309, 781
Dayan, Assaf 648
Dean, Bill 529
Dean, Isabel 604
Dean, Ivor 736
Dean, Jimmy 186
Dean, Vaughan N. 352
Deane, Charles 182, 695
Deane, Robert 188
Deane, Shirley 845
Dearden, Basil 19, 80, 288, 412, 469, 478, 586, 632, 644, 801, 806, 837
De Banzie, Brenda 351, 515, 571, 744
Debar, Andrée 310
De Benedetti, Aldo 657
Decae, Henri 68, 524
De Carellis, Aldo 606
Decker, Diana 38
Deckers, Eugene 418, 587, 654
Deeley, Michael 23, 379, 618
Deeming, Pamela 143
De Gallier, Alexis *see* Gallier, Alex
Degermark, Pia 432
Deghy, Guy 12, 140, 208, 473, 476
De Grunwald, Anatole 335, 413
De Grunwald, Dimitri 703
De Havilland, Olivia 413
Dehn, Paul 160, 269, 302, 501, 524, 557, 689
Dehner, John 68

De Koker, Richard *see* Simmons, Richard Alan
Delany, Pauline 11, 601
De Lautour, Charles *see* Endfield, Cy
Delerue, Georges 152, 538
Delgado, Roger 77, 341, 733, 740
Dell, Edith 176
Dell, Jeffrey 148
Delon, Nathalie 817
De Los Rios, Waldo 505
Del Prete, Duilio 606
De Marco, Arlene 171
De Marney, Derrick 197, 474, 662
De Marney, Terence 168
De Mendoza, Alberto 14
Dempster, Austin 432, 558
Dempster, Hugh 574
Dench, Judi 154
Denham, Maurice 10, 100, 139, 205, 212, 360, 565, 651, 679, 755, 799
Denison, Michael 122, 236
Denning, Richard 22
Denny, Susan 600, 664
Denton, Geoffrey 766
De Pommes, Felix 628
De Rouen, Reed 316, 454, 493, 508, 669, 771
De Sarigny, Peter 514
Desmond, Robert 286
Desmonde, Jerry 724
Desny, Ivan 543
De Souza, Edward 300, 437
De Toth, Andre 787
Deutsch, David 55
De Villiers, John 726
Devlin, J.G. 24
De Wolff, Francis 49, 116, 277, 343, 414
De Wolfe (Production Music Library) 135, 167, 365, 394, 470, 479, 523, 539, 711
Dexter, Brad 509
Dexter, William 168
Diamond, Arnold 74, 190, 327, 462
Diamond, Margaret 339
Diamond, Marian 304
Dickinson, Desmond 6, 10, 37, 81, 181, 247, 274, 374, 408, 442, 484, 492, 500, 512, 557, 716, 826, 835
Dickinson, Thorold 645
Dickson, Paul 176
Diffring, Anton 107, 130, 203, 204, 221, 332, 351, 368, 402, 464, 555, 654, 661, 770, 818
Dignam, Basil 176, 377, 649, 737, 750
Dignam, Mark 154
Dillman, Bradford 104, 298, 550
Dillon, Robert 546
Dines, Gordon 64, 97, 104, 288, 425, 459, 586, 645, 665
Dinsdale, Alan T. 125, 761
Dix, William 510
Dixson, Bill 726
Dmytryk, Edward 356
Dobie, Alan 489, 653
Doderer, Joop 357
Dodson, Eric 285
Doermer, Christian 726

Doleman, Guy 45, 161, 279, 378, 567, 751, 785
Domergue, Faith 449, 675, 761
Donaggio, Pino 195
Donald, James 80, 387, 512
Donally, Andrew 194, 375
Donat, Peter 626
Donlan, Yolande 63, 213, 383, 737
Donnenfeld, Bernard 402
Donner, Clive 467, 646, 667
Donner, Richard 630
Donovan, Terence 842
Doonan, Anthony 56
Doonan, Patric 53, 331, 363
Doonan, Tony 306, 536, 600
Dor, Karin 234, 844
Doran, James 378
Doré, Alexander 391
Doré, Edna 487
Dorléac, Françoise 45, 136, 820
Dorne, Sandra 9, 27, 287, 439, 556, 585, 642, 743, 750
Dorning, Robert 136, 440, 457
Dors, Diana 37, 139, 315, 409, 428, 479, 571, 629, 735, 775
Dotrice, Karen 745
Dotrice, Michele 13
Dotrice, Roy 785
Douglas, Angela 246, 466, 499
Douglas, John O. 479
Douglas, Johnny 30, 106, 108, 151, 334, 490, 766, 771, 802
Douglas, Katya 278, 397, 494
Douglas, Kirk 96
Douglas, Paul 284
Douglas, Robert 527
Douglass, Stuart 635
Dowling, Joan 504, 586
Down, Lesley-Anne 20, 70, 252
Doyle, David 119
Drache, Heinz 76, 106, 117
Drake, Betsy 374
Drake, Ronald 398
Drake, Tom 150
Dregorn, Lea 417
Dresdel, Sonia 71, 113, 171, 742
Drinkel, Keith 842
Driscoll, Frank 386
Driscoll, Patricia 102, 839
Dromgoole, Patrick 156
Dryhurst, Edward 352, 704
Dubin-Behrmann, Josef 12
Dudley, Ernest 16
Duering, Carl 208, 225, 714
Duff, Howard 684
Duffell, Peter 373, 568
Duhig, Tony 283
Dullea, Keir 78
Dunbar, Robert 155, 453, 482, 676, 721, 740
Duncan, Archie 125
Duncan, Peter 417
Duncan, Trevor 359, 377, 422, 428, 449
Dunham, Joanna 74, 142
Dunn, Geoffrey 197
Dunn, Valentine 398
Dunning, Ruth 142, 347, 793
Dunnock, Mildred 687
Dupont, René 496

Durant, Maurice 502
Durbridge, Francis 731, 800
Duringer, Annemarie 123
Durrant, Roberta 550
Duryea, Dan 192, 746, 809
Duvall, Robert 209
Dwyer, Leslie 47, 111, 345, 389, 477, 671, 697
Dyall, Valentine 63, 314, 338, 385, 526, 573, 631, 701, 721
Dyce, Hamilton 791
Dyke, John Hart 17
Dyneley, Peter 164, 227, 700, 740, 827
Dysart, William 410
Dyson, Reginald 50

Eades, Wilfrid 804, 843
Eady, David 236, 319, 367, 798
Earl, Clifford 24
Easdale, Brian 308, 576
East, John 663
Eastham, Richard 669
Eastwood, Clint 818
Eastwood, James 124, 177, 268, 422, 457, 773, 793, 840
Eaton, Shirley 59, 150, 292, 302, 367, 718, 732, 815
Eaton, Wallas 101, 146
Ebbinghouse, Bernard 2, 5, 24, 25, 98, 115, 156, 172, 199, 205, 233, 255, 258, 282, 368, 424, 437, 443, 491, 513, 516, 543, 549, 567, 583, 610, 612, 616, 651, 660, 677, 709, 759, 762, 784, 798, 811, 825
Ebbins, Milton 552, 630
Eddington, Paul 457
Eden, Mark 54, 282, 562, 567, 638
Edgar, Graham 165, 550
Edge, Francis 46, 336
Edwardes, Olga 669
Edwards, Alan 192, 289, 530
Edwards, Bill 592
Edwards, Blake 727
Edwards, Bob 183
Edwards, Ethel 398
Edwards, Glynn 290, 334, 584, 618, 672
Edwards, Henry 515, 621
Edwards, Hilton 93
Edwards, Kenneth 747
Edwards, Meredith 79, 225, 249, 281, 433, 475, 477
Edwards, Olga 46
Edwards, Vince 315
Egan, Peter 84, 324
Eggar, Samantha 118, 607, 810
Eggerickx, Marianne 87
Eggers, Fred 609
Eisinger, Jo 353, 518
Ekberg, Anita 10, 376, 450
Ekland, Britt 203, 220, 290, 461, 520, 828
Eland, Mike 323
Eldridge, John 554, 586
Eles, Sandor 13, 312
Elfers, Konrad 279, 373
Elg, Taina 744
Elliott, Alison 399
Elliott, Denholm 68, 283, 328, 466, 522, 615, 626, 723

Elliott, Peter 642, 813, 840
Ellis, Jacqueline 2, 334, 513, 667, 771
Ellison, Tim 27, 348
Elmes, Guy 4, 26, 125, 256, 533, 705, 707
Elms, Albert 9, 74, 176, 372, 420, 485, 548, 643, 706, 747, 750, 836, 838
Elphick, Michael 252
Elphinstone, Derek 16
Elton, Eileen 402
Elton, Philip 600
Elton, Ray 671
Elvey, Maurice 349, 411, 742
Elvin, June 631
Emanuel, Ronald 18
Emary, Barbara K. 389, 640
Emmott, Basil 54, 71, 74, 131, 307, 386, 428, 563, 582, 609, 647, 675, 715, 763, 766, 768, 769, 809
Endersby, Clive 241
Endfield, C. Raker see Endfield, Cy
Endfield, Cy (Hugh Raker, C. Raker Endfield, Charles De Lautour, Jonathan Roach and Jonathan Roche) 321, 326, 366, 382, 419, 470, 553, 641
Engel, Fred 785
Engel, Samuel G. 518
English, Richard 39
Englund, George 476
Epstein, Julius 607
Erickson, Paul 219, 307, 395, 465, 525, 647, 655, 749, 769
Eshley, Norman 58, 350
Estella, Alfonso 122
Estridge, Robin 67, 100
Evans, Barry 187
Evans, Clifford 23, 224, 232, 291, 319, 572, 678, 683, 711, 785, 806
Evans, David 411, 477, 742
Evans, Donna 296
Evans, Edward 143
Evans, Michael 53, 669
Evans, Peggy 85, 495
Exton, Clive 198, 347, 521
Eytle, Tommy 508

Fabian 732
Fahey, Brian 54, 71
Fairbanks, Douglas, Jr. 99, 692
Fairchild, William 215, 512
Fairfax, Deborah 276
Fairfield Parlour 231
Fairhurst, Lyn 766
Fairlie, Gerard 85
Faith, Adam 481, 514
Faithfull, Geoffrey 36, 47, 109, 142, 182, 257, 314, 385, 396, 397, 406, 444, 464, 471, 498, 503, 545, 564, 573, 591, 603, 617, 631, 634, 643, 655, 664, 695, 697, 704, 756, 790, 824
Falconer, Alun 133, 370, 453, 514, 792
Falconer, Robert 396
Falk, Rossella 483
Fallon, Terence 592
Fancey, E.J. 7, 257, 261, 385, 655, 738, 770
Fancey, Negus see Negus-Fancey, Olive

Fanning, Rio 592
Farebrother, Violet 267
Fargo, James 283
Farhi, Moris 592
Farmer, Suzan 580
Farnon, Robert 31, 103, 191
Faroughy, Ahmed 11
Farr, Derek 24, 26, 200, 212, 448, 504, 768, 800
Farrar, David 80, 207, 411, 433, 531
Farrell, Charles 171, 337, 488
Farrow, Mia 58, 137, 170
Faulds, Andrew 595
Faulkner, Keith 445, 715
Faulkner, Trader 30, 398, 498
Fawcett, Diana 93
Fay, Chris 775
Faye, Janina 196
Feller, Catherine 439, 499
Fellows, Don 688
Fellows, Robert 292
Fenemore, Hilda 1, 246, 715
Fenemore, Stephen 841
Fennell, Albert 13, 308, 566
Fenton, Bernie 465, 763
Fergusson, Guy 299
Ferrari, Otto 325
Ferraz, Catharina 440
Ferrer, Mel 70, 215
Ferrer, Tony 797
Ferris, Paul 110, 580
Ferzetti, Gabriele 547
Fiander, Lewis 723
Field, Alexander 508
Field, Harry 168, 726
Field, Jon 283
Field, Shirley Anne 323, 767
Fielding, Fenella 546
Fielding, Jerry 43, 710
Fielding, Marjorie 103
Filmer-Sankey, Patrick 683, 776
Finch, Jon 183, 272
Finch, Peter 242, 554
Fine, Harry 273, 578
Finlay, Frank 20, 161, 311, 387, 496, 618, 668, 716, 786, 831
Finn, Catherine 161
Finney, Albert 311, 501, 521
Firbank, Ann 156
Fischer, Kai 765
Fischer, O.W. 821
Fisher, George 173
Fisher, Gerry 12, 58, 70, 390, 639
Fisher, Steve 434, 746
Fisher, Terence 60, 235, 249, 259, 336, 338, 343, 396, 408, 409, 463, 497, 674, 684, 694, 702, 708, 832
Fisz, S. Benjamin 321, 533, 641
Fitzgerald, Geraldine 411
Fitzgerald, Walter 512
Fleischer, Richard 58
Fleming, Brandon 27, 142, 259, 287, 678
Fleming, Ian 372, 405, 440, 608, 813, 838
Flemyng, Gordon 255, 407, 677
Flemyng, Robert 52, 55, 91, 160, 456, 602
Flood, Gerald 276, 672
Forbes, Bryan 141, 158, 351, 412, 638

Forbes, C. Scott 579
Forbes, Meriel 335
Forbes-Robertson, Peter 517, 637
Force, Lewis J. *see* Shonteff, Lindsay
Ford, Derek 49, 637, 716
Ford, Donald 49, 716
Ford, Glenn 755
Ford, Roy 661
Foreman, John 252, 435
Forrest, Anthony 399
Forsyth, Brigit 519
Forsyth, Frank 54
Fortescue, Kenneth 355
Forwood, Anthony 50, 253, 463
Foster, Barry 272, 583, 618, 722, 786, 831
Foster, Dianne 434, 693
Foster, Dudley 516, 612
Foster, Maurice 21, 387
Fowler, Harry 36, 66, 109, 189, 634, 662, 814
Fox, Edward 43, 94, 152, 509, 691
Fox, James 208
Fox, John 280, 296, 781
Foxwell, Ivan 602
Frame, Grazina 563
Franciosa, Anthony (Tony Franciosa) 243, 251
Francis, Derek 25, 132, 240, 334, 451, 513, 798
Francis, Freddie 161, 360, 491, 521, 534, 565, 597, 760, 772, 796
Francis, Jeremy Lee 415
Francis, Kevin 580
Francis, Nina 165
Francis, Sandra 757
Francis, Silvia 526
Franco, Jess (Jesus Franco) 59, 92
François, Helene 767
Frank, Charles 411
Frankel, Benjamin 113, 200, 265, 312, 413, 426, 433, 438, 458, 480, 512, 518, 546, 557, 674
Frankel, Cyril 782, 799
Franklin, Gretchen 35
Franklin, Pamela 13, 510, 741
Franklyn, John 13
Franklyn, William 136, 141, 582, 673, 734
Frankovich, Mike J. 265, 438
Franks, Chloe 826
Franz, Arthur 356
Fraser, Bill 154, 469
Fraser, Colin 724
Fraser, John 636, 716
Fraser, Liz 563
Fraser, Ronald 243, 293, 802, 831
Fraser, Shelagh 580, 631
Frears, Stephen 311
Frechter, Colin 648
Frederick, Lynne 636
Fredericks, Scott 162
Freeman, Denis 4
Freeman, Ernie 203, 208
Freeman, Mona 35, 184
Fregonese, Hugo 654
Freiberger, Fred 812
French, Harold 266, 345, 458
French, Leslie 557

Frend, Charles 425
Friedman, Seymour 224, 629
Friend, Philip 38, 111, 178, 185, 280, 676, 707, 813
Fröbe, Gert 14, 302, 779
Frontiere, Dominic 70
Fuchsberger, Joachim 234
Fuest, Robert 13
Fuggel, James 223
Fuller, Patricia 816
Furneaux, Yvonne 131, 352
Furie, Sidney J. 378, 509
Furst, Joseph 186, 231, 328, 545, 736
Fusek, Vera 223, 306

Gabor, Zsa Zsa 459
Gabriel, John 120, 285, 600, 658, 660
Gael, Anna 723
Gaffney, Liam 712
Gale, John 466
Gale, Richard 475, 825
Galleani, Ely 606
Gallier, Alex (Alexis De Gallier) 22, 114, 138, 623
Galloway, Lindsay 199, 258
Galloway, Pamela 475
Gallu, Samuel 418, 452, 736
Gamley, Douglas 41, 171, 338, 436, 517, 609
Gampu, Ken 283
Gardenia, Vincent 251
Gardner, Arthur 70
Gardner, Ava 90
Gardner, Caron 168
Gardner, Hy 292
Garner, Rex 495
Garnett, Tony 368, 616
Garrison, Joy 129, 707
Gartside, Ernest 122, 123, 411, 742
Garvarentz, Georges 300, 323, 779
Gasson, Hilary 691
Gastoni, Lisa 74, 232, 238, 374, 444, 700, 807, 840
Gates, Tudor 151, 273, 780
Gauge, Alexander 35, 73, 125, 201, 301, 337, 349, 588, 753
Gawthorne, Peter 573
Gay, John 324
Gayford, John 395
Gaylor, Anna 654
Gayson, Eunice 408
Gee, Donald 791
Gee, Prunella 830
Geeson, Judy 37, 70, 183, 194, 198, 209, 227, 244, 304, 315
Gell, William 452, 734
Geller, Harold 391
Genn, Leo 39, 106, 187, 276, 308, 732, 765
George, George W. 529, 786
George, Götz 59
George, Susan 187, 231, 273, 432, 699, 710, 764
Georges-Picot, Olga 580
Gerard, Malcolm 472
Gerber, Jack 536
Gerhard, Roberto 645
Germaine, Mary 112, 182, 257, 262, 307, 349, 532
Gibbs, Gerald (Gerry Gibbs) 23,

48, 77, 111, 126, 174, 179, 267, 340, 377, 453, 523, 528, 555, 593, 627, 693, 711
Gibbs, Sheila Shand 398
Gibson, Alan 127, 304
Gibson-Smith, Ian 570
Gielgud, John 214, 298, 357, 496, 501, 639
Gifford, Alan 264, 757, 807
Gilbert, James 585
Gilbert, Lewis 91, 218, 303, 486, 634, 690, 844
Gilbert, Philip 3
Gill, Robert 82
Gill, Tom 419
Gilliat, Leslie 220, 614
Gilliat, Sidney 220, 267, 692
Gilling, John 53, 56, 65, 97, 101, 146, 163, 201, 216, 222, 275, 284, 291, 376, 400, 434, 450, 537, 564, 596, 605, 693, 743, 749, 753, 808, 819, 822, 832
Gilman, Martin 241
Gilmore, Denis 792
Gilmore, Peter 64, 271
Gilpin, Toni 240
Giltinan, Donal 98, 156, 811
Gingold, Hermione 507
Ginsberg, Donald 419, 774
Giovanni, Paul 828
Gish, Lillian 557
Gladwin, Joe 521
Glaister, Gerard 115, 567, 651, 660
Glass, George 507
Glass, Paul 78
Glendenning, Candace 260
Glendinning, Hone 475, 477, 635, 657, 748
Glover, Brian 778
Glover, Bruce 186
Glover, Julian 10, 154, 375, 407, 736
Glyn-Jones, John 667, 672
Goddard, Paulette 702
Goddard, Ralph 600
Goddard, Willoughby 367, 431
Godfrey, Derek 312, 317
Godsell, Vanda 69, 86, 109, 151, 344, 367, 406, 824
Godwin, Frank 589
Goehr, Walter 362
Goetz, Hayes 85, 345
Goldbeck, Willis 753
Goldblatt, Harold 478
Golden, Michael 150, 619, 631
Goldie, Wyndham 641
Goldman, William 469
Goldner, Charles 207, 362, 645
Goldoni, Lelia 360, 736
Goldsmith, Jerry 68, 90, 252, 489, 604, 639
Goldstone, Richard 755
Gomez, Arthur 177, 219, 429
Goode, Frederic 168, 696, 726
Goodhart, Geoffrey 27, 259, 287, 348, 678
Goodliffe, Michael 184, 213, 383, 447, 461, 543, 576, 744, 780, 784, 823
Goodman, David Zelag 708, 710
Goodwin, Harold 334, 771

Index of Names

Goodwin, Richard 170, 501
Goodwin, Ron 10, 114, 165, 227, 272, 384, 397, 441, 460, 492, 494, 500, 503, 568, 818, 821, 833
Gordon, Colin 345, 393, 422, 625, 653, 715, 742
Gordon, David 706
Gordon, Dorothy 354
Gordon, James B. 248
Gordon, Leon 345
Gordon, Nora 329, 528, 585
Gordon, Richard 94
Goring, Marius 40, 72, 103, 129, 179, 181, 238, 332, 458, 622, 717, 776, 792, 821
Gorman, Shay 83, 229
Gorrie, Alan 241
Gossage, John 238, 284, 408
Gotell, Walter 277, 690, 776
Gottlieb, Morton 670
Gough, Michael 37, 52, 86, 282, 348, 482, 528, 815
Gould, Elliott 403
Gould, Heywood 68
Goulder, Stanley 666, 780
Graham, Arthur 57, 232
Graham, David 133, 394
Graham, Kenny 527, 819
Graham, Ranald 722
Graham, Winston 531
Grahame, Gloria 303, 456, 533
Grahame, Margot 795
Grainer, Ron 19, 521, 550, 625, 842
Granat, Frank 786
Granger, Stewart 129, 265, 644, 782, 827, 831
Granik, Jon 590
Grant, Arthur 89, 123, 141, 213, 238, 244, 322, 383, 389, 546, 565, 640, 685, 706, 708, 733, 792, 807, 820
Grant, Gilly 110
Grant, Lee 375
Grant, Moray 147
Grant, Peter 9
Grant, Stanley 512
Grantham, Mark (M.M. McCormack) 120, 149, 226, 246, 285, 405, 440, 526, 649
Gray, Allan 145, 411
Gray, Barry 133
Gray, Carole 76
Gray, Charles 177, 186, 227, 248, 452, 469, 524, 844
Gray, Coleen 237, 362
Gray, Donald 79, 261, 562, 761
Gray, Elizabeth 415, 542, 725
Gray, Elspet 385
Gray, Janine 564
Gray, Nadia 129, 462, 509, 531, 794
Gray, Peter 394
Gray, Sally 224
Gray, Steve 228
Gray, Vernon 299
Gray, Willoughby 1
Grayson, Diane 58
Grayson, Godfrey 149, 226, 237, 329, 372, 405, 600, 686, 839
Greatorex, Wilfred 538
Greco, Juliette 821
Green, Danny 22, 367, 400, 404, 682

Green, Garard 217, 488, 596
Green, Guy 345, 351, 433, 531, 589, 617, 673, 683
Green, Janet 113, 230, 425, 433, 632, 801
Green, Mick 648
Green, Nigel 128, 159, 234, 378, 441, 455, 582, 583, 834
Green, Philip (Phil Green) 179, 223, 292, 412, 455, 469, 504, 554, 566, 581, 632, 644, 659, 801, 806, 834, 841
Greene, David 147, 361, 639, 699
Greene, Graham 559
Greene, Howard 616
Greene, Max 518, 720, 777
Greene, Richard 40, 59, 92, 122
Greenwood, Jack 2, 5, 24, 25, 86, 98, 114, 115, 116, 128, 156, 172, 177, 199, 205, 233, 255, 258, 268, 282, 368, 424, 429, 437, 441, 443, 457, 460, 467, 513, 516, 543, 549, 567, 568, 583, 610, 612, 616, 651, 660, 667, 677, 709, 759, 762, 784, 793, 798, 811, 825, 833, 840
Greenwood, Joan 242
Greenwood, John 15, 288, 305
Greenwood, Paul 276
Greenwood, Rosamund 498
Greeves, Vernon 402
Gregg, Christina 71, 126, 196, 789
Gregg, Everley 523
Gregg, Hubert 249, 742
Gregg, Olive 570
Gregory, Celia 8
Gregory, David 286, 334, 465
Gregory, Johnny (John Gregory) 286, 364, 525, 650, 664, 672, 715
Gregory, Nigel 399
Gregory, Rowena 666
Gregory, Thea 253, 301, 596, 678
Gregson, John 82, 236, 273, 274, 524, 683, 763, 795
Greifer, Lewis 89, 455
Grellis, Brian 244
Grenfell, Joyce 266, 546
Grennell, Aiden 221
Gréville, Edmond T. 310
Greville-Bell, Anthony 579, 735
Grey, Monica 790
Greyn, Clinton 618
Griffin, Josephine 352, 456, 589
Griffith, Hugh 153, 326, 826
Griffith, Kenneth 84, 107, 307, 331, 347, 453, 563, 575, 611, 720, 746, 752, 769, 831
Griffiths, David 300
Griffiths, Howard 414
Griffiths, Jane 157, 199, 281, 308, 365, 655, 739, 750, 770, 775
Griffiths, Leon 691
Griffiths, Lucy 739
Grigg, Thelma 400
Grindrod, Phil (Philip Grindrod) 121, 124, 130, 184, 189, 349, 359, 393, 398, 449, 588, 601, 628, 700, 712, 805
Grizzard, George 251
Grodin, Charles 214
Guard, Dominic 1

Guarnieri, Ennio 90
Gudrun, Ann 746
Guest, Val 15, 21, 63, 72, 213, 278, 322, 383, 624, 737, 812, 820
Guillermin, John 153, 170, 514, 555, 671, 768, 827
Guinness, Alec 242, 404, 559, 602, 633
Gunning, Christopher 304, 317
Gur, Alizia 527
Gurney, Rachel 279, 282, 587
Gutowski, Gene 136
Guttenberg, Steve 68
Guy, Alan 296
Gwillim, Jack 616, 649
Gwynn, Michael 646, 688
Gynt, Greta 182, 266, 363, 488, 615, 623, 748, 822, 833

Hafner, Ingrid 188, 255
Hagen, Uta 68
Hager, Peter 394
Hagleton, Lewis J. 110
Hagman, Larry 209
Haigh, Kenneth 160
Haines, Patricia 516, 549
Haines, Patricia 241, 410
Hakim, Andre 456
Hale, Elvi 443
Hales, Gordon 610
Hall, Brian 427
Hall, Cameron 366, 570
Hall, Henry 27
Hall, Peter 579
Hall, Robert 843
Hall, Willis 447
Hallatt, May 299
Hallett, Neil 773, 839
Halliday, Peter 188, 241, 436, 725
Hallinan, Susan 221
Halward, Christine 386
Hama, Mie 844
Hamama, Faten 81, 658
Hamer, Robert 242, 430, 633
Hamilton, Guy 186, 279, 302, 423, 447, 461, 615
Hamlett, Dilys 183
Hamlisch, Marvin 690
Hammond, Marcus 819
Hammond, Nora 348
Hammond, Peter 121, 675
Hammond, Roger 282
Hampshire, Susan 431, 521, 782, 804
Hampton, Orville H. 401
Hampton, Susie 241
Hanbury, Victor 167, 406, 539, 617
Hancock, Sheila 521
Handl, Irene 79
Hanley, Jenny 260
Hanley, Jimmy 47, 603
Hannaford, David 640
Hannen, Nicholas 748
Hanslip, Ann 235
Hanson, Barry 427
Harareet, Haya 644
Hardin, Ty 37
Hardtmuth, Paul 185
Hardy, Laurence 837
Hardy, René 779
Hardy, Robert 37, 689, 842

Index of Names

Hardy, Robin 828
Hardy, Sophie 729, 782
Hare, Robertson 562, 653
Hargreaves, L.Z. *see* Vetter, Charles F.
Harker, Gordon 26, 640
Harker, Jane 658
Harlow, John 62, 144, 174
Harper, Barbara S. 3, 588
Harper, Gerald 403, 709
Harper, Kenneth 6
Harrington, Curtis 826
Harrington, Jean 162
Harrington, Ramsey 120
Harris, Dean 202
Harris, Graham 520
Harris, James B. 34
Harris, Johnny 269
Harris, Julius W. 423
Harris, Lionel 199
Harris, Richard (actor) 90, 283, 390, 831
Harris, Richard (screenwriter) 24, 361, 424, 437, 443, 549, 715
Harris, Robert 604
Harris, Vernon 88, 218, 303
Harrison, Howard 699
Harrison, Joan 103
Harrison, Kathleen 91, 200, 654
Harrison, Maurice 155, 189
Harrison, Norman 83, 368, 424
Harrison, Rex 426
Hart, Ben R. 143
Hart, Diane 221, 551
Hart, Peter 54
Hartford-Davis, Robert 49, 134, 247
Hartley, Neil 154
Hartley, Richard 403
Hartnell, William 148, 150, 177, 200, 204, 265, 321, 359, 381, 548, 581, 615, 762
Harvey, Frank 141, 331, 430, 652, 744
Harvey, James *see* Harvey, Walter J.
Harvey, Jean 11
Harvey, Jimmy *see* Harvey, Walter J.
Harvey, Jimmy W. *see* Harvey, Walter J.
Harvey, John 50, 161, 434
Harvey, Laurence 82, 137, 303, 398, 529, 625, 634
Harvey, Verna 17, 61
Harvey, Walter J. (Walter Harvey, James Harvey, Jimmy Harvey, Jimmy W. Harvey) 3, 42, 50, 60, 72, 88, 112, 138, 169, 171, 175, 211, 219, 235, 253, 256, 281, 297, 316, 334, 346, 381, 391, 395, 400, 401, 409, 454, 488, 497, 499, 508, 525, 539, 553, 561, 600, 608, 621, 623, 629, 656, 682, 694, 702, 739, 740, 746, 773, 814, 822, 832, 845
Harwood, Johanna 193
Harwood, Ronald 231
Hashimoto, Shinobu 842
Haslett, Matthew 296
Hassall, Imogen 491
Hatch, Tony 723
Hauer, Rutger 830

Havelock-Allan, Anthony 557
Hawkesworth, John 752
Hawkins, Frank 369, 395, 663
Hawkins, Jack 267, 335, 412, 425, 469, 692, 735, 741, 787, 817
Hawkins, John 767
Hawksworth, John 578
Haworth, Jill 318
Hawthorne, Nigel 723
Hawtrey, Charles 671
Hay, Alan 202
Hayden, Jane 399
Hayden, Linda 228, 436
Hayden, Sterling 165
Haye, Helen 6
Hayers, Sidney 20, 107, 165, 183, 210, 439, 550, 575, 611, 805, 823
Hayes, Alfred 203
Hayes, Patricia 61
Haygarth, Anthony 791
Hayles, Kenneth R. (Kenneth Hayles) 28, 57, 249, 250, 327, 572, 694, 721
Hayne, Murray 616
Haynes, Stanley 62, 144
Hays, Geoffrey 726
Haystead, Mercy 172, 671
Hayter, James 85, 319, 363, 561, 587, 628, 703, 744
Hayward, Louis 629
Hazell, Hy 63, 393, 400, 532, 694, 827
Heal, Joan 591
Hearne, Reginald 211, 650, 664, 695
Heath, Eira 285
Heath, Joan 188
Heck, Carl 257
Hedison, David 423, 540
Hedley, Jack 513, 799
Heffer, Richard 577
Heflin, Van 452
Heinz, Gerard 333, 353
Hellaby, Andrew 688
Heller, John G. 111
Heller, Lukas 86, 341, 513
Heller, Otto 208, 279, 362, 378, 404, 458, 469, 509, 576, 765, 800, 801, 837
Heller, Paul 778
Hellman, Marcel 207
Helm, Carina 261
Helpmann, Robert 602
Hemmings, David 191, 269, 319, 390, 496, 563, 590, 691, 791, 810
Hempel, Anouska 202
Hendel, Kenneth 187
Hendry, Gloria 423
Hendry, Ian 17, 290, 293, 375, 735
Heneghan, Patricia 133
Henley, David 129, 707
Hennessy, Peter 155, 229, 264, 416, 482, 676, 721, 757
Henney, Del 710
Henreid, Paul 463
Henry, Kenneth 145
Henson, Basil 98, 199
Henson, Gladys 80, 142
Henson, Nicky 542, 577
Hentschel, David 691
Hepburn, Audrey 645

Herbert, Percy 198, 247, 831
Hermanos Deniz Cuban Rhythm Band 559
Heron, Joyce 662
Herrmann, Bernard 220, 519, 786
Hershey, Barbara 778
Heslop, Charles 411, 640
Hessler, Gordon 95, 215, 410, 505
Hewer, John 18, 714
Hewitt, Enid 678
Hewitt, Sean 44
Heyward, Louis M. 505
Heywood, Alan 197
Heywood, Anne 176, 263, 489, 796, 799, 806
Heywood, Pat 491
Hibbert, Geoffrey 219
Hickox, Douglas 70, 668, 735
Hickson, Joan 163, 331, 588, 652, 758
Higgins, John C. 185, 248
Higgins, Ken 630, 703
Hildyard, Jack 61, 308, 335, 382, 483, 599, 731, 831
Hill, Arthur 489, 631, 634
Hill, Benny 379
Hill, Douglas 517, 584
Hill, Jacqueline 62
Hill, James 716
Hill, Rose 27
Hill, Walter 435
Hill-Bowen, William 434
Hiller, Wendy 94, 355, 501
Hillier, Erwin 99, 207, 352, 473, 507, 602
Hilton, Tony 316, 815
Hinde, Madeline 247
Hinds, Anthony 50, 88, 112, 169, 239, 253, 256, 281, 297, 343, 346, 400, 401, 409, 565, 621, 629, 682, 708, 746, 822, 832
Hines, Ronald 210, 334
Hird, Thora 433, 753
Hirst, Robert 536
Hitchcock, Alfred 272
Hobson, Valerie 808
Hodge, Bill 143
Hodge, Jonathan 215, 803
Hodges, Ken 20, 21, 140, 157, 197, 217, 236, 248, 270, 286, 289, 387, 530, 577, 611, 687, 788
Hodges, Mike 290, 598
Hoffman, Dustin 8, 710
Hoffmann, Robert 21
Hogan, Brenda 756
Hogarth, Michael 143
Holden, Jan 22, 226, 592, 708, 838
Holley, Bernard 162
Hollingsworth, John 16
Holloway, Stanley 477, 732
Holm, Ian 390
Holm, Sonia 603, 743
Holmes, David 231, 410, 819
Holmes, Milton 473
Holt, Patrick 9, 105, 267, 287, 294, 301, 315, 479, 502, 525, 556, 650, 694, 702, 721, 743, 765
Holt, Seth 139, 510, 541, 730
Homeier, Skip 535
Homolka, Oscar 45, 227, 279, 352, 727

Index of Names

Hopcraft, Arthur 8
Hope, Gary 44, 110, 415
Hope, Vida 238
Hopkins, Anthony 390, 432, 817
Hopkins, Antony 91, 654
Hopkins, Joan 200
Hopkins, John 496, 751
Hopkins, Julie 416
Hoppe, Marianne 732
Hordern, Michael 305, 332, 345, 387, 435, 484, 522, 685, 689, 735, 818
Horne, Derek 84
Horner, Penelope 181
Horney, Brigitte 782
Horsley, John 28, 65, 73, 163, 174, 201, 366, 434, 449, 475, 525, 554, 605, 610, 650, 697, 704, 755, 758, 840
Hoskins, Bob 427
Hough, John 231
Houghton, Don 661
Houston, Charles 140, 564
Houston, Donald 135, 141, 182, 204, 250, 259, 294, 406, 453, 462, 716, 719, 818
Houston, Glyn 217, 564, 617, 677
Houston, Renee 136, 561, 760, 769
Hoven, Adrian 373
Howard, Arthur 553
Howard, Eldon 38, 102, 306, 329, 333, 372, 420, 485, 548, 649, 686, 747, 789, 813, 836, 838, 839
Howard, Elizabeth Jane 799
Howard, Joyce 657
Howard, Peter *see* Koch, Howard
Howard, Ronald 18, 30, 46, 64, 120, 200, 257, 327, 348, 394, 439, 440, 485, 503, 507, 528, 539, 686, 829
Howard, Trevor 96, 113, 214, 324, 376, 421, 447, 484, 580, 705, 779
Howard, Vanessa 491, 679, 816
Howell, Peter 788
Howells, Ursula 3, 132, 291, 425, 491, 664, 737, 769, 788, 814
Howerd, Frankie 347, 404, 624
Howman, Karl 228
Hubschmid, Paul 279, 490, 729
Hudis, Norman 73, 130, 171, 232, 264, 330, 344, 464, 572, 704, 814
Hudson, Vanda 391, 714
Hughes, Gary 326
Hughes, Ken 48, 69, 121, 346, 375, 422, 428, 589, 761, 768, 829
Hughes, Peter 592
Hughes, Roddy 314, 631
Huke, Bob 166, 796, 799
Hulbert, Jack 479, 686
Hulke, Malcolm 416, 445
Hume, Alan 31, 407, 579, 778, 804
Hume, Kenneth 342, 628
Hunka, Sasa 323
Hunnicutt, Gayle 269, 271, 648, 687
Hunt, Gareth 415
Hunt, Marsha 190
Hunt, Martita 78
Hunt, Peter 298, 547
Hunter, Alastair 758
Hunter, Ian 212, 312
Hunter, Jeffrey 123
Hunter, John 515, 621
Hunter, Russell 84

Hunter, Tab 780
Hunter, Thomas 356
Huntington, Lawrence 122, 163, 164, 166, 280, 366, 601, 707, 781
Huntley, Raymond 49, 340, 372, 408, 409, 426, 720, 731
Hurst, David 622
Hurst, Veronica 26, 67, 157, 291, 295, 414
Hurt, John 191
Hussey, Olivia 94, 170
Huston, John 32, 435
Hutchinson, Harry 206
Hutchison, Ken 165, 710, 723
Huth, Harold 52, 339, 585
Hutton, Brian G. 529, 818
Hutton, Robert 444, 580, 642, 664, 844
Huxtable, Judy 187, 597
Hyatt, Charles 271
Hyde, Kenneth 621, 685
Hyer, Martha 132, 680
Hylton, Jane 79, 107, 164, 180, 526, 647, 805, 845
Hyman, Kenneth 733

Ibbetson, Arthur 214, 239, 412, 494, 648, 810, 817, 818
Illing, Peter 211, 225, 346, 362, 376, 382, 449, 572, 642, 821
Iman 357
Imi, Tony 540
Innes, Charmian 146
Innes, George 311
Ireland, Anthony 523
Ireland, Jill 177, 391
Ireland, John 236, 297, 303, 608, 697, 764
Irving, Penny 44, 354
Ismael, Zoreen 663
Ives, Burl 559
Ives, Douglas 789

Jack, Collette 520
Jackson, Dan 39, 319
Jackson, David 399
Jackson, Freda 24, 408
Jackson, Gordon 55, 57, 139, 167, 173, 180, 378, 449, 591, 626, 747, 789
Jackson, Pat 196, 653, 815
Jacobi, Derek 357, 544
Jacobs, Alexander 668
Jaeger, Frederick 240
Jaffe, Carl 131, 197, 225, 339, 566, 692
Jaffrey, Saeed 830
Jago, Jo 79
James, Clifton 423, 461
James, Donald 418
James, Sidney 218, 222, 242, 256, 297, 321, 346, 400, 450, 566, 815
Jane, Topsy 481
Janni, Joseph 483
Jarre, Maurice 118, 435, 524
Jarrott, Charles 759
Jason, Rick 238
Jayne, Jennifer 50, 109, 219, 360, 836
Jayston, Michael 194, 375
Jeans, Ursula 522
Jeavons, Colin 181, 183
Jeffrey, Peter 165, 304, 544, 816

Jeffries, Lionel 47, 231, 330, 344, 397, 492, 800, 826
Jenkins, David 16
Jenkins, Megs 500, 645, 752
Jenkins, Patrick 281
Jerrold, Mary 662
Jessel, Patricia 482
Jessop, Peter 119, 260, 276, 350, 354, 417, 636
Jobert, Marlène 96
John, Derek L.L. 223
John, Rosamund 515, 556, 662
Johns, Glynis 686, 692
Johns, Harriette 149, 474
Johns, Mervyn 124, 210, 213, 250, 350, 377, 514, 546, 800, 824
Johns, Stratford 595, 788
Johnson, Fred 235
Johnson, Katie 355, 404
Johnson, Laurie 13, 183, 752
Johnson, Noel 567, 725
Johnson, Nunnally 426
Johnson, Rafer 407
Johnson, Richard 81, 119, 139, 159, 213, 324, 401, 533, 679, 785
Johnson, Van 6, 41
Johnston, Margaret 293, 597, 639
Johnston, Oliver 25
Johnston, Peter 180
Jones, Barry 113, 627, 652, 744
Jones, Christopher 432
Jones, Emrys 163, 549, 650
Jones, Evan 279, 483
Jones, Freddie 20, 304, 390, 668
Jones, Griffith 3, 232, 325, 395, 635, 709
Jones, Jack 119
Jones, Jacqueline 268
Jones, Jennifer 32
Jones, Jonah 173, 216, 249, 366, 419, 470, 511
Jones, Ken 29, 545, 571
Jones, Kenneth V. 81, 355, 374, 466, 665, 796, 826
Jones, Mary 42, 551, 758
Jones, Peter 336
Jones, Quincy 137, 160, 379
Jonson, Brian 17
Jordan, Bill 168
Jordan, Kerry 264
Jordan, Patrick 20, 111, 175, 188, 217, 443, 451, 465
Jordan, Richard 533
Jordan, William 696
Joseph, Robert L. 741
Josephs, Wilfred 64, 84, 89, 161, 197, 239, 340, 530, 783, 788
Joyce, Paddy 294
Joyce, Yootha 239
Judd, Edward 17, 97
Junkin, John 392
Jürgens, Curt 19, 326, 690
Justice, James Robertson 52, 100, 234, 312, 323, 503, 557, 654, 782, 808
Justin, John 86, 310, 342, 686, 731
Justini, Carlo 374, 665

Kadison, Ellis 736
Kahn, Ronald J. 491

Index of Names

Kandel, Aben 37
Kanner, Alexis 132, 304
Kanter, Jay 245, 803
Kaper, Bronislau 633
Kaplan, Sol 689
Karam, Mia 784
Karlin, Miriam 133, 268
Karloff, Boris 309
Kash, Murray 292, 643
Kasher, Charles 279
Kastner, Elliott 1, 43, 214, 392, 540, 817, 818
Kath, Katherine 459
Katz, Peter 195
Katz, Robert 90
Kaufman, Joseph 362
Kaufmann, Christine 505
Kaufmann, Maurice 150, 239, 250, 273, 294, 451, 647, 811
Kavanagh, Denis 261, 738
Kavanagh, Kevin 166, 718
Kay, Gilbert L. 642
Kay, Sydney John 564
Keach, Stacy 691
Kean, Georgina 399
Keating, John (Johnny Keating) 371, 618
Keats, Viola 789
Keeffe, Barrie 427
Keegan, Barry 258, 840
Keel, Howard 263
Keen, Diane 722
Keen, Geoffrey 37, 41, 164, 180, 198, 235, 267, 297, 331, 351, 358, 401, 415, 425, 430, 439, 478, 486, 541, 542, 589, 610, 633, 646, 690, 768
Keen, Malcolm 267, 554
Keiley, Virginia 488, 556
Keir, Andrew 1, 153, 400, 407, 721
Keir, David 671
Keith, Alan 429
Keith, Sheila 119, 276, 350, 354
Kelland, John 240
Kelly, Clare 13, 698
Kelly, Dermot 180
Kelly, Hugh 77
Kelly, James 54, 520, 763
Kelly, John 682
Kelly, Michael 174, 420
Kelly, Renee 634
Kelly, Sean 285
Kemp, Jason 725
Kemp, Jeremy 21, 231, 233, 699, 785
Kemplen, Ralph 685
Kendall, Henry 808
Kendall, Kay 463, 712, 832
Kendall, Suzy 20, 106, 245, 578
Kennaway, James 478, 806
Kennedy, Arthur 366, 503
Kennedy, George 170, 356
Kenney, James 11, 287, 325, 536
Kent, Howard 658
Kent, Jean 35, 41, 309, 434, 835
Kentish, Elizabeth 843
Kernan, David 240, 286
Kerr, Bill 588
Kerr, Deborah 507
Kerr, Richard 247
Kerry, James 296
Kerwin, Maureen 468

Kessel, Joseph 524
Kesten, Bob 394
Keyes, Evelyn 622
Keymer, Gordon 399
Khambatta, Persis 830
Kiel, Richard 486, 690
Kieling, Wolfgang 12, 797
Kier, Udo 228
Kimmins, Anthony 480
Kinberg, Jud (Judson Kinberg) 118, 648
King, Ann 27
King, Dave 427
King, Denis 722
King, George 212
King, Paul 701
Kingsley, Ben 245
Kingston, Frank 465
Kinnear, Roy 160, 390
Kinnoch, Ronald 79, 81, 224, 643
Kinski, Klaus 106, 254, 560, 718, 772
Kirby, Bill 787
Kirchin, Basil 21, 271, 361, 699
Kirk, Phyllis 617, 734
Kirwan, Patrick 178, 237, 384
Kitzmiller, John 193
Klee, Richard 364
Klinger, Michael 290, 298, 598, 764
Knapp, Terence 793
Knef, Hildegard 442, 490
Knight, David 4, 116, 230, 433, 534
Knight, Esmond 576, 693
Knight, John 437
Knight, Shirley 390
Knight, Vivienne 293
Knott, Frederick 409
Knowles, Bernard 28, 566
Knox, Alexander 9, 99, 374, 447, 483, 522, 554, 597, 599, 660, 787, 837, 844
Koch, Carl 523
Koch, Howard (Peter Howard) 377
Koch, Marianne 117, 166, 179
Kogan, Ephraim 236
Kohn, John 118, 243, 735
Komeda, Krzysztof 136
Kopp, Rudolph G. 85
Koscina, Sylva 159, 341
Koslo, Paul 764
Kossoff, David 123, 351, 353, 614
Kotto, Yaphet 423
Koumani, Maya 189, 325, 591, 790
Kovacs, Ernie 559
Krasker, Robert 15, 118, 128, 312, 413, 625, 692
Krasne, Philip N. 67
Kratina, Dick 251
Krein, Michael 740
Kretzmer, Herbert 765
Kruger, Christiane 375
Kruger, Hardy 55, 520, 831
Kruse, John 20, 210, 321, 611
Kulick, Barry 668
Kurnitz, Harry 442
Kydd, Sam 18, 115, 155, 249, 327, 603, 624, 672, 777, 808

Laage, Barbara 310
La Bern, Arthur 2, 157, 270, 368, 759, 798

Lacey, Catherine 676
Lacey, Jacqueline 2
Ladd, Alan 320
Ladd, Alan, Jr. 245, 803, 810
Laffan, Patricia 224, 325
Lafont, Bernadette 96
La Frenais, Ian 96, 387, 558, 803
Lageard, Theo 475, 477
Lake, Alan 271, 584, 725
Lamb, Charles 551
Lambert, Peter 74
Lamble, Lloyd 27, 287, 307, 401, 463, 596, 721, 749
Lamont, Duncan 79, 475, 498, 532, 564, 570, 731, 756
Lampell, Millard 55
Lancaster, Burt 90
Lanchbery, John 46, 53, 163, 174, 201, 216, 275, 537, 743
Lanchbury, Karl 637
Landau, Richard 297, 497, 684
Landen, Dinsdale 583
Landi, Marla 4, 206, 301, 337, 343, 498
Landone, Avice 216, 286
Landry, Gerard 531
Lane, Arthur 832
Lang, Gordon 16, 185, 363
Lang, Harold 38, 82, 112, 430, 460, 497, 565, 570, 629
Lang, Howard 149, 327, 372, 526
Lang, Robert 252, 529
Lange, Claudie 132
Langley, Norman 187, 271, 451
Langova, Sylva 368, 422
Langslow, Brian 285
Lansbury, Angela 403
Lapotaire, Jane 127
Lapresle, Robert 18, 135, 506
Larraz, José Ramón (José Larraz, Joseph Larraz) 300, 637
Lassally, Walter 570
Latham, Philip 688
Latimer, Hugh 289, 527, 620, 682
Latimer, Jonathan 827
Latimer, Michael 451
Launder, Frank 267, 614, 692
Laurence, Charles 131
Laurence, Zack 17
Laurenson, James 20
Laurie, John 237, 502, 537, 774
Laurimore, Jon 804
Lavagnino, Angelo 328, 341
Lavi, Daliah 538, 679, 732
Lavis, Arthur 95, 192, 338, 399, 472, 527, 578, 614, 780
Law, John 619
Law, Michael 669
Lawford, Peter 345, 552, 630
Lawrence, Delphi 28, 57, 60, 204, 240, 268, 299, 549, 653, 706
Lawrence, Marc 395, 461
Lawrence, Quentin 89, 455, 583, 811
Lawrence, Sheldon 130, 429, 464, 600, 697, 765, 773
Lawrence, Shirley 180, 642
Lawson, Anne 199, 405
Lawson, Gerald 206
Lawson, Sarah 420, 475, 530, 532, 549, 676, 747, 748

Index of Names

Lawson, Wilfrid 321
Lazare, Gaston 125
Lazenby, George 547
Lea, Andrea 352
Leach, Rosemary 233
Leaver, Philip 284, 393, 684
Le Beau, Betty 781
Lebeau, Madeleine 80
Lebor, Stanley 324
Le Borg, Reginald 229, 256
Lee, Belinda 230, 265, 497, 624, 646
Lee, Benny 525
Lee, Bernard 4, 32, 41, 80, 85, 115, 116, 132, 141, 186, 193, 242, 277, 302, 423, 453, 461, 480, 486, 541, 547, 568, 614, 644, 660, 689, 690, 751, 796, 825, 841, 844
Lee, Christopher 9, 31, 39, 59, 76, 92, 106, 179, 181, 183, 234, 343, 461, 569, 573, 730, 733, 736, 765, 770, 776, 797, 828
Lee, David 140, 210, 799
Lee, Jack 104
Lee, Margaret 254
Leech, George 117, 490
Leech, Richard 206, 425, 612, 733, 809
Leeds, Charles A. 35, 232, 270, 310, 448, 470, 493, 535, 719
Lefebvre, Rolf 123
Lefevre, Pierre 352
Leggatt, Alison 838
Leib, Vlado 658
Leigh, Andrew 259
Leigh, Constance 695
Leigh, Laurie 270, 465
Leigh, Suzanna 64, 159, 161, 247, 717
Leigh-Hunt, Barbara 272
Leigh-Hunt, Ronald 7, 110, 233, 257, 316, 340, 385, 655, 819
Leighton, Margaret 85, 303, 335, 731, 778
Leighton, Michael 386
Leister, Frederick 35, 105, 621
Le Mesurier, John 48, 56, 57, 62, 144, 146, 153, 155, 258, 341, 343, 379, 380, 383, 421, 460, 469, 560, 585, 630, 758, 820
Lemkow, Tutte 469
Lemont, John 274, 307, 659, 834
Lenska, Rula 162
Lenya, Lotte 277
Lenz, Kay 569
Leppard, Alex 637
Le Sage, Bill 246, 285, 333, 405, 600, 608, 714, 773, 789
Leslie, Desmond 701
Leslie, Eddie 210
Lesser, Julian 629, 822
Lesslie, Colin 141
Lester, Henry E. 716
Lester, Mark 231, 520, 606, 826
Lester, Michael 606
Lester, Richard 390
Lestocq, Humphrey 431, 582, 739, 789, 792
Lettieri, Al 598
Levene, Philip 165, 183
Leversuch, Ted 7, 728
Levinson, Barry 375

Levis, Carroll 176
Levison, Ken 436
Levitt, Alfred 787
Levitt, Gene 39
Levy, Jules 70
Levy, Ori 648
Lewis, Bernard 790
Lewis, Duncan 5
Lewis, Fiona 558, 803
Lewis, Gillian 614
Lewis, Jerry 552
Lewis, John Martin 619
Lewis, Michael J. 214, 540, 569, 626, 735, 791
Lewis, Ronald 278, 383, 646, 730
Lewiston, Dennis (Denis Lewiston) 228, 691
Lexy, Edward 301, 528, 671
Leyton, John 636
Li, Lily 661
Licudi, Gabriella 387, 421
Lieven, Albert 108, 147, 166, 172, 178, 179, 181, 772
Liles, Ronald 138, 211, 286, 656, 664
Lind, Gillian 196, 244
Linden, Jennie 534
Linder, Cec 61, 302, 371, 382, 683, 798
Linder, Leslie 58
Lindo, Olga 632
Lindsay, Helen 567
Lindsell, Stuart 596
Lindstrom, Bengt 446
Lindup, David 661, 687
Linehan, Barry 172, 616
Linzee, Lewis 766
Lipinski, Stanley 728
Lippert, Robert L. 338, 498, 527, 609
Lister, Francis 336
Lister, Moira 203, 305, 419, 586
Litvak, Anatole 524
Livesey, Jack 574
Livesey, Roger 377, 412
Llewelyn, Desmond 666
Lloyd, Euan 831
Lloyd, Jeremy 166
Lloyd, Sue 360, 371, 378, 542
Lloyd, Suzanne 609, 825
Lloyd, Ted (cinematographer [Edward Lloyd]) 56, 101, 146, 342
Lloyd, Ted (producer) 188, 294, 772
Locke, Harry 389, 445, 513
Locke, Philip 233, 368
Lockhart, Calvin 476, 538
Lockwood, Julia 676
Lockwood, Margaret 91, 332, 777
Lockyer, Malcolm 159, 254, 560, 732, 797
Loder, John 643
Lodge, David 706, 759
Lodge, Jean 2, 145, 169, 229, 249, 385
Loegering, Mark 707
Logan, Gary 357
Logan, Richard 357
Lollobrigida, Gina 32, 837
Lom, Herbert 6, 14, 33, 80, 99, 274, 321, 374, 403, 404, 458, 480, 505, 512, 518, 560, 571, 607, 615, 622, 692, 822
Lombardo, Lou 626
Loncar, Beba 67, 679

Long, Reginald 169, 419
Long, Robert 148
Long, Stanley A. 394
Longden, John 9, 50, 400, 474, 839
Longdon, Terence 109, 515, 562, 609
Lonsdale, Michael (Michel Lonsdale) 87, 152, 486
Lord, Jack 193
Lord, Justine 5, 368, 517
Loren, Sophia 90, 251
Lorimer, Enid 250, 834
Lorraine, Guido 737
Lorre, Peter 32, 200
Lorys, Diana 681
Losey, Gavrik 8
Losey, Joseph (Joseph Walton) 55, 128, 377, 483, 760
Lott, Barbara 188, 791
Loussier, Jacques 476
Love, Bessie 541
Lovegrove, Arthur 465, 508
Lovell, Dyson 564
Lovell, Raymond 693
Lowe, Arthur 403, 553, 735
Lowe, Barry 89
Lowitsch, Klaus 544
Lubin, Arthur 265
Lucas, Leighton 742
Lucas, William 71, 75, 83, 151, 181, 433, 465, 575, 589, 595, 766
Lucisano, Fulvio 61
Luckwell, Bill 11, 66, 175, 221, 313, 316, 325, 488, 499, 601, 623, 790
Luckwell, Kay 790, 814
Luke, Keye 489
Lukschy, Wolfgang 373, 783
Lumet, Sidney 160, 501
Lumley, Joanna 547
Lumsden, Geoffrey 340
Lundigan, William 145
Lung, Ti 661
Lustgarten, Edgar 459
Lutyens, Elisabeth 439, 565, 597, 736, 780
Lyel, Viola 721
Lynch, Sean 372
Lynley, Carol 78, 94, 139
Lynn, Ann 49, 485, 508, 581, 714, 715
Lynn, Jonathan 375
Lynn, Robert 98, 117, 369, 490, 788, 802

Maben, Alvys 702
MacArthur, James 34
MacCorkindale, Simon 170, 613
Macdonald, Aimi 542
MacDonald, David 9, 82, 434, 774
Macdonald, Philip 103
MacDougall, Ranald (Quentin Werty) 476
MacDougall, Roger 288
MacGinnis, Niall (Niall McGinnis) 320, 384, 455
MacGowran, Jack 55, 136, 481
MacGregor, Jock 11, 221, 454, 499, 601
MacIntosh, Fraser 67
Mackay, Fulton 311, 363
Mackendrick, Alexander 404
MacKenzie, John 427, 791

Index of Names

Mackenzie, Mary 111, 401, 470, 769
MacKenzie, Robert 57
MacKenzie, Ross 61
Mackie, Philip 114, 115, 116, 441, 543, 660, 784, 796
MacKinnon, Allan 36, 50, 62, 105, 301, 337, 349, 629, 662, 756
MacLaren, John 190
MacLaren-Ross, J. 393, 700
MacLean, Alistair 599, 817, 818
MacNaughtan, Alan 65, 199
MacOwan, Norman 147, 794
MacQuitty, William 370
MacRae, Duncan 835
Madden, Peter 192, 837
Maddern, Victor 93, 106, 133, 232, 408, 627, 665, 706, 712, 755
Maddow, Ben 489
Madison, Leigh 329, 508
Madrid, José Luis 681
Magee, Patrick 128, 247, 513, 593, 612, 638
Maher, Terry 414
Mahoney, John 487
Maibaum, Richard 186, 193, 277, 302, 461, 547, 690, 751
Maine, Charles Eric 225, 761
Mainwaring, Dan 95
Maitland, Marne 72, 163, 190, 208, 242, 460, 461, 471, 564, 609, 708, 733, 807
Makeham, Eliot 237
Malandrinos, Andrea 695
Malden, Karl 45
Malin, Edward 669
Malleson, Miles 343, 576, 777
Mallet, Tania 302
Mallik, Umesh 313, 454
Malmsten, Birger 446
Mamangakis, Nicos 417
Manahan, Sheila 652
Mandel, Johnny 8
Mango, Alec 680, 811
Mankiewicz, Joseph L. 670
Mankiewicz, Tom 90, 186, 209, 423, 461
Mankowitz, Wolf 820
Mann, Abby 588
Mann, Anthony 137
Mann, Stanley 118, 509, 626, 699, 735, 837
Mannheim, Lucie 40
Manni, Ettore (Red Carter) 61
Mannino, Franco 32
Mansfield, Jayne 97, 765
Mansfield, Keith 729
Manulis, Martin 208
Maranne, André 789
Maraschal, Launce 761
Margo, George 393, 464
Margolin, Arnold 626
Markham, Barbara 354
Markovic, Milorad 67
Marks, Alfred 274, 386
Marks, Leo 112, 576, 786
Marks, Louis 455
Markstein, George 544, 618
Marle, Arnold 72, 131, 262, 307, 422
Marlowe, Derek 137
Marlowe, Hugh 410, 518

Marlowe, Linda 44, 364, 452, 517, 725
Marlowe, William 12, 618
Marner, Richard 820
Marquand, Serge 87
Marquis, Max 715
Marriott, Anthony 161
Marsden, Betty 231
Marsh, Carol 440, 631
Marsh, Garry 201, 386, 434, 682, 808
Marsh, Jean 209, 233
Marsh, Reginald 656, 664
Marshall, Bryan 361, 427, 690, 727
Marshall, C.P. Hamilton 765
Marshall, Frank 246, 285, 313
Marshall, George 39, 207
Marshall, Herbert 812
Marshall, Roger 255, 282, 612, 651, 677, 736, 788, 816, 825
Marshall, Tom 399, 611
Marshall, Zena 25, 56, 134, 146, 163, 193, 216, 635, 724, 798
Marson, Ania 599
Martel, Gene 190
Martelli, Carlo 95, 192, 498, 824
Martin, Charles 642
Martin, George 83, 423, 598
Martin, Jean 152
Martin, John (actor) 813
Martin, John (producer) 40
Martín, Maria 7
Martin, Troy Kennedy 379, 723
Martinelli, Elsa 466
Martinson, Leslie H. 243
Marx, Sam 207
Maskell, Trevor 467
Maskell, Virginia 453, 720
Maslansky, Paul 231
Mason, Bert 24, 25, 63, 86, 114, 115, 172, 225, 258, 424, 441, 443, 493, 513, 543, 568, 583, 651, 660, 667, 677, 759, 770, 789
Mason, Edward J. 400
Mason, Herbert 91
Mason, Hilary 195
Mason, James 68, 160, 208, 214, 373, 435, 442, 468, 496, 540, 569, 703
Massey, Anna 272, 432, 576
Massey, Daniel 94, 269, 387
Massie, Paul 413, 557, 632
Matania, Clelia 195
Maté, Rudolph 587
Mather, Berkely 193
Matheson, Judy 260, 637
Matheson, Richard 239
Mathews, Carole 22, 700
Mathews, Kerwin 29, 462
Mathieson, Muir 107, 326, 815, 837
Matthews, A.E. 479
Matthews, Christopher 58
Matthews, Francis 132, 405, 492, 600, 649, 729, 838
Matthews, James 731
Matto, Jeanne 167
Mature, Victor 251, 376, 428
Mauban, Maria 82
Maule, Annabel 140
Maurey, Nicole 353, 620, 633, 799, 812
Maurstad, Alfred 794

Maxwell, James 604, 771
Maxwell, Lois 186, 193, 220, 277, 302, 330, 396, 401, 423, 461, 463, 486, 547, 572, 690, 751, 792, 844
Maxwell, Paul 108, 270, 452, 656
Maxwell, Peter 57, 177, 188, 364, 431, 650, 724
May, Hans 224, 622
May, Jack 44, 517, 593, 595, 771
Mayaro, Greta 495
Maycock, Peter 313
Mayer, John 139
Mayersberg, Paul 191
Maylam, Tony 613
Maynard, George 369, 386, 472, 593, 603, 620, 675
Mayne, Ferdy 33, 42, 62, 77, 82, 133, 164, 178, 219, 250, 297, 333, 371, 418, 438, 458, 511, 658, 686, 740, 749, 750, 810, 817, 818, 836, 845
Mazhar, Ahmed 81
Mazurki, Mike 518
McAlinney, Patrick 608
McAnally, Ray 245, 432, 499
McCabe, John 244
McCallin, Clement 621
McCallum, David 321, 391, 646, 806
McCallum, John 430, 588, 777, 794, 835
McCallum, Neil 95, 192, 382, 530, 548, 665, 809
McCarthy, Michael 18, 135, 506, 554, 655, 770
McCarthy, Neil 545
McClory, Kevin 751
McCormack, M.M. see Grantham, Mark
McCormick, John 801
McCowen, Alec 272, 760, 768
McCrea, Joel 622
McDermott, Brian 255, 667
McDermott, Hugh 175, 385, 438, 459, 777, 845
McDowall, Betty 155, 211, 380, 381, 757
McDowell, Malcolm 569
McEnery, Peter 94, 801
McFarland, Olive 274
McGillivray, David 276, 350, 354, 636
McGivern, William P. 70
McGoohan, Patrick 321
McGrah, Neville 164
McGrath, John 45
McGuffie, Bill (William McGuffie) 97, 431, 792
McHattie, Stephen 764
McIntosh, Alex 811
McIntosh, Ellen 205, 666, 784
McKenna, T.P. 205, 270, 579, 710, 803
McKenna, Virginia 191
McKern, Leo 21, 41, 341, 760
McLaglen, Andrew V. 540, 831
McLaren, John 102
McLeod, Bill see McLeod, William
McLeod, Gordon 88
McLeod, William (Bill McLeod) 83, 295, 504
McNaught, Bob 305
McNaughton, Fred 66

Index of Names

McShane, Ian 271, 604, 668, 803
McSharry, Carmel 416
Meade, Walter 389
Meadows, Stanley 392, 437, 564
Medwin, Michael 26, 100, 308, 311, 400, 426, 521, 657, 682, 684, 731, 783
Meek, Joe 240
Megahy, Francis 271
Meheux, Phil 427
Meillon, John 81, 156, 172, 545
Meisner, Günter 373
Melachrino, George 212, 284
Melford, Jack 120, 219
Melford, Jill 299, 493, 497
Mell, Marisa 108, 469
Mellinger, Michael 603, 747
Mellor, James 517
Melly, Andrée 40, 338, 541
Melnick, Daniel 710
Melvin, Murray 392
Melzack, Julian 764
Menges, Chris 311
Mercieca, Victor 598
Meredith, Andrew *see* Bryant, Chris and Scott, Allan
Merino, Manuel 59, 92
Merrall, Mary 238, 307, 411, 824
Merrill, Gary 15, 95
Merritt, George 523
Merrow, Jane 21, 95, 183, 317
Mervyn, William 492
Messina, Chick 143
Metzger, Radley 94
Meyen, Harry 779
Meyer, Hans 613
Michael, Ralph 149, 500
Michell, Keith 227
Michelle, Ann 354
Michi, Maria 606
Middleton, Guy 226, 237, 438, 515, 742
Middleton, Noelle 601, 800, 843
Mikell, George 40, 151, 203, 333, 381, 395, 592
Mikhelson, Andre 189
Milbourne, Olive 553
Miles, Bernard 632, 754
Miles, Sarah 43
Miles, Vera 41
Milland, Ray 103, 215, 283, 298, 340, 347, 627
Miller, Albert G. 686
Miller, Arnold Louis 394, 767
Miller, David 33, 315
Miller, Dusty 722, 723
Miller, Hugh 35
Miller, Jan 641
Miller, John 294
Miller, Magda 643
Miller, Mandy 641, 673
Miller, Martin 284, 368, 464
Miller, Peter 54, 165, 183, 550, 763
Miller, Sheila 767
Miller, Sigmund 382
Millington, Mary 584
Mills, Freddie 218, 396
Mills, George 134, 666
Mills, Hayley 165, 220, 752, 786
Mills, Hugh 52, 674

Mills, Jack 672
Mills, John 43, 288, 356, 430, 480, 745, 752, 768, 778, 800
Milnes, Bernadette 126, 454
Milroy, Vivian 135
Mimieux, Yvette 476
Minter, George 775
Miranda, Isa 192
Mirren, Helen 427
Mitchell, Cameron 792
Mitchell, Charles 11, 221
Mitchell, James 84, 371
Mitchell, Leslie 305
Mitchell, Stephen 480
Mitchell, Warren 19, 83, 371, 747
Mitchell, Yvonne 384, 632, 752
Mitchum, Robert 43, 447
Moffatt, Geraldine 290
Moffatt, Graham 640
Mohner, Carl 84, 97, 323
Mollison, Henry 101
Molloy, Mike 357
Monash, Paul 158, 627
Monette, Richard 44
Monkman, Francis 427
Monlaur, Yvonne 107, 733, 759
Montagu, Ivor 408
Montague, Lee 255, 441, 644
Montez, Conchita 520
Montgomery, Bruce 76, 100, 230, 310, 719
Montgomery, Doreen 502, 511, 551, 635, 758, 843
Moody, Jeanne 472
Moody, Ron 194, 500
Moon, George 313
Moore, Eileen 180, 480
Moore, Kieron 153, 293, 308, 326, 412, 463, 605, 750
Moore, Michael 701
Moore, Peter 705
Moore, Roger 132, 298, 423, 461, 486, 540, 690, 831
Moore, Ted 186, 193, 194, 277, 284, 302, 355, 376, 384, 423, 450, 461, 481, 594, 751
Moore, Terry 108, 589
Morahan, Tom 104, 425
More, Kenneth 113, 476, 744, 841
Morell, Andre 89, 301, 331, 343, 376, 456, 476, 641, 652, 737
Morey, Hal 7, 261, 620, 738
Morgan, Charles 89, 603
Morgan, Guy 212, 295, 339, 448, 515
Morgan, Patti 66
Morgan, Stanley 116, 197, 568, 609, 780
Morgan, Terence 266, 417, 578, 581, 657, 659, 693, 737, 775
Morley, Robert 10, 32, 341, 357, 413, 494, 546, 679, 716, 735, 782, 817
Morley, Royston 24
Morrell, Penny 472
Morricone, Ennio 356
Morris, Artro 699
Morris, Edna 15
Morris, Ernest 38, 211, 333, 526, 548, 556, 609, 656, 664, 714, 747, 750, 773, 836
Morris, Lana 48, 361, 485, 603, 711

Morris, Oswald 32, 82, 103, 269, 435, 456, 461, 544, 559, 670, 689
Morris, Reginald H. 496
Morris, Wayne 130, 131, 287, 307, 470
Morris, Wolfe 114
Morris-Adams, Richard 87
Morrison, Greg 436
Morrison, Kenneth D. 634
Morrison, T.J. 207
Morrow, Jeff 344
Morrow, Jo 559
Morse, Barry 537, 590
Morse, Helen 8
Mort, Patricia 24, 759
Mortimer, John 78, 312, 625
Mortimer, Penelope 78
Mortimer, Trisha 636
Morton, Clive 39, 114, 473, 531
Morton, Hugh 185, 262
Mosley, Bryan 290
Moss, Gerald 177, 188, 268, 364
Moss, Paul F. 242
Moss, Robert 642
Mottram, Anna 417
Mount, Peggy 216
Mower, Patrick 96, 550
Moxey, Hugh 845
Moxey, John Llewellyn (John Moxey) 106, 172, 205, 233, 612, 709, 784
Muir, David 491
Muir, Jean 714
Mullard, Arthur 27
Mullen, Barbara 288, 665, 799
Muller, Geoffrey 833
Muller, Robert 837
Mulock, Al 29, 171, 282
Mulvey, Anne 601
Munden, Maxwell 27, 348
Munro, Caroline 690
Munro, Janet 326, 639
Munro, Pauline 709
Munro, Stanley 782
Murcell, George 133, 600
Murphy, June 612
Murphy, Mary 225, 377
Murray, Barbara 15, 137, 148, 167, 275, 342, 506
Murray, Pete 226, 773
Murray, Stephen 23, 310, 471, 705
Murton, Lionel 143
Musel, Robert 104
Myers, Andy 780
Myers, Peter 388, 673
Myers, Stanley 1, 87, 119, 276, 350, 354, 392, 533, 558, 636, 668, 810, 830

Nader, George 541, 718
Nagy, Bill 4, 29, 69, 111, 134, 138, 292, 302, 431, 452, 460, 525, 655, 773
Naismith, Laurence 101, 398, 456, 754, 787, 812
Napier, Russell 46, 56, 69, 169, 422, 448, 511, 702, 758, 833
Narizzano, Silvio 239, 606
Nascimbene, Mario 820
Nasht, John 683, 776
Nat, Marie-José 215
Nation, Terry 13, 347
Navarro, Robert (Bob Navarro) 62, 662

Index of Names

Neagle, Anna 459
Neal, Patricia 519, 569
Neame, Ronald 456, 544
Nebenzal, Harold 830
Needham, Gordon 359, 536
Negus-Fancey, Olive (Negus Fancey) 562, 592, 663
Neil, Peter 173, 474
Nelson, Gene 184, 761
Nelson, Gwen 196
Nelson, Ralph 830
Nelson, Sidney 155, 189
Nelson-Keys, Anthony 89
Neri, Rosalba 92
Nero, Franco 606
Nesbitt, Cathleen 674, 782, 803
Nesbitt, Derren 296, 370, 371, 397, 416, 445, 509, 538, 584, 688, 715, 801, 818
Nesbitt, Frank 192, 809
Nethercott, Geoffrey 2, 825
Nettleton, John 13, 410
Neve, Suzanne 25
Neville, John 716
Nevinson, Nancy 614
Newbrook, Peter 49
Newell, Patrick 300, 530
Newfield, Sam 281, 401
Newlands, Anthony 106, 268, 360, 677, 784
Newley, Anthony 355, 408, 450, 587
Newman, Barry 245
Newman, Joseph M. 362
Newman, Nanette 158, 236, 563, 638
Newman, Paul 435
Newth, Jonathan 842
Newton, Sally 16
Ney, Marie 528, 657, 719
Neylin, James 601
Nicholas, Paul 58, 816
Nicholl, David 600
Nicholl, Don 217
Nicholls, Anthony 352, 653
Nichols, Dandy 5, 196
Nicholson, James H. 826
Nicholson, Nora 135, 142, 337, 774
Nicol, Alex 235, 291, 346, 473, 704
Nicolai, Bruno 14
Nicolaysen, Bruce 569
Nielsen, Leslie 527
Nieto, José 6, 122
Nightingale, Michael 110, 458
Nimmo, Derek 117, 341
Nissen, Brian 440
Niven, David 170, 312, 533, 820
Niven, David, Jr. 209
Noble, Patsy Ann (Trisha Noble) 168
Noiret, Philippe 19, 524
Nolan, Lloyd 203, 292
Nolbandov, Sergei 481
Norden, Christine 50, 88
Nordish, Louis 487
Norman, Leslie 481, 522
Norman, Monty 193
North, Frank 299
North, Virginia 159
Norton, William 70
Ntshona, Winston 831

Nuyen, France 447
Nykvist, Sven 604
Nystrom, Carl 33

Oaksey, John 154
Oates, Simon 198
O'Brian, Hugh 732
O'Brian, Melody 394
O'Brien, Pat 396
O'Brine, Manning (P. Manning O'Brine, Paddy Manning O'Brine) 396, 431, 444, 493, 792
O'Connolly, Jim (James O'Connolly) 37, 217, 240, 334, 656, 672, 771
O'Connor, Robin 584
O'Conor, Joseph 51, 577, 701, 842
O'Dea, Denis 426
O'Dell, Denis 775
O'Dell, Ronnie 728
O'Donnell, Cathy 212
O'Donnell, James see Wilson, Michael
O'Donovan, Danny 1
O'Farrell, Bernadette 401
O'Ferrall, George More 308
O'Flynn, Philip 313, 804
Ogden, Edward 465
Ogilvy, Ian 703
O'Grady, Tony see Clemens, Brian
O'Hara, Gerry 12, 282, 466
O'Hara, Maureen 438, 559
O'Herlihy, Dan 727, 734
O'Keefe, Dennis 185, 237, 402, 628
O'Leary, Liam 701
Oliver, Anthony 133, 138, 433, 737
Olivier, Laurence 68, 78, 670
Olsen, Olaf 774
Olson, James 127
O'Malley, Michael 44
O'Mara, Kate 418
O'Neill, Maire 701
Onions, S.D. 280, 495, 649, 669, 707
Opatoshu, David 312
Orme, Geoffrey 174, 319, 389
Ornadel, Cyril 187, 260, 451, 680, 717
Orr, Buxton 229, 309, 809
Ortolani, Riz 61
Osborn, Andrew 60, 146, 497, 657, 684
Osborn, David 99, 159, 466, 484, 577, 679, 696
Osborne, John 290, 764
Osborne, Tony 247, 642
Oscar, Henry 190, 643, 685
Oscarsson, Per 137, 220
O'Shea, Ethel 605
O'Shea, Milo 735
Osmond, Hal 548
Osmond, Lesley 101
Ostrer, Bertram 308, 566
O'Sullivan, Richard 308, 318, 705, 834
O'Toole, Peter 153, 524, 590
O'Toole, Stanley 68, 691
Oulton, Brian 479, 685
Owen, Alun 128
Owen, Bill 119, 659
Owen, Clare 211, 656

Owen, Cliff 545, 593
Owen, Reg (Reginald Owen) 150, 502, 511, 575
Owen, Yvonne 682
Owens, Patricia (Pat Owens) 135, 506, 809
Oxley, David 16, 343

Paal, Alexander 112, 463
Pack, Charles Lloyd 126, 258, 363, 539, 704
Paddick, Hugh 811
Padget, Elizabeth 313
Page, Anthony 1, 403
Paice, Eric 416, 445
Paige, Anne 704
Pakeman, Kenneth 40
Palance, Holly 119
Palance, Jack 450
Pallos, Steven 96, 181, 185, 237, 382, 535, 628, 820
Palmer, Ernest (Ernie Palmer) 22, 319, 325
Palmer, Lilli 68, 426, 505, 520, 538, 639
Palmer, Terry 64
Paltenghi, David 225
Paluzzi, Luciana 751
Pantera, Malou 700, 773
Papas, Michael 417
Papworth, Keith 181
Paramor, Norrie 274
Parely, Mila 60
Parke, Macdonald 143
Parker, Cecil 242, 404, 716, 796
Parker, Clifton 104, 320, 353, 370, 646, 730, 731, 744
Parker, Cyril L. 728
Parker, Kim 790
Parker, Mary 339
Parker, Suzy 104
Parkins, Barbara 31, 599
Parkinson, Austin 162, 296
Parks, Larry 753
Parks, Michael 540
Parkyn, Leslie 75, 107, 180, 210, 439, 445, 653, 754, 823
Parrish, Robert 208, 468, 622
Parry, Gordon 477, 528, 719, 775
Parry, Natasha 135, 148, 268, 293, 477
Parslow, Ray 436, 680
Parsons, Jack 95, 126, 140, 192, 197, 229, 289, 410, 416, 498, 527, 530, 609, 780, 809
Parsons, Nicholas 492, 688
Partos, Frank 587
Partridge, Derek 798
Partridge, Michael 738
Passmore, Henry 173
Pastell, George 57, 163, 164, 277, 328, 364, 414, 462, 642, 708
Patch, Wally 314, 488, 631, 650
Paterson, Bill 415
Patisson, Danik 765
Patrick, Nigel 123, 227, 266, 305, 355, 370, 384, 412, 435, 450, 594, 632
Patten, Frank 465
Patterson, Lee 75, 93, 100, 124, 164,

Index of Names

264, 303, 380, 393, 460, 570, 675, 685, 757, 823
Paul, John 75, 198, 805
Pavel, Anika 300
Pavey, Anthony 65
Pavey, Stanley (Stan Pavey) 293, 310, 344, 448, 622, 624, 737
Pavlow, Muriel 230, 503, 512, 754, 821
Paxton, John 355, 376, 594
Payne, Cy 562, 663
Payne, Laurence 134, 739
Paynter, Robert 43, 251
Pays, Howard 142, 391, 793
Payton, Barbara 256
Peacock, John 698
Peake, Lisa 472
Peake, Michael 30, 329, 464, 714
Pearson, Colin 44, 725
Pearson, Johnny 387
Pearson, Richard 24, 96, 144
Peck, Brian 210, 651
Peck, Gregory 68, 489
Peckinpah, Sam 710
Peirce, Douglas 173
Pelissier, Anthony 531, 754
Pellatt, John 431, 792
Peluffo, Ana Luisa 628
Pendrell, Anthony 56, 342
Penhaligon, Susan 350
Penington, Jon 23, 206, 236, 319, 367, 421
Pennington-Richards, C. 178, 266, 697
Penrose, John 342
Peppard, George 227
Perceval, Hugh 615
Perceval, John 623
Perceval, Robert 635
Percival, Norman 142, 837
Perier, Etienne 817
Perinal, Georges 153
Perkins, Anthony 501, 540
Perry, Anthony 365
Perry, Desmond 313
Perry, Linette 646
Perry, Vic 761
Perschy, Maria 92, 254, 505
Pertwee, Jon 63, 542
Pertwee, Michael 528, 552, 630
Pescarolo, Leonardo 61
Peters, Lorraine 487
Peters, Luan 260, 271, 451
Peters, Scott 292
Petrovitch, Michael 688
Pettet, Joanna 524, 618
Phillips, Conrad 107, 151, 157, 177, 196, 268, 313, 364, 409, 498, 503, 644, 696, 706, 724, 823, 824, 834
Phillips, Gregory 361
Phillips, John 263
Phillips, John I. 138, 211, 334, 364, 525, 650, 656, 664, 672
Phillips, Leslie 284, 419, 466
Picazo, Angel 728
Piccioni, Piero 599
Piccoli, Michel 469
Pickup, Ronald 745
Pidgeon, Walter 85
Pierson, Frank R. 432

Pike, John 839
Pilon, Daniel 70
Pinter, Harold 602
Piper, Frederick 95, 224, 335, 358, 612
Piperno, J. Henry 11, 221
Pitcher, George 821
Pithey, Wensley 396
Pitt, Ingrid 828
Pittock, Michael 681, 819
Platt, Victor 443, 568, 583
Pleasence, Donald 51, 107, 136, 209, 322, 371, 524, 590, 659, 720, 764, 778, 815, 844
Plummer, Christopher 191, 496, 524, 538, 687, 779
Plunkett, Patricia 504
Plytas, Steve 736
Poe, James 34
Pohlmann, Eric 4, 53, 60, 72, 81, 82, 113, 124, 179, 218, 266, 281, 287, 297, 330, 332, 341, 351, 353, 426, 450, 454, 464, 527, 594, 656, 664, 746, 747, 807, 820
Poitier, Sidney 34, 830
Pol, Talitha 607, 811
Polanski, Roman 136
Poll, Martin 529
Pollock, Ellen 301, 359, 429, 824
Pollock, George 397, 492, 494, 500, 503, 704, 732
Pomeroy, John 206
Ponti, Carlo 90
Porter, Eric 84, 152, 317, 324, 392, 745
Porter, Nyree Dawn 441, 649
Portman, Eric 34, 82, 158, 455, 507
Poston, Tom 546
Potter, Martin 304
Powell, June 728
Powell, Michael 576, 639
Powell, Norman S. 519
Powell, Peter 356
Powell, Robert 745
Power, Hartley 16
Powers, Stefanie 127, 239
Prador, Irene 673
Pratt, Mike 17
Pravda, George 326, 583
Pravda, Hana-Maria 13
Preminger, Otto 78, 357
Presle, Micheline 55
Preston, Robert 112
Preston, Trevor 520
Prévost, Françoise 575
Price, Dennis 141, 267, 318, 338, 397, 495, 504, 539, 581, 587, 598, 732, 735, 756, 801, 815
Price, Stanley 298
Price, Vincent 436, 735
Priggen, Norman 575, 595
Prior, Allan 550
Probyn, Brian 371, 661, 698
Protat, François 764
Proudlock, Roger 48, 669, 671, 685, 737, 756
Pryse, Hugh 588
Pudney, Alan 202
Pulman, Jack 227
Purcell, Noel 305, 804
Purcell, Roy 162, 445

Purdom, Edmund 484
Pursall, David 10, 123, 397, 492, 500, 503, 644, 764
Pyne, Natasha 436, 824

Quarry, Robert 436
Quayle, Anthony 97, 209, 459, 496, 716, 727
Quéant, Gilles 531
Quentin, John 604
Quested, John 569
Quigley, Godfrey 157
Quinn, Anthony 468, 569
Quinn, Derry 782
Quinn, Tony 66, 306, 623, 655
Quitak, Oscar 770

Race, Steve 134
Racette, Francine 191
Rae, John 42
Raffael, Erika 713
Raft, George 224, 362
Raglan, James 262
Raglan, Robert 102, 325, 329, 369, 605, 813, 839
Raikes, Robert 3, 420
Raines, Cristina 626
Raines, Ella 448
Rains, Claude 458
Rajna, Thomas 382
Raker, Hugh see Endfield, Cy
Rakoff, Alvin 132, 571, 776
Ralli, Giovanna 158
Rampling, Charlotte 87
Randall, Tony 10, 560
Randall, Walter 316
Randell, Ron 39, 295, 339, 488
Ransohoff, Martin 58
Rapper, Irving 15
Rassimov, Ivan 61
Rathony, Akos 181
Raven, Simon 791
Rawi, Ousama 51, 298, 356, 590, 598
Rawley, Peter 604
Rawlings, Margaret 33, 317, 535
Rawlinson, A.R. 47, 77, 111, 286, 555, 574, 634, 682
Rawsthorne, Alan 263, 456
Ray, Aldo 153, 373, 384, 665
Ray, Andrew 222, 841
Ray, Philip 149
Ray, Ted 222
Raymond, Cyril 196, 527, 627
Raymond, Gary 772
Raymond, Jill 701
Raynor, Molly 635
Re, Gustavo 92, 728
Read, Jan 60, 309
Read, John 133
Redgrave, Corin 817
Redgrave, Michael 21, 304, 308, 522, 760
Redgrave, Vanessa 8, 31, 501
Redmond, Liam 189, 249, 288, 297, 331, 428, 570
Redmond, Moira 383, 397, 418, 467, 534, 568, 582, 660, 805
Reece, Brian 88
Reece, Dizzy 541
Reed, Carol 442, 559, 625

Index of Names

Reed, Donna 39, 827
Reed, Les 552
Reed, Maxwell 35, 53, 69, 113, 148
Reed, Michael 180, 210, 240, 439, 547, 560, 569, 592, 595, 771
Reed, Myrtle 229
Reed, Oliver 14, 19, 43, 387, 565, 648, 668, 764
Reed, Tracy 162, 437
Rees, Angharad 317
Rees, John 364
Rees, Llewellyn 843
Rees, Yvette 780
Reeve, Geoffrey 87, 599
Reeves, Kynaston 671
Reggiani, Serge 645
Regin, Nadja 205, 280, 543, 677, 707
Reid, Alastair 519
Reid, Beryl 19
Reid, Dorothy 265
Reid, Trevor 291, 474, 511
Reisser, Dora 825
Reisz, Karel 521
Reizenstein, Franz 107, 823
Relph, Michael 19, 288, 412, 469, 478, 632, 644, 801, 806, 837
Remberg, Erika 86, 107
Remick, Lee 324, 625
Rennie, Michael 63, 717
Renoir, Claude 690
Renzi, Eva 279, 729
Retford, Ella 657
Revill, Clive 19, 51, 78, 203, 243, 392, 483, 538
Rey, Fernando 728
Reyes, Gene 681
Reynolds, Charles 29, 56, 101, 146, 292, 342
Reynolds, Harry 200
Reynolds, Peter 27, 48, 74, 97, 173, 286, 333, 409, 428, 454, 563, 601, 671, 840, 843
Rhodes, Brian 116, 457, 467
Rhodes, Christopher 754
Rhodes, Joan 386
Rhodes, Marjorie 295, 317, 841
Rice, Joan 429, 585, 693
Richards, Aubrey 378
Richards, C. Pennington 344
Richards, Martin 68
Richards, Robert 49
Richardson, Ralph 335, 432, 559, 826, 837
Richardson, Tony 154
Richfield, Edwin 47, 62, 69, 71, 83, 182, 250, 257, 327, 424, 482
Richmond, Anthony 26, 195, 209
Richmond, Fiona 228
Richmond, Harold 363, 532, 748
Richmond, Irene 534
Richmond, Susan 135
Ridgeway, Philip 724
Rienits, Rex 18, 131, 539, 617, 829
Rietty, Robert 129, 323, 759
Rigby, Edward 103
Rigg, Diana 19, 547, 735
Rilla, Walter 81, 166, 284, 307, 362, 692, 769, 795, 802
Rilla, Wolf 47, 81, 406, 539, 581, 834

Ripper, Michael 60, 88, 155, 161, 381, 491, 561, 819
Ritch, David 706
Ritchie, June 726
Ritt, Martin 689
Roach, Jonathan see Endfield, Cy
Robards, Jason 505
Roberts, Charles 221
Roberts, Ewan 255, 567, 617, 771
Roberts, Meade 139
Roberts, Rachel 501
Roberts, Sidney 704
Robertson, Cliff 194, 469
Robertson, Dale 117, 330
Robins, Toby 282, 509
Robinson, Alan 511
Robinson, Douglas 7
Robinson, Harry 248, 273, 347
Robinson, Joe 7, 700
Robinson, John 314
Robson, Flora 194, 269, 494
Robson, Mark 320, 594
Robson, Michael 745
Robson, Zuleika 611
Roc, Patricia 103, 348, 359
Rocco, Gustavo 6
Roche, Jonathan see Endfield, Cy
Roddick, John 172, 199, 567, 610, 616
Roderick, George 261
Rodgers, Ilona 630
Rodney, June 18
Rodriguez, Aurelio 642
Rodway, Norman 11, 499, 578, 601
Roe, Willy 584
Roeg, Nicolas 166, 195, 369, 802
Roffey, Jack 340
Rogan, Beth 120, 372
Rogell, Albert S. 35
Rogers, Eric 20, 611
Rogers, Erica 338, 550, 616
Rogers, Ginger 33
Rogers, Howard Emmett 85, 345
Rogers, Maclean 22, 257, 314, 385, 464, 573, 574, 631, 845
Rogers, Paul 104, 432, 741
Rogers, Peter 20, 611, 676, 757, 800
Rohm, Maria 14, 59, 108, 254, 718
Rolfe, Guy 10, 336, 555, 708, 843
Romain, Yvonne (Yvonne Warren) 274, 610, 672
Romanus, Richard 626
Romero, Cesar 401, 712
Ronane, John 666, 680, 687
Ronay, Edina 527, 725
Ronet, Maurice 468
Rooney, Mickey 598, 783
Roper, Brian 295
Roquette, Suzanne 797
Ros, Edmundo 592
Rosay, Francoise 278
Rose, David E. 248, 340, 353
Rose, George 93, 380, 769
Rose, Reginald 831
Rose, William 362, 404
Rosen, Al 780
Rosenberg, Max J. 139, 161, 436, 597, 816
Ross, Annie 698
Ross, Hector 163, 280, 363, 693
Ross, Kenneth 152, 544

Rossen, Steven 778
Rossiter, Leonard 158, 558
Rota, Nino 170, 705, 794, 795
Rotha, Paul 93
Roundtree, Richard 215, 283
Rouve, Pierre 703
Rouvel, Catherine 468
Rowland, Roy 292
Rowlands, Patsy 151
Roy, Ernest G. 77, 218, 314, 555, 573, 574, 631, 634
Rubin, Edward 446
Rubin, Mann 809
Rubinstein, John 68
Rule, Janice 311
Runacre, Jenny 435
Rupp, Sieghardt 254
Russell, Iris 16, 205
Russell, Ken 45
Russell, Kennedy 389, 640
Russell, Ray 338
Russell, Robert 202
Russell, William 42, 610, 660
Rustichelli, Carlo 48
Rutherford, Margaret 492, 494, 500, 503, 624
Rutland, John 83
Rutledge, Rusty 446
Ryan, Kathleen 628, 841
Ryan, Madge 361, 834
Ryan, Robert 129
Ryder, Paul 294, 369, 472, 593
Rydon, Ryck 102, 157, 201

Saad, Margit 128, 583
Sabela, Simon 298
Sachs, Leonard 232, 438, 444, 543, 582, 707, 730
Sachs, Tom 403
Sachse, Salli 718
Saint-Amant, Marcella 590
St. Helier, Ivy 299
St. John, Betta 9, 673
St. John, Jill 186, 421, 668
Sakata, Harold 302
Sale, Richard 438
Salew, John 235, 365, 506, 528, 620, 659
Salkow, Sidney 498
Sallis, Peter 109
Saltzman, Harry 45, 186, 193, 277, 302, 378, 423, 461, 547, 844
Salzedo, Leonard 35, 297, 702
Samson, Ivan 845
Samuel, Phil C. 305, 594
Sanda, Dominique 435
Sanders, George 81, 198, 220, 602, 827
Sandford, Christopher 187
Sands, Leslie 172, 552
Sangster, Jimmy (John Sansom) 127, 159, 233, 244, 360, 374, 380, 462, 510, 534, 565, 673, 730, 733, 762, 772, 826
Sansom, John see Sangster, Jimmy
Sarafian, Richard C. 269
Sarsfield, Michael 506
Sasdy, Peter 198, 317
Saunders, Charles 36, 46, 56, 101, 138, 142, 146, 150, 169, 219, 250,

Index of Names

289, 301, 337, 391, 395, 474, 502, 508, 511, 551, 635, 758
Saunders, Stuart 93, 440, 834
Savalas, Telly 19, 373, 547, 606
Saville, Philip 38, 122, 306, 495, 523, 548, 711, 747
Saville, Victor 85
Scaife, Edward (Ted Scaife) 33, 335, 353, 421, 476, 615, 668, 787
Scala, Gia 787
Scarpa, Renato 195
Schaffner, Franklin J. 68, 203
Schell, Catherine (Catherine Von Schell, Catherina Von Schell, Katharina Von Schell) 12, 51, 84, 547, 772
Schell, Maria 544
Schell, Maximilian 160, 544, 607
Schifrin, Lalo 209, 421
Schiller, Frederick 402, 566
Schmid, Helmut 388, 593
Schneck, Stephen 373
Schnee, Thelma 242
Schneer, Charles H. 227
Schneider, Romy 558, 779
Schönherr, Dietmar 490, 802
Schrecker, Frederick 470
Schroeder, Ernst 442
Schumann, Erik 787
Schurmann, Gerard 34, 425, 787
Schuster, Hugo 79, 349
Schwiers, Ellen 796
Scott, Adrienne 261, 738
Scott, Alex 612, 664
Scott, Allan (Andrew Meredith) 195, 687
Scott, Avis 253
Scott, Janette 546, 565
Scott, John (Johnny Scott, Patrick John Scott) 12, 37, 198, 324, 577, 703, 716, 718, 804
Scott, Ken 498
Scott, Lizabeth 598, 812
Scott, Margaretta 127, 408, 838
Scott, Patrick John *see* Scott, John
Scott, Peter Graham 3, 42, 75, 180, 224, 327, 717
Scott, Sandu 238
Scott, Zachary 124, 449, 832
Scully, Denis 388
Scully, Terry 517
Searle, Francis 88, 112, 157, 189, 217, 249, 270, 286, 287, 396, 400, 465, 493, 495, 515, 525, 553, 596, 621, 682, 694, 790, 822
Searle, Humphrey 6, 39
Sears, Ann 93, 402, 405, 443, 792
Sears, Heather 49, 665
Seddon, Jack 10, 123, 397, 492, 500, 503, 644, 764
Segal, George 602, 626
Seiber, Matyas 99, 185, 237, 484
Sekka, Johnny 837
Sellars, Elizabeth 77, 112, 153, 266, 288, 358, 382, 408, 430, 514, 528, 605
Sellers, Peter 404, 514
Seltzer, Walter 447, 507
Semple, Lorenzo, Jr. 243
Serafin, Enzo 705

Serato, Massimo 195
Serret, John 620, 730
Sessak, Hilde 442
Sesselman, Sabina 369
Seton, Bruce 11, 73, 130, 157, 174, 212, 270, 325, 488, 574, 790, 805, 814
Setton, Maxwell 33, 41, 265, 428, 768
Sewell, Charles 640
Sewell, George 290, 318, 392, 618
Sewell, Vernon 50, 125, 145, 147, 262, 386, 445, 472, 603, 620, 675, 680, 715, 793, 840
Seyler, Athene 355, 807
Seymour, Carolyn 311, 791, 842
Seymour, Jane 423
Seyrig, Delphine 51, 152
Shaffer, Anthony 1, 170, 272, 670, 828
Shaftel, Josef 407, 648
Shakespeare, Joan 168
Shakespeare, John 399
Shamata, Chuck 590
Shaps, Cyril 600, 608
Sharif, Omar 390, 524, 727
Sharman, Maisie (Stratford Davis) 167, 449
Sharp, Anne 57
Sharp, Anthony 115, 187, 350
Sharp, Clive 680
Sharp, Don 31, 76, 84, 234, 324, 560, 595, 599, 729, 745, 804
Sharp, Leonard 495
Sharpe, Edith 89
Sharples, Robert 386, 472, 593, 620, 675
Shaughnessy, Alfred 127, 260, 330, 339, 365, 721
Shaw, Christine 116
Shaw, David 450
Shaw, Denis 40, 176, 306, 349, 372, 380, 420, 485, 536, 623, 838
Shaw, Julie 713
Shaw, Maxwell 543
Shaw, Peter 687
Shaw, Richard 120, 130, 150, 325, 439, 454, 814
Shaw, Robert 277, 763
Shaw, Roland 698
Shaw, Susan 189, 398, 406, 586, 695, 707, 724, 756, 829, 835
Shaw, Vee King 661
Sheard, Michael 613
Shearer, Moira 576
Sheen, Martin 90
Shefter, Bert 410
Shelley, Barbara 54, 164, 172, 219, 493, 676, 707
Shelley, Norman 56
Shelton, Joy 88, 218, 366, 477, 566
Shenson, Walter 473
Shepherd, Cybill 403
Shepherd, Elizabeth 54
Sheppard, Morgan 715
Sheridan, Dinah 53, 537, 574
Sheridan, Margaret 185
Sherrier, Julian 696
Sherriff, R.C. 522
Sherwin, Derrick 2
Sherwood, William 206
Sheybal, Vladek 45, 158, 277, 371, 403, 418, 599, 607, 648

Shields, Tim 410
Shillo, Michael 827
Shine, Bill 189, 348
Shingler, Helen 238, 389, 621
Shonteff, Lindsay (Lewis J. Force) 44, 110, 241, 414, 415, 517, 542, 688, 718, 725
Siddons, Alathea 695
Siddons, Harold 445
Sieff, Percy 802
Siegel, Don 51
Signoret, Simone 160
Silva, Henry 609
Silva, Maria 681
Silva, Simone 178, 222, 712, 740
Silver, Christine 337, 506
Silver, Leon 417
Sim, Gerald 498, 638
Sim, Sheila 522
Simcoe, Benjamin 64
Simmonds, Annette 53, 275
Simmons, Anthony 570, 760
Simmons, Bob 306, 728
Simmons, Jean 80, 113, 194, 265, 674
Simmons, Richard Alan (Richard De Koker) 390
Simpson, O.J. 90, 251
Sinatra, Frank 509
Sinclair, Charles 99
Sinclair, Hugh 103, 389, 463, 515, 537, 748
Sinclair, Joshua 300
Sinclair, Peter 131, 551, 813
Sinden, Donald 152, 230, 481, 754, 803
Singer, Campbell 258, 295, 335, 401, 682
Singleton, Mark 120, 221, 285, 499, 525, 536, 568, 649
Skriver, Ina (Christina World) 300
Skutezky, Victor 504, 841
Slaney, Ivor 60, 235, 253, 256, 281, 342, 346, 388, 401, 497, 628, 629, 684, 746, 774
Slater, John 256, 386, 742, 806
Slavin, Martin 67, 138, 211, 369, 563, 582, 656, 658
Slesar, Henry 505
Slezak, Walter 783
Sloan, John R. 33, 41, 269, 384, 544, 587, 627
Sloan, Michael 17
Sloane, Olive 652, 840
Slocombe, Douglas 80, 107, 243, 379, 403, 468, 618, 730, 741, 775
Smart, Patsy 228
Smedley-Aston, Brian 228
Smedley-Aston, M. (E.M. Smedley Aston) 545, 706, 736, 788
Smethurst, Jack 437
Smight, Jack 392
Smith, Brian 246, 616
Smith, Constance 366, 753
Smith, Cyril 63, 79, 148
Smith, Greg 745
Smith, Jack 579
Smith, Maggie 170, 541
Smith, Mitchell 778
Smith, Murray 119, 187, 648
Smith, Neville 311

Index of Names

Smith, Putter 186
Smith, Ray 563
Smith, Shelley 752
Smith, Wilbur 298
Smyrner, Ann 802
Snell, Peter 31, 304, 324, 680, 717, 828
Snowden, Alec C. 69, 121, 124, 184, 225, 359, 377, 393, 422, 449, 700, 761
Sofaer, Abraham 82, 389
Soldati, Mario 705
Solon, Ewen 3, 36, 380, 823
Somerfeld, Helga 783
Somers, Julian 358
Somers, Julie 169
Somlo, Josef 731
Sommer, Elke 14, 159, 533, 550
Sommerly-Gade, Felix 728
Soskin, Paul 331
South, Harry 713
Spalding, Harry (Henry Cross) 498, 527
Sparv, Camilla 21, 538
Spear, Eric 26, 42, 125, 190, 262, 301, 398, 474, 495, 662, 707, 712, 724, 765, 829
Spence, Johnnie 418
Spencer, Frank 50, 88, 112, 147, 169, 400, 409, 621, 682, 822
Spencer, Marian 638, 641
Spenser, David 680
Spenser, Jeremy 796
Spicer, Bernard 11
Spiegel, Sam 524
Spies, Adrian 476
Spillane, Mickey 292
Spoliansky, Mischa 207, 477, 827
Springsteen, R.G. 131, 647, 769
Spurgin, Anthony 150
Squire, Anthony 204
Squire, Ronald 265
Stafford, Brendan J. (Brendan Stafford) 16, 26, 105, 132, 150, 212, 250, 327, 339, 502, 532, 551, 574, 596, 659, 701, 834
Stafford, John 4, 705
Stainton, Philip 91
Staiola, Enzo 362
Stallich, Jan 323
Stamp, Terence 118, 483
Stampe, Will 437
Stander, Lionel 90, 136, 137, 598
Standing, John 209, 597
Standing, Michael 804
Stanley, Kim 638
Stapley, Richard *see* Wyler, Richard
Stark, Graham 630, 738
Starr, Freddie 691
Stassino, Paul 210, 443, 484, 708, 751, 767, 798, 820
Steel, Anthony 15, 100, 218, 323, 446, 472, 724
Steel, Edward 67
Steel, Pippa 703
Stefano, Joseph 507
Steiger, Rod 4, 324
Stepanek, Karel 82, 144, 248, 414, 448, 622, 647, 692, 742, 814
Stephen, Susan 144, 346, 608

Stephens, Martin 833
Stephens, Robert 104
Stephenson, Pamela 119
Steppat, Ilse 547
Sterke, Jeannette 199, 627
Sterling, Joseph 111
Sterndale, Martin 391
Sterne, Gordon 102, 280
Stevens, Craig 418
Stevens, Dorinda 289, 301, 527, 530
Stevens, George 726
Stevens, James 177, 268, 812
Stevens, Mark 434
Stevens, Ronnie (Ronald Stevens) 635
Stevens, Vi 650
Steward, Ernest 76, 84, 100, 106, 159, 234, 324, 328, 341, 538, 552, 575, 581, 646, 653, 679, 732, 744, 783, 795
Stewart, Alexandra 466, 468
Stewart, Donald Ogden 484
Stewart, Hugh 430, 531
Stewart, Jack 147, 319, 386
Stewart, James 43
Stewart, Marjorie 470
Stewart, Richard 145
Stewart, Robert Banks (Robert Stewart) 25, 205, 467, 516, 568, 583, 667, 796
Stewart, Robin 318
Stock, Nigel 230, 522, 524, 626, 762, 801
Stockwell, Dean 550
Stoll, Gunther 92
Stolz, Clarissa 424
Stone, Bernard 437
Stone, David 326
Stone, John 485, 556, 750
Stone, Marianne 23, 525, 572
Stone, Philip 516
Stone, Sid 9
Stoney, Kevin 457, 549, 608
Stoppard, Tom 357
Storaro, Vittorio 8
Stott, Wally 432, 817
Stovin, Jerry 677
Stranks, Alan 88
Strasberg, Lee 90
Strasberg, Susan 328, 730
Strasburg, Ivan 542
Stratton, Inger 509
Stratton, John 425, 709
Straus, Barnard 529
Strauss, Alfred 488
Stretton, George 52
Stribling, Melissa 36, 135, 412, 502, 539, 627, 644, 829
Stritch, Elaine 687
Stross, Raymond 458, 622, 796, 799
Strueby, Katherine 212
Struthers, Ian 294, 402
Strutton, Bill 21
Stuart, John 291, 643
Stuart, Josephine 711
Stuart, Leone 240
Stubbs, Una 577
Stümpf, Günther 669
Sturges, John 209
Style, Michael 273

Subotsky, Milton 139, 161, 194, 436, 597, 816
Sukman, Harry 509
Sullivan, Barry 356, 447
Sullivan, Francis L. 518
Sullivan, Sean 285
Summerfield, Eleanor 235, 249, 312, 409, 433, 497, 535, 625, 742
Summers, Jeremy 151, 254, 797
Sumner, David 561, 766
Sumpter, Donald 517
Surtees, Robert L. 118
Suschitzky, Wolfgang 93, 290, 735
Sutcliffe, Clare 361
Sutherland, Donald 31, 191, 195, 209, 239, 252, 496
Sutton, Dudley 542, 552, 584, 810
Suzman, Janet 51
Swann, Fred A. 758
Swanson, Maureen 439, 740
Swanwick, Peter 173, 177, 502, 781
Sweet, Dolph 245
Swinburne, Nora 700
Sydney, Basil 320
Sydney, Derek 444, 833
Sykes, Eric 397, 421, 735
Sykes, Peter 347
Sykora, Ken 570
Sylvester, William 54, 206, 349, 368, 369, 545, 589, 614, 702, 726, 821, 841
Syms, Sylvia 139, 296, 340, 727, 801
Syson, Michael 244

Tabori, Paul 9, 190, 197, 253, 439, 463, 488, 684, 714
Tafler, Sydney 18, 27, 37, 56, 66, 101, 124, 184, 218, 262, 297, 310, 425, 506, 555, 629, 634, 690, 719, 829
Talbot, Kenneth 29, 198, 204, 292, 315, 317, 466, 479, 580
Tallier, Nadine 776
Tamba, Tetsuro 844
Tamiroff, Akim 421
Tamiya, Jiro 842
Tamm, Mary 544
Tammes, Fred 87
Tani, Yoko 567, 581
Tanner, Gordon 548
Tansley, Derek 405
Tapley, Colin 112, 120, 185, 217, 539, 693, 749, 829, 832
Tarloff, Frank 203
Tarlton, Alan 223
Tashlin, Frank 10
Tate, Nick 415
Tate, Reginald 224, 477, 645
Taube, Sven-Bertil 209, 283, 599
Taylor, Brian 405, 782
Taylor, Donald 181, 204, 523, 711
Taylor, Elizabeth 529
Taylor, Gilbert (Gil Taylor) 34, 103, 136, 272, 278, 326, 331, 452, 593, 652, 736, 841
Taylor, Jack 7, 655
Taylor, John C. 44, 110
Taylor, Kenneth 41
Taylor, Kent 647, 769
Taylor, Larry 134, 292, 392, 394, 431

Index of Names 439

Taylor, Richard 69, 121, 124, 184, 225, 429, 761
Taylor, Robert 353
Taylor, Rod 421, 476, 538
Taylor, Totti Truman 175, 838
Taylor, Valerie 236
Teakle, Spencer 126, 289, 681
Temple-Smith, John 3, 42, 46, 97, 250, 295, 327, 336, 553, 596
Templeton, William 200, 477
Tenser, Tony 198, 318
Terris, Malcolm 252
Terry, Ray 250, 295, 327
Terry-Thomas 397, 473, 560
Tetzel, Joan 320
Tetzlaff, Ted 755
Teynac, Maurice 531
Thamar, Tilda 470
Thaw, John 156, 255, 407, 722, 723
Thawnton, Tony 838
Then, Tony 725
Theodorakis, Mikis 236
Thomas, Gerald 676, 757, 800
Thomas, Nina 154
Thomas, Peter 772, 782
Thomas, Rachel 95
Thomas, Ralph 100, 113, 159, 328, 341, 533, 538, 679, 744, 795
Thompson, Derek 427
Thompson, J. Lee 489, 504, 569, 607, 752, 841
Thompson, Marshall 643
Thomson, Alex 94, 245, 283, 361, 519, 699
Thorburn, June 174, 226, 337, 471, 591, 773
Thorn, Ronald Scott 278
Thorne, Anthony 674
Thorne, Gary 176
Thorne, Ken 157, 390, 471, 561, 590
Thornton, Frank 365, 386
Thorp, Richard 784
Thorpe, Richard 353
Thulin, Ingrid 90, 607
Tierney, Gene 518
Till, Eric 810
Till, Jenny 736
Tilsley, Reg 318
Tilvern, Alan 99, 138, 656, 665
Tindall, Hilary 842
Tingwell, Charles 492, 494, 500, 503
Toal, Maureen 313
Tobias, Oliver 533
Tobin, Bud 584
Todd, Ann 247, 308, 357, 730, 760
Todd, Richard 43, 99, 117, 141, 166, 374, 514, 542, 717, 795, 799
Tomelty, Joseph 320, 322, 594, 761, 775
Tomlinson, David 85, 194, 421, 674
Tonti, Giorgio 606
Toone, Geoffrey 211, 442, 493, 733
Torch, Sidney 166
Toren, Heller 255
Toren, Marta 458
Tourneur, Jacques 103
Tournier, Jean 152, 486
Tovey, Roberta 766
Towb, Harry 493
Towers, Harry Alan (Peter Welbeck) 14, 59, 76, 92, 106, 108, 117, 166, 234, 254, 490, 560, 718, 732, 783, 797, 802
Townley, Toke 624
Toye, Wendy 731
Trace, Christopher 793
Train, Jack 95
Travers, Alfred 592, 678
Travers, Bill 125, 265, 712
Travers, Susan 561
Trell, Max 320, 408
Trestini, Giorgio 195
Trevarthen, Noel 25, 226, 762
Trevor, Austin 513
Trevor, Howard 491
Trevor-Davis, John 619
Tronson, Robert 240, 441, 443, 513, 543, 549, 614, 771
Trooger, Margot 772
Trosper, Guy 689
Troubridge, Andrea 348
Trubshawe, Michael 623
Truman, Michael 293
Truman, Ralph 522, 685
Trumbo, Christopher 70
Trytel, Bill 790
Tu, Francisca 489
Tuchner, Michael 245, 803
Tucker, Burnell 151
Tucker, Forrest 72
Tucker, Hubert 165
Tufano, Brian 713
Tully, John 206, 236, 367
Tully, Montgomery 29, 109, 124, 155, 182, 184, 185, 189, 225, 253, 297, 359, 381, 393, 429, 440, 449, 457, 460, 535, 561, 591, 700, 739, 746, 789, 824
Tunberg, Karl 413
Tunick, Irve 402
Turkel, Ann 90
Turner, Anna 793
Turner, John 49
Turner, Lana 580
Turner, Tim 309, 523, 585
Turner, Yolande 418
Turpin, Gerry 158, 638, 816
Tushingham, Rita 356, 698
Twist, Derek 238, 585
Tynan, Kathleen 8
Tynan, Kenneth 541
Tyzack, Margaret 333, 614

Underdown, Edward 30, 32, 148, 369, 424, 605, 712, 739, 772, 787, 808
Unger, Kurt 599
Unsworth, Geoffrey 19, 113, 200, 252, 304, 321, 375, 501, 754, 791, 821
Ure, Mary 478, 818
Urquhart, Robert 71, 140, 352, 418, 432, 494, 573, 726, 774, 843
Ustinov, Peter 170

Vadim, Roger 52
Valentine, Anthony 295
Valentine, Val 305, 615, 737
Valk, Frederick 256, 647
Valli, Alida 705
Vallone, Raf 356, 379
Van Bergen, Ingrid 181
Vance, Charles 595
Vance, Leigh 51, 132, 274, 581, 659, 834
Van Eyck, Peter 179, 673, 689, 796
Van Eyssen, John 3, 55, 467, 485, 568, 748, 770
Van Nutter, Rik 751
Varley, Beatrice 26, 47, 167, 530, 537, 574
Varnals, Wendy 623
Varnel, Max 102, 221, 306, 420, 485, 499, 536, 601, 608, 616, 649, 813, 838
Vaughan, Peter 214, 231, 239, 315, 435, 452, 509, 672, 710, 729, 785
Vaughan-Hughes, Gerald 639
Veale, John 109, 217, 270, 535, 589
Veitch, Anthony Scott 117
Vendell, Veronique 802
Ventham, Wanda 168
Ventura, Viviane 29
Verner, Gerald 774
Verney, Guy 262
Vernon, Anne 755
Vernon, John 51, 70, 245
Vernon, Richard 2, 89, 116, 341, 660, 712
Vernon, Valerie 173, 297
Versini, Marie 76
Versois, Odile 100, 571
Vetter, Charles F. (L.Z. Hargreaves) 29
Vicas, Victor 123
Vich, Vaclav 388
Victor, Charles 85, 184, 216, 275, 295, 585, 615, 629, 835
Vidler, Julia 202
Vidon, Henry 393
Vigo, David 175, 623
Villechaize, Herve 461
Villiers, David 86
Villiers, James 64, 114, 293, 494, 510, 558, 679
Vinter, Gilbert 532, 748
Vittes, Louis 229
Vitti, Monica 483
Vivian, James 125
Voight, Jon 544
Von Kotze, John 254, 718, 797
Von Krogh, Britta 696
Von Schell, Catherina *see* Schell, Catherine
Von Schell, Catherine *see* Schell, Catherine
Von Schell, Katharina *see* Schell, Catherine
Von Sydow, Max 215, 602

Wade, Michael 428
Waescher, Aribert 442
Wakabayashi, Akiko 844
Wales, Ken 727
Walford, Ann 299
Walker, Maggie 637
Walker, Pete 119, 187, 260, 276, 350, 354, 451, 636, 713
Walker, Zena 98, 140, 217, 410, 465, 771, 780
Walkley, Byrl 640
Wallace, Hedger 833

Index of Names

Wallach, Eli 251
Waller, David 579
Walsh, Dermot 23, 62, 65, 74, 97, 125, 211, 217, 262, 275, 327, 523, 562, 663, 711, 724, 781, 833, 836
Walsh, Kay 91, 213, 358, 729
Walters, Thorley 410, 503, 597, 614, 720, 786
Walton, Joseph see Losey, Joseph
Wanamaker, Sam 128, 139, 227, 248, 447, 480, 641, 648, 687, 689
Ward, Edmund 12, 304, 804
Ward, James 414, 681, 819
Ward, Julian 145
Ward, Michael 101
Ward, Simon 165, 194, 361
Ware, Derek 592
Ware, Kenneth 407
Warne, Derek 399
Warner, David 191, 579, 710, 745
Warner, Jack 26, 194, 218, 383, 404, 794
Warner, Richard 406, 513, 549, 660
Warr, Terry 637
Warren, Barry 192
Warren, Betty 674
Warren, Kenneth J. 714, 839
Warren, Yvonne see Romain, Yvonne
Warrender, Harold 669, 755
Warwick, Gina 318
Warwick, John 105, 122, 145, 224, 493, 515
Warwick, Norman 431, 781, 843
Washbourne, Mona 91, 118, 146, 269, 521, 704, 816
Waterhouse, Keith 447
Waterman, Dennis 273, 526, 722, 723
Waters, Jan 766
Waters, Russell 140, 169, 467, 828
Watford, Gwen 192
Watkin, David 842
Watling, Dilys 83
Watling, Jack 144, 257, 258, 301, 420, 510, 676, 734, 758, 825
Watson, Diana K. 180
Watson, Jack 255, 390, 457, 540, 561, 576, 636, 699, 831
Watson, John 66, 175
Watson, Wylie 657
Watt, Harry 665
Wattis, Richard 60, 413, 566
Watts, Gwendolyn 239
Watts, Queenie 636
Waxman, Harry 122, 139, 220, 242, 301, 337, 351, 430, 433, 474, 510, 520, 632, 644, 782, 786, 794, 828
Wayne, John 70
Wayne, Ken 677
Wayne, Naunton 103, 200, 332
Webb, Alan 252, 741
Webb, Clifton 456
Webb, William 202
Webber, Andrew Lloyd 311, 544
Webber, Robert 360
Webster, Harry 157
Webster, Joy 663, 697
Webster, Martyn C. 77
Weintraub, Fred 778

Weis, Heidelinde 452
Welbeck, Peter see Towers, Harry Alan
Welch, Ed 745
Welch, Raquel 243
Welchman, Harry 212
Welland, Colin 710, 722
Welles, Orson 777
Wellesley, Gordon 197, 308, 439, 807
Wells, Frank 299
Wells, Ingeborg 101, 201, 349
Wells, Jerold 86, 142, 583
Wells, Win 606
Welsh, John 104, 121, 534
Wenzel, Horst 717
Werner, Oskar 689
Werty, Quentin see MacDougall, Ranald
Weske, Brian 391, 536, 564
West, Anita 364, 656, 658
West, Brian 626
West, Timothy 8
Westerby, Robert 33, 35, 82, 179, 438, 683, 719, 768
Westergren, Hakan 446
Weston, Leslie 216
Wetherell, Virginia 451, 713
Wheatley, Alan 109, 174, 185, 336, 346, 419, 471, 684, 763, 822
Wheeler, Paul 87, 604
Whelen, Christopher 117, 234
Wherry, Daniel 808
Whitaker, David 194, 315, 584, 717
White, Carol 286, 445, 514, 691
White, Daniel 59
White, Jeremy 487
White, Leonard 23, 406, 617
White, Valerie 62
White, Wilfrid Hyde 52, 94, 207, 269, 332, 413, 421, 477, 480, 560, 718, 732, 734, 800
Whitelaw, Billie 75, 179, 272, 311, 322, 529, 575, 786
Whiteley, Jon 358, 812
Whiting, Margaret 370
Whitman, Stuart 661
Whitsun-Jones, Paul 86, 840
Whittingham, Jack 80, 358, 586
Wickert, Tony 563
Wickes, David 722
Wickham, Jeffry 604
Wicking, Christopher 505
Widmark, Richard 31, 34, 501, 518, 594, 648
Wiener, Jack 209
Wigan, Gareth 791
Wilcox, Herbert 459, 777
Wilcox, John 161, 320, 360, 418, 480, 489, 534, 597, 661, 785
Wild, Katy 161
Wilde, Colette 116, 525, 595
Wilde, Cornel 39
Wilding, Michael 141, 507, 777
Wiles, John 429, 460, 793, 833
Wilhelm, Theodore 663
Wilhelm, Wolfgang 645
Wilkes, John 720
Wilkinson, Arthur 101, 419
Williams, Billy 45, 529

Williams, Brock 150, 289, 291, 363, 474, 475, 508, 532, 697, 748
Williams, Cedric 237, 259, 287, 585
Williams, Charles 843
Williams, Derick 196
Williams, Edward 204
Williams, Emlyn 15, 41, 810
Williams, Harcourt 411, 755
Williams, Hugh 237
Williams, Jill 649
Williams, Michael 154
Williams, Norman 455, 581, 659, 834
Williams, Peter 711, 788
Williams, Richard 102
Williams, Treat 209
Williams, Wendy 246
Williams, William H. (W.H. Williams) 125, 135, 145, 262, 506, 712, 829
Williamson, Cecil H. 7
Williamson, Lambert 131, 266, 307, 647, 685, 769
Williamson, Malcolm 127
Williamson, Nicol 357, 830
Williamson, Paul 175, 610, 623
Williamson, Tony 529
Willis, Ted 79, 406
Willman, Noel 4, 128, 512, 514
Willoughby, George 12, 729
Wilmer, Douglas 76, 572, 791, 797
Wilmer, Geoffrey 261
Wilson, Gerald 251
Wilson, Gwenda 142
Wilson, Ian 13, 273, 347
Wilson, James (Jimmy Wilson) 2, 5, 38, 66, 98, 102, 120, 149, 156, 176, 190, 199, 205, 226, 233, 246, 255, 282, 306, 329, 368, 372, 420, 437, 440, 485, 516, 526, 536, 548, 549, 556, 567, 610, 612, 616, 686, 709, 714, 747, 750, 758, 762, 784, 798, 811, 813, 825, 836, 838, 839
Wilson, Manning 651
Wilson, Maurice J. 109, 310, 381, 471, 561, 591, 739, 824
Wilson, Michael (James O'Donnell) 787
Wimperis, Arthur 85
Windsor, Barbara 716, 765
Windsor, Frank 17
Winfield, Gilbert 548
Winn, Derek 66, 130, 325, 488, 814
Winner, Michael 43, 251, 387, 460, 562, 663
Winter, Donovan 162, 296, 781
Winter, Vincent 757
Winters, Shelley 826
Wintle, Julian 18, 75, 107, 148, 180, 210, 358, 439, 445, 653, 823
Wise, Herbert 762
Wiseman, Joseph 193
Withers, Googie 518, 588
Withers, Margaret 734
Witty, Christopher 416, 469
Witty, John 485, 678
Wolfit, Donald 310, 353, 448, 594, 615, 770
Wood, Annabella 637
Wood, Christopher 486, 690

Wood, John 552
Wood, Lana 186
Wood, Mary Laura 46, 226, 330, 344, 704, 794
Woodbridge, George 112, 256, 523
Woodthorpe, Peter 360
Woodville, Catherine 114, 129, 370
Woodward, Edward 84, 248, 668, 828
Wooland, Norman 310, 470, 526, 535, 615
Wooldridge, John 52, 123, 238, 408, 835
Woolf, John 152, 544
Woollard, Robert 619
Wootten, Rosemary 580
Wootton, Roger 688, 725
Worker, Adrian D. 39, 374
World, Christina *see* Skriver, Ina
Worth, Brian 22, 28, 73, 155, 555, 733
Worth, Irene 557, 633, 645
Wrede, Casper 604
Wrenn, Trevor 637
Wrestler, Phillip 134
Wright, Jennifer 197
Wright, Jenny Lee 436

Wright, Maggie 552
Wright, Tony 24, 236, 256, 367, 388, 654, 685, 754
Wyatt, Tessa 688
Wyatt, Yvette 823
Wyer, Reginald (Reg Wyer) 4, 230, 332, 336, 370, 445, 463, 515, 554, 674, 684, 774, 806, 812
Wyeth, Katya 698
Wyldeck, Martin 521, 609, 761, 767
Wyler, Richard (Richard Stapley) 329
Wyler, William 118
Wyman, Frank 767
Wymark, Patrick 128, 597, 818
Wynn, Keenan 30, 375, 447
Wynne, Gilbert 110, 517
Wynter, Mark 318

Yama, Conrad 489
Yates, Pauline 516
Yates, Peter 618
Yeldham, Peter 421, 490, 560, 732, 783, 802
Ying, Liu Ya 661
York, Michael 501, 613, 699
York, Susannah 208, 298, 392, 639

Yorke, Bruce 388
Yorke, Doris 259
Young, Aida 317
Young, Arthur 287
Young, Felicity 126, 270, 289, 562, 823
Young, Freddie (Frederick A. Young, F.A. Young) 39, 85, 160, 727, 755, 844
Young, Joan 410
Young, Leon 38, 372, 420, 485
Young, Leonard 542
Young, Les 688, 725
Young, Raymond 169
Young, Terence 6, 193, 277, 751, 765, 779, 794
Young, Tony 175, 325, 588, 623
Yule, Ian 550

Zampi, Mario 657
Zaza, Paul 496
Zetterling, Mai 30, 52, 178, 236, 382, 455, 545, 581, 594, 615
Zichy, Theodore 64, 197, 530
Ziemann, Sonja 388, 473
Zinnemann, Fred 152
Zittrer, Carl 496

Index of Film Titles

This index refers to page numbers and points to the reviews/synopses for the 845 main films. (Alternate titles are covered in the Filmography.)
Additional film titles appear in *italics*.

Absolution 135
Accidental Death 301
Account Rendered 86
Across the Bridge 266
Act of Murder 303
Action of the Tiger 320
Action Stations 251
Agatha 112
Alias John Preston 121
The Alphabet Murders 169
Ambush in Leopard Street 216
Amsterdam Affair 164
And Soon the Darkness 145
And Then There Were None 103
Another Man's Poison 63
The Armchair Detective 177
Assassin 42
Assassin for Hire 253
The Assassination Bureau Limited 327
Assault 145
Assignment K 36
Assignment Redhead 319
At the Stroke of Nine 266
Attempt to Kill 294

Backfire! 295
Baffled! 411
Bang! You're Dead 74
The Bank Raiders 206
Barbados Quest 173
Battle Beneath the Earth 326
The Bay of Saint Michel 323
Bear Island 314
Beat the Devil 315
Beautiful Stranger 254
The Bedford Incident 283
Before I Wake 78
Behind the Headlines 187
Berserk 142
The Betrayal 268
Beyond Mombasa 318
Beyond the Curtain 23
Beyond This Place 92
The Big Chance 205
The Big Sleep 184
Big Zapper 184
Billion Dollar Brain 32
Black Orchid 68

The Black Rider 189
Black 13 201
The Black Torment 126
Black Widow 59
The Black Windmill 329
Blackmailed 231
Blackout 242
Blind Corner 102
Blind Date 93
Blind Man's Bluff 63
Blind Spot 242
Blind Terror 148
The Blood of Fu Manchu 309
Blood Orange 194
Blowup 3
The Blue Lamp 3
Blue Movie Blackmail 238
The Blue Parrot 157
The Body Said No! 58
Bomb in the High Street 218
Bond of Fear 264
Booby Trap 265
The Boy Cried Murder 283
The Boys from Brazil 335
The Brain Machine 245
Brannigan 165
The Break 248
Break in the Circle 317
Breakaway 174
The Breaking Point 213
Breakout 255
The Brides of Fu Manchu 308
The Broken Horseshoe 253
Bunny Lake Is Missing 105
Burnt Evidence 262

Cage of Gold 230
Cairo 217
Cairo Road 155
Calculated Risk 280
Callan 42
Calling Bulldog Drummond 177
Candidate for Murder 295
Caravan to Vaccarès 314
A Case for P.C. 49 156
Cash on Demand 277
The Cassandra Crossing 286
Cast a Dark Shadow 79
The Castle of Fu Manchu 309

Cat and Mouse 269
The Cat and the Canary 111
Catacombs 124
Catch Me a Spy 40
The Challenge 210
Change Partners 305
Chase a Crooked Shadow 267
Checkpoint 319
Chelsea Story 61
The Child and the Killer 273
Circle of Danger 62
Circle of Deception 24
Circumstantial Evidence 66
Circus of Fear 106
Circus of Horrors 138
City of Fear 33
Clash by Night 282
Clegg 182
Cloak Without Dagger 20
Cloudburst 314
The Clouded Yellow 259
Clue of the New Pin 293
Clue of the Silver Key 293
Clue of the Twisted Candle 291
Coast of Skeletons 307
The Collector 126
The Comeback 134
Compelled 213
Confession 78
Contraband Spain 246
Count Five and Die 21
The Counterfeit Plan 252
Counterspy 17
Cover Girl Killer 136
Crescendo 119
The Criminal 212
The Crooked Road 194
The Crooked Sky 251
Cross Channel 246
Crossplot 328
Crossroads to Crime 161
Crosstrap 277
Crow Hollow 63
Cul-de-Sac 227

A Dandy in Aspic 37
Danger by My Side 249
Danger Route 37
Danger Tomorrow 94

442

Index of Film Titles

Danger Within 91
Dangerous Afternoon 236
Dangerous Assignment 188
Dangerous Cargo 201
Dangerous Voyage 316
Dark Interval 120
The Dark Light 199
The Dark Man 259
Date at Midnight 192
Date with Disaster 205
Dateline Diamonds 219
The Day of the Jackal 285
The Day They Robbed the Bank of England 210
Dead Cert 257
Dead Lucky 186
Dead Man's Chest 305
Dead Man's Evidence 26
Deadfall 220
Deadlier Than the Male 53
The Deadly Affair 34
The Deadly Bees 106
The Deadly Females 257
Deadly Nightshade 16
Deadly Record 92
Deadly Strangers 152
Death Drums Along the River 306
Death Goes to School 68
Death Is a Woman 249
Death of an Angel 62
Death on the Nile 171
Death Over My Shoulder 269
Death Trap 298
The Delavine Affair 186
Delayed Action 254
Delayed Flight 282
The Depraved 86
The Desperate Man 192
Desperate Moment 262
The Devil's Agent 26
Devil's Bait 276
The Devil's Daffodil 247
Devil's Point 196
Diagnosis: Murder 110
Dial 999 263
The Diamond 250
Diamonds Are Forever 47
Die Screaming, Marianne 284
Dilemma 280
The Diplomatic Corpse 185
Diplomatic Passport 245
The Disappearance 111
Do You Know This Voice? 240
Dr. No 45
Dominique 135
Don't Look Now 132
Don't Talk to Strange Men 140
Doomsday at Eleven 279
Doomwatch 164
The Double 300
Double Confession 57
Double Exposure (1954) 179
Double Exposure (1976) 241
The Double Man 34
Doublecross 20
Downfall 302
Dublin Nightmare 90
Duel in the Jungle 317
Duffy 220

The Eagle Has Landed 333
Echo of Barbara 225
Echo of Diana 27
Eight O'Clock Walk 74
80,000 Suspects 280
11 Harrowhouse 222
Embassy 40
The Embezzler 234
Emergency 261
Emergency Call 260
The End of the Line 87
Endless Night 131
Enter Inspector Duval 162
Escape by Night 188
Escape in the Sun 264
Escape Route 16
Escapement 197
Escort for Hire 97
The Executioner 39
Exposé 134
The Eyes of Annie Jones 101
Eyewitness (1956) 265
Eyewitness (1970) 284

Face in the Night 204
Face of a Stranger 303
The Face of Fu Manchu 307
Face the Music 72
Faces in the Dark 123
The Fake 250
Family Doctor 88
Fanatic 118
Farewell Performance 101
The Fast Kill 221
Father Brown 180
Fathom 325
Fear in the Night 119
Fear Is the Key 313
Feet of Clay 96
The Fiction-Makers 3
The Fiend 149
The File of the Golden Goose 253
Final Appointment 185
Find the Lady 203
The Firechasers 411
Firepower 335
The First Great Train Robbery 223
Five Days 262
Five Golden Dragons 311
Five to One 302
The Flanagan Boy 69
Flannelfoot 72
Flat Two 296
The Flaw 77
The Flesh and Blood Show 108
The Flesh Is Weak 3
Flight from Vienna 20
The Floating Dutchman 157
Floods of Fear 320
The Flying Scot 205
Footsteps in the Fog 234
Forbidden Cargo 244
Foreign Exchange 412
Fortune Is a Woman 196
The Fourth Square 293
Fragment of Fear 107
Freedom to Die 216
Freelance 284
Frenzy 149
Fright 147

The Frightened City 225
The Frightened Man 200
Frightmare 151
From Russia with Love 46
The Full Treatment 115
Funeral in Berlin 32
The Fur Collar 193

The Gambler and the Lady 223
Game for Three Losers 305
Game for Vultures 335
The Gamma People 191
Gang War 226
Gaolbreak 216
The Gelignite Gang 180
The Gentle Gunman 315
The Gentle Trap 225
Get Carter 228
The Gilded Cage 245
The Girl Hunters 181
Girl in the Headlines 163
The Girl in the Picture 191
The Girl on the Pier 232
Give Us Tomorrow 287
The Glass Cage 77
Gold 329
The Gold Express 189
The Golden Lady 53
The Golden Link 158
Golden Salamander 3
Goldfinger 46
The Good Die Young 202
Goodbye Gemini 127
Grand National Night 71
The Great Van Robbery 160
The Green Buddha 317
The Green Scarf 76
Grip of the Strangler 121
Guilty? 81
Gumshoe 183
Guns of Darkness 279
A Guy Called Caesar 226

Hammer the Toff 172
Hammerhead 56
The Hand 95
Hands of the Ripper 129
The Haunted House of Horror 143
The Heart Within 247
Hell Below Zero 316
Hell Drivers 255
Hell Is a City 161
Hell Is Empty 283
Hennessy 331
Hidden Homicide 89
Hide and Seek 28
The Hideout 196
The High Bright Sun 324
High Jump 208
The High Terrace 81
High Treason 259
Highly Dangerous 15
Highway to Battle 24
The Hi-Jackers 218
Home at Seven 65
Home to Danger 62
The Hornet's Nest 202
The Horror of It All 102
The Hostage 265
Hostile Witness 107

Index of Film Titles

Hot Enough for June 29
Hot Ice 200
The Hound of the Baskervilles 175
Hour of Decision 191
The Hour of 13 66
The House Across the Lake 74
The House in Nightmare Park 110
The House in the Woods 87
House of Blackmail 232
House of Mortal Sin 153
House of Secrets 251
The House of the Arrow 157
The House of the Seven Hawks 322
House of Whipcord 150
How to Murder a Rich Uncle 84
The Human Factor 44
The "Human" Factor 333
Hunted 260
The Hypnotist 121
Hysteria 118

I Start Counting 144
I'll Get You for This 249
I'm a Stranger 65
Impact 194
The Impersonator 139
Impulse 76
In the Wake of a Stranger 225
Incident at Midnight 299
Information Received 215
The Informers 163
Innocent Bystanders 40
Innocent Meeting 271
Inside Out 332
Intent to Kill 271
The Internecine Project 110
Interpol 159
The Intimate Stranger 80
The Ipcress File 31
The Italian Job 220

Jack the Ripper 136
Jackpot 211
Jet Storm 275
Jigsaw 162
Johnny Nobody 96
Johnny on the Spot 75
Johnny, You're Wanted 247
The Jokers 219
Journey into Nowhere 279
Judgment Deferred 188
Juggernaut 286
Jungle Street 215

Kaleidoscope 257
The Key Man 204
Kil 1 256
Kill Her Gently 270
Kill Me Tomorrow 266
Kill or Cure 181
A Killer Walks 120
Killer's Moon 153
King of the Underworld 2

The Lady Craved Excitement 242
Lady in the Fog 188
Lady of Vengeance 82
The Lady Vanishes 112
The Ladykillers 203
The Lamp in Assassin Mews 99

The Large Rope 73
The Last Grenade 329
The Last Man to Hang 81
The Last Page 232
The Last Shot You Hear 107
The Late Edwina Black 60
The League of Gentlemen 211
Libel 93
Licensed to Kill 50
Licensed to Love and Kill 52
Life in Danger 274
The Lifetaker 134
The Limbo Line 37
The Limping Man 233
Links of Justice 90
The Liquidator 56
Little Red Monkey 19
Live and Let Die 47
Locker Sixty-Nine 298
The Long Arm 159
The Long Dark Hall 61
The Long Good Friday 230
The Long Haul 224
The Long Knife 255
The Long Memory 69
The Long Shadow 26
The Looking Glass War 39
Lost 264
The Lost Hours 65

The Mackintosh Man 41
Madame Sin 411
Madhouse 133
The Main Chance 303
Malaga 244
The Malpas Mystery 292
Man Accused 94
Man at the Carlton Tower 293
The Man Between 17
Man Detained 295
Man from Tangier 252
The Man in the Back Seat 277
The Man in the Middle 192
Man in the Middle 281
The Man in the Road 21
Man in the Shadow 84
The Man Inside 271
Man of Violence 328
The Man Outside 35
The Man Upstairs 271
The Man Who Couldn't Walk 212
The Man Who Finally Died 27
The Man Who Never Was 21
The Man Who Was Nobody 291
The Man Who Watched Trains Go By 120
The Man Who Wouldn't Talk 22
Man with a Gun 197
The Man with the Golden Gun 48
Maniac 116
Mantrap 178
Marilyn 3
Mark of the Phoenix 21
The Marked One 237
Maroc 7 325
Marriage of Convenience 291
The Marseille Contract 330
Masquerade 324
The Master Plan 19
Master Spy 27

A Matter of Choice 281
A Matter of WHO 162
Meet Mr. Callaghan 179
Meet Mr. Malcolm 71
The Mercenaries 326
Midnight Episode 61
The Mind Benders 124
Miss Tulip Stays the Night 77
Mr. Denning Drives North 64
Mister Jerico 411
Mix Me a Person 100
Model for Murder 91
Modesty Blaise 52
Moment of Danger 210
Moment of Indiscretion 91
Moonraker 49
More Deadly Than the Male 92
Morning Call 238
The Most Dangerous Man in the World 39
Mousey 411
Mozambique 309
Mumsy, Nanny, Sonny & Girly 127
Murder Ahoy 169
Murder at Scotland Yard 2
Murder at Site Three 181
Murder at the Gallop 168
Murder at 3 A.M. 70
Murder by Decree 176
Murder by Proxy 74
The Murder Game 104
Murder in Eden 252
Murder Most Foul 169
Murder on the Orient Express 170
Murder Reported 187
Murder She Said 11, 168
Murder Without Crime 231
Murders in the Rue Morgue 108
Mystery Junction 63

The Naked Edge 123
Naked Fury 208
The Naked Runner 35
The Nanny 118
The Narrowing Circle 79
The Net 17
Never Back Losers 295
Never Let Go 255
Never Look Back 64
Never Mention Murder 304
Night, After Night, After Night 144
Night and the City 223
The Night Digger 128
Night Hair Child 130
Night Must Fall 141
The Night My Number Came Up 263
The Night of the Full Moon 18
The Night of the Generals 142
Night of the Prowler 100
Night Train for Inverness 276
Night Train to Paris 30
Night Was Our Friend 120
Night Watch 131
Night Without Pity 217
Night Without Stars 243
The Night Won't Talk 67
A Nightingale Sang in Berkeley Square 223
Nightmare 117

Index of Film Titles

No Road Back 204
No Safety Ahead 208
No Trace 60
Nobody Runs Forever 164
Noose for a Lady 70
North Sea Hijack 336
Nowhere to Go 207
No. 1 of the Secret Service 52
Number Six 296

The Odessa File 330
Offbeat 161
The Old Dark House 100
On Her Majesty's Secret Service 47
On the Run (1957) 225
On the Run (1962) 299
One Away 333
One Jump Ahead 186
One More Time 327
One Way Out 159
Operation Amsterdam 321
Operation Diplomat 253
Operation Murder 80
Orders to Kill 269
Otley 38
Our Man in Havana 23
Our Man in Marrakesh 311
Out of the Fog 140
Out of the Shadow 193

The Painted Smile 226
Panic 218
Paranoiac 117
Park Plaza 605 179
The Partner 301
Partners in Crime 293
The Passage 288
The Passing Stranger 202
Passport to Shame 255
Passport to Treason 181
Paul Temple Returns 172
Paul Temple's Triumph 172
Payroll 215
Peeping Tom 138
Penny Gold 110
The Penthouse 127
Perfect Friday 221
Persecution 133
Piccadilly Third Stop 212
Pit of Darkness 215
A Place to Go 3
Playback 297
The Playbirds 153
Police Dog 158
Pool of London 243
Port Afrique 81
Port of Escape 263
Portrait of Alison 247
Power Play 334
The Price of Silence 235
The Primitives 216
A Prize of Arms 216
A Prize of Gold 318
The Professionals 212
Profile 76
The Psychopath 141
Pulp 229
Puppet on a Chain 313
The Pursuers 278

A Question of Suspense 98
The Quiller Memorandum 33

Radio Cab Murder 202
Ransom 331
Recoil 200
Redneck 222
Repulsion 3
Return from the Ashes 127
Return of a Stranger 140
The Return of Mr. Moto 163
Return to Sender 299
Revenge 146
Ricochet 300
The Riddle of the Sands 335
Ring of Spies 28
The Ringer 66
The Rivals 300
River Beat 157
Robbery 219
Robbery with Violence 208
Rogue's Yarn 82
The Rossiter Case 61
Rough Shoot 17
Run a Crooked Mile 412
The Runaway 29
The Runaway Bus 73
The Running Man 280
Russian Roulette 43

The Safecracker 206
Sail into Danger 247
The Saint's Return 179
Salt & Pepper 327
Salute the Toff 172
Sapphire 161
The Scapegoat 91
Scarlet Thread 199
The Scarlet Web 195
Schizo 134
Scream—and Die! 150
Séance on a Wet Afternoon 240
Sebastian 36
The Second Mate 242
The Secret 246
The Secret Door 28
The Secret Man 23
The Secret Partner 236
Secret People 15
The Secret Place 204
Secret Venture 19
The Sellout 43
Sentenced for Life 94
Serena 99
The Set-Up 299
Seven Days to Noon 258
Seven Keys 237
Seven Thunders 267
Shadow of a Man 77
Shadow of Fear 28
Shadow of the Past 58
Shadow of Treason 323
The Shakedown 235
The Share-Out 296
Shatter 331
She Shall Have Murder 60
Shoot to Kill 193
The Sicilians 226
The Siege of Pinchgut 274
The Silent Playground 280

The Sinister Man 294
Sitting Target 229
The Six Men 156
Sleuth 131
Smart Alec 62
Smokescreen 197
The Snorkel 89
So Long at the Fair 59
Soho Incident 224
The Solitary Child 88
Solo for Sparrow 298
Solution by Phone 73
Some Girls Do 54
Some May Live 36
Somebody's Stolen Our Russian Spy 51
Someone at the Door 57
Something to Hide 3
SOS Pacific 275
Spaceways 70
The Spaniard's Curse 87
The Spider's Web 96
The Spiral Staircase 152
The Spy Killer 412
Spy Story 43
The Spy Who Came In from the Cold 33
The Spy Who Loved Me 49
The Squeeze 241
Stage Fright 3
State Secret 258
The Steel Key 315
Stolen Assignment 185
Stolen Time 233
Stop-over Forever 282
Stormy Crossing 83
Straight On Till Morning 150
The Strange Affair 237
The Strange Awakening 88
Stranger at My Door 230
The Stranger Came Home 75
Stranger in the House 107
A Stranger in Town 191
The Stranger's Hand 18
Strangers' Meeting 86
Stranglehold 124
The Stranglers of Bombay 322
Strangler's Web 305
Straw Dogs 285
The Straw Man 195
Street of Shadows 68
Strip Poker 227
Strip Tease Murder 97
Strongroom 278
A Study in Terror 175
Subterfuge 38
Sumuru 311
The Surgeon's Knife 85
Suspect 25
Suspended Alibi 82
Sweeney! 167
Sweeney 2 167
The Switch 249
The Swordsman 184
The Syndicate 325

The Tamarind Seed 42
Tangier Assignment 245
Taste of Excitement 283
Taste of Fear 115

Index of Film Titles

The Teckman Mystery 19
Ten Little Indians 102
10 Rillington Place 3
The Terror of the Tongs 323
That Woman Opposite 82
Theatre of Blood 109
Theatre of Death 105
They Can't Hang Me 20
They Never Learn 159
The Third Alibi 97
Third Party Risk 317
The Third Secret 125
The Third Visitor 59
13 East Street 157
The 39 Steps 271
The Thirty-Nine Steps 272
36 Hours 72
Three Crooked Men 206
Three Steps in the Dark 70
Three Steps to the Gallows 244
Three Sundays to Live 86
Thunderball 46
Tiger Bay 274
Tiger by the Tail 189
Tiger in the Smoke 319
Time Bomb 262
Time Is My Enemy 233
Time Lock 266
A Time to Kill 233
Time to Remember 296
Time Without Pity 83
Timeslip 190
To Have and to Hold 300
Tomorrow at Ten 239
Tomorrow Never Comes 286
Too Hot to Handle 236
Torment 3
Touch of Death 279
A Touch of the Other 183
Town on Trial 136
Track the Man Down 189
The Traitor 84

The Traitors 26
Traitor's Gate 218
Transatlantic 214
Tread Softly 65
Tread Softly Stranger 206
The Treasure of San Teresa 322
Trent's Last Case 67
Trial by Combat 333
Triple Cross 34
Troubled Waters 126
The Trunk 97
The Trygon Factor 219
24 Hours to Kill 310
The 20 Questions Murder Mystery 3
The £20,000 Kiss 298
A Twist of Sand 326
Twisted Nerve 142
The Two-Headed Spy 23
Two-Letter Alibi 98
Two Wives at One Wedding 236

Undercover Girl 192
Unman, Wittering and Zigo 129
The Unstoppable Man 239
Urge to Kill 137

Valley of Eagles 259
Vendetta for the Saint 3
Venetian Bird 178
Vengeance 100
The Vengeance of Fu Manchu 308
The Verdict 302
The Very Edge 141
The Vicious Circle 85
Victim 236
Victim Five 309
Villain 229
The Violent Enemy 328
Violent Moment 123
Violent Playground 160
Visa to Canton 322
The Voice of Merrill 68

Walk a Tightrope 101
The Walking Stick 221
We Shall See 302
The Weapon 265
Web of Suspicion 92
West of Suez 320
What a Carve-Up 98
What Became of Jack and Jill? 131
When Eight Bells Toll 312
Where Eagles Dare 312
Where the Bullets Fly 50
Where the Spies Are 55
Whirlpool 321
Whispering Smith Hits London 178
The White Trap 274
Who Killed the Cat? 106
Who Was Maddox? 302
Whoever Slew Auntie Roo? 129
The Whole Truth 90
The Wicker Man 165
Wide Boy 232
The Wilby Conspiracy 331
The Wild Geese 334
Wings of Danger 244
The Witness 210
Witness in the Dark 275
The Woman in Question 59
A Woman of Mystery 192
Woman of Straw 125
A Woman Possessed 90
A Woman's Temptation 208
Wrong Number 209

The Yellow Balloon 261
Yellow Dog 41
You Can't Escape 79
You Only Live Twice 46
You Pay Your Money 320
Your Witness 3

www.ingramcontent.com/pod-product-compliance
Ingram Content Group UK Ltd.
Pitfield, Milton Keynes, MK11 3LW, UK
UKHW011911190225
455321UK00020B/234